UNDERSTANDING DEVELOPMENT

Sandra Scarr
University of Virginia

Richard A. Weinberg
University of Minnesota

Ann Levine

Under the General Editorship of
Jerome Kagan
Harvard University

Harcourt Brace Jovanovich, Publishers
San Diego   New York   Chicago   Atlanta   Washington, D.C.
London   Sydney   Toronto

To our children:
Brett and Eric
Karen, Phillip, Rebecca, and Stephanie
who have taught us about human development
from infancy to adulthood
and
about a species made up of distinctive individuals.
Thank you for growing up to be yourselves.
And to our spouses:
James Walker, Gail Weinberg, and Stacy Holmes
Who could ask for anything more?

Cover photo: Jean-Claude Lejeune, Stock Boston.
Illustrations by John Odam

Text Credits

Ablex Publishing Corporation. Table 10-2, from R. Plomin and J. C. DeFries, "Genetics and Intelligence: Recent Data," *Intelligence, 4,* 1980. Adapted by permission of the publisher.

American Psychological Association. Figure 10-2, from R. J. Sternberg, "Who's Intelligent?" *Psychology Today,* April 1982. Reprinted with permission from *Psychology Today* Magazine. Copyright © 1982 by the American Psychological Association.

Ann Arbor Institute for Social Research. Page 440, table, adapted from S. G. Timmer, J. Eccles, and K. O'Brien, "How children use time." In F. T. Juster and F. P. Stafford (Eds.), *Time, goods, and well-being.* Ann Arbor, Mi.: Institute for Social Research, University of Michigan, 1980. Reprinted by permission.

W. H. Freeman and Company, Publishers. Table 5-1, adapted from "The Origins of Personality," A. Thomas, S. Chess, and H. G. Birch. *Scientific American,* August 1970. Copyright © 1970 by Scientific American, Inc.

Harcourt Brace Jovanovich, Inc. Table 8-4, adapted from *The Longest War: Sex Differences in Perspective,* Second Edition, by Carol Tavris and Carole Wade. Copyright © 1984 by Harcourt Brace Jovanovich, Inc. Table 7-1, from *Psychology and Language: An Introduction to Linguistics* by Herbert H. Clark and Eve V. Clark. Copyright © 1977 by Harcourt Brace Jovanovich, Inc. Reproduced by permission of the publisher.

Harper & Row, Publishers, Inc. Figure 1-5, from *One Boy's Day: A Specimen Record of Behavior* by Roger G. Barker and Herbert Wright. Copyright © 1951 by Roger G. Barker and Herbert F. Wright. Reprinted by permission of Harper & Row, Publishers, Inc.

Harvard University Press. Table 7-2, from *Early Language* by P. A. de Villiers and J. G. de Villiers, 1979. Page 173, from Dan Stern, *The First Relationship: Infant and Mother,* 1977. Reprinted by permission of the publisher.

Continued on page 639.

PREFACE

Developmental psychology is changing. Many books are still rooted in ideas that have been discarded in the mid-1980s. This textbook is based on current theory and research, in which two of the authors, Sandra Scarr and Richard A. Weinberg, are participants. Most developmentalists have now accepted a cognitive view of complex learning, even while retaining a healthy respect for simple conditioning. Most espouse a biological view of the basic processes of development, grounded in the science of genetics and the theory of evolution, while crediting experience with an important facilitating role. They see social and emotional development both as an expression of the human developmental pattern, with all the variability that implies, and as a product of the individual's personal history of encounters with the social environment. They have discarded old dichotomies of nature and nurture, innate versus learned, body and mind in favor of an integrated view of how all of these factors work together to make our species human and individuals unique.

This text sets forth a modern synthesis that incorporates biological and social knowledge about every aspect of human development. We do not drop genetics after the first two chapters; nor do we ignore social events in the beginning chapters. Rather, the book weaves a coherent story for students about the biosocial wonders of human development from conception to adolescence.

Understanding Development is organized chronologically *and* topically. Each of the sections on infancy, the preschool years, middle childhood, and adolescence contains chapters on perceptual-cognitive development and social-emotional development, as well as a chapter on

another set of topics especially important to that phase of development. The section on early childhood includes a chapter on language; the section devoted to middle childhood contains a chapter on intelligence and creativity; the section covering adolescence includes a chapter on physical growth and sexuality. By combining the "whole child" approach of a chronologically structured text with a topical organization within each period of development, this book reflects the best of both pedagogical worlds.

We have created a number of special aids to understanding development. Seven *Profiles* featured between chapters are in-depth interviews of prominent investigators by Ann Levine, not excerpts from previously published articles. We believe that these interviews offer students a unique opportunity to visit with some of the leading developmental psychologists in the field. Their accounts of how they became involved in their particular area, what they find most challenging about their work, and what interests them most today constitute a personalized, informal history of modern developmental psychology. Urie Bronfenbrenner recounts the multicultural childhood that led to his interest in human ecology; Robert McCall tells why he is devoting his time to communicating scientific findings to mass audiences; Mary Ainsworth describes how she "discovered" attachment and methods for studying its development; Willard Hartup makes an eloquent statement on the long-overlooked importance of peers in a child's development; John Flavell reevaluates Piaget's theory of cognitive development in light of his own and other contemporary research; Carol Gilligan explains the feminist critique of theories of moral development; James Marcia describes how he devised empirical measures of Erikson's concept of identity and what he has found.

Boxed *Insights* offer case histories, cross-cultural perspectives, commentary, and applications of ideas and topics discussed in the text. Important terms, highlighted in boldface type, are defined in the text and in a glossary at the end of the book. Each chapter contains a summary and an annotated list of suggested readings. Most chapters conclude with a *Highlights Chart* that gives an overview of developments in the area and age range covered in the chapter. The wall chart enclosed with each copy of the text is designed to help students visualize the intertwining threads of cognitive, social-emotional, and physical development, from conception to adulthood. The set of ethical standards for research with children published by the Society for Research in Child Development makes up the appendix.

The test file, study guide, and instructor's manual for *Understanding Development* focus on a grasp of the major concepts in the text as well as on factual knowledge.

Throughout, our goal has been to make sophisticated ideas easy to understand. We believe that students who are majoring in psychology and considering a career in the field will find the book informative and provocative. We also believe that students who are majoring in business, nursing, English, or another field and are taking developmental psychology as a required course or elective will come away with a deeper appreciation of children, parenthood, friendships, and cognition as these grow and change over the years.

This book arises from a fifteen-year collaboration between two of the authors, Sandra Scarr and Richard A. Weinberg, whose work in developmental behavior genetics and clinical research with schoolchildren, respectively, has produced more than thirty coauthored projects.

Understanding Development is a culmination of our joint thinking, discussions, and synthesizing of developmental psychology. In 1983 we began a fortunate association with writer Ann Levine, whose background in sociology has prompted us to direct more attention to social problems and practical applications.

We thank everyone at Harcourt Brace Jovanovich who helped to turn our dog-eared manuscript into an attractive, stylish book: Marcus Boggs, who supported this project enthusiastically from his first days in San Diego; Craig Avery, our hard-laboring manuscript editor; and the art and production staffs. Judith Greissman, the HBJ alumna who convinced us to write a textbook, has been friend and editor to all of us for many years. We thank Jerome Kagan, General Editor in psychology, for his helpful reviews of early drafts of the manuscript. And we thank the subjects of our profiles for their honesty, humor, insights, and advice.

Sandra Scarr
Richard A. Weinberg
Ann Levine

Acknowledgments

The following people have provided invaluable insights and suggestions for improving the text, and for this we offer our thanks.

Nora Newcombe, Temple University; Stanley Kuczaj, Southern Methodist University; Thomas Berndt, Purdue University; Marc Bornstein, New York University; Gerald Gratch, University of Houston/University Park; Tiffany Field, University of Miami Medical School; Robert Sternberg, Yale University; Linda Smith, Indiana University; Jonathan Baron, University of Pennsylvania; Jeffrey Fagen, St. John's University; Theodore Wachs, Purdue University; Jeanne Brooks-Gunn, Educational Testing Service; John L. Roche, Cape Cod Community College; Chadwick Karr, Portland State University; Willard Hartup, University of Minnesota; Melinda Small, Bowdoin College; Nancy Eisenberg, Arizona State University; Dale Blyth, Ohio State University; Fred Wilson, Appalachian State University; Elizabeth Douvan, University of Michigan; William H. Cunningham, Western Kentucky University; Katherine Nelson, City University of New York Graduate Center; Carol Eckerman, Duke University; Rochel Gelman, University of Pennsylvania; Susan Harter, University of Denver; and Jerome Kagan, Harvard University.

CONTENTS

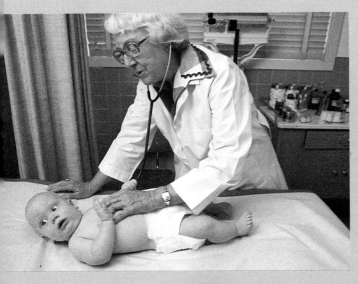

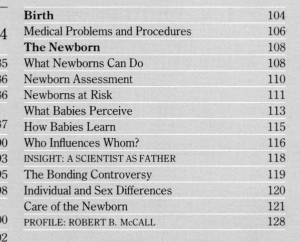

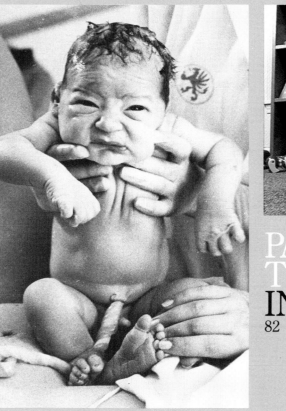

PART
TWO
INFANCY
82

PART THREE
THE PRESCHOOL PERIOD
216

PART FOUR
THE MIDDLE CHILDHOOD YEARS
340

CHAPTER 12
COMING OF AGE

PART
FIVE
ADOLESCENCE
TO ADULTHOOD
494

UNDERSTANDING DEVELOPMENT

*[Development] is a constant process of
transformation, of reconstruction. . . . There are
stages, and phases, and a perpetual knitting together
of what happens, and happened.
—Arnold Gesell, 1928*

The science of developmental psychology has come of age in the 1980s. New and sophisticated research techniques have pushed the boundaries of developmental psychology back to the earliest days of infancy and even earlier, to the prenatal period. The image of the infant as a passive, helpless creature has been replaced by the view that infants are competent social partners, equipped with cries, smiles, and expressions that few adults can ignore. The infant's new status as a social actor has prompted interest in infant temperament and the ways in which babies influence their own experiences. During this period, psychologists have also begun to question the belief that early childhood experiences have irreversible effects on later development.

The "cognitive revolution" that swept through psychology in the 1960s provided new theories and techniques for studying social and emotional development, as well as the development of language and ideas. Research on social cognition, or children's understanding of other people's motives and behavior, added a dimension to the portrait of the school-age child. Psychologists now recognize the positive influence of peers in a child's development—friendships that in the past were often overlooked or dismissed as being harmful.

Most important, the debate over nature vs. nurture that for decades divided developmental psychologists into opposing camps has been largely resolved. Most psychologists have abandoned the one-sided, deterministic views that a child is *either* a product of the environment *or* a prisoner of his genes. Rather, they see development as a result of the interplay between nature *and* nurture, between biological characteristics and experience in a particular family, neighborhood, and culture.

Part 1 of this text traces these developments, beginning with the history of childhood and child psychology in Chapter 1 and ending with a contemporary, biosocial view of "becoming human" in Chapter 2.

PART 1
PRINCIPLES OF
DEVELOPMENT

1

Human beings change dramatically as they progress from birth to adulthood. How and why development occurs—and the roles heredity and environment play in this process—have long been subjects of controversy. A debate between two leading psychologists of the 1920s is a fitting introduction to the comparatively new branch of science known as developmental psychology.

In 1928, the psychologist John B. Watson (1878–1958) issued a warning to parents who were affectionate and demonstrative toward their children:

All we have to start with in building a human being is a lively squirming bit of flesh, capable of making a few simple responses such as movements of the hands and arms and fingers and toes, crying and smiling, making certain sounds with its throat. Parents take this raw material and begin to fashion it in ways to suit themselves. This means that parents, whether they know it or not, start intensive training of the child at birth. (1928, pp. 45–46)

Watson had been studying infants in the laboratories and the newborn nursery of Johns Hopkins Hospital. He was convinced that nothing about a child's development could be taken for granted: Character, personality, and behavior were the results of learning and experience. The environment parents provide determines who their child will become.

Watson described the many ways in which parents can spoil a child's development. He was particularly concerned about "coddling": hugging, kissing, and other displays of affection. Too much mother love would turn a child into a social "invalid." Feeding a baby on demand, picking her up when she cries, were to him "dangerous experiments." Instead, Watson recommended an impersonal, "scientific," emotionally antiseptic approach to raising children:

THE ROOTS OF DEVELOPMENTAL PSYCHOLOGY

Treat them as though they were young adults. Dress them, bathe them with care and circumspection. Let your behavior always be objective and kindly firm. Never hug and kiss them, never let them sit on your lap. If you must, kiss them once on the forehead when they say goodnight. Shake hands with them in the morning. Give them a pat on the head if they have made an extraordinary good job of a difficult task. Try it. In a week's time you will find how easy it is to be perfectly objective with your child and at the same time kindly. You will be utterly ashamed of the mawkish, sentimental way you have been handling it. . . . (1928, pp. 81–82)

Watson held parents wholly responsible for their children's development—an awesome task. In turn, he promised that, with proper

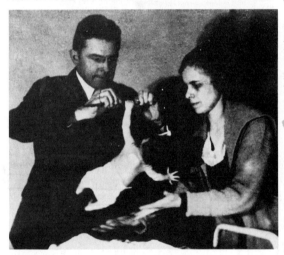

Watson believed that an infant is born with only a few simple reflexes and emotions, and that the developing child's talents, personality, and character are the result of learning. Here Watson is shown testing the grasping reflex.

training, parents could make of their children whatever they wished. Only half in jest, Watson claimed:

Give me a dozen healthy infants, well-formed, and my own specified world to bring them up in and I'll guarantee to take any one at random and train him to become any type of specialist I might select—doctor, lawyer, merchant, chief, and yes, even beggar-man and thief, regardless of his talents, penchants, abilities, vocations, and the race of his ancestors. (1924, p. 104)

Watson's promise that "scientific" child-rearing could work wonders appealed to the democratic ideal that every child has a chance to become a genius or a millionaire.

In the same year the psychologist Arnold Gesell (1880–1961) painted an entirely different portrait of the developing child. According to Gesell, infants are neither as helpless nor as impressionable as they seem. They do require basic care; but unless they are mistreated or are seriously malnourished, Gesell believed, children develop according to nature's plan.

Every normal child is born with a genetically programmed timetable and blueprint for development. Many skills are the result of *maturation*, or physiological and neurological growth, not acquired through learning. What parents do or fail to do is of little consequence.

All things considered, the inevitableness and surety of maturation are the most impressive characteristics

Gesell saw development as the unfolding of the child's natural or innate abilities and devoted much of his career to charting maturation. Here Gesell is shown in his laboratory at Yale University.

of early development. It is the hereditary ballast which conserves and stabilizes the growth of each individual infant. . . . If it did not exist the infant would be [the] victim of a flaccid malleability which is sometimes romantically ascribed to him. His mind, his spirit, his personality would fall a ready prey to disease, to starvation, to malnutrition, and worst of all to misguided management. (1928, p. 378)

Infants are endowed by nature with self-propelled maturation and protected by nature from parental blunders.

With his colleagues at Yale, Gesell established norms or standards for physical growth and behavioral development in the first 5 years of life. He was one of the first psychologists to use motion pictures to analyze behavior and to use twins as controls. For example, if a twin who had been trained in the manner of Watson began to walk at about the same age as one who had not, Gesell reasoned that walking must be the result of maturation, not learning. After many years of studying children, Gesell could state with authority that the average 6-month-old reaches for objects, the 9-month-old babbles in consonant-vowel combinations ("ma-ma," "ba-ba"), the 2-year-old stacks blocks, and the 3-year-old can name many parts of the body.

Gesell's standards, refined in the Bayley Tests of Mental and Motor Development (see Chapter 4) and the Denver Development Screening Test, are still in use today. They enable pediatricians to identify children who lag far behind most of their age-mates and who may require special care or treatment. Gesell was careful to point out, however, that each child's rate of development is different, that these differences are normal, and that the rate itself does not predict a child's future accomplishments. The baby who walks ahead of schedule will not necessarily win a footrace at age 8. Nor is the early talker destined to become the state debating champion at age 16. Slow developers have just as good a chance of becoming winners as those who develop more quickly. For Gesell, each child is on his or her own schedule of development that must be understood and respected:

The inborn tendency toward optimum development is so inveterate that [the baby] benefits liberally from what is good in our practice, and suffers less than he logically should from our unenlightenment. Only if we give respect to this inner core of inheritance can we respect the important individual differences which distinguish infants as well as men. (1928, p. 378)

Gesell advised parents to sit back and relax.

Writing in the same year, Watson and Gesell presented diametrically opposed versions of child development and entirely different prescriptions for parenting (Scarr, 1984). Watson's baby is an unformed ball of clay that parents must shape to their wishes. Gesell's baby is a robust biological organism, equipped by evolution to develop into a normal adult and a unique individual. According to Watson, rearing a child is like building a house. The builders—the parents—determine whether the house will be large or small, Colonial or Tudor in style. How sturdily the house is built depends on how much the builders invest and whether they pay careful attention to architectural details and furnishings. Once the foundation is laid, however, it is difficult to change the basic plan. Poor habits established in early childhood are difficult to correct. Gesell, on the other hand, suggested that raising a child is more like planting a tulip garden. All the parents as gardeners must do is to plant the bulb in good soil, water it, and wait for spring. The height, color, and shape of the flower has already been determined by heredity. The gardeners can affect how well the tulip grows by tending it carefully or carelessly, but they cannot change its basic form. Similarly, the basic pattern of a child's development is determined at conception. For Gesell, good parental care can allow the child to become the best possible version of herself.

The one point on which these two psychologists agreed was that child development is worthy of scientific study. This was a revolutionary idea in the 1920s. The days when most parents would look to experts for advice in child-rearing lay in the future. Indeed, psychologists knew very little about what the infant could see and hear, why toddlers can be so negative, or how 4-year-olds think. These discoveries also lay in the future.

How did children find their way from the nursery to the laboratory? Where do contemporary psychologists stand in the Watson–Gesell debate? The first part of this chapter traces the roots of developmental psychology in social history. The second part describes how developmental psychologists think and work today. The final section previews topics and issues that will be explored in depth in later chapters of this book.

A Model of Development

Human development begins with a single cell, the fertilized egg, which is smaller than the period at the end of this sentence. Within hours of conception, this cell begins to divide and multiply. At four days, it is a cluster of three to four dozen cells known as a "mulberry." By four weeks, the embryo has a distinct head, heart, liver, digestive tract, and tail. At four months, the fetus can kick, make a fist, turn its head, squint, frown, and swallow, although it is months from using this behavior to adapt to independent life.

Biologists have charted the day-to-day progress of the embryo and fetus, identifying stages of development, substances that direct and disrupt growth, and the overall plan that produces specific organs and functions at the proper time. In much the same way, developmental psychologists chart the progress of a human being from birth through infancy, childhood, and adolescence to adulthood.

The psychologist Heinz Werner (1948) saw the development of the embryo and fetus as a model for other aspects and stages of development. For Werner, all development depends on two processes. The first is *differentiation:* cells that are identical at conception develop into different body parts, each with its specific form and function (such as the heart and liver). The second process is *integration:* the various parts of the body interconnect, producing a more complex and flexible organism—one that can kick and frown, for instance. Human development is more than simple growth or change over time. The shape of a rock changes over time because of erosion, but rocks do not develop. Simple organisms such as algae or sponges grow larger, but each new cell is a duplicate of the parent cell; there is no differentiation or reorganization of newer cells. These organisms do not develop, either. By contrast, early human cells produce, not their own kind, but an enormous variety of highly specialized cells that perform diverse functions. In Gesell's words, development is

a constant process of transformation, of reconstruction. The past is not retained with the same completeness as in the tree. The past is sloughed as well as projected, it is displaced and even transmuted to a degree which the anatomy of a tree does not suggest. There are stages, and phases, and a perpetual knitting together of what happens and happened. [Development] is a process of constant incorporation, revision, [and] reorganization. . . . The reorganization is so pervading that the past almost loses its identity. (1928, p. 22)

Like physiological growth, behavioral development is an orderly sequence of changes. All infants creep before they stand, stand before they walk, and walk before they run. Language development reveals a similar pattern. Most normal children babble at about 6 months, begin to use single words between 11 months and 14 months, start putting two words together by the end of their second year, and produce complex sentences at age 3. All children progress from sound to sense at about the same time and in much the same way. There is even an orderly sequence in the development of play. Infants amuse themselves by mouthing, squeezing, and banging their toys or anything else they can grasp. At around 1 year their play becomes more imitative and social. The infant puts her doll in its bed, rather than in her mouth or on the back of a toy dump truck. During the second year she begins to engage in symbolic play, pretending that a wooden block is a boat and that the living room carpet is a lake. Elaborate games of make-believe emerge at about the same age in all children, regardless of their society, culture, or living circumstances.

As a general rule, development proceeds from simple, general, or global acts to differentiated and integrated sets of activities. For example, the child progresses from one-word utterances that apply to many different situations to complex accounts of specific experiences; from one form of locomotion (creeping) to balanced pirouettes, gymnastics, or end-runs on the football field. The development of moral judgment also illustrates this progression. Small children have simple, broad notions of right and wrong. They tend to judge behavior in terms of concrete consequences. A child of 4 or 5 considers that a boy who steals an apple because he is poor and hungry is as "bad" as a boy who steals an apple for fun. Older children are more likely to judge a person's behavior in terms of his or her intentions. A child of 10 or 11 considers motivations and recognizes different degrees of wrongness. Most adolescents begin to judge behavior in terms of abstract ideals. They reason about hypothetical situations as well as actual occurrences. Indeed, adolescents often frustrate adults with their idealistic attacks on the Establishment and logical arguments for what

seem to be impractical and unrealistic plans.

The adolescent who argues that stockpiling nuclear arms to prevent war is illogical has come a long way from the fertilized egg. The full story of the changes a person undergoes on that journey must wait for later chapters. The key point here is that **development** is an orderly, cumulative sequence of changes that leads to increasing differentiation, integration, and complexity. This applies to intellectual, emotional, and social development as well as to physical and motor development—or so psychologists believe today.

A History of Childhood

The concept of development and the belief that children are different and special are relatively modern ideas. In the Middle Ages, childhood as we know it did not exist. This does not mean that children were universally neglected or disliked. Adults simply did not think of childhood as a unique and important stage in life (Aries, 1962).

The period from birth to age 6 or 7 was seen as a biologically necessary prelude to the socially important business of adulthood. Youngsters graduated from early childhood directly into adulthood. As soon as they were able to perform useful tasks, they were put to work alongside adults and expected to earn their keep. Wealthy families sent their sons to work as pages in the households of their kinsmen; peasants sent their children to work in the fields or apprenticed them to craftsmen or tradesmen. Most children did not marry until they were sexually mature, at puberty, but in all other ways their immaturity was ignored. No one sought to shield them from the facts of life. In the Middle Ages children were seen as miniature, imperfect adults.

William Shakespeare is widely regarded as the greatest interpreter of the human condition in the English language. Yet children are conspicuously missing from his plays. When Shakespeare does refer to children it is to evoke an image of foolishness and incompetence:

> All the world's a stage,
> And all the men and women merely
> players.
> They have their exits and their entrances,
> And one man in his time plays many parts,
> His acts being seven ages. At first the
> infant,
> Mewling and puking in the nurse's arms.
> Then the whining school-boy, with his
> satchel
> And shining morning face, creeping like
> snail
> Unwillingly to school.
>
> . . . .
>
> Last scene of all,
> That ends this strange eventful history,
> Is second childishness and mere oblivion,
> Sans teeth, sans eyes, sans taste, sans
> everything.
> (As You Like It, 2.7. 138–65)

The Discovery of Childhood

Ideas about children began to change during the Renaissance. The English philosopher John Locke (1632–1704) was one of the first to include children in his speculations on human nature. Locke's position anticipated that of Watson. He described the infant's mind as a blank slate, or *tabula rasa,* on which experience would write. He believed that the early years were a formative period and assigned parents—not God or nature—responsibility for shaping the child's character. It was their duty to teach the child reason, self-restraint, and respect for authority. Locke advocated strict but humane treatment of children. A half-century later the Swiss-French philosopher Jean-Jacques Rousseau (1712–1778) painted a radically different picture. Like Gesell almost two centuries later,

Rousseau believed that children develop according to nature's plan. Left to their own devices, they seek opportunities to learn and draw the proper lessons from their experiences. According to Rousseau, instruction was largely irrelevant. The parent's duty was to protect the child from corrupting influences and unnecessary interference. For different reasons, both Locke and Rousseau held that children have their own particular needs and abilities, and that they should be valued for what they *are* as well as for what they will become.

Some children profited from these new ideas. In the seventeenth and eighteenth centuries, upper- and middle-class youngsters began to spend more time in schoolrooms and less time in the adult world. But children of the lower classes did not gain their freedom from fields, mines, and factories until the twentieth century. The child labor laws that removed young people from the labor force, and the school attendance laws that put them into classrooms, were not enforced until the early 1900s in the United States. Thus childhood—as a time to learn, explore, and play—was an idea before it became a reality for many young people.

The Rise of Adolescence

While childhood was first discovered during the Renaissance, adolescence is a twentieth century invention. Puberty, the physiological changes that occur in the early teens, is universal; but adolescence, the psychological and social changes accompanying puberty, is not. Some traditional societies hold rites of passage to mark the transition from childhood to adulthood; in others the change is gradual and smooth. But few institutionalize an in-between stage.

In stable agricultural societies, where occupations are passed from parent to child, one generation merges into the next. Industrialization opens a gap between the experiences of parent and child, creating a new period of occupational training and choice. In advanced technological societies this period has been extended as more young people pursue advanced education and remain financially dependent on their families into their twenties.

Rousseau is credited with first identifying the "symptoms" of adolescence: "He becomes deaf to the voice he used to obey; he is a lion in fever; he distrusts his keeper and refuses to be controlled" (Kessen, 1965, p. 93). But it was the American psychologist G. Stanley Hall (1844–1924) who made adolescence a household word when he published his ambitious *Adolescence: Its Psychology and Its Relations to Physiology, Anthropology, Sociology, Sex, Crime,* *Religion, and Education* in 1904. Hall also played a major role in establishing the science of child-rearing in the United States.

The Science of Child-rearing

The roots of developmental psychology lie in the late nineteenth century. When Charles Darwin (1809–1882) published *The Origin of Species* in 1859, he established a turning point for psychologists as well as for biologists (Kessen, 1965). Darwin had amassed evidence that humans are part of the natural order and subject to the same natural laws as other species. It was only a matter of time before scholars would begin to draw parallels between the evolution of humankind

and the development of a child. In 1877 Darwin published his observations of his son William Erasmus, or "Doddy" (see Figure 1-1). It was not an ordinary "baby book," for in it Darwin was seeking common threads in the behavior of humans and other animals. Doddy's animated behavior as a newborn provided missing links. His reflexes seemed to echo an earlier stage of evolution. The idea that *ontogeny* (the development of the individual) *recapitulates* (or repeats) *phylogeny* (the evolution of the species) captured the attention of the scientific community. Many psychologists and biologists in the late nineteenth century viewed the child as a natural museum of the history of humankind (Borstelman, 1983). The infant's behavior was seen as a living record of our species' evolutionary history. This view of development was discredited around the turn of the century. The developing embryo and child do not recapitulate evolution. But the belief that studying children was a valid part of the search for laws of human behavior took seed.

While scientists continued to debate the nature of the child, nonscientists began translating concern for child welfare into concrete programs (Siegel & White, 1982). Numerous orphanages, adoption agencies, and foster care programs were established across the United States in the 1860s, in the belief that all small children have a right to basic care. The first Society for the Prevention of Cruelty to Children was created in 1874, with branches in New York and Massachusetts. In the 1880s concern for small children was extended to youth in the form of juvenile courts and training schools intended for young people whose families had failed them in one way or another. In the 1890s child-savers and health workers focused on establishing milk programs and building open-air playgrounds for the urban poor. The pressure to

During the first seven days various reflex actions, namely sneezing, hiccoughing, yawning, stretching, and of course sucking and screaming, were well performed by my infant. On the seventh day, I touched the naked sole of his foot with a bit of paper, and he jerked it away, curling at the same time his toes, like a much older child when tickled. The perfection of these reflex movements show that the extreme imperfection of the voluntary ones is not due to the state of the muscles or the coordinating centers. At this time, though so early, it seemed clear to me that a warm soft hand applied to his face [evoked] a wish to suck. This must be considered as a reflex or an instinctive action, for it is impossible to believe that experience and association with the touch of his mother's breast could so soon have come into play. (Darwin, 1877)

Darwin and his son "Doddy."

In the Renaissance, children were seen as miniature adults.

Figure 1-1 Darwin's Baby Diary

enforce child-labor and compulsory-education laws mounted.

By the turn of the century, a number of groups had developed strong interests in children: scientists who sought to legitimize child study; educators who dreamed of colleges for teachers; school administrators who wanted standardized tests to help them manage the growing number of elementary and high-school students; social workers who sought scientific data and lines of communication to their colleagues around the country; clinical psychologists, whom Freud had convinced that early childhood was a critical period in psychological development; and, most of all, parents, who needed encouragement and company in a changing world. But there was no forum where these diverse groups could meet to exchange information and ideas. The child-study movement lacked organization and structure.

G. Stanley Hall gave the movement momentum. The first American to earn a Ph.D. in psychology, the first American to study in Wilhelm Wundt's psychology laboratory in Germany, and the first president of the American Psychological Association, Hall convened the first National Child Welfare Congress at Clark University in 1909. There he announced plans to create a children's institute whose members would engage in research, run a school and health clinic, and "coordinate science and social activism for children" (Siegel & White, 1982, p. 280). Although the institute at Clark University did not materialize, Hall's plan provided a model for others. The first actual child-research center was established in Iowa in 1917 (Sears, 1975). Cora Bussey Hillis, a housewife and mother, had been campaigning for a child-study center for over a decade. The many successes of science in medicine and engineering around the turn of the century had convinced Mrs. Hillis and others that a science of child-rearing was both necessary and possible. If scientists could help farmers raise better corn and hogs, she asked, why couldn't they help parents raise better children?

The child-study movement came into its own in the 1920s. Major centers for research were founded at the Fels Institute, the Universities of California and Minnesota, and Yale and Columbia Universities. Courses in child development were introduced at many schools. The basic aim of these institutes was to improve the lives of small children by educating them and their parents.

Through most of history, children had been seen as servants to their parents, families, and communities. Society tried to rid them of their childish deficiencies and hurry them into adulthood. The contrary view—that communities, families, and parents should serve the best interests of the child—has only been taken seriously since the last century, and for the most part in the United States (Borstelmann, 1983). The child-study movement arose from this dramatic shift in attitude toward the young.

Developmental Psychology Comes of Age

The creation of child-study centers in the 1920s did not produce a new branch of psychology overnight. Indeed, developmental psychology did not establish itself as an independent field of study until the 1950s (Kessen, 1965). Before then child study was considered to be a stepchild of general psychology. Only those in the fields of education and home economics seemed to appreciate the revolution in thinking about children: often, courses in child development were taught in these departments rather than in the department of psychology. One reason for this was that psychology in the United States from the 1930s to the 1950s was dominated by

The class of 1911, South Pittstown, Pennsylvania. Until the 1920s there was no law against putting young children to work in mines, factories, or fields.

behaviorists and by psychoanalysts; neither school dealt directly with the developing child. As we will see later in this chapter, behaviorists were interested in discovering universal principles of learning that transcend differences in species, age, or circumstance. Psychoanalysts focused on the echoes of early childhood experiences in adult personality. Studying child development itself was not considered to be serious psychology.

This attitude would soon change. In the late 1950s, American psychologists discovered the Swiss psychologist Jean Piaget's (1896–1980) theory of cognitive development. Piaget was interested in how people come to understand the world. Systematic observation of his own three children had convinced him that children are active learners, not passive recipients of adult teachings; that intellectual development begins in infancy and continues into adolescence; and that during the course of development there are major, qualitative changes in the way children think. Jerome Bruner's studies at Harvard confirmed the view that children actively seek to make sense of their worlds. Piaget, Bruner, and other developmental psychologists not only challenged many popular assumptions about children, they also pioneered the field of cognitive psychology.

Once psychologists began to think of small children as active learners, it was almost inevitable that they would discover the "remarkable infant." Newborn babies can see, hear, smell, and respond to what they perceive. Twenty-five years ago no responsible psychologist would have made this statement. But William Kessen and his students at Yale, Lewis P. Lipsitt at Brown, Robert Fantz at Case Western, and many others contributed to the image of the infant as an aware, capable, and social being. The question many psychologists ask today is not how parents influence babies, but how babies influence their parents.

The "remarkable infant" raised questions about how much of human behavior is inborn. In the late 1950s and the 1960s, a number of social scientists became interested in the evolutionary origins of human behavior. Linguist Noam Chomsky of the Massachusetts Institute of Technology and others began to study language from an evolutionary perspective. Are humans "wired" for speech? Reports on apes who had been taught sign language—including one named Nim Chimpsky—provided a counterpoint to observations of small children. The British psychologist John Bowlby developed an evolutionary interpretation of attachment and loss in children, work that was extended in this country by Mary Ainsworth and her colleagues. Harry Harlow's studies of "mother love" in rhesus monkeys addressed a similar question: What is the adaptive function of affection?

Sociobiologists went several steps further. In the tradition of Konrad Lorenz, who had studied the biological roots of aggression, Harvard biologist Edward Wilson and others proposed that *all* social behavior is biologically determined in humans as well as in other animals. This view was not a return to older theories that simplistically labeled all behavior as instinctive. Rather, sociobiology is a renewed appreciation for the evolved nature of all learning, including learning to be social in human ways. Still other psychologists began investigating the genetic basis of individual and group differences in intelligence as measured by IQ tests.

The changing role of women in our society also challenged developmental psychology. The idea that girls are "sugar and spice and everything nice," destined to play with dolls and become full-time mothers, is being replaced by the belief that one's gender should not determine one's toys, interests, vocational choices, or income. Are masculinity and femininity the product of nature (Gesell's view), nurture (Watson's view), or the interaction of the two (a more

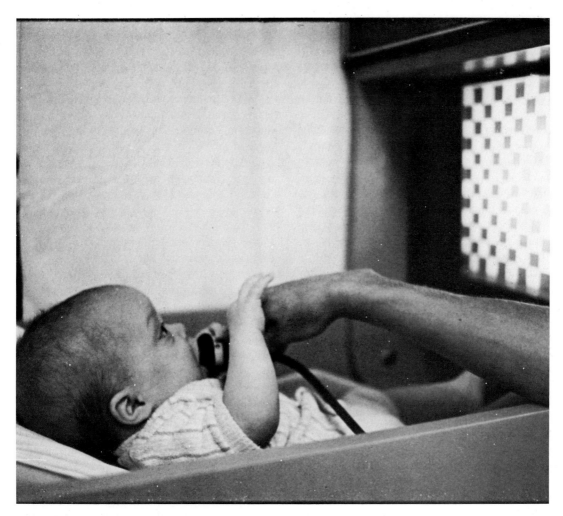

The word *infant* comes from the Latin word for
"without speech." Babies cannot tell researchers
what they see and hear, and until the 1960s
psychologists knew little about the infant's world.
Then researchers invented a number of ingenious
methods for discovering whether infants can perceive
patterns, distinguish meaningful communications
from meaningless noise, or tell their mother from
another person. Here researchers are testing
whether a baby will suck harder to bring a
checkerboard pattern into focus.

contemporary view)? Newborns and small children are major sources of information about sex similarities and differences. Moreover, the fact that women are moving from the kitchen and the car pool to the boardroom and the operating room—as surgeons instead of nurses—has resulted in new family lifestyles, such as dual-career marriages and households in which the husband stays at home. How do children fare in these families? Many researchers are now focusing their efforts on the father's role in his child's development and on the impact that divorce and single-parenthood have on children.

In short, many new frontiers in development psychology opened in the 1960s and 1970s. Both cognitive psychologists and evolutionary psychologists challenged the extreme environmentalism of the 1950s. The concept of the child as being a blank slate, as being merely a product of his or her environment, was shattered. Today, developmental psychologists see the child as an *active* learner, who may be genetically predisposed to learn certain things at certain times, and as an active social partner, who has a natural ability to evoke emotional responses from adults and an inborn disposition to form attachments to them. Current research emphasizes the growing child's competencies. Moreover, these new ideas have influenced psychologists who are not directly concerned with children. Developmental psychology has come into its own.

The Age of Kids

Like the miniature adult of the Middle Ages, Locke's child of reason, and Rousseau's child of nature, the new image of the child matches the times.

The cognitive revolution in psychology occurred during a national panic over the focus of education. When the United States lost the "race to space" to the Soviet Union, America blamed its schools: Children were not receiving adequate training in mathematics and physical sciences; the next generation of scientists and technicians was studying poetry and human relations. In the late 1950s "sputnik[1] fever" led the federal government to pour millions of dollars into science curricula that would interest young people in physics, engineering, and other "hard" sciences. The interest in cognitive development within psychology reflected these concerns.

Soon the spotlight shifted from turning third-graders into scientists to molding brilliant preschoolers. Some educators attempted to use behaviorism and learning theory to accelerate the development of language and thought in small children. Others looked to Piaget and Bruner for inspiration. New kindergartens were designed to provide children with structured stimulation. Play was encouraged, not because it was fun for children, but because it was good for their minds. A new industry was born: edu-

[1] On October 4, 1957, the USSR launched Sputnik I, the first artificial earth satellite.

Head Start, a massive program to provide poor and minority children with medical care and preparation for school, illustrates how dramatically ideas about children had changed by the 1960s. Lady Bird Johnson, the First Lady, was a longtime advocate of aid to underprivileged children.

cational toys. No nursery was complete without a musical, multicolor mobile. Revised baby and child-care books guided parents in their efforts to turn their toddlers into geniuses (Clarke-Stewart, 1978). (This marketing trend continues today with ads that imply that parents who do not provide their 3-year-olds with a computer are not taking proper care of their children's development.) Middle-class children were not the only ones to be affected by these ideas. Project Head Start was a massive preschool intervention plan to provide economically disadvantaged children, often those of minorities, with comprehensive health and educational services. President Lyndon Johnson made this project a cornerstone of his War on Poverty.

The nationwide interest in children's rights is another legacy of this period. Child advocacy groups, such as the Children's Defense Fund, have called attention to research on such problems as the extent and prevention of child abuse, providing handicapped children with mainstream education rather than special classes, and, in general, the task of offering children the emotional, social, and educational opportunities that foster optimal development.

When historians attempt to describe the preoccupations, interests, and focus of American society during the second half of the twentieth century, they might choose terms such as "The Age of Aquarius," "The Nuclear Age," "The Age of Lost Innocence"—or they might label our times "The Age of Kids."

Our concern with children and their development sets us apart from other times and cultures. Never before have so many profession-

als—from psychologists to politicians—been so concerned with children. In some ways, kids have never had it so good. Children in developed nations are better protected from disease and abuse than at any time in the past. (There are tragic exceptions, however. See Insight: Who Is for Children?)

The Age of Kids is not over. If anything, it has just begun. The closer professionals and politicians look at the needs of children, the more they recognize what remains to be done. We have come a long way from the view of youngsters as "little adults." Today we appreciate the significance of different periods of the lifespan, for we have discovered that infants, children, and adolescents each have distinctive ways of thinking and being. One of the major discoveries of the Age of Kids is that child behavior needs to be understood in its own right.

Contemporary Theories of Development

The goal of developmental psychology is to describe and explain the changes that occur on the route from infancy to adulthood and to suggest ways in which adults who live and work with children can apply this information to real life situations.

In the 1930s and 1940s, the early days of developmental psychology, the emphasis was on description: establishing accurate timetables of human development and accurate measures of individual differences. In the 1950s and 1960s, developmental psychologists began to move beyond description and measurement and tackled the hows and whys of development. New voices joined the debate between Watson and Gesell as the study of youngsters became more sophisticated and specialized.

Five distinct approaches to developmental psychology emerged from this latter period. These theoretical schools differ in the behavior they seek to explain. *Psychobiological* approaches focus on the biological underpinnings of relatively simple or abnormal behavior. *Behaviorist* theories emphasize events in the person's immediate environment that might explain his or her observable behavior. *Structuralist* approaches infer rules in the person's mind that shape, or structure, his or her behavior. *Psychodynamic* theories look to biological and social events to explain subjective experiences and interpersonal behavior. The *ecological* perspective uses information about the person's socioeconomic, cultural, and physical setting to analyze behavior. A full explanation of child development depends on all five approaches.

Psychobiological Approaches

Psychobiologists study the biochemistry of behavior. Ten or fifteen years ago, many psychologists rejected studies of the relation between human biochemistry and human behavior as simplistic. This attitude has changed, and psychobiologists have earned a respected place in developmental psychology. It may be true that the human mind and heart cannot be reduced to a series of biochemical reactions. But it is equally true that one cannot understand the mind and heart without understanding how the brain works.

The adult brain has billions of cells organized into networks that transmit impulses via biochemical changes. The groundwork is laid during prenatal development, but these networks continue to form over the first few years of life. The speed of neural conduction increases rapidly, and experiences are coded and stored in the brain. Without these biological changes, infants would never come to think and act like adults.

The biological reasons for some types of behavioral development are clear. Infants do not perceive the world as adults do. Newborn babies can detect shapes, but the fine details of their environment are blurred. They cannot rec-

Insight

WHO IS FOR CHILDREN?

Marian Wright Edelman of the Children's Defense Fund reports (1981) that at the beginning of the 1980s:

- Over 17 percent of American children— 10 million youngsters—are poor. This figure includes one in every six preschoolers.
- Only a sixth of the nation's poorest children receive the health care to which they are legally entitled; less than a quarter are served by Head Start; only a half million youngsters receive mental health care.
- Seven out of ten teenage mothers receive no prenatal health care.
- The debate over day-care standards drags on. Meanwhile, the nation will need at least 1 million more day-care places and 1.6 million more day-care workers before the end of the decade.

Edelman continues:

We have a long way to go. At the moment, children are the easiest people in America to ignore. They do not vote, lobby, or make campaign contributions. Demographers tell us to expect more childless couples, fewer children, later childbearing, and an increasingly older population. Inflation, unemployment, and uncertainty about the future have fueled fear and selfish instincts. Calls for preventive services like child care to help families with parents who work, are single, are teenagers, or [who] simply cannot cope are immediately attacked by some claiming to want to protect the family. Competition for scarce resources has pitted human services proponents against each other rather than against the political untouchables that are the real budget breakers. Amidst protestations of "Who can be against children?" too few people are *for* children when it really matters. (p. 111)

Edelman cites a number of myths that create obstacles to programs for children and families.

- *Myth 1:* "Only other people's children have problems." This usually means poor, minority, non-English-speaking youngsters. In fact, white youngsters are more often arrested for vandalism, drug abuse, running away, or drunken driving.
- *Myth 2:* "Families are self-sufficient; they should take care of their own children." No family is totally self-sufficient. All families need the services of doctors, teachers, housekeepers or baby sitters, and perhaps unemployment compensation or student loans, from time to time.
- *Myth 3:* "Child advocates want the government to take control over the lives of families and children." No one favors government intrusion. But the fact is that government programs and policies (tax laws, school decisions, and so on) already affect families. The aim of child advocates is to see that these programs help children and strengthen families.

Edelman concludes that developmental psychologists have a special responsibility for children.

We must become fiscally hard-nosed and ensure the most cost-effective use of our service dollars. We must also become more willing to hold ourselves accountable for the level, quality, and responsiveness of services provided; to monitor or be monitored; and to ensure compliance with emerging professional and legislative expectations. . . . More of us must join together in a network for children and work both within states and nationally to become a strong voice for positive policies for children. (p. 114)

ognize their parents' faces, or respond to a smile, until their eyes and brains mature. (Newborns have 20/200 vision.) Infants of less than 9 or 10 months cannot walk because their nerve–muscle connections are not sufficiently mature to allow independent, coordinated stepping. When the nervous system matures, however, they walk without instruction. Adolescents "fall in love"; children do not. One reason adolescents pine is that sex hormones are surging through their bodies.

The biological basis for other types of behavioral development are less clear to psychologists. No amount of coaching will induce infants of less than a year to speak in meaningful phrases. Yet at about 12 months all normal babies begin learning their parents' language. Why does it occur at this age? No one knows. Which brain structures control attention and memory? To what extent are the differences in behavior between men and women stimulated by hormones? These and many other questions have yet to be answered.

Many studies of abnormal behavior, especially of mental retardation and severe psychological disorders, point to biochemical imbalances in the brain. Too much or little of an essential substance will cause abnormal brain development. In some instances the causes are genetic; in others disease or injury upset the biochemistry of the nervous system. Drugs or diet may help to restore these biochemical balances. Such discoveries about abnormal behavior provide clues to the psychobiology of normal development.

Biological studies are often helpful in identifying some of the causes of our behavior. But they seldom, if ever, tell the whole behavioral story. Infants would not walk if they had no opportunities to practice. Toddlers would not talk if they never heard a language. Adolescents would not fall passionately in love unless their environments provided models of, and opportu- nities for, romance. Biological explanations are often necessary, but rarely are they sufficient, for explaining behavioral development.

Behaviorist Approaches

Behaviorists study observable activities and their causes and consequences in the immediate environment. Although pioneered by the Russian psychologist Ivan Pavlov (1849–1936), behaviorist approaches are in large part a twentieth century American "invention." Through the 1900s, most psychologists defined their field as the study of mental experience. Most research took the form of introspection: the psychologist observed and recorded his or her own feelings and thoughts. In the 1920s, Watson and others rebelled against this subjectivity. A true science, Watson argued, is the study of behavior, or activities that can be observed. And, according to Watson, all behavior is *learned*, including love, hate, fear, laughter, identity, and self-esteem, as well as academic knowledge and skills. The environment determines who and what the infant will become. As elaborated by B. F. Skinner, Albert Bandura, and others, behaviorist theories dominated American psychology for almost half a century.

The simplest form of learning is **classical conditioning,** or learning to associate a new stimulus with an existing response. When a newborn is stroked on the cheek, he turns toward the touch and prepares to suck. This is an automatic or *unconditioned response* (UR). Over the first weeks of life, this experience is paired repeatedly with the feeling of being picked up, the sound of his mother's voice, the sight of her breast or a bottle, and other stimuli. At 3 weeks the infant doesn't wait for a touch on the cheek, but opens his mouth when he sees a bottle. This is a *conditioned response* (CR), which is based on a learned association. The same process can be seen in older children and adults. Just as 3-year-old Maria reaches out to play with a teddy bear, a loud crash of thunder frightens her. She cries and runs to her mother for comfort. After a short time she returns to the teddy bear. A second thunderclap terrifies her. She flees to her mother's side and later refuses to go near the bear, even though the sun is shining. Maria's fear of the thunderclap is an unconditioned response; her fear of the stuffed bear, a condi-

tioned response. This pattern of learning is diagrammed in Figure 1-2.

Conditioned responses may be *generalized,* or extended to other, related stimuli. A child who has been frightened by a dog may become fearful of all dogs and other animals. An adolescent boy who feels he has been humiliated by one girl may become defensive with all girls and withdraw from dating.

A somewhat more complex form of association called **operant conditioning,** entails learning that behavior has consequences. A 5-month-old girl is lying in her crib, twisting, kicking, and cooing. Her behavior is spontaneous; she is operating on the environment for the fun of it. Then she notices that the mobile above her head moved when she kicked. She kicks again and produces the same response. Delighted by the twirling mobile, she kicks and kicks again. Simply put, people (and other organisms) tend to repeat behavior for which they have been rewarded (see Figure 1-3). The technical term for rewards is *reinforcement.* Reinforcement may take the form of tangible payoffs, such as candy for a toddler who used the toilet or flowers for a date, or intangible returns, such as attention, praise, an interesting experience (such as the dancing mobile), or the pure satisfaction of accomplishing a difficult task. Behavior that is not reinforced—that produces no response—is unlikely to be repeated. It has been *extinguished.*

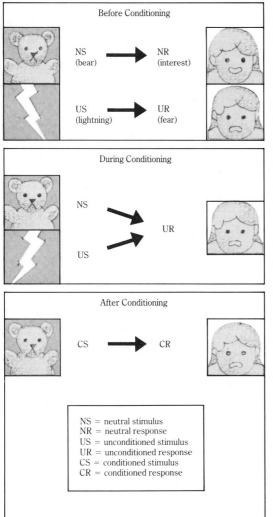

NS = neutral stimulus
NR = neutral response
US = unconditioned stimulus
UR = unconditioned response
CS = conditioned stimulus
CR = conditioned response

Figure 1-2 Classical Conditioning

Operant conditioning has many practical applications. Teaching machines and programmed learning texts, for example, reinforce learning in the form of immediate feedback. Operant conditioning may also be used to affect social behavior, such as that of a young boy who does not participate in group activities in kindergarten. If the teacher rewards his occasional attempts at group play by praising him and putting an arm around his shoulders, but ignores him when he stands alone in a corner, the child will begin to join the group more often. By rewarding *successive approximations,* or behavior that increasingly resembles a goal, one can shape desired behavior. In this way pigeons have been taught to play Ping-Pong (Skinner, 1960) and children taught language and cognitive skills (Semb, 1972). Using these principles to change human behavior is called *behavior modification.*

Social learning theorists such as Albert Bandura add that children also learn by *imitating* models and receiving rewards, sometimes vicariously. Children will copy the behavior of a *model* who rewards them, of models they admire, and of models who themselves are rewarded. ("That boy was praised for using the potty, *I* will be, too.")

Behaviorists do not believe it is necessary to describe what is going on inside the person in order to explain development. Neither do they consider the individual's wider socioeconomic environment. According to their view, the child is a product of the *immediate* environment.

Figure 1-3 Operant Conditioning

Structuralist Approaches

Just as behaviorist approaches were a rebellion against the excessive introspection of early psychology, so structuralist approaches began as a rebellion against the excessive environmentalism of behaviorists. Structuralists see behaviorist explanations as overly mechanistic: put a stimulus in the machine, pull the reinforcement

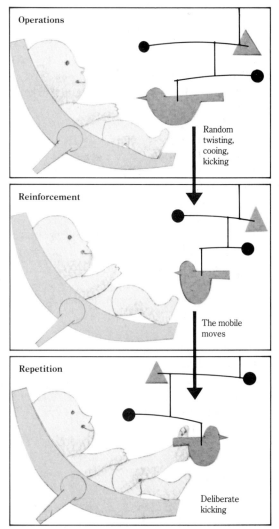

lever, and out pops a response. Structuralists argue, first, that conditioned associations explain only the simplest forms of human learning. In their view, when a person is presented with new information—a stimulus—he or she compares it to information stored in the memory, thinks about possible reactions, and then organizes a response. Simply put, something happens between the stimulus and the response. Second, structuralists argue that the behaviorist view is essentially *non*developmental: It does not acknowledge changes in the structure or organization of a person's thought and behavior. Behaviorists see the complex behavior of adults as the accumulation of simple behaviors, or a change in the *quantity* of behavior from childhood to adulthood. Structuralists see the development from child to adult as the achievement of new levels of organization and functioning, or a change in the *quality* of behavior.

The development of simple empathy illustrates structural change. Two-year-olds often comfort dolls, stuffed animals, and even chairs and ashtrays that have been dropped or hit. They operate on the rule, "If it hurts me, it hurts other things." Five-year-olds may pretend to comfort a teddy bear, but they know it is only a toy. Moreover, they exclude ashtrays and other objects from the realm of pretend-hurt. Through observation and experience, they have learned that feeling hurt is usually accompanied by crying, yelping, mewing, or other sounds. They have developed a rule for distinguishing between the animate and the inanimate: "If it can make noise, it can feel hurt." Later they discover that words can also injure and, still later, that people can pretend to feel hurt or not hurt. Reinforcements alone do not explain these reorganizations of understanding.

Structuralism has developed in three broad traditions. The *cognitive* tradition, whose chief exponents are Jean Piaget and Jerome Bruner, is concerned with the development of rules for information processing and problem solving. It focuses on changes in the way children understand the physical and social world and resolve such moral problems as what-and-who-feels-hurt. The *linguistic* tradition, represented by Noam Chomsky and Roger Brown, is dedicated to explaining language development. Human speech, according to this tradition, is so astoundingly complex that children *must* have rules to produce phrases they have never heard and to understand other people's speech. The *ethological* tradition, represented by Konrad Lorenz, Nikko Tinbergen, and the new sociobiologists, is concerned with behavioral development. As a species, we humans have evolved perceptual and conceptual ways of coping with the environment. Rules for behavior are adaptive.

Structuralists from these three traditions share the beliefs that behavior is rule-guided, that rules change with development, and that development proceeds from both maturation and experience. The child develops as a result of actively engaging and exploring his environment, searching for stimulation, and screening, organizing, interpreting, and storing experiences.

Psychodynamic Approaches

Some ideas and feelings are not rational; that is, they do not seem sensible or reasonable to other people. Many highly successful adults feel depressed. Some adolescents feel that their well-intentioned parents are their worst enemies. Some popular children live in constant fear of rejection. Emotions, and the ideas behind them, have a strong influence on our daily lives.

Sigmund Freud (1856–1939), the founder of psychoanalysis, traced these emotional dispositions to the early years of life. He believed that infants are born with powerful sexual and aggressive drives that must be civilized. The focus of sexual energy changes as the child moves from infancy to adolescence. Freud described four stages of psychosexual development: oral, anal, Oedipal, and genital. At each stage the child must learn to gratify his desires in socially acceptable ways. Social standards of conduct are internalized in the conscience. Parents tell the child, "Thou shalt not"; later he forbids himself to do what society condemns. The conflict between the conscience, which Freud called the *superego,* and inner drives, which he called the *id,* creates a coping, adapting part of the personality called the *ego.* A strong ego allows a person to monitor his behavior and to reconcile what he wants to do with what he should do. The control of aggression illustrates this development. Young children tend to strike out directly at those who anger them. They hit, kick, and bite. Older children learn to express anger by insulting, teasing, and swearing. They may feel like physically destroying the other person, but they express their feelings in a socially acceptable manner.

Freud held that unresolved conflicts between the id and the superego result in anxiety.

To control anxiety, we develop *defense mechanisms.* We redirect id energies into socially acceptable channels (sublimation), give logical explanations for illogical acts (rationalization), and blame others for our own unacceptable feelings (projection). Many unpleasant, ego-threatening experiences are never recorded in conscious memory; this is called repression. But they remain in the unconscious. The idea of the unconscious was one of Freud's most important contributions to psychology. The *unconscious* consists of feelings and experiences that people cannot easily admit to themselves. For example, a mother who is very angry with a colicky baby who cries day and night may not be aware of her anger. She may tell herself and everyone else what a sweet, helpless, blameless creature her baby is. She has developed what Freud called a "reaction formation": that is, hate manifested as love. She may drop the baby on occasion, "accidentally" stick him with diaper pins, and often fail to hear him crying. Thus her anger

shows itself in her behavior. A healthier adaptation would be to admit to herself how angry the baby makes her. This requires a strong ego: mothers are not supposed to feel hate for their infants.

Other theorists have elaborated on Freud's theories. Erik H. Erikson (1963) has proposed a psychosocial theory of personality development that extends over eight stages of the life cycle. Like Freud, he believes that each stage is characterized by a central problem. But Erikson sees these crises as psycho*social*, not psychosexual: the result of social interaction rather than the product of conflict between the id and the superego. As the growing person develops new capabilities and interests, society demands new standards of conduct. (See Figure 1-4.)

Other contemporary followers of Freud have focused on the adaptive, intellectual functions of the ego. Robert White (1960), for example, highlighted our inherent curiosity and exploratory nature. He proposed that a basic motive—the drive to be competent and master one's environment—guides child development. The need to be effective and learn from the environment is added to the primary instincts, sex and aggression, as a driving force of behavioral change.

Ecological Approaches

Like Erikson, ecologists stress the role of the individual's social environment in the development of behavior. Like behaviorists, they pay little attention to what is happening within the person (the focus of the psychodynamic and structuralist approaches). But they go well beyond the behaviorist conception of the environment.

Urie Bronfenbrenner (1977; Bronfenbrenner & Crouter, 1983) sees the developing child's environment as a "nested arrangement of structures, each contained within the next." The *microsystem* is the network of relationships and the physical settings a child is involved with every day. Bronfenbrenner stresses the need to study reciprocal and overlapping influences within this "nest." For example, how does the relationship between the mother and the father affect each parent's handling of the child, and how does the infant's behavior affect their relationship? How does TV influence, not only the child, but the family? Family members often watch a TV show together. Does this increase interaction—that is, does the show give them a common experience to discuss? Or does watching TV decrease interaction—that is, does each person watch and respond in private?

The *mesosystem* is the different groups and settings around the child at different stages of development. The family, and perhaps a babysitter or grandparent's home, are the infant's whole world. The 12-year-old's world includes

In 1909, G. Stanley Hall (seated, center) invited psychologists from all over North America and Europe to a convention at Clark University. One of his guests was Sigmund Freud (seated, left). Although personally impressed with the man, most psychologists resisted Freud's views of child development. Swiss psychologist Carl Jung is seated at right. Standing are (from left) A. A. Brill, Ernest Jones, and Sandor Ferenczi.

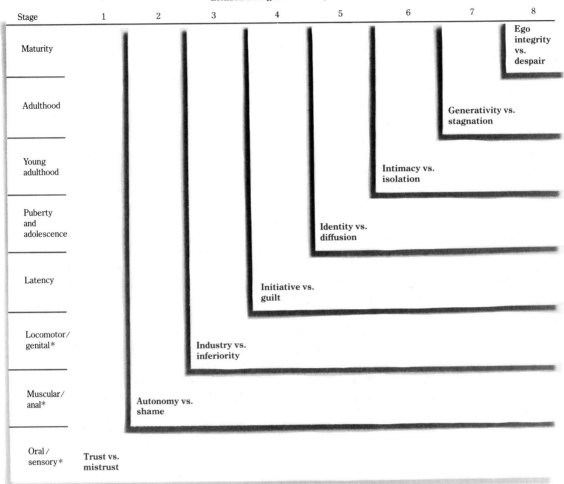

Erikson's Stages of Development

| Stage | 1 | 2 | 3 | 4 | 5 | 6 | 7 | 8 |

Maturity — Ego integrity vs. despair

Adulthood — Generativity vs. stagnation

Young adulthood — Intimacy vs. isolation

Puberty and adolescence — Identity vs. diffusion

Latency — Initiative vs. guilt

Locomotor/ genital* — Industry vs. inferiority

Muscular/ anal* — Autonomy vs. shame

Oral / sensory* — Trust vs. mistrust

Figure 1-4 Erikson's Eight Ages of Man

*Note that Erikson used Freud's terms for stages of psychosexual development, but added more general characteristics (sensory, muscular, locomotor).

(Adapted from Erikson, 1963)

school, friends, the local shopping center, perhaps church groups and summer camp, as well as the family. Bronfenbrenner suggests that there have been too few studies of how the *same* person behaves in different settings and adapts to new social roles and activities.

The *exosystem* is composed of social structures that affect the child's life directly or indirectly: the world of work, the mass media, the school system, and transportation facilities. For example, whether a mother reads to her child depends on if she works, the hours of her job, how much time she spends commuting to and from work, whether someone else helps with cleaning and cooking, her social and recreational life, the value she places on reading, and innumerable other influences on her daily life.

The *macrosystem* is the norms and values of the culture that establish a "blueprint" for social behavior: the cultural ideas and ideals that people in a society take for granted. In our society, for example, we exempt young children from a number of social responsibilities. For instance, we think it is unfair to ask a 10-year-old child to care for his 5-year-old sister or an aging grandparent in the afternoon when his mother is working. No one proposes a "curriculum for caring" in the schools, in which elementary schoolchildren, under supervision, would care for the babies of working mothers. In other societies and cultures, however, adults assume that children will spend much of their time helping to raise their brothers and sisters. The macrosystem creates boundaries to children's lives. It also tends to blind psychologists to alternative patterns of development. (See the interview with Urie Bronfenbrenner at the end of this chapter.)

The Role of Theory

Generating theories is a crucial element of psychological inquiry. A theory is like the lens of a camera. Without a lens, a camera would record a blur of light. The lens defines the field of vision and provides the focus. Without theory, developmental psychology would be a collection of biographical anecdotes. Facts do not speak for themselves. Theories tell psychologists which facts are important, how they are related to one another, and what conclusions can be drawn from them.

Some psychologists use a variety of lenses in their research and writing, changing theoretical views to adapt to different problems and situations. Others approach every issue by filtering their observations through the same lens. Pictures of the child's development taken by those who use one lens—say, behaviorism or psychodynamics—sometimes strike others as being distorted images of reality. Each of the approaches described here helps to explain development. In coming chapters, we shall draw on all five views to present a full picture of how development occurs.

Contemporary Research Strategies

Theory and research are intertwined in all sciences. The aim of research is not only to collect accurate and useful information, but also to test theories. The tests developmental psychologists use are similar to those of all scientists.

The scientific method rests on four basic rules of inquiry. The first requirement is that scientists must confine themselves to studying *observable behavior*. For psychologists, this often means establishing operational definitions for the behavior they wish to study. Abstract concepts such as attachment, intelligence, and self-esteem must be translated into concrete measurements. For the purposes of a study, a researcher might define attachment in terms of the number of times a small child seeks physical contact with his mother during a ten-minute observation period. She might define intelligence as a score on a standard IQ test. This does not mean that the psychologist believes that there is

Insight

SIMPLEMINDED VS. MUDDLEHEADED

According to Paul H. Meehl (1972) of the University of Minnesota, psychologists are prone to being one of two opposite types: the simpleminded or the muddleheaded. (These terms come from a famous dinner conversation between philosophers Alfred North Whitehead and Bertrand Russell.) The simpleminded are hypercritical, superscientific, intellectually cautious, and dull. They are exceedingly careful researchers, but "tend to have a difficult time discovering anything interesting or exciting." The muddleheads, in contrast, are uninhibited, imaginative, socially conscious, and inaccurate. They have not learned to think scientifically or even to value scientific reasoning. Muddleheads "have a tendency to discover a lot of interesting things that are not so." The simpleminded demand data; muddleheads trust "gut feelings." Meehl continues:

> I have never been able, despite my . . . "simpleminded" training, to decide between the two evils. At times it has seemed to me that the best solution is . . . the political one, namely, we wait for clever muddleheads to cook up interesting possibilities and the task of the simpleminded contingent is then to sift the wheat from the chaff.
> (p. 934)

But he adds that although the simpleminded may be cured of their unscientific traits—by personal experience, exposure to bright intellects who hold opposing beliefs, or the feeling of security brought on by simply growing older—the prognosis for the muddleheaded is poor.

nothing more to attachment than physical contact, or that all aspects of intelligence can be measured by a test. These are working, or operational, definitions.

A second requirement is that the measure be *reliable,* or produce consistent results. If a child receives approximately the same score on a test the first time she takes it as when she is tested again six months or a year later, if she obtains the same score on different forms of the test, or if she receives the same score on odd- and even-numbered items in the test, the measure may be considered reliable. Another criterion for psychologists is interobserver reliability. Do two researchers or observers scoring the same test or interpreting the same interview arrive at the same conclusions? If not, the operational definitions of the study may be imprecise.

A third requirement is that the form of measurement be *valid:* it must measure what the researcher claims it measures. For example, the hairs on your head can be reliably counted, but this would not be a valid measure of intelligence. Bald men can be geniuses. One test of validity is prediction. Does a score on a math aptitude test predict how well a youngster will do in math classes? If it does—most youngsters with high scores on the test earn high grades—the test can be said to have *predictive validity*.

The fourth requirement, and the ultimate test of scientific findings, is *replication*. Replication is duplication. The results of a scientific study should be reported in such a way that allows other researchers to repeat the study with other subjects at other times and places. If the same or similar results are found in both studies, the conclusions are more likely to be believed.

Following these basic rules for scientific inquiry, developmental psychologists have assembled a rich assortment of techniques for studying behavior: naturalistic observation, the experiment, correlational studies, and clinical studies. Each of these has strengths and weaknesses. The strategy a researcher chooses depends on the question he or she wants to answer. (For the ethical standards governing research using children, see the appendix.)

Naturalistic Observation

One technique for gathering information on development is to observe children in their everyday settings and record what they do or say. Roger Barker and Herbert Wright's *One Boy's Day* (1951) is a classic of naturalistic observation. Barker and Wright attempted to record everything a single boy did on a single day in

April. It took a team of researchers to keep up with the child; the results filled an entire book. (See Figure 1-5.) Baby biographies also fall into this category. Darwin (1877) and Piaget (1963), among others, attempted to observe their children from a scientific point of view. (See Figure 1-1.) More often, researchers study a group of children and limit themselves to one aspect of behavior. For example, Dianne McGuinness (1985) and colleagues spent 100 hours observing preschoolers during free play. Each child was monitored for twenty-minute periods. A team of fourteen judges classified everything the child did into predetermined categories. McGuinness found clear sex differences in behavior. Girls spent twice as much time in activi-

---

Before school
8:19 [A.M.]

[Raymond] darted to some park benches near the bandstand.

He pulled a small green bench out from several others and tipped it over so that the back was on the ground.

He dashed back to the walk and returned, making a running leap as if to jump over the bench.

Seeing that he couldn't quite make it, he put his hands on the perpendicular seat of the bench and just vaulted over it with his hands helping him.

He looked over at me when he hopped over the bench and called, "I can't do it the other way," as if he had hoped to jump it but just hadn't been able to make such a high leap. He smiled happily and didn't seem apologetic. . . .

In school
8:54 [A.M.]

Raymond started to draw an outline on the blackboard, making a series of quick short marks, each roughly overlapping the previous one. He was quick and enthusiastic in drawing. What he drew was a goonlike figure consisting of a head and a long snout.

Then he drew a chin almost as long as the snout.

At the back of the neck he drew a large hump.

After drawing the rough outline, he gave the figure a cursory glance.

Raymond looked over at Clifford Grinnell who was making a drawing on the blackboard next to him.

Clifford came to the blackboard after Raymond, watched him, then started a drawing of his own.

Raymond showed interest in Clifford's drawing.

Suddenly Raymond went "Baa, baa," and laughed aloud. This laugh wasn't exactly a humorous one but it seemed to release some exuberance.

Clifford informed Raymond, "I'm going to draw a steamboat." He rapidly drew a rough outline of a boat and then a few inches of water underneath it.

Raymond watched closely.

When his companion had finished drawing the water, Raymond looked back thoughtfully at his own drawing.

He picked up some chalk from the chalk tray and played with it for a second.

(Barker & Wright, 1951)

Figure 1-5 One Boy's Day: Raymond Birch, Age 7, on April 26, 1949

ties organized by a teacher; boys, twice as much time in unsupervised play, such as construction. Girls often spent twelve minutes at a single activity, compared to eight minutes for boys. In a single twenty-minute period, boys engaged in an average of 4.5 different activities; girls, in 2.5 different activities. Boys interrupted an activity three times more often than girls did. McGuinness suggests that the routines and structure of a traditional classroom fit girls, but place unnatural constraints on boys.

The advantage of naturalistic observation is that it allows psychologists to study phenomena as they occur in the real world. The uninterrupted stream of behavior of a group of preschoolers on a playground may reveal unexpected patterns that teachers or parents, who are responsible for maintaining order, would not see. But there are obvious disadvantages. The method is time-consuming and expensive. Observers must be trained to use the recording system reliably. An experiment may take half an hour, but a study of naturally occurring aggression can take months to complete. Moreover, there is always the danger that the observer's presence will alter behavior. However, psychologists who conduct observational studies are often surprised to discover how quickly children and adults forget their presence. It is not unusual to see preschoolers fall over a seated observer much the way they would stumble over a misplaced block or truck.

The Experiment

The term "experiment" conjures up images of white-coated scientists hovering over bubbling test tubes or cages of rats in a laboratory. But it is the procedure, not the uniform or the setting, that distinguishes this technique from others. Experiments can take place anywhere.

An experiment allows a researcher to control a situation so that the effects of one or a few variables can be measured. Suppose research-

ers are interested in the effects of TV violence on children's behavior. They might show an *experimental group* of 5-year-olds an episode from a typical police story, put them in a room with a Bobo doll (a doll that bounces back like a punching bag when hit) and other toys, then observe the children through a two-way mirror as they play. (See Liebert & Barn, 1972.) Suppose they find that many of the children beat up the doll. How do the researchers know that the TV episode influenced the children's behavior? Perhaps the children didn't like the other toys. To eliminate this possibility, the researchers show a *control group* of 5-year-olds a nonviolent TV show and observe the behavior in the same playroom. Then they compare the behavior of the experimental group to that of the control group. If the children in the experimental group hit the doll harder and more often than those in the control group, the researchers may tentatively conclude that the TV show influenced the children's behavior. The children in the experimental group may have been more aggressive to begin with, however. To guard against this possibility in advance, the researchers assign the children to the two groups at random, perhaps by flipping a coin. This ensures that whatever differences exist among the subjects are distributed evenly between the two groups. As a final precaution, the researchers may ask graduate students who do not know the purpose of the experiment to score the children's behavior. This is known as the "blind" technique. All of these procedures are designed to rule out alternative explanations of the children's behavior.

When psychologists conduct an experiment, they are not interested in only the twenty children who took part in the study, or the *sample*. They hope to make generalizations—about all 5-year-old Americans or all 5-year-old boys, for example. The breadth of a generalization depends on the extent to which the sample represents the entire population under study. If all of the children in the sample are middle-class, or urban, or male, the sample will be biased because the results of the study cannot be applied to *all* 5-year-olds. A common bias in psychological research is that subjects are usually volunteers, often college students, or children who are "volunteered" by their parents. This means that they are unlikely to represent everyone in the population to be studied. Many people do not volunteer for anything!

The strength of the experiment is that it enables researchers to eliminate outside factors that might contaminate the results. If researchers conducted a study of aggression in a child's home, the knowledge that his mother is in the next room might influence his behavior. This strength is also a weakness. Many psychologists question whether findings obtained in a laboratory can be generalized to real-life situations. For example, the fact that a little girl doesn't pummel a Bobo doll in the laboratory does not mean that she treats her own toys gently or never gives in to the impulse to beat up a younger brother. She might be very aggressive in other situations. Urie Bronfenbrenner, a critic of reliance on experiments, once commented that "much of American developmental psychology is the science of the behavior of children in strange situations with strange adults" (1974, p. 3). (See the Profile at the end of this chapter for Bronfenbrenner's explanation of this statement.)

Correlational Studies

In some cases a psychologist wants more than description, but it would be unethical or impractical to carry out an experiment. Researchers who suspect that there is a relationship between mothers-to-be who smoke and low birth weights would not ask 100 pregnant women to smoke two packs a day so that they could see how the babies turned out. A psychologist who is interested in whether parents who were abused as children abuse their own children obviously cannot select 50 children at random for abuse.

Instead, the researcher conducts a correlational study using data on existing groups. A **correlation** is a relationship between variables—between a mother's smoking and her infant's birth weight, or between being an abused child and becoming an abusive parent. Although the mathematics are a bit difficult, the principle is simple: Measure two (or more) variables to see if they are related. For example, there is a high correlation between a student's scores on the Scholastic Aptitude Tests (the S.A.T.s) and his or her grade point average as a freshman in college. There is no correlation between a student's grade point average and his or her shoe size.

COINCIDENCE OR WHAT?

HOWARD L'S ANXIETY LEVEL

THE PRICE OF PEANUT BUTTER

Correlation does not prove cause and effect, as the Insight on page 34 explains.

Insight

CORRELATIONS, NOT CAUSE AND EFFECT

Two factors are correlated when changes in the value of one are associated with changes in the value of the other. For example, high S.A.T. scores are associated with a high grade point average in college; low S.A.T. scores with a low grade point average.

A correlation coefficient ($r =$) is a numerical expression of the degree of association between two variables. A correlation of $+1.00$ means that high values of A always occur with high values of B; a correlation of $+.60$ means that high values of A and B often occur together; a correlation of $+.30$ means that high values of A and B occur more often than by chance; a correlation of 0, that there is no relation between the two variables.

Correlations may be positive or negative. A positive correlation such as $+.60$ means that if you find A (high S.A.T. scores), you are likely to find B (a high grade point average). A negative correlation such as $-.60$ means that if you find high levels of A (obesity), you are *un*likely to find high levels of B (regular exercise).

A high correlation between two variables does not mean that one causes the other. Often the cause lies in a third, unmeasured variable. Suppose you found a high negative correlation between the price of coffee and the birth rate. When the price of coffee rises, the birth rate declines. You might conclude that coffee stimulates sexual appetites. When coffee becomes a luxury, couples are less likely to drink coffee and then conceive children. In fact, the relationship between the two is caused by a third variable, economic insecurity. Coffee prices soar and birth rates drop when inflation threatens the economy.

Correlational studies sample existing groups and describe the differences among them. Using this approach, a psychologist would compare the birth weights of babies of women who did smoke during pregnancy with those of women who did not smoke but who were like the former in other significant ways, such as age and social class. The researcher who is concerned about child abuse might interview known child abusers about their past.

Correlational studies supply important information on behavior and developmental events as they occur in the real world. But they do not tell a researcher anything about cause and effect. The fact that two variables usually occur together does not mean that one causes the other, any more than the fact that a rooster crows at sunrise means that the rooster causes the sun to rise. Often what one finds are "clouds of correlations" (Scarr, 1985). For example, children who have been exposed to lead in their environment often show behavior problems. It is tempting to conclude that exposure to lead causes brain damage. But exposure to lead is not distributed evenly through the population. Poor and minority children are more likely than are other children to live in old buildings whose walls are covered with lead paint. They are also more likely to live near lead smelters and in areas with heavy traffic congestion. Thus, they are more likely than are middle-class children to be exposed to high levels of lead. But they are also more apt to suffer from malnutrition and child abuse, and to have poorly educated parents, absent fathers, and many siblings. All of these conditions are associated with low IQ and poor motor skills. It is almost impossible to isolate the effects of lead in this cloud of variables.

PIAGET: Do you know what a lie is?
CLAI: It's when you say what isn't true.
PIAGET: Is 2 + 2 = 5 a lie?
CLAI: Yes, it's a lie.
PIAGET: Why?
CLAI: Because it isn't right.
PIAGET: Did the boy who said that 2 + 2 = 5 know it wasn't right or did he make a mistake?
CLAI: He made a mistake.
PIAGET: Then if he made a mistake, did he tell a lie or not?
CLAI: Yes, he told a lie.
PIAGET: A naughty one?
CLAI: Not very.
PIAGET: You see this gentleman [a student]?
CLAI: Yes.
PIAGET: How old do you think he is?
CLAI: Thirty.
PIAGET: I would say 28. [The student says he is really 36.] Have we both told a lie?
CLAI: Yes, both lies.
PIAGET: Naughty ones?
CLAI: Not so very naughty.
PIAGET: Which is the naughtiest, yours or mine, or are they both the same?
CLAI: Yours is the naughtiest because the difference is bigger.
PIAGET: Is it a lie, or did we just make a mistake?
CLAI: We made a mistake.
PIAGET: Is it a lie all the same, or not?
CLAI: Yes, it's a lie!
    (Piaget, 1932)

Clinical Studies

A *clinical study* is a psychological assessment of an individual child. This assessment usually includes personal interviews, a battery of intelligence, aptitude, and personality tests, and interviews with family members, teachers, a pediatrician, and others who can provide data on the child's developmental background. The clinician may also observe the child at home, in classrooms, in structured play settings, and perhaps in a hospital.

In most cases, clinical studies are undertaken when parents or others believe that a child might require psychotherapy or other forms of treatment. But studies of individuals can also generate hypotheses about the development of all children. Freud's theory of personality development, discussed earlier in this chapter, was based on intensive case studies, for example. Piaget's theory of cognitive development, discussed in Chapter 4, was based on intensive interviews of children. Piaget did not ask each child a series of standardized questions. Rather, he pursued a topic until he felt sure that he understood what the child was thinking. (See Figure 1-6.) During an interview, his attention was focused on one child. Ultimately, however, he was interested in how all children think.

The advantage of the clinical study is depth. The researcher is not limited to a particular set of observations or to predetermined questions,

Figure 1-6 Piaget Interviews a Child

but can use a variety of probes to learn how the subject thinks or feels. This advantage is also a disadvantage. The interviewer may read thoughts or feelings into the subject's responses, or lead a subject toward answers that fit a particular theory. Because the observations or questions are not standardized, it is difficult to make exact comparisons of different subjects. Nevertheless, clinical studies are a source of valuable and interesting hypotheses that can be tested by other methods.

Longitudinal vs. Cross-sectional Studies

Developmental psychologists face a special problem in research design: measuring consistency and change over the lifespan. There are two basic strategies for studying age-related changes in behavior: the longitudinal study and the cross-sectional study.

In a *longitudinal* study, researchers focus on one group of people and study their behavior over a period of time. One of the most ambitious projects of this type was the Fels Longitudinal Study, launched in 1929. Researchers followed 750 individuals from childhood to middle age. But a longitudinal study need not cover half a lifetime. A researcher might study a group of children at birth, at 6 months, at 1 year, at 2 years, and at 5 years.

The major advantage of this research strategy is that it allows psychologists to study developmental changes over time in the same group of individuals. They can observe subjects at a young age and then when they are older, note the relationships between their behavior at the two ages, and chart the stability or changes in behavior patterns.

Unfortunately, this method has critical disadvantages. Longitudinal studies require a long-term commitment of the researcher and the research organization. The study must be carefully designed and planned, and the researcher must know what specific measures he or she will use at each stage of research. It is difficult to anticipate research methods and interests over a twenty year period. The sample size must be large enough to compensate for subjects who lose interest or move out of the researcher's grasp. A more important concern is that a subject's participation in the study may influence his or her development. Indeed, the longitudinal study may be a form of treatment intervention: being studied, measured, and evaluated on repeated occasions can affect subjects' behavior. Moreover, subjects in longitudinal studies are all members of the same cohort. A **cohort** is a group of people of the same age who are exposed to similar cultural environments and historical events at the same stage of their development. The changes one observes in a cohort may be due to the times rather than to development. It was one thing to be a college student in the 1950s, another to be going to school during the 1960s and the Vietnam war. Conclusions based on a group of subjects who were graduated from college in 1955 might not apply to other groups.

The alternative to a longitudinal study is a *cross-sectional study,* in which a researcher studies groups of people of different ages at the same point in time. For example, a psychologist might place groups of 2-, 4-, and 6-year-olds in a room where there are more children than toys and observe what happens. The psychologist might ask 4-, 10-, and 14-year-olds, "What is a lie?" The success of this approach depends on selecting children who are alike in other characteristics, such as socioeconomic status and preschool experience.

A major problem with cross-sectional studies is that subjects who are of different ages may also be members of different cohorts. Here again, differences in behavior and attitudes may reflect their different experiences, not their different chronological ages. Sports provides an example of this. In 1976, a 10-year-old girl swam the 100-meter freestyle in a time that would have earned her a gold medal in the men's Olympic event in 1900 (Cairns & Cairns, 1983). This does not mean that girls have caught up with men in this sport. Swimming techniques and training procedures have improved dramatically in recent years. Both males and females swim faster today than they did in 1900. They also think and feel differently as a result of changes in eating habits, child-rearing styles, school systems, and many other factors. Cohort effects such as this present the biggest problem to researchers who are interested in changes over long time spans. A comparison of 15-year-olds and 50-year-olds will not tell us how those teenagers will see life in middle age. The cohort effect can be minimized by using groups whose ages are within 4 or 5 years of one another.

As an alternative to longitudinal or cross-sectional studies, K. Warner Schaie (1965) recommends combining the two in a *cohort-sequential* study. For example, a psychologist might give an IQ test to a cross section of age groups, then follow these groups over time until their ages overlap. This research design is shown in Table 1-1. A comparison of test scores for the same group at different ages yields a measure of developmental change, A. A comparison of different groups at the same age yields a measure of generational change, B. A psychologist can then compare these two measures. This design is not foolproof, but it does eliminate some of the flaws found in cross-sectional and longitudinal studies.

The Plan and Themes of This Book

The story goes that a group of blind men came upon an elephant and tried to describe what it was. Each approached the animal from a different direction. One ran into the elephant's side and declared that it was a wall. One found the tail and proclaimed that it was a snake. The third man examined the elephant's leg and announced that it was a pillar. Although each man gave an accurate description of one part of the animal, the sum of their descriptions did not produce a picture of the whole elephant.

Developmental psychologists face similar problems in their efforts to describe and explain the whole person. In both theory and research, developmental psychologists must wear blinders. Attacking all of the problems of human development at once is impossible. Out of practical necessity, most developmental psychologists concentrate on one of five domains: biological and physical growth, perceptual and cognitive functioning, language, personality and emotion, or social interaction (see Table 1-2). For the same reasons, research usually focuses on two, or perhaps three, age groups. The aim of a developmental textbook, however, is to present the whole person: to show how one phase of

---

Table 1-1   A Cohort-Sequential Study of IQ

Year of Birth	Age at First Test (1980)	Age at Second Test (1985)	Age at Third Test (1990)
1960	20	25	30 A
1965	15	20	25
1970	10	15	20 B

development builds upon previous phases and how different domains of behavior are related.

The organization of this text reflects the conventions of the field. The book is arranged chronologically, with an introductory section and sections on infancy (birth to age 2), the preschool years (ages 2 to 6), middle childhood (ages 6 to 12), and adolescence (ages 12 to about 18). Our discussion of the young person at each phase is divided into chapters on cognitive development (and related physical, perceptual, and motor development) and chapters on emotional and social development. We stop at many points along the way to show how intellectual and social development and thoughts and emotions relate to one another.

We have included special chapters on human nature in Part 1, the beginnings of life in Part 2, language in Part 3, intelligence and creativity in Part 4, and physical and sexual development in Part 5.

At the end of some chapters are interviews with distinguished developmental psychologists whose work has been considered in the text. They explain how they became interested in their areas of developmental psychology. They describe major influences on their work and suggest where they believe the field is heading.

Table 1-2 Dimensions of Study in Child Development

Dimension of Behavior	Psychological and Biological Functions	Examples of Research Topics
Biological and physical growth	Skeletal growth and physiological changes (height, weight, sexual characteristics, brain development, gross and fine motor control: running, using tools, writing with a pencil)	The prerequisites for learning how to walk, climbing stairs, tying shoelaces; the effects of hormones on skeletal growth and sexual development; fetal development
Perceptual-cognitive functioning	Perceptions of the environment (through sensory organs: eye, ear, hand, nose, mouth, body movement); selection, processing, retention, and use of information from the environment; and generation of rules for understanding what has been learned	Infant perception; the development of intellectual processes and cognitive styles; how children learn to read, find their way in space, hear different pitches and rhythms in music
Language	Expressing and receiving information (communicating) through representative symbol systems (such as the alphabet) that are oral, written, and gestural	The development of rules of grammar; how children acquire language symbol systems in their early years
Personality and emotion	Emotional state; means of expressing feelings, interests, and attitudes; personality and identity	The development of attachment; the effects of maternal separation on a child's affective state; the patterns of development of autonomy, initiative, and various personality characteristics (introverted, assertive, outgoing); the development of vocational interest patterns
Social interaction	Interpersonal exchanges, relationships, and roles in the variety of social contexts in which children and youth function (whole family, parents, siblings, peers, classrooms, community); the process of socialization	The development of friendship patterns in young children; child rearing practices

There are six running themes in this book, issues that developmental psychologists continue to discuss and debate. We alert you to these issues here and state where the authors stand.

Mind–Body Dualism

The Greek physician Hippocrates discovered the importance of the brain in the fourth century BC. Hippocrates recognized that the brain controls others organs and parts of the body. He also described this organ as "the interpreter of consciousness." During the Middle Ages, however, theologians insisted that the mind or soul was separate from the body. Psychologists and biologists are still struggling to put the two back together again. Their difficulty is compounded by the lack of knowledge about the connections between the physical, neurochemical transmission of impulses in the brain and the rich mental life of human beings.

Can the relatively simple neurochemistry of the brain really be the source of our admirably complex thoughts? In the early days of psychology, many scientists argued that conscious thought is much too elegant to be explained by mere physiology. Some went so far as to ignore or even deny any connection between brain processes and mental life. Others who accepted the physical basis for all behavior went so far as to reduce thought to a mere by-product of brain activity. Neither position is satisfactory. This book assumes that brain activity does underlie mental life, but that thought is organized on a level that cannot be explained by brain activity alone.

Maturation vs. Experience

The maturation–experience debate concerns itself with how much of human thought and behavior is inborn and revealed naturally in development and how much is learned from the environment. All psychologists would agree that some environmental features, such as food and water, are necessary for development to occur. But there is controversy about how much *specific* experience is necessary for babies to walk, for example, or for toddlers to talk. As we saw at the beginning of this chapter, Arnold Gesell believed that children mature and develop new behaviors with very little specific learning. In contrast, John B. Watson argued that experience is everything: children can become beggars, lawyers, or textbook authors, depending on what they are taught.

The maturation–experience controversy is resolved when we recognize a simple principle: Both maturation, or readiness to learn, and experience, or opportunities to learn, are necessary for learning. Alone, neither is sufficient for learning. Language is an example of this principle. No amount of training (experience) will help a 2-month-old child to speak; the child is too immature, both physiologically and neurologically. But no 2-year-old, whose level of maturation prepares him for speech, will learn to talk unless he interacts with people who speak to him. Experience is also necessary for language development. Together, maturation and experience are sufficient for learning to speak.

Heredity and Environment

To what extent are individual differences caused by heredity (the fact that no two people other than identical twins have identical genes)? To what extent are such differences caused by environment (the fact that no two people, including twins, have identical experiences)? This is not a debate about whether genes *or* environment determine behavior; clearly, both do. It is an argument about what makes people different from one another. Consider two 3-year-old girls, one verbally fluent, the other speaking only in two-word sentences. Why are their levels of development so different? The fluent child probably has intelligent parents who frequently talk and read to her; the other child may not be so fortunate. The first child has both the genes and the environment for rapid development of verbal skills; the second child has neither. Only by studying children who have not been reared by their biological parents—adopted children—or by studying relatives of different degrees, such as identical and fraternal twins, can we estimate the relative importance of hereditary and environmental differences among people. (*Identical,* or monozygotic, twins develop from a sin-gle fertilized egg and have the same genes. *Fraternal,* or dizygotic, twins develop from two ova that are fertilized at the same time. Genetically, they are no more alike than other siblings.) Thus the heredity–environment controversy is not an either-or issue. Instead, it resolves into a question of how much each contributes to individual differences. (We examine this issue in more detail in Chapter 2.)

The Human and Humans

As members of the human species, people are all very much like one another—compared to, say, chimpanzees. All humans who are not physically or mentally impaired have two arms, two legs, an upright posture. These traits are typical of our species. All normal humans learn to talk, count, and feel strong emotional bonds to other people. These behavioral traits are also typical of our species. As individuals, however, we differ from one another in important ways. Some of us are more sociable or generous than others are, some are more musically talented, some are taller or fatter, and some are longer-lived. When we describe the average person as more sociable than a gorilla, we must remember that individuals vary within a species.

The dual concern with average patterns of development and with individual variation leads to debates between the *idiographic* approach to child development, which seeks to explain indi-

Studies of identical twins are an important source of information on the degree to which intelligence, temperament, interests, vulnerability to mental disorders, and other traits are inherited.

vidual differences, and the *nomothetic* approach to development, which seeks general rules that apply to all people. Champions of the study of individual differences argue that no account of average traits can really capture the richness and diversity of humankind, or even characterize a single person adequately. "The average person" is an abstraction that distorts our understanding of human behavior. Those who promote the study of general laws of behavior argue that focusing on individual variations prevents us from seeing the forest for the trees. Both views are correct. It is true that the abstract average may not represent any individual very well. But it is also true that attending to all the details of human variation may prevent us from seeing common themes and causes. To understand development fully, we must look at the human animal and its species-specific traits as well as at individual humans in all their variety.

Normal and Abnormal

Normal developmental variation is a very important concept. There are many patterns of development that produce "normal" adults, by which we mean adults who see themselves and are seen by others as adequately functioning members of society. The various routes to this goal are the many individual variations on developmental themes found in all areas of behavioral development.

Some babies walk independently at 9 months; others, who will also walk normally, do not do so until 18 months. Some children talk in short sentences at 18 months; others, whose speech will later turn out to be quite normal, do not talk well until they are nearly 3 years old. The causes of these differences in the rate of development are not clear to researchers. The point is that humans can vary in many ways and still develop into normal members of the species.

Normality is defined in two ways: with statistics and by consensus. The statistical definition of normality is based on frequency: those patterns of development that occur most frequently in a population are considered normal. The consensual definition, on the other hand, depends on agreement among observers about what is desirable at various ages. Suppose the 3-year-olds in a population average 33 inches in height, and 95 percent vary from 27 inches to 37 inches. A height of 33 inches is statistically nor-

Psychologists are interested in both the common patterns of human development and variations on the human theme.

mal for that population. But we know that the average height of well-fed 3-year-olds is 37 inches. Hence, 33 inches is not "normal" in the sense of being desirable: the children are smaller because they are malnourished.

The concept of *abnormality* also has two definitions, exactly mirroring the definitions of normality. Abnormality is defined statistically as those patterns of development that occur infrequently. For example, a few children have IQ scores so low that they are below those of 97 percent of other children. These few are considered retarded, or abnormally low in IQ. Another few children have IQ scores above those of 97 percent of other children. By a statistical criterion, they have "abnormally" high IQ scores. But on a consensual basis, usually high IQ's are not considered abnormal in the sense of undesirable; unusually low IQ's are. High-scoring children are more often well adapted to their social worlds than normal children; low-IQ children are less often well adapted than normal children.

For other behavioral characteristics, it is undesirable to have extreme or infrequent values at *both* ends of the scale. To be so introverted as to fear being with other people, or so extroverted as to be miserable without constant companionship, are both undesirable and statistically infrequent conditions; that is, they are abnormal by both statistical and consensual criteria. Keep these distinctions in mind when you read about "the average child."

Stages or Phases?

The last debate among developmental psychologists concerns the very nature of development. Some psychologists view development as a continuous process by which an individual's behavior becomes more complex and mature as the result of the gradual accumulation of new responses and knowledge. To them, human growth occurs without a reorganization of the individual's capacities. Behaviorists, for example, hold that the same principles of learning apply regardless of the developmental status of the learner. According to this view, development takes the form of a smooth curve.

Other psychologists see development as a sequence of distinct stages, each of which entails important changes in the way the child thinks, feels, and behaves. Although the rate of development varies from child to child, the order of the stages in the developmental journey to maturity is the same for every person. Freud described emotional development from the infant to the toddler as a transition from the oral to the anal stage. Piaget proposed a shift from concrete thought, which depends on immediate perceptions, to a more formal, abstract form of thinking in adolescence. Erikson suggests that an individual progresses through the Eight Ages of Man (see Figure 1-4).

"Pop, am I experiencing a normal childhood?"
(Drawing by Lorenz; © 1984, The New Yorker Magazine, Inc.)

The metamorphosis of the butterfly from larva to winged insect is a biological example of the stage concept. According to this view, human development takes the form of sudden steps up the ladder of development.

How useful is the stage concept? We agree with John Flavell (1982), who says that stages cannot be seen as sudden shifts in development. True, there are changes in the ways children think and behave, but they are less dramatic and less mysterious than metamorphosis. Unlike the butterfly, children do not suddenly grow new intellectual or social wings. Most of what is new depends on earlier skills: running depends on walking, two-word sentences on one-word utterances, and multiplying on addition. In our view, development is not entirely continuous. Some periods entail more rapid change than others. But neither is development a series of metamorphoses. Development at any period evolves from what went before, with a little reorganization and the addition of a few new elements. Different levels of development might be better described as phases than as stages.

The mind–body dualism, maturation–experience, and heredity–environment controversies spring up repeatedly in the study of developmental psychology. We can resolve these problems by recognizing that people are organisms that learn from experience. But they have evolved to learn certain things more easily than others. And differences among people in what they learn are probably due to both genetic and environmental differences.

Developmental psychology is the study of consistency and change over the lifespan. While growing up, each person changes in important ways yet remains fundamentally the same person. To understand this, we must look at the typical human and at individual humans, and at normal and abnormal variations, during each phase of development.

SUMMARY

1. Development is more than growth. It is an orderly sequence of cumulative changes that leads to more complex and better organized behavior patterns.

2. The concept of development is a relatively modern one. In the Middle Ages children were seen as miniature, imperfect adults. The idea that children are different and special dates to the Renaissance. Most children were not treated as special until the early twentieth century, however. Adolescence is a modern, twentieth century phenomenon.

3. Developmental psychology has its roots in Darwin's theory of evolution (which provided a metaphor for development), the child welfare movement at the turn of the century, and the child study movement led by G. Stanley Hall. In the early days of the discipline, the emphasis was on developing a science of child-rearing.

4. Developmental psychology matured in the 1950s and 1960s, when American psychologists discovered Piaget's studies of cognitive development, "the remarkable infant," and new applications of evolutionary theory. These advances influenced, and were influenced by, the social and political climate. Our times might be described by historians as "The Age of Kids."

5. Developmental psychology today draws on five distinct theoretical traditions:
   (a) Psychobiologists study the biological underpinnings of behavior: the brain, the biochemistry of maturation, the genetic

contributions to mental disorders, and so on.

(b) Behaviorists, who dominated psychology in the United States in the 1940s and 1950s, study the impact of experience on behavior. They emphasize the roles of conditioning and imitation in development.

(c) Structuralists include cognitive psychologists, linguists, and ethologists, who focus on the internal representation and reorganization of behavior over the course of development.

(d) Psychodynamicists base their approach on Freud's theory of unconscious motivation—the struggle between the id, the superego, and the ego—and on the development of defense mechanisms.

(e) Ecologists investigate the role of the social environment in individual development. They see the social environment as including everything from the immediate physical setting to age-old traditions.

6. Like all scientists, developmental psychologists are concerned with the reliability, validity, and replication of research.

7. The basic research techniques in developmental psychology are naturalistic observations (studying behavior in its real-world setting), experiments (the controlled manipulation of a situation), correlational studies (analyzing the relationships among different variables), clinical studies (individual case histories), longitudinal studies (examining the same group of subjects over a period of time), and cross-sectional studies (examining subjects of different ages at the same point in time).

8. Students of developmental psychology should be alert to six recurring issues: the philosophical legacy of mind–body dualism; the importance of both maturation (an inborn trait) and experience (learned from the environment) to human development; the correlation of heredity and environment in the creation of individual differences; the complementary study of individuals and average patterns; the distinction between statistical and consensual definitions of normal and abnormal development; and the debate about whether the same mechanism of development occurs at every age (the behaviorist's view) or whether development occurs in stages that are different and more complex with age.

FURTHER READING

Cook, R., & Campbell, D. T. (1979). Boston, MA: Houghton Mifflin. *Quasi-experimentation. How to do science in an imperfect world.* No better guide to research strategies on important social issues could be written.

DeLone, R. H. (1979). *Small futures: Children, inequality, and the limits of liberal reform.* New York: Harcourt Brace Jovanovich. A product of the work of the Carnegie Council on Children, this book examines the social inequalities that hamper children today. DeLone proposes changes that must be made before kids have an equal chance in society.

Kagan, J. (1984). *The Nature of the child.* New York: Basic Books. Historical and contemporary views of the child, which will astound readers with how much our views of children change with the times.

Sears, R. R. (1975). *Your ancients revisited: A history of child development.* Chicago: University of Chicago Press.

Sommerville, J. (1982). *The rise and fall of childhood.* Beverly Hills, CA: Sage. This brief paperback is a concise review of the history of childhood throughout civilization and summarizes changing views about the child's place in society.

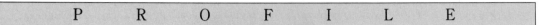

Urie Bronfenbrenner
Jacob Gould Schurman
Professor of
Human Development
and Family Studies and of Psychology
Cornell University

ANN LEVINE: Dr. Bronfenbrenner, how did you first become interested in psychology?

URIE BRONFENBRENNER: I'll answer that on two levels—the manifest and the latent. The manifest is pretty clear. I grew up on the grounds of what was called an institution for the "feeble-minded" in the 1920s: 3,600 morons, imbeciles, idiots—and me. These were my friends and companions. My father was a physician, a neuropathologist. In those days it was hard for a Russian immigrant to establish a private practice. You got a job at a state institution. We lived at Letchworth Village in upstate New York—a marvelous place, really. The superintendent, a New England granite type named Charles Sherman Little, believed that an institution should be a community. Every patient—the "boys" and "girls" as they were called, although they ranged in age from three to eighty-three—had some responsibility. There were farms, bakeries, shops, small factories that produced rugs and this or that, horses and wagons driven by the inmates to deliver supplies. On the Fourth of July there was a parade with a float from every cottage.

Two things that happened at Letchworth stand out in my mind. Some of the kids who were sent there didn't belong in a home for the mentally retarded. A judge would say, "I don't know what to do with this one. . . . Let's send him up to Letchworth; being in the country will be good for him." My father would examine them when they arrived and see that they were not mentally retarded. His problem was to get them tested before the institution had its effect, for then they would be stuck there for life. The Binet* was the hand of God. It was the only way he could get them out.

* The first modern intelligence test and the forerunner of today's IQ tests; see chapters 4 and 10.

The second thing that happened was that the inmates worked in the physicians' homes as maids and helpers. I was brought up by Hilda and Anna and Marilyn. These were my caregivers. They were supposed to be mentally retarded. But, when they worked in our homes, their IQs would go up. So you can see the beginnings of an interest in development right there.

What was more important, I think, was that my parents prepared me to intellectualize these experiences. This is the latent level. Letchworth Village was in Rip Van Winkle country. (Remember the little people? I've seen them.) My father, who had a degree in zoology and was a magnificent observer, took me for walks in the woods. His theme on those walks was the interplay of organisms and environments. He would stop and point up to a magnificent green caterpillar with red horns, yellow stripes. A little while later he'd point to another one. "How did you find it?" I'd ask. "I can't see them." "Don't look up," he'd say, "look down. Wet feces." He would point to a straight line of trees and ask me how that happened. I didn't know. "Chance, little one, chance. The wind blew them against a fence." My mother was a lover of literature, art and music, and there was none of that at Letchworth. Psychologically, she never came to the United States. She lived in her own world of Russian literature. I learned to read and write Russian before English, and read all the great Russian poetry and novels with my mother. You know what Russian novels are about: human development. Do you remember how *Anna Karenina* begins? "All happy families are alike: every unhappy family is unhappy in its own way."

Continued

I became the translator of America for my parents because I picked up English, went to school, and made friends. The school was in a town five miles away. The blacks and Italians and Irish Catholics who worked in the brick factories lived along the river; the Presbyterians and Methodists were up on the hill. There weren't any other Jews in town. My father said, "They have something here called Sunday school. But my best friend was Bill Brophy, and I spent a lot of time with his family and their priest Father Rogers. Through the accidents of circumstance, I had a multicultural childhood.

AL: A very American childhood.

UB: Yes, only in America do you find this kind of mix. Then, when I was an adolescent, my father contracted tuberculosis and was sent to a sanitorium. I became the de facto head of the household. There wasn't much money, but fortunately I won a scholarship to a university named Cornell. I'd never heard of it.

AL: What were your plans for college? Had you thought about studying psychology?

UB: I arrived on campus wide-eyed and innocent. It was the first time I'd left home. I didn't have a plan. By chance, I got a lot of exposure to psychology. The psychology department at Cornell was Titchener-oriented in those days, centered around analyzing mental experiences. But Frank S. Freeman, a professor of psychology, and Ethel Waring in the college of home economics brought Kurt Lewin to Cornell. Lewin was working on his field theory. Freeman had written a text called *Individual Differences* that was ahead of its time, in my judgment. He pointed out, very early in the game, that the gene–IQ correlations psychologists were looking at were confounded by environmental factors. That was in the 1930s; I was in the class of 1938. He had intellectualized what I had seen at Letchworth. I understood him and he recognized this. He became my mentor, not just my professor.

Freeman used his influence to send me to his teacher at Harvard, Walter Fenno Dearborn, for graduate work. Dearborn had written one of the first books on the development of intelligence. He was a marvelous, dry, crisp New England aristocrat with a razor mind and a gen-

tle humor. He would say things like, "Bronfenbrenner, if you want to understand something, try to change it." Or "He's a chip off the old block, not just because he was knocked off it, but because he knocked around with it." He would look at the psychology of the day, chuckle, and say, "It's not quite so simple." Dearborn's specialty was reading, and I became his clinical assistant. There was no textbook in those days on how to deal with reading problems. He believed that they weren't simply reading problems, they were problems of the family and the environment.

But psychology at Harvard then was too departmentalized for me. So I went out to the University of Michigan to study with Willard Olson. He was a progressive educator who believed that a student should teach himself. I would ask his permission to do this or that, and he would say, "I think this is what you want to do." I took courses in statistics in the math department, courses in anthropology, whatever I liked. The only requirement was that I pass an examination and do a thesis. How lucky can you be?

AL: A charmed life.

UB: Yes, it was. By now the United States was involved in World War Two. I was drafted the day after I had my Ph.D. exam and sent to an army/air force classification center to work under Major Shaffer—Lawrence Shaffer of "adjustment" fame at Columbia University. We were supposed to do psychometric analysis, classifying navigators and the like. Terribly dull stuff. So I wrote to the adjutant general and said, "I'm a psychologist, I speak Russian, and I'm stuck here pushing buttons. What kind of an army is this?" Pretty brash for a G.I. But I got orders to report to the Office of Strategic Services in Washington to do secret work. What was the secret work? Every day I went to the Library of Congress and read six-month-old issues of *Pravda* behind locked doors. Later I was sent to Station S. Who was there? Harry Murray, Ted Newcomb, Kurt Lewin, Edward C. Tolman, David Levy. There I was, a fresh Ph.D., quarantined with America's top psychologists and sociologists. But I asked to get out of there because there was a war going on. I became a clinical psychologist at an army hospital, and ended up as Assistant Chief for the Veterans Administration's clinical program for about a year. Then I taught at Michigan for a short time, and went back to Cornell.

AL: Your comparative study of the United States and the Soviet Union, *Two Worlds of Childhood,* is a classic. Could you summarize the differences between these two worlds, for children?

UL: The Russians have a word, *vospitanie,* which doesn't translate very well into English. It means upbringing, building character, becoming cultured. *Vospitanie* is a national hobby. Everyone is preoccupied with children. They are given the best clothes, the best food available. Adults speak to children wherever they are, and see themselves in the role of aunt or uncle to all children. I recall one time when my wife and I were walking along a park with our two youngest children, Katie, who was ten, and Steve,

who was about four. Suddenly we saw a gang of teenage boys running toward us. We didn't know what was going to happen. Well, they scooped up Steve and passed him from boy to boy, teasing us all the while. "We don't want to give him back." Imagine, adolescent boys who loved small children and knew how to handle them! Russian children grow up surrounded by affectionate adults, but also under constant surveillance. Adults feel they have a right to love—and to correct—any child. This pattern of upbringing develops a lot of conformity.

You can see the effects in nursery school. If you go to a nursery school in the United States, you see kids running around all over the place. If there's a fence, they try to climb it. In Soviet nursery schools you see something I call "the magic circle." The children stay within a

certain radius, as if there were a fence around them when there's not. To a degree, the magic circle reflects events in Soviet society. In periods when there are a lot of arrests, when Soviet–American relations are strained, the circle gets smaller. It's fascinating. In the higher grades, this magic circle is institutionalized. The peer group—"the collective," as they would call it—is responsible for its own discipline. In our society, peers and adults are often seen as opposing forces. Kids encourage nonconformity. In Soviet society, the peer group is an instrument of adult socialization.

AL: How was a book on Soviet society received in this country?

UB: Let me tell you the positive response first. I gave a talk at the Institute of the Council of Child Health and Development and used my observations in the Soviet Union to make the case that we ought to pay more attention to small children in this country. The next thing I knew, I had an invitation to tea at the White House. Lyndon Johnson was president at the time. He was called away, but his wife, Lady Bird, and his two daughters were fascinated by my slides. I remember one of the girls saying, in all innocence, "Mommy, we should do something like this here." Remember, these were slides of communist day-care facilities! Years later, Lady Bird told me that her interest in Head Start (and she became its patron) began with our conversation.

A short time later, Sargent Shriver asked Bob Cook, who was head of pediatrics at Johns Hopkins, to set up a planning committee for a preschool program for poor children. I was on that committee. Ed Zigler has written about the history of this. They called us the Bobbsy twins because we were so uppity and full of impossible ideas. But there were other, wiser heads who looked at the political and financial realities. Finally we recommended to Shriver that the government try Head Start on an experimental basis. But Shriver, bless him, said to me, "Urie, I know you characters, you are always unsure. Well, I'm confident. We're going to write Head Start across the face of this country so that no president, no congress can ever destroy it." Those were his words. I wish it were so.

Continued

I should be ashamed to admit this, but I was one of those who said that Americans will never accept Head Start, that it will be seen as interfering with families and with schools, that we'll be lucky to enroll 500 kids. Well, we had 500,000 children the first summer.

AL: And the negative response to *Two Worlds*?

UB: I was branded a communist. I was quoted—on the floor of the Senate and, needless to say, in the press—as saying "The family is defunct; the nation needs to move toward a system of communal child-rearing." In fact, the quotation was from a speech by an old Bolshevik that I had translated because the Communist Party had disciplined *him* for trying to destroy the family!

AL: Let me ask you about another controversial statement. In 1974 you wrote, "much of American developmental psychology is the science of the strange behavior of children in strange situations with strange adults for the briefest possible period of time."

UB: Now I did write that; you aren't misquoting.

AL: Would you explain what you meant?

UB: I felt that, at the time, too many of our ideas about development were based on laboratory studies that had little to do with the child's everyday world. In many studies (although by no means all), both the task and the participants were unfamiliar. Being taken to a strange room and asked to play a game with a strange adult has no social meaning to a child. It's unreal. Theory and research tended to be unidirectional: how the experimenter (or parent or teacher) influenced the child, with little attention to how the child influenced the other person. There was little sense of process or interaction. Most theory and research focused on two-person systems, or dyads. A researcher would look at the relationship between *A* and *B* (say, the mother and child), but rarely at how *C* (the father, a second child, a grandparent or neighbor) affected the relationship between *A* and *B*. In real life, nearly all households and settings include more than two people. Most important of all, we were ignoring the social contexts: the home itself, the neighborhood, the school room, the TV set, the parent's work situations, government policies. . . . Clearly these variables affect how and with whom children spend their time. We weren't paying attention to the ecology of development.

AL: Ecology is usually seen as a branch of biology. How do you define *human ecology*?

UB: As the study of mutual accommodations between the developing person and the changing contexts, both immediate and broader, in which that person lives. In the 1970s, I proposed a conceptual framework for describing systematically the various parts of the environment.* It's like one of those nested Russian dolls. The inner doll is the developing human being. The next doll is the immediate setting; the physical environment and the people the child is interacting with now. The next doll is the community as it influences activities and relationships . . . and so on.

AL: Is the social context still being ignored?

UB: To the contrary. The whole area has mushroomed in the last decade. Let me give you some examples. We used to attempt to isolate genetic effects on a child's development. Now we see genetic effects as mediated by the family.

AL: The way inherited tendencies are expressed depends on how the family reacts to the child's temperament and abilities.†

UB: Yes. We have good information on how different kinds of day-care affect children of different ages. But we don't know very much about indirect effects. Suppose day-care enables the mother to take a full-time job or to go back to school. How does this alter relationships within the family? There is an enormous amount of research on the influence of family background on a child's performance in school. But we don't know very much about how the child's behavior and performance in school affects the family, the way teachers evaluate the parents, and so on. We still tend to see things as a one-way street.

AL: What about the world of work?

UB: The interesting thing here is that researchers have treated mothers' and fathers' job situations as separate worlds. The mother being *employed* was thought to be damaging, and the father being *unemployed* was thought destruc-

* See text pp. 27, 29.
† See Chapters 2 and 5.

tive. We've learned that neither of these effects is as simple and direct as we thought. Rosabeth Kanter introduced the important concept of "work absorption"—how much of one's physical and mental energy are taken up by work.

AL: It's one thing if your mother and father have nine-to-five jobs and another if they are involved in high-pressure careers.

UB: Exactly. Again, there are the indirect effects. My colleagues and I found that career women tend to have very positive images of their daughters—to see their three-year-old as a competent little woman who will follow in their footsteps. They are not as confident about their sons. But mothers who work part time tend to have very positive images of their sons. Why?

We don't know as much about these indirect or second-order effects as we should.

AL: You seem to be saying that there has been progress, *but*. . . . What is the "but"?

UB: Studies of the social context are commonplace today. There is even a whole new area of research, the child and social policy. This is what I called for in 1974. I should be applauding, but I'm not. We used to have too many studies of development without context. Now I think we have too much research on context without development. The emphasis has shifted from the developing person to the analysis of organizations, the history of policies, the structure of programs. The child is all but invisible. It's a case of "the failure of success."

What's in a Smile?

The Evolutionary Perspective
Ontogeny and Phylogeny
What Is Human Nature?
The Theory of Evolution
The Human Family Tree
The Role of Genes in Evolution
INSIGHT: THE MECHANISMS OF HEREDITY

Genetic Influences on Development
Genotypes and Phenotypes
Gene Action
Genes and Human Development

Environmental Influences on Development
What "Environment" Means
The Essentials: Loving Care
Early Experience
INSIGHT: RECOVERY FROM ABUSE AND NEGECT
What Is a Normal Environment?
INSIGHT: THE GARCIA EFFECT
How People Shape Their Environments

You are standing over the crib of a friend's 4-month-old. You find yourself cooing at the baby. You smile; he grins back immediately, wriggles a little, waves his arms and legs, almost inviting you to pick him up. His soft cooing sounds and big smiles follow one another, and your attention remains riveted on him.

What has happened here? That's easy, you say: When adults smile at babies, babies smile back. In part, that is correct. But there is much more to understand about you and that baby, because there is a vast human history behind this simple interchange. Understanding what happened requires that we look at the smile, and development itself, from an evolutionary perspective. This chapter begins with an analysis of a smile, considers the origins of human nature, and examines the roles genes and environments play in development.

What's in a Smile?

You smiled at the baby and the baby smiled back. This apparently simple exchange can be explained on different levels. The immediate causes of the baby's smile were your expression and his happy state. Your smile caused a reciprocal smile in this 4-month-old. If the baby were less than 2 months old, chances are that he was just dozing with his eyes open. (Babies can sleep with their eyes open.) If he were a year old, his smile probably meant that he knew you or that there was a familiar person nearby to reassure him. If he were older than 2, the smile could have conveyed many more meanings, although it probably meant pleasure at seeing you. Smiling, like other behavior, changes over the course of development.

The development of smiles begins at birth. A newborn is most likely to smile when he is drowsy. It is difficult to evoke a response to your smile in babies less than 6 weeks old. Early smiles are the baby's responses to internal states. Psychologists call these reflex smiles. After 6 or 8 weeks babies respond more often to a smiling face than to their internal states, and they begin to prefer human faces as stimuli for

BECOMING HUMAN: HOW GENES AND ENVIRONMENTS WORK TOGETHER

their smiles. By 4 months babies have become smiling machines. The smile of an adult reliably produces a return smile in an otherwise contented baby, just like pushing a button. After about 6 months infants become more discriminating. They smile only at familiar people and may even cry when a friendly stranger approaches them. By 2 to 3 years children become deliberate smilers who can decide what they want to communicate to adults about their feelings. They can even use smiles to deceive, a feat that infants cannot manage.

Smiles tell you something about the child's personal history. Suppose the baby has been well taken care of by attentive parents. He has not been ill very often, his food agrees with him, and he is a healthy, normal infant who has several months of good experiences with other humans. This baby is more likely to smile at you than is a sickly or maltreated baby, whose personal history has given him less to smile about.

Smiles tell others how we feel. Babies do not understand the meaning of these messages as adults do, but they smile nonetheless. Why? Babies are programmed to reward their caretakers by communicating pleasure and satisfaction. Many human expressions occur early in the baby's behavior as part of our species' repertoire of communications. Adults respond to infant smiles with pleasure and feel rewarded for their good care of the baby. To be touched by an infant's smile is to feel an irresistible urge to smile back, pay attention, and pick up the adorable tyke. That tug on your heartstrings is programmed in you!

Smiles are part of an evolved behavioral system between babies and their caretakers that keeps them attending to one another. Mothers and fathers are attracted and rewarded by their babies' smiles. They develop a bond of attachment to their young, partly because of smiles. Very ill or listless babies who smile infrequently do not evoke the same degree of at-

tachment in their parents as do those who are more lively smilers. Their parents are more likely to abuse or neglect them (Starr, n.d.).

Darwin pointed out in *Expression of the Emotions in Man and Animals* (1965) that the newborn's smile is the result of an evolved set of neural connections between facial muscles and the lower portions of the brain. Although human facial expressions are especially flexible and complex, as far as we can tell, nearly the same thing occurs in all higher mammals. Later in human development the higher regions of the brain mature and take over much of the control of expressions. Smiling changes from an automatic response to one that is voluntary, or almost so. Think how often we smile when we do not want to, in socially embarrassing situations or when we wish to hide our amusement over an unfortunate event. Thus smiling is a programmed form of communication that appears in all normal members of our species.

Understanding a smile depends on knowing the immediate situation, the developmental stage of the smiler, his or her personal history, and the evolutionary program for the species. A smile is no simple event!

The Evolutionary Perspective

An *evolutionary perspective* views the development of an individual over the seventy or eighty years of the human lifespan against the backdrop of the evolutionary history of the human species. **Ontogeny,** the development of an individual, is shaped by **phylogeny,** the evolution of the species. As our analysis of a smile showed, to understand one you must understand the other.

Ontogeny and Phylogeny

From an evolutionary perspective, individual development—ontogeny—is the story of a biological organism growing and changing in collaboration with its surroundings. The genetic program

Smiles change over the course of development. Newborns smile reflexively, even in their sleep; infants smile at anyone and everyone; older children smile for private reasons.

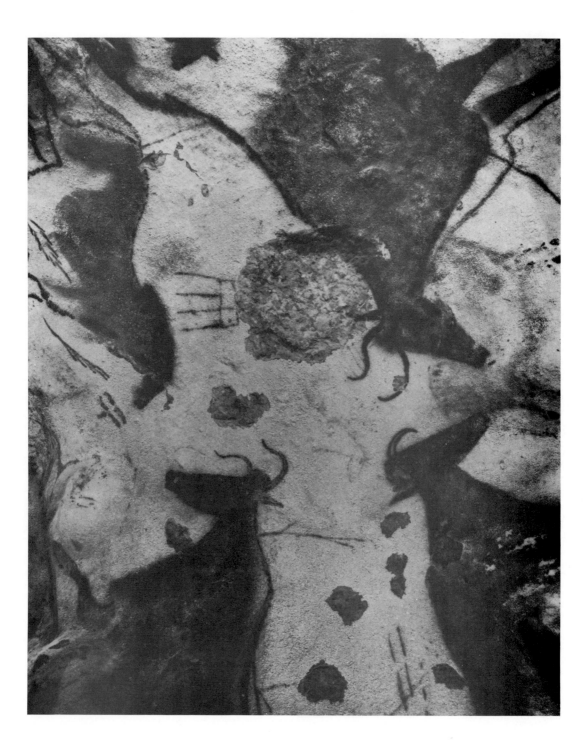

a child inherits from her parents determines certain traits, such as blood type, and helps to establish certain capabilities, such as perfect singing pitch. The environments a growing person experiences—her personal history—help to determine the direction and speed of her development. If she has been well nourished physically, socially, and intellectually, she is probably developing faster and reaching higher levels than is a poorly nourished brother or sister. On the other hand, the emotionally or intellectually deprived child may be on a developmental track toward instability or mental apathy. The person's own past and present environments determine which of her developmental potentials are realized.

Her developmental potential is in turn a product of the evolutionary history of the species—phylogeny. Unless something goes radically wrong, the individual's development follows a characteristically human path. Thus every normal human is born with two eyes, one nose, and two upper and lower limbs. There are many variations on the basic human physique. Some of us are tall, some short; some are thin, some fat. But the basic pattern is the same. We all learn to think, speak, smile, and interact with other people in recognizably human ways. Normal genes in normal human environments produce human beings within a narrow range of physiology, appearance, and behavior.

Our evolutionary heritage establishes both potentials and limitations. We do not have wings like birds or gills like fish. But we have the brains and hands, as well as the social organization and technology, to build planes, spaceships, submarines, and aqualungs. These abilities are part of human nature.

What Is Human Nature?

The evolutionary perspective has concrete answers to age-old questions about human nature that bypass debates about whether humankind is good or evil, pure or corrupt, moral or immoral. From this view, what we are today is a function of what we have evolved to be. As primates—the classification we share with apes and monkeys—humans enjoy conceptual intelligence, flexible learning abilities, long care of our young, and family living, among other characteristics. But we are, as we keep telling ourselves, unique.

Bipedal locomotion (walking on two feet instead of four) and opposable thumbs are two of the characteristics that define our species. More remarkable are humankind's ways of dealing with experience. Our unique abilities to use experience arise from the large cortex of our brains, which is more than twice the size of that of our nearest primate relatives. This neocortex is our thinking and language apparatus. With it we can think about ourselves, believe in ideals,

Using symbols is part of being human. Fifteen thousand years ago, artists in Lascaux, France, captured the spirit of the animals they hunted in their paintings. Are the markings around the animals religious symbols? a hunting calendar? the artist's signature? We do not know, but we can be sure that they were meaningful.

solve complex problems, and talk about the world. As far as we know, no other species has this unique set of assets.

Symbolic thought and language allow us to carry meaning beyond immediate experience. We can transport our experiences across time and space, communicating them to others who were not present when an event occurred. We can tell our children about experiences they have not yet had, ask questions of travelers from far away, joke about the future, and share our innermost thoughts with a lover.

Our ability to transport meaning across time and space is the foundation of culture. A culture is the accumulated knowledge of a people, passed on in various forms to those of the next generation. Culture is one of the distinguishing traits of the human animal. No other animal can *accumulate* experience over many generations. Museums and libraries are monuments to the uniquely human ability to record our history, preserve our thoughts and insights, and develop new technologies.

Many of our thoughts fall into three categories: ideas about the environment, ourselves, and "What does it all mean?" We have applied thought to physical problems in the environment, such as how to build shelter, catch game, and cross rivers, for many thousands of years. Our technological ingenuity is unsurpassed. Other animals do solve practical problems, of course, such as how to run down and throttle their dinner. But humans take problem-solving one step further, devising alternative ways to solve problems and evaluating the possible consequences of each. "Aha," we say to ourselves, "if I set the oven at 500 degrees, then the turkey will cook in an hour and a half. On the other hand, if I set the oven at 300 degrees and baste the turkey every half an hour, then it will be juicier." *If . . . then, if . . . then.* The same kind of reasoning can be applied to more complex problems, such as how to launch a satellite

into space or how to comfort a heartbroken adolescent. We contemplate the alternatives, size up the consequences, and weigh the costs and benefits of each course of action. We delay action while we think about alternative solutions. If we fail to find a satisfying answer, we can turn to the written record of our ancestors, who discovered solutions to many problems. In this particular case, we would consult a cookbook to find out how to cook the turkey.

We use the same strategies to think about ourselves. As far as we know, no other animal wonders what is to become of itself and tries out alternative ways of being. Human consciousness of self enables us to watch ourselves doing and being.

Finally, we wonder about what life means. We find purpose and direction in our lives that can be described as values, religious beliefs, philosophies, and the like. The large cortex that contemplates physical problems and self-knowledge also struggles to understand the human's place in the universe itself.

From an evolutionary perspective, our ability to think abstractly and to use language makes humankind very different from any other species. In other aspects of human nature, such as the attachment between mother and child, social-group living, sharing, cooperation, and sensory capacities, we are not fundamentally different from our primate or even mammalian relatives.

A look at our uniquely human qualities suggests that we are unusually capable of creating and solving problems; that we use our intelligence to try to understand ourselves and the meaning of life; that we communicate these thoughts through symbolic speech; and that we transmit our accumulated culture to our offspring to give them a head start on the problems of living. The theory of evolution explains how we became what we are and how other species became what they are.

The Theory of Evolution

Although some of the details have been since corrected, Darwin's original concept of evolution, published more than one hundred years ago in *Origin of Species* (1964), has withstood the test of time. The theory rests on five important premises:

1. *Like begets like.* Reproduction is a stable process, so that offspring resemble their parents. (Dogs do not give birth to kittens, and poodle parents have poodle pups).
2. *No two individuals are exactly alike, however.* There are variations among individuals in every population of sexually reproducing organisms, and some of these variations are inherited (that is, they are transferred from parent to offspring via genes).
3. *The number of individuals in a population that survive to reproduce usually is small compared to the number born.*
4. *Which individuals survive and reproduce is determined by natural selection.* Individuals that are better adapted to their environment—better able to find food, avoid danger, and attract mates—produce more offspring than other individuals do. Their offspring inherit these favorable genetic variations and pass them on to their own offspring.
5. *Species change because environmental opportunities change.* A trait that helps a species adapt to one environment may be useless, or maladaptive, in another. A change in the climate, an invasion of grazing or hunting animals, the spread or decline of forests, the evolution of a new

The peppered moth is a classic example of natural selection. In the mid-nineteenth century, these moths were light in color, which made them almost invisible to predators when they settled on the lichen-covered trees and rocks around Manchester, England. One mutant black moth was captured in 1845. When industrialization spread across England, however, pollution killed the lichen and the trees and ground were covered with soot. By the end of the century, 99 percent of the peppered moths were black. Pollution controls instituted in this century have cleaned up the environment. Today, most of the moths are light-colored.

strain of bacteria, or other environmental over others. Natural selection is the mechanism by which environments alter the gene pool.

Evolution is an ongoing process of adjustment to changing circumstances. Individual variations provide the raw material for evolution; environmental conditions put these variations to the test.

The Human Family Tree

There is no obvious beginning—or end—to the story of human evolution. For convenience, we might start about 200 million years ago, when the first mammals appeared. The earliest mammals were small, rat-sized, warm-blooded omnivores (they could eat almost anything). Dinosaurs were most active during the day; mammals took advantage of this fact to hunt insects and snatch buds and fruit at night. When dinosaurs became extinct about 65 million years ago, the mammals divided into two dozen or more different lines, including carnivores (meat-eaters), herbivores (plant-eaters), animals such as whales and bats, and primates.

Primates were distinguished from other mammals by the fact that they were "generalists" (they did not specialize in hunting or grazing or evolve fangs or hoofs) and by the fact that they lived in trees. Life in the trees favored flexible arms, five digits for gripping branches, eyesight over smell to locate food, and an upright or semiupright posture. Over time the primate line divided into four branches: the prosimians (or premonkeys), which are most like the earliest primates; the monkeys, which are more active, curious, and flexible than their ancestors were; the apes, large, tailless, and intelligent creatures that are represented today by chimpanzees, gorillas, orangutans, and gibbons; and, about three or four million years ago, our ancestors the hominids, who walked upright and

were brainier and handier than any primate before them. Modern humans (*Homo sapiens,* or "wise man") evolved about 250,000 years ago.

The course of human evolution is often represented as a diagram of a tree, with the trunk representing the earliest primates and the branches showing the lines leading to the primate groups alive today. (See Figure 2-1.) A more accurate picture would be two trees (Sameroff, 1983). One would represent the evolution of primates. The other would diagram the evolution of other animals and plants and the changes in climate that created (and withdrew) adaptive opportunities at different times.

Without trees—real trees—there would have been no reason for, hence no selection of, primates. If the forests that supported an abundance of tree-dwelling primates had not receded four or five million years ago, there would have been no evolutionary incentive to adapt to life on the open grasslands—the path our ancestors took. Just as the development of a child reflects his environments, so the evolution of our species was shaped by the environments of our ancestors.

The Role of Genes in Evolution

Genes play a dual role in evolution. They provide the glue that, despite our varied personal experiences, makes us all human across many generations. They direct the cells of the embryo to become a human being instead of a frog or an oak tree. They help to establish common modes of thinking, communicating, and socializing. Our survival, as individuals and as a species, depends on this genetic code. Imagine what would happen if some humans had developed genetically so that they used wolf-threat postures to declare war, while others responded only to bird shrieks as a result of *their* heredity; if some people attempted to make friends by licking and pawing while others considered a direct stare a form of sexual assault. Shared patterns of verbal

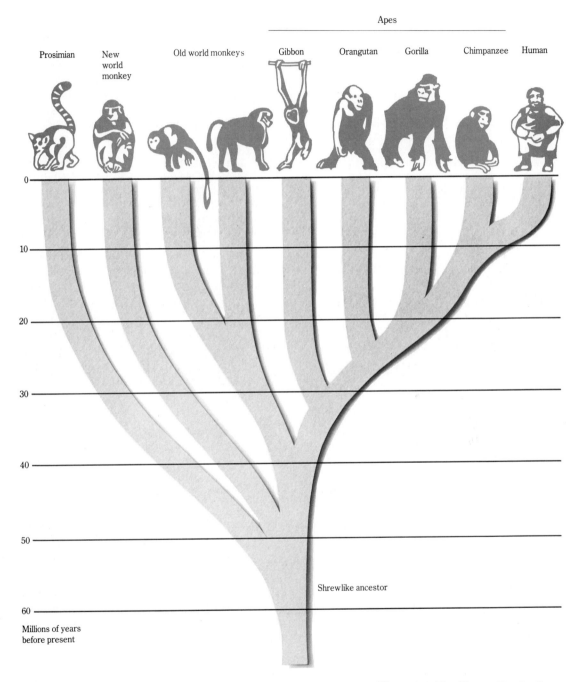

Figure 2-1 The Human Family Tree

THE MECHANISMS OF HEREDITY

The traits parents pass on to their offspring are encoded in the *chromosomes*—long, threadlike strands of genetic material found in the nucleus of the cell. Our cells have 23 pairs of chromosomes, which contain a complete set of genetic instructions for the development of a human being.

Meiosis, the production of ova and sperm, creates cells with only half the usual number of chromosomes (see A). In the first phase of meiosis (I), the pairs of chromosomes line up and exchange bits of genetic material—a phenomenon known as *crossing over*. Suppose, hypothetically, that a gene for blue eyes is linked to a gene for brown hair on one chromosome in the pair, and a gene for green eyes is

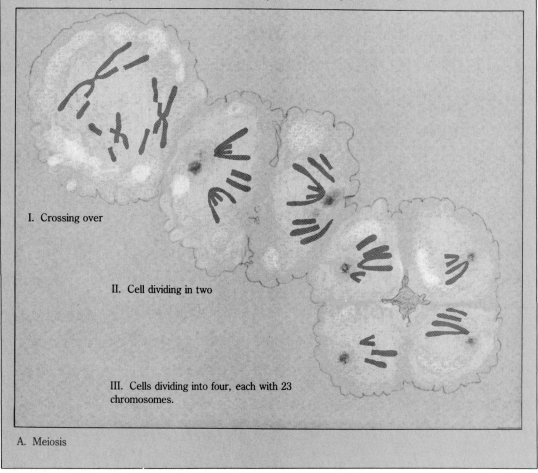

I. Crossing over

II. Cell dividing in two

III. Cells dividing into four, each with 23 chromosomes.

A. Meiosis

linked to a gene for red hair on the other. The gene for blue eyes may cross over and link up with the gene for red hair, and the gene for green eyes may link up with the gene for brown hair. These "new" chromosomes, with their new combinations of genetic instructions, then separate and migrate to opposite ends of the nucleus. In the second phase of meiosis (II), this cell divides in two and the "new" chromosomes duplicate themselves. In the third phase (III), these daughter cells divide, producing four cells with only one set of 23 chromosomes. These are the sex cells, or gametes.

At fertilization, the 23 chromosomes in the mother's ovum are joined to the 23 chromosomes in the father's sperm. The outcome of this union depends on which genes from each parent are matched with one another. In some cases visible traits appear to be a mix because a number of genes from the mother and the father affect the trait. For example, the child of a black father and a white mother will have tan skin. Other genes are *dominant* or *recessive*. For example, the gene for brown eyes is dominant over the gene for blue eyes, which is recessive. A child who inherits the gene for brown eyes from both parents will have brown eyes. But so will the child who inherits the dominant gene for brown eyes from one parent and the recessive

gene for blue eyes from the other. Only if he inherits the recessive gene for blue eyes from both parents will he have blue eyes (see B).

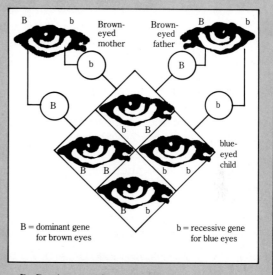

B = dominant gene for brown eyes   b = recessive gene for blue eyes

B. Dominant and Recessive Genes

Crossovers during meiosis, and re-pairings during fertilization, account for some of the tremendous variety in the human species.

and nonverbal communication ensure that both the sender and the receiver understand the message most of the time. If the range of human variations were not kept relatively narrow by our genes, reproduction would become impossible. Genes keep us in line—the human line.

At the same time, genes provide the raw material for evolution by creating variations among individuals. The ultimate source of variation is *mutation,* a random change in the genetic code. Most mutations are slight or harmful, but a few prove adaptive. A second source of variation is *genetic recombination.* During meiosis, the production of sperms and eggs, the genes that a parent inherited from his or her own parents are reshuffled, producing new combina-

tions of genes. At fertilization, the genes from one parent pair off with those from the other As a result, each individual inherits a unique genetic program. (The only exceptions are identical twins, who come from a single fertilized egg that split.) A third source of variation is *gene flow,* a redistribution of genetic material caused by the migration of individuals from one population and environment into another.

Without genetic variation, there would be no evolution. If human beings were carbon copies of one another, everyone would be suited for the same niches. Imagine a society in which everyone could write poetry, but no one could fix cars, or one in which everyone wanted to care for children, but no one wanted to hunt or shop for groceries. Without some specialization and cooperation, there could be no society. The expression, "It takes all kinds" applies not only to people in societies, but also to evolution.

In short, genes affect the ways we are *like* and *un*like one another. They contain the general inheritance of the species, which makes us all human, and the specific inheritance of our parents, grandparents, and great-grandparents, reshuffled to make us individuals.

Genetic Influences on Development

Development is the process whereby a person's **genotype** (the set of genes he inherits) comes to be expressed as a **phenotype** (observable characteristics and behavior). The development of a person's particular phenotype is *not* determined directly by his genes. What each of us becomes is only one of many possible outcomes.

A person with "tall" genes will be taller than someone with "short" genes if they grow up in the same environment. But if the first person receives poor nutrition early in life and the second is well nourished as a child, they may be the same height as adults. The fact that Sam is 5 ft. 10 in. tall, of average intelligence, gregarious, and musically talented are only some of the possible characteristics he might have developed, depending on his experiences.

Genotypes and Phenotypes

Some genotypes, such as eye color and blood type, are expressed directly in the phenotype. The environment does not affect them. But most phenotypes are the result of transactions between different genes and between genes and the environment. For example, the genes that produce clinical diabetes in some people are not expressed in others because of modifying effects in the latter's environment or because of the genes' combination with other genes. Skin color provides an example of this. The expression of skin color is affected by the amount of sunlight received shortly before measurement. The same genotype will be expressed as a darker phenotype near the equator and a lighter phenotype at greater distances from the equator. This does not mean that skin color is less

Basketball star Wilt Chamberlain and jockey Eddie Arcaro are variations on the human theme. Genes account for both the similarities and the differences in members of our species.

genetically determined in Scandinavia than in equatorial Africa. Rather, many genotypes for skin color are less fully expressed in climates with little sun. And some produce pale phenotypes in all sun conditions. A person who has normal genes for skin color, but who also has one pair of genes that blocks the production of melanin, will lack pigmentation and be an albino.

Presumably the same principle of expression applies to intellectual, social, and emotional behavior. For example, we know that the intellectual skills measured by IQ tests are influenced by heredity. The more closely related two people are—the more genes they share— the higher the correlation between their IQ scores. Siblings are more likely to have similar IQs than cousins are, and identical twins are more intellectually alike than brothers and sisters. Of course, close relatives are likely to grow up in the same or similar environments. One way to test the heritability of IQ is to compare the IQs of adopted children with those of their biological parents and also with those of their foster or adoptive parents. The correlation in IQ scores between adopted children and their biological parents is usually higher (about +.35) than that between these children and the parents who raised them (from .00 to +.16) (Skodak & Skeels, 1949; Honzik, 1957, 1983; Scarr & Weinberg, 1983).

These correlations do not mean that the youngsters' IQ scores match those of their biological parents. In fact, the average IQ scores of these children are closer to the average of their adoptive parents than to that of their biological mothers. In one study the average IQ of natural, black mothers was estimated to be 86; the average IQ of their children who had been raised in white, middle-class homes was 106—above the national average for black *or* white children. Clearly, the environment influences the expression of intellectual potential (Scarr & Weinberg, 1976).

Genotypes establish a *reaction range*, a range of possible responses to different environments. This concept is illustrated in Figure 2-2. If three children are reared in similar environments, a child with a great deal of natural ability (genotype A) scores higher on an IQ test than a child with average ability (genotype B) or one with limited ability (genotype C). But if child A grows up in an unstimulating environment and child B in an intellectually enriched environment, the second child will probably perform better on IQ tests than the first child. According to one estimate, genotypes establish a reaction range of about 25 IQ points (Scarr-Salapatek, 1975). Where a person falls within this range depends on her upbringing and experiences.

Gene Action

The basic principles of genetics have become part of common sense. Farmers have long known that if they sow wheat they will harvest

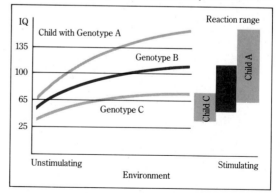

Figure 2-2 Hypothetical Reaction Ranges for IQ
(Adapted from Gottesman, 1963)

wheat, not barley, and that if they breed a prize bull with a fine cow they are more likely to get a prize calf than if they breed poor-quality livestock. But it is only in the last fifteen or twenty years that scientists have discovered what genes are and begun to understand how they work.

The nucleus of every cell in the human body contains 23 pairs of chromosomes. Chromosomes are long strands of DNA (deoxyribonucleic acid) which resemble a twisted ladder. The chromosomes provide a complete set of instructions for the development of a unique human being. Chromosomes direct activities in the cell by attracting RNA (ribonucleic acid) molecules. RNA serves as a messenger, carrying genetic instructions out of the nucleus into the surrounding cytoplasm of the cell, which contains the raw materials for synthesizing many different enzymes, hormones, and other proteins. A **gene** is a section of the chromosome that controls a specific aspect of the production of a particular protein. This much is known; beyond this point is speculation as to how genes actually work.

Delbert Theissen's model of the pathway from DNA to behavior—from genotype to phenotype—is shown in Figure 2-3. Theissen hypothesizes that RNA messengers transcribe the genetic code and carry it to the cytoplasm, where it is translated into enzymes and hormones, which direct the development and behavior of the organism. Although scientists are a long way from detailing every step in this process, we can make some educated guesses based on current research.

Geneticists once thought that each gene was related to specific features of the phenotype (height, eye color, and so on). They now suspect that there are at least three distinct types of genes: structural genes that direct protein synthesis, operator genes that turn structural genes on and off at different times, and regulator genes that activate or repress the operator genes (Jacob & Monod, 1961; Lerner, 1968; Martin & Aimes, 1964; Scarr & Kidd, 1983). Most of the structural genes are found in a wide variety of species and function in approximately the same way in all of them. Structural genes provide the fundamental identity among living things (and biochemical evidence for the theory of evolution, which holds that all living things are descended from a common ancestor). Regulator genes, which modify basic biochemical processes, are probably responsible for the differences among species and among individuals (Theissen, 1972).

Scientists used to think that genes controlled biochemical activity in the cell. They now see biochemical activity as the result of dynamic transactions between genes and the environment within the cell. When a cell divides, each

Genotype   Phenotype

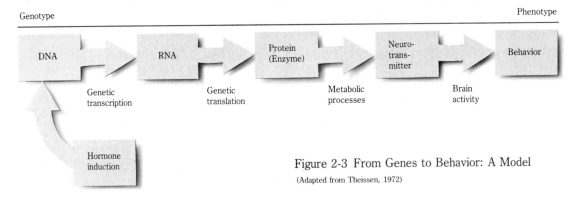

Figure 2-3 From Genes to Behavior: A Model
(Adapted from Theissen, 1972)

daughter cell takes cytoplasm from a different area of the mother cell. Hence, the genes in each daughter cell have a somewhat different environment. Chemicals in that environment activate certain genes; these genes alter the environment by producing different chemicals; these chemicals inhibit that set of genes and activate another set. The process is reciprocal: genes and their cytoplasmic environment alter each other's compositions and activities (Sameroff, 1983). Thus, even at the most primitive biological level, genes interact with the environment.

Scientists have only begun to understand the biochemistry of gene action. Many important questions remain. For example, each cell in the human body originates from the same fertilized egg and carries the same genetic information. What causes some cells to develop into the brain and others into blood? Why do some genes become active and others become inactive at different stages in the life cycle? (Some hereditary diseases do not affect people until young adulthood or middle age.) How does protein synthesis at the cellular level relate to intellectual or emotional behavior? The pathway from genotype to phenotype is still uncharted territory.

Genes and Human Development

When we step back from the microscope and look at the whole child again, certain patterns emerge. A human genotype creates potentials and sets limits on development, but it does not establish a single route to one phenotypic endpoint. Rather, there are many possible paths and outcomes. Some aspects of human development are not strongly controlled by the genes: environmental influences and individual differences guide the child's path. Other aspects of development are strongly controlled. Unless something highly unusual happens, all children follow the same developmental path. C. H. Waddington's "landscape," shown in Figure 2-4,

illustrates this (Waddington, 1957, 1966). The ball at the top of the hill represents the developing phenotype. It rolls through valleys of varying widths and depths, which represent genetic influences on development. At some points a slight breeze in the environment (a minor illness, a good or bad teacher) can send the phenotype into another channel of development. At other points the walls of the channel are steep, so that a major environmental storm (a devastating illness or accident) is required to change the course of development. **Canalization** is the genetic restriction of development to one or a few phenotypic outcomes. The more highly canalized a developmental path is, the less likely that the phenotype will stray from the normal path for its species. There are some developmental paths that all members of a species follow unless they are exposed to severely atypical environments.

Robert McCall (1981) has applied this model to mental development. McCall argues that up to about the age of 2, mental development is channeled by the genotype through a deep valley that restricts the child to a narrow range of phenotypic outcomes. A strong environmental wind may blow the ball off course, but the steep walls of the valley usually force it back. Individual differences are minimal during this period: all normal infants acquire object permanence, the ability to form mental images, and other basic human cognitive skills. (We will describe these in detail in Chapter 4.) All normal children begin to understand and produce words and sentences (the subject of Chapter 7). After age 2, this valley branches out into different developmental pathways that reflect the child's unique genetic heritage. The walls of these channels are not as steep as they were earlier; the developing child becomes more vulnerable to the shifting winds of experience. As a result of unique genetic and environmental circumstances, individual differences become more ap-

Figure 2-4 Waddington's "Landscape" of Development

(Adapted from Waddington, 1957)

parent and more significant. Almost all children acquire speech, but some are more fluent than others. Only a few children will become poets.

The actual phenotype is the expression of the genotype in a set of environments over the lifespan. It is tempting to conclude that heredity sets limits on development, while environments determine the extent of development. Neither view is entirely true. There are constant transactions between the genotype and the environment over the course of development. Under different environmental conditions, the same genotype may become different phenotypes; under the same environmental conditions, different genotypes may become different phenotypes; and under different environmental conditions, different genotypes may result in the same phenotype (Ginsburgh 1966, 1968, 1971). (See Figure 2-5.) There is no simple, one-to-one correspondence between the two.

Environmental Influences on Development

Advice on how to rear children changes with the times. In the 1920s Watson and other experts pictured children as impulsive little creatures who needed stern training. Mothers were warned not to spoil their offspring with too much hugging and kissing. In the 1950s children were seen as fragile flowers who would thrive only in the hothouse of unconditional love. The slight-est frustration might thwart their emotional development. Today parents are being advised once again to say what they mean and enforce the rules. The pendulum has swung back and forth between permissiveness and law-and-order. The one point on which three generations of child experts seem to agree is that the environment parents provide for their children influences the youngsters' development.

What "Environment" Means

Developmental psychologists would agree that the environments a child experiences affect the rate and course of development. But as Joachim Wohlwill (1973) has pointed out, psychologists have not always agreed on what the term "environment" means. To illustrate contrasting theoretical positions on the nature of the environment, Wohlwill described four models:

1. *The hospital bed.* The person is a passive recipient of stimulation, over which he has little control, and to which he makes few discriminating responses—like a patient

Ordinary rearing

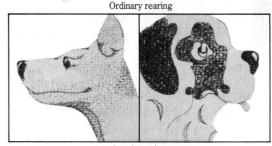

Attack rearing

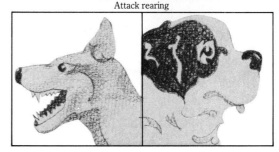

Figure 2-5 Gene–Environment Interactions Doberman Pinschers reared to be pets can be gentle with their owners; those reared to be attack dogs become vicious on command. But no amount of training can turn a Saint Bernard into an attack dog.

immobilized in a hospital bed. Events keep happening to him: nurses enter the room, take his temperature, wheel him out for X-rays, and bring him food, whether or not he is hungry. In this model, the stimulation is passively received from the environment.

2. *The amusement park.* In this model the person is surrounded by an array of intense and varied stimulations. She can choose what to attend to: whether to take one ride or another, whether to eat popcorn or cotton candy. But once she has made her choice—for example, by climbing into a roller coaster car—she has little control over what stimulation she receives. As Wohlwill says, in bumper cars even skillful drivers have little control over the jarring bumps and collisions. Everyone gets his or her share of jolts—precisely the attraction of the ride.

3. *The swim-meet.* This is the pure model of the environment as an opportunity to act. As soon as the gun sounds, the person dives into the water and swims as fast as possible. His experience is under his own control. The water provides the opportunity to swim, regardless of the behavior of other swimmers or of other environmental stimuli.

4. *The tennis match.* In tennis each player's actions depend on continuous interaction with an ever-changing environment. There is a tight "feedback loop" between the opponents, each of whose responses determines the other player's next opportunity. If the opponent hits the ball low over the net and short, the player must run forward to retrieve the ball and send it back over the net. On the other hand, if the opponent misses the shot or returns a high lob, the player's behavior will be entirely different. And the opponent's

behavior is similarly determined by the interchange. In this model, the environment affords opportunities to respond actively, and one's responses change the nature of the environment.

There are appropriate uses for all of these models of the environment. The tenth-grader who goes from geometry class at 9:45 A.M. to history class at 10:30 A.M. can be an example of a hospital bed experience. She isn't given a choice where to go or what she will see and hear. The preschooler watching "Sesame Street" has made his selection from the amusement-park world of TV; what happens to him while he watches has already been determined by the program's writers. The child riding his bicycle alone as fast as he can down a hill has a swim-meet experience. And finally, the girl talking to her best friend on the telephone experiences a tennis match: what each one says is contingent on what was said before and determines the direction of the next remark.

All of us experience environments in all of these forms throughout our lives. Many arguments in psychology have been based on the advocacy of one model of the environment to the exclusion of others. Behaviorists, for example, tend to see life as a hospital bed, while structuralists tend to use the swim-meet model. The authors of this book accept all of these models but emphasize the tennis match and the view that people structure their own experiences and change their environments as they act on them. Even in a hospital bed, people interpret their experiences and code them for memory storage in ways that give them meaning. Even if they cannot act to change the environment, they are not entirely passive recipients of environmental treatments.

Learning is an active process. The sensory reception of patterns of stimuli is only part of the process. Memory is not a tape recorder that transcribes an exact copy of whatever sounds occur in the environment. People give events meaning in the process of storing them in memory. And they interpret or reinterpret what they remember when they retrieve events from memory (Bower, 1979). The external environment provides light waves, sound waves, and other forms of physical stimulation. The brain molds and gives meaning to these experiences.

Different people pay attention to different aspects of their environment. Naturally, there are strong, unavoidable stimuli such as very loud noises that will impinge on everyone within earshot. But some people respond to such stimuli with fear, some with annoyance, and some with a calm determination to think of something else until the disturbance goes away. In most cases people have a choice of whether or not to attend to stimuli and how to interpret their meaning. Have you ever seen someone running down a busy street at full speed? Social psychologists have shown that if the runner is a black youth, many people see him as a thief escaping from the scene of a robbery. If he is a well-dressed, middle-aged man, people may assume that he is late for an important appointment. If the person is an attractive young woman, people look behind her for the man in pursuit! In each case the physical stimulus is simply a person running down the street. But observers interpret, and remember, their experiences with this stimulus very differently depending on the meaning they give to the event.

Our discussions of environments assumes that there is some active interplay between the individual and the environment at every stage of development.

The Essentials: Loving Care

Children need loving attention at every stage of their development. Every baby requires milk, baths, affection, opportunities and encouragement to learn, and a thousand other particulars

in their everyday environment if they are to develop in the best possible ways.

Social contact may be as important as nutrition. In a classic series of experiments, Harry Harlow separated rhesus monkeys from their mothers shortly after birth and raised them in isolation for six months (Harlow, 1958; Harlow & Suomi, 1970). The infant monkeys spent most of their time huddled in a corner of their cage, clutching their own body and rocking back and forth. They were then given a choice between two artificial wire "mothers," one equipped with a bottle and one covered with foam rubber and soft terry cloth but no bottle. The baby monkeys chose the "contact comfort" of the cloth mother over the mother with food. They preferred warm mothers to cool mothers and mothers that rocked to mothers that were immobile. But these surrogates did not compensate for the loss of "mother love," in Harlow's phrase. As adults, monkeys reared with artificial mothers did not interact normally with other monkeys but responded to ordinary events with exaggerated fear or extreme aggression. They did not make appropriate responses to sexual approaches. The few females that did mate tended to abuse or neglect their own infants. For monkeys, then, normal development depends on social contact in the first six months of life.

For obvious reasons, one would not conduct similar experiments with human infants. But psychologists have studied children whose parents kept them in an attic or back room and gave them only minimal care. These children do not learn to walk or talk or interact with other people in normal human ways. When they are discovered, they are usually small for their age, uncoordinated, and apathetic (Clarke & Clarke 1977). In 1945 René Spitz studied babies who were living in an orphanage where they received food and medical care but little personal attention. Their scores on mental tests taken at 1

year of age suggested that most were retarded. They rarely smiled or cried and made no effort to talk. Wayne Dennis (1973) found similar developmental retardation in infants in an orphanage in Iran. These babies were deprived not only of mothering, but of almost any kind of stimulation. They spent most of their time lying on their backs in their cribs, without toys or even pictures on the walls. They had few opportunities to interact with anyone or anything. Although these particular studies have been questioned, there is no doubt that isolation in an unstimulating environment retards a child's motor, intellectual, and social development. Infants need attention and interaction.

Some studies show that continuity is also essential for normal development. In the orphanages Spitz and Dennis studied, nurses changed shifts and hours often, so that no one nurse was responsible for all the care of a particular baby. The ratio of infants to caregivers was about eight to one. The continual turnover of personnel in such institutions makes it difficult for children to form attachments to particular people (Bowlby, 1969). There is evidence that children who are cared for impersonally by many people may have personality disturbances in adolescence (Cadoret, 1976; Crowe, 1972). When children learn that no one in particular cares for their welfare, some learn that they need not care for others.

Early Experience

Psychologists are divided on the importance of early experience to later development. Some think that only a few bad experiences can disrupt normal development. These psychologists often stress the importance of early experience in determining the course of development; in other words, "As the twig is bent, so grows the branch." Other psychologists conclude that most children are quite resilient and will be seriously disturbed only by major traumas or persistently evil environments.

Both views are probably correct. Some few individuals are not very robust or hardy; they need high-quality environments at all times, or they are pushed away from the normal course of development toward mental illness, retardation, or social deviance. These are the people who are most often referred to psychologists, psychiatrists, and social workers. We feel that most people can endure hardships and less-than-optimal amounts and combinations of environmental "nutrients" for long periods without permanent damage. If their later circumstances are more supportive of normal growth, they catch up and follow a normal developmental path (Brim & Kagan, 1980).

Support for this position comes from Ann and Alan Clarke's review (1977) of case studies of children whose early environments were wretched by any standard, but who were res-

The importance of cuddling is part of our primate heritage, as Harry Harlow demonstrated in his classic experiments with infant rhesus monkeys. Here an infant manages to reach a bottle without losing contact with its terry cloth "mother."

Insight

RECOVERY FROM ABUSE AND NEGLECT: A CASE STUDY

Jarmilla Koluchova reported the amazing case of identical twin boys, whose mother died shortly after they were born (Clarke & Clarke, 1977). Their father placed them in a children's home. When they were about 18 months old, he took them to live with his new wife, their two older sisters, and two of the stepmother's children. There were six children altogether in the household, the oldest of whom was 9. The parents moved into a neighborhood where no one knew them.

The father, who was below average in intelligence, was inarticulate and passive. His wife ruled the home. Her own mother had reared her two children in their early childhood; she had little experience with or interest in small children. She fed the twins, but otherwise she left their care to their father, who worked on the railroad and was often away from home.

The central figure in this tragedy was the stepmother. Later investigations revealed that she was a person of average intelligence but was egocentric and lacking in feelings for others. Her disinterest soon developed into active hostility toward the twins. The boys grew up in almost total isolation. They lived in a small, empty, unheated room, slept on a plastic sheet on the floor, and were locked in the cellar for long periods. They were often severely beaten. The twins were not allowed into the main living rooms of the apartment or out of the house. The other children in the family were forbidden to talk to them or play with them. A few building blocks were their only toys. They had no sunshine, fresh air, or exercise, and they often shared inadequate food.

When discovered at age 6, the boys appeared to be about 3 years old. They hardly walked and seemed to be severely mentally retarded. A physician suspected abuse and reported them to authorities in August, 1967. In December of that year, the parents were charged with criminal neglect and the twins were placed in a home for preschool children. They remained in the home for nearly two years, making steady progress in motor, speech, and intellectual development, and then they were enrolled in a school for the mentally retarded. In the summer of 1969 they were placed in a foster home with two middle-aged sisters who, according to case workers, gave the twins patient, devoted attention. By the end of the 1969–70 school year, they had outstripped their mentally retarded classmates and were placed in second grade in a normal school. Although they were about three years behind their age-mates in schoolwork, both now scored in the normal range of intelligence tests.

In the short space of four years, the twins made giant strides in intellectual and social development, speech, and social relations. They rose from the level of intelligence of a 3-year-old to that of an 11-year-old in this short period. No one can say what intellectual level they would have attained had they been raised in a normal environment from the beginning—given their family history, an average IQ is the best prediction. Yet they reached this milestone, despite horrifying early experiences.

cued and placed in warm, supportive care. When discovered, all of the children were below normal in motor, mental, speech, and social development. But within a few years, all but one child recovered to a normal level of functioning. The one exception is the case most often cited by American social scientists, a child named Anna who was studied by Kingsley Davis. Although Anna made progress in some areas, she did not attain normal levels of intelligence. But her mother was mentally deficient and she may have been retarded herself.

These children were not typical because all of them were removed permanently from their wretched surroundings. In most cases of early deprivation, abuse, or neglect, the quality of the children's environments remain poor throughout their growing years. When they leave a hospital or an enriched day-care center, they go home to the same or similar parents, neighborhoods, and schools. They are rarely transported from slums to palaces, except in fairy tales; few children are Cinderellas. Thus the seemingly long-term effects of early deprivation are better described as early *and continuing* deprivation (Sameroff & Chandler, 1975).

What Is a Normal Environment?

Psychologists know a good deal about how to distort development and what makes a bad environment. What is a normal environment? In our view, it is that range of environments that was typical for humanity during the period when we evolved as a species. For most of human history, our ancestors gathered wild plants and hunted wild game for a living. Hunting and gathering were the mill in which natural selection pounded the grist of the human body and mind (Mayr, 1970; Fishbein, 1976). For millions of years, human beings lived in nomadic bands of ten to fifty males, females, and children in groups of several nuclear families that may or may not have been related to one another. Ac-

cording to Harold Fishbein (1977), the crucial elements in our adaptation to the hunter-gatherer way of life were: 1) cooperative hunting by men, 2) the sharing of food among members of the band, 3) the manufacture of tools, 4) husband–wife reciprocity, with each partner contributing an essential part to their survival and that of their young, 5) symbolic communication through language, and 6) rule-giving and rule-making.

Through most of human history, infants were carried and cared for by their mothers for the first three years, mainly because the mothers nursed them. And mothers with infants were always part of a larger human group that helped to support mother and infant (Scarr-Salapatek, 1975). Nearly all children had peers with whom to play and learn. Peer groups allow children to try out many forms of behavior that could be dangerous if tried with adults. Angry fights, sex games, arguing with and challenging authority can be safely played out with age-mates but not with adults. Adults showed children how to be acceptable grown-ups: how to work, choose a mate, accept responsibilities toward kin and society, and evaluate their own experiences.

All humans pass on their culture to their young and provide opportunities for intellectual, social, and moral development. Youngsters must be taught these special human adaptations, or the group would not survive into the next generation. But teaching the young these essential human skills turns out to be simpler than one might expect. Evolution has provided children with brains that are ready to learn. Even without formal instruction, children come to understand and communicate their experiences. Of course, children must first be exposed to a human language. They must have opportunities to measure things, to weigh them in relation to other objects, to test the strength of various materials. They must observe how adults be-

Left: !Kung mothers keep their babies with them at all times and nurse them whenever they whimper. *Above*: In the Soviet Union, many infants spend their days in a collective nursery. Healthy infants can thrive with many forms of care.

have in relation to each other. And it certainly helps if they are told the traditional stories of proper behavior and the consequences of improper behavior. (Every culture has its *Grimms' Fairy Tales* to illustrate good and bad behavior.) Socialization—the process of learning the values and rules for behavior of the culture in which one is born and will live—is part of a normal human environment.

How cultures socialize their children varies greatly. Some societies separate their children into same-sex groups by the age of 6. The men teach the boys, and the women teach the girls, how to be true Ashanti or Hopi, for example. In the United States, children typically stay with an adult man and woman, usually their biological parents, until late adolescence or early adulthood. We do not rear our children communally in groups. On Israeli kibbutzim, however, children are reared in mixed-sex groups, divided by age, in children's houses where they are supervised by women whose job it is to care for all the children of the kibbutz. Although the children visit their parents in the evenings and on weekends, they spend most of their time in these children's groups.

The variety of child-care arrangements in the world sometimes obscures what they all have in common. In all of these societies (indeed, in all societies), the children are given opportunities to learn how to be an adult in their culture, and they are taught the culture by adults who care for them and protect them. None of these children are neglected or abused by the standards of evolutionary history. Although some psychologists in the United States would question the early separation of children from their biological parents, there is no evidence that these variations in child-rearing produce any better or worse results than our own typical practices (Beit-Hallahmi & Rabin, 1977). Indeed, anthropologists would tell us that it is atypical among the world's cultures for children to be isolated with their mothers for most of the day, as most small children in middle-class

Insight

THE GARCIA EFFECT

Common sense holds that innate of inborn behavior and learned or acquired behavior are distinct categories. Behavior is *either* innate *or* learned. A series of learning experiments with rats by John Garcia and his colleagues (Garcia & Koelling, 1966) showed that this distinction is false. Garcia followed the classic avoidance-conditioning model: he gave the rats water to drink, punished them while they were drinking, but warned them with a signal before the punishment began. According to learning theory, the rats would soon learn to stop drinking right after the signal. They would acquire an avoidance response.

Garcia divided the rats into four groups. One group was given a noise-and-light signal followed by an electric shock. The second group was given water with a distinctive flavor followed by artificially induced nausea. (The nausea was caused by X rays, not by something in the water.) In the third and fourth groups the punishments and signals were reversed: the rats in group three were given a noise-and-light signal followed by nausea, and the rats in group four were given flavored water followed by an electric shock.

The rats in groups one and two developed an avoidance response as expected. But the rats in groups three and four defied learning theory. No matter how often they were punished, they did not make the association between signal and punishment and continued to drink. Were the rats in the first two groups brighter than those in the second two groups? No, the animals were genetic equals. Garcia concluded that while it is easy to teach a rat to associate noise-and-sound with a shock, or taste with nausea, it is very difficult to teach the same rat that a taste signals shock or that a sound signals nausea. It is as if rats had a "genetically coded hypothesis" in their brains that runs something like this: "When I feel sick to the stomach, it must be something I ate." Moreover, rats adhere so strongly to this hypothesis that they ignore evidence that the nausea was caused by a light-and-sound signal. Similarly, when rats feel shock they don't "think" that this might have been caused by something in the water. In short, rats are genetically predisposed to learn some things more easily than others.

Rats are not alone. Martin Seligman (Seligman & Hager, 1972) recalls a familiar experience. For dinner one night he had his favorite dish: filet mignon with béarnaise sauce. Six hours later he became violently sick with the flu. He recovered, but he also acquired a permanent distaste for béarnaise sauce. Why, he asks, did he associate the nausea with the sauce he had eaten six hours earlier and not with the table setting, his dinner companion, or the opera he was listening to when he became ill? The Garcia effect is his answer: Evolution "prepared" or "directed" him to make this particular association.

As biologist Julian Huxley put it, "even the capacity to learn, to learn at all, to learn only at a definite stage of development, to learn one thing rather than another, to learn more or less quickly, must have some genetic basis" (1965).

America were during the 1950s and 1960s.

Normal human environments provide growing children with close contact with mothers, other adults and peers, and with tools and material culture. This gives them opportunities to learn to manipulate objects, to form social bonds, and to acquire a human language. Equally important, children have an evolutionary bias toward acquiring these forms of behavior—what

geneticist Theodore Dobzhansky (1967) called a *bias toward human educability.*

How People Shape Their Environments

We often assume that the environment is something *out there,* something that happens *to* people and over which they have no control—the hospital bed. But there is a difference between the environment to which people are exposed

Because of their own characteristics, people evoke different responses from others and therefore experience different environments.

Passive genotype–environment correlations are
strongest in infancy.

and the environment they actively experience (Scarr & McCartney, 1983). The meaning of events changes with development. The child who has "caught on" that things have names, and who demands to know the names for everything, experiences a different verbal environment than the one he experienced earlier. His parents and others have been talking to him since birth. But because *he* has changed, his world has changed. The meaning of events also varies from person to person, as we pointed out earlier. One child is thrilled by a visit to a family who owns a large German shepherd; another is terrified. Their experiences depend not only on what is out there but also on what is within them. To some extent, people (including children) create their own environments.

Most developmental psychologists consider the impact of environments on genotypes. Let us also consider the impact of genotypes on the environments the growing child experiences. Often genotype and experience are intertwined. Robert Plomin and his colleagues (1977) have described three types of genotype–environment correlations: passive, evocative, and active. *Passive* genotype–environment correlations result from the fact that parents provide both genes and environments for their offspring. There is a similarity between what each of us is as a person and what we do as parents. To some extent, what we are depends on our genotypic differences from other people. To that extent, the environment we provide our children also depends on genetic differences. Reading illustrates this. Children whose parents read to them often do well in school. We could conclude that reading to children enhances intellectual development. But parents who read to children are people who enjoy reading and who read well. Their children are not only exposed to books, they also inherit "genes" for reading skills. These children are likely to become book lovers for both genetic and environmental rea-

sons. This passive genotype–environment correlation might be called the "double whammy effect." Children who have intellectually stimulating environments also tend to have intelligent parents—a double dose of advantage.

Evocative genotype–environment correlations result from the fact that genotypically different individuals evoke different responses from their social and physical environments. Cheerful, outgoing children are more likely to engage other people in social interaction than are sober, inactive children. They experience a friendlier environment. In school, cooperative, attentive children are more likely to receive pleasant instruction from the teacher than are uncooperative, distractible children. Children who are well-coordinated physically are more likely to be invited to join a game and so get more athletic practice than clumsy children do. Talented youngsters also get more positive feedback from the racquet, or the piano, than less talented children do. The instruments respond to their touch.

The third type of genotype–environment correlation results from *active,* niche-picking behavior. People seek out environments that they find compatible and stimulating. Each of us selects the people and things we want to learn more about, become involved with, and dedicate ourselves to. The choices we make in sports, school, relationships—in life—reflect the motivational, intellectual, and emotional elements of our genotypes.

The relative importance of these three types of genotype–environment correlations changes over the course of development. Most of the infant's environment is provided by adults. When those adults are the infant's biological relatives, the kinds of experiences they offer—lullabies, loud rock music, or silence—are correlated with the infant's genotype. Infants can select what they pay attention to, but they cannot do much seeking out or niche-building. Hence, passive genotype–environment correlations are more important for infants and small children than for older children, who can range beyond their family's influence.

The importance of active genotype–environment correlations increases with age as children develop the skills and are given opportunities to choose environments. A 2-year-old plays with whomever her mother invites to play; a 6-year-old makes her own friends in the school playground; an adolescent can meet people from other schools and other parts of town. Evocative genotype–environment correlations are important throughout the lifespan. The way infants respond to handling affects the way they are treated, just as the way adults behave toward others affects how others respond to them.

We do not mean to suggest that genotypes *determine* environments. Rather, individuals with certain genotypes are *more likely* to receive certain kinds of parenting, evoke certain responses from others, and seek out certain experiences. What feelings they evoke in others depends in part on those other people; what aspects of the environment they select for special attention depends on what is available. Genotypes and environments combine to produce human development, and genetic and environmental *differences* combine to produce *variations* in development.

Both the shared genetic heritage of our species and the shared features of normal human environments determine what behavior humans have in common. Development is the expression of our genotypes in the contexts of our environments. Constant transactions between the developing person and the environment determine a person's development. As we have seen, an evolutionary perspective emphasizes the role of both genes and environments in programming the development of human behavior and in determining the differences between people. Viewing both the species-typical themes and the individual variations on those themes are essential in understanding how children develop from infancy to adolescence.

SUMMARY

1. What's in an infant's smile? Information on the baby's current condition, developmental status, personal history, and the evolutionary history of the species. The impulse to smile back is programmed in us.
2. The development of the individual (ontogeny) is shaped by the evolution of the species (phylogeny).
3. Human beings have much in common with apes and monkeys, our closest relatives. What makes us unique is not only our ability to walk on two feet and use our hands to make tools, but also our ability to think about alternative solutions to problems and to communicate thoughts, experiences, and beliefs through language.
4. Human nature, like human anatomy, is the product of natural selection. We are mammals and primates who took a separate evolutionary path about three million years ago.
5. Genes account for the continuity in a species (such as common modes of communication) and also for individual variation in a species. The three main sources of genetic variation are mutation, meiosis, and gene flow.
6. From an evolutionary perspective, development is the process whereby an individual's genotype (the set of genes inherited from one's parents) is expressed as a phenotype (observable traits). A few genes (such as those for eye color and blood type) are expressed directly: the environment does not affect them. But in most cases genes establish a reaction range, or a set of potential responses to environmental conditions.

7. Recent discoveries in biochemistry indicate that transactions between genes and the environment begin at the cellular level. But much of the biochemistry of development (why some cells become blood and others bone) remains a mystery.

8. Some aspects of development are more highly canalized—that is, under stronger genetic control and less subject to environmental influence—than others are. The development of speech in its early stages is an example.

9. For development psychologists, there are four contrasting models of the environment: (a) the hospital bed, in which the person lies passively, (b) the amusement park, in which the person can choose experiences, (c) the swim meet, in which the environment is an opportunity to perform, and (d) the tennis match, in which the person engages in interplay with a changing environment.

10. All psychologists would agree that infants need social contact, stimulation, and continuity of care. But the impact of early experience has been exaggerated: Children can recover from early isolation and neglect.

11. A "normal environment" can be described in evolutionary terms as one in which an infant has close contact with his mother, experience with other adults and children, opportunities to explore and experiment, and exposure to a culture and language.

12. Heredity and environment together influence development, for three reasons: (a) the experiences parents provide their children reflect the parents' own genotypes, (b) different people evoke different responses from others, and (c) people actively choose the environmental niches they find comfortable and interesting.

13. The statement that genes establish limits on development, while environments determine the extent of development, is based on half-truths. Each influences the other.

FURTHER READING

Boakes, R. (1984). *From Darwin to behaviorism.* New York: Cambridge University Press. A fine history of how theories about human behavior have changed from the mid-nineteenth to the mid-twentieth centuries.

Dobzhansky, T. (1960). *Mankind evolving.* New Haven, CT: Yale University Press. A classic and still important tale of the evolution and genetics of the human species.

Ghiselin, M. (1984). *Triumph of the Darwinian method.* Chicago: University of Chicago Press. Not all science is done in a laboratory or with experimental methods. This book describes the logic of observational, evolutionary science.

Konner, M. (1982). *The tangled wing: Biological restraints on the human spirit.* New York: Holt, Rinehart & Winston. A contemporary evolutionary account of human nature that synthesizes biological and psychological research on rage, fear, lust, and other common and uncommon experiences.

A million, million spermatozoa
    All of them alive
Out of their cataclysm but one poor Noah
    Dare hope to survive
And among that billion minus one
    Might have chanced to be
Shakespeare, another Newton, a new Donne
    But the One was Me.
—Aldous Huxley, "Fifth Philosopher's Song"

Most people find older babies adorable. Put a 9-month-old cutie in an ad and adults take notice. Newborns are not so cute, with their red and wrinkled skin, tremulous movements, and pitiful cries. For the first two months or so babies seem totally helpless. But a closer look reveals that new babies have ways of getting adults to attend to their needs. Babies in the first few weeks also perceive much of the world around them.

From 2 months to 12 months, the infant changes dramatically. The first changes adults notice are smiles and attentive looks. Then come advances in mobility: from lying to sitting to creeping to standing alone. Less observable are babies' abilities to make discoveries about their environments, to recognize familiar people and objects, to socialize and form attachments, and to direct their own behavior. It is in the middle of the first year that adults find babies so lovable, because typically they have the rounded appearance, high forehead, and miniature facial features that attract adults of all primate species to their young.

From 12 to 18 months, babies explore wherever possible with little concern for adult views of appropriate hunting grounds. Toddlers bear constant watching, both for their own safety and for the sake of the household. In this period, infants seem to develop a mind of their own. They begin to resist their parents' requests and may begin to throw temper tantrums. With curiosity great, they cruise around the house looking for interesting things and places to explore. By this point, babies can remember where favorite items are kept; they no longer forget about an object that has temporarily disappeared. Words become signals for action, expressions of feelings, and comments on the state of the world. "Muk" (milk) and "cookie" are obvious requests for the parent to provide some nourishment. "No" is a clear refusal to comply, something they often practice in inappropriate contexts. Toddlers also use idiosyncratic expressions such as "whazat?" or "der" as queries about the names of objects while pointing at the things the adult is being asked to name. Vocabulary development is usually slow from 12 to 15 months, but it can explode toward the end of infancy. Toddlers are even more adorable than younger infants. Those cherubs in Renaissance paintings are actually overweight toddlers!

This section covers development from conception to cherubim, a remarkable tale of cell division. The processes of development are far more interesting than simple cell division—we must explain how a single fertilized cell comes to walk and talk.

PART 2
INFANCY

CHAPTER

At the beginning, the body consists of only one cell; by the time of birth, it has two hundred billion cells. When you, gentle reader, were a single cell you weighed about fifteen ten-millionths of a gram; at birth (if you were a seven-pound baby), you weighed 3,250 grams. In those nine months, you gained two billion times. You began as a spherical egg that could have been lost in a pinhole; you soon became hollow and then long and narrow. Sometime in the third week of life (Chinese reckoning),[1] your heart began to beat; was that not a great day in your career? You had the beginnings of a brain before you had hands, and of arms before legs; you developed muscles and nerves and began your struggle; in the darkness you faced strange perils, and you came at last to the threshold of the world. (Corner, 1944, pp. 1–2)

More development, more differentiation and growth, occurs in the first nine months of life than in any other period in the human lifespan. In this chapter we track prenatal development,

[1]The Chinese reckon age from the date of conception, not from the date of birth.

describe birth and some of the controversies surrounding it, and introduce the neonate—a tiny, dependent creature who still surprises psychologists.

The First Nine Months

The idea of prenatal development is a comparatively modern one. Up to the nineteenth century, most people believed that the fetus was a preformed, miniature human being who grew larger and larger during pregnancy but did not change in any significant ways. Where did this "little person" come from? This question was the focus of heated debate in the 1600s. Some biologists maintained that the female's egg contained a tiny but functioning human being; all that the male's sperm did was to stimulate growth. Many others argued that this miniature person was in the head of the sperm and that the womb merely provided a home in which the little one could grow (Needham, 1969) (see Figure 3-1). These arguments were

FROM FETUS TO NEWBORN

laid to rest in the early nineteenth century when the new science of embryology gave both parents credit for the beginnings of life. But is was not until 1944 that scientists actually observed the union of the parent cells. Thanks to sophisticated photographic techniques developed in the 1950s and 1960s, we are the first generation to have a clear picture of our own early development (Flanagan, 1962).

Conception

The development of a new human being begins when a male's sperm pierces the cell membrane of a female's ovum, or egg. The human female is born with about 200 million immature ova. Starting in puberty, one of her two ovaries releases a ripe egg about every 28 days. The egg falls into the Fallopian tube and begins a slow journey of four to five days to the uterus. In most cases the trip is uneventful and the egg disintegrates when it reaches the womb. The human male begins to produce sperm in adolescence, at the rate of about 200 million a day. During sexual intercourse, a man ejaculates between 20 million and 500 million sperm into the woman's body. Only a few hundred sperm cells make their way through the cervix, into the uterus, and up to the Fallopian tube, where a ripe egg may or may not be waiting. Only one sperm can penetrate the egg's membrane.

Within hours of meeting, the sperm and egg fuse to become a new cell, called a **zygote,** in which 23 chromosomes from the mother link to 23 from the father. The newly fertilized egg begins its journey down the Fallopian tube. In the uterus the zygote takes the form of a hollow ball, called the *blastocyte.* About six or seven days after fertilization, the outer layer of this blastocyte begins to grow root-like extensions, called *villi.* The villi push into the lining of the uterus like the roots of a growing plant into the soil (see Figure 3-2 on pp. 88–89). The villi become the placenta, which will nourish the developing infant for the next eight and a half months. The inner cells become the embryo.

The Embryo

When the zygote is firmly attached to the wall of the uterus—about two weeks after conception—it is called an **embryo.** The next six weeks of prenatal development are marked by *differentiation* of tissue into specialized layers. One layer of cells (the ectoderm) will develop into skin and nerves, another (the mesoderm) into muscle and bones, and another (the endoderm) into the internal organs. The amniotic sac, a protective covering in which the embryo floats like a tiny toy in a glass ball, takes shape. And the placenta begins to function. The *placenta* is a disc-shaped organ that enables the embryo to obtain oxygen and nutrients from the mother's bloodstream and dispose of carbon dioxide and other wastes. The placenta connects

Figure 3-1 A Homunculus   In the seventeenth and eighteenth centuries, many biologists believed that the man's sperm contained a tiny but complete human being (called a "homunculus"). The mother's only role in conception was to serve as an incubator.

Insight

THE BRAVE NEW WORLD OF HIGH-TECHNOLOGY FERTILIZATION

There is more than one way to conceive a child today. *Artificial insemination* is the simplest technique when the husband is infertile and cannot produce sufficient sperm. The physician inserts a donor's sperm into the fertile wife by syringe. Between 10,000 and 20,000 American babies are conceived this way each year. If the wife is infertile, a couple may opt for *surrogate motherhood*. The couple contracts to pay a fertile woman to be artificially inseminated with the husband's sperm. This woman carries the baby and delivers it to the couple when it is born. *In vitro fertilization,* or fertilization in an artificial environment, is used when a woman's Fallopian tubes are damaged. The first "test tube" baby was born in Britain in 1978. In this procedure, physicians surgically remove a number of eggs from the woman's ovaries, fertilize them with the husband's sperm in a petri dish, and implant one or more of the embryos in the wife's uterus. Perhaps 1,000 babies have been conceived this way since 1978, several hundred in the United States. The latest technique is *surrogate embryo transfer*. It is designed for women who cannot conceive but can carry a fetus. A fertile surrogate is artificially inseminated with the husband's sperm, then four or five days later the embryo is flushed from the womb of the surrogate and implanted in the wife's womb. To date, two babies have been conceived this way.

As a result of these new techniques it is possible for a child to have five parents: the woman who donated the egg, the man who donated the sperm, the woman who carried the embryo after in vitro fertilization, and the couple who contracted and paid for these procedures and will raise the baby.

Traditionally, legal parentage has been defined in terms of biological relationships. Alternative techniques for conception raise a host of bioethical questions. If a couple who had a child by artificial insemination with a donor's sperm get divorced, what rights does the husband have regarding the child? Should single women who want to raise a child by themselves be given artificial insemination? What if a surrogate mother decides to keep a baby, or the couple who contracted for the child decide that they don't want it? Should a woman who feels pregnancy would damage her career, or a woman who is afraid of the pains of childbirth, be allowed to contract a surrogate mother? What are the embryo's rights? In vitro fertilization may result in several embryos, which may be frozen and kept for use if the first implantation does not take. Do these embryos have a right to be born? Who should decide? In one recent case, a wealthy Los Angeles couple were killed in a plane crash, leaving two frozen embryos behind. Do those embryos have a right to be born? If they are, should they inherit the couple's fortune? What are the rights of the prospective parents? Should couples be permitted to "shop" for donors, selecting their future child's probable eye and hair color, intelligence, temperament, and talent for music and sports?

The list of moral dilemmas created by high-technology fertilization could go on for pages. Some scientists and legal experts have taken sides. On one side are those who feel the new technology is undermining the ideals of love, marriage, family, and lineage, and that artificial conception should not be permitted under any circumstances. On the other side are those who believe that infertility destroys many more families than does medical fertilization. They argue that decisions of the United States Supreme Court on contraception and abortion have guaranteed Americans procreative freedom. In the words of one legal scholar, these decisions allow "the freedom to reproduce when, with whom, and by what means one chooses." (Otten, 1984)

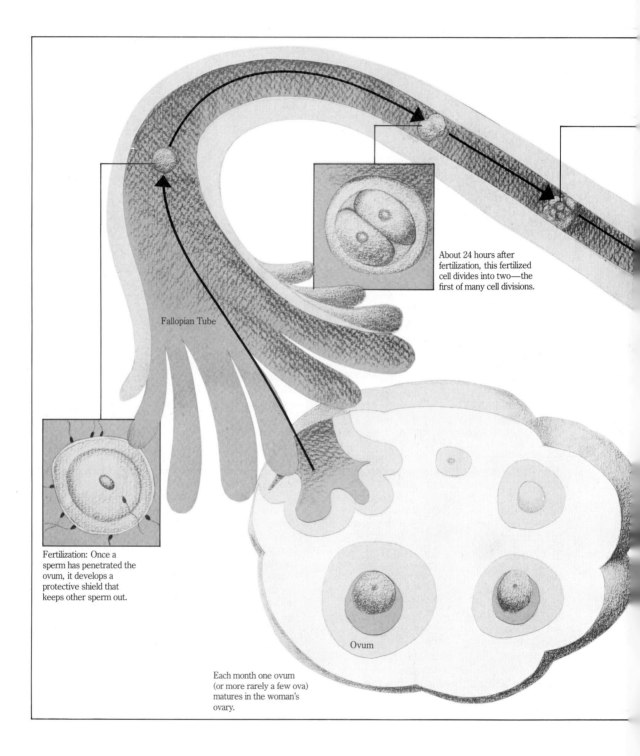

About 24 hours after fertilization, this fertilized cell divides into two—the first of many cell divisions.

Fallopian Tube

Fertilization: Once a sperm has penetrated the ovum, it develops a protective shield that keeps other sperm out.

Ovum

Each month one ovum (or more rarely a few ova) matures in the woman's ovary.

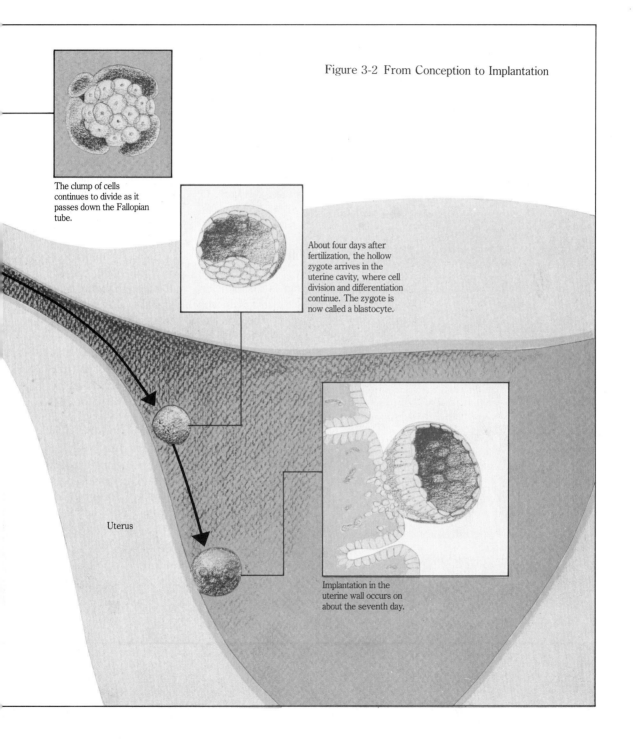

Figure 3-2 From Conception to Implantation

The clump of cells continues to divide as it passes down the Fallopian tube.

About four days after fertilization, the hollow zygote arrives in the uterine cavity, where cell division and differentiation continue. The zygote is now called a blastocyte.

Uterus

Implantation in the uterine wall occurs on about the seventh day.

blood vessels from the mother to those of the embryo through membranes that prevent many harmful substances from reaching the embryo. The embryo has its own blood supply.

At one month the embryo does not look very human. The tip of its developing spinal cord sticks out like a tail, and the folds of tissue that will become its chin, cheeks, jaw, and outer ear look like gills. But it has a head and the beginnings of eyes, ears, a mouth, and a brain; a rudimentary liver, digestive tract, and kidneys;

A month-old embryo, greatly enlarged. The fluid in the amniotic sac is like a warm water bed, cushioning the tiny embryo from sudden movement or shock.

and arm and leg "buds." Its heart has already begun to beat, pumping blood through the villi. In time, the umbilical cord will take over for the villi. But for now, the embryo is "all heart": in proportion to the rest of its body, the embryo's heart is nine times as large as it will be in adulthood.

The embryo grows about one millimeter a day, but its development is not uniform. Each organ system has its own program, and different parts of the body develop on different days.

The Fetus

At about two months after conception, the embryo is an inch long and recognizably human. The basic systems of life are already established. The brain sends signals to other organs; the stomach produces some digestive juices; blood cells are being manufactured; and bone cells are beginning to form. The embryo (from the Greek word for "swelling within") has become a **fetus** (from the Latin word for "offspring" or "little one").

The embryonic phase is marked by differentiation of organ systems. The fetal period is marked by the development, coordination, and maturation of those systems. The nervous system and reproductive organs are formed. Hair, fingernails and toenails, sweat glands, and taste buds are finishing touches to the basic forms and functions that appeared in the embryo. Development is uneven, however. The respiratory system, which is designed for the air-breathing newborn and not the aquatic life of the fetus, is the last to mature. Premature infants often suffer from respiratory problems because their lungs are not fully developed.

Behavior—that is, self-initiated movement—increases steadily in the fetal period. Halfway to birth, a fetus of 20 weeks swallows, hiccups, spontaneously opens and closes its eyes, frowns, stretches and flexes its limbs, sleeps and wakes, and may even suck its thumb. A fetus born prematurely at 24 weeks may be able to breathe temporarily in a shallow way and may emit thin cries. By about 28 weeks, a fetus is "viable": it *may* survive outside the womb. By this time, its nervous, circulatory, and respiratory systems may function, but only with considerable aid from an incubator and a respirator. (We discuss premature babies later in this chapter.) The full-term fetus uses the additional time to acquire an insulating layer of fat under its skin and to develop more fully its muscle tone, sensory systems, wake–sleep cycles, sucking digestion, and other preparations for independent existence.

There is some evidence that the fetus is capable of simple learning (Macfarlane, 1978). In one series of experiments, fetuses of about 38 weeks were exposed to a bright light shown through the mother's abdominal wall. Fetal activity increased, indicating that the light was an unconditioned stimulus (one that evokes a response without learning). Then a tone was sounded just before the light was turned on. After a number of pairings of the tone and the light, the fetuses responded to the tone alone, a case of classical conditioning. No one knows how much "learning" occurs naturally. These experiments do not confirm the folk belief that if

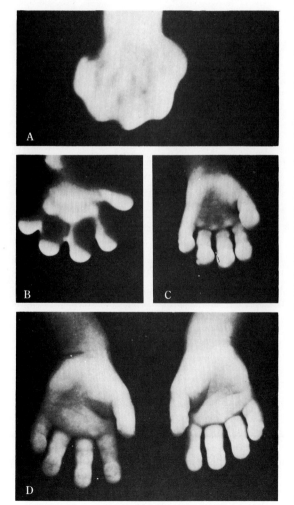

The Development of the Hand. The hand begins as a "plate" with finger ridges in the fifth and sixth weeks (A and B); develops fingers and a thumb between the seventh and eighth weeks (C); and assumes mature form in the third month (D).
(Flanagan, 1962.)

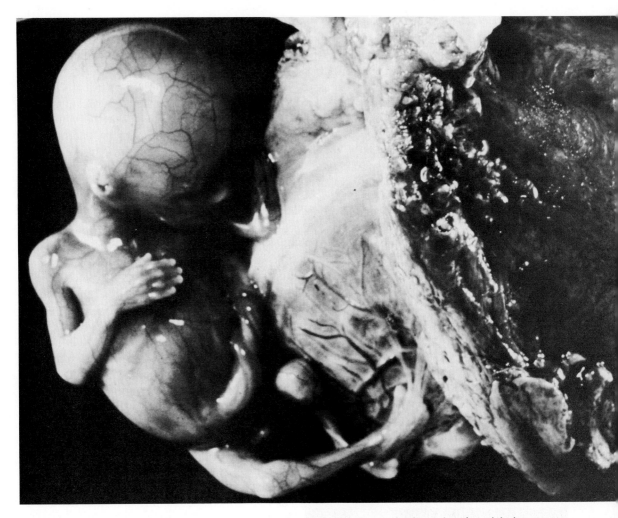

In the fourth month, the embryo's weight increases sixfold. It gains 5 inches or more in length, reaching half what its height will be at birth. This growth spurt depends on the nourishment the embryo receives through the placenta.

an expectant mother listens to classical music for nine months, her child will grow up to be a great composer or conductor!

From the mother's perspective, the most significant changes in the later stages of pregnancy are increases in the size and activity of the fetus. The embryo that measured one inch and weighed a quarter of an ounce at 8 weeks very likely weighs 6 to 8 pounds and measures 18 to 22 inches at 40 weeks. In the ninth month its quarters are cramped, and its limbs stick into the mother's rib cage, diaphragm, and abdominal wall. The mother is almost constantly aware of the fetus now. When she sits or lies down, it squirms to get into a comfortable position. Loud noises startle the near-term fetus; the rocking movement when she walks soothes it (Macfarlane, 1977).

Boy or Girl?

Sex differentiation is one of the more interesting chapters in the story of prenatal development. Sex is determined by the X and Y chromosomes. Females have two X chromosomes, hence all of the mother's ova contain an X chromosome. Males have an X and a Y chromosome, so their sperm may contain either an X or a Y chromosome. The father "decides" the sex of the child. If the sperm that penetrates the egg contributes an X chromosome, the child will be female (XX); if it contributes a Y chromosome, the child will be male (XY). But the child's reproductive system, secondary sex characteristics, and future love life are not prescribed the moment X meets X (or Y). The translation of a sex genotype into a phenotype is a complex story, and one that beings in utero.

The fact that an embryo has two X chromosomes or an X and a Y has little effect on the first stage of sexual development. For the first six weeks after conception, the embryo is "unisex." The only way to determine its sex is to examine its chromosomes. All embryos develop tissues that will become gonads (either testes or ovaries), tissues that will become external reproductive structures (either a penis and scrotum or a clitoris and labia), and two sets of ducts that will become internal reproductive organs. (The latter organs will develop into either seminal vesicles and the prostate gland in the male or Fallopian tubes, the uterus, and vagina in the female). (See Figure 3-3.)

Physiological differentiation begins in the second stage of sexual development. At about 7 weeks, a gene or genes on the Y chromosome sends a signal to the embryo's unisex gonad to develop into testes. A week or so later, the testes begin producing two hormones: testosterone, which stimulates the development of the male ducts, and another hormone called Mullerian Inhibiting Substance (MIS), which blocks the development of female ducts. If the embryo does not receive this signal, testosterone and MIS are not produced and the embryo develops female reproductive organs, beginning with the ovaries at about 10 weeks. In the third stage, testosterone stimulates the development of testicles and a penis. If this hormone is not present in sufficient quantities, the embryo develops a clitoris and vulva. In the fourth and final stage, testosterone inhibits the rhythmic cycles of the two "master glands," the hypothalamus and the pituitary.

Notice that nature's basic plan seems to be to produce a female. The development of a male requires two extra steps. The first requirement is a Y chromosome from the father. If the Y is somehow misplaced, leaving a single X chromosome, the embryo will develop into a female—a rare condition known as *Turner's syndrome*. The second requirement is testosterone. If the embryo and fetus do not produce or cannot use this hormone, development will follow the female pattern, in spite of the XY genotype.

Genes do not control sexual development the way a puppeteer controls the movements of

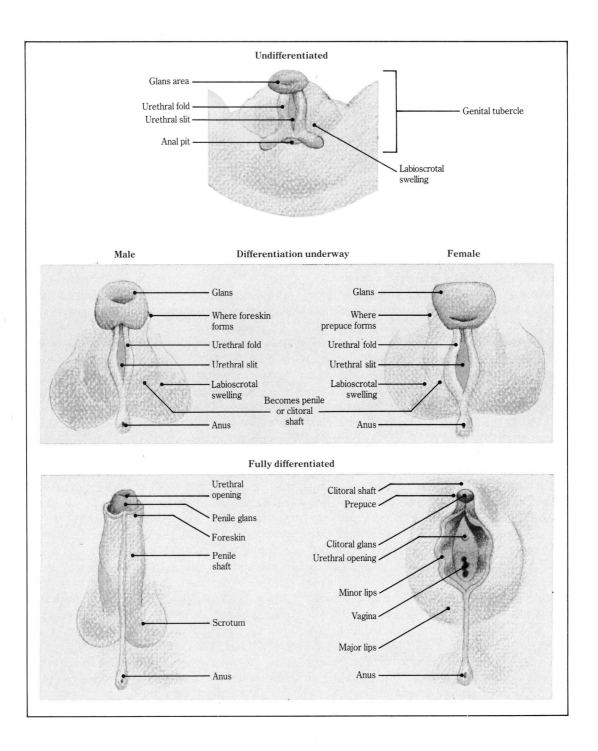

the Muppets. A gene is more like the director of a Broadway play, who has to contend with a variety of pressures from inside and outside the group of actors. Genes direct the first two stages of sexual development, after which hormones take over. The fact that an embryo has an XX or XY genotype does not guarantee that a baby will be born a normal male or female.

The stages in sexual development can be seen as a series of hurdles or gates (Lamb & Campos, 1982). Each gate has its own key. Once passed, the gate is permanently closed. Whatever developments took place at that stage cannot be reversed. But the next gate requires a different key. For example, a genetic defect called *testicular-feminizing syndrome* prevents the tissues of a male (XY) fetus from responding to testosterone and MIS. The embryo develops testes. But because it does not respond to male hormones, it develops female external genitalia. This condition is rare.

Another problem is all too common. In the 1950s and 1960s, hundreds of thousands of women were given the hormone DES (diethylstilbestrol) to prevent miscarriage. Only later did physicians discover that DES stimulated the production of testosterone. When women carrying female (XX) fetuses were given this treatment in the third trimester of pregnancy, their daughters were born with normal ovaries. That gate had been locked. But the next gate was still open, and many females developed masculine-looking external genitalia. More recently researchers have discovered that DES also increased the risk that daughters would develop cervical or vaginal cancer later in life and that sons would be sterile. Most infants are "normal," both sexually and otherwise, at birth. But such accidents can and do happen during prenatal development.

Genetic Hazards

About one in every three or four pregnancies ends in spontaneous abortion, or "miscarriage" (Freire-Maia, 1970). Most such miscarriages occur in the first month or two after fertilization; the mother may not even know that she was pregnant. Three-fourths to four-fifths of all miscarriages are the result of genetic or chromosomal abnormalities. Spontaneous abortions are a form of natural selection, which reduce the number of genetic defects in the population.

There is some evidence that male fetuses are more likely to be aborted spontaneously than are female fetuses (Beatty & Gluechsohn-Waelsch, 1972; Kopp & Parmelee, 1979). The reason for this is unknown. But this finding squares with the fact that females are more likely to survive infancy and generally live longer than their male contemporaries. Biologically, males seem to be the weaker sex.

Figure 3-3 Prenatal Sex Differentiation   For the first six weeks of prenatal development, it is impossible to tell the sex of an embryo through visual examination. Both male and female sex organs develop from the same primitive "sex bud."

Some fetuses with genetic abnormalities survive the prenatal period and are born with mild to severe problems. In some cases their genetic disorder is the result of an accident: The chromosomes in their mother's egg did not separate completely during meiosis, or one or more sections were stretched or broken. In *Down's syndrome,* for example, the fertilized egg has a whole extra chromosome or a piece of one. Down's syndrome is called "Trisomy 21" because the person has three twenty-first chromosomes instead of two. Children with this genetic abnormality are usually short and stocky, with round faces and "oriental" eyes (the reason why they are sometimes called "mongoloids"). Many are born with heart defects and other problems; some do not survive their teens. Most show moderate to severe mental retardation, although this depends in part on their environment (Edgerton, 1979). Babies reared at home receive more stimulation and develop more normally than those who are institutionalized in infancy. Down's syndrome has been linked to the mother's age. About 1 in 1,500 babies born to women under age 30 have this disorder. The risk increases to 1 in 750 for women 30 to 40 years old and 1 in 100 for women 40 to 45 (Frias, 1975).

Some disorders are sex-linked. In these cases, a child inherits a defective gene on the X chromosome. *Hemophilia* is an example. Women can carry hemophilia but rarely suffer its effects. A daughter (XX) who inherits the defective gene on the X chromosome from her mother usually inherits an X chromosome with a normal, dominant blood-clotting gene from her father. If she inherited the defective gene from *both* parents, she would suffer the effects. But men with hemophilia rarely live long enough to have children; even a minor injury can cause them to bleed to death. A son (XY) is not protected by a second X chromosome.

The royal houses of Europe illustrate this pattern of inheritance, as shown in Figure 3-4. Queen Victoria of England carried the genetic defect. One of her sons, three of her grandsons, and six of her great-grandsons developed hemophilia, including the son and heir of the last tsar of Russia. The royal house of England escaped the disease.

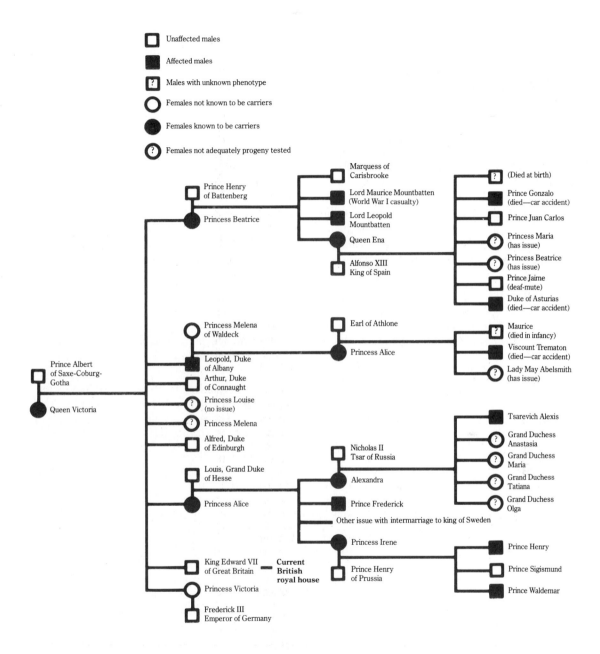

Figure 3-4 Hemophilia in Queen Victoria's Line
(Curtis, 1975)

Other genetic defects are not sex-linked, but occur because of a recessive gene on other chromosomes, as in *sickle-cell anemia.* A child who inherits the sickle-cell gene from *both* parents—a **homozygote**—develops a painful blood disorder which often leads to heart or kidney failure and early death. The parents and other children who have one normal gene and one defective gene—called **heterozygotes**—rarely experience even mild symptoms. In homozygotes, all of the red blood cells are curved into a sickle shape and carry very little oxygen. In heterozygotes only some of the cells are sickled. This trait is most often found in populations who live or once lived in the tropics. There is some evidence that heterozygotes are better able to resist malaria than are individuals who do not have the sickle-cell trait; in half-doses, this "defect" is adaptive.

PKU, or *phenylketonuria,* is a mental disorder that results from a recessive gene. A child who inherits PKU from both parents does not produce an enzyme that converts the amino acid phenylalanine into tyrosine. As a result, phenylalanine builds up in the blood stream. While small amounts are normal and harmless, high concentrations are toxic enough to kill nerve and brain cells. If untreated, homozygotes suffer irreversible brain damage. Fortunately, this malady can be treated effectively by eliminating phenylalanine from the diet. The child still carries the PKU genes but shows few of their harmful effects. (Many states now require that all newborns be screened for PKU.) When the child reaches adulthood, he or she can eat a normal diet, because the mature central nervous system resists the toxic effects of phenyl-

alanine. But if the adult is a woman and she becomes pregnant, the high levels of this amino acid in her blood stream will affect the neurological development of her fetus. PKU causes mental retardation in the fetus even though this fetus does not have PKU. In other words, this disease is genetic and environmental at the same time.

Environmental Hazards

The environment is rarely, if ever, a "silent partner" in child development. This is as true of prenatal development as it is of later stages in the child's life. The genetic program arranges and times the progression of embryonic and fetal development leading to a normal newborn— *if* the intrauterine environment supports the growth processes. But it can cause damaging changes in the normal course of development by pushing genetic programs into errors or by failing to evoke the right change at the right time. Because genes must be turned on and off at specific times to begin the next step in development, the necessary environment must be available at the right time. Different environmental hazards present different risks to different organ systems at different times.

The main source of contact with the outside world for the embryo and the fetus is through the mother's bloodstream. As explained earlier, her blood does not flow through the veins of the fetus. Rather, it flows into the placenta, which breaks down large molecules into particles that are small enough to pass through the walls in the fetus' umbilical cord. The placenta has been described as a protective wall, shielding the fetus from harmful substances. To some extent this is true. It does prevent most bacteria from reaching the fetus. But the placenta is more like a barnyard fence than a wall: it keeps horses out but lets mice slip through.

DISEASES Some of the most harmful of these substances are viruses. Syphilis organisms invade the fetal brain and may cause blindness and other abnormalities. Toxiplasmosis, a disease women contract from eating raw meat or from handling cat litter, can result in a baby with an abnormally large or small skull. Rubella or German measles, which is a relatively mild disease in adults, may cause blindness, deafness, brain damage, and heart disease in the fetus. The extent of the damage and the risk to the fetus depend in part on timing. Those parts of the fetus that are developing when the disease attacks are most vulnerable.

As a general rule, the earlier the fetus is exposed, the greater the harm. Viruses that cause serious damage during the embryonic period generally have less serious effects after the first trimester, when the basic structures of the organ systems, including the brain, have been formed.

DRUGS Medications that are good for the mother can be harmful to the fetus. In some cases, the effects are mild. For example, some babies whose mothers took the antibiotic tetracycline during their pregnancy have stained tooth enamel. In other cases, the effects of drugs on the fetus are severe. Thalidomide was a tranquilizer that had been tested on pregnant mice with no side effects. In the 1960s thousands of women who took thalidomide gave birth to deformed babies. The damage to the fetus depended on the stage of pregnancy during which the drug had been taken. If a mother had used thalidomide 34 to 38 days after conception, the baby was born without ears. If she had taken it between 38 and 46 days, the baby was born with malformed arms. If she had taken it between 40 and 46 days, the baby was born with deformed legs. If the mother had taken the drug 50 days after conception, however, it had no effect on the baby's development. The "gates" had been closed (Saxén & Rapola, 1969).

Babies born to mothers who are addicted to heroin may go through painful withdrawal in their first days of life. Often they are irritable as infants and have poor attention spans later in childhood. They may remain small for their age through childhood, even though they have good appetites (Kolata, 1978).

Prescription and nonprescription drugs are not the only hazards. If the mother takes an alcoholic drink, some of the alcohol reaches the fetus; if she smokes a cigarette, some of the nicotine enters the fetal bloodstream. How harmful are these social drugs during pregnancy? The babies of alcoholic mothers are often born with *fetal alcohol syndrome*. They are small for their age, have misshapen heads and facial features, and may be mentally retarded. Some have cleft palates, heart or kidney damage, and eye or skeletal defects as well (Streissguth, Landesman-Dwyer, Martin, & Smith, 1980). Estimates are that about 1 in 1,500 babies born in the United States each year has fetal alcohol syndrome (Smith, 1978). Alcoholic mothers are not the only ones who are endangering their babies. There is evidence that

PRENATAL DIAGNOSIS AND TREATMENT OF DEFECTS

New techniques for detecting genetic defects before birth may make it soon possible to identify—and someday treat—nearly all disorders caused by faulty genes. The first diagnostic breakthrough, *amniocentesis,* came in the early 1970s. In this technique, doctors insert a syringe through the mother's abdominal wall and into the uterus to draw out some of the amniotic fluid surrounding the fetus. The fetal cells that have been shed into this fluid are then grown in a culture. Medical technicians can analyze their chromosomal makeup and detect such abnormalities as Down's syndrome.

Amniocentesis is usually accompanied by *ultrasonography,* a procedure in which sound waves are bounced off the fetus. These echoes form dots on a screen, making a picture of the developing embryo called a *sonogram.* By examining sonograms physicians can find visible abnormalities, predict complications in childbirth, and clarify the age of the fetus. Amniocentesis and ultrasonography have already become standard procedures with older mothers and high risk cases. By using these two techniques, medical researchers have been able to detect more than 190 genetic aberrations and hereditary disorders within the first twenty weeks of life.

Amniocentesis does have drawbacks, however. There is not enough amniotic fluid to test safely until the sixteenth week of pregnancy, and the cells must be cultured for three to four weeks before they can be analyzed. The results are not known until the fifth month of pregnancy, when the fetus is relatively large. If the tests show that the baby has a serious genetic disorder, the mother must then decide whether to give birth to a severely handicapped child or to abort a fetus whose movements she may already be able to feel.

To overcome these physical and emotional problems, a new technique called *chorionic villus biopsy* (CVP) is being tested at medical centers in the United States and Europe (Schmeck, 1983). In this procedure the physician removes a small amount of tissue from the fetal villi. CVP can be performed as early as the tenth week of pregnancy. Because the test is performed directly on fetal tissues, rather than on the amniotic fluid, the results are almost immediate and perhaps more accurate. This method has already been used successfully to test for sickle-cell anemia and other disorders.

Today these prenatal diagnostic methods are done to make sure that there is no genetic abnormality in the fetus and to permit an abortion if one is found. Medical researchers see another, brighter prospect for the future—the possibility that most genetic defects can be treated and corrected in the womb. Ultrasonography has already made fetal surgery possible. In 1981 surgeons at the University of Colorado inserted a drainage tube into a 24-week-old fetus to treat hydrocephalus, an accumulation of cerebrospinal fluid in the brain cavity. Other surgeons have been able to correct minor malformations of the heart and urinary tract before they become fatal to the unborn child. Researchers are working on techniques for diagnosing and treating jaundice and anemia, which are vitamin and enzyme deficiencies.

The most revolutionary possibilities for the future treatment of genetic defects lie in the analysis of DNA. Once researchers began to break the DNA code, they were able to decipher the recipes for dozens of vital proteins and manufacture the genes for them synthetically. Since genetic defects occur when this code is out of sequence, the discovery of DNA has also helped to find the underlying causes of many disorders that had not previously been considered hereditary. Dr. Arno G. Motulsky, director of the Center for Inherited Diseases at the University of Washington in Seattle, calls the latest genetic research "a big leap forward" for preventive medicine:

Diabetes, high blood pressure, allergies, peptic ulcers—these and many other diseases of middle life are now being found to

have genetic determinants. By finding out what these are, we can begin to identify populations at much higher risk for various disorders, and then direct preventive measures at these people in a more concentrated way. (McAuliffe & McAuliffe, 1983)

It may also be possible to prevent Down's syndrome and other genetic disorders by repairing genes.

heavy drinking (more than 45 drinks a month or 5 drinks on the same occasion) increases the risk of birth defects. Smoking has been associated with a higher risk of miscarriage, difficult delivery, and low birth weight (Babson, Pernoll, Benda, & Simpson, 1980).

With social drugs it is difficult to establish cause and effect. Women who drink a lot are more likely to smoke, to take prescription and nonprescription drugs, and to eat poorly than nondrinkers are. In fact, studies of the effects of alcohol or cigarettes on the fetus may be measuring the effects of several interacting drugs, plus unknown factors. What is certain is that smoking and having more than two drinks a day are not *good* for the fetus or for the expectant mother. They are not good for anyone.

INCOMPATIBILITY So far in this section, we have described outside environmental influences on the fetus. Prenatal development also depends on the mother's general health and ability to nurture a fetus—the internal environment. For many reasons, some women do not provide a nourishing and safe environment. Poor placental connections can starve the fetus of the food and oxygen required for optimal development. Diabetic or prediabetic mothers who have unusually high levels of blood sugar often bear infants who are overweight, immature, and have difficulty breathing. If a diabetic mother takes insulin, the fetus may suffer liver damage or other abnormalities. In other cases, the mother and the fe-

tus have incompatible blood types. The mother's body may build up antibodies that invade and attack the fetal blood cells, causing anemia and, in some cases, damage to the liver or brain.

DIET The fetus depends on the mother for nutrition. As recently as ten years ago, many physicians put expectant mothers on strict diets in the belief that they should not gain more than 8 or 9 pounds during pregnancy. This notion was based on a study of pregnant women in Germany during World War I, a high percentage of whom had babies who were mentally retarded. Physicians believed this was because they had gained too much weight during their pregnancy. In fact, these women were suffering from a disease called *toxemia*. The symptoms of toxemia are high blood pressure, sudden weight gain due to water retention, and protein in the urine. The women in the German study looked overweight and had retarded babies because of the disease, not because they had eaten too much. Yet the belief that gaining weight during pregnancy was bad persisted, even after this study was disproved. Today most physicians recommend that a woman whose weight is normal when she becomes pregnant gain about 3 pounds a month, or 24 to 30 pounds before delivery. In general, a pregnant woman should eat the same kinds and variety of foods as any other person her age, but more of them. The fetus receives only as much food as he or she can *share* with the mother. Extreme malnutrition in utero and in the early

Insight

OLD AND NEW WIVES' TALES

Not far in the past, many of a baby's traits were attributed to events in the mother's pregnancy. According to one old wives' tale, if a pregnant woman was frightened by an animal, her baby would bear the marks of that animal. Birthmarks that looked a little like animals "proved" the case. The mother's experiences while pregnant could have good effects too: "Listen to classical music and your child may compose like Mozart." "Keep calm, don't get upset, and your baby will have a pleasant disposition."

Today these notions seem absurd. No one believes seriously that if a pregnant woman is frightened by a horse her baby will be born with a birthmark in the shape of a horse. But there is evidence that fear or stress can affect the fetus. Moreover, we know that the fetus is able to learn some simple associations, for example, between a tone and a light. Who knows whether listening to music can enhance the baby's later appreciation of music? The music would have to be quite loud to penetrate the wrappings around the fetus and to compete with the gurglings of the mother's innards. But it is not impossible.

There are many "new wives' tales" to replace the old. In the 1940s and 1950s, expectant mothers felt guilty if they gave in to their craving for an afternoon snack, extra helpings at dinner, or a bite to eat before they went to bed. Today many women fear that if they have a cup of coffee in the morning or a glass of wine with dinner, or if they occasionally take two aspirin for a headache, they are causing irreparable harm to their fetus. There is some truth to these fears. No responsible physician or developmental psychologist would recommend overeating, indulging in every urge for sweets, or drinking coffee all day or martinis every evening. But millions of babies born to women who didn't know these habits were bad for the fetus survived the traumas.

Recent discoveries about the harmful effects of drugs and diseases on fetal development make it easy to exaggerate the vulnerability of the fetus. Many healthy, happy, intelligent adults were conceived and born under the most adverse conditions. A whole generation of Europeans, now in their forties, were born to mothers who endured the constant stress and frequent food shortages of World War II. The fetus is well-protected from any number of dangers that attack infants and older babies directly. Many more babies are born healthy than not.

years of life may retard development. But judging from the healthy adult offspring of a generation of American women who starved themselves on doctor's orders, most children recover (National Natality Survey, 1980).

STRESS Does a pregnant woman's emotional state affect her fetus? A classic series of studies indicates that it does (Sontag, 1941, 1944). A woman who is continuously anxious and upset secretes epinephrine, which stimulates the fetus Fetuses of mothers who are under prolonged stress may be ten times as active as those of calmer mothers (Sontag, 1966). Some

researchers claim that anxiety has long-term effects, and that infants of nervous mothers are given to colic, excessive crying, and the like. But mothers who were anxious before delivery are more likely to handle their infants in an uncertain manner, creating problems for the baby after delivery. The infant's behavior may be a reaction to her postnatal behavior, not her prenatal state.

How Genes and Environments Interact
It is often difficult to know precisely why a newborn has been damaged in pregnancy, because

genetic and environmental causes interact. Some infants seem to inherit a genetic vulnerability to developmental defects; the maternal environment may or may not trigger an abnormal response.

In PKU and other genetic disorders mentioned earlier, scientists have a fairly clear picture of why the disorder occurs, how it is trans-mitted, and how the environment affects it. But these few cases stand out sharply from the many disorders in which no cause-and-effect sequence has been determined.

There is a large body of research that implicates genes in a variety of cognitive and psychological disorders (Scarr & Kidd, 1983). More than 150 known gene defects have been associ-

Ideas about pregnancy change with the times. At the turn of the century, many physicians advised pregnant women not to exert themselves; today most physicians recommend that women continue to exercise through most of their pregnancy. Laws and company policies that require a woman to stop working several months before her baby is due have also been challenged.

ated with mental retardation (Anderson, 1974). Stuttering, dyslexia (difficulty in learning to read despite normal intelligence and conventional instruction), schizophrenia, and affective disorders (manic and depressive illnesses) are some of the illnesses that run in families. A child who has one of these problems is far more likely to have a relative with the same problem than chance would predict. However, these disorders do not follow clear patterns of inheritance (as does hemophilia, for example). There is no known biochemical malfunction in most of them (as there are in sickle-cell anemia and PKU). Moreover, scientists cannot easily separate the effects of genetic transmission from those of cultural transmission or socialization. For example, is the child of a schizophrenic mother more likely to become schizophrenic because of genes he inherited from his mother or because of the way she relates to him?

In most cases there is no simple, one-to-one relationship between genotype and phenotype. Many disorders are *polygenic*—that is, they result from the combined effects of a number of genes. Often, a child inherits not a disease but a *vulnerability* to a disorder. Whether his "vulnerable" genotype is expressed as a disorder depends on the environment. Here, the environment can be anything from the mother's diet during pregnancy, to family dynamics, to the neighborhood and sociocultural influences on the parents and child. If there were a single gene for stuttering—chances are there isn't—this might be expressed in different ways. A heterozygote for stuttering (one who has received a "stuttering gene" from only one parent) might show no symptoms if she were reared in a relaxed environment. If she were raised in a chaotic, stressful environment, however, she might have frequent speech blocks. On the other hand, a homozygote for stuttering (one who had received such a gene from both parents) might stutter badly if she were reared in

an "average" environment, but show fewer symptoms if she were raised in an exceptionally supportive environment. Moreover, the effects of both genes and the environment change over time. The child might stop stuttering because the gene "turns off" during childhood or adolescence. Her family situation might improve, lowering her anxiety. She may make new friends or benefit from speech therapy. (See Insight on stuttering in Chapter 7.)

Figure 3–5 illustrates this schematically. Some individuals are all but invulnerable genetically. They would thrive in almost any prenatal or postnatal environment. Others are genetically vulnerable. They may achieve nearly optimal levels of development in supportive environments, but they would sink in nonsupportive environments. The curve shows that there are many degrees of developmental outcome between these two extremes.

Birth

Birth normally occurs about nine months after conception, give or take a few weeks. But it is impossible to predict the exact date. Scientists still do not know what triggers birth. The distended uterus begins to contract, at first in widely spaced intervals, then more and more frequently as labor progresses.

The goal of labor is to deliver the infant from a sealed womb through the vagina, or birth canal, and out into the world. The first stage of a normal labor consists of repeated contractions that pull open the cervix, the narrow opening from the vagina into the uterus, which has been sealed by a mucous plug during the pregnancy. The criss-crossed uterine muscles pull and tug open the cervix to the 10 cm or 12 cm width required for the infant's head and body to pass through. This stage of labor usually takes seven or eight hours for first deliveries. Later births are usually shorter. The second stage of labor is the actual birth. After the infant's head has

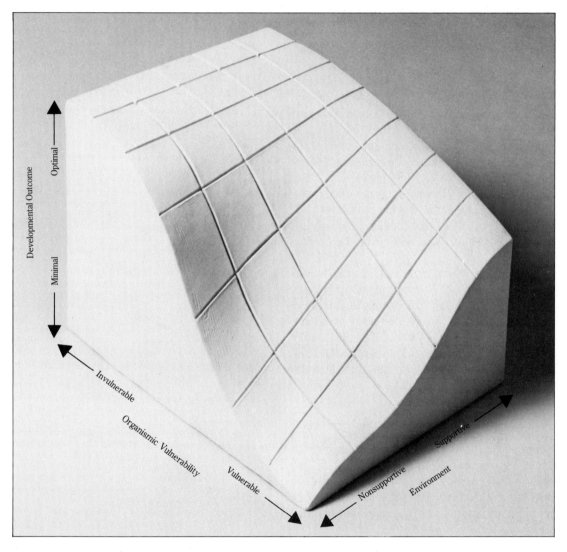

Figure 3-5   A Model of Developmental Outcomes
(Adapted from Horowitz, 1982)

passed into the birth canal, the uterine contractions push the rest of the body out of the womb. With help from these involuntary contractions, the infant is finally eased out of the vaginal opening. The waiting physician or midwife holds the infant lower than the delivery table to assure that the blood in the umbilical cord drains into the infant, then ties off the cord and cuts it a few inches from the infant's abdomen. In the third stage, the uterus continues to contract, expelling the placenta, the fetal membranes, and the remainder of the umbilical cord. The crisscrossed muscles of the uterine wall then contract firmly to cut off the bleeding that occurs after the placenta is torn away from the uterine wall.

What is the birth process like from the infant's point of view? No one knows, of course, but it is likely to be a strenuous experience. Although he is compressed for many hours under extraordinary pressure, the infant usually emerges alert and awake. He may gaze around the delivery room, cry a little, and remain awake for more hours just after delivery than he will for several days thereafter.

Medical Problems and Procedures

Some babies need help coming into the world. Most fetuses shift position in the week or two before birth so that their head rests against the opening of the uterus. But some babies are born feet first or bottom first. Breech births, as these

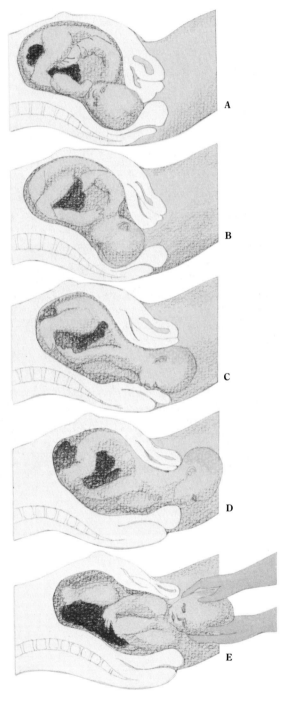

The Birth Process. At the end of the first stage of labor, the baby's head presses against the cervix (A). In the transitional stage, the cervix is fully dilated (B). The head moves through the vagina until it emerges completely (C and D). The top shoulder emerges next (E), after which the rest of the body simply slides out.

are called, prolong and complicate delivery. During some births, the placenta detaches from the wall of the uterus or the umbilical cord is twisted or squeezed, cutting off the baby's supply of oxygen before his head has emerged and he is able to breathe for himself. *Anoxia,* or lack of oxygen, is a leading cause of brain damage in newborns and can result in cerebral palsy, or lack of muscle control. The extent of the damage depends on when anoxia occurs, how long it lasts, and the general health and maturity of the baby.

The sonograph and other fetal monitoring devices enable hospital staff to detect and even anticipate anoxia and other birth complications. If the baby is threatened, physicians can perform a Caesarian section (or "C-section"), delivering the baby through an incision in the mother's abdomen. This technique is also used if the mother cannot deliver the baby because her pelvis is contracted or the baby is too large. Caesarian births save babies' and mothers' lives. But like all other interventions in childbirth, they carry risks. Babies who have not gone through the birth trauma are less alert at birth and more likely to develop respiratory problems than are normally delivered babies.

Parents have become active participants in childbirth in recent years. Fathers are invited into the delivery room, something that was seldom allowed twenty years ago, and in some instances help with delivery. Many couples prepare for the event in advance by taking classes in childbirth. The Lamaze method, for example, teaches expectant mothers how to relax, concentrate on breathing, and help push their baby into the world. It teaches fathers how to assist their mate, physically and psychologically. Some couples choose natural childbirth in the more personal environment of their home, with the assistance of a midwife. Many believe that the journey through the birth canal is traumatic enough without exposing the neonate to the brightly lit, often noisy hospital delivery room and maternity ward (Leboyer, 1975). Given the possible complications in delivery described above, most physicians do not recommend childbirth at home.

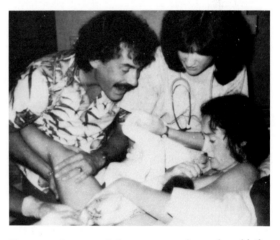

In most cultures and times, women have given birth alone, with the help of female kin, or, in modern societies, a physician. Today birth is becoming a family affair.

The "medicalization of childbirth" is an established fact. About 98 percent of American babies are born in hospitals. But the way physicians and hospitals handle delivery has changed in recent years. Fifteen or twenty years ago, birth was treated as a surgical procedure. Doctors routinely gave women general anesthesia to ease labor pains. As a result, the mother could not participate in the birth process, and many babies were delivered with the aid of forceps. Head and neck injuries were not uncommon. Many doctors also used drugs to induce labor at a time convenient to the parents and physician, or to speed up the process. Because this made labor more painful, these women were often given extra doses of barbiturates. Today, physicians realize that any drug given to the mother also affects the child. Once the umbilical cord is cut, the newborn metabolizes drugs in his own system. And a newborn's metabolism is slower than that of an adult. When mothers were given general anesthesia and painkillers shortly before delivery, their babies were sleepy and unresponsive for several days after birth. The depressing effects of such drugs can last for the first two months of life (Brackbill, 1979; Brazelton, 1969). These treatments are still used—but only when they are necessary to protect the mother or child, not for convenience.

The Newborn

From the time the fetus's head emerges from his mother's birth canal, he can look around while the rest of his body is being delivered. Even before his physical tie to his mother is cut, he is adapting to his new environment with eyes and lungs he never used before. When he is held upside down and tapped on the bottom, he cries for the first time, expelling excess fluid from his lungs. Laid beside his mother, he waves his arms and kicks, behavior he "practiced" in the womb.

Newborn babies are not what most people would consider cute. Most emerge from the birth canal red and battered. The skull, still flexible to permit passage into the world, may be elongated or even pointed. The features are often flattened or twisted. Some newborns are completely bald; others are covered over most of their bodies with a downy hair called *lanugo*. Most are bow-legged and pigeon-toed from their cramped quarters inside their mother. Their movements look jerky and uncoordinated. They may be wall-eyed (their eyes focusing outward instead of forward). Only a parent could describe this just-delivered baby as beautiful. But newborns are not as helpless as they appear.

What Newborns Can Do

The newborn is equipped with an array of *reflexes,* or automatic responses, that organize the baby's behavior in the first months of life. She responds to certain stimuli in regular, predictable ways. When you run a finger down her spine, she moves her rump from side to side in a swimming motion. If you stroke the sole of her foot, the toes fan upward (the *Babinski reflex*). Stroke her cheek and she turns her head in that direction and opens her mouth, as if she expects a nipple; this is the *rooting reflex.* Tap her gently on the forehead and she closes her eyes. If she is lying on her back and you put a rod in her hands, she grabs it; if you lift the rod, she holds tight and may even be able to support her own weight for a few moments (the *grasping reflex*). If she feels she is about to fall, her arms may reach out in what looks like an embrace (the *Moro reflex*). When you hold her under the arms and lower her to a firm surface, she will usually move her legs up and down as if she were walking (the *stepping reflex*).

Some reflexes are adaptive, such as rooting and sucking. The newborn does not have to learn to begin feeding. Some reflexes

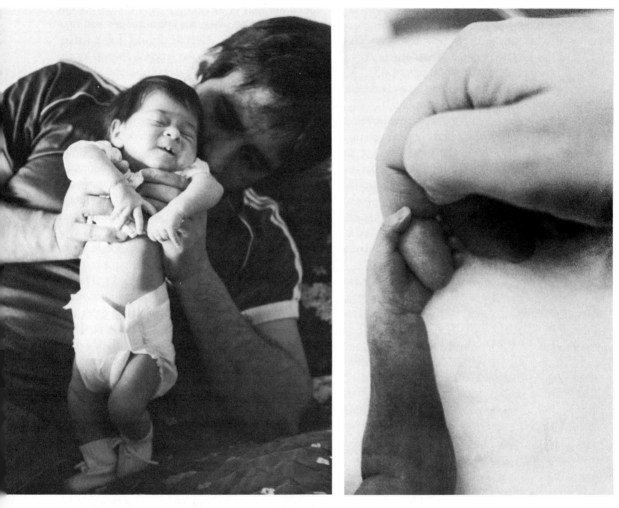

The stepping reflex (left) and grasping reflex (right) are part of the equipment the newborn brings into the world.

are probably left over from our evolutionary past. For example, the grasping and Moro reflexes are adaptive for a newborn who must cling to the mother's chest when she is traveling, as most nonhuman primate infants do. And some reflexes, such as stepping, are precursors of behaviors that develop later in life.

Reflexes disappear as the baby develops voluntary control over her body and behavior. If reflexes persist beyond the first five or six months, it is a sign that the infant's brain and nervous system are not developing in a normal way.

From the caretakers' point of view, aspects of newborn behavior that are not controlled by reflexes seem to be unorganized. Newborns

Table 3-1   States of Arousal in Newborns

State of Arousal	Behavior
Quiet sleep (non-REM sleep)	Full rest; low muscle tone and motor activity; eyelids closed and eyes still; regular breathing
Active sleep (REM sleep)	Increased muscle tone and motor activity; facial grimaces and smiles; occasional eye movements; irregular breathing
Periodic sleep	Intermediate between non-REM and REM sleep: bursts of deep, slow breathing alternating with bouts of rapid, shallow breathing
Drowsiness	More active than non-REM sleep but less active than REM or periodic sleep; eyes open and close; eyes glazed when open; breathing variable
Alert inactivity	Slight activity; face relaxed; eyes open and bright; breathing regular
Active alertness	Frequent diffuse motor activity; vocalizations; skin flushed; irregular breathing
Distress	Vigorous diffuse motor activity; facial grimaces; red skin; crying

(Wolff, 1966)

spend sixteen or seventeen hours a day sleeping. They wake when they are hungry and fuss until they are fed. Alert and quiet for a while, they then become drowsy and fall asleep again. Unfortunately for their caretakers, the sleeping patterns of newborns are highly unpredictable. They shift back and forth between various states of sleep and arousal frequently and irregularly. Moreover, the distinction between sleep and waking is not clear-cut in newborns. Compared to older children and adults, neonates spend more time in active sleep (rapid-eye-movement or REM sleep, which indicates that the cortex is working) and less time in quiet sleep (non-REM sleep, when the sensory systems are resting.) Newborns also spend more time in a drowsy, half-awake state—and more time in active distress (see Table 3-1). The infrequent and brief moments of quiet alertness in the lives of newborns are perhaps the most important times for development (Lamb & Campos, 1982). It is during these interludes that infants visually explore their environment, examine their parents' faces, gaze at the mobile over the crib, and gradually learn that their behavior has an effect on the world.

Newborn Assessment

The first thing parents ask is whether their new baby is healthy. Virtually all hospitals give the newborn, or *neonate,* a simple test devised by Dr. Virgina Apgar, one minute and again five minutes after birth (see Table 3-2). The newborn's heart rate, breathing, body tone, circulation, and reflexes are all tested, and the baby is given a score of 0, 1, or 2 at each measurement. If the total score is 7 or better, he or she is not in danger; if the score is below 4, the infant is in critical condition. (A useful way to remember the content of this test is to think of the letters of the author's last name as: *A*ppearance, *P*ulse, *G*rimace, *A*ctivity, and *R*espiration.)

Table 3-2 The Apgar Scale

Characteristic	0	1	2
Heart rate	Absent	Slow (below 100)	Rapid (over 100)
Respiratory effort (breathing)	Absent	Irregular, slow	Good: baby is crying
Muscle tone	Flaccid, limp	Weak, inactive	Strong, active
Color (circulation)	Blue, pale	Body pink, extremities blue	Entirely pink
Reflex irritability	No response	Grimace	Coughing, sneezing, crying

(Apgar, 1953)

There are some questions the Apgar scale cannot answer. Can the baby see and hear? Is he or she very irritable or very unresponsive? Is brain function normal? Neonates do not respond to light, sounds, or other stimuli the way an adult or even an older infant does. Blind babies seem to "look around," as if they were inspecting their new environment. The vibrations of a loud tone may startle a deaf baby but produce no response in a neonate with normal hearing. Newborns have a way of shutting out unpleasant stimulation by going into "defensive" states.

One of the most widely used tests of the baby's overall well-being is T. Berry Brazelton's Neonatal Behavioral Assessment Scale. It is a test of newborn adaptation and is based on social responses as well as reflexes. Twenty reflexes and twenty-six "behavioral responses" are tested. The examination begins when the infant is asleep and measures everything from the response to a scratch on the foot, a light in the eyes, or a cloth partially covering the face, to the response to a human face and voice and cuddling. The Brazelton scale is particularly useful in identifying babies who need special care.

Newborns at Risk

Most babies are born about 280 days, or 40 weeks, after the mother began her last menstrual period. If the baby is a week or two off schedule, there is nothing to worry about. Most full-term babies need a few days to adjust to life outside the womb. It takes time for them to coordinate their reflexes so that they can breathe or suck without spitting up or hiccupping. But *preterm* babies, who spent less than 38 weeks in the womb, require more time to adjust and need more professional care. Respiration, digestion, temperature regulation, and other vital functions are not fully mature until shortly before birth. Many preterm babies experience respiratory distress because they do not produce enough *surfactin,* a substance that aids in transporting oxygen into and carbon dioxide out of the lungs. Their breathing may be irregular or unreliable. If born six weeks or more before term, they usually require intravenous feeding. They have not developed an insulating layer of fat, and must be kept in a warm isolette, or incubator, until they can maintain a body temperature of 98°F on their own. The earlier a baby is born, the less likely he is to survive; if he does survive, the more likely he is to have permanent problems.

Some babies are small and immature at birth even though they spent a full 40 weeks in the womb. These babies are called *small-for-dates.* Because of maternal malnutrition or disease, poor placental connections, or other problems, they are not completely developed.

Small-for-dates experience the same problems as preterm babies. Any newborn who weighs less than 1,500 grams, or about 3¼ pounds, at birth faces a struggle to survive. The lower an infant's birth weight is, the less likely he is to survive and the more likely he is to encounter developmental difficulties, however long the period of gestation.

TREATING PREMATURE BABIES The medical prognosis for preterm and small-for-date babies is much better today than it was ten or even five years ago. Hospitals with special neonatology units now estimate that they can save 80 percent of babies born weighing 2.2 to 3.2 pounds, and 50 percent of those who weigh only 2 pounds. As recently as the mid-1970s, 80 percent of these babies died (*The New York Times News Service*, April 5, 1981). More and more premature babies are surviving with less and less damage than ever before. Nevertheless, these infants are at risk. Perhaps a third of them show signs of delayed physical or mental growth.

One possible explanation of slower development is that preterm babies are deprived of normal environments. They spend less time in utero than other babies do, and after birth they are often kept in "isolation" for weeks. Until recently, physicians believed that premature babies are fragile and, therefore, should not be disturbed. Such babies were handled as little as possible and shielded from the sights and sounds that surround other newborns. There is some evidence that creating stimulating environments for these babies may improve their chances of survival. In one experiment (Burns, Deddish, Burns, & Hatcher, 1983) preterm babies were placed on an oscillating waterbed designed to recreate the rhythmic environment of the womb and were played tapes of a mother's heartbeat. These babies did not grow any faster than preterm babies kept in conventional isolettes. But four weeks after birth, their sleep and waking cycles were more mature than those of control babies, and they received significantly higher scores on Brazelton's measures of motor organization, or coordination. In another experiment (Scarr-Salapatek & Williams, 1973), the nurses in a maternity ward for preterm babies were instructed to take the babies out of their isolettes for feeding and to spend time rocking them, talking to them, and the like. Mobiles were placed in their isolettes. At 1 week these babies scored lower than a control group of preterm babies on the Brazelton scale. But at 4 weeks they scored significantly higher than the other group. They had also gained more weight than the control babies had. Follow-up treatment administered after the infants left the hospital seemed to produce lasting gains in the babies' first year.

Interpretation of these studies is controversial, however. Many psychologists agree that the postnatal environment is important. But others believe that development in the first

Figure 3-6 Major Causes of Infant Mortality in the United States
(*Healthy People*, 1979)

weeks of life is largely the result of maturation, not stimulation. Parmelee (1981) argues that the development of the human nervous system during the first 40 weeks after conception is almost entirely under genetic control.

SOCIAL CLASS AND INFANT VULNERABILITY Some premature babies gain weight quickly and catch up with their peers by about 5 months (Tanner, 1974). But others do not. Every year about 14 in 1,000 American babies die before they reach their first birthday (Calhoun, Grotberg, & Rackley, 1980). Infant mortality rates are directly related to socioeconomic status. Black mothers (who are often poor) are twice as likely as white (middle-class) mothers to lose their babies. (See Figure 3-6.) Teenage mothers are also more likely to lose their infants. But these two categories overlap: young mothers are often poor, and poor women often become pregnant when young. Women in both of these categories are more likely than other women to suffer from protein, vitamin, and/or mineral deficiencies, untreated infections, and emotional stress during pregnancy. They are less likely to seek prenatal care and are more likely to give birth to preterm or small-for-date babies. Medical treatment may enable their infants to survive the first weeks of life and to begin catching up. But when mother and baby leave the hospital, they return to the same environment that created problems during prenatal development. Mothers of babies who need the most attention may be those least equipped to provide attentive care.

What Babies Perceive

Psychologists once thought that newborns just ate and slept, and that months would pass before they began to make sense out of the world. But a growing body of research shows that babies see more, hear more, and perhaps understand more than anyone had ever suspected.

Before 1960, most parents and professionals believed that newborns were virtually blind. They knew that neonates reacted to light, but assumed that they could not perceive such things as shape, distance, and motion. The fact that a newborn's eye movements look uncoordinated supported this belief. The results of experiments conducted by Robert Fantz and Thomas Bower took psychologists by surprise. Fantz (1963) argued that newborns are not only capable of perceiving different patterns (such as a bull's-eye or checkerboard), but recognize and prefer a drawing of the human face to other figures. Bower's experiments (1974) suggested that an infant can recognize an object even when it is some distance away (and appears smaller) or when it is tilted (and looks different in shape).

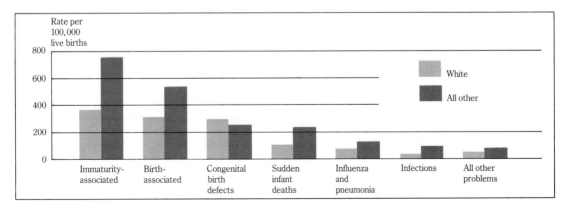

These findings implied that infants can make sophisticated perceptual distinctions from birth. Today most psychologists think that Fantz and Bower exaggerated the newborn's visual skills. But they did open the eyes of psychologists to what newborns can perceive. (We discuss these experiments and perceptual development in more detail in Chapter 4.)

Newborns do see, but not as clearly as adults do because they cannot adjust their focus. An image 8 to 10 inches from a baby's face looks as clear to him as it would to an adult; beyond that point his vision is blurred. An optimistic estimate is that neonates have 20/200 vision— that is, they can see an object 20 feet away about as well as an adult with good vision can see an object 200 feet away. Infants are several months old before they can coordinate the movement of their eyes and look at something with both eyes at the same time. This ability, called *binocularity,* gives humans three-dimensional vision. But newborns can look with one eye at a time. Indeed, they actively seek visual stimulation, and by two months they are developing systematic strategies for scanning their world (Haith, 1979). Newborns may perceive color, although this is uncertain (Bornstein, Kessen, & Weiskopf, 1976).

Newborns can hear. But because their eardrums are flaccid, they cannot detect higher and lower sounds that adults and older children can hear. Indeed, they seem to be tuned into sounds within the range of the human voice. In 1971 Peter Eimas and colleagues published reports of studies which showed that newborns can not only distinguish speech from nonspeech sounds, but also can make fine distinctions between consonants (such as "*ba*" and "*pa*"). Infants *may* recognize their mother's voice within days of birth (DeCasper & Fifer, 1980).

There is no doubt that newborns can taste and smell. Babies are born with a "sweet tooth." Lewis Lipsitt (1977) and others have shown that babies prefer a sweet drink to a liquid that is tasteless or salty. They may sleep better if the nursing mother eats a candy bar before the evening feeding. Newborns react to different tastes much as adults do. When given something sweet, they smile and lick their lips; something sour makes them purse their lips, wrinkle their nose, and blink their eyes; something bitter makes them stick out their tongue and spit (Steiner, 1977). (See Figure 3-7.) Newborns also show strong likes and dislikes for odors. When tested with foods, babies in one study had a strong positive response to the smell of butter and bananas, a positive or indifferent reaction to vanilla, and some dislike of fish. All the babies rejected the smell of rotten eggs (Steiner, 1977). No one knows why newborns prefer the smell of bananas to that of vanilla, for example. The point is that babies come

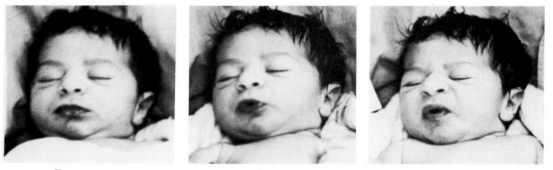

Face at rest   Sweet   Bitter

into the world with all sensory systems functioning (Lipsitt, 1977).

Studies of circumcision (surgical removal of the foreskin of the penis) indicate just how resiliant the newborn is (Gunnar, Malone, & Fisch, 1985). The operation is performed without anesthesia, and babies show all the biochemical signs of stress. They cry intensely. Yet moments after the operation is completed, they are able to nurse and interact with their mothers. If permitted, they fall into a deep sleep which seems to help them recover from the experience.

How Babies Learn

Studies of perception show that newborns are aware of their surroundings. But can they use their senses to learn anything in the first months of life? The answer is a qualified yes. Newborns are capable of making associations between events and remembering sensations, but their short attention span limits how much they can learn.

When neonates are presented with a repeated sound or visual pattern, they pay increasingly less attention to it. This progressive decline in response to the same stimulus presented repeatedly is a simple form of learning called **habituation.** Newborns also respond to both classical and operant conditioning. If a baby is presented with a nasty smell (a piece of cotton

dipped in essence of rotten egg, for example), he turns his head away—an unconditioned response. If an experimenter rings a bell just before exposing the baby to the unpleasant smell and repeats this several times, the newborn does not wait for the smell before turning his head. He turns away as soon as he hears the sound—a conditioned response. This type of learning is called classical conditioning, or learning new associations. If an experimenter rewards a baby with milk or sugar water for sucking harder on a nipple, the baby learns to use more pressure to obtain the reward. This is operant conditioning, or learning new behavior. Although these examples of learning are primitive, they show that newborns are neurologically capable of making connections between events.

Newborns also have the beginnings of memory. In 1941 Dorothy Marquis studied two groups of babies who were accustomed to three- or four-hour feeding schedules in the first eight days of life. During this time, babies in both groups became more active and began to cry as their usual feeding time approached. On the ninth day, Marquis shifted the three-hour babies to a four-hour schedule. When three hours passed, the babies in this group became upset. This suggests that infants in the first two weeks of life "remember" such events as scheduled feeding. However, the three-hour group

Figure 3-7 Newborn Response to Bitter and Sweet The newborn's preference for sweet tastes and dislike for bitter liquid may be an evolved response that encouraged our ancestors to choose sweet, nutritious fruits and reject potentially poisonous foods; we do not know. But we are certain that humans demonstrate these preferences at a very early age.

(Ganchrow, Steiner, & Daher, 1983)

simply may have eaten less at each feeding and were more hungry after the same interval than the four-hour group. But there is other evidence for memory.

Lewis Lipsitt (1977) and his colleagues at Brown University (Crook & Lipsitt, 1976; Kobre & Lipsitt, 1972) capitalized on the fondness of newborns for sweet tastes. Babies who were fed a sweet liquid sucked faster and had higher heart rates than those fed the same amount of water. When the researchers fed the sweet-tasting liquid first, then the water, the babies decreased their sucking to a level below that of the water-only group. But when they fed the water first, then the sweet liquid, the babies increased their sucking rate to a high level. In this brief period, the newborns "remember" what came before and seemed to react to the second liquid as a disappointment or a pleasant surprise. The newborns could also discriminate between more and less sweet liquids by sucking and savoring the sweeter ones longer.

Infants may remember their mothers by smell. Aidan Macfarlane (1978) showed that newborns learn to pick out their own mother's breast smell. Two breast pads were placed against the infant's cheeks. One pad was from the mother and one pad was clean or from another mother. After the first few days of life, the baby turned more often toward her own mother's odor than to that of the other pad. By ten days, each of the infants definitely preferred the smell of her own mother.

An experiment by Anthony DeCasper and William Fifer (1980) demonstrates that even 3-*day*-olds can learn. Small babies suck on nipples in bursts and pauses; every baby has his or her own rhythm. The researchers began by determining each baby's normal sucking rhythm. Once they established this, the researchers divided the infants into two groups. Babies in group A were rewarded by the sound of their own mother's voice when they increased the

pause between sucking bursts. Babies in group B were rewarded the same way when they decreased the pause. Remarkably, eight of the ten babies learned to change their sucking patterns so that they would hear their own mother. Later the procedure was reversed. Babies in group A were rewarded for short pauses and babies in group B for long pauses. The newborns in both groups again learned quickly which sucking pattern produced their own mother's voice. When played the sound of another woman's voice, however, they did not respond. Neither did they respond to the sound of their fathers' voices, even when they had had early and extensive experience with him. DeCasper and Sigafoos (1983) suggest that the baby's hearing the mother's voice and heartbeat from the womb may influence his postnatal learning.

Whatever the source of infant preferences, it is clear that some learning is possible in the first weeks and months of life. But one of the major difficulties in getting newborns to learn is that they are seldom fully awake; even when alert, they rarely pay attention to whatever the experimenter wants. As we discuss in later chapters, one of the major changes in intellectual functioning during childhood is the child's growing ability to focus on a task. In newborns, this ability is virtually absent. Demonstrations that infants can learn owe more to the inevitability of the stimuli—a baby cannot "close his ears" as a child can—and to the cleverness and persistence of the experimenters than to the infant's cooperation. Infants might be able to learn much more than we realize—if we could somehow hold their attention.

Who Influences Whom?

Humans are social animals from birth. When a newborn is distressed, nothing quiets him more than being picked up and held (Korner, 1974). The most effective position for soothing a new baby's crying is holding him upright against the adult's chest so that his eyes can peer over the adult's shoulder. This gives the baby the double pleasure of warm contact and visual stimulation. Rocking the baby or swaddling him in a blanket are also effective pacifiers, as mothers have known for centuries. Sucking on a nipple, whether it gives food or not, quiets a baby. Most of all, newborns like company.

In the first weeks after birth, babies spend many of their waking moments learning about people, especially the people who care for them every day. They learn to recognize their mother's voice, as noted above. And although they cannot see very clearly, they may remember the faces they see most often. When given a choice, a 2-week-old infant prefers looking at her mother to looking at a female stranger (Carpenter et al., 1968). (This preference changes later in the first year. Apparently, babies get bored looking at their mother's face and prefer looking at someone new!) Responding to people is as natural to a baby as sleeping or sucking.

Everyone knows that the newborn baby is a helpless, defenseless creature who is totally dependent on adults for survival. When we compare a tiny, naive neonate to a mature, sophisticated adult, it seems absurd to ask who influences whom. John Bowlby (1969) was one of the first to suggest that the baby plays an active part in the attachment that develops between a mother and a newborn. It is no accident that most adults find babies irresistible. Evolution

has equipped the newborns with powerful means of attracting adults to them. Adults respond, sometimes in spite of themselves.

Researchers have found consistently that babies initiate 50 percent to 80 percent of all mother–infant interactions (Als, 1975; Bell & Harper, 1977; Moss & Robson, 1968; Schoggen, 1963). The infant's cries and other signs of distress dictate the mother's actions in this period. Her attention is focused on the infant's needs; she is attuned to the baby's signals and probably lends far greater meaning to them than developmental psychologists do. She does not try to socialize, educate, or push the baby toward goals she holds desirable; caregiving and relieving the infant's discomfort are her primary aims.

One of the most effective ways newborns attract adults is by crying. Few adults fail to

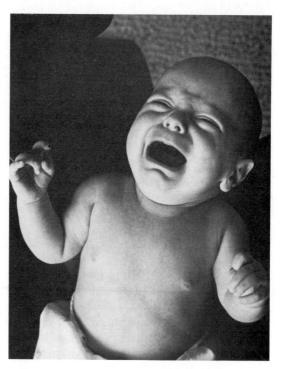

A baby crying is one of the most compelling sounds on earth. The urge to comfort a distressed newborn, like the compulsion to return a baby's smile, is programmed in adults.

Insight

A SCIENTIST AS FATHER

Anthropologist and physician Melvin Konner (1982) describes his experience and observations as a new father:

> When my firstborn daughter was six weeks old we went to the pediatrician with her for the usual scheduled visit. My general impression as a scientist—that newborn babies all looked the same and were quite unappealing, much less appealing, say, than a Barbie doll, or a pony—was confirmed for me by my experience as a father. Not only that, but this one was one of those that did not sleep. . . .
>
> Anyhow, there we were, the three of us, in the bosom of medical wisdom, and I wanted an answer to a question. So I held the baby up to the light, squinted at the physician out of one bloodshot eye, and made my statement starkly and clearly: "Tell me, Doctor" I said. "You've been in this business a long time." (I now glanced meaningfully at the baby.) "She's ruining my life. She's ruining my sleep, she's ruining my health, she's ruining my work, she's ruining my relationship with my wife, and . . . and . . . and she's ugly. . . . Why do I like her?"
>
> The physician, a distinguished one in our town, and a wise and an old and a virtuous man, seemed most unbaffled by the problem.
>
> "You know"—he shrugged his shoulders—"parenting is an instinct and the baby is a releaser."
>
> "Doctor," I said. "That's one of the worst clichés from one of my own worst lectures!" . . . I took my leave of the doctor (without giving vent to any violent feelings) and sank back into my misery of love: a desperation of affection for a tiny, whining monster that was making a constant assault upon my nerves.
>
> The adoptive parents of another newborn we knew (they went through the same feelings in almost exactly the same way) found a wonderful way to describe it. It was, they said, like nothing so much as the short end of a one-sided adolescent love affair. You whined, you gazed, you mooned around, you dreamed orgies of tenderness, you saw, in your mind's eye, decades of future mutual love, dignified, courtly, publicly known. Meanwhile you suffered every known variety of emotional abuse, neglect, rejection, anguish, and humiliation. If you managed somehow to steel yourself for an hour, to become convinced that you could stay on an even keel, you were thrown a scrap—here an appropriately timed belch, there a split second of eye contact—and you tumbled back down into the well with glazed walls, stewing in your [own] affectional juices. This set you up nicely for the next diaper change when, almost literally, you would have more offal dumped on your pitiful head. (p. 291–92)

Konner reasons:

> Since the newborn human infant is incapable of love, it is essential that its mother and father make up for its deficit; if they don't, the infant will lose its life, and the parents, their reproductive success. Later in infancy, the child's emotional capacities grow, and the parent starts to get something out of the deal. (p. 293)

respond to a baby's cries of distress. It is an irritating, inescapable sound. Ann Frodi and colleagues (1978) found that a mother's heart rate and blood pressure rise when her baby cries, as does the father's. A hungry cry can make a mother's temperature rise and her milk flow (Lind, 1971). When parents pick up a screaming infant, it is as much to calm themselves as it is to calm the child. Most mothers (80 percent) and many fathers (45 percent) are able to identify their baby on the basis of cries alone (Green & Gustafson, in press). And most parents are able to tell why the baby is crying: whether he is hungry, in pain, or simply angry (Wolff, 1969).

The baby's social responsiveness is a second source of power over adults (Duchowny, 1974; Korner, 1974). When babies are awake and alert, parents become alert and excited. A newborn's visual explorations hold a special fascination for mothers, even before a baby is mature enough to maintain eye contact. The baby's emotional responses, especially smiles, are a parent's reward for interrupted sleep and hours of care. Parents are also influenced by how well they can soothe their baby. Easing the newborn's discomforts is the major challenge in the first few months of his life. A mother's success or failure in consoling her newborn has a major impact on her sense of competence as a mother. A baby who quiets easily will make a mother feel good about herself; an irritable baby who is difficult to calm may evoke frustration in some parents, additional attention from others.

Studies of parents' responses to different babies suggest that preterm or small-for-date babies, and babies with Down's syndrome or similar problems, are doubly disadvantaged (Starr, Dietrich, Fischoff, Cerenise, & Zweier, 1984). Their cries are more irritating than those of other babies, and they are more difficult to calm. They are less alert and respond more slowly to visual or auditory stimulation. They are not as ready to become "social partners" and offer parents fewer tangible rewards. These studies also show that normal babies are far from helpless; parents are easy to condition.

The Bonding Controversy

When does the "romance" between parent and infant begin? Marshall Klaus, John Kennell, and others have argued that the first hours after birth are critical in establishing a mother–infant bond (Klaus, Jerauld, Kreger, McAlpine, Steffa, & Kennell, 1972). Klaus and Kennell were concerned about the practice of separating mothers from newborns in the hospital. Fifteen years ago, premature babies were isolated from their mothers in incubators for days or even weeks after delivery. Mothers of healthy babies were allowed a glimpse of their newborn after delivery, brief contact six to twelve hours later for identification, and then twenty- to thirty-minute visits about every four hours for feeding during the time she and the baby were in the hospital. Was this routine good for infants? good for mothers?

Klaus and Kennell compared fourteen first-time mothers who followed the usual hospital routine with fourteen mothers who were given an hour of contact with their naked newborns shortly after delivery and five hours of extra contact with them every day in the hospital (Klaus et al., 1972). All were single mothers from low socioeconomic backgrounds. They found that when the mothers returned to the hospital for a routine checkup a month later, those who had been allowed early contact seemed more attached to their babies than the other mothers were to theirs. The former were more attentive during the pediatric examination, soothed their babies more, and engaged in more fondling and face-to-face interaction. One year later, they still seemed more concerned about their infants than were the mothers in the control group; also, they reported being reluctant to leave the infant with a babysitter or to return to work (Kennell, Jerauld, & Wolfe, 1974). In a follow-up study, researchers observed five mothers from each of the previous groups when the children were ages 1 and 2 years. Mothers who had had early contact asked more questions, issued fewer commands, and used more complex sentences with their child. Tests of the same children again at age 5 years indicated that they had somewhat better language skills (Ringler, Trause, & Klaus, 1978).

Klaus and Kennell were convinced that mothers who have close physical contact with their baby immediately after birth establish a special bond with their infant. Separating the mother and child, even for a few hours, weakens that bond. "There is a sensitive period in the first minutes and hours of life during which it is necessary that the mother and father have close contact with their neonate for later optimal development" (Kennell & Klaus, 1976, p. 14). One might call this the "epoxy theory" of mother–child attachment (Klaus, 1978). If mother and newborn are together during the early, critical period when the "glue" is still wet, they establish an unbreakable bond. If contact is delayed, the glue on each person hardens and no secure bond between them is established. Klaus and Kennell hold that separating a mother from her infant makes mild or severe neglect and child abuse more likely.

Klaus's and Kennell's studies and articles have had an important and positive effect on hospital procedures. Obstetricians and maternity ward staff are more flexible about routines, and they pay more attention to parents' wishes in most hospitals today than they did ten or fifteen years ago. But many psychologists disagree with their reasoning. The concept of bonding is borrowed from the literature on animal behavior. There is clear evidence of bonding in other species. For example, if a mother goat is separated from her kid for an hour or more after birth, she will actively reject it, using her head and horns to butt it away. If she is with her kid during that critical hour, she will use her head and other parts of her anatomy to keep the kid from harm. Like other herding animals, all nanny goats give birth at about the same time. If a mother couldn't recognize her kid, its chances of survival would be lowered. Human mothers and babies do not have this problem.

Mother rats are biochemically attached to their young. The hormones that prepare a mother rat or mouse for lactation also prime her to care for her young. She licks them, fetches them if they wriggle away from the nest, and protects them from intruders. This behavior is largely an automatic response. She doesn't have to think about what she feels toward her off-spring. Human mothers can and do think about their babies. Their thoughts and feelings about motherhood begin before birth and continue long after.

The evidence for an early, critical period in human mother–child relations is weak at best. Some researchers have found that early contact has positive effects, but many others have not (Lamb, 1982). Klaus and Kennell themselves found significant differences of behavior because of bonding on only 5 of some 75 measures of maternal interest. These differences might be the result of chance. They might reflect the combined effects of early contact, "rooming in" (that is, having the baby close most of the time), and nursing—not early contact alone. Or this appearance of bonding might be the indirect result of extra attention from the medical and nursing staff, who knew these mothers were under observation. Perhaps extra attention was especially important to poor, single mothers.

Early contact may, indeed, have some short-term positive effects on some mothers in some circumstances (Entwistle & Doering, 1981). Certainly, it is a delightful, memorable experience for many, but it is apparently not necessary. Fathers who were not present at delivery, mothers who required special medical attention during and after delivery, and parents who adopt babies ten days or six months after birth nevertheless establish close relationships with their children. The term "bonding," which is still used in the popular press, exaggerates and oversimplifies human attachments to newborns. (In this chapter's Profile, Robert McCall discusses the problems of communicating scientific findings through the media.)

Individual and Sex Differences

From the moment of conception, babies are different from one another in almost every possible way. By the time of birth, environmental influences have combined with genetic differences present at conception to produce a unique individual. Some newborns are relatively active, some quieter. Some are quick to respond to lights, sounds, and pinpricks; others are slow to respond. Some respond in a prolonged or vigorous way; others become slightly aroused, then quiet again. Some need to be held for a long time when they are distressed; others regularly become quiet without being picked up. How parents react to a baby depends in part on the behavior of the baby, in part on their own personalities, expectations, and experience. (How different parents react to different babies is discussed in Chapter 5.)

Are male and female newborns different? Parents think so. Jeffrey Rubin and colleagues (1974) asked parents for their first impressions of their newborn babies. The hospital staff had rated the 30 babies in the study alike in muscle tone, color, irritability, and even size. Parents of girls described their babies as soft, fine featured, delicate, weak, and passive. Parents of boys described their babies as firm, large-featured, strong, hardy, and alert. The fathers in this study were somewhat more likely to perceive their newborn as "all boy" or "all girl," but mothers generally agreed. Many similar studies suggest that sex differences in the early months, like beauty, are largely in the eyes of the beholder.

Anneliese Korner does not deny the impact of sex stereotypes on parents' treatment of their young. But she believes (1974) that the differences in behavior of male and female infants caused by hormones also influence parents. Female newborns tend to be more sensitive to touch than male babies are. This might cause mothers to hold them more gently. Male babies are more likely to startle than females are. Perhaps mothers hold them tightly to restrain and calm them. Female babies are more likely to smile spontaneously. This may prompt mothers to spend more time talking to them and gazing at their faces. Sex stereotypes are, for Korner, the primary reason why parents treat males and females differently from birth. But "behavioral sex differences of infants themselves may also exert a subtle influence on the caregiver" (1974, p. 113).

Care of the Newborn

Although the newborn baby is not as helpless as she seems, she requires a good deal of care. Many months will pass before she establishes herself as an independent organism. Precisely what she needs is the subject of ongoing debates.

NUTRITION The most important factor in the newborn's physical growth and development is adequate nutrition. The most obvious nutritional source in the early months is mother's milk. Today as in the past, most women in the world breast-feed their babies. In modern Western societies, however, breast-feeding has gone in and out of style. In the 1920s and 1930s some physicians recommended that mothers bottle-feed their newborns, on the grounds that it was more sanitary and that infant formulas could be designed to fit the baby's particular needs. Women who breast-fed infants were considered old-fashioned. Today the pendulum has swung the other way, and many physicians are urging a return to breast-feeding. A recent article in a respected popular magazine (Marano, 1979) argued for breast-feeding. The author quoted scientists who believe that the antibodies the newborn receives through breast milk are essential to the neonate's health. A bottle-fed baby, they claim, is an "immunological orphan." (The fetus absorbs antibodies all through its prenatal development, but this protection is lost a few months after birth.) Some experts claim that although formula-fed babies gain weight faster—a positive effect—they are more likely to become obese or have high levels of serum cholesterol

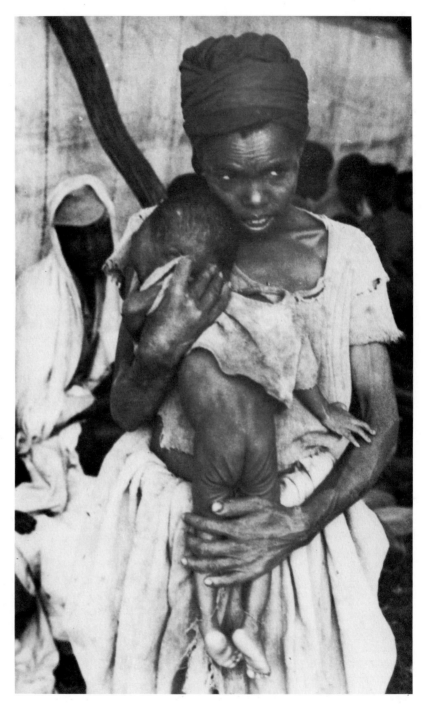

Newborns and their mothers need adequate food to thrive. Infants can recover from early deprivation if they receive good nutrition in later months. Unfortunately, in many parts of the world starvation is not a temporary condition. This mother and child are victims of the drought in East Africa.

as adults. Others argue that breast-feeding is essential to maintaining the mother–infant bond and may reduce the likelihood of child abuse or neglect. The problem for most women today is that they work outside their homes. Many cannot afford or do not want to take off several months from their jobs or careers. A careful analysis shows that babies are not seriously affected when they are bottle-fed. There is no firm evidence that either breast- or bottle-feeding enhances the baby's well-being more than the other (Horowitz, 1982). The one important exception is in developing nations, where breast-feeding is preferable to bottle-feeding because impure water and lack of refrigeration may introduce harmful substances into infant formulas.

Babies who are being nursed or fed a balanced formula do not need solid food until they are 1 year old. But many physicians recommend introducing baby foods at 3 or 4 months; some, as early as 2 weeks. When solid food becomes a significant part of the infant's diet, caretakers must provide the right amounts of proteins, iron, and other nutrients. Severe and prolonged malnutrition has been associated with mental as well as physical retardation. Malnourished infants perform poorly on virtually all psychological tests. *Kwashiorkor,* or protein deficiency, can cause swollen bellies and spindly limbs. Such extreme conditions are usually found in countries plagued by famine, drought, war, and economic upset. But most children can recover mentally and physically when adequate nutrition is restored. If they do not, it is usually because of other, complicating diseases (Lloyd-Still, 1976).

Equally troubling is a syndrome called *failure to thrive.* In these cases, a baby who was normal and healthy at birth is admitted to the hospital four to eight months later in a weak, apathetic condition. The baby has not gained weight and does not respond to people. Some-

times physicians discover a medical cause, such as a metabolic problem that prevents the infant from absorbing nutrients; many times they do not. Once in the hospital, the infant gains weight, becomes increasingly alert, and begins to smile. For these infants, their failure to thrive can only be attributed to the caregivers' neglect or ignorance of infant care.

SCHEDULING AND CUDDLING The caregiver whose baby is alert and socially responsive, is gaining weight, and is otherwise thriving must at some point begin to exercise control over the infant's demands. Like breast-feeding versus bottle-feeding, *scheduling* infants has been controversial. As recently as the 1960s, most physicians and infant-care books recommended putting babies on a regular schedule almost as soon as they were born: "Feed the baby every four hours. If she is asleep, wake her. If she cries and fusses between feedings, let her cry." The theory behind scheduling was that caregivers who fed their babies whenever the babies were hungry and picked them up whenever they cried were "spoiling" them. Early training was considered essential for establishing lifelong habits. A spoiled infant would grow up to be a household tyrant.

Today most developmental psychologists would give the following advice: "Comfort the baby when he cries; feed him when he is hungry. Play with him when he is awake; 'spoil' him as much as you can." Why? Studies of both cognitive and social development show that a baby must learn that he has an effect on his environment and, therefore, can have some control over his own experience (Lewis & Goldberg, 1969).

Babies should know that they can make things happen. The fact that feeding and cuddling are contingent on the newborn's behavior is almost as important to his development as care itself. Parents and caregivers can accom-

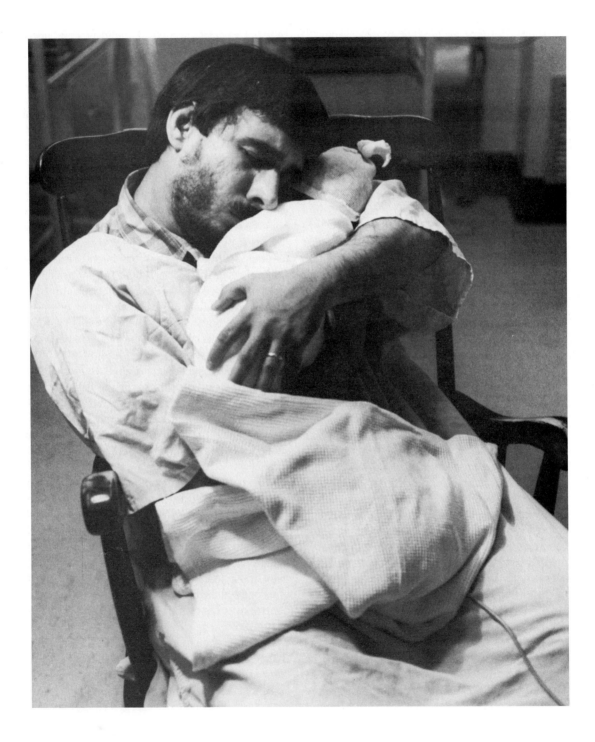

plish this by being responsive to the baby, and by encouraging frequent associations between crying and being picked up, sucking and obtaining nourishment, gurgling and hearing another voice reply. There is some evidence that babies who cannot predict if or how their behavior will affect their caregivers are slower to develop than those whose caregivers react to their demands with relevant actions (Vietze, Abernathy, Ashe, & Faulstich, 1978).

Infants must experience the benefits of self-motivation, apart from the rewards of good caregiving. Babies thrive where there are many opportunities to watch, touch, and manipulate things for themselves. Babies who are restricted in their play and put on rigid schedules from birth may be apathetic. Repeated frustration teaches them that their own actions do not matter.

THE FATHER'S ROLE What role does the father play in the newborn's life? Popular thought has it that men are not very interested in small babies. This is not so. In *Fathers* (1981), Ross Parke surveys the small but growing literature on paternity. Parke begins with the prenatal period. Everyone knows that women can be moody during pregnancy. Expectant fathers also undergo psychological changes. They may worry about their wives' aches and pains more than their wives do. Fathers may be more conciliatory in disputes with their wives than they are at other times and, like their wives, may turn to their own parents (especially their mothers) for emotional support. When present at delivery, fathers are even more likely than mothers to describe the birth as a "peak experience." (This is not surprising: They did not go through physical pain or take dulling drugs.) When visiting their babies in the hospital in the first few days after the birth, fathers are as nurturant and stimulating with their newborn as mothers are. Their presence seems to increase the mother's interest in the baby. At home, in the weeks following birth, they become as good at reading the baby's signals as mothers are.

There are differences between fathers and mothers, however. Fathers usually spend more time playing with their newborn and less time feeding them or otherwise caring for their needs. One reason may be that they have less time to spend with the baby than the mother has and they want to get the most out of that time. Similarly, working mothers also spend proportionately more time playing with their babies. Another reason fathers play more may be that the presence of a baby brings out stereotyped sex roles in a marriage. Many couples slip into a more traditional pattern when they have a child. Even if they consciously planned to share child care, both may unconsciously believe that feeding, bathing, diapering, and such are "women's work" or that the mother is more competent in these areas. Some mothers do not consider

Much of the research on parents and newborns emphasizes the differences between fathers and mothers: "Fathers make better playmates." But fathers are also capable of great tenderness.

themselves especially feminine or maternal and do not claim special expertise in handling their babies. Fathers of these babies are likely to devote more time to basic infant care than are other fathers.

Fathers and mothers also have different styles of playing with an infant. While mothers emphasize verbal play, fathers seem to prefer physical play. They like to get a baby excited—and usually do. Brazelton (1979) finds that at 2 or 3 weeks babies display a brighter attitude (they are more wide-eyed and playful) toward the father than they do toward the mother. Apparently, a distinct and special bond is formed between father and infant in the first weeks and months of life.

Already the child has come a long way from the single cell produced by the union of the mother's egg and father's sperm. But his developmental journey has only begun.

SUMMARY

1. Development begins at conception, with the union of a sperm and ovum, each of which contains half a set of human chromosomes. About two weeks after conception, this zygote attaches to the wall of the uterus, and the embryo as it is now called, begins to form basic body structures and organ systems. At two months these systems have begun to function and the developing organism is now called a fetus. The fetal period is marked by growth, increasing coordination, the beginnings of behavior, and possibly some simple learning.

2. Sex differentiation illustrates that genes do not so much determine the course of prenatal development as trigger a series of biochemical reactions that depend on the right ingredients at the right time.

3. Genetic hazards to development include the inheritance of an extra chromosome (as in Down's syndrome, most common in children of older mothers), a defective gene on the X chromosome (as in hemophilia), and certain recessive genes (as in sickle-cell anemia).

4. Environmental hazards to development include diseases (such as syphilis) and drugs (large amounts of alcohol as well as medicine) which penetrate the placental membrane, and a poor or incompatible intrauterine environment. PKU—an inherited disorder which can be cured through diet yet sill transmitted to offspring—shows how genes and the environment interact.

5. In most cases it is impossible to determine the exact cause of a disorder. The child inherits a vulnerability (to diabetes or schizophrenia for example) which diet, experience, or some other element of the environment may or may not activate.

6. The "medicalization of childbirth" remains controversial. Some procedures may be harmful or unnecessary, such as routine use of general anesthesia. Others save lives, such as fetal monitoring.

7. The Apgar and Brazelton scales are tools for identifying newborns at risk. Preterm and small-for-date babies have a much greater chance of surviving today than they did even ten years ago. Stimulating environments and human contact may help these babies catch up. The infant's chances are in part a function of social class.

8. The newborn's behavior is organized and adaptive. Newborns are equipped with a number of reflexes, or automatic responses. They can see and hear (though not as clearly as they will later), smell and

taste. And they demonstrate the beginnings of learning and memory (for example, they can remember their mother's voice).

9. Newborns are social actors, capable of attracting adults by crying, establishing eye contact and other social responses, and quieting when they are held.

10. Studies that suggested intimate contact immediately following birth establishes a critical bond between a mother and child have been discredited. But early contact can be delightful.

11. Individual differences are present from birth; so are sex differences, although perhaps only in parents' imaginations.

12. To develop and thrive, babies need good nutrition (and they probably benefit from nursing, although this is not necessary). They need responsive care. Satisfying an infant's demands will not produce a spoiled child. Newborns also enjoy playing with the father, who has his own style of handling infants.

FURTHER READING

Apgar, V., & Beck, J. (1972). *Is my baby all right?: A guide to birth defects.* New York: Trident. An excellent resource about genetically and environmentally produced defects.

Boston Women's Health Book Collection, The. (1984). *The new our bodies, ourselves: A book by and for women.* New York: Simon & Schuster. An excellent guide to women's health needs and approaches that are not as widely known or practiced as one might think.

Lamaze, F. (1970). *Painless childbirth: The Lamaze method.* New York: Pocket Books. A good introduction to natural childbirth, directed toward the expectant mother.

Nilsson, L. (1977). *A child is born.* New York: Delacorte/Seymour Lawrence. A stunning photographic account of prenatal development.

ANN LEVINE: Dr. McCall, what first got you interested in psychology?

ROBERT B. MCCALL: I remember being asked the same question at my doctoral orals. My answer was that in high school I read a book on ESP by J. B. Rhine, who was at Duke University. I asked my biology teacher if I could do a special project on ESP, and he said yes.

At this point, one member of my doctoral committee said, "Strike one!" But another asked me to go on.

Robert B. McCall
Senior Scientist and
Science Writer,
Boys Town

I told them that I began showing a standard ESP card deck to people. There are twenty-five cards with five different symbols. You show the person the back of the card and ask them which symbol is on the front. By guessing alone, a person should average about five right answers. Well, I found someone who averaged twenty out of twenty-five on several thousand trials. He was way above anyone I'd read about in Rhine's book. I wrote to Rhine, who told me I should put the subject in another room. He wouldn't do it, which made me suspect that he was picking up cues from the back of the card. But when I put him in the third row of the class, about fifteen feet away, he still got thirteen out of twenty-five right.

"Strike two!" The second strike was for not using proper controls in that experiment. I never went back to studying ESP. But I did pass my doctoral exam.

AL: So you began taking psychology courses as an undergraduate?

RBM: Psychology was my major before I walked in the door.

AL: Then you got your Ph.D. in experimental psychology at the University of Illinois.

RBM: Right. As a graduate student, I did somewhat "radical" experiments with rats. My advisor was J. McV. Hunt, a clinician who became a developmentalist. At that time he was interested in intrinsic motivation, curiosity, and the magnitude of discrepancy between what you already

know well and a stimulus you now experience. We found that a modest discrepancy, something that is different but not too different from the familiar, is most interesting . . . to rats.

After I graduated I spent a year with Jerome Kagan at Harvard as a National Science Foundation postdoctoral fellow. Jerry was also interested in the distribution of attention. We ended up doing studies of infants that were essentially similar to what I had done with rats. I went to the University of North Carolina for two years. Then I took over the job Jerry Kagan had once held at the Fels Research Institute, as chairman of psychology. I was there for nine years. Then, in 1977, I came to Boys Town as a senior scientist and science writer.

AL: What exactly does a "senior scientist and science writer" do?

RBM: I have two responsibilities. One is to communicate research and professional advice on children, youth, and families to the general public. That means working on popular books, national newspaper and magazine articles, and TV and radio productions. The second is to maintain my standing as a scholar. I haven't collected any new data for some years, but I analyze data, write professional papers,* and serve on the editorial boards of seven psychological journals.

AL: Why did you decide to leave research and academia and specialize in public communications?

RBM: Because I had the chance; that's the short answer.

An old high school friend, Thomas Gregory, saw an article I wrote for *Science* magazine and wrote me. He was vice president of a small documentary film company that had produced a series of ninety-second news features on medi-

*See, for example, McCall's analysis of the canalization of intelligence, text p. 65.

cine for distribution to local commercial TV stations. He was interested in producing a series on child development. When he saw my article he remembered that I had wanted to be an actor (among other things) during high school. Now he saw me as a performer who had picked up academic credentials—public clout. On my next trip to California we got together, and he explained what he had in mind. I told him that no psychologist could say anything in one to three minutes. He said physicians could, and they're no more articulate than psychologists. That evening we met our wives for drinks in the Bank of America Building. Fifty-two stories above the San Andreas Fault, he turned to me and said, "Tell me about some finding that really interests you." I did and he said, "That was fascinating, it's useful, and it took only a hundred and thirty-eight seconds!"

So Gregory and I began looking for funding. One foundation after another told us, "It's a terrific idea, it should be done, but we can't fund you. We only support research and service programs." TV spots didn't qualify as either. Then I heard that Boys Town was starting a new center for the study of youth development and wrote to them. They wrote back that they had planned a whole division for just the sort of programs we were proposing. Within a year and a half, Gregory and I were both at the center.

Why did I accept their offer? I thought there were a lot of good scientists around, but few who could communicate to the general public, and fewer still who wanted to. And then there was the lure of the mass media. . . . But it wasn't as big a decision as it sounds. I went to a research institute, not a popular magazine or a TV station.

AL: You've spent most of your adult life, some fifteen years or more, as a researcher and a teacher. Now, at Boys Town, your job is to reach a mass audience. How did you get started?

RBM: I had a lot of help and incredible luck. We hired two consultants to help us with the print media: Maya Pines and Patrick Young, both highly respected science writers. The first thing they told me was that it is very difficult to get published in a popular magazine if you have never published in a magazine before. So you have to do something to break this Catch-22. It turns out that it is much easier to publish a popular book. I had already started a book on infants. We decided that if that were promoted properly, a few magazines would pick up exerpts and I would acquire magazine credits. Lo and behold, that is what happened. Harvard University Press sent galleys to *Parents* magazine, and *Parents* happened to be looking for someone to write a column on birth to age one. On the basis of the galleys and no other information, they gave me the column. Until I started writing, they thought I was an M.D.! A column is every journalist's dream. And here I was, a beginner at popular writing. (My writing teacher and editor, Holly Stocking, who is a trained journalist, must have been frosted.)

The book and the column paved the way to talk shows, on radio and TV, which we were also aiming for. Here, I had Gregory and his staff to coach me. I remember the first time he took me into the studio at Boys Town. He sat me in front of a camera and, without skipping a beat, asked, "What's normal development, doctor?" I said, "Damn it, how do you expect me to answer that?" He said calmly, "You can't use that word on the air, doctor. Try again." I was lucky. How many scientists have a media coach? Not many.

So you can see, it was mostly fortuitous, a matter of chance.

AL: Luck doesn't help if you don't have the knowledge and skill to use it.

RBM: Well, you need both.

AL: What are your goals as a science communicator? What do you hope to accomplish?

RBM: I have two goals, really. The first is the obvious one: to contribute to the welfare of children, youth, and families. I think that, in some small way, giving people information they can use in their own decision-making and in meeting their responsibilities as parents and child-care workers contributes to that.

We academics tend to assume that the media and the public want us to tell parents what to do: ten rules for child-rearing, five rules for toilet training, and so on. But if you give people a how-to, the only ones who are likely to use it are those who already agree with you. There are other ways. You can give people information that is pertinent to decisions they have to make without telling them what to do. Benjamin Spock and Arnold Gesell, especially,

Continued

were popular for just this reason.* Gesell didn't tell you to do anything; he didn't believe that what you did would make much difference anyway. Rather, he told you what to expect. Parents got great relief from knowing about the "terrible twos." Gesell didn't tell them how to "cure" a terrible two-year-old, but it was comforting to know that this was normal and they shouldn't be upset.

You can encourage good parenting. There are parents out there who are doing a good job and not getting rewarded for it. Seeing examples in print or on the TV that illustrate what they are already doing can make them feel that they are being good parents. Then, too, some people need help knowing whether they have a problem. You don't have to give them a solution; you help them decide whether they need help. And finally, there are people who feel better when they've heard about somebody else's problems. Somebody's always got it worse than you do.

AL: How do you know whether you are having an effect, whether you are reaching people?

RBM: In most cases you never know. If you present a program designed to help people stop smoking, let's say, you have a clear dependent variable. You can ask people if they have stopped and, if so, for how long. When you are simply providing information, people can take different behavioral routes. Suppose you produce a program on family therapy. You explain what it is, what kinds of problems it can help, which problems it can't help, and so forth. Some people who see the program will decide, "I never want to do that." Other people will think, "Gosh, maybe we ought to see somebody." Most people don't need it and never will. Others file it away and, ten years later, when problems arise, pull it out of their mental file. They may not remember the program at all, but they have a positive attitude toward therapy.

All of this is particularly true of television. TV doesn't communicate facts very well. You can't cut out a TV program and pin it up on the wall. But TV does communicate, even create,

attitudes and feelings about things. The electronic media don't tell people what to think so much as what to think about.

AL: You said you had two main goals. What is the second?

RBM: I would like to demonstrate that scholars can go public without prostituting the material they want to communicate. Good science writers know this; they do it every day. Academics often think it can't be done. They are so convinced that journalists will oversimplify or sensationalize their research, or just "get it wrong," that they refuse to cooperate. And this creates a self-fulfilling prophecy, because nonscientists and pop scientists *will* say it. Often they do get the research wrong, which confirms the researcher's belief that the press and the media are not to be trusted.

But I must say that my colleagues have been very supportive of what I'm doing. Some have said they were pleased that "one of us" was doing this. I expected some flack; I haven't gotten much. But I'm not sure how much respect I'm accorded.

AL: Does the fact that psychology is a behavioral science cause special problems with the media?

RBM: Definitely. For one thing, everybody fancies himself or herself a psychologist. If what you have to say doesn't square with their experience, you lose credibility. At the same time, if your findings confirm what the journalist or the public already believes, it isn't news. Physicists and biologists don't face these problems. With behavioral sciences, journalists tend to favor the novel or even the odd study. As a result, more bad behavioral science gets into the mass media. An off-the-wall theory of subatomic particles goes unnoticed. But a bizarre theory of sexual development has "human interest."

There's another problem. The scientific writing community developed alongside the space program. Many of the best scientific writers and editors use physics and astronomy, medicine and biology, as reference points. They don't think that behavior needs "translating"; they're still debating whether psychology is a science. So the media cover children, delinquency, and the like, but not from a scientific viewpoint. Talk show hosts tend to see me as a Dr. Spock type rather than a Carl Sagan, Jonathan Miller, or Jacob Bronowski scientist type.

*The author of one of the most widely read books of advice for parents ever written, Dr. Spock urges parents to trust themselves and their child. Spock was an early advocate of what became known as "permissive" child-rearing: the belief that children should be allowed to express their feelings. If parents follow their own "instincts," everything will turn out fine.

For a discussion of Arnold Gesell's work, see Chapter 1 of this text, especially pp. 6–8.

AL: You have written dozens of popular articles and appeared on scores of radio and TV talk shows. What have you learned about dealing with the mass media? What would you advise a psychologist whose work attracts media attention?

RBM: One public relations professional advised a client, "If 'Sixty Minutes' calls, hang up. At best you'll be raped; at worst you'll be killed."

Seriously, I do think there are some basic principles for dealing with the mass media. The most important is to select topics that are intrinsically interesting so that you don't have to hype. One of the glories of our discipline is that people are already interested in what we study; you don't have to sell the subject. Social scientists are about forty percent more likely to be contacted by the press than are scientists from other disciplines. But this has dangers. If people really care about what you're working on, by definition it's going to generate controversy. The safety of the ivory tower is that no one cares what you are doing in there.

A second rule is to talk only about the topics you specialize in. If a question is not in your area, refer the reporter to someone else, unless the interview is for a local paper and you are the "local professional" or it's a live show. Even then, don't be afraid to say, "I don't know." But you should say *why* you don't know.

Dealing with live interviews requires special skills. You have to learn how to handle scientifically naive questions. Developmental psychologists are often asked for personal advice or diagnosis. The best way to handle this is to discuss the general issue. For example, a parent asks, "My baby is fifteen months old and doesn't walk yet. Should I be worried?" You can answer this by saying, "Between ten and twenty percent of babies don't walk at fifteen months. Most of them turn out fine. But if you are worried, see your pediatrician." You haven't said yes or no, but you have given her information.

Be prepared for questions that are impossible to answer. On one show, the interviewer said, "We have thirty seconds. Which is more important in intelligence, environment or heredity?" It was a morning show for housewives, so I said, "It's like baking bread. Which is more important, the flour, the yeast, or the oven temperature? You can't have bread without all of these."

And you should have some dodges ready, for questions you don't want to answer. "Yesterday we interviewed the parents of the first test-tube baby. What kind of psychological problems is that child going to have?" I said I didn't know because this baby was the first. It's okay to say you don't know, especially if you give a reason ("It's the first"). Or you can rephrase a question into something you can answer. Once I was asked, "When does a baby first love its parents?" Now, you don't want to be pedantic and say that it depends on how you define love. So you subtly change the subject. "To love someone you have to be able to recognize them and remember them from day to day. Now, a baby first recognizes. . . ."

AL: Many large corporations hold workshops and seminars for executives who are called on by the press, to teach them how to communicate in different media. Would you recommend something similar for scientists?

RBM: I would, and I have. A number of professional associations have taken steps in this direction. The American Psychological Association published a media guide to help psychologists prepare press releases. Developmental psychologists held a one-day seminar for science writers in which they presented recent advances in research. The American Association for the Advancement of Science sponsors internships for advanced science students who want to work in the mass media. And workshops and symposia on the media are appearing at our conventions. All of these things are useful.

AL: Has your experience as a science communicator changed your thinking or attitudes?

RBM: I'm certain it has. When you write for magazines you have to step outside your own area of expertise. You might do an article on teenage pregnancy one month, disobedient eight-year-olds the next month, detecting abnormal development the next. You lose depth, but you gain breadth. I think I'm more aware of relationships between different areas than I was before. And I'm more interested in "relevant" topics and applications. If I were to go back to research, I think I'd concentrate on the problems of older kids and adolescents.

AL: Are you glad you put one foot outside the ivory tower?

RBM: Yes. But I've tried to keep the other foot in it.

Studying Cognitive Development: Three Approaches
Psychometrics
Piaget's Theory
Information Processing

Perceptual Development
Using One's Senses
Memory and Learning
Maturation, Experience, or Both?

Motor Development
Body and Brain
INSIGHT: CRIB DEATH: A COGNITIVE VIEW
Standing on Two Feet
Developing Finesse

The Sensorimotor Stage: The Dawn of Awareness
Cognition as Adaptation
Substages of Sensorimotor Development
INSIGHT: THE IMITATION CONTROVERSY
The Object Concept
The Infant's Construction of Reality

The Search for Infant IQ
The Bayley Scales of Infant Development
Assessing Infant Intelligence Tests
INSIGHT: THE SUPERBABY SYNDROME

Individual Variations and Species Similarities
Genetic Influences
Environmental Influences
An Evolutionary View of Sensorimotor Intelligence

Cognitive Motivation: Intelligence and Affect

Further Reading

The baby awakens. Two months old, she is making the transition from neonate to infant. As a newborn she drifted in and out of sleep around the clock. Now her awake states are more mature. She lies in her crib, gazing at the play of morning light on the wall. When her father appears and bends over the crib, she wiggles with delight. She studies his face intently as he picks her up. As he carries her out of the room, the shiny black eyes of the light brown teddy bear on the dresser catch her attention. The sounds and smells of the kitchen are vaguely familiar; she recognizes the feel of her infant seat. She begins pursing her lips and sucking in anticipation of a meal. She is willing to wait—but not too long. Her mother delivers the first spoonful of cereal just in time. After the cereal, her mother moves the baby to her lap to nurse. A month ago, her mother had to turn her head or stroke her cheek to get her into position. Now the baby finds the nipple by herself. After a gentle burping, her mother carries her back to her room. Her mother talks and smiles as she changes the baby's diaper; the baby smiles and gurgles back.

You are witnessing the beginnings of awareness. The baby is still entirely dependent on adults, of course. But signs of the dramatic changes she will undergo in the next twelve to eighteen months are already apparent. She is aware of her surroundings and beginning to recognize recurring sights, sounds, smells, and sensations (perceptual development). She is maturing physically and neurologically and beginning to gain some control of her body (motor development). She is curious (cognitive development). She responds to people and they respond to her (social development).

The term **cognition** refers to the mental processes (perceiving, remembering, using symbols, reasoning, and imagining) that human beings use to acquire knowledge of the world. For the infant, cognitive development is a journey through unmapped territory. At birth everything is new and strange to the baby. It will be many years before she thinks as an adult

THE BEGINNINGS OF MIND

does. But the infant is well equipped for the trip. She can see and hear, smell and taste, grasp and suck. The knowledge of the world she acquires during infancy builds on her perceptions and actions.

Psychologists approach mental development from different angles. Some are interested in measuring intellectual advances, some study changes in the structure of thought, and some focus on thought processes. We begin this chapter by looking at these three approaches to the study of cognition. Then we look at what perceptual and motor development contribute to cognitive development. Finally, we consider the relationship between thinking and motivation, which is important at every age.

Studying Cognitive Development: Three Approaches

Our discussion of cognitive development in this and later chapters draws on three distinct theoretical traditions and bodies of research: psychometrics, Piagetian theory, and information processing. Although the three often overlap, each has its own history and special concerns (Siegler & Richards, 1982).

Psychometrics

The measurement of human characteristics is called **psychometrics**. One branch of psychometrics, intelligence testing, was pioneered at the turn of the century by Alfred Binet and his colleague Théodore Simon. The French government asked Binet to devise a test that would identify slow learners so that they could be given special education. The first intelligence test, published in 1905, was a general scale designed to measure all facets of intellectual ability. Questions on word knowledge, spatial relationships, reasoning, and immediate memory were ranked in order of difficulty. A child's score depended on how far up this ladder he could go and how he compared to other children

his age. The Binet test was elaborated and refined by two American psychologists—Lewis Terman and, later, David Wechsler[1]—for evaluating school-age children and adults. Arnold Gesell and his colleagues at Yale University and Nancy Bayley at the University of California constructed the first intelligence tests for infants. Revised and updated versions of these tests are still in use today.

For psychometrics, the central questions are: How can intelligence be measured, or quantified? What intellectual skills do most children of a given age exhibit, and what tasks identify children who are advanced or slow for their age? How can tests be used to predict future achievement, especially academic success? What is the correlation between a child's score and those of his parents and siblings? between his score and his socioeconomic position? between his score and his personality traits?

Psychometricians use the enormous body of data accumulated in over 75 years of ability testing to evaluate individual and group differences in intelligence and chronological changes in intellectual abilities. Psychometrics is a pragmatic approach to cognition. Psychologists who work in this field have been more concerned with developing reliable measures of mental competence and growth than with discovering why children develop intellectually. For the Swiss psychologist Jean Piaget, "why" was most important.

Piaget's Theory

Piaget's first job as a postgraduate student in psychology was as an intelligence tester for Alfred Binet. Piaget had studied philosophy and had earned a degree in biology before he enrolled at the Sorbonne in Paris to study psychology. This eclectic background gave him an unusual slant: he found children's *wrong* answers

[1] Wechsler developed alternative measures of intellectual ability in reaction to Binet. (See Chapter 10.)

to test questions as interesting as their correct responses. Piaget began observing his own three children at play, presenting them with simple scientific and moral problems, and asking them how they arrived at their ideas. This *méthode clinique* led Piaget to a theory of the evolution of logic. He identified four distinct stages in cognitive development: the sensori-motor stage, the preoperational stage, the concrete-operational stage, and the formal-operational stage. In doing so, he traced the adolescent's capacity for abstract reasoning to its origins in infant behavior.

It would be only a slight exaggeration to divide the history of cognitive psychology in the United States into two periods: Before Piaget and After Piaget. Before Americans discovered Piaget, descriptions of cognitive development were based on learning theory. According to this view, the infant is a passive, helpless being whose behavior and thinking are shaped by the environment. (See Chapter 1.) In contrast, Piaget viewed the child as an active learner and the architect of his own learning experiences. Cognitive development is the result of the child using his own skills to make sense of his experiences. The environment is still important in Piaget's theory, for interaction with the environment leads to qualitative changes in the way the child thinks. But adults cannot arbitrarily structure the child's thinking and behavior. The direction of cognitive development is genetically predetermined and lies within the child. Learning also plays a role in Piaget's theory. But learning and cognitive development are not synonymous. Piaget reserved the term *cognition* for the mental rules that govern a person's understanding of, and relation to, the external world.

Whereas psychometrics focuses on quantitative changes in intellectual abilities, Piaget focused on *qualitative* changes in intellectual abilities. Intelligence tests assess what children know (the product); Piaget's games and interviews probed how children think (the process). Whereas psychometrics is concerned with individual and group differences, Piaget sought *universal* patterns.

The central questions for Piagetians are: How do children come to understand the basic principles of time, space, and cause and effect that organize adult thinking? What is distinctive—that is, "nonadult"—about the child's understanding of these phenomena? Is the child's reasoning about one area of experience (*Which jar has more candies?*) similar to her reasoning about other areas (*Why does the sun shine? Why is it wrong to steal?*)? How do children in different stages of cognitive development learn from experience, and how does experience change the way they learn?

Information Processing

The main weakness of both the psychometric and Piagetian approaches is that they do not account for the specific processes involved in intelligent behavior (Siegler & Richards, 1982). Psychometricians may tell us that knowing the capital of Thailand at age 10 predicts grade point average in high school; Piagetians may show that children discover in late infancy that objects have an existence of their own. But neither approach tells us precisely what it takes to accomplish these mental feats. This is what the information processing approach tries to do.

The information processing approach to cognitive development is the detailed, step-by-step analysis of cognitive processes. The focus is on how people acquire information (perception and attention), store and retrieve information (memory), and use this information to deal with the present or to plan for the future (problem solving). The approach is based on an analogy between the human mind and a computer (see drawing.) Like a computer, people have "programs" for receiving, storing, retrieving, transforming, constructing, and otherwise manipulating information. The aim of the information processing approach is to discover what these programs are and how they work. While psychometricians use test scores as a data base and Piagetians rely on observations and interviews, psychologists who study information processing devise experiments to measure small units of thought, such as eye movements, reaction times, and lists of words recalled. They may reanalyze the tasks studied by psychometricians and Piagetians, but in minute detail.

Information processing raises a new set of questions: Are the differences in thinking between children and adults due to limits on: (a) children's capacity for handling information? (b) the speed at which they process information? (c) their knowledge base (what is already in the memory) and/or (d) their "programs" for learning? How do perception, attention, memory, and problem-solving strategies change over the course of development?

We begin our investigation of the intellectual achievements of infancy by looking at the most basic form of information-processing: perception. Next we show what motor development contributes to the infant's growing awareness. We consider Piaget's analysis of infant intelligence in detail. Then we turn to measurements of infant IQ and what they tell us about the origins and nature of human intelligence.

Perceptual Development

All of our information about the world comes to us through our senses. We can read because our eyes register the patterns of light on a page; listen because our ears pick up vibrations in the atmosphere. What we perceive are not patterns

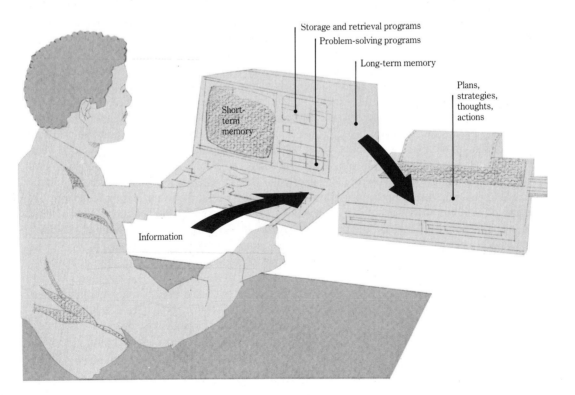

of light, but words and pictures; what we hear are not vibrations, but voices, music, or the ticking of a clock. Thus **perception** is the recognition and *interpretation* of sensory stimuli.

Until very recently, we didn't know how much infants perceive, or what captures their attention. When William James (1950) described the infant's world as "one great blooming, buzzing confusion," his guess was as good as anyone's. In the late 1950s, however, Robert Fantz (1961) and other psychologists developed a number of ingenious techniques for measuring infant preferences. In one procedure, the infant is placed in a seat which supports his head. He is shown two stimuli—such as a plain gray card and a card with black and white stripes. A camera records the reflection in the baby's eyes. If he looks at one card more than at the other, the researcher can infer that he discriminates between the two (sees that one is different from the other) and that one interests him more than the other. In a more sophisticated version of this experiment, a special camera records the infant's eye movements, telling the researcher exactly which parts of the picture draw his attention (Banks & Salapatek, 1983).

Another set of procedures uses sucking patterns or heart rates as measures of attention. The infant is exposed to a picture (or sound or smell) while he is sucking on a pacifier. On first exposure, the rate at which he sucks drops, indicating that the picture has attracted his attention and he has temporarily lost interest in the nipple. If he is shown the same picture (or played the same sound) over and over, he resumes sucking with his original vigor. This tells the researcher that the baby has become habituated (see Chapter 3). In plain language, the infant is bored. If he regains interest in the picture after a rest period, he has become dishabituated. Similarly, a deceleration in heart rate indicates that the infant is paying attention, an acceleration means that he is startled, and no change means that he is uninterested or habituated.

The infant's preferences tell us two things about his perceptual world. First, he is able to discriminate between two stimuli. If the baby could not discriminate a gray card from one with black and white stripes, or between a bull's-eye and a drawing of a face, he would not pay more attention to one than to the other. Second, preferences tell us what attracts the infant. For example, a baby who has become habituated to a melody played on a clarinet sucks more slowly on the pacifier when he hears someone singing the same tune. We can assume from his action that he can discriminate between the instrument and the human voice. If he takes longer to habituate to the voice than to the instrument, we can infer that he is more interested in the voice (Pick & Pick, 1970). He *may* be genetically predisposed to tune into human sounds.

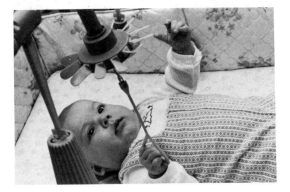

Crib mobiles appeal to the infant's fascination with movement and help the child to discover that he can make things happen in the world around him.

Using One's Senses

Countless experiments based on infant preferences show that infants start to appreciate the variety of shapes, colors, and patterns in their visual environment at about 2 months (Banks & Salapatek, 1983). Certain developments stand out. Up to about 3 months, infants prefer familiar to unfamiliar sights. Novelty does not attract them. They like to look at something they have seen before. After the age of 3 months, this preference reverses. When infants are shown the same figure over and over, their attention wanders. When they are shown something new, their interest "recovers." The same is true for sounds and smells. There is some evidence that infants find *moderate discrepancy* (or a slight change) interesting. Once infants have acquired an image or scheme for something, an addition, deletion, or rearrangement of the elements captures and holds their attention (Kagan, 1984; McCall, Kennedy & Applebaum, 1977). A 4-month-old, who has an image of her parents' faces, is fascinated by a face in which the eyes and nose are rearranged; a 6-month-old, who has an image of dolls, stares at a doll whose head is in the wrong place. Something totally unfamiliar—a butterfly, for example—does not have the same appeal for infants, but fascinates a 2-year-old (see Figure 4-1). Interest in novelty and discrepancy are clearly adaptive: they lead infants to pay attention to new material, which gives them new opportunities to learn about their worlds.

Neonates are attracted by *motion;* they are more interested in moving objects than in stationary ones. But they do not seem to distinguish between two- and three-dimensional figures. At 3 to 4 months infants begin to show special interest in graspable objects. They are not yet very good at reaching out and grabbing things that attract them. But they are attracted to those features of the environment that invite activity (Fantz, Fagan, & Miranda, 1975).

Babies under 2 months tend to look at the *outlines* of figures rather than at internal details.

Held securely on an adult's shoulder, babies are free to visually explore a world that is all new to them. This is one of their favorite positions.

Figure 4-1 Discrepancy and Interest

Their attention is captured by angles, edges, and contrast. Shown a square, they focus on one corner; shown a picture of a human face, they examine the hairline or the chin. Parents often comment that babies do not "look them in the eyes" or "recognize" them during the first month of life, and this is the reason (see Figure 4-2). Older babies scan the entire figure and inspect internal details, such as their father's eyes and nose. They prefer complex figures to simple ones; this suggests that as babies develop they are able to take in more visual information at a single viewing.

The infant's ability to make perceptual discriminations increases with every month. By 6 months, babies remember facial features of particular people, the arrangement of elements in a pattern, and the shape and color of a figure (Cohen & Gelber, 1975). Even 4-month-olds recognize changes in shape and color. If they have become bored with a blue triangle, their interest revives when they are shown a red circle. They do not respond to changes in a single dimension, however: a change in color only, from a red triangle to a blue triangle, or in shape only, from a blue circle to a blue triangle, does no impress them. By 8 or 10 months, they do notice a change in shape *or* color; this indicates that now they perceive these as different dimensions.

These forms of perceptual development have clear social implications. Babies are attracted to human faces from birth. The reason is not necessarily that babies are predisposed to respond to their parents, or even to members of their own species. It is that neonates are attracted to motion, angles, and contrast. The adult face, with its mobile features—exaggerated by much eyebrow-raising and nodding in conversation with an infant—is one of "the most successful attention-getting devices in the infant's world" (Goldberg, 1982, p. 39). But small babies are not very discriminating. A new mother who is ecstatic when her baby first smiles at her soon discovers that the child smiles at anyone and everyone (when he is in a receptive mood). Not until the baby is about 6 months old can he distinguish among people and select individuals for special attention.

Memory and Learning

Infant preference studies show that the 3-month-old is becoming an active learner as well as an active observer. Babies become habituated to an image or sound because it is familiar, and this means that they remember it (Cohen, 1979). The image or sound has not only registered on the infant's senses, it has remained in her mind. Improvements in memory during in-

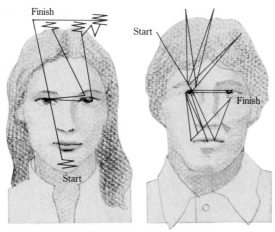

1-month-old child   2-month-old child

Figure 4-2 Visual Scanning in Infants   At one month the child is attracted to eyes and edges; at two months the infant has begun to examine internal detail.

(Maurer & Salapatek, 1976)

fancy are rapid. A baby younger than 2 months old can only retain information about a pattern for a few minutes. By the age of 2 months, an infant who has been shown a pattern for two minutes can remember it a day later. By 5 or 6 months, an infant who has been exposed to a face or other figure for only two minutes can remember it two weeks later (Cohen & Gelber, 1975). The infant may not process information as efficiently as she will in later months, but she *stores* information, which is a first step.

Using her perceptions and memory, the infant is developing a set of expectations about the environment. T. G. R. Bower and colleagues created an optical illusion of a solid object within the baby's grasp (Bower, Broughton, & Moore, 1971). Even neonates were surprised when they reached out and found only thin air. The illusion violated their expectations about the location of objects in space. Babies expect visual and auditory information to be synchronized. In one experiment infants were simultaneously shown a film of a bouncing kangeroo and a film of a donkey dancing. At the same time, they were played an audio soundtrack that was synchronized with only one of the films. The infants preferred the synchronized film (Spelke, 1978).

One recent discovery about very early cognition is that infants may have a rudimentary grasp of concepts (Cohen, 1979). In the standard perceptual experiment, the infant is exposed to the same image until he becomes habituated; then he is shown a new image. In a concept experiment, the infant is shown a number of different members of the same category, such as human faces; then he is shown members of a different category, such as animals. For example, Leslie Cohen and co-workers (1979) showed one group of 30-week-old infants pictures of the same female face photographed from different angles. Another group was shown pictures of different female faces. When the babies had become habituated, they were shown pictures of a new female face. The babies in the first group showed renewed interest, suggesting that they recognized the new face as different from the same face shown from different angles. Infants in the second group did not respond, implying that they were bored with female faces in general.

How infants arrive at such rudimentary concepts is not known. What is clear is that infants are not simply watching the passing parade in their environment. From a very early age they are organizing their perceptions. As Fantz has suggested, this is the age at which infants "learn by looking" (Fantz, Fagan, & Miranda, 1975).

Maturation, Experience, or Both?

Is perceptual development primarily the result of maturation? Or is it a product of experience and learning? There is one quite simple way to find out: compare babies who were born at full term to infants who were born prematurely. The babies were conceived at the same time physiologically, but the premature babies have had more experience in the outside world. Fantz and colleagues did just this (Fagan, Fantz, & Miranda, 1971). At 11 months after conception, full-term and premature babies had similar responses to preference tests. This suggests that maturation is more important than experience in early perceptual development. The exception was that the "more experienced" babies—those who had been born premature—preferred solid, three-dimensional forms to flat, two-dimensional pictures.

Studies of depth perception address the same maturation–experience question: Do infants perceive depth at birth, or do they have to learn the fear of falling? The classic device for testing depth perception was developed by Eleanor Gibson and Richard Walk (1960). The *visual cliff* is a large table with a plexiglass top and protected sides (see Figure 4-3). On half of the table there is a checkerboard pattern right under the glass; on the other half (the "deep" side) the checkerboard is several feet below the glass. When Gibson and Walk placed 8- to 12-month-old infants at the center of the table, most of them refused to crawl over the "cliff" to their mothers. Gibson and Walk concluded that infants are naturally afraid of heights. However, later studies showed that when 6-month-olds were placed on the cliff side, their heart rates decelerated, indicating interest but not fear. When 8-month-olds were placed on the deep side, their heart rates accelerated, indicating arousal and distress (Campos, Hiatt, Ramsay, Henderson, & Svejda, 1978). Why were the infants fearful at 8 months but not at 6 months? Joseph Campos points out that most babies begin crawling at about 8 months. Thus fear of heights emerges when the infant is becoming more independent—and more likely to get into dangerous situations. Campos and his colleagues (Campos, Svejda, Bertenthal, Benson, & Schmid, 1981) compared infants who had been crawling for about three weeks to infants of the same age who had not begun to move around on their own. The mobile infants were wary of the deep side of the cliff; the premobile

infants were unconcerned. Providing infants who hadn't crawled on their own with "walkers" seemed to accelerate the development of fearful reactions. This suggests that there is more to the fear of heights than simple maturation. Infants may need some experience of locomotion to perceive depth accurately.

Gordon Bronson (1974) has suggested that there is a shift from the second to the primary visual system in infancy. The **second vision system** is a primitive, phylogenetically older system that is controlled by the midbrain, the section of the human brain that is most like the brains of lower animals. It tells the baby *where* objects are located in the environment. The **primary visual system,** which evolved more recently, is controlled by the neocortex, the gray matter in the human brain that is associated with language, attention, memory, and spatial understanding. (See Figure 4-4.) The primary visual system tells the baby *what* something is. For the first six to eight weeks of life, the baby's vision is guided by the second system and oriented toward movement and edges, which are necessary for location. After eight weeks the infant's vision is guided by the primary system, which orients him toward curves, inner details, and the finer discriminations necessary for identification. This is a maturational explanation of perceptual development.

Eleanor Gibson (1969) adds a cognitive twist. Gibson reasons that the most important

Figure 4-3 The Visual Cliff   Eleanor Gibson and Richard Walk invented the visual cliff to test depth perception in infants. Current research indicates that fear of heights develops at about the same time as the ability to creep, whether or not an infant has experienced a frightening fall herself.
(Gibson and Walk, 1960)

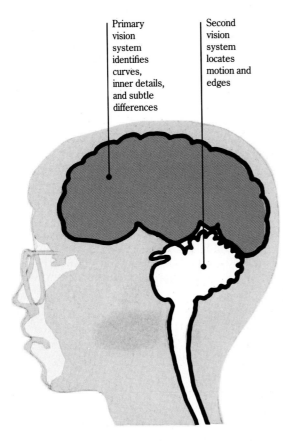

Primary vision system identifies curves, inner details, and subtle differences

Second vision system locates motion and edges

Figure 4-4 The Primary and Second Visual Systems Bronson proposes that the second vision system in the midbrain locates motion and edges, while the primary visual system in the neocortex identifies curves, inner details, and subtle distinctions.

perceptual development in infancy is discrimination. The stimuli that an infant receives through the eyes, ears, and other receptors provide all of the information needed to identify objects. To use this information, however, the infant must develop the ability to scan and direct his gaze intentionally, not just reflexively; to inspect the inner as well as the outer components of figures; to see interrelationships—to perceive parts and wholes; and to decide what is relevant and what is not. Feature analysis, as Gibson calls this, is not "simple perception"; it is cognitive activity.

Infants do not learn by looking alone. Motor development is an important subplot in the story of the infant's cognitive awakening.

Motor Development

Parents often record motor developments in their baby diary. The days the infant is able to roll over, sit without support, creep, stand, and walk alone are developmental milestones. These are achievements in *gross motor skills,* or movements involving the whole body or a large segment of it. *Fine motor skills,* or movements requiring precision and dexterity (such as reaching and grasping), also improve during infancy. Both are important for the infant's cognitive development. Independent locomotion enlarges the infants' world, creating opportunities for new and varied experiences of her own choosing. When she learns to crawl, she no longer depends on adults to take her where she wants to go or to bring her the toys she wants to investigate. The hand is an extension of the intellect in infancy. The baby's intellectual grasp is enhanced by her ability to grasp things in her hands, weigh their properties, and discover what she can and cannot do with them.

Body and Brain

Many of the changes in behavior during infancy are the result of brain maturation. It is useful to think of the brain as having three layers. The **brain stem,** which sits at the junction of the head and neck, controls such vegetative functions as automatic breathing, digestion, and heartbeat. The brain stem is essentially mature at birth. Without it, the neonate could not survive. The **midbrain,** which wraps around the brain stem, regulates such reflexes as startling and withdrawing from painful stimuli, awakeness, the senses, emotions, and other behaviors that are not voluntary. The midbrain is well developed at birth, but it does not reach adultlike levels for several months. The **neocortex,** or outer layer of the brain, controls thinking, decision-making, motor coordination, and speech. The neocortex is hardly functioning at birth and does not mature fully until puberty. About 90 percent of brain growth is achieved by 6 years of age, however.

For the first few months of life, the baby's behavior is controlled by the lower, subcortical layers of the brain. His actions are regulated by reflexes, or automatic responses. As described in Chapter 3, when a newborn is held by the arms and lowered to the ground, he moves his legs up and down as if he were walking. Newborns also reach and grasp objects, such as an adult's finger. This, too, is an involuntary reaction, like a sneeze or a hiccup.

Curiously, these behaviors disappear in early infancy, then reappear after a "silent period" (Bower, 1974). Stepping disappears at about 3 months and reappears at about 6 months; the reach-and-grasp reflex disappears at about 4 weeks and reappears at about 20 weeks. This suggests that there are two stages in early motor development: reflexes are inhibited, and connections between the higher centers of the brain and the muscles are established. Thus when the infant gains voluntary, cortical control of his body, the behaviors reappear in different forms. The newborn's "steps" are haphazard; mature walking is flexible and adjusted to the walking surface. The newborn's reach is a hit-or-miss swipe at something he sees; once started, it is not subject to correction. Five-month-olds direct their aim with their eyes and are able to adjust the path of their arm. During the silent period, infants acquire coordination and control.

Standing on Two Feet

Walking upright on two feet is a distinctively human trait. Other primates stand and walk on occasion, but they revert to all fours when they need to move quickly or to cover long distances. The ability to balance the body in an upright position and move on two legs without other support lays the foundation for many human skills, such as running, skipping, jumping, and dancing. Most significantly, bipedal locomotion frees the hands for other activities, such as running with a spear or a brief case, or walking with a baby and a bag of groceries.

Infants develop locomotion in the regular sequence shown in Figure 4-5. For the first five months or so, infants are horizontal, unless of course they are held by an adult or an infant seat. Most babies are able to sit by themselves at 6 months—a seemingly minor accomplishment, but one that opens new horizons for visual exploration. Before this age, they could only see what was put in front of them; now they can look around. Within another month or two they can crawl on their bellies, creep on

Insight

CRIB DEATH:
A COGNITIVE VIEW

Each year, crib death (or sudden infant death syndrome) takes the lives of as many as 10,000 babies in the United States alone. As far as doctors can tell, there was nothing physically wrong with these babies. When they are discovered, there are no signs of pain or struggle. They simply stopped breathing.

Lewis Lipsitt (1977) believes that crib death is in part the result of a learning disorder. Crib deaths peak between 2 and 4 months of age. Ninety percent occur before 6 months of age, and 99 percent before a child's first birthday. The first months of life are a period of rapid neurological growth. Between 2 and 4 months, the reflexes the newborn brought into the world begin to disappear, supplanted by learned responses that are controlled by the higher brain centers. Lipsitt suggests that infants who succumb to crib death have not made the transition from reflexive behavior to learned defensive maneuvers. When they start to choke, they do not cry (behavior that would open their respiratory passages). When they accidentally pull a blanket over their faces, they do not turn their head or push it away, as other babies do.

A retrospective study of crib deaths in Providence, Rhode Island, revealed that many victims had minor disorders at birth. Their Apgar scores were a little below average, they were slightly below normal in weight and length, they required treatment and remained in the hospital longer than normal babies do, and so on. They were not perfectly healthy, but there was nothing alarming about their condition. Lipsitt hypothesizes that such minor disorders may inhibit or delay learning. Babies who are less active, less visually alert, weak, and generally less aware of their environment have fewer learning experiences than normal babies do in their waking hours. As a result, they do not know how to react to temporary obstructions to normal breathing that occur when they are asleep or when they have a slight respiratory infection. Apparently insignificant early problems are "compounded by the failure of experience to prepare the infant for later threats to its survival."

Through comparisons of infants who stop breathing to infants who survive their first year, Lipsitt and others hope to identify infants at risk in advance so that sudden, tragic, early deaths can be avoided.

their hands and knees, or even "bear walk" on their hands and feet. By 9 months they are making active efforts to stand up. By 10 or 11 months many infants can walk with support. Most take their first stiff-legged, flat-footed solo steps at about 1 year. Another year will pass before they can walk steadily and smoothly and run without falling.

Most babies begin walking at 1 year. But infants vary considerably in their rate of motor development. Some go directly from sitting to walking at 9 or 10 months, skipping the crawling phase. Others do not even try to stand before 18 or 20 months, making their parents wonder if they will ever walk. The rate at which infants acquire motor skills has no bearing on their coordination and agility at a later age. The last baby on the block to walk may well be the first across the finish line in a race at age 6.

Developing Finesse

The human hand, with its opposable thumb and precise grip, is a unique organ. In maturity, we can touch the thumb to each of the other fingers to form a strong, highly flexible grip. The development of full use of the hand takes years, however. Six-year-olds struggle to print their first letters, while 10-year-olds work on improving their penmanship. Even so, there are remarkable improvements in voluntary control of the hand and the coordination of hand and eye movements in infancy.

Voluntary reaching begins at about 5 months. The 5-month-old's aim is much better than that of the newborn. She is still slow to grasp an object once she has made contact, but reaching and gripping are now separate skills. By 6 months most babies can reach and grasp in any direction, from any posture. They can also let go. By 8 or 9 months they can adapt their grasp to the shape of the object, but they still do not anticipate its weight, even if they have held the object before. If given something light, like a feather, an infant's hand flies up; if given something heavy, it sinks (see Figure 4-6). This is one reason why peas, spoons, and other things litter the floor around the high chair. Not until infants are about 1 year old do they learn to adjust their arm tension and grip strength.

Finger control is even slower to develop than the use of the hand. A 6-month-old can only hold something if it fits neatly into her all-hand grasp. With concentration, a 9-month-old can pick up small things like peas or buttons. But the full thumb–forefinger opposition that enables a child to turn a doorknob or unscrew a lid does not emerge until about age 2. Fine finger control continues to improve through childhood and beyond. Adolescents devote hours to improving

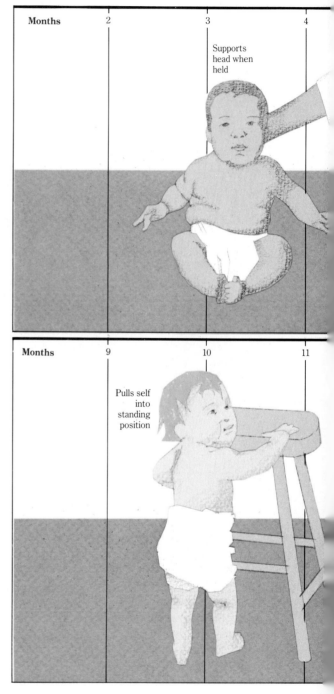

Figure 4-5 Motor Development in Infancy

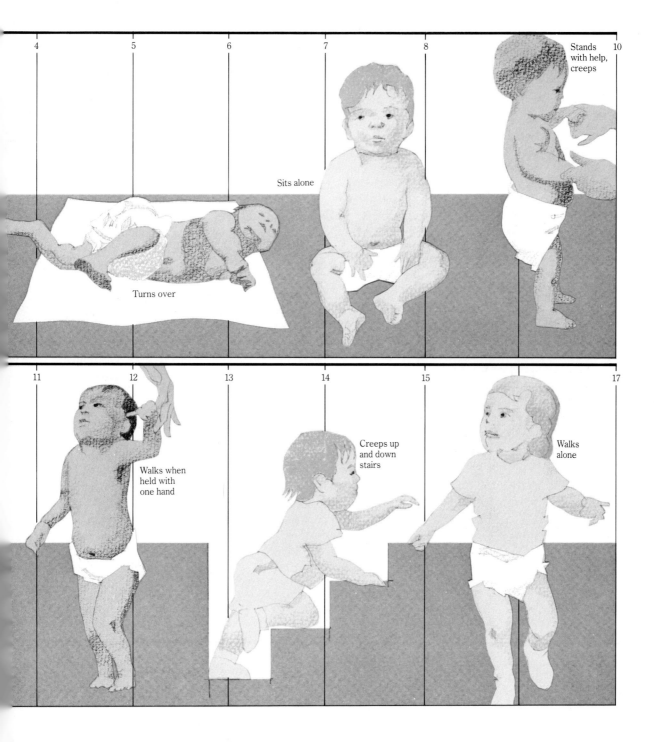

4 5 6 7 8 Stands with help, creeps 10

Sits alone

Turns over

11 12 13 14 15 Walks alone 17

Walks when held with one hand

Creeps up and down stairs

their ability to play the piano, throw a baseball, or wire a circuit board.

The 18-month-old is quite different from what he was at 8 weeks. The reason is not simply that he is grasping his toys and standing on his own two feet. He has already made giant strides in cognitive development as well. Fine and gross motor development have allowed him to become an active experimenter and an independent explorer. His knowledge of his surroundings, and of himself, has expanded and changed as a result. He has begun to think.

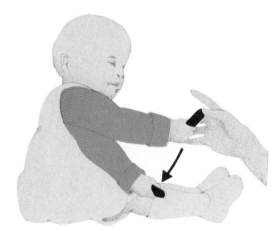

The Sensorimotor Stage: The Dawn of Awareness

It may sound absurd to talk about a young infant "thinking." After all, a baby does not think as an adult does. Adult thinking is based on symbolic representation. Language, which is one symbol system, frees us from the here and now. We can talk about objects and events that are not present in the immediate environment. We are able to store mental images in memory, retrieve them, and manipulate them. We can recall an event that took place months ago, compare it to recent events, change the characters or the action, and imagine a happier ending—all in our heads. Even a 2-year-old infant has practical knowledge about the people and objects in her world and can communicate her specific likes and dislikes effectively. The 2-month-old infant does not yet possess these skills. But according to Piaget, small babies do possess the beginnings of *sensorimotor intelligence*. The infant "knows," in the sense that he recognizes and anticipates recurring events; he "thinks," in the sense that he uses his eyes, hands, and mouth in regular, systematic ways. These preverbal strategies that babies use for dealing with the sights, sounds, and objects they encounter in their environment Piaget called schemes. A **scheme** is a sensorimotor action the infant repeats when faced with the same or similar opportunities. When presented with a nipple, for example, the newborn responds by sucking.

Figure 4-6 Flying Objects   Infants need time and experience to learn how to adjust the tension of their arm to the weight of an object. Given something light as a feather, their arm flies up; given something heavier, their arm drops.
(Bower, 1974)

When something is put in her hand, she grasps it.

Schemes are the motor equivalent of concepts. They organize the baby's world into categories: *things I can suck, things I can hit,* and so on. Over infancy, these simple sucking and grasping schemes are elaborated and combined into more sophisticated patterns. At 6 months the infant puts anything into her mouth that she succeeds in grasping; this is a grasp-and-suck scheme. Babies use such schemes to explore their worlds. They try sucking, licking, hitting, squeezing many things, discovering that some objects are hard, others soft, some cold, others warm. Later in development internal, mental operations replace many of these external, physical actions. Mental arithmetic replaces physical counting (adults don't need to use their fingers); hypotheses (thinking, "If . . . then") replace concrete experiments. But schemes remain useful. Infants apply a hitting scheme to rattles and high-chair trays; older children and adults use a hitting scheme with hammers and tennis rackets.

The infant's knowledge-in-action is similar to the "thinking" intelligence adults use when they brush their teeth or start a car (Flavell, 1984, 1977). Over his first two years the infant elaborates and refines the reflexes that organized his earliest experiences, applying them to a wider range of situations and combining them into more complex patterns. By the end of his second year he will have developed a number of practical, present-oriented, action-based ways of learning and solving problems. What makes the infant progress? What motivates cognitive development?

Cognition as Adaptation

Piaget viewed cognition as a form of adaptation or adjustment to the environment and part of our species' biological heritage. He broke down cognitive adaptation into two reciprocal processes: assimilation and accommodation. **Assimilation** is the process of taking in experiences by fitting them into the schemes or concepts one has already mastered. When the baby sucks on her fist, the edge of a blanket, or her mother's ear, she is assimilating new material into a scheme she developed for nursing. When you decide that the odd-looking wedding present you received from your aunt is a pickle dish, you are assimilating it into one of your existing categories. You have transformed the incoming information to conform to your present mental structures. One of the best examples of assimilation is make-believe, in which the child ignores the physical characteristics of an object and treats it as if it were something else. In her mind the broom has become a horse.

Accommodation means changing one's schemes or concepts to take into account new

Sucking is a form of assimilation, and one of the ways babies learn about their world—including their friends.

information. Suppose a baby is kicking her feet randomly one day and notices that the brightly colored mobile above her crib moves. She kicks, and it moves again. After several repetitions, she develops a new scheme: kick-to-make-it-move. She has expanded her behavioral repertoire to accommodate new information about what makes things move. The incoming information has transformed her mental structures. Adults do this, too. For example, when your image of homosexuals changes as a result of meeting several self-proclaimed gays who are not effeminate and do not work as hairdressers or interior decorators, you have accommodated your prior conception of homosexuals to new information. (If you decide that they are exceptions to the rule that all homosexuals are effeminate and artistic, however, you are assimilating new information into your existing stereotypes.) Imitation is a pure form of accommodation: the child adjusts her behavior to match another person's actions.

Piaget explains the evolution of more mature ways of thinking this way. Human beings seek *equilibrium,* or balance. When a child is satisfied with his current mode of thinking—when he is able to assimilate most of what he encounters into his existing schemes—he is in a state of equilibrium. When he becomes aware of shortcomings in his patterns of thought, he experiences disequilibrium. The conflict between his internal mental structures and external events—between what he expects and what happens—throws him off balance. When he adopts a new, more sophisticated approach, accommodating new information, his equilibrium is restored. For example, a baby has developed a scheme for holding large rubber balls. The scheme works, and she is at equilibrium. One day she clasps a balloon the way she usually hugs balls, and it explodes in her face. Her equilibrium is upset. When she accommodates this information by learning to adjust her grip, her

equilibrium is restored. The new scheme leads her to new discoveries, new experiences. In time the new scheme also leads to information that doesn't fit, and she is forced to accommodate again. In this way a child's thinking and behavior gradually become more adaptive.

Substages of Sensorimotor Development

Piaget divided the sensorimotor period into six substages (see Figure 4-7). We refer to them hereafter as stages.

STAGE 1 (THE FIRST OR SECOND MONTH) At this age, depending on the infant's maturity, reflexes organize most of the newborn's interactions with the world. Some of the early reflexes, such as Babinski and Moro, disappear as cortically controlled behavior develops. Other reflexes, such as rooting, sucking, and reaching, are transformed from subcortical to cortical behaviors by their continual use as the baby interacts with the world. For example, babies learn to suck differently on an artificial nipple than on the breast, adapting their sucking behavior to the characteristics of their environment. They also learn to track moving objects more smoothly with their eyes. Although at first these may seem to be trivial adaptations, they are precursors of later, more noticeable accommodations and assimilations.

Even in the first three weeks, babies come to expect certain coordinations among perceptual events, such as sights and sounds. Although they cannot locate a sound accurately by looking in the correct direction, they are surprised and even distressed when a sound they expect to come from one direction comes from another. In a clever experiment, Aronson and Rosenbloom (1971) had mothers talk to their babies from behind a glass screen. Speakers were located directly in front of the baby and three feet to his left and right. At first the mother's voice came from the front, where she stood. Later her

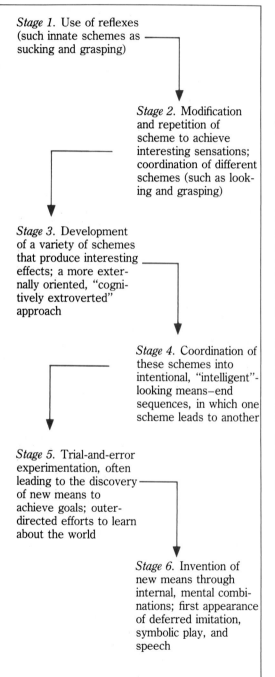

Stage 1. Use of reflexes (such innate schemes as sucking and grasping)

Stage 2. Modification and repetition of scheme to achieve interesting sensations; coordination of different schemes (such as looking and grasping)

Stage 3. Development of a variety of schemes that produce interesting effects; a more externally oriented, "cognitively extroverted" approach

Stage 4. Coordination of these schemes into intentional, "intelligent"-looking means–end sequences, in which one scheme leads to another

Stage 5. Trial-and-error experimentation, often leading to the discovery of new means to achieve goals; outer-directed efforts to learn about the world

Stage 6. Invention of new means through internal, mental combinations; first appearance of deferred imitation, symbolic play, and speech

voice was displaced to either the left or right. The babies were upset; moving mouths and voices are supposed to come from the same place! This experiment implies that even in the first few weeks, infants expect coordination between sensory experiences.

STAGE 2 (ABOUT 2 TO 4 MONTHS) In this period the infant refines and elaborates on existing schemes and integrates simple schemes into more complicated behaviors (Flavell, 1985). Through continuous practice, the baby refines sucking, looking, listening, and swallowing. He learns to consume cereal and drink from a cup and to scan stationary objects as well as track moving figures. Much of the fine-tuning of simple schemes depends on maturation of the brain. But experience with challenging new foods to swallow and new sounds to locate surely plays a role in these developments.

More significant is that the baby begins to coordinate different schemes. When he hears a sound, he turns and looks; he opens his mouth when he senses he is being held in the nursing position; he brings whatever he happens to grasp up to his eyes or mouth for investigation. The baby's behavior looks more purposeful, but at this age an infant does not have intentional motives.

STAGE 3 (ABOUT 4 TO 8 MONTHS) If a baby in this stage happens to do something that produces interesting results, such as kicking the mobile over her crib, she will do it again—and again and

Figure 4-7 The Sensorimotor Period: Six Substages
(Adapted from Flavell, 1985)

again. Piaget called this a *secondary circular reaction*. This response also could be described as operant conditioning: when immediate reinforcement follows a spontaneous activity, the baby repeats the activity. In this case, the mobile moves interestingly when the baby kicks it, so she kicks it again to make it move.

In stage 2 the baby was primarily interested in her own body and in exercising sensorimotor schemes. She sucked for the sake of sucking and grasped for the sake of grasping. In stage 3 the baby is more interested in the properties of objects in the world around her. She is more "cognitively extroverted" (Flavell, 1985, p. 30). But she does not seem to distinguish between her own body and its actions and the objects and events around her. If her rattle drops to the floor, she keeps shaking her arm as if the action alone produced the sound.

The first attempts at imitation are another sign of the infant's interest in people and events other than herself. If an infant is cooing and her mother imitates her, she will coo back. According to Piaget, the infant will only imitate someone who is imitating her in this stage. Other psychologists disagree (see Insight: The Imitation Controversy).

STAGE 4 (ABOUT 8 TO 12 MONTHS) In this stage, babies are more purposeful. They try out schemes in order to have an effect on their environment. They combine schemes into sequences in order to reach a goal. Some schemes serve as means for others. In stage 4 a baby removes a barrier to get to a toy. He wants to throw, bounce, mouth, hit, and subject the toy to other schemes—not just to exercise his skills, but to find out more about it. The stage 4 baby can also anticipate events that do not depend on his own immediate behavior. When his mother walks towards the door, he responds to the signal that she is about to leave by crying or creeping after her. Such goal-oriented behavior

indicates that the infant has begun to distinguish between himself, other people, and things in his world.

The baby is now a skillful imitator of events he cannot see himself perform, such as sticking out his tongue or frowning in imitation of his mother. More important is that now he can imitate behavior and sounds that have not been part of his repertoire. For example, if an adult pushes a new toy car along the floor while saying "Rmm-rmm!," a stage 4 baby can imitate the action and the sound, "Rmm-rmm," which he never did before. This advance in sensorimotor skill is particularly important, because the baby can now learn by imitation.

Play—that is, practicing sensorimotor schemes for the sheer fun of it—becomes prominent in this period. Babies bang blocks together over and over, laughing with glee at the exercise of this well-learned, easy-to-perform scheme. For Piaget, play is pure assimilation (Millar, 1968): the baby is "taking in" the world. Piaget argues that accommodation (changing one's schemes to adapt to the external world) does not occur in play. Flavell (1977) and others believe that much learning occurs during these playful encounters. We agree: Infants in the fourth sensorimotor stage learn from *both* play and imitation.

STAGE 5 (ABOUT 12 TO 18 MONTHS) By now the baby is a skillful, purposeful experimenter with the materials at hand (or mouth). She explores the properties of objects by trial and error, systematically testing different approaches as if she were thinking, "Let's see what would happen if . . ." (Flavell, 1977, p. 30). Different babies have different routines. A typical action sequence with a new toy might be: hit it with the hand, bang it on a table, drop it on the floor, roll it over, chew its small end, try to fit the large end in the mouth, pull at its outer cover, squeeze its middle, and so on, until many action

Insight

THE IMITATION CONTROVERSY

About ten years ago Olga Maratos, a Greek graduate student who had been testing 7-week-old babies, went to see Piaget to tell him how her work was progressing.

> "Do you remember what I am doing?" she said. "I am sticking out my tongue at the babies, and do you know what they are doing?"
>
> "You may tell me," Piaget murmured.
>
> "They are sticking their tongues right back at me! What do you think of that?"
>
> The venerable professor puffed on his pipe for a moment as he contemplated the challenge to his theory. "I think that is very rude," he said. (*Time*, 1983)

Piaget held that babies are not capable of imitating an invisible act (that is, something they cannot see themselves doing) until late infancy. To imitate the rude gesture described above the infant must be able to encode what he saw in memory, translate this visual perception into motor commands, and then execute these commands. Piaget believed that small babies are not capable of coordinating these different schemes. Imitation does not develop until the child is able to form mental images, around 18 months.

Maratos and others have challenged this. In 1977 Andrew Meltzoff and M. Keith Moore reported that 12- to 20-*day*-old infants imitated an adult model sticking out his tongue, opening his mouth, pursing his lips, and wiggling his fingers. More recently, Tiffany Field and her collaborators (Field, Woodson, Greenberg, & Cohen, 1982) reported that neonates with a mean age of 36 *hours* imitated an adult's happy, sad, and surprised facial expressions. Meltzoff and Moore now report that 1- to 3-day-olds imitate an open mouth expression and tongue protrusion (1983). These experiments were recorded on videotape. But other researchers (Hayes & Watson, 1979; Jacobson, 1979; McKenzie & Over, 1982) have not been able to replicate their findings. Critics suggest that the newborns in Meltzoff and Moore's studies may have been responding to other stimuli, such as a nearby bottle. Another possibility is that these expressions, which are part of the baby's natural repertoire, occurred by chance. The debate continues.

Perhaps Piaget and his critics are each half right. It may be that an adult model can trigger expressions which a newborn performs spontaneously under the right conditions but which require time and experience for the infant to control well enough to use in other contexts.

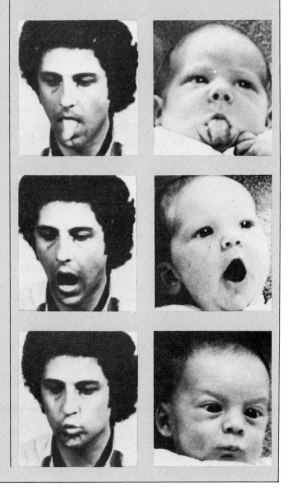

schemes have been applied to many aspects of the toy, all in the service of discovering the properties of this new thing. The baby is flexible enough in her approach to these routines to put together new action sequences and to try varied approaches to the same goal. For example, if there is a barrier between a stage 5 baby and a desirable object, she may try one time to crawl around the barrier, another time to climb over it, and still another time to remove the barrier. Even if the initial attempt to crawl around the barrier is successful, she may vary the approach, seemingly for the sheer pleasure of exploring the variety of solutions to such problems. Through such trial-and-error approaches, she may discover a new action pattern and practice it over and over for the sheer fun of it.

Stage 5 is the last "pure" sensorimotor stage. The baby still deals only with the here and now. She cannot yet imitate events that have occurred earlier or elsewhere. And she is "imprisoned" in her own cognitive world by her limited ability to communicate.

STAGE 6 (ABOUT 18 TO 24 MONTHS) The transition between sensorimotor and conceptual intelligence takes place in the last sensorimotor stage. In most ways, however, stage 6 is really the beginning of representational intelligence and preoperational thought, which occur in the preschool years. The dramatic changes in stage 6 are the baby's ability to represent objects and events in thought by symbols—other objects and events that stand for the originals—and to act on the basis of those symbols. The baby can now contemplate a problem, pause to think, and then act to solve it—without the trial and error that characterized stage 5 problem-solving. The baby in stage 6 is able to visualize his own actions and thus to use *mental* trial and error. Toddlers in stage 6 have not mastered symbolic thought. But they do seem to have mental images and apparently are able to use them in solving problems.

It is in stage 6 that infants begin to comprehend the flow of human speech and to talk in sentences. Their first words may occur a little before 12 months and are usually repeated syllables such as "mama" and "dada" (see Chapter 7). Vocabulary development accelerates rapidly in the middle of the second year. And around 18 months, infants begin to use simple words in flexible combinations that are primitive sentences, such as "allgone cookie," "allgone milk," and "eat cookie."

The symbolic value of language to transport experience across time and space cannot be overestimated. There are, however, other symbolic representations. One of Piaget's favorite examples was of his daughter, Lucienne, at 18 months. She had observed an age-mate, the child of a family friend, throw a full-blown temper tantrum. The next day Lucienne imitated the boy's crying, kicking tantrum with some

Infants practice sensorimotor schemes with whatever happens to be available. Piaget's great insight was to realize how these apparently meaningless activities contributed to cognitive development. The "nouvelle cuisine" shown here is an example.

glee—a feat that required her to have stored her experience and to have retrieved it. *Deferred imitation* is a symbolic act. Actions that the infant has observed but not imitated at the time can be reproduced in detail at a later time. Our baby can now crawl around on all fours, panting and saying "Woof, woof!" even though no dog is present. Sally tries on Mommy's shoes and says, "Bye-bye, Sally," while heading for the front door. Sally is clearly imitating Mommy's departures for work, although Mommy is sitting on the sofa and reading at the time.

The stage 6 child can even invent new means to desired ends through mental manipulations. For example, when faced with a clear lucite box with a tricky latch and a toy inside, the stage 5 infant is likely to try out his varied action schemes in trial-and-error fashion: banging the box on the floor, shaking it, hitting the box with another toy, and so forth, until he discovers that the latch will open when turned 90°. The stage 6 baby is more likely to turn the box around in his hands, look at it intently, finger the latch, and then try manipulating it before successfully opening it. No longer does the baby need to try out all of his schemes; he can imagine what might happen if he tried this or that and eliminate some schemes before trying them. In other words, he "uses his head" to open the box.

As the stage 6 child develops into the full-fledged symbolic thinker in the preschool years, the symbols he uses bear less and less physical resemblance to the *referents,* those objects and events to which the symbols refer. Lucienne's temper tantrum was very similar to the one she had seen the day before, but an older toddler can gallop a broomstick for a horse and move sticks through the water for boats.

The Object Concept

Adults take much of the physical world for granted. We know that people and other objects are separate entities. You are one thing, the book you are reading is another thing, and the desk on which it is resting is something else. We do not confuse our own perceptions (seeing or touching an object) with the physical existence of the object. When you misplace your glasses, you know that they are *somewhere,* even though you cannot find them. Further, we know that the behavior of objects can be independent of our interactions with them. The pen you left on your desk does not necessarily await your return. It may roll onto the floor while you are out of the room, or someone may borrow it. The reason we enjoy magic shows is that we know it is impossible for a rabbit to appear in an empty hat; there must be a trick.

One of Piaget's most surprising discoveries was that these basic facts of life are not at all obvious to the baby. Indeed, it takes almost two years for an infant to discover that objects have an existence of their own. Many other researchers have confirmed what is called the **object concept,** or object permanence (Harris, 1983).

For the infant in sensorimotor stages 1 and 2, out of sight is not only out of mind, it is out of existence. A baby at this age tracks a moving object with his eyes. But if it disappears behind a screen, he loses interest almost immediately. If a magician covers a rabbit with a hat, then removes the hat to reveal an empty table, the baby is not the least bit surprised. Infants under 4 months do not believe that a toy that has been covered by a cloth continues to exist, even when they watched as it was covered (Charlesworth, 1966). Their awareness of an object depends on visual contact; they do not form a lasting image of it in their minds. (See Figure 4-8 on p. 157.) Further, if you take a toy from a baby at this age and place it on a table or book within his view, he does not pursue the toy. The infant seems to believe that the objects merge with one another, so that the toy no longer exists as a separate entity to be grasped (Bower, 1974).

In stage 3 (about 4 to 8 months), infants become very good at tracking moving objects with their eyes and reaching for things to grasp. If a spoon falls from their high-chair tray to the floor, they bend over to look for it. If an object is slowly covered by a moving screen, they wait for it to reappear. If they have watched a toy train enter one end of a tunnel and exit from the other, or a ball disappear into one porthole in a screen and reappear from another, they anticipate the reappearance and track the object's invisible path (Anglin, 1969; Nelson, 1971). They have some awareness of object permanence, if the disappearance of the object is slow.

A stage 3 baby retrieves a toy that is hidden under a transparent cup. She reaches for a toy dog that is partially covered so that she can see only its head. But if the toy is covered completely while she is reaching, her arm drops. If the toy is covered while she is holding it, she lets go! The infant searches for a missing object with her eyes, but not with her hands. She still does not credit the object with a permanent, ongoing existence.

In stage 4 (ages 8 to 12 months), the infant begins to do what most adults assumed he could do all along: he retrieves an object that has been hidden in front of his eyes. Now the baby is surprised if the toy he saw disappear under a cloth is not there when he lifts the cover (a trick played by William Charlesworth in 1966). But does the infant *really* understand that an object is still there when he cannot see it? Some researchers think not (Flavell, 1985; Gratch,

1975). If you try this, you will see why. Put two cloths on the floor in front of the baby. Hide a toy under the one on the right. The infant retrieves it without a moment's hesitation. Now hide the toy under the cloth on the right, slowly bring it out into the open, then hide it under the cloth on the left. Make sure the baby is watching your actions. The baby will search for the toy under the cloth on the right, where it first disappeared, not the cloth on the left, where it last disappeared! Flavell (1985) suspects that the reason for this behavior is that the baby is not really searching for objects yet. Rather, he has developed a motor habit of reaching for the toy in one place and simply repeats this scheme. In other words, he is playing a reaching game, not a searching game.

The stage 5 baby (ages 12 to 18 months) can follow an object through a series of *visible* displacements without getting lost. He searches for the toy where it last disappeared. But he can only do this if he is able to see each step in the game of hide-and-seek. If you put a toy in a cup, cover the cup with a cloth, tip the toy onto the table, and pull out the empty cup, he is bewildered.

Finally, in stage 6 (ages 18 to 24 months) the infant is able to trace the disappearing toy through a sequence of *invisible* displacements. He can imagine the trip from cup to cloth to table (and much more complicated series), even though he cannot see each step. He is so *sure* that the object is there somewhere that he grins

Figure 4-8 Object Awareness   At the beginning of the sensorimotor period, "out of sight is out of mind." The 6-month-old in the top row of photographs is fascinated by the toy elephant. When it is hidden behind a screen, however, she acts as if it ceased to exist. She has not yet developed the object concept. When an object is hidden from the older infant in the bottom row of photographs, he immediately crawls behind the screen to look for it.

in anticipation of the search. And he delights in playing the same tricks on the researcher (Flavell, 1985). The baby has begun to use symbolic representations and clearly has an image of the toy in his mind. (See Figure 4-9.)

The full development of the object concept takes the infant nearly two years. This is not surprising when one considers how much information about the nature of the world is required by the child to make inferences about "fellow objects" outside her perceptual grasp. Understanding that objects have a permanence apart

Figure 4-9   Development of the Object Concept

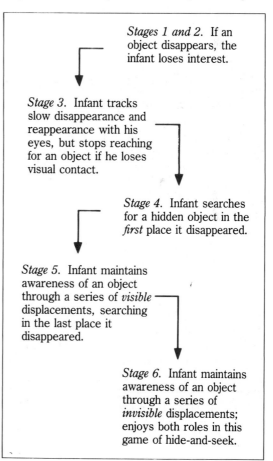

Stages 1 and 2. If an object disappears, the infant loses interest.

Stage 3. Infant tracks slow disappearance and reappearance with his eyes, but stops reaching for an object if he loses visual contact.

Stage 4. Infant searches for a hidden object in the *first* place it disappeared.

Stage 5. Infant maintains awareness of an object through a series of *visible* displacements, searching in the last place it disappeared.

Stage 6. Infant maintains awareness of an object through a series of *invisible* displacements; enjoys both roles in this game of hide-and-seek.

from her own existence, her location in space, and her behavior is a major step toward understanding the physical world.

The child's cognitive journey has only begun. But she has come a long way from the point at which we first met her, at the beginning of this chapter. She is aware that objects have an independent existence and has a sense of her own separate identity. She knows much about the properties of objects in her everyday environment; she has a rudimentary understanding of cause and effect. She explores and experiments purposefully. And she has begun to receive and communicate information by means of symbols, both words and play.

The Infant's Construction of Reality

Underlying Piaget's description of sensorimotor development is a particular view of human nature. Piaget was concerned with the age-old philosophical question of how human beings come to understand the properties of objects and the basic principles of space, time, and causality that organize adult thinking. Do babies automatically see cause and effect? Is sensorimotor development the result of brain maturation? Or do babies acquire these understandings through observation and experience? Piaget reconciled these two views: Maturation brings babies into contact with new experiences. For Piaget, action is the basis of knowledge. Each child constructs reality—that is, constructs an understanding of how the world works— through his own physical efforts. In a sense, each child rediscovers the wheel. For Piaget, "the mind neither copies the world, passively accepting it as a ready-made given, nor does it ignore the world, . . . creating a private mental conception of it out of whole cloth. Rather, the mind builds its knowledge structures by taking external data and interpreting them, transforming them, and reorganizing them" (Flavell, 1977, p. 6).

The rate at which individual babies progress, through Piaget's stages of sensorimotor development varies. Moreover, the baby's progress in different cognitive skills (the object concept, means–ends relations, imitation) may be uneven. One infant achieves an understanding of visibly displaced objects several weeks before he shows evidence of grasping means–ends relations (for example, using a string to pull a desired object toward him) or is able to imitate adult vocalizations. Another baby imitates adult vocalizations before he searches for hidden objects.

Stage theorists (See Chapter 1) such as Piaget argue that for the child to make the transition from one stage to the next, these skills must be coordinated (Fischer, 1980). Ina Uzgiris (1976) has studied coordinations in infant learning. She found, for example, that infants in stage 6 of the object concept (searching for hidden objects through several invisible displacements) soon begin to show social influences on their actions. Earlier, they treated blocks, stuffed animals, and their mother's shoes in similar ways: banging, dropping, pulling, and otherwise manhandling them to discover their properties. Now, in stage 6, they treat things in socially approved ways. They push cars along the floor, put strings of beads around their necks, not into their mouths, and hug dolls instead of banging on them. At about this time, babies begin to imitate actions they cannot see themselves performing.

Uzgiris argues that these diverse skills all spring from the development of the same new mental structure and reflect infants' new awareness of the relationship between actions and outcomes. She admits that each child's development within a stage may occur in a different order, but she believes that all of the infant's achievements are consolidated or synchronized at the end of that stage and the beginning of the next. (Not all psychologists agree, as we will see in Chapter 9.)

The Search for Infant IQ

In the 1920s, at about the same time that Piaget was playing hidden-object games with his children, Arnold Gesell, Nancy Bayley, and other American psychologists also began testing infants. Gesell and his co-workers at Yale wanted to establish standards of normal behavioral development that would parallel the existing scales for normal physical growth. Bayley and her colleagues in the Berkeley Growth Study wanted some way to measure intellectual changes with age and individual differences among babies. Both were pioneers in the development of infant intelligence tests.

Interest in tests that *predict* a baby's intellectual future increased in the 1940s. The number of adoptions had risen dramatically, and the usual age of adoption had dropped from one year to six months (Brooks & Weintraub, 1976). Prospective parents wanted to know how smart a baby was likely to be, or at least whether the baby was normal.

Measures of infant intelligence have always been controversial. Intelligence tests for older children and adults rely on responses to verbal or written questions. Infants do not have symbolic intelligence or language to communicate their thinking. The only way to assess infant intelligence is to observe what babies *do*. Researchers had to redefine infant intelligence in terms of behavior. But would behavioral measures of infants tap the same mental functions assessed in standard intelligence tests? Would the infant tests be useful in diagnosing mental retardation? Could they predict an individual child's probable course of development? Such a test might be reliable and yield a valid measure[2] of the infant's *current* developmental status, yet it might not predict *future* intellectual success or failure. Many psychologists were skeptical of infant intelligence testing. Florence Goodenough

likened the search for intelligence in infancy to the attempt to predict the growth of a man's beard in babyhood. Male hormones, the important determinants of beard growth, and symbolic reasoning, what we usually call "intelligence," are simply not present in infants.

Here we look at the Bayley scales (1969), which are generally regarded as the most carefully researched measure of infant intelligence.

The Bayley Scales of Infant Development

The Bayley scales are divided into three sections: the Mental Scale, the Motor Scale, and the Infant Behavior Profile. The Mental Scale is designed to assess perception, memory, learning, and problem solving, including the ability to find hidden objects; vocalization and response to verbal instructions; and early signs of the infant's ability to generalize and classify. The Motor Scale is designed to measure control of the body and coordination. It emphasizes gross motor skills, the absence of which are often associated with mental retardation. The Infant Behavior Profile is designed to assess the impact of attention, motivation, and sociability on the infant's performance.

After nearly 30 years of experience with infant assessment, Bayley selected several hundred items and tried them out on a representative pool of 1,300 infants ages 2 to 30 months. Items were graded at the age at which half of the infants passed the question successfully. For example, item 108 is placed at the 13-month level because half of the 13-month-olds in the standardization sample could place one peg in a hole in a pegboard, but fewer than half of the 10-month-olds and more than half of the 15-month-olds could do this. Then items were arranged in order of difficulty, beginning with the easiest. Test-makers felt that, rather than mix easy and difficult items as in an experiment, they could keep the child motivated to continue the test by allowing him to succeed early before

[2]A test is considered *reliable* if it is internally consistent. A test is considered *valid* if it measures what it is intended to measure—in this case the infant's developmental status.

Age in months	Item
0.1	Responds to sound of bell
1.6	Turns eyes to light
2.0	Visually recognizes mother
2.8	Simple play with rattle
3.8	Inspects own hands
4.4	Eye–hand coordination in reaching
5.0	Reaches persistently
6.2	Playful response to mirror
7.9	Says "da-da" or equivalent
8.1	Uncovers toy
9.1	Responds to verbal request
9.7	Stirs with spoon in imitation
10.1	Inhibits on command
11.3	Pushes car along
12.0	Turns pages of a book
12.5	Imitates words
13.8	Builds tower of 2 cubes
14.3	Puts 9 cubes in cup
14.6	Uses gestures to make wants known

Figure 4-10 Selected Items from the Bayley Mental Scale

he began to fail and perhaps lose interest in the test materials. Selected items from the Bayley Mental Scale are shown in Figure 4-10.

Scores on the Bayley scales are based on the number of items successfully passed. The examiner consults tables in the test manual to compare the infant's score to those of others the same age. For example, responsiveness to test materials increases dramatically during the first year for most infants. To determine if a particular 4-month-old with a score of 3 is unusual for her age, the examiner can find in the tables that her score, on a scale of 0 to 9, is typical for age 4 months.

Assessing Infant Intelligence Tests

The Bayley scales and other infant intelligence tests are useful in identifying children with severe developmental problems (Broman, Nickolas, & Kennedy, 1975; Werner, Bierman, & French, 1971). Babies with test scores one standard deviation[3] below the mean in their first

[3]*Standard deviation* is a measure of the variability of scores made on a psychological test. It is a useful tool because it describes the proportion of scores that will be found for a population under any part of the normal curve (68 percent of all scores lie between the mean and one standard deviation above or below the mean).

two years are many times more likely to be considered mentally retarded in later years than children who score at or above the mean in infancy. However, infant tests have not been successful in predicting intellectual achievements within the normal range. The correlation between a child's IQ score at the beginning of school (age 6) and in adolescence is quite high. But the correlation between infant intelligence test scores and scores on preschool IQ tests—a much shorter time span—is disappointingly low (see Figure 4-11).

Recent studies by J. F. Fagan and others suggest that there may be a way to assess intelligence in infancy, however. One component of childhood and adult intelligence is cultural knowledge. On IQ tests this is assessed primarily through vocabulary tests. Obviously one cannot give an infant a vocabulary test. But a second component of childhood and adult intelligence is inquisitiveness. Individuals who are oriented toward learning, who continually scan their environments for information, are more intelligent than those who are not learning-oriented. This component of intelligence can be measured in infancy by assessing the baby's responses to visual novelty. Fagan (1984) reviewed fifteen studies that compared preference for novelty between 4 and 7 months of age to school-age IQ. The mean correlation was .45— much higher than that found with the Bayley scales.

Although still in the experimental stage, Fagan's work suggests that one can assess infant intelligence—and predict future intellectual performance—if one uses the right measures. Other psychologists feel that infant tests will never yield accurate predictions because the nature of intelligence changes over the course of development (Siegler & Richards, 1982). In other words, what it means to be intelligent at age 10 is quite different from what it means at 6 months or 2 years. We believe the truth lies between these views. Perhaps some components of intelligence are present from birth. But a full assessment of intelligence must take into account the intellectual changes every child undergoes between infancy and adolescence.

Individual Variations and Species Similarities

Some babies find a hidden object easily at 9 months (Piaget's stage 4); others do not make this step until 10 or 11 months. Some infants walk and talk at 12 months; others are still crawling on all fours and babbling at 18 or 20 months. These variations are all within the normal range. There is no cause for parents to celebrate or despair: the infant who can say "bye-bye" at 11 months will not necessarily grow up to be a poet, nor will the infant who is speechless at 20 months remain unable to speak forever.

What causes individual variations in the rate of early cognitive development? In some cases of mental retardation it is possible to pinpoint the genetic disorder or environmental conditions that are causing the problem. Within the normal range of development, however, it is much more difficult to identify cause and effect.

Genetic Influences

Many single-gene and chromosomal abnormalities clearly defeat normal intellectual development. Tay-Sachs disease is a hereditary disorder that causes progressive deterioration of the brain over the first two years and early death. PKU causes permanent damage to the brain if not treated with a limited diet (see Chapter 3). Down's syndrome infants are slower in their intellectual, social, and motor development than normal infants. There are no exaggerated abnormalities in their development in infancy or later; they simply develop more slowly and do not reach normal adult cognitive levels. Individuals with Down's syndrome typically have very pleasant personalities, but they rarely live outside institutions because they cannot become economically independent (Cicchetti & Sroufe, 1978).

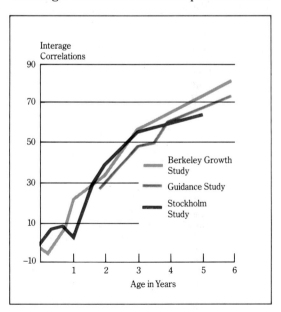

Figure 4-11 Predicting IQ   Analysis of three separate longitudinal studies found a negative correlation between scores on infant intelligence tests and IQs on the Standard-Binet at 8 years old. The predictability of IQ increases over the preschool years and remains steady from age 4 or 5 on.
(Honzik, 1983)

Within the normal range, however, genetic differences among infants seem to have less effect on intelligence than they do at later ages. There is little or no relationship (a correlation of 0 to .05) between a child's score on an infant test and the parents' IQ scores. After age 3, the child's IQ increasingly resembles those of the parents, whether or not the parents are rearing the child (Skodak & Skeels, 1949) (see Figure 4-12). The correlation between the infant intelligence scores of brothers and sisters is about .20 during infancy, but much higher later in life (Scarr-Salapatek, 1976). Infant test scores for fraternal twins, who have no more genes in common than nonfraternal brothers or sisters, have high correlations of between .50 and .70. This indicates that the environment has a powerful effect at this age (Wachs & Gruen, 1982). Being born of the same pregnancy *and* being reared at the same time by the same parents may well explain why these twins are more alike than other siblings.

Environmental Influences

Extreme environmental deprivation may also slow mental development. As a growing biological and social organism, the infant has certain minimum environmental requirements for normal development. Malnutrition severe enough to retard physical growth, and to require hospitalization, is clearly a threat to mental development as well (Honzik, 1983). If deprivation lasts

Figure 4-12 Parents' Education and Child's IQ The correlation between a child's IQ and his or her parents' education (indirect measures of their intelligence and social class) are low before age 2 but climb at age 4

(Honzik, 1957)

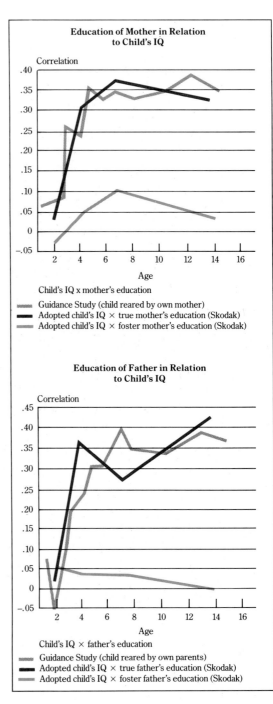

Insight

THE SUPERBABY SYNDROME

Some parents are not content to leave their infants' cognitive development to chance. They begin listening to classical music before the baby is born; they read books, take seminars, and earn "professional parenting" certificates; they flash reading and arithmetic cards at their 3-month-olds; they take their 6-month-olds to regular gym workouts. French lessons begin when the child is 10 months old; Suzuki violin lessons begin when the child is 2. In Tucson, parents enroll their infants in a programming course at Small Bytes Computer School at 2½. They are raising what one writer called "the gourmet baby."

The leading spokesman for starting education at birth is Glenn Doman, the founder of the Better Baby Institute and the author of *How to Teach Your Baby to Read, Teach Your Baby Math,* and *How to Multiply Your Baby's Intelligence.* Among other claims, Doman holds that "our individual genetic potential is that of Leonardo, Shakespeare, Mozart, Michelangelo, Edison, and Einstein." With training, he claims, any baby can be a superbaby. At a recent meeting at the Institute, a 4-year-old veteran of Doman's training program identified characters from Shakespeare's "The Merchant of Venice." Then he constructed sentences in Japanese and translated them into English and French. When Doman was asked why he hadn't published his procedures and results, he responded that creating a control group would be too costly.

Doman is not alone. Other recent entries into the book market for parents include Eric Johnson's *Raising Children to Achieve,* Muriel Schoenbrun Karlin's *Making Your Child a Success* (subtitled "Career Guidance from Kindergarten to College"), and *How to Maximize Your Child's Potential,* which advises parents to think about what they want to "accomplish" with babies, "capitalize" on events in a toddler's life, and remember that "input precedes output." (These books are reviewed by Goodman, 1984.)

Most consumers of superbaby programs are successful couples who postponed parenthood until their 30s. Older and wealthier than most new parents, they are convinced that there are lessons for everything. Their own identities are grounded in their achievements, and they want their baby—often their only baby—to be a high achiever, too. They approach parenthood in much the same way they approach their careers: planning ahead and working overtime. Their child must be prepared, they feel, for the quality preschool program that leads to the right nursery school that feeds into the prestigious kindergarten. In the words of one parent, "You have to start them young and push them toward a goal. They have to be aware of everything—the alphabet, numbers, reading. I want to fill these little sponges as much as possible" (*Newsweek,* 1983).

Perhaps 6-month-old babies can learn to distinguish a painting by Picasso from one by Renoir. No doubt some 3-year-olds can learn to play with a computer. Does this mean they will be more intelligent or creative at age 5 or 50? The best evidence says no. Infants learn from almost any experience: playing with kitchen utensils or with dirt, manipulating old standbys such as jigsaw puzzles and wooden blocks, or taking trips to the supermarket and the playground. The danger of the superbaby syndrome is that parents who are intent on raising the smartest kid on the block may neglect the child's social and emotional development.

more than four months, or if it occurs in the first months of life, the infant may be severely retarded, even if he or she is well fed later on (Cravioto & Delicardie, 1970). The infant's brain and nervous system are not complete at birth but continue to develop over the first months and years of life. Cortical development is about half-complete at 6 months. Deprivation of food before this point comes at the most dangerous time. But severe malnutrition at any point in the first two years of life can cause permanent intellectual damage.

In addition to nourishment, the child also needs "food for thought," or cognitive stimulation. Continual neglect of infants can have bad effects on their mental development as well as on all other forms of growth. Given good treatment, however, most infants recover. Babies reared in institutions that offer only minimal physical care and little stimulation have lower scores on tests of infant intelligence and motor development than children raised normally (Dennis & Najarian, 1957). White and Castle (1964) described the sterile environment of the infants they studied in a Massachusetts institution. The babies were kept spotlessly clean, but they lay on their backs in cribs, staring at the white ceilings all day with nothing to see, reach for, or manipulate. No wonder these babies were retarded in mental and fine motor behaviors! When they were provided with mobiles and reachable objects, their development quickly came up to normal levels. In another study, Kagan and Klein (1973) observed infants in Guatemalan villages who spent most of their first year in dimly lit huts with their faces covered to ward off the "evil eye." Mothers rarely spoke or interacted with their babies, except to care for them physically. These Guatemalan babies were extremely passive, and tests of infant development showed that they were retarded. Nevertheless, both the institutionalized infants and those studied in Guatemala caught up to normal rates of development when their circumstances changed. In the Guatemalan village, after their first year babies were allowed out of the hut and into the social group; their rate of development increased, leaving no residue of passivity or retardation later.

Infants are surprisingly resilient. They seem to be protected from variations in the environment, unless conditions are extremely bad and continue for an extended period.

The Clarkes' review (1977) of severely isolated children indicates that most respond well to later improvements in their environments and have no long-term effects of their early deprivation. Unless the early conditions are far beyond normal for the species, improvements in later environments will compensate for the early problems.

Except in extremely harsh conditions, environmental effects on an infant's cognitive development are difficult to establish. We do know

A 2- to 3-year-old chimp is as intelligent as a 2- to 3-year-old child (and a good deal more agile). One of the earliest studies of chimpanzees' problem-solving skills (shown here) found that chimps are capable of insight learning, or suddenly seeing the solution: pile up the boxes to get the bananas. By age 4, however, the child has left the chimp behind.

that social class differences relate to intellectual differences in childhood and adolescence. On the average, the lower the socioeconomic status of the family, the lower the child's IQ score. *But there is no relationship between developmental level in infancy and social class.* Based on a review of the extensive research literature on social class and infant development, Mark Golden and Beverly Birns (1976) concluded that "social class differences in infant [intelligence] or sensorimotor intelligence probably do not exist. . . . Clear-cut, consistent, pervasive differences in intellectual performance on a variety of measures emerge somewhere between 18 and 24 months of age" (p. 343). It is not until symbolic representation and language skills emerge to define intelligence that social class differences arise among children.

Nevertheless, certain qualities of parent–child relationships do affect intellectual development within the normal range. In four detailed longitudinal studies from infancy to maturity, the behavior of mothers toward their infants was observed and rated. Boys who had warm, close relationships with their mothers as babies earned higher IQ scores in later childhood than did boys with less affectionate mothers. But girls were hardly affected at all by variations in mothering within the normal range (Kagan & Moss, 1962). No one knows why this is true.

We do not mean to confuse readers by citing studies of fraternal twins that suggest the environment shapes sensorimotor development, research on social class differences that indicate the environment is not as important in infancy as it is later, and then evidence that the mother–infant relationship can influence IQ. The data themselves are confusing. Indeed, many aspects of infant intelligence seem to defy explanation. Why should this be?

An Evolutionary View of Sensorimotor Intelligence

The studies we have reviewed here suggest that sensorimotor intelligence is qualitatively different from the symbolic intelligence of older children and adults. It may be that sensorimotor intelligence evolved much earlier in our primate history, and that it is more firmly established (or canalized) in the genetic blueprint for human development, and less subject to individual variation (Scarr, 1983). There are two main lines of evidence for this view.

The first comes from primate studies. Human and nonhuman primate infants, especially the great apes, have similar patterns of intellectual development. Like human infants, apes are born curious. They seem to be programmed to learn by observing, imitating, and exploring within a social context. In the first three years of

life, apes acquire virtually all of the presymbolic skills Piaget discovered in infants: the object concept, imitation, cause-and-effect relations, means–end reasoning, and so on. A 3-year-old chimp performs about as well as a 3-year-old child on tests that do not require language. But despite extensive tutoring, no chimp can match the conceptual understanding or problem-solving skills of a 4-year-old child. Just as humans and apes took different evolutionary paths at some distant point in prehistory, so human and ape youngsters part company intellectually at age 3 to 4. It is at this age that children are acquiring the linguistic skills and cultural knowledge that we commonly associate with human intelligence.

A second line of evidence for the earlier evolution of sensorimotor intelligence comes from infants themselves. The similarities in sensorimotor development of infants overshadow the differences. The *rate* at which individual infants develop does vary. But the *level* of attainment is universal. All normal babies acquire all sensorimotor skills—just as all normal youngsters learn to speak, become attached to at least one caregiver, achieve sexual maturity, and die in old age. The same cannot be said for other human attainments. All normal humans do not develop the same level of formal logic, learn a second language, become attached to a member of the opposite sex, or exhibit musical talent. These developments depend on each person's heredity and environment. They are subject to considerable variation among individuals. Higher attainments, such as becoming a grand master at chess, are within our species' potential; however, they are not part of the basic program.

In short, infants seem predisposed to learn certain schemes and combine them in flexible, innovative ways. In order to develop sensorimotor skills, all that they need are the materials and opportunities to learn; the basic "programs" are within them. This is not to say that the environment has *no* effect on cognitive development in infancy. The same evolutionary forces that produced infants equipped to learn also produced caregivers who are equipped to teach and environments with many chances for a child to experiment and explore. Viewed from this evolutionary perspective, sensorimotor intelligence is as basic to human nature as is sociability.

Cognitive Motivation: Intelligence and Affect

The boundaries between skill and motivation—between what an individual can do and what she wants to do—are not sharp at any age, but they are particularly weak in infancy (Yarrow & Pederson, 1976). Being "smart" on an infant test depends on the level of a baby's understanding of the world and her effect on it. But it also depends on the attention, persistence, cooperation, and other social-emotional characteristics the baby brings to the test.

Infant tests reflect the close connection between intelligence and affect (mood and emotions) in the sensorimotor period. In one study, the Bayley Mental and Motor scales results for a group of 6-month-olds were analyzed into clusters of items based on similar performance. The authors of the study, Yarrow and Pederson (1976) called the three most important clusters (1) goal directedness, (2) visually directed reaching and grasping, and (3) secondary circular reactions (the babies' repeated actions to produce interesting results). In each of these clusters, the items measure not just cognitive understanding but persistence, purposefulness, and intention in the behavior of the babies (see Table 4-1). These three clusters had high correlations with the total scores on the Bayley Mental Scale and with each other. From this we can conclude that babies' performance on infant intelligence tests cannot be evaluated without considering many personality and motivational traits that help determine whether or not the

Table 4-1   Clusters Derived from the Bayley Scales

Cluster Name	Reliability		Item No.	Age Placement (Months)	Description
1. Goal directedness	0.82	Mental scale	60	5.0	Reaches persistently
			71	5.7	Pulls string, secures ring (?purposeful)
			80	7.1	Pulls string to secure ring (purposeful)
			82	7.6	Attempts to secure three cubes
			96	10.5	Unwraps toys
		Motor scale	25	5.6	Attempts to secure pellet
2. Visually directed reaching and grasping	0.92	Mental scale	37	3.1	Reaches for ring
			46	3.8	Closes on dangling ring
			49	4.1	Reaches for cube
			51	4.4	Eye cooperation in reaching
			54	4.6	Picks up cube
			63	5.2	Lifts cup
			64	5.4	Reaches for second cube
			70	5.7	Picks up cube directly and easily
			73	5.8	Lifts cup by handle
3. Secondary circular reactions	0.92	Mental scale	66	5.4	Bangs in play
			72	5.8	Enjoys sound production

(Adapted from Yarrow & Pederson, 1976)

babies will pass all the test items.

Indeed, facial expressions alone determine an infant's level of performance on the infant scales. Jeannette Haviland (1976) analyzed the Bayley Mental and Motor Scales at several age levels to assess how many items required or typically used the baby's affect or emotional expressions in their scoring. She found that during the first three months 40 percent of the test items cannot be assessed without including the baby's affect, 58 percent of the items probably are assessed with affect, and only 2 percent of the items (head turns) can be scored without including affect. By eight months, 57 percent of the items do not need the baby's affect in order to be assessed, and only 25 percent of the items require the infant's affective response or are usually assessed based on affect. Scoring the Bayley items for infants in the first year of life depends on the baby's emotional expressiveness that the examiner can observe. A baby who is obviously not interested in the materials, lacks persistence, or is excessively fearful cannot pass many of the Mental Scale items.

Furthermore, the baby's positive response to the test is one of the best predictors of later IQ test scores (Birns & Golden, 1972). Similarly, Haviland has shown that in many observations, Piaget and other cognitive developmentalists depend on an infant's affect to understand his or her response. Examples of these observations include a child's showing surprise when a hidden object is not where he evidently thought it would be, and an infant's showing curiosity and persistence in searching for hidden objects. In the first example researchers inferred the child's expectation of where the object was located from the surprised affect, and in the second example they inferred the child's understanding that the object was not gone forever from the show of persistence and curiosity in the search. Reading the emotional expressions in a baby's face and behavior is a major source of information about the child's cognitive understanding.

A baby's eagerness to explore the environment and a lack of fearfulness influence his many opportunities to learn. Feeling secure in the parents' love and protection greatly affects a baby's intellectual achievements. Chapter 5 is devoted to understanding infants' emotional and social development, which interacts with cognitive development at every step in the first two years.

SUMMARY

1. The study of cognitive development draws on three distinct schools of thought: psychometrics, the measurement of intelligence and quantitative analysis of changes over the course of development; Piagetian theory, which deals with qualitative changes in the way children think as they develop; and information processing, which deals with the specific processes that make up intelligent behavior (such as attention and memory) and how these change.

2. Perception is more than simply registering sensation; it involves interpretation.

3. Our knowledge of infant perception is based on techniques pioneered by Fantz in the late 1950s. We now know that neonates are attracted to motion, angles, and contrast—all of which are found in a human face. By five or six months, if not before, infants recognize people and objects they have seen before and may even recognize classes of objects. Infants at this age prefer to look at new objects.

4. Perceptual development is the result of both maturation and experience. Studies with the visual cliff show that experience contributes to depth perception; fear of heights develops at about the same time as locomotion. But improvements in visual scanning and discrimination over the first year also reflect a shift from the second to the primary visual system, or maturation.

5. In the first year of life, reflexes disappear and the infant begins to acquire voluntary, cortical control of her body. She holds her head up, sits, creeps, and eventually stands. She learns to adjust her reach and grasp to the object she desires.

6. Piaget saw the infant's discovery that motor actions are related to sensations as the dawn of intelligence. During the sensorimotor stage (birth to about age 2) the infant develops schemes, or action patterns. When the child is unable to assimilate new experiences into these schemes, he must develop new strategies to accommodate them. Cognitive development (at all ages) results from the reciprocal processes of assimilation and accommodation.

7. Piaget divided the sensorimotor period into six substages: (1) applying reflexes, (2) modifying and repeating schemes, (3) interest in effects, (4) coordinating different schemes, (5) deliberate experimentation,

and (6) inventing new schemes mentally. (The last stage is seen in deferred imitation and symbolic play.)

8. The most important development of the sensorimotor period is the object concept, or object permanence: learning that an object out of sight is not out of existence. The 2- or 3-month-old baby loses interest if an object is hidden; the 18- or 20-month-old infant is sure the object is somewhere and delights in hide-and-seek.

9. Piaget saw the infant as an active learner who constructs an understanding of the world by acting on it. He held that although the rate of development varies, all children progress through the same stages of cognitive development in the same order.

10. Infant intelligence tests are designed to establish standards of normal cognitive development in the first two years of life. They are useful in identifying mental retardation, but they do not predict how intelligent a normal baby will be at age 8 or 18.

11. It is virtually impossible to pinpoint the causes of individual variations within the normal range for cognitive development in infancy. There is little or no correlation between an infant's IQ and the IQs, education, or social class of his parents. Environmental deprivation may retard mental development, but most children recover with later care.

12. Sensorimotor intelligence appears to be more firmly established in the genetic blueprint for human development than are more advanced cognitive skills. The fact that apes exhibit similar patterns of curiosity suggests that sensorimotor intelligence evolved early in our primate history.

13. Infant intelligence is in part a reflection of interest and affect, or motivation.

FURTHER READING

Brazelton, T. B. (1969). *Infants and mothers: Differences in development.* New York: Dell. This is an excellent book for new parents or people who plan to have a child. Brazelton looks at differences among normal infants during their first year of life. He draws composite profiles of active, average, and quiet babies.

Bower, T. G. R. (1977). *The perceptual world of the child.* Cambridge, MA: Harvard University Press. This easy-to-read book highlights the major perceptual development during the first few years.

Lewin, R. (1975). Starved brains. *Psychology Today, 9*(4), pp. 29–33. This brief summary explains the effect of malnutrition on the development of children's brains.

Sroufe, A. (1977). *Knowing and enjoying your baby.* Englewood Cliffs, NJ: Prentice-Hall. This engaging book by an important child development researcher highlights the emotional development of the infant and how parents can be responsive to their children.

Sutton-Smith, B., & Sutton-Smith, S. (1974). *How to play with your children (and when not to).* New York: Hawthorn. This book summarizes what children are likely to be doing at different ages from birth to age 13 and how adults can stimulate play. It considers the role of the father in children's play and differences in play between boys and girls.

Perception (vision)

Attracted by motion, edges, contrast
<1–2 mos.>

Perceives change in shape-and-color
<4 mos.>

Interest in novelty
<3 mos.>

Recognizes specific people
<6 mos.>

Perceives change in shape *or* color
<8–10 mos.>

Scans internal details
<3–4 mos.>

Perceives depth
<6 mos.>

Fears heights
<7–9 mos.>

Motor skills

Lifts chin when prone
<6–8 wks.>

Lifts chest
<3–4 mos.>

Sits without support
<6–8 mos.>

Pulls to standing position
<10–13 mos.>

Rolls over
<2–5 mos.>

Voluntary reaching
<5 mos.>

Stands with help
<6–10 mos.>

Stands alone
<11–14 mos.>

Sits with support
<4–6 mos.>

Transfers object from one hand to the other
<6–7 mos.>

Creeps
<7–9 mos.>

Adjusts grasp to object
<8–9 mos.>

Walks with support
<9–13 mos.>

Cognition
Piaget's Sensorimotor Stage

Uses reflexes as schemes
(Stage 1)

Repeats and modifies schemes to achieve interesting sensations
(Stage 2)

Develops a variety of schemes to achieve interesting effects
(Stage 3)

Coordinates schemes in means–ends sequences
(Stage 4)

Development of object concept:
Does not search if object disappears

Search for objects depends on visual contact

Looks for object in first place it disappeared

| 1 | 2 | 3 | 4 | 5 | 6 | 7 | 8 | 9 | 10 | 11 | 12 |

Age in months

HIGHLIGHTS OF PHYSICAL AND COGNITIVE DEVELOPMENT, BIRTH TO 24 MONTHS

< > onset or peak

Walks
alone
< 12-15 mos. >

Climbs
stairs
< 17–22 mos. >

Runs
< 20–24 mos. >

Kicks ball
< 22–24 mos. >

Walks
backward
< 14–22 mos. >

Walks
well

Uses various
coordinated
schemes
in systematic
trial-and-error
experiments
(Stage 5)

Uses internal images to conduct
mental experiments; deferred
imitation, symbolic play, and
speech
(Stage 6)

Follows a series of invisible
displacements, indicating mastery
of the object concept

Traces object through visible displacements

| 13 | 14 | 15 | 16 | 17 | 18 | 19 | 20 | 21 | 22 | 23 | 24 + |

In *The First Relationship* (1977), Dan Stern describes watching a mother feed her 3-month-old son.

While talking and looking at me the mother turned her head and gazed at the infant's face. He was gazing at the ceiling, but out of one corner of his eye he saw her head turn toward him and [he] turned to gaze back at her. This had happened before, but now he broke rhythm and stopped sucking. He let go of the nipple and the suction around it broke as he eased into the faintest suggestion of a smile. The mother abruptly stopped talking and, as she watched his face begin to transform, her eyes opened a little wider and her eyebrows raised a bit. His eyes locked on to hers, and together they held motionless for a moment. The infant did not return to sucking and his mother held frozen her slight expression of anticipation. This silent and almost motionless instant continued to hang until the mother suddenly shattered it by saying "Hey!" and simultaneously opening her eyes wider, raising her eyebrows further, and throwing her head up toward the infant. Almost simultaneously, the baby's eyes widened. His head tilted up and, as his smile broadened, the nipple fell out of his mouth. Now she said "Well hello! . . . heello . . . heeelooooo!" so that her pitch rose and the "hellos" became longer and more stressed on each successive repetition. With each phrase, the baby expressed more pleasure, and his body resonated almost like a balloon being pumped up, filling a little more with each breath. The mother then paused and her face relaxed. They watched each other expectantly for a moment. The shared excitement between them ebbed, but before it faded completely, the baby suddenly took an initiative and intervened to rescue it. His head lurched forward, his hands jerked up, and a fuller smile blossomed. His mother was jolted into motion. She moved forward, mouth open and eyes alight, and said, "Ooooooo . . . ya wanna play do ya . . . yeah? . . . I didn't know if you were still hungry . . . no . . . noooo . . . no I didn't. . . ." And off they went. (p. 3)

This was one moment in an infant's emotional and social development—an early step in the "courtship dance" between mother and child.

THE SOCIAL ANIMAL

Infants are social and emotional creatures. They respond to contact and care from the start. They signal their distress with crying, their contentment with snuggling, and otherwise make their feelings known. Newborns are anything but shy. At 3 months, this infant is beginning to read his mother's signals and to express joy at engaging her attention. He is a gregarious little fellow at this stage: he likes people, whoever they are. If he is like most babies, he will begin to develop a special attachment to his mother and father at 7 or 8 months. The beginnings of love are also the beginnings of fear. At 12 months, he may cling desperately to his mother and sob hysterically when she puts on her coat to go out, even though he knows the baby-sitter well. No two infants are exactly alike, however. Some are friendlier and easier to soothe than others are, and some more passionate in their attachments.

Do infants have distinct "personalities" or temperaments? Do they have emotions, or must they *learn* to feel joy, fear, love, grief, and rage? At what point do they become attached to other people? How important is mother love in their development? When do they begin to develop an image of themselves? The emotional repertoire and social behavior of a 2-year-old are much different from those of a 3-month-old. This chapter traces the infant's emotional and social development and shows how developments in perception, cognition, and even motor skills affect an infant's feelings and relationships.

Infant Temperament

Differences among babies are apparent from birth. One newborn baby in the hospital nursery is peaceful and still, while another kicks and squirms in her crib. One reacts immediately and loudly to a sudden noise; another seems oblivious. One adapts easily to change, as in bathing and diapering; another fusses in protest. Where do these differences come from? Do they last?

The New York Longitudinal Study (NYLS)

One of the first empirical studies of infant characteristics was launched in the late 1950s by Alexander Thomas, Stella Chess, and their colleagues in the New York Longitudinal Study, or NYLS (Thomas & Chess, 1977; Thomas, Chess, Birch, Hertzig, & Korn, 1963). The researchers followed 140 middle- and upper-middle-class children from birth to adolescence. In the first few years of the study they concentrated on parents' reports of their infants' reactions to a variety of situations. Thomas and Chess found distinct differences among infants in nine characteristics shown in Table 5-1 on page 176. Ongoing observations indicated that the differences were consistent and stable over time.

The original aim of the NYLS was to investigate the infants' "reactivity," or physiological responsiveness. After several years Thomas

Differences in activity, sensitivity (reactivity), and soothability are visible from birth. The question is whether these temperamental qualities are stable over the course of development.

and Chess concluded that they were observing variations in behavioral style, or temperament. They defined **temperament** as individual differences in the intensity and duration of emotional responses that influence personality development and social relationships.[1]

Thomas and Chess identified three types of temperament. *Easy* babies (about 40 percent of their sample) were playful, regular in body functions, and adaptable. They approached new situations with interest and were moderate in their responses. In contrast, *difficult* babies (10 percent of the sample) were negative, irregular, and unadaptable. They withdrew from new situations and had intense reactions. The third type, *slow-to-warm-up* babies (15 percent of

the sample) were low in activity and mild in their responses. They tended to withdraw from new situations and needed time to adapt to change. The remaining 35 percent of the children were not rated high or low on any of the dimensions measured. The NYLS found that difficult infants were most likely to have problems with their parents, school, and peers later in their development; easy infants were the least likely to have problems later.

These findings challenged prevailing views of early emotional and social development. Through the 1950s, theory and research focused on the impact of different environments on the baby (Wachs & Gruen, 1982). The assumption was that "good" environments had uniformly positive effects on all babies and that "bad" environments had uniformly negative effects on all babies. Thomas and Chess demonstrated that there is no such person as "*the* baby." Infants vary in their responses to people

---

[1]Recently, however, Jerome Kagan (1984) and others have begun to think that temperament is just what Thomas and Chess originally thought it was: the result of individual levels of physiological arousal in babies faced with the same or similar experiences.

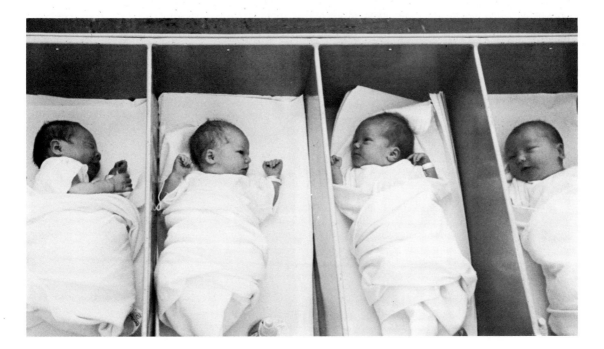

Table 5-1 Temperamental Differences Among 6-Month-Old Infants

Temperamental quality	Rating	6 months
Activity level Proportion of inactive periods to active ones	High Low	Tries to stand in tub and splashes. Bounces in crib. Crawls after dog. Passive in bath. Plays quietly in crib and falls asleep.
Rhythmicity Regularity of hunger, excretion, sleep, and wakefulness	Regular Irregular	Is asleep at 6:30 every night. Awakes at 7 A.M. Food intake is constant. Length of nap varies; so does food intake.
Distractibility The degree to which extraneous stimuli alter behavior	Distractible Not distractible	Stops crying when mother sings. Will remain still while clothing is changed if given a toy. Stops crying only after dressing is finished. Cries until given a bottle.
Approach/withdrawal The response to a new object or person	Positive Negative	Likes new foods. Enjoyed first bath in a large tub. Smiles and gurgles. Does not respond when spoken to, withdraws physically, looks frightened, or cries.
Adaptability The ease with which a child adapts to the environment	Adaptive Not adaptive	Previously disliked new foods; now accepts them well. Does not cooperate with dressing. Fusses and cries when left with sitter.
Attention span and persistence The amount of time devoted to an activity, and the effect of distraction on the activity	Long Short	Watches toy mobile over crib intently. "Coos" frequently. Sucks pacifier only for a few minutes and spits it out.
Intensity of reaction The energy of response, regardless of its quality or direction	Intense Mild	Cries loudly at sound of thunder. Makes sucking movements when vitamins are administered. Does not kick often in the tub. Does not smile.
Threshold of responsiveness The intensity of stimulation required to evoke a discernible response	Low High	Refuses fruit he likes when vitamins are added. Hides head from bright light. Eats everything. Does not object to diapers being wet or soiled.
Quality of mood The amount of friendly, pleasant, joyful behavior as contrasted with unpleasant, unfriendly behavior	Positive Negative	Plays and splashes in bath. Smiles at everyone. Cries when taken from tub. Cries when given food he does not like.

(Adapted from Thomas, Chess, & Birch, 1970)

The infant's social and emotional development do
not depend on the infant's temperament or the
mother's personality and skill,
but on goodness of fit.

and events. What is a good environment and good parenting for one baby may be a poor environment and unhelpful parenting for another baby. The key to healthy development is *goodness of fit* between the child's temperament and the demands made on the child in her home environment. "If the two influences are harmonized, one can expect healthy development of the child; if they are dissonant, behavioral problems are sure to ensue" (Thomas, Chess, & Birch, 1970, p. 108). An energetic, extroverted, noisy child who cannot sit still will test the patience of parents who enjoy quiet evenings spent reading and listening to classical music. Parents who are always ready for a party, love a practical joke, and enjoy arguing would find the same child a welcome addition.

Temperament and Experience

In Chapter 2 we suggested that, to some degree, individuals create their own environments. The concept of temperament illustrates this. The infant's disposition affects the way adults care for him. The same mother handles different babies differently (as any 14-year-old with a younger brother or older sister will loudly proclaim). Suppose a mother is lively and outgoing, adapts quickly to change, sleeps well, enjoys her food—in short, is an "easy mother." She is likely to find it highly rewarding to care for an infant who is as even-tempered and responsive as she is. But she may find an infant who is slow to warm up, who lacks her energy and sociability, disappointing to care for. She devotes extra time and effort to this child in an

attempt to "pep him up." The same mother may unintentionally overstimulate a third baby, who objects to tickling and games of peek-a-boo, and make him more difficult than he already is. All her efforts to soothe him fail. In time she decides that the only way to handle him is to let him cry until he is exhausted; plunge him into his bath despite his vigorous protests; let him go hungry if he refuses food. This mother lets the first baby determine his own schedules for sleeping, eating, and playing; pushes the second baby; and withdraws emotionally from the third. Thus different infants elicit different styles of care from the same parent.

At the same time, different infants react differently to the same treatment and environment. Imagine a mother who tiptoes around the baby's room, speaks softly, and holds the baby gingerly. A baby who is slow to warm up may blossom in this environment; so might a highly reactive baby. But an easy baby might languish from low levels of interaction and stimulation. How this infant experiences the environment depends in part on her own temperament.

Temperament affects the infant's experience in two ways: infants with different temperaments elicit different responses from others, and infants with different temperaments have different reactions to the same environment or event. Reactions to a stranger illustrate these two types of influence (Rothbart & Derryberry, 1981). At 6 or 7 months most infants become suspicious of people they do not know.[2] But the intensity of this reaction varies from infant to infant, as shown in Figure 5-1.

"His Father's Temper"

Where do temperamental differences come from? Relatives often comment that an infant

has "his father's temper" or "her mother's smile," implying that temperament is inherited. This homespun observation now has scientific support: Evidence of the heritability of behavioral disposition is accumulating. With the assistance of the National Mothers of Twins Club, Robert Plomin and his colleagues compared identical (monozygotic) and fraternal (dizygotic) twins (Buss & Plomin, 1975). They found that correlations in emotionality, activity, and sociability were an average of .55 for identical twins—and zero for fraternal twins. This means that fraternal twins are no more alike in temperament than are two children chosen at random from the population. Identical twins are not identical in temperament, but in some ways they are similar. Other research (Goldsmith & Gottesman, 1981) confirms this. If one identical twin is extroverted, the other is likely to be so; if one has a poor attention span and is easily distracted from a task, the chances are good that the other twin is the same.

This does not mean that temperament is "genetically determined," however. Temperament is better seen as a *bias* towards being easy or difficult, introverted or extroverted, gleeful or grumpy (Kagan, 1984). Whether a bias in one direction or another is actualized depends in part on experience. A child with a tendency toward introversion, for example, might be quite friendly at age 5 or 15 if he grows up in a warm, supportive, outgoing family. His bias toward introversion may only show when he is under stress.

Is Temperament Stable?

Will a child who is friendly and outgoing at 6 months be the same at 6 years? Is temperament stable over time? There is some evidence that it is—but only some. In one study (Kagan, Reznick, Clarke, Snidman, & Garcia-Coll, 1984), children who were identified as extremely inhibited or fearless at 21 months were observed

---

[2]We will examine stranger anxiety again when we discuss the development of fear later in this chapter.

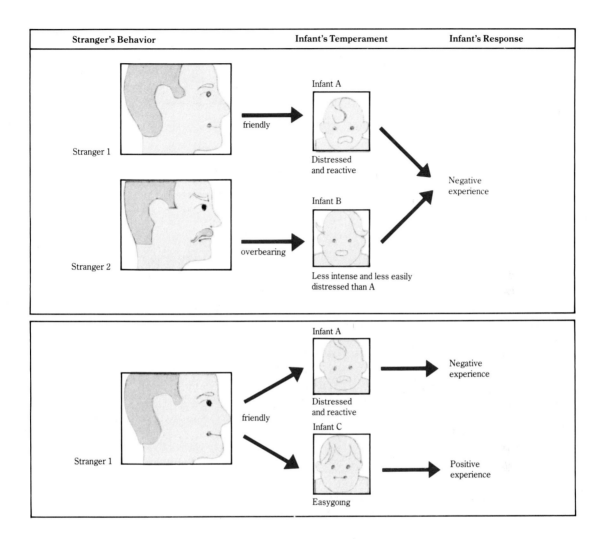

Figure 5-1 Interactions with a Stranger: Three Scenarios   Child A is highly reactive and easily distressed. He has an experience with a stranger who smiles, speaks softly, and does not force himself on the infant. Nevertheless, Child A is distressed by the experience.

Child B is less intense and less easily distressed. But she has an experience with a loud, overbearing stranger who upsets her.

Although Child A and Child B had objectively different experiences, both were afraid of the strangers.

Child C, who is easygoing, meets the nice stranger Infant A met. Although he has the same objective experience as Infant A had, his subjective experience is quite different. His smiles and eye contact with the stranger show that he is not afraid of a friendly stranger.

Insight

INFANT BEHAVIOR AND MATERNAL CARE IN JAPAN AND THE UNITED STATES

Comparisons of infants in Japan and the United States made in the 1960s (Caudill & Weinstein, 1969) found significant differences in temperament between the two. American babies were more physically active, vocal, and playful than their smaller Japanese peers. Some psychologists attributed this to inborn genetic differences; others, to cultural differences in infant care. American mothers responded to infant distress with play; Japanese mothers were more inclined to rock their babies and lull them to sleep.

Much has changed in the last decade in the United States and Japan. Both countries have experienced rapid economic development, urban crowding, a decrease in the number of children per family, and an increase in the percentage of mothers who work. Moreover, many middle-class Japanese mothers look to the United States—and translations of Dr. Spock—for models of infant care.

Have maternal and infant behavior changed as a result? Otaki, Durrett, and Pennebaker (in press) compared urban, middle-class mothers and their 3- to 4-month-old firstborn from the United States and Japan. They found that Japanese mothers spend more time with their infants, largely because Japanese homes are smaller and most infants do not have a separate bedroom. But there were no observable differences in the way today's Japanese mothers and American mothers care for their babies (bottle-feeding and breast-feeding, diapering, bathing, and so on). There were no significant differences in the ways they played with the infants (the amount of kissing, chatting, lulling, looking). Moreover, the differences between babies from the two countries seemed to have "disappeared." In fact, the Japanese babies in this study were more playful and vocal than were their peers in the United States.

The researchers did find that in the sample of American babies, the female infants were more vocal—and protested longer and louder when distressed—than were the male infants. The reverse was true in the sample Japanese babies: the males were more vocal. The researchers suggest that this is because Japanese mothers see a small boy's protests as foreshadowing his dominant role in adult society. In contrast, American mothers expect girls to be chatty and boys self-contained.

This study underscores the importance of considering the cultural context of early infant–mother interaction.

again around their fourth birthdays. Three-quarters of the inhibited children were still withdrawn, but none of the fearless children had become shy. When observed with an unfamiliar child their same age and sex, the extremely inhibited children rarely attempted to approach the other child and reacted passively when that child seized their toys. The uninhibited children, in contrast, were active, gleeful, and sometimes aggressive. When tested by an unfamiliar woman, the extremely inhibited children were quiet and obedient. The uninhibited children frequently interrupted the adult, laughed, and voiced their own opinions freely. In another study of 89 children, seven boys who were rated as extremely inhibited at age 3 remained introverted, passive, and shy through adolescence and into adulthood (Kagan & Moss, 1962).

Given the small numbers involved in the two studies, the results should be seen as tentative. Other research suggests that temperament can and does fluctuate (Lewis & Starr, 1979).

A Critique of the NYLS

Like other ground-breaking studies, Thomas and Chess' research has drawn criticism. Some psychologists question the very concept of temperament. In their view, to say that each baby has a particular behavioral disposition or style implies that the infant responds the same way in all contexts, regardless of the other actors or the context. A withdrawing baby will withdraw from new toys as well as new people, at home and in a laboratory. This may not be true.

Other psychologists point to flaws in the research design. Thomas and Chess measured infant temperament indirectly, by interviewing parents. The parents' attitudes toward the infant influenced both their description of the child and their handling of her. Temperamental differences may exist only in the eye of the beholder.

In addition, the terms Thomas and Chess used to describe temperamental types ("easy," "difficult," and "slow-to-warm-up") imply value judgments. Which type of baby would you want? The answer is an easy one. These labels may also be misleading. Parents may find an 8-month-old easy because they can easily distract her from prohibited, dangerous activities. Later in development, the same child may have problems because she does not concentrate on homework or other tasks. Moreover, categories derived from a white, middle-class sample of children may not apply to children of other ethnic groups and socioeconomic classes. For example, lower-class Puerto Ricans often consider highly desirable the traits Thomas and Chess label "difficult." To them, the baby has *machismo* (Korn, 1978).

Thomas and Chess' description (1977) of the "difficult" child is particularly controversial. They suggest that about one child in ten is just plain contrary: irritable, irregular, intense, unadaptable, and unhappy, through no fault of the parents. These are the infants who still wake up crying two or three times a night at 12 months, who absolutely refuse to get dressed at age 2 or 3, and who resist any effort to soothe or control them. Thomas and Chess suggest that parents who attempt to change such children will only make them more difficult; what these children need most is patience.

This prescription has the positive effect of taking the blame off parents who might otherwise feel the child's misbehavior is a reflection on them and attempt to "beat sense" into the difficult child. But the diagnosis of "difficult" may also function as a self-fulfilling prophecy. Parents, teachers and others may expect a particular child to *be* difficult and, because of the way they treat the child, get what they expect. The easy child's experiments with painting walls or playing doctor may well be labeled "creativity" and "curiosity." But the same behavior from a so-called difficult child may be taken as evidence that he is incorrigible. The latter child is given a label he has to live up to, or live down.

Raymond Starr and others (Starr, Dietrich, Fischhoff, Ceresnie, & Zweier, 1984) have hypothesized that some of the children whom Thomas and Chess would label as difficult suffer from subtle developmental abnormalities that are not detected on the usual infant tests. If these children were diagnosed as mildly handicapped, their parents might attribute irritating or slow behavior to the handicap. But because they are assumed to be normal, the child is considered to be a "bad" baby. Starr believes that such children are high risks for child abuse.

Despite such controversies, Thomas and Chess paved the way for other researchers (Buss & Plomin, 1975; Goldsmith & Campos,

Insight

CHILD ABUSE: MOTHERS AND INFANTS AT RISK

Every year an estimated 1.5 to 2 million American children are beaten, burned, neglected, or otherwise abused. As many as 2,000 are killed by their parents. Research on child abuse has either focused on the psychological characteristics of the parents or on socioeconomic stresses on the family. Most psychological studies take data after the fact, which makes it difficult to distinguish between cause and effect. The parent may be interviewed after an abused child has come to the attention of authorities. There is no way of knowing whether a parent beat the child because he or she was emotionally disturbed, or the parent became emotionally disturbed after the beatings. Sociological studies suggest that parents who are under constant stress, who struggle for the necessities of life and live from crisis to crisis, are most likely to abuse a child. But the fact is that the vast majority of poor parents do *not* hurt their children. Byron Egeland's study was designed to overcome these two difficulties in research methods (Egeland, Sroufe, & Erickson, 1983; Egeland, 1979).

Egeland has followed 275 mothers who received prenatal care at the Maternal and Infant Care Clinics in Minneapolis. The families have been studied in great detail, beginning in the last weeks of pregnancy, continuing into the child's preschool years. All of the mothers were considered at risk for child abuse and neglect. All were poor, most were on welfare, and 60 percent were not married when they gave birth. When she was about 36 weeks pregnant, each woman was given a battery of tests designed to measure personality traits (aggression, dependency, impulsivity, and the like) and attitudes toward motherhood (such as whether the woman had wanted to become pregnant, and whether she felt competent about meeting a baby's needs). The infant's temperament was assessed at birth and again at 3 months (Egeland wanted to determine if there were something about certain children that provokes abuse). The mothers were observed feeding and

playing with their infants in their homes at 3 and 6 months, and rated for feeding skill, sensitivity, and so on. The researchers also looked for evidence of abuse and neglect on these visits.

The most surprising finding was how many infants were mistreated. The Minneapolis health department estimates that 1 percent to 2 percent of children seen in public health centers have been abused or neglected. Egeland found that 10 percent of the babies he observed were grossly mistreated.* This suggests that many of the children who are in danger never come to the attention of health or social workers and go untreated and unprotected.

Egeland compared 26 "inadequate" (abusive and neglecting) mothers to 26 women whom the home visitors rated as "good" mothers. The most striking differences were in age, marital status, and education. The mean age at birth was 24.5 years for the good mothers and 19.3 years for the inadequate mothers. Only 30 percent of the good mothers were single at delivery, compared to 70 percent of the inadequate mothers. The good mothers reported that their families and, in most cases, the babies' fathers were supportive. Many of the inadequate mothers were on their own. All of the good mothers had completed twelve years of school and all had attended childbirth classes. Most of the inadequate mothers had dropped out of high school before they became pregnant. Only 30 percent of them had attended childbirth classes.

Egeland also found differences in the mothers' feelings for and interest in their newborn. Maternity ward nurses reported that the good mothers were prepared for childbirth. They had planned where the baby would sleep and had purchased the necessary equipment. Most of the inadequate mothers had not done so. The good mothers had a better understanding of newborns. They recognized an infant's need for both attachment and autonomy. Home observers found that they were sensitive to the baby's

*When abuse or neglect was detected, the researchers immediately reported the case to child protection agencies.

signals and cues. Feeding and play were reciprocal activities—something the mother did *with*
the baby, not *to* the baby. The good mothers
were also able to accept their own ambivalent
feelings about pregnancy and motherhood.

The inadequate mothers misinterpreted the
meaning of newborn behavior. For example,
when newborns cry they are expressing dislike
or discomfort; they may be hungry, want attention, or have a stomachache. The inadequate
mothers did not understand that crying was a
signal of discomfort. Many of them interpreted
the cry as criticism: "She thinks I don't know
how to care for a child," or "My baby doesn't
like me." Many of these mothers had been
abused or neglected themselves as children. As
adults, they still had a strong need to be cared

for. This interfered with their ability to
nurture and care for a child. They had difficulty
maintaining their own identity and were both
frightened by a small infant's demands and disappointed by the infant's responses. Not sensitive
to the baby's states, moods, or interests, they
delivered care in a highly mechanical fashion.

This study shows that child abuse is most
likely to occur when the mother is young, poorly
educated, lacks social support and mothering
skills, and has a personal history of abuse and
neglect. Of course, mothers are not the only
ones who abuse children. Like other researchers, Egeland was unable to enlist fathers in the
study. He and his colleagues have continued to
follow the children, who are now enrolled in
school.

1982; Rothbart & Derryberry, 1981). Psychologists working in this area of development may
not agree on exactly what they mean by temperament or on how to measure it. But they do
agree that there are individual differences in
emotional reactions among babies, and that
these differences seem to be present from
birth.

Each baby's temperament reflects his or
her unique genetic background. The capacity to
feel and express emotions is part of our common
human heritage.

Emotional Development

Sometimes we infer what a person is feeling
from the facial expression, tone of voice, or
body language; at other times, the person's
train of thought is the clue to how he feels.
Sometimes we identify emotions from what a
person does (giving a bear hug, for example) or
from what they do not do (such as refusing a
handshake). We all know that adults and older
children can feign emotions: delight when someone else gets the job or marries the person you
wanted, for example. Sometimes we betray
ourselves, letting our fear or anger or love show
when we want to appear "cool." Whatever form
emotions take, they serve the two basic func-

tions of motivation and communication. Emotions motivate by energizing us, alerting us to
certain information in the environment, and tun-
ing us to respond in certain ways. (When we are
angry, we are not likely to listen to reason.) The
expression of emotions communicates to other
people how we are likely to behave and, in turn,
allows us to guess what they might do.

Much social information travels along emotional channels. Thus **emotions** are feelings
that motivate us and communicate a wide range
of nonverbal messages between us and others
(Lamb & Campos, 1982, p. 109).

Do Infants Have Emotions?

Do babies have feelings? Parents say they do. In
one series of interviews, 85 percent of the
mothers of 1-month-olds said that their babies
expressed anger; 58 percent reported fear; 74
percent, surprise; 95 percent, joy; 34 percent,
sadness; and 99 percent, interest (Johnson,
Emde, Pannabecker, Stenberg, & Davis,
1982). But mothers can hardly be considered
unbiased observers. They want to think that
their infants are happy, interested, and responsive.

There is less biased evidence that infants
have emotions. Carroll Izard has been studying

the facial expressions of infants for almost ten years (Izard, Huebner, Risser, McGuinness, & Dougherty, 1980; Trotter, 1983). He and his colleagues at the Human Emotions Laboratory at the University of Delaware have videotaped hundreds of infants responding to such events as being handed an ice cube, having their favorite toy taken away, and being reunited with their mother. In each case, the tape of the infant's facial expression is analyzed and scored numerically using the Maximally Discriminative Facial Movement Coding System, or MAX. Izard's aim is to see whether distinct emotions can be recognized from changes in the infant's facial expressions alone. Scorers of the videotapes are not told anything about the context or what the baby is responding to. Izard also investigates whether different people, such as mothers, nurses, and college students, see the same emotion in a baby's face. They often do—more often than if they were guessing. (See Figure 5-2.)

Less research has been done on vocal expressions of emotions in infancy. But one in-depth study of crying indicates that babies can send clear messages in this way as well. After observing and recording infants in their homes, Peter Wolff (1969) identified three distinct cries: the hunger (or basic) cry, characterized by rhythmic, repetitive vocalization; the anger cry, characterized by long and loud vocalization; and the pain cry, characterized by a sudden,

Joy: Mouth forms smile, cheeks lifted, twinkle in eyes.

Surprise: Brows raised, eyes widened, mouth rounded in oval shape.

Anger: Brows drawn together and downward, eyes fixed, mouth squarish.

Distress: Eyes tightly closed, mouth, as in anger, squared and angular.

Interest: Brows raised or knit, mouth may be softly rounded, lips may be pursed.

Sadness: Inner corners of brows raised, mouth corners drawn down.

Disgust: nose wrinkled, upper lip raised, tongue pushed outward.

Fear: Brows level, drawn in and up, eyelids lifted, mouth retracted.

Figure 5-2 Infant Facial Archetypes
(Izard, 1980)

long cry followed by a long silence as the infant holds her breath, followed by another wail. Later he played the tapes in the baby's homes. Wolff found that young infants get their emotional message across. Even inexperienced mothers could distinguish between different cries. When he played a tape recording of an infant's pain cry, the anxious mother rushed to the baby's room (a test that evoked anger from many of the mothers). Mothers were slower to respond to their babies' cries of anger and hunger.

Not all developmental psychologists would agree that these facial and verbal expressions are emotions in the usual sense of the term. When adults get angry, it is because they feel that they have been wronged: that someone or something has deprived them of their legitimate rights. Infants do not have a concept of legitimacy. Izard's critics consider calling an infant's protests "anger" roughly equivalent to claiming that a dog is depressed because he didn't come running the instant his master opened the door. Their argument is largely over words, however. Most psychologists would agree that infants are able to communicate different feelings or states to their caregivers. Most would also agree that these states affect or motivate the infant's behavior: a baby cannot nurse or study her mother's face when she is crying. We consider *emotion* the best term for these motivating and communicable states.

Some emotions seem to be present at birth. Neonates express distress, interest, and disgust (when presented with a bitter taste or noxious smell). Other emotions, such as joy and fear, appear at more or less predictable times in the development of every normal child.

Joy and Laughter

The emergence of social smiling is a milestone in the infant's development because smiling serves the adaptive function of drawing adults to her. Few adults can resist an infant's bright-eyed, toothless grin, as noted in Chapter 2. To review: Newborns produce what look like smiles in their sleep, but not when they are awake. These are not real smiles, because they are not voluntary. Social smiling emerges at between 6 and 8 weeks. Most 2-months-olds smile at anyone or anything. The sight of a human face reliably evokes expressions of pleasure—but so do bull's-eyes, bells, and other interesting non-human stimuli (Emde & Harmon, 1972). Two-month-old babies like faces—probably because of the contrasts and motion in adult facial expressions, not because they have a special interest in fellow humans (see also Chapter 4). Their smiles are indiscriminate. By 3 or 4 months, infants do show a preference for faces. But an infant this age is promiscuous: she smiles at anyone who approaches her. Familiar objects also evoke pleasure. At 5 or 6 months, babies begin to save their smiles for familiar people. They usually greet caregivers with a broad grin. But friendly strangers may elicit no response, or even distress.

Thus smiling begins as a reflex, develops as a response to stimulation, then gradually becomes associated with pleasant experiences, familiar objects (including faces), valued people, and later with delight in fooling Daddy or in solving a problem (Sroufe & Waters, 1976). Perceptual and cognitive development are part of this process.

There are parallel changes in the infant's sense of humor (Waters, Matas, & Sroufe, 1975). If a mother dangles a cloth from her mouth, a 5- or 6-month-old will stare soberly at the cloth, take it from her mouth, examine it, and bring it to his mouth. The game is interesting to him, but not funny. A 9- or 10-month-old looks at his mother and the cloth, brightens, breaks into peals of laughter, grabs the cloth, then tries to shove it back into her mouth, laughing all the while. He has enough experience now to sense that his mother is doing something silly. (We will say more about the development of humor in Chapter 6.)

Fears

Fear is the expression of distress in the absence of physical pain. It, too, follows its own developmental timetable (Scarr & Salapatek, 1970). Neonates and young infants are startled by loud noises, sudden appearances or disappearances, and "looming" objects. But the startle response is reflexive and brief. For the first six months, infants are essentially fearless. Over the next six months, however, they become increasingly wary. One example of this is the visual cliff, discussed in Chapter 4. When young infants are placed on the deep side of the visual cliff, they show interest but not distress. Fear of heights develops at about the same time as does independent locomotion (Bertenthal, Campos, & Barrett, 1983), between 7 and 9 months. The intensity of the infant's fear of heights increases with age. In one study, none of the 18- to 24-month-old infants would cross to the deep side. Similarly, young infants find an adult wearing a mask interesting. Many older infants react with fear. They do not distinguish between a mask of a happy, smiling bear and a mask of a horned monster. Masks produce fright, whether the masks are friendly or mean (Scarr & Salapatek, 1970).

Up to about 6 months, infants are generally friendly to strangers. It may take a little longer for a new babysitter to get a smile from the infant than it does for his mother, but the chances are good that he will warm to her. Then, almost without warning, between 6 and 8 months infants begin to whimper, cry, and even sob when someone unknown comes too close or tries to pick them up. *Stranger anxiety* is quite common. By 8 or 9 months, infants are anything but sociable with people they do not know.

Separation protest (sometimes called separation anxiety) appears at about the same age. Rather suddenly, infants are afraid of being separated from their parents or another well-known caregiver. Up to 6 months, infants may cry when their mother or father suddenly stops playing and leaves the room. But if another person steps in, they stop crying and recover quickly. As long as the action continues, they are content; any playmate will do. Similarly, infants under six months old want to be held and rocked when they are distressed, but anyone can do the rocking. At 6 or 7 months this changes: The infant protests vigorously and refuses to accept substitutes if his familiar caregiver leaves him. Studies of adoption provide clear illustration of the onset of separation protest. When infants under 6 months are placed in new homes with adoptive parents, they show few if any signs of being upset. When infants older than 6 months are given up for adoption, they are often extremely distressed and take weeks or months to adjust to a foster family (Yarrow & Goodwin, 1973).

Infants vary in the intensity of their fear of strangers and of separation, and in the duration of this phase of emotional and social development. But both phases appear to be universal (see Figure 5-3).

Like joy, the development of fear is intertwined with perceptual, cognitive, and motor development. Whereas startles and cries of pain are physiological reactions, fear is a psychological response that indicates that the infant attaches some meaning to the situation (Waters, Matas, & Sroufe, 1975). For an infant to be afraid of strangers, she must have more or less clear mental images of the people she knows. Forming mental images is one of the major steps in Piaget's theory of sensorimotor development (see Chapter 4). If she insists on her mother and father as caregivers and protests their departure, she must have some sense of "person permanence"—the emotional equivalent of object permanence (Bell & Ainsworth, 1972).

Reading Faces and Voices

Parents, developmental psychologists and others recognize and respond to infants' emotional communications. Is this a monologue, with infants doing all of the signaling and adults all of the interpreting? Do infants read the emotional messages of adults?

Infants respond to vocal messages earlier than they do to facial messages. Newborns react to the sound of another newborn crying by crying themselves (Sagi & Hoffman, 1967; Simner, 1971). If one baby in the maternity ward wails, the others soon join the chorus. It would be an exaggeration to describe contagious crying as empathy, but it does indicate that small infants respond to sounds of distress from another human being. Young infants also hear emotional overtones in their mothers' voices (Mehler, Bertoncini, Barriére, & Jassik-Gerschenfeld, 1978). At 6 weeks, the infant can distinguish his mother's voice from that of another woman if the mother speaks in a normal tone of voice. But if she speaks in a monotone, without any affect or feeling, the mother becomes a stranger to the infant. He does not react. This is not to say that a newborn knows whether his mother is feeling happy or sad, frustrated or triumphant. But he is attuned to emotional overtones.

There is clear evidence that by 8 or 9 months infants are reading faces and voices. How the infant responds to strangers at this age depends in part on the mother's emotional communications. In one experiment with mothers and infants (Boccia & Campos, 1983), mothers were asked to respond to a stranger who en-

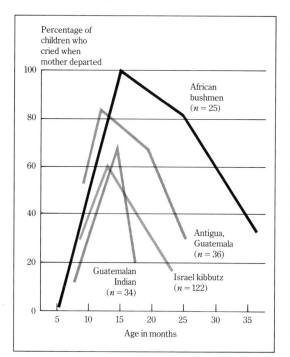

Figure 5-3 Separation Protest in Four Cultures
Children of different societies react with different intensities to fear of separation from their mothers. Whereas African bushman children were most prone to tears, children from Israeli kibbutzim cried the least. But all the children passed through this stage of fear.

(Kagan, 1974)

tered the room either by frowning and uttering an abrupt, unfriendly hello, or by issuing a cheerful greeting and smiling broadly at the stranger and at the baby. Infants whose mothers acted wary at the stranger's appearance were fearful. Their heart rates accelerated, they refused to smile, and often they fussed and cried. Those whose mothers acted happy to see the stranger were more interested than afraid.

James Sorce and colleagues (Sorce, Emde, Campos, & Klinnert, 1981) conducted a modified version of the visual cliff experiment with 1-year-olds. To make the situation ambiguous, the deep side of the cliff was raised from about 40 inches to 12 inches, a little more than the height of a stairstep. The mother was asked to attract the infant to the center of the table by smiling and dangling an interesting toy. When the baby reached the cliff, some of the mothers were asked to express alarm; others, to encourage the baby with smiles. As they approached the cliff, the infants typically looked at the drop,

then looked to their mothers. Fifteen of the twenty infants whose mothers smiled crawled across the deep side. Not one of the 17 babies whose mothers's looked afraid ventured across; most of these backed away in haste.

The videotapes of this experiment (Figure 5-4) illustrate social referencing. *Social referencing* is using emotional cues from significant others to regulate one's own behavior in uncertain situations (Lamb & Campos, 1982). The infants searched their mothers' faces for emotional information and used it to orient their own behavior. Emotional communication between the mother and infant has expanded to include third parties or events in the environment—in this case, the visual cliff.

The infant's attention to social cues is clearly adaptive. Social referencing creates opportunities for the infant to learn vicariously. The infant doesn't have to discover through painful experience that heights are dangerous or that fire burns. Rather, he learns to avoid these dangers by observing his parents' emotional reactions to near-misses. Perhaps one reason why infants protest separation from parents is that they are losing a valuable source of information.

Theories of Emotional Development

Where do emotions come from? Why do smiles, separation protest, and other expressions of

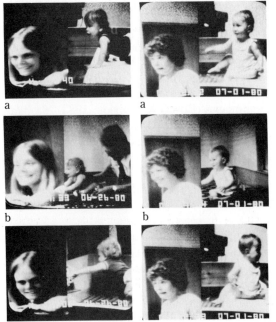

a a

b b

c c

Figure 5-4 Reading Emotions These photographs illustrate the adaptive value of reading emotion messages—and perhaps why the inexperienced infant is distressed when his mother departs. The 12-month-old infant on the left (a) reaches the edge of the visual cliff and looks down; (b) looks up to the mother who is smiling broadly; and (c) proceeds confidently across the cliff. The infant on the right, also 12 months old, (a) looks down when she reaches the visual cliff; (b) looks up to her mother, whose face expresses intense fear; and (c) backs away from the deep side in hasty retreat.

(Sorce, Emde, Campos, & Klinnert, 1981)

emotion develop when they do? There are at least three schools of thought on these questions (Lamb & Campos, 1982). Learning theorists, as one would guess, hold that emotions are learned through reinforcement and imitation. Ethologists maintain that emotions are part of our species' genetic program for survival. Cognitive psychologists argue that emotional development depends on intellectual development. Here we will analyze the strengths and weaknesses of each of these theories, then look at a recent synthesis.

Learning Theory

Learning theory holds that emotions, like all other behavior, are learned. According to this view, infants come into the world with a set of simple responses—what behaviorist John Watson (1930) called reactions X, Y, and Z. Infants respond in different ways to cuddling, loud noises, and restriction such as swaddling. But the expression of emotions and the attachment of feelings to different people and situations—*or translating reactions into emotions*—are the result of learning. Knowingly or unknowingly, parents and others teach infants how and what to feel. The notion that responding whenever an infant cries is spoiling the baby is based on this view.

In one of his most famous experiments, Watson demonstrated that infants can be taught fear through classical conditioning (Watson & Raynor, 1920). When little Albert first came to Watson's laboratory, he enjoyed playing with a friendly white rat. On subsequent visits Watson sounded a loud gong soon after Alfred began playing with the animal. Watson reported that after a few repetitions of this experience, the infant began to whimper the moment he saw the rat. He claimed that the child's distress soon spread to the way he responded to other furry white things—including Watson's hair! Yvonne Brackbill (1958) reported that operant condi-

tioning could increase or decrease smiling. Four-month-olds who were picked up, cuddled, and talked to when they smiled spontaneously began to smile more often—and cry less. Social learning theorists such as Albert Bandura (1969) emphasize the role of imitation in emotional development.

Learning theory helps to explain why infants become afraid of, or attached to, different people and situations. (No wonder little Alfred feared Watson!) It shows how rewards and punishments can affect the frequency and intensity of the baby's emotional responses. But learning theory does not explain timetables of emotional development. Why do all normal infants begin to smile at about 6 weeks of age? We know that social smiling is not the result of imitation, for blind babies, who never see a smile, begin smiling at this time also (Fraiberg, 1974). Why do infants suddenly become wary of strangers? Their parents are not afraid of most strangers; infants do not learn this through observation or reinforcement. Indeed, 8- or 9-month-olds frequently embarrass their parents by pouting or crying when the mother's favorite aunt tries to pick them up. Learning theory does not explain the *onset* of emotions: where they come from, and why they appear when they do.

Ethological Theory

Ethologists focus on the evolutionary origins and genetically programmed aspects of emotion. Charles Darwin pioneered this approach in *The Expression of Emotions in Man and Animals* (1975). Darwin observed, first, that smiles, frowns, looks of disgust, and other human expressions of emotion are universal. They have the same meaning and are used in the same ways by members of primitive and literate societies. (Contemporary cross-cultural research by Ekman & Friesen, 1972, and Izard, 1971, supports this.) Second, Darwin saw similarities between the facial expressions and gestures of humans and those of the great apes, which presumably reflect our common ancestry. Third, he argued that the expression of emotions is adaptive. For example, by assuming a submissive posture, an animal can prevent attack by a more powerful member of its species. Individuals who know when to give in and who can communicate this stand a better chance of survival than those who do not. Darwin suggested that an angry face in humans might serve a number of adaptive functions. The lowering of the eyebrows and narrowing of the eyes shield the eyes from direct sunlight and may improve vision. The flaring of the nostrils may promote rapid intake of oxygen. The open mouth may be left over from a time when our distant ancestors attacked with their teeth. In Darwin's words, "We may suspect . . . that our semi-human progenitors uncovered their canine teeth when preparing for battle as we still do when feeling ferocious or when merely sneering at or defying someone without any intention of making a real attack with our teeth" (1975, pp. 251–52). Darwin saw the expression of emotions as part of our species' evolutionary heritage.

Carroll Izard (1977), a contemporary disciple of Darwin, agrees. In his view, just as the ability to discriminate different tastes is inborn, so is the ability to experience and react to different emotions. Izard has used his studies of facial expressions in infants (see p. 184) to chart the development of emotions (see Table 5-2). He

Table 5-2   Izard's Timetable for Infant Emotions

Expression of Fundamental Emotions	Approximate Time of Emergence
Interest Neonatal smile* (a half-smile that appears spontaneously and for no apparent reason) Startled response* Distress* (in response to pain) Disgust	Present at birth
Social smile	4–6 weeks
Anger Surprise Sadness	3–4 months
Fear Shame/Shyness/Self-awareness	5–7 months 6–8 months
Contempt Guilt	2nd year of life

*The neonatal smile, the startled response, and distress in response to pain are precursors of the social smile and the emotions of surprise and sadness, which appear later. Izard has no evidence that they are related to inner feelings when they are seen in the first few weeks of life.
(Trotter, 1983)

argues that different emotions emerge when they help the child to adapt to a new situation. The newborn expresses only interest, distress, and disgust. *Interest* is adaptive because it causes the newborn to pay attention to the environment and thus promotes cognitive development. The expression of *distress* is adaptive for summoning caretakers. *Disgust* mobilizes the infant to expel noxious substances that might threaten her survival.

In the expression of emotions humans betray their primate origins. Shown here is the tense-mouth expression typical of dominant males (and heads of state).

Anger emerges at about the same time as voluntary motor activity. Anger would not be adaptive for an infant because she is not physically mature enough to deal with a disagreeable situation; an older infant may be capable of pushing something unpleasant away. According to Izard, *fear* appears just before locomotion. Fear would not be adaptive for a baby, who has no means of fleeing the threat; an older infant is mobile.[3] Fear also serves the adaptive function of making the infant more cautious in her independent explorations of the environment.

Ethologists stress the reciprocal nature of emotional communication. An infant's cry is not simply a venting of internal distress; it is a signal to caregivers that something is wrong and must be changed. The genetically programmed expression of distress is adaptive because adults are programmed to respond to the infant's signal. Both partners are disoriented when their emotional communication does not conform to the human norm. One- to 3-month-old infants are upset when their mothers sit very still, speak in a monotone, and keep a blank face, making themselves emotionally unavailable (Cohn & Tronick, 1982). Mothers report that they are distressed by the bland facial expression of blind babies (Fraiberg, 1974) and the slow responses and muted smiles of babies with Down's syndrome (Emde & Brown, 1978).

Ethologists offer hypotheses about the evolutionary origins of emotions and why they emerge in infancy. But they leave unanswered the question of *how* infants' emotions change.

Cognitive Theory

Cognitive theory deals with how emotions develop and change. One of the first cognitive theories of emotional development grew from a study of spontaneous expressions of fear in chimpanzees. Donald Hebb (1946) hypothesized that repeated experiences create memory traces in the chimpanzee brain in the form of neurological circuits. Discrepancies, or slight changes in experience, upset these circuits. When a chimp encounters something that is similar enough to previous experiences to activate this neurological circuit, but not similar enough to complete the circuit, normal mental functions are derailed. The chimp is scared. Hebb maintained that something unlike anything the chimp had ever seen before, or something familiar, would not produce this effect.

Jerome Kagan has expanded and revised Hebb's theory and applied it to infants (Kagan, Kearsley, & Zelazo, 1978). For Hebb's neurological circuits, Kagan substitutes schemes, or mental images.[4] In the first weeks of life, the infant has no memories or expectations; everything is new. She responds to new people and events with interest. (This is the stage of indiscriminate smiling and sociability.) As her schemes become more elaborate and she grows older, she begins to develop hypotheses about the environment, or simple rules about what goes with what. When something violates her expectations and she has no ready response, she is afraid.

Infants are interested in strangers at 3 or 4 months, but they are fearful of them at 8 or 9 months. At the younger age, their schemes are not fixed and discrepancies do not upset them. When they are older, their rules say that a familiar adult should be there to protect and comfort them. As demonstrated by the visual cliff, and by their responses to strangers, the onset of fear reflects cognitive development. An infant's perception of people and objects becomes more accurate with age. She has a growing store of memories, and she engages in more careful

---

[3]Izard's timetable for the emergence of fear is earlier than that of other researchers, perhaps because he concentrates on facial expressions.

[4]Kagan's use of the term "scheme" is similar, but not identical, to Piaget's. Piaget stressed the internalization of motor habits. A child can use a scheme to think about an activity without actually performing the activity: The action becomes the thought. Kagan emphasizes the child's comparison of present experiences with *memories* of past experiences.

comparisons of what she sees with what she expects. She cries when her expectations are not met.

This theory predicts that the development of an emotional response takes the form of an inverted U (see Figure 5-5). For example, when faced with a novel task, the infant is sober. Discrepancy interests him more than novelty does. After some exposure, he tries to fit the new experience into his existing schemes. As he begins to comprehend the task, his smiling increases. The effort to understand it is rewarding and pleasant. The harder he works at it, the more he smiles. Once he has mastered the task, however, his interest and smiling decrease. If he fails to assimilate or accommodate the new information, however, he is distressed. The same pattern occurs when the infant is exposed to new people, places, and things.

Cognitive theories emphasize the roles of perception, memory, and the infant's active efforts to understand the environment in emotional development. The infant is not portrayed as a blank slate on which parents and others inscribe emotions (learning theory) or as a creature whose expressions of joy and fear are ticked off by a genetically powered biological clock (ethological theory).

The main criticism of cognitive theories is that they imply that the development of emotions is all in the infant's head. Emotions are mostly a form of cognition. Cognitive theories tend to ignore temperament on one hand, and the context on the other. They do not explain why different infants at the same cognitive level react to the same event in different ways (Campos, Hiatt, Ramsay, Henderson, & Svejda, 1978; Scarr & Salapatek, 1970). Nor do they explain why the same infant responds to the same event in different ways on different occasions (Sroufe, Waters, & Matas, 1974). Being dropped from a height may elicit panic or glee, depending on the situation. If a strange adult puts on a mask, most infants cringe and turn away. If the mother puts on the same mask, most laugh. Moreover, infants are much more likely to react negatively to a stranger in an unfamiliar laboratory than they are in their homes. Cognitive theories of emotion do not explain these different responses.

A Synthesis

In a recent article, Joseph Campos, Karen Barrett, and their coauthors (Campos, Barrett,

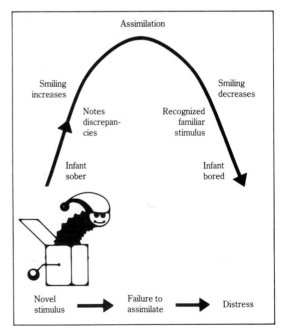

Figure 5-5 The Curve of Smiling

Table 5-3   Five Basic Emotions: A Synthesis of Cognitive, Ethological, and Learning Theories

Emotion	Goal	Perception	Action Tendency	Adaptive Functions
Joy	Any significant object	Goal is perceived or anticipated	Approaching with increased energy	Reinforces successful actions; leads to rehearsal of new skills and willingness to accept new challenges; sends social message to others to join the action
Anger	Any significant object	Obstacle to attaining goal, which will not easily be removed	Elimination of obstacle	Restores progress toward the goal; changes other people's behavior; and (later in development) revenge.
Sadness	Securing or maintaining contact with a person or object	Goal is unattainable	Disengagement	Conserves energy; eventually leads to redirection toward new goals; elicits nurturance from others.
Fear	Survival and (later in development) maintaining self-esteem	Protective action must be taken	Flight, withdrawal	Survival; avoiding pain; alerting others to avoid situation or to help
Interest	Involvement in a task or event	Information to be gathered	Gathering and processing information	Acquires information from the environment; communicates to others a willingness to start a relationship and consider joint action

(Adapted from Campos, Barrett, Lamb, Goldsmith & Stenberg, 1983)

Lamb, Goldsmith, & Stenberg, 1983) offer a new theory of emotional development that synthesizes the three views presented here. Campos and Barrett see emotional growth as a special form of information processing that relates to *goals and strivings*. In their view, people do not react emotionally to a situation or event unless they feel that they have something at stake. This applies to infants as well as to adults. Adding goals and strivings to the emotional equation explains why an unexpected snowfall produces joy in one person (she wants to go skiing), anger in another (he wants to watch football, not shovel the sidewalk), and fear in another (he has to drive 200 miles and does not have snow tires on his car). The infant's varied emotional responses in different contexts and at different stages of development are brought on by her goals and strivings at these different times. As the infant's goals change, so do her emotions.

Campos and Barrett agree with cognitive theorists that whether an infant responds emotionally, and how he responds, depend on his understanding or "appreciation" of the situation. For example, an infant will not fuss when he sees the baby-sitter unless he realizes that this means his parents are going out that evening. But in their view, emotions are more than "cold cognition." They agree with ethologists that some emotions are universal, have a long evolutionary history, and are genetically programmed. These emotions became part of our species' program because they are adaptive. But Campos and Barrett add that socialization or learning can alter emotions in significant ways.

Campos and Barrett identify five basic emotions: joy, anger, sadness, fear, and interest (see Table 5-3). These emotions originate in biological goals: in striving to breathe, to obtain food, and otherwise to maintain physical integrity. Present in rudimentary form in the early months of life, these emotions become more complex over the course of development.

One reason emotions change is cognitive development. A newborn may express anger when she is swaddled and prevented from exercising motor reflexes; an 8-month-old is angered when her mother puts the ring of keys she was happily banging on the floor out of reach (a physical obstacle); a 4-year-old is angered when her father tells her to send her imaginary playmate home (a symbolic obstacle); a 10-year-old is angered by an insult (a more highly symbolic and complex obstacle); and so on. The infant's emotions also change as a result of socialization. Every culture has rules about the expression of emotions, such as when it is and is not appropriate to display emotions ("don't laugh in church") and who should and should not express certain emotions ("big boys don't cry"). Socialization modifies existing emotions and creates new ones. Shame, guilt, envy, and depression—complex emotions that involve comparisons of the self with others—reflect the development of socialized goals. In short, Campos and his colleagues emphasize the interplay among biological factors (innate emotions and

temperament), cognitive development, and socialization in emotional development.

Social Development

We asked a mother we know how she felt about her week-old son. "I'm in love!" she exclaimed. Already she was enthralled by the courtship dance described at the beginning of this chapter. At 6 weeks, her son had become an active partner in the dance, rewarding her care and attention with smiles and gurgles. But many months would pass before he returned her special affection. And it would be years before he began to make friends.

Babies are not very interested in other babies. During the first two years of life, the infant's social world is comprised of adults. His first social relationships are with the people who care for him. They are his first playmates, his first loves, and perhaps his first enemies. In western societies his caregivers are usually (but not always) his parents, especially his mother. In this section we look at the development of attachment in infants, consider the importance of mothers and fathers, then analyze the impact of day-care on a small child's social and emotional development.

Attachment in Other Species

In some species, the young become attached to their mothers shortly after birth. This is called **imprinting**. Baby swans, chickens, sheep, llamas, and other animals who follow their mothers at birth are genetically programmed to latch onto the first moving object they see. Under normal conditions this is their mother. Her image becomes so imprinted on their minds in the sensitive period after birth that it cannot be erased. They follow her, and only her, wherever she goes. Konrad Lorenz (1970) demonstrated imprinting by presenting himself to a gaggle of goslings at this critical time. They treated Lorenz as a Mother Goose in their youth, following him and ignoring other geese. When they reached maturity they were sexually attracted to humans rather than to members of their own species. Lambs, calfs, baby gnus, and other animals whose survival depends on their ability to move with a herd within hours after birth and to identify their own mother are similar. In the nursery rhyme, Mary's little lamb followed her to school—clearly a case of mistaken imprinting. Humans are *not* like sheep or goats.[5] Infants of our species form attachments more gradually, and the strength and duration of these attachments varies from infant to infant.

The Development of Attachment in Human Infants

In humans, **attachment** is an enduring emotional tie to a specific person. We can say that an infant is attached to someone when (1) he stays close to the person, (2) becomes distressed when he is separated from that person, (3) shows joy and relief when the person returns, and (4) is oriented toward that person when they are not interacting—he watches that person's movements, listens for the person's voice, and attempts to capture his or her attention whenever he can (Maccoby, 1980). Attachment may not be "love" in the mature sense of caring for another person, but it is certainly desire and longing.

John Bowlby (1969) has identified four phases in the development of attachment:

Phase 1. Indiscriminate sociability (birth to 2 months). The newborn uses cries to attract adults to her. She uses rooting, grasping, and, by the middle of her second month, smiling and vocalizations to keep adults near her. She is predisposed to initiate and respond to social interaction. But she uses her charms indiscriminately. As long as someone responds to her, she is content.

---

[5]Sheep, geese, and other species whose young are mature enough to follow their mothers shortly after birth are called *precocial* animals. Robins, cats, rats and other species whose young stay in a nest under their mothers' or parents' care and protection until they are mature enough to venture forth are called *altricial* animals. Humans are more like robins than like geese.

Konrad Lorenz with several of his imprintees. If humans were programmed this way, babies might develop into adults who fall in love with mobiles or teddy bears.

Phase 2. Discriminating sociability (2 to 6 months). The infant begins to discriminate among people, to recognize her caregivers, and to show a preference for them. These changes are subtle. She soothes more easily when they hold her and smiles more often at them. She adds playful behavior to her repertoire for holding a favored adult's attention. But she is still friendly to other people.

Phase 3. Specific attachments (7 to 24 months). The emergence of intentional behavior and independent locomotion lead to phase 3 and enduring, affectionate attachments to specific people. For the first time, the infant protests when a person to whom she is attached leaves her. Her caregivers are no longer replaceable; she knows whom she wants and makes her preferences known. For the first time, she can use her newly acquired mobility to stay close to attachment figures. She creeps or crawls to follow her mother or another valued person around the house. Her behavior is more purposeful and goal-directed. She uses her motor abilities deliberately, to influence others.

Phase 4. Partnerships (over 24 months). Relationships in phase 3 are limited by what Piaget called egocentrism (see Chapter 6). According to Bowlby, on or around her second birthday the child begins to understand that other people have different needs and desires, which she begins to take into account. Soon, language will help her to negotiate mutually agreeable plans with her mother or another person—but only when she wants to. Attachments gradually give way to the more mature relationships Bowlby calls "goal-corrected partnerships." The child becomes more willing and better able to interact with peers and unfamiliar adults.

Variations in Attachment

All babies form attachments in the second half of their first year. But the intensity of this bond varies from infant to infant. Mary Ainsworth and her colleagues (Ainsworth, Blehar, Waters, & Wall, 1978) devised a research procedure called the *Strange Situation* to assess differences among infants in the quality of attachment. In this procedure, a mother and her infant are taken to an observation room that is well supplied with toys.[6] The mother puts the infant on the floor, sits in a chair, and allows him to explore. After a few minutes, a strange woman enters the room and engages the mother in conversation. Observers note how the child reacts to the stranger's presence. Then the stranger approaches the child and attempts to play with him. The mother slips quietly out of the room, leaving her handbag on the chair as a sign to the infant that she will return. Observers note how the infant reacts to her departure and how he greets her when she returns. The stranger

[6]The procedure has also been used with fathers.

This infant demonstrates John Bowlby's phase 3. According to Bowlby's theory, attachment to one or a few caregivers, separation protest, and fear of strangers during this stage of development are part of the genetic program for becoming human.

Table 5-4 Summary of Episodes of the Strange Situation

Number of Episode	Persons Present	Duration	Brief Description of Action
1	Mother, baby, and observer	30 seconds	Observer introduces mother and baby to experimental room, then leaves.
2	Mother and baby	3 minutes	Mother is nonparticipant while baby explores; if necessary, play is stimulated after 2 minutes
3	Stranger, mother, and baby	3 minutes	Stranger enters. Minute 1: stranger silent. Minute 2: stranger converses with mother. Minute 3: stranger approaches baby. After 3 minutes mother leaves unobtrusively.
4	Stranger and baby	3 minutes* or less	First separation episode. Stranger's behavior is geared to that of baby.
5	Mother and baby	3 minutes** or more	First reunion episode. Mother greets and comforts baby, then tries to settle him again in play. Mother then leaves, saying "bye-bye."
6	Baby alone	3 minutes* or less	Second separation episode.
7	Stranger and baby	3 minutes* or less	Continuation of second separation. Stranger enters and gears her behavior to that of baby.
8	Mother and baby	3 minutes	Second reunion episode. Mother enters, greets baby, then picks him up. Meanwhile stranger leaves unobtrusively.

(Campos et al., 1983)
*Episode is curtailed if the baby is unduly distressed.
**Episode is prolonged if more time is required for the baby to become reinvolved in play.

leaves and the mother settles him back into play. Then she leaves the room again, this time calling "bye-bye." The stranger enters the room and attempts to interact with the infant. Then the mother returns. Unless the infant is too upset to continue, observers watch and record the child's responses to eight episodes of departure and reunion (see Table 5-4).

Ainsworth found three different patterns of response to the mother's presence or absence. *Securely attached infants* (about 60 percent of her sample) use their mothers as a base for exploration. They stay close to them for the first few moments, but soon begin to explore the room and its toys. They move back toward their mothers when the stranger enters the room, but usually smile at the stranger from the safety of their mother's side. They are upset when their mothers leave. Some cry; some become immobilized, holding a toy but not playing

with it. When their mothers return, they greet them with joy and obvious relief. Some infants do not fully trust their mothers, however. *Ambivalently attached infants* (about 20 percent of the sample) are reluctant to explore the room or play with the toys. Some cling to their mother's side, hiding from the stranger. They are intensely distressed when their mothers leave, but difficult to soothe when they return. Some push her away angrily. *Avoidant infants* (about 10 percent of Ainsworth's sample) are also somewhat slow to explore. What distinguishes them from the other infants is that they avoid their mothers when they return, ignoring their greetings. Some are friendlier to the stranger than to their mothers. While ambivalent infants seem to be afraid that their mothers will never return—and angry at them when they do—avoidant infants almost seem afraid of their mothers.

This research challenged the common assumption that an infant who is "tied to his mother's apron strings" will grow into an immaturely dependent adult. Ainsworth argues that attachment *promotes* autonomy. Ideally, attachment figures provide a secure base from which the child can explore the world and learn ways of coping with it. They also give the child a safe haven when he feels uncertain or threatened.

Ainsworth traced the origins of ambivalent and avoident attachment, to disturbed parent–infant partnerships. In one study, she and her colleagues observed 26 white, middle-class mother-and-infant pairs in their homes during the infants' first year (Ainsworth, Bell, & Stayton, 1971). Mothers were rated for sensitivity (defined as whether they responded to their infant's signals or let their own wishes and activities dictate schedules, acceptance (whether they accepted being "tied down" by the infant or resented the infant's demands), cooperation (whether they respected the baby's autonomy or imposed their own will on the child), and accessibility (whether they were usually aware of what the infant was doing or too preoccupied with their own activities to notice). Researchers gave particular attention to the mother's style of feeding the infant.

Ainsworth concluded that securely attached infants had consistently sensitive, responsive mothers. The mothers were alert to the baby's signals, moods, and preferences; let the baby stop to play during a meal if he wanted to; and accepted interruptions and frustrations as part of being a mother. The mothers of ambivalently attached and avoidant infants tended to be rejecting, interfering, or inconsistent in their treatment. The concept of "sensitive responsiveness" is an important one. Ainsworth argued that mothering is not something a woman does *to* the baby, but that it is a reciprocal process, an active dialogue between mother and infant.

Other researchers have investigated how different patterns of attachment affect cognitive and social development. For example, Leah Matas and colleagues (Matas, Arend, & Sroufe, 1978) presented 2-year-olds with difficult problems for children their age. Those who had been rated as securely attached as infants were enthusiastic about the task, listened to directions, tolerated failure, and asked for help when they needed it. In contrast, those who had been rated as ambivalent or avoidant ignored directions, quickly became frustrated with the task, got angry at their mothers or at the materials, and gave up. The first group approached learning as a game, not a test, and performed better. There is some evidence that these effects carry over into later years and other areas of development. Waters and colleagues (Waters, Wippman, & Sroufe, 1979) found that children who had been securely attached as infants were better adjusted to school at 5 years than their insecure peers were. According to their teachers and other observers, they were popular, outgoing, empathetic, and high in self-esteem. Children at age five who had been insecurely attached as infants were hesitant and shy or hostile and aggressive—in short, less socially competent.

The moral of this research is clear: Mothers have a direct impact on the child's development. Ainsworth and her colleagues clearly believe that some styles of mothering are good—and that others are not. (A profile of Mary Ainsworth appears at the end of this chapter.) While this is undoubtedly true, some psychologists disagree with their analysis of attachment.

A Critique of Attachment Theory

One critic of attachment theory is Jerome Kagan (1984), who sees a number of flaws in the use and interpretation of the Strange Situation. One "troublesome fact," according to Kagan, is that the quality of attachment is not very stable. In

Insight

THE IMPORTANCE OF MOTHER: A FREUDIAN VIEW

To Freudian psychologists, the mother–infant relationship is not just the most important relationship in the infant's life, it is the *only* important tie. In Freud's words, it is "unique, without parallel, established unalterably as the prototype of all later love relationships . . . for both sexes" (1949, p. 48). This view has had a profound impact on both the practice of clinical psychology and social policy in the United States. For example, Aid to Families with Dependent Children, or welfare, is based on the belief that infants and small children need full-time mothers.

Contemporary Freudians focus on ego development in infancy. The ego is the part of the personality that organizes perceptions, cognition, emotions, and social behavior. The ego mediates between the id (sexual and aggressive drives, which are present from birth) and the superego (moral and ethic imperatives, which develop in later childhood). Freudians hold that the mother plays a pivotal role in ego development. She is the one who gratifies the infant's longings (for food, contact, and so on) on one hand, and frustrates his desires (by weaning, toilet training, and so on) on the other. It is through interaction and identification with the mother that the infant learns to cope with reality. The child's future mental health depends on his relationship with his mother in infancy.

Margaret Mahler's theory of separation and individuation (Mahler, Pine, & Bergman, 1975) illustrates this view. Mahler's theory is based on clinical observations, not experimental data. Most developmental psychologists would disagree with her timing of attachments and description of the consequences of different patterns of attachment. But she has had a major influence on the practice of psychoanalysis.

Autistic Phase (birth to 2 months). The infant is dominated by internal sensations. She can distinguish between pleasure and pain, tension and relief, but little else. The infant's developmental task in this stage is to recognize the mother's role in reducing tension. Failure to accomplish this task results in autism, or the inability to distinguish between internal states and external events.

Symbiotic Phase (2 to 5 months). The infant develops a feeling of symbiosis, or mutual dependency, with the mother. She experiences herself and her mother as one organism, and assumes that her wishes are as all-important to her mother as they are to her. The developmental task in this stage is to establish "mutual cuing," a reliable pattern of emotional expression and response. Failure to accomplish this task can lead to a distorted sense of reality, parasitic relationships, and panic and rage when others do not gratify the individual's every need.

Separation-Individuation (5 to 36 months). Mahler describes this stage as a "second birth experience." The child has two developmental tasks: recognizing that other people are not part of the self, or separation, and developing an identity as an autonomous person, or individuation. The first step is for the infant to distinguish the mother from other people and to develop a preference for her. The next step occurs when independent locomotion enables the infant to practice moving away from the mother, and also to seek her out for "emotional refueling." Between 15 and 22 months, the infant's wish to be independent but her need for security lead to a rapprochement. She seems more attached to her mother than she was before. If the mother is consistently available, the infant will be able to internalize a stable image of the mother that she can recall in the mother's absence. The infant also comes to accept the fact that her needs and wishes and those of her mother sometimes conflict. If the child fails to achieve separation and individuation, she enters a lifelong struggle between the desire for fusion with another person and fears of annihilation by that person.

one study (Thompson, Lamb, & Estes, 1982), half of the infants tested in the Strange Situation at 12 and 18 months changed classification.

A second problem is that the Strange Situation may measure differences in temperament, not differences in the quality of attachment. Infants who are not easily frightened might have a very close relationship with their mother. Yet they might not cry when she leaves or feel a need to scramble to her side when she returns. These easygoing, independent youngsters would probably be considered insecurely attached or classified as "avoidant." The infants Ainsworth and her colleagues classify as "ambivalent" might be those Thomas and Chess called "difficult": infants who are upset by almost any new situation. They may be in such an extreme state of distress, and so busy sobbing, that when their mother returns they are unable to accept comfort. But the reason lies in their own temperamental vulnerability, not in their relationship with their mother. Kagan cites studies in West Germany and Japan that suggest that one of the best predictors of responses to the Strange Situation is measurement of temperament at 10 days of age.

Kagan also objects to the implied value judgments in Ainsworth's system of classification. Children who do not cry in the Strange Situation (and therefore would be classified as avoidant) may have developed adaptive coping strategies for dealing with stress. The reason they do not cry may be that their mother encourages independence and self-control, not that the mother is rejecting. Many of the studies that use the Strange Situation as a measure of attachment do not assess the mother's attitudes and behavior. In one study that did (Hock & Clinger, 1981), mothers of securely attached infants complained that their child was not very self-reliant but added that they felt they were irreplaceable in their infant's life. The mothers of infants rated as less securely attached were more likely to have professional careers and to encourage self-reliance and control of fear in their child. Children of these mothers had had more experience with unfamiliar settings and people. Kagan questions the implication that early independence is harmful to the child or a measure of a poor relationship between mother and child.

Finally, Kagan suggests that a procedure in a strange setting that takes an average of six to eight minutes is not a fair sample of a "history of interaction between mother and infant comprising over a half-million minutes in the home" (1984, pp. 62–63). But he adds that "the concept of attachment remains useful and should not be abandoned" (p. 63).

Mother Love: Myths and Facts

If attachment is a vital part of human development, what is the impact of *de*tachment on small children? Put another way, how important is "mother love"? A number of researchers (for example, Goldfarb, 1943) have found that children who had been placed in institutions as infants score lower on intelligence tests than those who had been placed in foster homes. The institutionalized children are slow to speak, had difficulty reading, and showed other symptoms of mental retardation. Other researchers trace antisocial, delinquent behavior in adolescents to a history of "broken homes" and frequent or prolonged separations from the mother.

John Bowlby has argued that even temporary separations could cause psychological harm. He found that children who are hospitalized go through three stages of mourning. The first stage is protest. The child is angry and distressed, and rejects the efforts of other adults to comfort him. The second stage is despair. The child is apathetic and withdrawn, as if he has given up all hope of being reunited with his parents. In the third stage despair gives way to detachment. The child no longer seems to care about his family. Bowlby sees this as a defense mechanism that may prevent the child from ever caring deeply about anyone. The child defends himself from abandonment by becoming psychologically detached: If he doesn't care, being abandoned won't hurt.

In 1951, Bowlby wrote that "mother love in infancy and childhood is as important for mental health as are vitamins and proteins for physical health." This quotation is from a monograph published by the World Health Organization that was designed to call attention to deplorable conditions and "crass indifference [to children's] sensitivities" in hospitals and other institutions. Taken out of context, Bowlby's statement on mother love is easily misread. Freudian psychologists do hold that the mother is uniquely important to the infant's emotional and social development; Bowlby does not. He and Ainsworth agree that an infant needs to form an attachment to a responsive, caring, available adult. In most cases this is the child's mother. But the attachment figure need not be the child's biological mother; it need not be the person who cares for him; and it need not be female. The father, a grandparent, an adoptive or foster parent, or a nanny can serve just as well. Bowlby holds that infants are predisposed to form one primary attachment (a tendency which he calls "monotropy"). But he does not maintain that an infant has one and only one "true love." Most infants have a hierarchy of attachment figures. One person may be the infant's favorite haven of safety, but others can stop in when she or he is not available. Despite Bowlby's qualifications, he and other psychologists are often interpreted as saying that an infant needs his mother 24 hours a day, day in and day out.

In *Maternal Deprivation Reassessed* (1981), the British psychiatrist Michael Rutter updates

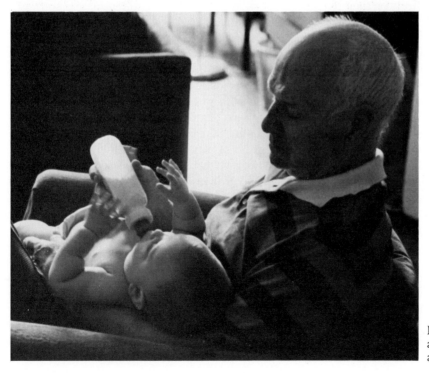

Mothers are not the only adults who can serve as attachment figures.

Bowlby's monograph with contemporary research. What psychologists once saw as symptoms of a single syndrome caused by maternal deprivation they now see as distinct problems, some of which have little to do with the mother. It is true that infants who are placed in institutions in their first year may become intellectually retarded. The primary reason for their retardation is not separation, but that some institutions do not provide adequate perceptual and linguistic stimulation. Infants are not exposed to the varied sights, sounds, and smells found in a home. Nurses do not have much time to play with and talk to each baby. Stimulation is necessary for cognitive growth; care by one's biological mother is not. Children reared in foster homes from infancy can show normal intelligence at 8 years, even though some have been exposed to as many as 80 surrogate parents (Tizard & Hodges, 1978). This highly disrupted upbringing can have ill effects on their psychosocial development, but apparently not on their intellectual growth.

Mourning is not an inevitable consequence of hospitalization. About one in twenty preschool children who require hospitalization do show signs of the "acute distress syndrome" that Bowlby compared to mourning. But their distress is a response to the strange hospital environment and to the lack of opportunity to form new attachments (caregivers change shifts every eight hours and take days off) as well as to separation from their families. Children who are told what to expect and are familiarized with the people who will care for them in the hospital are not emotionally wounded by the experience (Ferguson, 1979).

Delinquency and conduct disorders can indeed be traced to broken homes. But here again, the problem is not separation from the mother or father as such. There is no evidence that the death of a parent leads to these behavioral problems. But discord and disharmony in the home before and after a divorce can contribute to such problems. The context in which the separation takes place, and the quality of care the infant receives thereafter, count for more than separation itself. Many British children were separated from their parents and sent to the countryside to escape the bombings of London during World War II. Few showed any of the disturbances commonly attributed to maternal deprivation (Rutter, 1981). In short, mother love can be (and usually is) important; but it is not indispensable.

Fathers and Other Playmates

Until ten or fifteen years ago, fathers were "missing persons" in research on infant development. Studies of fatherhood focused on the impact on the young child of the father's death or departure, not on his presence. The rediscovery of fathers has added interesting twists to the story of attachment.

Fathers are as enchanted by their first contacts with their red, wrinkled newborns as mothers are. One team of researchers (Parke & Sawin, 1980) observed fathers feeding their 3-month-olds. They used the same scales of sensitivity to rate fathers as Ainsworth used with mothers. Fathers responded to their infant's cues by adjusting the pace of feeding or the intensity of play—just as mothers do. It seems, however, that they rarely use this skill. When asked to demonstrate their competence for a researcher, fathers perform well. But under normal circumstances, most yield caretaking responsibility to their wives.

Do infants become attached to their fathers? Yes, they do. Infants begin to protest separation from their fathers at about 7 months—the same age at which they begin clinging to their mothers. At home, infants approach their fathers, smile at them, vocalize to them, and seek contact with and comfort from them as often as from their mothers (Lamb, 1977,

1979). When fathers are substituted for mothers in the Strange Situation, infants use them as a secure base for exploration and a safe haven when confronted with a stranger. They show distress when he leaves the room and relief when he returns. They much prefer the father to a strange female (Cohen & Campos, 1974). When both parents are present, however, they are more likely to seek comfort from the mother. In stress-free situations infants seem equally attached to both parents. When they are tired, frightened, or in a strange situation (such as the laboratory) they run or crawl to their mothers.

This is not to say that fathers are simply good mother substitutes. A number of studies have shown that fathers and mothers have distinct styles of parenting and provide their infants with different kinds of experience. T. Berry Brazelton and his colleagues (Yogman et al., 1977) watched parents interact with their infants, who were from 2 to 24 weeks old. Mothers spoke softly to their babies, repeating words and phrases in a rhythmic pattern. Fathers talked less and touched their babies more, as if trying to excite them. Thomas Power and Ross Parke (Parke, 1981) watched fathers and mothers play with the 8-month-old infants in a laboratory playroom. Even when they played the same games with the child, there were differences in style. Mothers used a more attention-getting approach, showing the infant a toy from a distance and moving it around to get her to watch. Fathers had a more physical approach and played more bouncing and lifting games, especially with boys.

Michael Lamb (1977) found similar patterns at home. Fathers engaged infants in more rough-and-tumble play and invented new and unusual games. Mothers were more inclined to conventional games such as peek-a-boo and pat-a-cake, simulating toy games such as look-and-see, and reading. Fathers who take on primary responsibility for infant care while their wives work adopt some of the mothers' games but still prefer physical play (Field, 1978). These differences are not lost on the infant. In one study (Clarke-Stewart, 1978), two out of three toddlers preferred to play with their fathers when given a choice. According to small children, the fathers make better playmates.

Do babies need to play with other babies? Apparently they do not. Infants are interested in one another. A 2-month-old stares at another baby; a 4-month-old touches another baby; an 8-month-old smiles at peers. In play laboratories, infants seem fascinated by their older siblings. They follow them around, pick up toys they have abandoned, and sometimes attempt to imitate the older child (Lamb, 1978). But this behavior is not true play. There is almost no communication or give-and-take between babies. In the first year of life and in most of the second, infants are adult-oriented. They treat other infants much the way they treat toys; adults are their favorite and most frequent playmates, both in day-care situations and at home.

Day-Care: The Pros and Cons

Many infants in the United States spend most of their waking hours during the first two years of life with their mothers; but many do not. The number of working mothers in the United States has increased eightfold since 1940. Nearly 65 percent of mothers of children aged six to seventeen work outside their homes, and more than 40 percent of mothers of children under age three hold full-time or part-time jobs. Where are their children? The latest available data show that 19 percent of these infants and toddles are cared for by baby-sitters in their own homes; 54 percent are in day-care homes or family care (typically, a group of four to six youngsters cared for by a neighborhood mother with young children of her own, or an older woman who enjoys having small children in her home); and 27 percent in day-care centers (formal centers that handle larger numbers of children and are more like nursery schools) (Roupp & Travers, 1982).

Fifteen or twenty years ago, day-care was considered a necessary evil at best; at worst, it was seen to be equivalent to placing one's child in an orphanage. Many parents and psychologists believed that care outside the home was bad for all small children. These early fears were exaggerated.

THE IMPACT ON COGNITIVE DEVELOPMENT The impact of day-care on a child's development depends on both the child's developmental level and the quality of the care. A study of child-care arrangements in Bermuda (Schwarz, Scarr, & McCartney, 1983) found that youngsters who had been enrolled at day-care *centers* before their second birthdays did not do as well intellectually as other children did. But children placed in child-care *homes,* or cared for by sitters in their own homes, did just as well as children with full-time mothers. After age 3 these effects were reversed. Three- and 4-year-olds in day-care centers did better than children who remained at home with their mother or a sitter and better than those who are in family care at this age. This suggests that infants and toddlers benefit from the frequent one-on-one interaction with an adult in their own or another home. Day-

care centers, which have one caregiver for about eight children, cannot provide this. But preschoolers benefit from the greater number of opportunities to interact with peers and more extensive facilities (such as better playgrounds and more toys) at day-care centers.

Other researchers have found that *high quality* day-care has little or no effect on intellectual development (Belsky, Steinberg, & Walker, 1982). Children who attend good day-care programs do not lose cognitive ground. But neither do they accelerate, even when they attend "cognitively enriched" programs. The only exception to this rule are children from economically disadvantaged homes: Day-care has positive effects on these children. In play sessions they make more spontaneous efforts to communicate with an adult by showing and naming objects than do other children from similar back-

Day-care requirements depend in part on the age of the child. Older children can be happy playing among themselves, but infants need adults.

grounds (O'Connell & Farran, 1982). Their intelligence test scores remain stable during childhood—in contrast to other poor children whose scores often decline in the preschool years (McCartney & Scarr, in press; Ramey, Dorval, & Baker-Ward, 1981).

THE IMPACT ON SOCIAL AND EMOTIONAL DEVELOPMENT Does enrollment in day-care affect attachments? There is no evidence that day-care workers replace parents in the child's affections. Day-care children are just as attached to their mothers as home-care children are. They stay close to their mother, go to her when they are distressed or bored, and seek her attention and help more often than that of the day-care worker when both are in the room. They do not greet the day-care worker in the morning with the joy they display toward their mother in the evening (Clarke-Stewart & Fein, 1983).

But does day-care affect the *quality* of mother–infant attachments? Here the evidence is not so clear. One early study (Blehar, 1974) indicated that 30-month-old day-care children avoided their mother on reunions and 40-week-olds were ambivalent (clinging and angry) in the Strange Situation. But subsequent studies (for example, Kagan, Kearsley, & Zelazo, 1978) found few significant differences between home-care and day-care children. One reason for the earlier finding may be that at the time of the study, most people disapproved of putting an infant in day-care. Perhaps the parents felt guilty and their infant's behavior reflected this. Another reason may be that the children in the earlier study had been in day-care for only five months. Children may go through a period of temporary distress when they are first enrolled in day-care, just as many children do when they start nursery school (Belsky, 1985). But most children adjust.

The exceptions to this rule are infants who are enrolled in full-time day-care before their first birthday (Schwarz, 1984). Some psychologists see their behavior as a sign of precocious independence: They "ignore" their mothers because they are accustomed to interacting with people and toys in her absence and are habituated to her coming and going. Others see the same behavior as a sign of emotional insecurity. Both may be right (Clarke-Stewart & Fein, 1983). Day-care may heighten avoidance and ambivalence in young and insecurely attached infants *and* speed up the development of independence in older and securely attached infants.

Day-care seems to have both positive and negative effects on social development (Belsky, 1985). One- and 2-year-olds with group experience are more likely to approach an unfamiliar child; 3-year-olds are more likely to play *with* other children, not just beside them. But the same children are also more likely to issue commands, enforce rules, demand attention, and physically or verbally attack another child. They initiate more positive, friendly interaction and also more negative, aggressive interaction than do children reared at home. Teachers often report that they are quarrelsome, disobedient, and uncooperative. They tend to be peer-oriented and ready to disobey an adult to win peer attention and approval.

These effects are not seen in Sweden, however (Gunnarson, 1978). Day-care children in that country are no more or less cooperative and compliant than other youngsters are. This suggests that it is not day-care that makes children more socially active, aggressive, and peer-oriented, but the kind of care they receive in a center. Day-care programs reflect the society and culture in which they are found. American day-care teachers may be more tolerant of disobedience and aggression and less inclined to set behavioral standards than are adults from other cultures. Chinese-American parents often report that their children become too aggressive in day-care (Kagan et al., 1978). Perhaps what they are saying is that their youngsters are becoming "too American."

VARIATIONS IN DAY-CARE All day-care programs are not alike. The size of the program, the ratio of caregivers to children, the amount of training the caregivers have had, the consistency of care (staff turnover), and the physical safety and attractions vary widely. An infant whose babysitter takes her to the playground and the supermarket, and is ready to play whenever she is, will have different experiences from an infant who spends the day with a neighbor who "warehouses" six or seven babies in her apartment; an infant who goes to a large, formally structured day-care center with 60 or 70 children; or one who is enrolled in a university-based program whose staff works hand in hand with the psychology department. The number of children in a day-care facility seems to have a direct impact, especially on young infants (Roupp & Travers, 1982; Schwarz et al., 1983). Centers with child populations of 50 or 60 emphasize rules and routine care; there are few opportunities for the infant to initiate activity or control his own activities. In smaller groups, caregivers are able to question and answer, praise and comfort each child. The infant is more likely to be involved in activities, to contribute ideas, and to persist at tasks, and less likely to be found in solitary activity or inactivity.

The criteria for good day-care are similar to those for home care: good nutrition and physical care, opportunities to explore in a safe environment, consistent care by the same one or two people, and care that is responsive. This means that no more than three or four small infants are assigned to a caregiver. What more—or less—does any baby need? Unfortunately, this level of care is beyond the means of many mothers. A woman who earns only $8,000 a year after taxes cannot afford to pay one-quarter of the caregiver's salary, plus associated expenses—a total of $3,000 to $4,000—particularly if she has more than one small child. But those women who can afford high-quality care or who qualify for government assisted programs can have more confidence.

Whether the child spends the day at home or elsewhere, alert parents will perceive changes in behavior toward the second half of the second year.

The Beginnings of Self-Awareness

Mothers on the South Pacific island of Fiji say that their children become more responsible after their second birthday. They have acquired *vakayalo* (sense or reason). Mothers in the United States talk about the "terrible twos" and the emergence of what their great-grandmothers called "willfulness." Although they disagree on the particulars, these mothers agree that there are major changes in a child's behavior toward the end of infancy.

In *The Second Year* (1981), Jerome Kagan focuses on three interrelated developments in children at this age: preoccupation with adult standards, mastery, and self-awareness. As infants approach their second birthdays, they begin to display concern about events and actions that violate adult norms. Some events bother them more than others. If an 18-month-old sees her mother put on a large red feathered hat, she is likely to laugh. But if she sees her mother or another child in a shirt spattered with ketchup, she becomes serious, frowns, and may exclaim "oh-oh." She distinguishes between two kinds of nonroutine events: those that are simply unusual, and those she associates with adult disapproval, such as dirty clothes, broken toys, forbidden foods, and toilet accidents. She has developed *normative standards,* which are cognitive representations of what is proper and good. Such standards evoke an emotional response.

Many of the 2-year-olds in one of Kagan's studies commented on a tiny crack in one of the toys, which had no effect whatever on the toy's function. But none of the children mentioned a crack in the paint on a cabinet door in the laboratory playroom. This subtle discrimination illustrates both cognitive and social development. The child who is disturbed by the crack in the toy must have a mental image of what is right and proper. She must be formulating simple hypotheses about cause and effect that lead her to the conclusion that someone produced the crack. And she must anticipate that adults will not to be happy with that someone. She responds emotionally because she associates this event with other events that evoked adult displeasure. Undoubtedly she has been scolded for breaking toys; she has also noticed subtle changes in a parent's tone of voice or facial expression. The realization that she herself may have provoked these responses alerts her to similar situations.

Kagan traces the so-called terrible twos to their uncertainties. The child is mature enough to be aware of adult standards but too inexperienced to know precisely what makes the adults she cares about angry. One 2-year-old boy dropped some clothes his mother had just ironed into the toilet. Without thinking, his mother struck him—something she had rarely done before. The boy cried bitterly and seemed quite frightened. Two days later he repeated the act, went to his mother, told her what he had done, and stiffened as if he expected a spanking. Kagan suggests that his behavior was neither rebellious nor hostile. The boy simply wanted to be certain that his actions had brought on the frightening experience of several days before.

Another development in the second year is the emergence of *mastery standards*. These are goals the child sets for herself, irrespective of adult approval or disapproval. When an 18- or 20-month-old succeeds in finding the last piece in a puzzle, building a tower, or fitting a dress onto a doll, she smiles. A 12-month-old may smile if something unexpected happens while he is playing or if someone joins his game. But he does not set goals for himself, persist in spite of difficulty, and smile when he succeeds. A 12-month-old will cry if someone interrupts his play or takes something away from him. But he will not cry if he finds he does not have the ability to build a tower or meet some other goal; the 18- or 20-month-old child will do so. The older child is aware of adult standards. Further, she has an image of what she ought to be able to accomplish and judges her activities in terms of her goals.

The demands the child makes on herself translate into trials for her parents. This is the age at which children begin to resist coercion and seek independence. They refuse to eat dinner, to put on their clothes, to come inside or go outside—as if refusing for the sheer pleasure of saying no. "I do it" becomes a familiar refrain.

The third development is the emergence of *self-awareness*. Michael Lewis and Jeanne Brooks (1978) pinpointed this shift in a series of experiments. The infant is placed in front of a mirror for a time. Then he is picked up and distracted while a researcher surreptitiously places a dot of bright red rouge on his nose. He is put back in front of the mirror. If the infant knows that he is looking at himself, he should be surprised. None of the 9- to 12-month-olds who were given the nose test reacted, but 25 percent of the 15-month-olds and 75 percent of the 24-month-olds immediately grabbed their noses. These researchers also found that when 1-year-olds are shown photographs of themselves and their families, they label the pictures "Mommy," "Daddy," and "baby." Not until they are approaching their second birthdays do they label the picture of themselves with their name and the pronoun "me."

Normative and mastery standards are also signs that the child is becoming aware of herself as a distinct and separate person. By age 2 the child is aware that *her* actions might be responsible for her mother's emotions and makes associations between different emotional episodes. She has ideas about *her* own competencies and feelings about what she ought to be able to do. She has an image of *herself*. Just as she experiments on the physical world, banging pots and mouthing keys, so she experiments on her social world, testing the limits of her own capabilities and her mother's patience. The smile of triumph when she puts the seventh block on her tower, the frown when she detects the crack in the toy, the recognition that the face in the mirror is hers are all signs that she is leaving infancy behind.

SUMMARY

1. Differences in emotional intensity and social responsiveness, or temperament, are visible from birth.

2. The New York Longitudinal Study (NYLS) was designed to assess the impact of temperament on development. Researchers Thomas and Chess identified three temperamental types: easy, difficult, and slow-to-warm-up. They emphasized the importance of parent–child compatibility, or goodness of fit.

3. Studies of twins provide some evidence of a genetic component in temperament. But stability of emotional style is difficult to establish.

4. Emotions are feelings that not only motivate the individual, but also communicate nonverbal messages to others.

5. Infants express distress, interest, and disgust from birth through crying and facial expressions. The development of joy and fear follow predictable timetables. Smiles develop from reflexes, to expressions of interest, to social smiles, to personal communication. The emergence of fear of strangers and separation protest between 7 and 9 months and 1 year demonstrates the impact of cognitive development on emotional responses: The baby is developing a sense of person permanence.

6. Infants respond to other people's expressions of emotion from an early age. They may use their mother's emotional signals as a guide to behavior in unfamiliar situations. This is called social referencing.

7. Psychologists disagree about the origins of emotions. Behaviorists see fear or joy as the result of conditioning. Ethologists view emotions as part of an evolved communication system that increases adaptability. Cognitive psychologists link emotional development to mental development and the child's growing ability to compare what she sees with what she expects. A synthesis of these views sees emotional growth as a special form of information processing that relates to goals and strivings.

8. In some species the young become attached to their mother, or a mother figure, during an early critical period of development. Imprinting, as this is called, is a genetically programmed response.

9. The development of enduring emotional ties in humans is a longer and more complex process than imprinting. Bowlby identified four phases in the development of attachment in humans: indiscriminate sociability, discriminating sociability (a preference for familiar people), specific attachments (to one or a few caretakers), and partnerships (or reciprocal relationships).

10. Ainsworth's Strange Situation was designed

to assess differences in the quality of children's attachments. This procedure suggests that securely attached infants use their caregiver as a base for exploration; ambivalently attached infants are sometimes clinging, sometimes angry; and avoidant infants are detached. Secure attachments promote autonomy. The disagreement between Ainsworth and her critics is based on whether secure attachments result primarily from the mother's responsiveness (Ainsworth's view), the infant's temperament (Kagan's view), or both.

11. Is a mother's love uniquely important to an infant? Many developmental problems that are associated with maternal deprivation are better explained in terms of lack of stimulation, lack of understanding, and family discord.

12. How important are fathers? Infants become attached to their fathers as well as to their mothers and may prefer them as playmates.

13. The impact of day-care on an infant's social development and intelligence depends on the quality of the care. High-quality day-care neither delays nor accelerates cognitive development for middle-class children. Disadvantaged children benefit from high-quality day care.

14. Children in day-care are as attached to their parents as other children are although they may go through a period of adjustment when they begin day-care. Children who have been in day-care may be slightly more aggressive in nursery school.

15. The child's second birthday heralds the development of normative standards, or caring what others think; mastery standards, or self-initiated goals; and self-awareness.

FURTHER READING

Erikson, E. (1963). *Childhood and society* (2nd ed.). New York: Norton. A classic in the field of child development and a literary contribution as well. Erikson describes the relationship between culture and personality in compelling terms.

Kempe, R. S., & Kempe, C. H. (1978). *Child abuse*. Cambridge, MA: Harvard University Press. Discusses neglect and sexual abuse and considers their prevention and treatment.

Scarr, S. (1984). *Mother care/other care*. New York: Basic Books. An excellent guide to changing conceptions of motherhood, children, and what kinds of rearing and care children need.

Stern, D. (1977). *The first relationship: Infant and mother*. Cambridge, MA: Harvard University Press. An appealing account of what those little evidences of humanity that young infants show can mean and how mothers can respond.

Stevens, J. H., Jr., & Matthews, M. (Eds.). (1978). *Mother/child/father/child relationships*. Washington, DC: National Association for the Education of Young Children. This is an edited volume of selected reports on significant research in parent–child relations. It also includes papers about critical issues in doing research and applying findings to professional practice.

Zigler, E. F., & Gordon, E. W. (Eds.). (1982). *Day-care: Scientific and social policy issues*. Boston: Auburn House. This edited volume by two well-known psychologists summarizes recent research on the effects of day-care and presents policy analyses on the delivery of day-care.

P R O F I L E

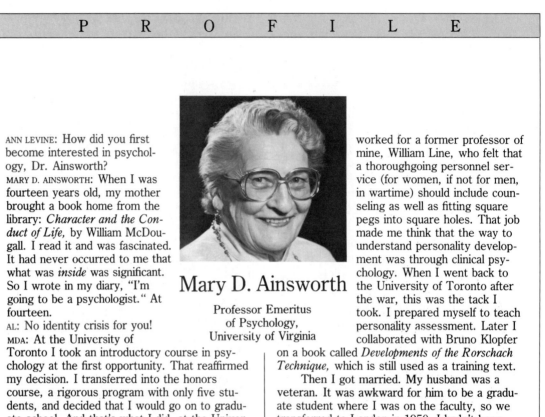

Mary D. Ainsworth

Professor Emeritus
of Psychology,
University of Virginia

ANN LEVINE: How did you first become interested in psychology, Dr. Ainsworth?

MARY D. AINSWORTH: When I was fourteen years old, my mother brought a book home from the library: *Character and the Conduct of Life,* by William McDougall. I read it and was fascinated. It had never occurred to me that what was *inside* was significant. So I wrote in my diary, "I'm going to be a psychologist." At fourteen.

AL: No identity crisis for you!

MDA: At the University of Toronto I took an introductory course in psychology at the first opportunity. That reaffirmed my decision. I transferred into the honors course, a rigorous program with only five students, and decided that I would go on to graduate school. And that's what I did, at the University of Toronto.

AL: What led you to developmental psychology?

MDA: I was always interested in personality development, rather than physiological psychology—sensation, perception and so forth. I had a professor named William Blatz whose theories intrigued me. He was almost the Doctor Spock of Canada in that period. His views took off from Freud, but he didn't dare acknowledge this. Psychoanalytic theory was absolutely taboo in provincial Toronto at that time. I did my dissertation—"The Concept of Security as a Basis for the Evaluation of Adjustment"—on a problem derived from Blatz's theories. And I took a faculty position at Toronto to continue my collaboration with him.

World War II came along a few months after I got my degree, and most of the faculty enlisted. Many ended up in personnel selection directorates. By 1942 I couldn't stand being out of the swim any more and joined the army. I worked for a former professor of mine, William Line, who felt that a thoroughgoing personnel service (for women, if not for men, in wartime) should include counseling as well as fitting square pegs into square holes. That job made me think that the way to understand personality development was through clinical psychology. When I went back to the University of Toronto after the war, this was the tack I took. I prepared myself to teach personality assessment. Later I collaborated with Bruno Klopfer on a book called *Developments of the Rorschach Technique,* which is still used as a training text.

Then I got married. My husband was a veteran. It was awkward for him to be a graduate student where I was on the faculty, so we transferred to London in 1950. I hadn't been there very long when a friend from the British army told me about an advertisement for someone with experience in psychological research and projective techniques, which I had. They also wanted someone who had worked with children, which I hadn't done. But they hired me anyway.

The job turned out to be with John Bowlby's research team, which was studying the effects of separation from the mother in early childhood on personality development. That really turned my career around—because I got interested in research with children, and because I got involved in direct observation of a naturalistic sort. That was quite different from constructing tests and having your knowledge of an individual filtered through a test.

AL: At that time [the early 1950s], psychology was primarily a laboratory science. I would think that observational studies were not considered quite "respectable." Is that true?

MDA: Yes. There was a fellow on the team named James Robertson who had trained as a social worker and later became a psychoanalyst. Jimmy had undertaken what was considered a pilot study of some sixty children between the ages of about one and three. All of them had experienced separation from the mother—in a sanatorium, an isolation ward for infectious diseases, or a residential nursery that kept children while their mothers had babies. (In those days mothers stayed in the hospital with their newborns for two weeks.) He observed the children in the separation environment, at the reunion with their parents, and at home as they picked up the threads of their lives. His data consisted of typed transcripts of his observational notes. Jimmy was very apologetic about this, because he thought it wasn't science. In academic psychologists' eyes it wasn't quantitative or systematic enough; in psychoanalysts' eyes it wasn't deep enough, it was just behavior. But I didn't see any reason why those data couldn't be treated quite objectively, by "counting noses"—how many children protested separation, how many cried, how long did they cry, how many did this or that when they returned home, and what variables seemed to make a difference in their behavior.

The study was never properly published. At one time we planned a book. Jimmy Robertson was going to write up the case studies; I was going to present my data analysis; and Bowlby was going to discuss the theoretical implications. We never wrote the book, but Bowlby cites the study in each of the three volumes of *Attachment and Loss.**

AL: Why did Bowlby consider this study so important? Did it change his thinking or yours?

MDA: Yes, I think it did. Bowlby did not believe that either learning theory or psychoanalytic theory—certainly not as constituted in the 1950s—could explain the children's responses to separation. He was groping for a new theory when he learned of Konrad Lorenz's work on imprinting.† The notion that the bond between mothers and their offspring is an evolved characteristic—part of human *nature,* if you will—got him started on a new theoretical track.

* J. Bowlby. *Attachment and Loss.* New York: Basic Books. Vol. I, *Attachment,* 1969; Vol. II, *Separation: Anxiety and Anger,* 1973: Vol. III, *Loss: Sadness and Depression,* 1980.
† See p. 195.

At first I was very skeptical. Some truths are self-evident: Babies become attached to their mothers because their mothers feed them. I didn't think you needed a new theory to explain this. Nursing is gratifying (the psychoanalytic view) and reinforcing (the learning view). But then I had an opportunity to study infant–mother dyads firsthand, in Ugandan villages. The picture of the helpless, passive infant the psychoanalysts and learning theorists had painted went right out the window. The babies were so active, so directed. I saw a lot of things that just didn't appear in existing theories. After that, the new approach Bowlby was taking began to make sense to me.

AL: Would you summarize the ethological explanation of attachment?

MDA: The basic notion is that certain behaviors have evolved as characteristic of the species. Proximity-promoting behavior, or what we call attachment behavior in humans, is an example. The young of some species cling to the parent. In other species they emit some sort of signal that lures the parent to them. The parents may be equipped with signals that attract the young, such as a mother hen clucking. So you find complementary systems in the adults and the young that promote proximity. These behaviors have evolved through the process of natural selection because they increased the chances of survival to reproductive age.

Bowlby thinks that the formation of attachment in humans is similar to imprinting in goslings and other precocial birds, but very much slower. The reason can be found in the characteristics of the species. Precocial birds are capable of locomotion at birth, but they can't protect themselves. If they weren't equipped with some mechanism that enabled them to be close to an adult, their chances of survival would be slim. Human babies don't need this mechanism at first because they can't stray. But once they are mobile, being able to achieve proximity becomes important—for the same reason as in goslings: protection. So perhaps it is no accident that the formation of attachment coincides with the emergence of locomotion. These things have been worked out in great detail for many species. Each is different. But the basic idea is that there is a genetic basis to attachment.

AL: How did you come up with the Strange Situation?

Continued

MDA: I'll have to backtrack here. My dissertation research focused on security/insecurity, as I said. Blatz maintained that parents who provide a secure base give a child the courage to brave the anxieties implicit in learning. This made sense to me. Then, in 1943 I think, I read a study by Jean Arensian entitle "Young Children in an Insecure Situation." It was similar to one of René Spitz's studies: the sample consisted of children whose mothers were inmates in a correctional institution. When these children were introduced to an unfamiliar playroom in the company of the mother or another familiar caregiver, they explored. When that person left, they were undone. I read this report and thought I'd like to do something with that someday.

In 1956, I was hired as a clinical psychologist by Johns Hopkins University in Baltimore. It took a while to sort out my life and my job so that I could get back to developmental research. When I began my longitudinal study of infant–mother dyads in the 1960s, I was primarily interested in comparing American babies to the Ganda babies I had observed. In their homes, the American babies seemed much less afraid of strangers and less distressed when their mother left the room than the Ganda babies had been. So I thought it would be interesting to observe the American sample in an unfamiliar situation that was somewhat stressful. Also, we had been studying these babies in their homes, which were all somewhat different. I wanted to see how they behaved in a standard situation. I intended this as part of a normative, comparative study. But as soon as I began to work with it, it became obvious that individual differences were the crux of the yield.

AL: Did the Strange Situation produce any surprises? behavior you hadn't anticipated?

MDA: It did. We had been following these kids for up to a year and knew their backgrounds. They behaved as we would have expected—with one major exception. Some of the children whom I thought would be quite anxious, because of their situation and behavior at home, showed far less anxiety than those with the most secure backgrounds. Instead of seeking to be close to their mothers when reunited after separation, they avoided them. It was very puzzling. Then I realized that they were behaving very much like the children we had studied in England. A long separation tends to evoke detachment in any child. These kids had not experienced a major separation, but they acted as though they had. When we went back to the data we had collected in the homes, the only thing we found that distinguished the backgrounds of the avoidant babies from those of other babies was that their mothers were on the rejecting end of an acceptance/rejection scale.

Mary Main, who was a graduate student then, became preoccupied with the issue of avoidance. When she reanalyzed our data, she found new variables that we hadn't noticed. For example, she discovered that the mothers of avoidant babies in one way or another showed an aversion to close physical contact. I remember one mother who just didn't know how to hold a baby. She would try to soothe the baby, but then get impatient, put it down, and let it cry. She once said, "I know I'm a lousy mother. I don't know how to do it—and small wonder. My mother was horrible. I never had good mothering as a child." But she was the only one who was open about this. Another time I saw a baby who was sitting in a high chair reach for the mother. She drew back and said "Don't touch me!" She immediately realized how this would look to an observer and began singing, "Don't touch me, don't touch me," trying to turn it into a game. When Mary Main went through the data with this idea in mind, she found a number of similar incidents, reported in passing.

AL: At the time you were working on this, the 1960s, mothers were being told not to pick up their babies every time they cried, not to spoil them, not to let them become "overdependent." The idea that attachment encourages independence, not dependence, was revolutionary, wasn't it?

MDA: I suppose it was. All of the mothers I studied had been exposed to this kind of advice. But the advice was contradictory. They were told that picking up the baby would spoil him. But they were also told that they should hold the baby during feedings. Anyway, despite "expert advice," we found that when a baby cried, the average mother in our sample would pick the baby up about 85 percent of the time. Some would apologize: "I know I'm spoiling

Mary Ainsworth's photograph of a Ganda woman holding her "securely attached" child.

him rotten." But that's what they wanted to do, and they did it.

I had never really swallowed the notion that comfort and reassurance work against independence. Neither had Blatz, and neither did Bowlby. He used the terms "attachment" and "self-reliance" to avoid the dependency/independence antithesis. My studies confirmed this. A baby needs a parent as a secure base from which to explore to explore the world and to learn.

AL: That brings up another controversy. The theory of attachment implies that a small child needs a mother who is available, not a working mother who sees the baby at breakfast and again at dinner. Do you think mothers who can afford to, financially and in terms of their career, should take six months or a year off to be with a child? Should society support them in this?

MDA: I think the question is too concrete. The same issue came up in 1951 when Bowlby said that a baby needs a continuous relationship. He certainly did not mean that a mother should *never* go out at night and leave the child with a baby-sitter! Many people misread him. Bowlby focused on mothers because they are usually the primary caregivers, in many species. But he never denied that there can be more than one attachment figure. I don't think I would go as far as Margaret Mead and say that a small child can have multiple attachment figures. Multiple sounds like many, and I don't think you can be attached to many people. But two, or a few, attachment figures, yes.

I believe that it is very important to have stability in child-care arrangements. But this is often difficult to achieve. One graduate student of mine is studying the quality of attachment a baby has to a family day-caregiver as compared to the mother. Not only was it difficult to assemble a sample in which the day-caregiver had been in the picture for at least four months and intended to remain for the three months required by the study; almost immediately the sample began to shrink because day-caregivers moved away, got married, became ill, and so

on. The student herself is a single mother with two children, one still an infant. She's found it very difficult to establish good, stable child-care arrangements for them. . . . So it's hard. The more money you have, the better your chances are of finding a good, long-term arrangement. Another solution, which you ofter find in homes of the poor, is a grandparent of other relative who shares child care with the mother.

AL: What about fathers? I once heard you quoted as saying, "Some of the best mothers I know are fathers."

MDA: I don't remember saying precisely that. But some of the fathers in my Baltimore study did seem to have better relationships with the baby than the mother did, even though they weren't at home as much. They just seemed to have the knack. There's a danger in this, though. When Daddy can do it better and the baby seems more attached to Daddy, it isn't very good for Mommy's morale. Some mothers are very jealous of their baby.

AL: What interests you most today? What would you like most to do when you retire from teaching?

MDA: I've gotten very interested in the notion of attachment over the lifespan. I think attachments, or affectional bonds, are important "from cradle to grave." Some people have a very disrupted, unhappy, anxious childhood, yet seem pretty well put together as adults. How can this be? One possibility is that somewhere along the line, someone gave them the security and understanding that is implicit in a good attachment. Bowlby talks about this in the third volume of *Attachment and Loss*. It's something I'd like to pursue. One of my students is investigating how the parent–child relationship affects the way college freshmen deal with being away from home for the first time. Robert Weiss is working along similar lines with marital separation.* I find my thinking very close to his. I am not about to undertake large-scale empirical studies. But I have the feeling that in the literature on friendship, marital relationships, separations and divorce, and geriatrics there is a good deal of data that can be interpreted along the lines of attachment theory. And that is what I'd like to do: a quite extensive review of the literature from different fields.

* See R. Weiss, *Marital/Separation*. New York: Basic Books, 1975; and *Going It Alone*. New York: Basic Books, 1976.

Smiles

Reflex smiles

    Social
    smiles
    <6–8 wks.>

    Special smiles
    for special
    people <5–6 mos.>

Fears

    Fearless

Separation protest (6–7 mos. to 24 mos.)

Fear of visual cliff <7–9 mos.>

**Expression of
emotions (Izard)**

Interest

    Smile

    Anger,
    surprise,
    sadness
    <3–4 mos.>

    Fear
    <5–7 mos.>

    Shame,
    shyness
    <6–8 mos.>

**Attachments
(Bowlby)**

    Indiscriminate
    sociability
    (0–2 mos.)

    Discriminate
    sociability
    (2–6 mos.)

Self-consciousness

No self-recognition in
nose test (9–12 mos.)

**Related perceptual,
motor, and cognitive
developments**

Recognizes
specific
people
<6 mos.>

Uses single words

    Attracted by motion,
    edges, contrast
    (as in human face)
    <1–2 mos.>

Begins to look for
hidden objects <4–8 mos.>

Creeps
<7–9 mos.>

| 1 | 2 | 3 | 4 | 5 | 6 | 7 | 8 | 9 | 10 | 11 | 12 |

Age in months

( ) age range
< > onset or peak
⌠ age extension beyond
⌡ that shown on chart

HIGHLIGHTS OF SOCIAL AND EMOTIONAL DEVELOPMENT, BIRTH TO 24 MONTHS

Deliberate smiles
<after 22 mos.>

Fear of strangers (8–9 mos. to 24 mos.)

Contempt, guilt
<after 24 mos.>

Specific attachments
(7–24 mos.)

Partnerships
<after 24 mos.>

Passes nose test
<24 mos.>

Normative standards
Mastery standards
<2nd birthday>

Puts two words
together

Begins to speak in
multiple-word
sentences

Walks alone
<12–15 mos.>

Capable of deferred imi-
tation, symbolic play,
and speech <12–18 mos.>

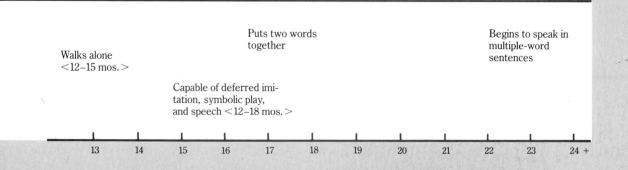

| 13 | 14 | 15 | 16 | 17 | 18 | 19 | 20 | 21 | 22 | 23 | 24 + |

4-YEAR-OLD: *There's no such thing as ghosts.*
6-YEAR-OLD: *I know.*
5-YEAR-OLD: *Yes, there are in London.*
4- AND 6-YEAR-OLDS: *How do you know?*
5-YEAR-OLD: *It's in the cyclopedia.*
4-YEAR-OLD: *But there are no dragons.*
5- AND 6-YEAR-OLDS: *You're right, no dragons.*
5-YEAR-OLD: *But Dracula is real and lives in London.*
4- AND 6-YEAR-OLDS: *You're right.*
—*Listen! The Children Speak (p. 18)*

Between the ages of 2 and 6, the unsteady, tentative toddler develops into a coordinated child. At the beginning of this period the youngster's social world is comprised almost entirely of adults; at the end she is making friends her own age. At age 2 her vocabulary is composed of a limited number of words; at age 6 she is holding conversations. Her thinking has advanced from sensorimotor associations to mental experiments and simple calculations of cause and effect. She knows that she is a girl and has definite opinions about her own and the opposite sex. She knows that it is wrong to take her baby brother's toys or play with matches. When another child is hurt, she wants to help.

It is easy to overestimate a 3- or 4-year-old's intelligence and intentions. Because preschoolers can talk, ask questions, deliver opinions, and defy adults (at least verbally), parents may assume that they understand more than they do. In fact, 3- and 4-year-olds are only beginning to distinguish between fantasy and reality. They rarely think ahead, have short attention spans, and are blissfully unaware of what they do and do not know. They are only beginning to gain control over their bodies and behavior.

It is also easy to underestimate the small child's abilities. A child who counts "one, six, ten" sounds as if he does not understand numbers. But closer questioning may reveal that he does understand the concept of numbers but uses the wrong words. A child who says, "Mommy goed to the store" or "Look at his foots" sounds ignorant of basic grammar. But closer examination reveals that this child has advanced from the vocabulary stage of language development to the rule stage. He could not make these mistakes if he did not know the English rule for forming the past tense and plural.

By age 4, if not before, many children are enrolled in a preschool program. But their cultural education begins much earlier. Parents and other caregivers are the child's first teachers. As this period of development draws to an end, however, playmates are becoming increasingly important in the child's life.

PART 3
THE PRESCHOOL PERIOD

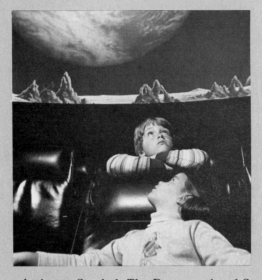

The preschool years, ages 2 to 6, are a time of rapid development. At age 1½ the child tottered across the carpet on wobbly legs. At 6 he can run, skip, jump, ride a tricycle, and turn somersaults in the air. He has graduated from a high chair to a to a place at the table with a knife and fork. He can button his own shirt, zip his own jacket, and tie his own shoes. He knows his way around the neighborhood. When he was 2 years old his attempts to stack blocks were haphazard. At 5 or 6 he can put together a puzzle, play a simple tune on the piano, draw a human figure, and even print his name. At age 1½ he spoke in one- and two-word telegrams. At 6 he understands most of what is said to him. He can name familiar objects, say how they are used, identify color and shapes, count, and perhaps tell time. He can and does express his own thoughts about broccoli, Aunt Susie's boyfriend, or God. The skills of language and thought are helping him to construct a picture of the world and to understand his place in it.

If you listen closely to children of this age, however, it is obvious that they do not perceive and interpret the world around them the way adults do.

Jim (age 2½) watched a jet streak across the sky and exclaimed, "Mommy, there's a rip in the sky!"

Karen (age 2 or 3) was delighted for first time she saw a sky writer. "What a smart cloud!"

Dora (age 4) looked up at some rippled clouds one morning and declared, "God sure didn't get the wrinkles out of the sky very good this morning."

Preschoolers have a long developmental journey before they are capable of thinking in mature ways. In this chapter we trace change in the child's ability to learn and make sense out of the world during the preschool period. We analyze and update Piaget's description of the preoperational stage of cognitive development, with help from studies of attention and memory. We consider what new motor abilities and artistic capabilities contribute to cognitive development. We

LEARNING ABOUT THE WORLD

look at the controversy over early education and at the special world of child's play. In the final section of the chapter we suggest that developments in all of these areas reflect a drive for competence that is part of our species' evolutionary heritage.

From Action to Symbol: The Preoperational Stage

Piaget called the second stage of cognitive development, which extends from age 2 to age 6 or 7, the **preoperational stage**. The preoperational thinker can use images and symbols, but does not have the logical abilities of older children. He can imagine the effects of sucking, banging, kicking, and other sensorimotor schemes. He does not have to see or do things directly to think about them. But he does not think as systematically as he will later.

The foundations of preoperational thought are laid in the late sensorimotor stage. The infant's discovery of object permanence is a cornerstone for later cognitive development. Something out of sight is not necessarily out of existence. Object permanence is the first step toward realizing that the physical world is not chaotic but operates according to rules.

A new kind of imitative behavior signals that the child is thinking in a new way. Imitations are reproductions of what the child sees and hears. Because they represent or stand for the actions of others, imitations are indirect evidence that the child is capable of creating internal, mental images. Whereas infants can copy what someone is doing in front of them, here and now, preschoolers perform *deferred imitation*. The 18-month-old who sits on the kitchen floor, stirring a pot while her mother cooks, is mimicking her mother. A 2½-year-old "cooking" on the toy stove in her room is reenacting something she witnessed earlier. She is able to do this because she has formed a mental image of her mother's behavior. Something out of sight is not out of mind. Make-believe carries this development one step further. The 3-year-old who pretends that a table is a castle, a stick a magic wand, and a tattered towel an elegant velvet cape demonstrates the rudiments of symbolic thought. Children's drawings are another attempt to reproduce symbolically perceptions that occurred earlier.

A **symbol** is something that stands for something else. A red light symbolizes "STOP"; a cross symbolizes Christianity; a flag symbolizes a nation. Spoken and written words are also symbols. The sound "dawg" and the written letters *d-o-g* stand for an animal. The word *dog* also represents general notions of a furry, four-legged, domesticated canine that apply to everything from toy poodles to Great Danes.

The acquisition of language is a major achievement of the preoperational stage. (We discuss language in Chapter 7.) Language provides human beings with an essential tool for mastering new knowledge, communicating thoughts and feelings to one another, and maintaining cultural heritages. With language, the preschooler can label objects, people, and events. Knowing the word *dog* makes it easier for her to think and learn about dogs. Language provides basic concepts that help the child to simplify, sort out, and group the many things in the environment. In time, the child will be able to distinguish between "books" and "comics," "same" and "different," "many cookies" and "few cookies." At the preoperational stage, the child's mental activity no longer depends on the here and now. She can think about the past and imagine the future.

In many ways, the preoperational stage is a transitional period. The child is developing numerous cognitive skills, but it will be some time before she puts them all together. This is why preschoolers can appear to be so smart to their

Piaget saw signs of cognitive development in activities other psychologists had dismissed as irrelevant. Make-believe is one of the first indications that a child has entered the preoperational stage.

parents one moment, and so stupid (or stubborn) the next. Reasoning with a 2-year-old is largely an exercise in futility. Piaget's description of the preoperational child suggests why.

Intuition

According to Piaget, one of the major achievements of the preoperational period is **insight learning**, or learning based on intuition. The preschooler can look at a problem and quickly deduce the solution ("Aha!"). An infant solves problems by trial and error, applying one scheme after another until he happens on one that works. The preschooler can solve a problem simply by considering the alternatives.

Insight learning may make the preschooler look clever. In fact, his thinking is still primitive. He runs through images in his mind but does not systematically plan a course of action for solving the problem. He may be able to sort pictures into different categories, or to find a shoe he mislaid the night before; but he cannot tell you how he did it. Preschoolers' solutions are "guesstimates." An older child has developed strategies for solving problems. She knows that it usually takes more than one try to get from a problem to a solution. A preoperational child does not understand this.

Egocentrism

Piaget found that the preoperational child is **egocentric**: He is unable to take the role of another person or view the world from other vantage points. Piaget does not mean that the preoperational child is selfish, in the sense of disregarding other people's wants and needs. Rather, the child does not know yet that other people *have* different wants, needs, and perspectives.

A 4-year-old subject is asked:
"Do you have a brother?"
He says, "Yes."
"What is his name?"
"Jim."
"Does Jim have a brother?"
"No."
(Phillips, 1969, p. 91)

Piaget demonstrated childhood egocentrism with an experiment (Piaget & Inhelder, 1963). He set up three mountains of different size and shape on a table. He encouraged a child to walk around the display and examine it from different angles. Then he asked the child to sit in one chair and put a doll in another. He presented the child with a series of pictures showing the mountains from different angles, and asked the child what the doll saw. Four- and 5-year-olds did not seem to realize that the mountains would look different from the doll's perspective. They always picked the picture that matched what they themselves saw. Six- and 7-year-olds realized that the doll had a different perspective, but they made numerous mistakes. It was not until

An anecdote about President Kennedy's daughter Caroline illustrates childhood egocentrism. One day 4-year-old Caroline was playing with her cousins when one of them announced, "Caroline, your daddy is the President." Caroline chuckled and replied in a disbelieving voice, "Oh, no, he *isn't*. He's my Daddy!" (*Listen!* 1979, p. 12)

age 9 or 10 that children consistently picked the correct picture.

Everyday examples of childhood egocentrism abound. Preschoolers say "me," "my," "mine," and "I" over and over: "*I* had it first." "It's *my* turn." "Let *me* do it." When a small child's mother is sick in bed, he may feel that "she doesn't want to play with *me; I* must have done something bad." If a preschooler's mother dies, the child may be angry: "she deserted *me.*" It is difficult for a child at this stage to believe that anything that happens in his life is *not* connected with his own wishes, feelings, and behavior (A. Freud, 1965).

Magical Thinking

Given this limited perspective, it is no wonder that children believe that they have magical powers—to make the sun follow them when they walk, to pull up the cover of night when it is time for bed, and to affect other forces in nature. Children take seriously such rhymes as "Rain, rain, go away" and "Step on a crack, you'll break your mother's back" (Pulaski, 1971).

Animism is the belief that inanimate objects have thoughts, feelings, and motives. It is an extension of egocentrism. For small children, the sun, wind, and fire are alive because they move and make us feel hot or cold; crayons, marbles, watches, and cars are alive because

they write, roll, tell time, or ride (Pulaski, 1971, p. 42). If they are alive, the child reasons, they must think and feel just as I do. Piaget recorded the following conversation with a 4-year-old:

"Oh, the sun is moving. It's walking like us. . . ."
"Where is it walking?"
"Why, on the sky. The sky's hard. It's made of clouds."
Then she discovered the sun was following them.
"It's doing that for fun, to play a joke on us. . . ."
"But does it know we're here?"
"Of course it does, it can see us!" (1962, p. 252)

The same child attributed human motives to objects closer to the ground. When she and Piaget missed a train one day, she was angry. "Doesn't the train know we aren't in it?" Later that day she declared, "The stairs are horrid, they hit me!" (p. 252)

Such fanciful explanations of natural phenomena and human accidents are examples of what Piaget calls **precausal reasoning:** the inability to distinguish between psychological and physical causes, between subjective experiences and objective events. For example, most small children are convinced that their dreams are real. Piaget says that this is why it is so difficult to calm a child who has awakened from a nightmare and to convince her that the mon-

In a letter to Maurice Sendak, author of *Where the Wild Things Are,* a 7-year-old asked, "How much does it cost to get where the wild things are? If it is not too expensive, my sister and I want to spend the summer there. Plese answer soon"

(*Listen!* 1979, p. 19).

sters in the dream do not really exist (1962). Preschoolers often say that their dreams come "from the night" or "from God." Some children at this age believe that the people they saw in a dream caused the dream, and that bad dreams occur because they have done something wrong.

Monique Laurendeau and Adrian Pinard (1962) questioned children aged 4 to 12 about their dreams. More than half of the 4-year-olds said that their dreams took place in their rooms, on the walls, or on their pillows. These youngsters said that they dreamed with their eyes open. By 7, the end of the preoperational stage, virtually all children distinguished between the subjective visions of their dreams and the objective sights they see when they are awake. The 7-year-olds said that dreams occur inside one's head and that nobody else can see them. Similarly, many 4-year-olds believe in Santa Claus; most 7-year-olds do not. For younger children, the line between fantasy and reality, the world outside and the world within, is blurred.

Preoperational children tend to believe that every event has a purpose (finalism) and that all things must conform to a grand pattern (artificialism). If it rains the day their family planned a picnic, there must be a reason. They also assume that events occurring together must be causally connected (phenomenalism). If Daddy comes home when it gets dark, one must cause the other. Preoperational children often ignore physical mechanisms in thinking about cause and effect.

Centering

Piaget saw the inability to consider more than one dimension at a time as another defining characteristic of preoperational thought. The preoperational child tends to *center attention* on a single, striking feature of whatever he is trying to think about, ignoring other important and relevant features.

The single-mindedness of the preoperational child is often difficult for adults to believe. Like small children, adults sometimes have difficulty waking from a dream. Furthermore, they may kick a stalled car as if this could make it get up and move (animism). But adults would never made the following mistake. An experimenter shows a preschooler two identical short, wide glasses filled with the same amounts of Kool-Aid. She asks the child if one of the glasses has more Kool-Aid than the other. The child says, "No, they're the same." With the child watching, the experimenter pours the Kool-Aid from one of the short, wide glasses into a tall, thin glass. She asks the child again if one glass has more Kool-Aid than the other. This time the child says, "Yes." She asks how the child knows this. He responds, "Because it's taller." Now she pours the Kool-Aid back into the original glass and repeats the question. Undaunted, the preoperational child says that the glasses have the same amount of liquid. (See Figure 6-1.)

This experiment has been tried hundreds of times, in a number of variations, with hundreds of children—all with the same results. (See Chapter 9.) Preoperational children do not understand **conservation:** the fact that certain properties remain the same, even though the shape or spatial arrangement has changed. (The property—in this case, the amount of liquid—is conserved.)

Piaget held that the main reason for this surprising mistake is that the preoperational child's thinking is centered. One dimension captures his attention. In the liquid experiment, it is the height *or* the width of the glass. An older child has a more holistic, decentered approach. He considers height *and* width, and the relationship between the two (a decrease in width offsets an increase in height.)

Centering is only one of several reasons for the conservation error. The preoperational child's thinking is *irreversible*: her mind only

works in forward gear. She cannot retrace her mental steps. If she could, she would imagine pouring the liquid back into the first glass and realize that the amount was the same. An older child can think the problem through. Also, the preoperational child pays more attention to *present states* (the liquid in the glass) than to *transformations* (pouring the liquid back and forth). A child at this age is like a camera that takes only still shots; older children and adults have minds that are more like movie cameras.

Hidden in this list of things the young child cannot do are two mental feats a 4- or 5-year-old *can* perform (Flavell, 1985). If the experimenter hides the glass of Kool-Aid behind a screen, the preoperational child knows that it still exists. The child mastered object permanence at the end of the sensorimotor stage. If the experimenter asks him whether the Kool-Aid she poured into the tall glass is the same Kool-Aid as before, he says that it is. He has learned to recognize *identity,* which is the fact that something can remain the same even though it looks different.

The distinction between identity and conservation is subtle but important. Identity requires a qualitative judgment: Is the Kool-Aid still Kool-Aid, or has it changed to ginger ale or milk? Conservation requires a further, *quantitative* judgment: Do the two glasses have the same *amount* of liquid? Older children (who are

Figure 6-1 The Liquid Conservation Problem

Insight

THE MEANING OF SANTA CLAUS

The belief in Santa Claus is one of the enduring myths of Western culture. However, some parents and psychologists wonder whether the belief in Santa Claus—and the inevitable disillusionment that follows it—is good for children. Two surveys of school children in Lincoln, Nebraska, taken about eighty years apart, explored what Santa Claus means to the developing child.

In 1896, Frances E. Duncombe, a graduate student at the University of Nebraska, set out to study just what children think about Santa Claus. How real is he? What superhuman qualities does he have? What happens when children learn that there is no Santa Claus, that he is only a myth? Duncombe surveyed 1,500 Lincoln schoolchildren, ranging in age from about 8 to 13. Nearly three generations later, three psychologists (Benjamin, Langley, and Hall, 1979) replicated her research by using the same questions, the same scoring system, and a comparable sample of 900 Lincoln public schoolchildren. Although the details of the Santa Claus story were much the same in both eras, the beliefs of the two generations showed some subtle and interesting differences.

Compared to their counterparts in 1896, children today are much less likely to attribute superhuman powers to Santa Claus. The authors of the recent study speculate that today's children, who are raised with Wonder Woman and Batman, find Santa a little tame as a superhero. Furthermore, they are more likely to see Santa as an everyday human being on street corners and in department stores.

In both surveys, nearly half the children realized the truth about Santa Claus through their own experience and observation. This finding is not surprising: children in this age group have passed from Piaget's preoperational stage of intellectual development—in which fantasy

and reality are the same—to the concrete operational stage, in which they are able to decide logically that Santa does not exist. As for the children who learned that "there is no Santa Claus" from others, today's children are twice as likely to hear the news from their parents as from other children.

Present-day children remembered feeling "sorry" or "cheated" more often than the children in 1896, but they were also more likely to think that the next generation should be taught to believe in Santa. Only 4 percent of the 1977 group, compared with 17 percent of the 1896 group, thought that children would behave better if they thought that Santa Claus would reward them. Members of both groups said that the best reason for passing on the myth was that it made children happy. "Let them believe in fairy tales and myths," wrote a fifth-grade girl in 1896. "It won't do them any harm, and little children find out soon enough that things are not as they are represented to be." Her 1977 counterpart agreed, saying, "I think children should have a little bit of their life believing someone besides parents care for them. (p. 39).

Fantasies like Santa Claus are an essential part of a child's development. Objections that the Santa Claus myth has been commercialized, and that Santa is used too often as a bribe, are certainly valid. Yet the negative aspects of this fantasy are overcome by its many positive effects. By representing the spirit of giving, Santa Claus serves a useful purpose by fostering the altruistic feelings of the holiday season. The rituals and traditions of Christmas and other celebrations are important: They bring the generations together, contribute to a sense of security, and celebrate a family's intimacy and uniqueness.

conservers) understand that some problems have precise solutions that involve some form of quantitative measurement. Younger children (nonconservers) lack "the cognitive equipment to do other than guess or make simple perceptual estimates" (Flavell, 1977, p. 85). Recognizing identities is a transitional stage that helps the child move from the discovery of object permanence to the mastery of conservation.

Appearance vs. Reality

Piaget held that preoperational children are seduced by appearances. The 4-year-old says that the tall glass has more Kool-Aid for the simple reason that it *looks like* more to her. Seeing is believing in this stage.

Research supports this characterization in part. Rheta De Vries (1969) studied children's reactions to a physical transformation. One by one, boys aged 3 to 6 were introduced to Maynard, a remarkably docile black cat, shown in Figure 6-2 (A). De Vries began the experiment by saying, "I want to show you my pet. Do you know what it is?" All of the boys answered correctly, "a cat." They were encouraged to play with the animal for a while. Then De Vries hid Maynard's front half behind a screen and strapped a highly realistic mask of a fierce dog with bared teeth onto the cat's head. While performing this transformation, she asked the boys to keep their eyes on the cat's tail so that they could see that she was not switching animals. "Now," she told them, "this animal is going to look quite different." She removed the screen, revealing the creature shown in Figure 6-2 (B). "Look, it has a face like a dog," she said. Then she asked each boy a series of questions that were designed to test the child's beliefs about identity: What kind of animal is it now: How do you know? Is it *really* a dog (or a cat)? Would it like to eat dog food, cat food, or birdseed? Can it bark? While the child watched, De Vries then unmasked Maynard and asked more questions.

De Vries rated the children on an 11-point scale, ranging from a score of 1 for children who believed that the cat had *really* become a dog to a score of 11 for those who said that a cat could *never* become a dog, even if De Vries used

Figure 6-2 Maynard the Cat Maynard, the exceptionally patient cat used in the De Vries experiment on identity, as himself (A) and disguised as a dog (B). (De Vries, 1969, p. 8).

magic. As shown in Figure 6-3, most of the 3-year-olds were completely taken in by the disguise. They believed Maynard had been so completely transformed that he now had the insides of a dog. Many of these children were afraid he would bite. In contrast, most of the 6-year-olds staunchly maintained that it was still the same animal. Clearly, they had mastered identity. Most interesting were the children in between. They said that a cat could not become a dog; but they could not deny what they saw—a fierce little dog.

In a recent series of experiments, John Flavell and his colleagues (1983a) probed deeper into the young child's difficulties in distinguishing between reality and appearance. Like De Vries, they found that preschoolers can be seduced by appearances. Often they center on what is perceptually striking, ignoring other evidence. But preschoolers also make the opposite mistake, identifying an object or event in terms of what they know and ignoring what they see at that moment. Preschoolers ranging in age from 3 to 5 years were shown such things as an imitation rock made of sponge. They were asked, "What is this *really, really?* Is it *really, really* a rock or *really, really* a piece of sponge?' They were also asked, "When you *look* at this with your *eyes* right now, what does it *look* like? (p. 102)" The 3-year-olds showed some ability to distinguish between reality and appearance,

but made numerous errors in both directions. They were just as likely to say the object looked like a sponge as to respond that it really, really was a rock. These experiments were conducted first at the Stanford University nursery school and later in China, at the Beijing University nursery school (1983b), with the same results.

Flavell concludes that the reason for this is not that preschoolers are seduced by appearances, but that they do not analyze the source of their mental representations. This is why small children often tell innocent "whoppers." They may not recall that the wicked dog or nice lady in the story they are telling is a figment of their imagination. By 5 or 6, most children know the difference between fact and fantasy.

Concrete vs. Abstract Thinking

Another characteristic Piaget associated with the preoperational child is her dependence on *concrete* mental images. The child's thoughts arc mental representations of experiences—snapshots of objects, people, places, and events she witnessed or heard about in a story—not abstractions. Piaget held that the preoperational child's cognition takes the form of a mental experiment. The child runs through a sequence of images in her mind in the same order that she or others might perform those actions in real life. Unlike the older child, the young thinker does not reorder, refashion, or otherwise manipulate

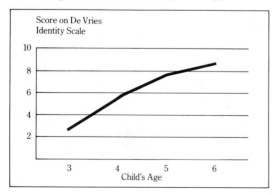

Figure 6-3 Seeing Is Believing   The youngest children in De Vries' experiment were deceived by appearance; the older children were mastering identity. (Adapted from De Vries, 1969)

these images. Sometimes the child stumbles on a solution immediately (insight learning). Often, however, the concrete mental experiment results in slow-paced thinking.

David, age 4, was riding with his grandmother to his new school for the first day. She noticed that he was very quiet for some time, deep in thought but relaxed. After some time he said, "Grandma, do you know how I 'figgered' out I would make friends at my new school?"

"Tell me, David, how do you plan to make new friends?" she asked.

Slowly David explained, "I'm just going to look around and watch for a while and when I see that someone needs some help I'm going to help him and then he'll be my friend!" (*Listen!* 1979, p. 13)

One can imagine David picturing the schoolyard in his mind, seeing groups of children, visualizing their activities, recalling an incident in which one child helped another, and proclaiming "Aha!" David kept at it until he saw a solution to his problem.

Whereas preschoolers think in specifics, older children and adults use generalizations and abstractions. Mature thinkers use concepts to sort objects, people, and events into prelabeled categories. A **concept** is a generalized idea or notion that applies to many cases. The concept of dogness, for example, applies to many different kinds of dogs and to many individual dogs. Concepts provide an economical way to deal with the innumerable things we encounter in a single day. If we can identify a particular object as a member of a category, we already know a great many things about that object that are not immediately perceptible. When presented with a new dessert, an adult knows even before he tastes it that it will probably be sweet and fattening, and that he will feel guilty if he eats too much of it. All of this information is contained in the concept *dessert*. Concepts are the building blocks of mature thought.

Small children's concepts reflect egocentric thought. When preschoolers are asked to say the first word that comes into their head, they respond to the word "bed" with "sleep," to "apple" with "eat." In other words, they define a concept in terms of what objects in that category can do for them (their function). Given the same task, older children are more likely to respond to the word "apple" with class associations. For example, to "apple" they respond with "fruit" (the word for a class of such objects) or "orange" (another member of the fruit class) (Nelson, 1978).

Learning concepts is one of the tasks of the preschool period, and children take an active part in it. When small children ask adults, "What's this?" "What's that?"—an inquisition that seems endless to us—they are asking what labels their culture places on objects and events in the environment. In this way they develop conceptual schemes for organizing their perceptions in terms of common traits (red things, round things, small things, many things). It will be some years before the child can handle more abstract concepts.

There are many words and concepts that the preoperational child cannot "picture," such as bravery, astronomy, and democracy. Language development expands the child's cognitive horizons. Learning numbers, musical notation, and other symbol systems releases the child further from the constraints of concrete thought.

A child is not preoperational today, concrete operational tomorrow. Developing children are in a constant state of flux and transition. The child who believes it is raining because the clouds are sad may also be conducting mechanical experiments on toy trucks. He may grasp conservation of some materials before understanding conservation of others. He attacks today's problems with preoperational mental tools. But the results of these efforts move him toward the acquisition of more mature cognitive skills.

How Young Children Think: Information Processing

Piaget's observations of children and his interpretations of cognitive development provide a broad framework for understanding how preschoolers think. But many of the details of preoperational thought remain to be filled in. The small child looks out of the window on an overcast day and declares that the sun stayed in bed because it wasn't feeling well. A 4-year-old girl watches a friendly adult poor milk from one glass into another, listens to the adult's question, and announces, "The tall glass has more." A 5-year-old boy rounds a corner, sees an unfamiliar German shepherd dog, turns, and runs. What has happened here? How does the child's mind work in these circumstances? To answer these questions, we turn to information processing, which was introduced in Chapter 4.

Harold Fishbein (1976) provides a vivid illustration of how the human mind processes information. The person:

1. receives information, [such as] patterns of light;
2. identifies that information—it's a dog;
3. stores information—stores in memory some representation of that dog;
4. operates on or elaborates on the information— that dog is larger than any other dog seen before;
5. makes decisions (which need not be conscious) about this information—that dog is dangerous;
6. acts on the decisions made about the informa tion—run like hell. (p. 86)

The beginning thinker is capable of performing each of the six steps in Fishbein's model, which uses reaction to a dog as an example. But the amount of information he is able to take in, the speed at which he processes the information, and the strategies he uses will change over the course of development (Siegler, 1983).

Research on attention and memory illustrate age-related changes in information processing. Gathering information (attention) and storing and retrieving information (memory) play critical roles in all kinds of learning. What do preschoolers notice? How much do they recall?

Attention

The young child is bombarded by sights, sounds, smells, physical contact with people and objects, and other forms of sensory stimulation. The environment is a three-ring circus with many competing attractions. The child cannot possibly pay attention to everything at once. At any time, he has to decide which information about objects and events is worthy of exploration and mental processing. *Attention* is a selective process (Gibson & Spelke, 1983; Pick, Frankel, & Hess, 1975). The child's understanding of the world depends in part on what attracts and holds his attention.

There are three basic changes in attention over the preschool period (Fishbein, 1984; Gibson, 1969). First, the young child is captured by whatever clamors loudest for his attention. What he notices depends more on the environment than on his own intentions. Older children are more investigative, less reactive. Second, the preschooler's attention often flits from one thing to another. Older children are more systematic and less random in their observations. Third, small children are not very selective. Older children are better able to isolate those features of an event or object that are relevant to the task at hand and screen out irrelevant information.

A study by Eliane Vurpillot (1968) illustrates these changes in attention. Vurpillot showed children aged 3 to 10 a series of simple drawings of houses. She presented the houses in pairs. On some trials, the two houses were identical; on others, some of the windows in one house had curtains, flower pots, or a bird cage but those in the other house did not (see Figure 6-4). Vurpillot asked the children to say whether the two houses were alike or different. Children of all ages performed well on trials with identical houses. But the ability to spot differences improved with age. Nine- and 10-year-olds made no mistakes.

Vurpillot was interested in right and wrong answers. But she also wanted to learn how the children arrived at their answers. A camera recorded their eye movements as they scanned the houses. The camera revealed clear developmental differences. The 3- and 5-year-olds looked at about seven windows in no particular order, then gave an answer. The older children

compared the windows systematically, row by row or column by column, not stopping until they had checked ten or more windows. They did not leap to hasty decisions; many rescanned the windows to check their decisions.

Preschoolers may not be very efficient at scanning the environment for relevant information or at screening out irrelevant information. But this does not necessarily mean that they have poor attention spans. Often small children become so absorbed in play that they do not hear a third or fourth summons to dinner. They may ask a parent or grandparent to read the same story over and over. Nor does it mean that preschoolers lack curiosity. Two researchers studied the reactions of preschoolers, first-graders, and second-graders to a series of games (Henderson & Moore, 1979). In one study, children were invited to play with a box that had eighteen drawers, each of which held something different (such as an airplane, a flashlight, a ring). In some ways, the preschoolers exhibited more curiosity than the older children did. They asked more questions and were more likely to handle the toys. The older children moved rapidly from one drawer to the next, as if driven by a "need to know."

John Wright and Alice Vlietstra (1975) summarize the changes in attention over the preschool period this way. Three-year-olds are *explorers*: They approach the environment in a playful way, moving rapidly from one thing to

Figure 6-4 Window Shopping   These are examples of the houses Vurpillot used in her study of visual scanning in children.   (Vurpillot, 1968)

another, and responding impulsively to whatever attracts them. They are motivated primarily by curiosity and easily distracted from a task. Six-year-olds are *searchers*: They investigate the environment in a more systematic, planful, task-oriented way. They establish goals for themselves and are more likely to stop and reflect before moving from one thing to another. Motivated by a need to know, they are less easily distracted. For example, a 3-year-old who can't find his toothbrush looks in one or two places where he usually finds it. Then he gets caught up in the game of looking and forgets what he was looking for. A 6-year-old who discovers that her toothbrush is not where she usually puts it is more likely to stop and think about where it might be. The older child has more control over her own attention.

Memory

We cannot study attention without considering memory at the same time. The two skills work hand in hand. Attention determines which information enters the human "computer." Memory determines which information stays in the system, how it is organized and "filed," and how it is retrieved later for use.

A **memory** is a person's mental record of an event. Like attention, memory is selective. Only some of the information available in the environment is attended to, and only some of what is noticed is remembered. Memory varies from situation to situation and from individual to individual (Perlmutter, 1980). As any trial lawyer knows, two people who witnessed the same event, such as a mugging, may record quite different images. One remembers that the mugger was tall; the other is convinced that he was short.

Study after study has shown that preschoolers have poor memories compared to older children and adults. They have a harder time remembering pictures or words, or the order in which items were presented on a memory test. When they are asked to remember a particular class of things (pictures of birds, for example, they are easily distracted by irrelevant material) (Pick, Frankel, & Hess, 1975). Preschoolers can *recognize* material they have encountered before (they can pick out pictures they have seen). But they have trouble *recalling* material (that is, naming pictures from memory).

There are several possible reasons for preschoolers' poor performance on memory tests. First, their memories are not *organized*. Adult memory is an extraordinarily complex filing system. One might compare the storage area of the human mind to a vast library, filled with endless shelves of information. To recall a particular ex-

Mitten clips, notes to teachers, and identity tags are some of the ways parents compensate for preschoolers' forgetfulness.

Insight

AMNESIA FOR EARLY CHILDHOOD

Adults usually cannot recall early childhood experiences. Most of our memories of the preschool years are secondhand: stories our parents or aunts and uncles told us when we were older.

Freud saw amnesia for early childhood as a classic example of repression. According to Freud, the small child's mental life is flooded with erotic fantasies that the adult superego finds unacceptable. To defend our self-esteem, we blockade early memories in the unconscious. The threat of recalling our early sex life is so great that we repress virtually all memories of this period.

Information processing offers an alternative explanation of amnesia for early childhood (White & Pillemer, 1979). It is obvious that small children have memories. They recognize people and situations, respond with surprise or fear when their expectations are not met, and so on. But they do not process memories as older children and adults do. Small children associate ideas and activities with the external event (sights, sounds, smells) or the internal state (fear, excitement, joy) that accompanies them. If a situation is repeated, they may recall fragments of associated ideas or activities. But they do not form these "memories" through conscious effort, and they cannot retrieve them at will. Recall depends on external or internal cues. When a preschooler is asked, "Do you remember what we did last Sunday?" she may think of church. The image of church may trigger the thought of a new hat. This thought may lead to one of Grandma, who said, "You look grown-up." That pleasant feeling recalls a trip to the zoo. In short, the child responds with a string of associations.

Around age 5, children begin to make deliberate efforts to encode experiences in memory so that they will be available in the future. They develop strategies for storing and retrieving ideas and events; they use words and concepts to organize their mental storehouse. Recall no longer depends on the context or on emotional cues. Asked about the previous weekend, the older child looks up Sunday in his mental file, finds that particular day, goes through the list of people and activities on that card, compares it to cards for other Sundays, and picks out what was special about last Sunday.

Adults have two separate memory "programs." The first is based on unconscious sensory and emotional associations; it develops in early childhood, beginning about age 5. The second is an organized "filing system," which develops later. Attempts to use this filing program to locate early childhood experiences usually fail; our mental computer replies, "Path not found." A random sight or smell, a feeling of joy or fear, may activate early associations. But we may not recognize these as memories or know why we feel as we do.

The views of Freud and of information-processing theorists are not incompatible. The existence of two separate kinds of memory might explain some of Freud's observations. It suggests how nonconscious memories might influence behavior. And it explains why free associations and dreams sometimes trigger early memories. When we are asleep or not monitoring our thoughts, the mature memory program is turned off.

perience or retrieve certain information, the child must search the shelves to find what she needs. If her memory collection is organized in a meaningful way, if it is cataloged, the search is much easier. Like a library arranged according to the Dewey decimal system, the memories of the older child and the adult are more accessible because they were shelved in an orderly fashion. We use concepts to categorize and label material, and this enhances our ability to recall that information later. Concepts are retrieval cues; they guide our search through stored memories. The preschooler's knowledge of concepts is limited. Her memory is more like a toy box than a library—a jumble of blocks, dolls, crayons, stones, shoelaces, and other treasures stored in no particular order. When she looks for something, she may or may not find what she wants.

A second reason for poor memory in preschoolers is that their information-processing *capacity* is limited (Brown, Bransford, Ferrara, & Campione, 1983; Case, Kurlind, & Goldberg, 1982). When faced with a memory task, an older child automatically begins grouping items in his mind, rehearsing the list of words, and applying other strategies to the task. He has a program or scheme for memorization. The younger child does not have such a scheme. She has to think about how she is going to learn the pictures or words. This uses up mental "space," leaving less room for actually storing information.

A third reason is that memory depends to some extent on the *knowledge base,* or the fund of previous knowledge (Flavell, 1985). The more you know about a subject, the easier it is to add new information to your memory store. Preschoolers' memories are limited, in part, because their general knowledge is limited.

Finally, there is growing evidence that *metamemory,* or knowing how memory works, is a critical factor in storing and retrieving information (Fishbein, 1984; Flavell, 1979; Flavell &

Wellman, 1977; Norman, 1969). Older children and adults have strategies for committing information to memory. Moreover, they have techniques for determining whether the information has been recorded. Preschoolers seem to lack such plans; their memory strategies seem haphazard.

We return to memory development in Chapter 9, where we discuss the intellectual revolution of middle childhood. The key point here is that although preschoolers remember much more than infants can, they are much less efficient than older children are.

Performance vs. Competence

The preceding description of preschool thought emphasizes the "babyishness" of preschoolers. Piaget and other cognitive psychologists tend to describe young thinkers in terms of what they cannot do. Preschoolers cannot imagine different points of view, cannot distinguish fantasy from reality, cannot understand conservation, cannot pay attention—the list continues. Indeed, the term *pre*operational implies deficiencies.

Rochel Gelman (1979) and others feel that preschoolers have been the victims of "bad press." In their view, too much emphasis has been placed on preschoolers' cognitive deficits and too little on their competencies. Gelman and Charles Gallistel (1978) suggest two main reasons why psychologists have underestimated preschoolers. First, most studies of cognitive development in childhood are based on comparisons of preschoolers and older children. The older child serves as the standard. The skills being measured are those he can usually perform. Gelman and Gallistel do not deny that young children fail a wide range of cognitive tasks that most older children perform with ease. Rather, they argue that using the older child as a standard diverts attention from what the younger child *can* do.

Second, the fact that many preschoolers perform poorly on cognitive tests does not necessarily mean that the young child is *unable* to think logically or to transcend egocentrism. Under limited demands, young children can actually use deductive reasoning (Hawkins, Pea, Glick, & Scribner, 1984). The problem may lie in the design of the experiment, not in the child. Under the right conditions, the child may be able to perform everything of which he is capable. This *competence/performance problem* occurs in all areas of psychological research. For example, a person may have certain areas of competence— such as jumping rope, singing a tune, reasoning deductively, or remembering a list of words— but not perform or demonstrate those skills in a given situation. The competence/performance problem is particularly significant in studies of young children (Briars & Siegler, 1984). A preschooler may fail a test because she is not accustomed to being asked certain questions, because she does not understand the meaning of certain words (*same* and *different*), or because she is not accustomed to the test situation or familiar with the test materials (Richards & Siegler, 1984).

New evidence indicates that preschoolers are not as cognitively inept as psychologists once believed (Gelman, 1979). The egocentrism of small children probably has been exaggerated (Black, 1981). In one experiment (Hughes, 1975), children were shown a table top divided into four sections or "rooms," by screens. A policeman was placed at the edge of one screen, a doll was put in one of the rooms and the child was asked whether the policeman could see the doll. Then a second policeman was put on the table and the child was asked to hide the doll from both officers. In another experiment (Flavell, Shipstead, & Croft, 1978) children were asked to hide a Snoopy doll behind a screen so that the experimenter could not see it from where she was sitting.

Like Piaget's three-mountain experiment, these studies were designed to test whether preschoolers understand other points of view. Whereas most small children "failed" Piaget's test, most "passed" the Snoopy and policeman tests. Why? For one thing, is it much easier to hide a doll than to *say* what another person sees. For another, Piaget's mountain task has little to do with the small child's everyday experience; he may not understand the point of it. The Snoopy and policeman dolls were familiar. The experience of hiding is also familiar: Most small children have tried to avoid the consequences of being naughty by hiding at one time or another. Given familiar materials, preschoolers showed that they were aware that other people see things from different points of view.

Preschoolers often give animistic answers to some questions, such as why the sun rises but practical, mechanical answers to others, such as why tires go flat (Gelman, 1978). They may demonstrate conservation on some tasks but not on others (Gelman, 1979). For example, unschooled Guatemalan children could not perform the usual Piagetian tasks. But they understood conservation as it applied to their farms (Lester & Klein, 1973). There is even evidence that children as young as 2½ have a rudimentary understanding of numbers (Gelman & Gallistel, 1978).

Studies of social perception lead to the same conclusion about preschoolers' cognitive abilities. Rochel Gelman and Marilyn Shatz (1977) observed the way 4-year-olds explained a toy to 2-year-olds, to children their own age, and to adults. With the 2-year-olds, the children used short, simple statements; with adults, they spoke in longer, more complex sentences. The conversations with 2-year-olds were limited to show-and-tell (statements designed to direct the toddler's attention to this or that). Conversations with adults included speculations and questions designed to confirm beliefs or seek information. It was clear to the team that these 4-year-olds were aware of the different mental capacities of the listeners.

In another study, Shatz (1973) asked 4- and 5-year-olds to help her select presents for a 2-year-old and for a child their own age. Resisting the (egocentric) temptation to pick something they themselves would like for a 2-year-old, they chose wisely. One child explained that she had rejected giving a letter-and-number board because 2-year-olds cannot read—hardly egocentric behavior. Janet Black (1981) reports that a mother took her 3-year-old to see a dog that someone wanted to give away. When she asked the child if she would like to have the dog for her own, the little girl was troubled. "But if we take Zoe, she [Zoe's owner] won't have a dog" (p. 51). Like adults, small children are sometimes egocentric, but they can also show empathy.

New research indicates that laboratory studies of memory may have underestimated the preschooler's abilities. Preschoolers are rarely required to engage in deliberate memorization, as are elementary school children. When asked to memorize a list of words or set of pictures, preschoolers may not understand why they are doing it or may not see that the task requires special effort (Flavell & Wellman, 1977). As a result, they perform poorly. Observations made outside the laboratory paint a different picture. Preschoolers have excellent memories for stories (Mandler, 1983). They learn all kinds of nursery rhymes and jingles on their own and almost never forget a parent's promise.

One team of psychologists (Todd & Perlmutter, 1980) studied 3- and 4-year-olds in their homes. The youngsters responded to questions about previous experiences in considerable detail and volunteered memories on their own. Only a small percentage of the incidents they recalled dealt with objects—the usual material for laboratory studies. Most of their mem-

ories were social: incidents involving themselves and other people. But most remarkable is the speed with which preschoolers learn new words (Carey, 1978). By the age 6, most children know about 14,000 words. To achieve this, they need to memorize ten or more new words a day between the time they start talking and their sixth birthday! In most cases, children only need to hear a word two or three times to understand what it means and how it is used. Poor memories, indeed!

This is not to say that preschoolers have the same cognitive abilities as older children have; they do not. Preschoolers may have some understanding of conservation or of other people's points of view. But their ability to apply this knowledge to different situations is limited. Faced with a new problem, an older child will compare it to problems he has faced before, then try a solution that worked in the past. The preschooler does not seem to generalize in this fashion. In this sense, he *is* preoperational.

Some cognitive skills may develop at an earlier age than Piaget believed. The boundaries between stages may not be as clear-cut as he suggested. Progress in different areas—concepts, measurements, social perception—may be uneven. Some children may be precocious in certain areas but slow in others. But Piaget's basic description of this stage remains useful. Children do acquire object permanence before they discover identities; they understand identities before they grasp conservation, and so on. To throw out Piaget on the basis of new data would be "throwing out the baby with the bath."[1]

The Thinker and the Doer: Perceptual and Motor Development

In her own way, the preschooler is a thinker. But it would be misleading to describe her as spending her days lost in thought! She is a whirl-

[1] See the profile of John Flavell at the end of Chapter 9.

wind of activity. Between the ages of 2 and 6, the child develops both fine and gross motor control. For the first time, she is able to investigate her environment on her own. She explores the boundaries of the playground on foot, a tricycle, or a scooter. She climbs a tree or boards a swing and surveys the horizons of her backyard from above. She builds a sprawling metropolis with her blocks and recreates the ocean with a pail of water in a sandbox. She also creates with crayons, paints, and, in time, a pencil.

Perceptual and motor advances in the preschool period have important consequences for the child's cognitive development. The "thinker's" quest for understanding is aided by the "doer's" active explorations. She is in perpetual motion, all the while learning by doing.

Piaget saw perceptual and cognitive development as separate but parallel. Through perceptual activity, the child gradually learns to correct distortions and to compensate for illusions. This process began in infancy. The baby perceives size, shape, and color as constant, even though things may look different from different angles or in different light. The 2-year-old boy may not know that three mountains look different from different perspectives, but he can recognize his teddy bear or the cookie jar from any angle. The 4-year-old boy knows that his father is tall even though he appears small when he is far down the block. *Perceptual constancy* develops hand-in-hand with object permanence.

Both are prerequisites for understanding identity and conservation. And both are established in the preoperational stage. Indeed, the preschooler's perceptual skills are more advanced than his thinking. He can't "think straight," but he can find his way around the neighborhood.

The preschooler's growing body awareness is an example of how perceptual and motor advances work together at this age. The preschooler knows the names of different parts of his body. His eager parents have been naming his foot, nose, and belly button ever since he was an infant in his bath. Now his activities and observations of other people lead him to make finer discriminations. He discovers that hands have five fingers, including a thumb, a baby finger, and even a "swear finger." He realizes that

The development of fine and gross motor control are two of the major tasks of preschool years.

the arrangement of fingers is the same no matter whose hand he examines. He sees that eyes are fringed by lashes and topped with eyebrows. He knows that while many parts of the body come in twos, we have only one nose and one mouth. "Tadpole" drawings are a universal sign of growing body awareness (see Figure 6-5).

All through the preschool period, children exercise new motor abilities, testing their limits and developing greater body control. Maneuvering through the playground and dealing with people and objects that stand in the way increases the child's awareness of physical prop-

erties and spatial relationships. The child picks up things and examines their shapes and sizes; tries to fit the pieces of a puzzle together; stuffs crayons back into their box; tries to squeeze her hand into a candy jar. With the aid of a few basic concepts, the preschooler begins to comprehend how the multitude of objects in his environment are organized. *Basic concepts* indicate the location of one object, person, or event in relation to others (Boehm, 1983). The child learns to place a ball *in front of* the teddy bear, to find the cookie that has fallen *under* the chair, to put his hands *over* his head, to give you the book

Argentina   The Philippines   Japan   China   Syria

Iran   Hong Kong   Denmark

Figure 6-5 "It's a Person!" At about age 4, children everywhere begin to draw tadpole figures that they label "Mommy," "a person," or "me." The child's first tadpole may be a happy accident—a circle with some protruding lines that is sufficiently humanoid to merit a human label. When the young artist discovers that he can regularly achieve this effect, he has entered the representation stage. The drawing stands for someone. Typically, youngsters draw tadpole after tadpole, delighted with their newfound ability. (Kellogg, 1969)

that is *on top* of the table, to tell you who is the *first* person in line, to take a seat *in the middle* of the row. Concepts dealing with size—biggest, smallest, fattest—also help the child to understand relationships among things.

The Boehm Test of Basic Concepts is used by school psychologists and educators as a guide for curriculum building, to plan educational experiences that foster the development of these concepts. Items from the Boehm Test are shown in Figure 6-6.

Adults and other children help the preschooler acquire these basic concepts. But as

.Now pick up your pencil.

Look at the animals. Mark the animal that is *next to* the rabbit. . . .

Look at the boxes and balls. Mark the box with the balls *inside* it. . . .

Look at the bowls of flowers. Mark the bowl that has *some but not many* flowers. . . .

Look at the children. Mark the child who is in the *middle*.

Piaget emphasized, to a large extent the child is "self-educated." In acting on the environment, she creates learning experiences that enhance her skills and general intellectual competence.

The Drawing: A Window to the Preschooler's World

Cognitive psychologists usually focus on the development of logic and the child's ability to solve scientific problems and understand scientific concepts such as conservation. The child's artistic abilities are often ignored—or left to clinical psychologists, who are interested in the child's feelings. But children are also artists and performers. Their songs and dances, stories and drawings, should be seen as important steps in mastering the use of symbols (Gardner, 1973; 1980).

Preschoolers love to draw. Drawing is a natural activity for children around the world (Kellogg, 1967). A crayon, a felt-tip marker, a paint brush, lipstick, even a stick, allows the child to make his mark on the world. To the chagrin of parents, these marks often end up on the wall, the pages of a book, or the child's clothes.

The popularity of drawing among preschoolers is only one reason for taking the child's artistic efforts seriously. Drawings are evidence that the child has a mental image of the world and wants to communicate this. They require the

Figure 6-6 Items from The Boehm Test of Basic Concepts

child to bring together many skills that are developing in this period. Perceptual, motor, and cognitive growth are all reflected in drawings. To translate mental images into graphics, a child must be able to integrate these different skills. A child's drawings are the proud product of a young thinker and doer. They deserve all the acknowledgment they receive in many American homes, in which children display artwork on the refrigerator door.

Drawing begins with scribbling straight or curvy lines that meander across the page (Day, 1978). Scribbling helps the child to develop a graphic vocabulary in much the same way babbling helps the child to develop the vocabulary of sounds necessary for speech. Early scribbles are the precursors of a symbol system that each child develops independently and uses in his or her own way. Spontaneously between the ages of 2 and 3 the child acquires the ability to make lines and shapes, crosses, circles, and so on. Once the child develops control over the production of lines, he is ready to make the leap into symbolism. The shapes and marks on the page stand for something else. At 3, a child will label a shape as "me" or "Mommy." A round shape may represent a whole person. As his perceptual and motor skills develop and his understanding of spatial relationships improves, the round shape will become a head on a human stick figure.

Gradually, the child's designs become recognizable to adults. By age 5 or 6, a child often draws a body and head with arms, legs, hands, feet, face, hair, and clothes in the appropriate places. She may add trees, a house, a ball, and other objects to the scene. The preschooler's drawings tend to be egocentric, with objects and other people in orbits around "me" like the planets around the sun. Eight- and 9-year-olds, who are more sophisticated and socially oriented, draw people and objects arranged horizontally along a baseline.

Five- and 6-year-olds often display a creativity that younger children lack and most older children lose (Gardner, 1973, 1980). They give free rein to their imagination. They are spontaneous in their production of visual images (and stories, dance, and other art forms) and in their responses to them. They exhibit many of the qualities we associate with adult artists (see Chapter 10). Their drawings are original and unconventional. They do not seem to feel the need to copy reality or to "draw by the rules." The main difference between the young artist and the mature one is that the preschooler is not in full command of his artistic faculties. His creations are not deliberate or intentional. Often the medium takes over: he is so mesmerized by the colors and patterns that he forgets himself. Only later does he think of a title or explanation of what he created. (See Figure 6-7.)

Figure 6-7 Expression and Inhibition Artistic expressiveness often peaks between ages 5 and 7. Children this age are uninhibited and creative in their stories, songs, and dances, as well as their drawing (see A). By age 8 or 9, many children have lost this flair. Concerned with achieving realistic, literal copies of what they see, older artists tend to produce such conventional drawings as that in B. (Gardner, 1980)

The uninhibited expressiveness of preschoolers often disappears during the school years. By age 10 or 11, children have become self-conscious and self-critical. If a child has not developed graphic abilities that satisfy her critical awareness, drawing is no longer fun. Children are most likely to develop artistic talents if they have intrinsic interest in a particular medium; if their environment offers opportunities and rewards for creativity; if they are alone much of the time and need to fill their world; and when unsettling experiences, such as the death of a cherished pet, stimulate a need to express strong emotions (Gardner, 1973). But many youngsters abandon art as a means of expression in middle childhood. The tragedy is that as adults, many of us continue to think and learn visually but do not have the skills to represent ideas graphically (Kellogg, 1967).

Drawings can be seen as a window to the world of children's thoughts and feelings. Children draw things that are significant to them. Ideas and concerns that otherwise may be hidden from adults are visible in their art. There is a wealth of developmental and psychological information hanging on the refrigerator door.

Ready, Set, Learn: Early Education

The label "preschooler" for children ages 2 to 6 is a misnomer in several ways. First, the young child has been an active student of his environment since birth. His whole world has been a classroom in which he learned many important skills from numerous instructors. Even if we limit the definition of *school* to a formal institution, many 3- and 4-year-olds go to day-care centers, nursery school, or other "preschool" educational institutions. Kindergarten for 5-year-olds has been incorporated into the national public education system. Many see it as a rehearsal hall where small children practice for their school debut in first grade. Others, however, consider early education serious business in its own right.

In the past, parents took responsibility for guiding the child's early development and for informal education in the home. Today, many Americans believe that all children should have preschool experience. Indeed, a popular magazine recently published an article on the intense competition to get 3- and 4-year-olds into the "right" nursery schools. The parents who were interviewed for the article were as nervous about their children's performance at admissions

Photographer David Seymour used art to document feelings in this photograph of a young survivor of the bombing of Warsaw during World War II. The photograph was part of a pictorial report on the effects of the war on European children, commissioned by UNESCO.

interviews for nursery school as parents of high-school students are about their children's Scholastic Aptitude Test scores. They spoke as though children who "made it" into the right nursery schools were assured of a bright future, and those who did not were doomed. Their concerns are only a slight exaggeration of a nationwide concern with giving children the right educational start.

Getting an Early Start

Like many other national enterprises, early education in the United States has been a melting pot of different ideas and interests. In the 1920s and 1930s a number of day-care centers and nursery schools were established in connection with child-study centers (see Chapter 1). Designed by developmental psychologists, these centers were laboratories for observation and study (Moore, 1977). During the Depression and again during World War II, the federal government sponsored play groups for small children—not because legislators believed that 3- and 4-year-olds needed a structured environment, but because it was a convenient way to employ out-of-work adults and to distribute food to hungry children. A "new wave" of nursery schools appeared in the 1940s and 1950s. They were modeled on new philosophies of child-rearing: the ideas of John Dewey, Sigmund Freud, Maria Montessori, and others (Weinberg, 1979).

Typical nursery schools of the 1950s emphasized the "whole child" (Moore, 1977). Teaching the children to get along with other children and adults, outside the home, was their primary goal. Encouraging youngsters to have fun was also a goal: Much of the day or morning was devoted to play, and children were provided with all sorts of dramatic props to stimulate their imaginations. There was some informal education in these nursery schools. Children were read stories and were encouraged to ask questions and to talk about what interested them (show-and-tell). Ideally, the youngsters left nursery school knowing "a little about a lot." But overall adjustment came first. The teacher–student relationship was modeled on the parent–child relationship, and the "curriculum" was an extension of the kind of informal learning opportunities offered in the home. The nursery schools of this period were a luxury available to those upper- and middle-class children whose parents could afford it.

Preschool education was extended to poor children in the 1960s. Countless studies had documented the impact of social class on intelligence tests, achievement tests, school performance, and by extension, adult occupations and income. Children from low-income families started school with less advanced cognitive skills than children from families with higher income, and this disadvantage remained over the school years. Why? According to what is called the cultural-deficit model, the very behavior that helped poor children to adapt to their everyday environments—the way they dealt with peers, related to authority, thought about the future—made it difficult for them to adapt to school. They "spoke a different language." The cycle of poverty—each new generation following the last onto the unemployment lines and welfare rolls—was attributed to the so-called culture of poverty. Poor minority children were socialized to fail in school and, by extension, in life.

A number of universities began designing and testing early-education programs for poor children. The hope was that early intervention with children (and in some cases parents) would compensate for cultural deficits, stimulate cognitive development, and enable low-income children to enter school on a more equal footing.

Project Head Start

Project Head Start was launched in 1964 as part of President Lyndon Johnson's War on Poverty.

Insight

"SESAME STREET": THE VIDEO EXPERIMENT

Parents and teachers are not the only agents of preschool education. In the past decade or so, television has become a leading preschool "teacher," responsible for millions of "pupils." "Sesame Street," a creation of the Children's Television Workshop, was a pioneer in this area. The program first appeared on educational TV channels in November 1969. To date, the program has been shown in some 50 nations. Its audience has included millions of children *and adults*. The Cookie Monster, Ernie, and other residents of Sesame Street have become household names. Big Bird—the program's 7-foot-tall, yellow-feathered mascot—even visited the People's Republic of China in 1979.

"Sesame Street" was designed to teach small children to recognize and name letters, numbers, shapes, and body parts; to count and tell time; and to classify objects by size, place, and function. Other TV programs had had similar goals. "Sesame Street" was unique because its creators borrowed the advertising techniques Madison Avenue uses to sell cereals and toys to children on TV to teach basic concepts. They used animation, jingles and rhymes, comedy, repetition, and quick changes in pace and style to "sell" knowledge and skills. The Children's Television Workshop did not claim that "Sesame Street" was a substitute for a good nursery school. They did hope to reach the millions of preschoolers who have no opportunity to attend nursery school, but do have access to TV.

Does "Sesame Street" increase preacademic achievement? Studies by the Educational Testing Service during the first and second years of the program found that, indeed, viewers did learn numbers, letters, and classification (Ball & Bogatz, 1972). The more children watched the show, the more they learned, especially if adults watched the show with them and talked about what they were viewing. Disadvantaged children were less likely to become

regular viewers than their more advantaged peers. But when they watched, they learned.

Does "Sesame Street" have lasting effects? Do disadvantaged children who have been exposed to the program do better in elementary school than they might otherwise? Apparently not. Sprigle (1972) compared "Sesame Street" graduates from low-income families to other children. Watching the program for one or even two years did not close the achievement gap. At the end of first grade, working-class children had significantly better vocabularies, arithmetic scores, and study skills than did low-income viewers. But disadvantaged children in a control group, who had been enrolled in a preschool program that emphasized social skills, did show significant gains. A fancy format and attractive characters are not a substitute for "caring, interacting, teaching, in-the-flesh adults" (Honig, 1983, p. 66).

Some critics have argued that "Sesame Street" may even be harmful. The rapid-fire presentation of short, entertaining fragments of learning material may foster a short attention span. The emphasis on rote learning and repetition of numbers and letters may interfere with the development of learning strategies. According to these critics, the program pays too little attention to social and emotional development: Learning by sitting on the floor and looking at "the tube" encourages passivity. But the creators of "Sesame Street" never claimed that their program should be the only meaningful show on children's television, or the only learning experience in a preschooler's life. There is no evidence that Big Bird and Ernie interfere with cognitive development. Children who watch the show with an adult do show intellectual gains. Even if they do not learn very much, most preschoolers *like* "Sesame Street."

It was a multipurpose program, designed to involve members of low-income communities in the planning of their children's education; to hire members of those communities as teachers and assistants; to provide children with nutritious meals and medical and dental care; and to help families and children cope with physical disabilities and personality problems. But the program's primary goal was to prepare economically disadvantaged children for school. Children in isolated rural areas and minority children were special targets for aid.

In contrast to the nursery schools of the 1950s, Head Start emphasized education—or more precisely, learning to learn. The curriculum usually included instruction in standard English and the use of basic concepts. Children were taught to classify objects and events in terms of temporal and spatial relationships ("before" and "after"; "distant" and "near"), size, color, and shape. They were taught to count. Some programs taught reading as well. Instruction was offered on an individual or small-group basis, and children were allowed to proceed at their own pace. Head Start centers were not like first-grade classrooms, but neither were they like home. Educators spent a good deal of effort instilling such habits as paying attention, listening to teachers, and following the rules.

The centers used a number of different models of parental involvement. Some programs were center based. In these, parents were informed about the program and, in some cases, participated in planning; but they were not involved in daily activities. Other programs were home based. Here, "parent educators" visited homes; provided toys, books, games, and other materials for use in the home; and trained parents (usually mothers) in techniques for promoting cognitive development. Other programs used a combined approach. But the goal was always the same: to give poor children a better chance to succeed in school.

From a relatively modest summer program, Head Start mushroomed into a major national effort (Collins, 1983). Over 8.3 million Americans are Head Start graduates. In these days of federal cutbacks, the Reagan administration requested more than a billion dollars for programs serving 1,200 communities and about 429,000 children in 1984. Project Head Start has turned out to be one of the most ambitious, influential, and controversial social programs in this country's educational history.

Conflicting Report Cards

The first evaluations of Head Start were not encouraging. A national study conducted by Westinghouse Learning Corporation and Ohio State University (Ciccirelli, 1969) indicated that children who had participated in Head Start performed better in school than did members of control groups who had not had preschool training. But the benefits were small and usually disappeared after two or three years in elementary school—the so-called fade-out phenomenon (Wolff & Stein, 1966). Other studies seemed to confirm this conclusion.

Response to these early reports was immediate and strong. Some psychologists, such as Arthur Jensen (1969), held that the apparent failure of Head Start demonstrated that education could not overcome innate intellectual deficits. Others, such as Urie Bronfenbrenner (1974), argued that it was absurd to think one could change the child without changing the family and community in which the child lived. For many legislators and for much of the public, the implication was clear: Head Start was an enormous waste of federal funds.

More recent reports paint a different picture, however. Two independent studies traced Head Start graduates through elementary school, and in some cases through high school (Lazar & Darlington, 1982; Schweinhart & Weikart, 1980). These researchers measured attitudes and behavior as well as test scores. Both teams found that early education had significant, long-lasting effects on low-income youngsters. The most recent report, issued by the Head Start Evaluation, Synthesis, and Utilization Project (Collins, 1983), found that the Head Start programs themselves have improved over the years. According to this report, Head Start graduates show immediate gains in basic cognitive skills and school readiness. They outperform other low-income children in elementary school, although they are still below the norm on standardized tests. They are less likely to be held back or placed in remedial classes, or to drop out of school. Some Head Start graduates may maintain this superiority on achievement tests in high school. According to this report, the children who benefit most from participating in Head Start are the most needy: children whose mothers have a tenth-grade education or less, who live in single-parent families,

or who had low IQs before they entered Head Start.

The Readiness Debate

Despite positive reports from Head Start in recent years, the debate over early intervention continues. Underlying the controversy over Head Start is the ongoing debate over the importance of early experience in a child's development. On one hand are those who maintain that the early years are critical (Bloom, 1964). According to this view, the ability to learn in later life depends on the quality and quantity of early learning experiences. Although many developmental psychologists find this claim extreme, they agree with Benjamin Bloom in principle concerning the need for early childhood learning experiences.

The early-intervention position is based on four basic assumptions (Goldhaber, 1979):

1. Children are malleable; their growth and development is shaped by their experiences.
2. Development is cumulative. If basic structures are not established in early childhood, later attempts to influence development are likely to fail. (No matter how well built the house, it will fall if it does not have a solid foundation.)
3. The earlier one intervenes in a child's development, the better.
4. Because performance in school plays a critical role in the individual's future opportunities in our society, the emphasis in early education programs should be on developing basic learning skills.

Extending this line of reasoning, Joseph McVicker Hunt (1961) compared the effects of "cultural deprivation" on the cognitive development of poor children to the effects of social deprivation on isolated laboratory animals, such as Harlow's monkeys (see Chapter 2). The harm of such deprivation could never be undone. Together, Bloom and Hunt provided much of the theoretical and empirical rationale for Project Head Start. Their views contributed to a sense of national urgency.

Other psychologists reject the belief that early experience is decisive. In their view, cognitive development follows a genetically programmed course. Children cannot benefit from learning experiences until they are cognitively ready to acquire new knowledge and skills. Readiness depends on the child's age and level of physiological development, especially brain development (Gesell, Ilg, & Ames, 1974). From this point of view, the level of maturity sets limits on the effects of teaching and practice. The child cannot benefit from instruction in reading, for example, if she is not yet "ready to read"—that is, if she has not yet reached the appropriate level of maturity for reading and comprehension.

The readiness approach is also based on four assumptions:

1. The genetic timetable is as important to the child's development as are environmental experiences, particularly in the early years.
2. Development is continuous. There is little evidence of "critical periods" in a child's cognitive development. If children who have been deprived of early learning experiences perform poorly in school in later years, it is because they remain in the same environments–not because they were intellectually "traumatized" in early childhood. (No matter how firm the foundation, a house that is shabbily built will not stand.)

3. Early intervention to improve cognitive skills will have little impact if it stops the day the child enters first grade.
4. The emphasis on developing cognitive skills in Head Start and other preschool programs is misplaced.

Developmental psychologists who emphasize readiness question both the urgency and the impact of early intervention. Some have argued that preschool training is not only ineffective, but potentially harmful. David Elkind (1981) and William Rohwer (1971) warn that extending formal education to early childhood—pushing children to learn at younger ages—may produce generations of cognitively "burned out" children. According to Rohwer, the prime period for training intellectual skills is adolescence, when the young person is capable of formal operations. Others simply believe that we have placed too much emphasis, and too high hopes, on early cognitive training.

A moderate view in this controversy emphasizes the *match* between the child's level of cognitive development and her educational experiences (Hunt, 1961). The child is not able to learn new things until she is equipped with certain prerequisite information and skills. The Russian psychologist Lev Vygotsky (1978) emphasized the **zone of proximal development**—that is, the zone of near or almost development (see Figure 6-8). These are the things a child can almost do, the things she can do with help. For example, a preschooler may not be able to complete a jigsaw puzzle on her own, but she is able to do it if her mother assists: "Try this one," "Look for a red piece," and so on. Teaching preschoolers is most effective when the adult deals with skills or ideas the child is beginning to grasp. But trying to teach a preschooler how to "add" together three piles of blocks will be useless if the child has not yet mastered basic counting skills. She must be aware that each object in a group must be assigned one and only one number word; be able to recite the number words in a consistent order (one, two, three); and so on (Gelman & Gallistel, 1978).

The young child can master many tasks once thought beyond her reach because of "immaturity." The child's readiness to benefit from many learning situations is limited only by the skills she already has. The challenge to early childhood teachers is to better understand the nature of the tasks young children must learn and the skills needed to assimilate new knowledge—whether it is the ability to tie one's own shoes, play with peers, follow instructions, tell time, write one's own name, or name the letters of the alphabet and associate them with sounds.

A moderate view emphasizes the importance of *continuity* between preschool and

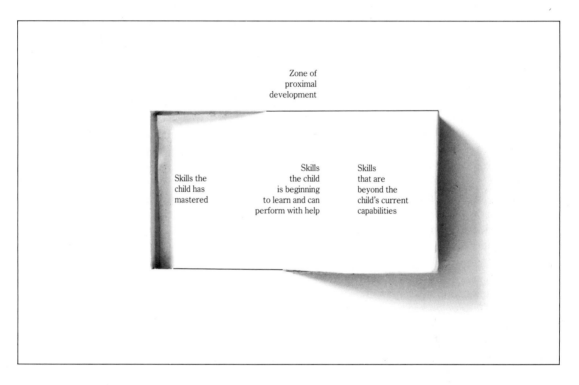

Figure 6-8 The Zone of Proximal Development Lev Vygotsky's zone of proximal development is any group of activities that a child can almost perform or can perform with help. Vygotsky distinguished these activities from those the child cannot yet perform even with help. (Based on Vygotsky, 1978)

ome and
luch evi-
chool are
an, 1976;
r parents
imes with
or the role
r children
h for first
table with
its in the
tional pro-
ect families
ing homes,
educational

materials, and teaching parents ____ to prepare their children. In multiethnic communities, they can set up bilingual and bicultural programs in areas where many children come from different ethnic backgrounds.

The transition from preschool to school programs is often abrupt. Despite the emphasis on cognitive development in some preschool programs today, most are informal. Children are allowed to choose their own activities, to move about the room as their interests dictate, to interrupt the teacher, for example. In contrast, most first-grade classrooms are formal in structure. The teacher decides what children should attend to; speaking out of turn is not allowed; getting up without permission is forbidden. The child who has become accustomed to self-directed learning is suddenly confronted with teacher-directed learning. Establishing lines of communication between preschool and elementary teachers eases the transition for children. Youngsters feel more comfortable in first grade if they meet their new teacher in advance, or their old teacher visits them in their new school. Keeping classes together, so that children who have been classmates before can help one another adjust to new demands, also contributes to continuity.

The moderate view also suggests that *expanding* the child's mental horizons is as important to future development as accelerating his cognitive growth—perhaps more so. Many education programs stress language and logic, facts and figures. But many psychologists believe that cognitive development also results from play, children's conversations with one another, their musings on life, death, and reality, and their concepts of good and evil.

One of the major goals of early education should be to make learning and mastery rewarding. In Rohwer's words, "The guiding principle of early education (preschool and elementary) should be to provide the child with repeated experiences of gratification resulting from intellectual activity" (1971, p. 338). This is not to say that teachers should forget about counting, spelling, multiplication tables and other "difficult" subjects. The educators' challenge is to match the task to be learned to the child's level of development and to engage the child's natural motivation for achieving competency.

Child's Play

We have called ages 2 to 6 the preschool period, to emphasize the social and cognitive developments that prepare a child for his or her first "job," that of student. But this period might also be described as the play years. Small children spend hour upon hour exploring, experimenting, being silly, chasing, shouting, pretending, and having fun.

What Is Play?

Play eludes precise definition (Vandenberg, 1978). After all, what do riding a tricycle, cuddling a teddy bear, wrestling, finger painting, playing Pac Man, and dressing up have in common? Many psychologists think Konrad Lorenz (1966) was wise to say, "Don't ask me to give a definition." We will not attempt to squeeze the concept into a single sentence. But we can highlight here some of the distinctive features of play (Rubin, Fein, & Vandenberg, 1983).

1. *Intrinsic motivation.* Play activities are spontaneous and freely chosen. Behavior that is motivated by a biological need, such as hunger or thirst, or by social demands does not qualify as play. (Dressing up as a space invader or a princess is play; dressing for church or a birthday party is not.)

2. *Attention to means.* Play is not a means to an end; it is an end in itself. Goals are self-imposed and can change at the whim of the player. A child might set out to build a tower, but find that using her blocks as barnyard animals is more fun. Freed from "the straightjacket of means–ends considerations," the child can combine familiar materials or actions in new ways (Rubin et al., 1983, p. 698). A youngster who has learned to zoom down a sliding board tries climbing up it. He fails, time after time—that's the fun of it.

3. *Pretense.* Much play involves make-believe. The child acts *as if* an object (a chair) were something else (a horse). Two children act *as if* they were warlords fighting for control of a planet. But both know that they aren't really warlords. The fight isn't serious, it's simulated.

4. *Active engagement.* Playing is active, often exaggerated behavior. Daydreaming, loafing, or lounging in front of the TV are not really play. The child is not actively engaged. Often play takes the form of "galumphing" (Miller, 1973)—silly, useless actions performed for their own sake.

5. *Freedom from external rules.* Play is spontaneous and free-form; games like checkers or baseball are played according to established rules. This distinction is not absolute, however. In make-believe, preschoolers strive to conform to the social norms for the role they are playing—and they expect others to do the same (Garvey, 1977). In games-with-rules, children may be more interested in running and shouting than in winning. Thus play may be governed by rules, and games may be intrinsically motivated.

In short, the difference between play and nonplay is largely subjective. For example, drawing letters may be play in one situation (such as trying out new magic markers) and work in another (such as a first-grade assignment). If the activity is voluntary, relatively spontaneous, open-ended, and fun, we would call it play.

Types of Play

A look at the different ways children have fun points out the functions of play in development. Like the young of many other species, young humans engage in all kinds of solitary *motor play*. Running, jumping, skipping, and "frolicking in the woods" are examples of action for action's sake. In species that are relatively mature at birth, motor play exercises skills that the animal already possesses. In humans, who are helpless at birth, motor play lays the foundation for later development of complex action patterns (Vandenberg, 1978). Children practice scaling the heights of the stairs or a mountain of snow, and jumping over puddles or logs, before they take on the challenge of climbing a jungle gym, jumping rope, playing hopscotch, or riding a bike. Jerome Bruner (1972) suggests that play enhances behavioral flexibility. At play, a child does not worry about the consequences of behavior. He plays with his own abilities, experimenting with small acts and new combinations of actions which may later be applied to serious business. Play expands the child's motor repertoire.

A second type of play is *object play*. Object play also occurs in other species. Puppies chew slippers and chase sticks; kittens toy with a ball of string or their own tails. But the ritualized play routines of lower animals do not compare to the flexible, manipulative object play of primates, especially humans. Object play enables children to learn about physical properties, spacial relations, and mechanics in an unthreatening situation: "If it's play, you can't fail." Free to experiment, the child can invent new uses for objects and devise new strategies for solving problems. This knowledge can be put to serious use at a later date. Bruner (1972) hypothesizes that our species' ability to use tools—and, through tools, to alter our environment—builds on early object play.

A third common type of play is *social play*. Play allows children to commit social blunders and engage in inappropriate behavior without paying the consequences. There is room for error. A child can excuse misbehavior by saying, "I was *only* playing." Preschoolers can use play to try on different social roles, mimic adult behavior, rehearse social relationships, review past experiences, and perhaps rewrite them. They can learn what might have happened if they had done this instead of that. Social play need not involve other people directly. Preschoolers engage in a good deal of solitary role-playing. They talk to themselves, to imaginary friends, and to dolls and teddy bears. (Adults also do this, but usually not when another person might overhear them.)

Make-Believe

Humans are the only animals who engage in pretend play or make-believe. A juvenile chimpanzee may attempt to play with a baby chimp in her group, but it does not treat a piece of wood *as if* it were a baby. A young chimp or gorilla may build a play nest, imitating adults, but it doesn't build sand castles based on fantasy worlds. A child may pretend that he is a gorilla; a gorilla does not pretend that he is a human.

Make-believe depends on symbols. In make-believe, children use objects to stand for other objects and pretend to be someone other

Rough-and-tumble play is a common pattern among mammals, especially young male mammals. Boys are no exception. Note the similarity between the chimp's "play grimace" and the expression of the boy at the bottom of the pile.

than themselves. Piaget (1962) described the development of make-believe, or what he called *symbolic play,* as an inverted U. Up to about age 18 months, play takes the form of repeating sensorimotor activities, with or without objects. Piaget called this *practice play.* Between ages 2 and 5 (the preoperational stage of cognitive development), children spend more and more time in symbolic play—the uniquely human *as-if* activity. By age 6 or 7 (the beginning of the concrete operations stage), symbolic play has declined and children are more interested in *games-with-rules.* At the beginning of this curve, play is usually solitary. Two children may engage in parallel activities, but there is little interaction or exchange. As the level of symbolic play increases, so does the amount of give-and-take, turn-taking, and cooperation between children. By the time children reach the game stage, most play is social. (See Figure 6-9.)

Contemporary research has revised this picture somewhat (Rubin et al., 1983). Pretend gestures appear rather suddenly as 12 to 13 months, in children of different cultures and social classes. The infants' actions mimic real-life activities (for example, sleeping or drinking). But they are separated from their usual contexts (in this case, bedtime or mealtime) and their usual outcomes (sleeping or a full stomach). At first, these gestures are directed toward the self (the child pretends he is sleep-

ing); later in the preschool years they are directed toward other people, real and imaginary. Infants use objects for their usual social purposes, such as a cup for drinking. Later they use substitute objects—such as a shell for a cup, a block for a pillow—and still later they engage in make-believe without props. Action sequences become more complex during the preschool years. The child begins by giving her doll imaginary milk from a cup. Later she will feed, bathe, and dress the doll in sequence.

The amount of time preschoolers devote to pretend play increases from age 3 to age 5 or 6 and then declines (Rubin et al., 1983). A look at the social contexts of make-believe reveals more complex patterns, however. Group games of make-believe increase during the preschool years, then decline in late kindergarten or early elementary school. Solitary pretend play peaks at about age 3, declines between ages 4 and 5, then seems to rise again at age 6 or 7. One reason may be that games-with-rules require new skills. The child may use solitary play to practice and consolidate these social skills when away from the group.

According to Piaget, the infant's solitary practice play is "pure assimilation": fitting new experiences into existing schemes. Peer play, however, often forces accommodation. When two children do not agree about the rules of the game, or about how they should play their re-

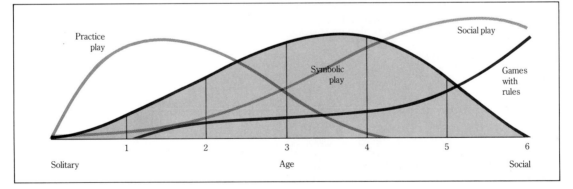

spective roles, they have to negotiate. Two 4-year-old boys are pretending to be father and mother:

> FATHER: So long, I'll see ya later. It's time to go to work.
> MOTHER: Hey, wait for me! I gotta go to work too!
> FATHER: Hey, my mom don't work . . . you stay here.
> MOTHER: Well my mom works . . . lotsa womens work ya know. My mom is a perfessor at the unibersity.
> FATHER: O.K. then, just hurry so we won't be late. Are you sure ya wanna work?
> (Rubin, 1980, p. 75)

The Role of Play in Development: A Proposal

Brian Vandenberg (1978) proposes a model sequence for the role of play in development: exploration → play → application. In other words, play occupies a pivotal position between the acquisition and use of information.

Exploration is cautious, gradual, controlled investigation of something new in the environment. Play, in contrast, is characterized by vigorous activity and spirited manipulations of objects. Caution is thrown to the wind! When children (or young animals) are exposed to something that they have never encountered before, or to something that violates their ex-

pectations, they explore before they play (Weisler & McCall, 1976). An experiment with nursery-school children illustrated the exploration-to-play phase of the sequence. Corinne Hutt (1976) brought children one at a time into a familiar room that contained a curiosity box. This one was red metal with brass legs, a lever with a bright blue handle, and various dials, buzzers, and bells. At first the children were cautious, serious, and intense. They explored the strange object tentatively. After several exposures, however, they attacked the box with glee. In the exploratory phase, the children seemed to be asking, "What does this object do?" In the play phase, the question changed to, "What can I do with this object?" The unspoken answer was, "Anything I wish."

The play-to-application phase of the sequence is illustrated by experiments on play and problem solving. In a typical experiment (Sylva, 1977), children were presented with a problem and the pieces of a solution. For example, they were asked to retrieve a piece of chalk that was beyond their grasp without getting out of the chair. They were given several short sticks and several clamps to do so. To reach the chalk, they had to clamp the sticks together. Children in the experimental group were given time to play with the sticks and clamps before they were presented with the problem; children in the control group were not given any time. In

Figure 6-9 The Curve of Make-Believe
(Based on Piaget, 1962)

Insight

MAKE-BELIEVE IN CROSS-CULTURAL PERSPECTIVE

Most Western psychologists assume that play is a natural and necessary part of growing up. Make-believe is assigned a special role in the development of both symbolic capacities and social understanding. Is make-believe universal? Do children everywhere pretend? Dina Feitelson's review of the cross-cultural literature (1977) suggests not.

In many small, preindustrial societies children imitate their elders, practicing for adulthood. But they do not transform adult activities into games of their own; they do not invent fantasy worlds or act out stories of their own invention. Rather, they copy adult behavior as literally as they can. Caring for a doll, or stalking lizards with a child-sized bow and arrow, is seen as serious preparation for adult work. In these societies adults often work near their homes or take children to their work. Children have numerous opportunities to observe how their parents and relatives make their livings, and they begin participating in the family livelihood as soon as they are able. Make-believe is unknown.

In six months of close observation of about forty children on the island of Manus in the South Pacific, Margaret Mead observed small girls playing house only once. Anthropologists who have studied rural communities in Africa and the Middle East report that children are silent observers who study adult life from the sidelines. Toys are rare and sometimes absent altogether. Children in rural Indian villages engage in a good deal of chasing, teasing, and galumphing. But in some African villages even this is discouraged.

Children's play seems to depend on four factors: (1) play space, an area that adults give to children for their own use; (2) legitimate time, or periods of free time in which children are not held responsible for child care or household chores; (3) play objects, or materials children can transform through imagination, often missing in arid zones or societies where there are too few household implements to spare; and (4) an atmosphere conducive to play. The last factor may be the most important. If adults do not consider play a legitimate activity, they are not likely to give children objects, free time, and space.

Cross-cultural studies suggest that make-believe does not develop spontaneously, but requires encouragement and perhaps modeling by adults. Feitelson concludes that "play, like all social behavior, is . . . part and parcel of the social relationships and cultural traditions of the society in which it occurs" (p. 13).

---

general, children who had an opportunity to play first solved the problem faster, with fewer hints, than those who had no opportunity to play with the materials. There is also some evidence (Dansky, 1980) that playful children, who are prone to fantasy and make-believe, are more creative than are nonplayful children.

Vandenberg summarizes what the exploration-to-play-to-application sequence contributes to the development of social competence in preschoolers and other social animals:

[For] social animals, the integration of an individual into the protective social unit requires that the animal learn the expected behaviors necessary for mature social interaction. The organism's approach to this novel situation is developmentally similar to its approach to a novel object. The animal must first *explore* the environment to ensure that it is safe. . . . Only after finding it safe will the animal then engage in social play. Through *play,* the animal masters the mature social behaviors that it then *applies* in a "serious" context. . . . Extensive social play is necessary for later successful social intercourse. (1978, p. 736)

It is no wonder that play flourishes in the preschool years, when social adaptation is one of the child's key challenges.

The Drive for Competence

Throughout the preschool period, children are learning to learn and to communicate more efficiently and more completely (Siegler, 1983). Whether in problem-solving or in artistic creation, the preschooler's growing ability to "use her head"—to represent objects, people, and events internally, in the form of images and symbols—is a major step toward more mature thinking.

What moves the child forward? One reason for cognitive development is maturation. Between the ages of one and two, the areas of the

The pride preschoolers take in fastening their shoes is an example of what Kagan calls mastery motivation and White terms the drive for competence.

brain that oversee motor activity and sensory input mature. Some biopsychologists (for example, Eichorn, 1970) have reported that the EEG (electroencephalogram) pattern, which reflects chemical activity in the brain, stabilizes just before one year of age. Most of the reflexes associated with brain immaturity disappear at this time. These findings support the notion that physiological changes in the brain lead to psychological reorganization of thought. The "wiring" of the brain may have reached sufficient maturity to permit new ways of processing information.

The evolutionary perspective suggests additional reasons for the child's newfound skills (Fishbein, 1984). As the child becomes more mobile, she needs better means of acquiring and processing information. She is not as protected by adults as she was when she was cradled and carried in infancy. Acquiring the rudiments of language, understanding instructions, and other advances in learning abilities improve her chances of survival. To keep up with others of the species, the child must change.

In a classic essay, Robert White (1959) proposed that evolution equipped humans with an inborn drive to deal competently with the environment. The *drive for competence* leads us to experiment and explore. The results of these experiences make us better able to adapt and survive.

Almost from birth, infants exert active efforts to understand the physical and social worlds and to have some power over them. The struggle for mastery begins with sucking, looking, and grasping, and continues with crawling and walking, language and thinking, "manipulating and exploring the environment" (White, 1959, p. 317). White's main point is that "competence is its own reward." Even young children strive to achieve mastery over their environments. Their persistence is often extraordinary. Children (and adults) pursue new challenges for the sheer pleasure of succeeding at a chosen activity.

Development in the preoperational period is part of an ongoing adaptive process. The preschool child is engrossed in learning language, constructing simple mental representations of the world, manipulating objects, and exercising his body. These activities not only produce immediate satisfaction, but also enhance the child's social competence.

SUMMARY

1. According to Piaget, the most significant advance of the preoperational stage is the ability to form mental images and use symbols. Deferred imitation is the first sign of this; the development of language is the cornerstone. Preoperational thinking is characterized by:
   a) intuition, or the ability to imagine solutions to problems without resorting to physical trial and error;
   b) egocentrism, or difficulty understanding that other people see things from different angles;
   c) magical thinking, or the belief that inanimate objects have thoughts and feelings, all events are motivated, and dreams are real;
   d) centering, or the inclination to focus on one dimension or feature, ignoring others, and to concentrate on present states rather than on transformations;
   e) the tendency to be seduced by appearances;
   f) dependence on concrete mental images.
2. Preschoolers process information differently than older children do. They tend to react rather than investigate; they are easily distracted by irrelevant information; and they seldom plan ahead mentally. Their ability to remember, and their understanding of memory, is poor compared to older children.
3. New research indicates that preschoolers are not as intellectually limited as this portrait implies. When tested "on their own grounds" (about familiar characters such as Snoopy or their own memory of everyday events), they demonstrate more advanced capacities. But they do not employ these skills in a regular, systematic way.
4. Observation and activity, perceptual and motor development, increase the preschooler's knowledge of her environment and understanding of basic concepts.
5. Drawing and other artistic activities are an important chapter in the child's mastery of symbols. Young artists usually advance from scribbles, to shapes they label as people or objects, to recognizable images and (too often) to self-consciousness and inhibition in middle childhood.
6. Most preschoolers have at least some experience with formal instruction. The interest in early education today can be traced in part to Head Start, a massive preschool program designed for poor and minority children. The

latest studies indicate that Head Start may improve achievement and attitudes toward school among the most disadvantaged.

7. The debate over preschool programs is part of an ongoing disagreement over the importance of early experience. Psychologists who support early intervention view the first four years as critical to cognitive development; those who emphasize readiness to learn argue that acceleration may destroy motivation. A moderate approach focuses on the match between a child's level of development and educational goals, continuity, and expanding intellectual horizons.

8. Play is an integral part of the preschooler's cognitive and social development. The young of many other species engage in motor play, object play, and social play, but only humans pretend. Make-believe increases during the preschool years, then declines as children take up games-with-rules. Play can be seen as an adaptive form of practicing behavior before applying it in serious contexts.

9. The preschooler's efforts to draw, swim, tell stories, understand how things work can be seen as an expression of a drive for competence that is part of our species' evolutionary heritage.

FURTHER READING

Boehm, A. E., & Weinberg, R. A. (1977). *The classroom observer: A guide for developing observation skills.* New York: Teachers College Press. This brief book describes how each of us can systematically and reliably observe children's behavior as a basis for planning educational programs and making other decisions about children.

Flavell, J. H. (1977). *Cognitive development.* Englewood Cliffs, NJ: Prentice-Hall, 1977. An excellent summary and evaluation of Piaget's theory and introduction to contemporary views of cognitive development.

Gardner, H. (1980). *Artful scribbles: The significance of children's drawings.* New York: Basic Books. This book takes children's artwork seriously, tying the development of drawing, from scribbles to abstract forms, to other aspects of child development.

Garvey, C. (1977). *Play.* Cambridge, MA: Harvard University Press. A beautifully written statement of the different forms of play and their role in children's physical, cognitive, social, and emotional development.

Singer, D. G., & Revenson, T. A. (1978). *A Piaget primer: How a child thinks.* New York: Plume. A clear, simplified introduction to Piagetian ideas that applies and gives focus to his work. This paperback draws on *Winnie the Pooh, Alice in Wonderland, Peanuts,* and other classic and popular literature for children to illustrate his views.

Zigler, E., & Valentine, J. (Eds.). (1979). *Project Head Start: A legacy of the war on poverty.* New York: The Free Press. This is a fascinating comprehensive history and analysis of one of our nation's largest social experiments. The book is informative in its historical perspective and treatment of Head Start's development.

Cognition: Piaget's Preoperational Stage

Deferred imitation
(e.g., tantrum)
<18–24 mos.>

Egocentrism   [Adjusts speech to baby]
[but not with Snoopy
or in speech to baby]

Relies on intuition and trial and error

Seduced by appearances
(phenomenalism)

Information processing

Attention: From "explorer" . . .
(reactive, random, nonselective)

Memory: Limited and disorganized   [but good memory for words,
(on school-like tasks)   jingles, and stories]

Drawing

Scribbles   Lines and shapes   Private symbols
(shapes that stand
for something)

Play

Practice play (repeated sensorimotor schemes)
<peaks at 3 yrs.>

Pretend gestures   Plays with
<10–12 mos.>   substitute objects
(stick for horse)

2   3
Age in years

HIGHLIGHTS OF COGNITIVE AND RELATED DEVELOPMENT IN THE PRESCHOOL PERIOD

< > onset or peak
[ ] qualifications
⩽ age extension beyond
⩾ that shown on chart

⩽ Conducts mental
experiments
< + 6 yrs. >

Animism ("The stairs hit me") and precausal reasoning

Grasps identity → ⩽ conservation

[Conservation only on limited,
familiar tasks]

. . . to "searcher"
(investigative, systematic,
selective)

Increases in organization,
capacity, knowledge base,
and metamemory

Attempts at realism   Socially oriented   ⩽ Inhibition
drawings   ⩽ <10–11 yrs. >

Games-with-rules
<6 yrs. on>

Make-believe (with, then without, props)
<peaks at 5–6 yrs. >

| 4 | 5 | 6 |

CHAPTER

7

There are many developmental milestones in the child's early years: the baby's first social smiles, his first drink from a cup, his first steps, his first ride on a tricycle, his first day in nursery school. But these achievements pale in comparison to the child's first words.

For the first year of life, infants are speechless. Parents and others can only guess about what they want, need, or think. At age 1, a child may have a small, idiosyncratic vocabulary. In *Conversations with a One-Year-Old,* Ronald Scollen (1976) reports that Brenda's vocabulary at this age consisted of three "words": "nene" (meaning milk, juice, or bottle, or sometimes mother or sleep), "awa" (I don't want), and "da" (for doll). At age 1, Brenda needed a translator to communicate with people outside her immediate family.

At three or four the same child will be a fluent speaker. Her vocabulary may be limited; her grammar may not be perfect; she may stumble over pronunciation. But she will be quite capable of making herself understood, errors and all. Indeed, most adults are charmed by a youngster's mistakes—as when a small child calls every man in a uniform "Daddy," asks for "pesgetti" (spaghetti), or declares, "His is gooder than mine." But no one enjoys learning how to speak more than the child herself.

Anyone who has struggled to learn a foreign language knows how difficult it is. Acquiring vocabulary is only a beginning: One must recognize subtleties of pronunciation and intonation, master the intricacies of grammar, learn what forms are polite or impolite in different situations, and more. *All* language is foreign to a baby. Yet without any formal instruction, all normal children master the language spoken in their environment in the space of four or five years.

Language development is remarkable—whether it is seen from the perspective of parents, who observe their child's growing competence, from the broader perspective of developmental psychologists, or from an evolutionary view of the human species. We begin this chapter by analyzing what makes human

COMMUNICATING
WITH LANGUAGE

languages unique, then turn to language development.

Language and Communication

Human beings do not have a monopoly on communication. Birds do it, bees do it, whales and chimpanzees do it (to paraphrase Cole Porter). No matter how solitary its daily existence may seem, every animal must get together with others of its kind occasionally if only to mate. If a creature were unable to communicate—unable to transmit and receive information—social contact would not be possible.

Billing and Cooing: The Basics of Communication

The forms of animal communication vary widely. Honeybees enact an intricate waggle dance that tells other members of their hive the exact location of pollen or of a new site for a hive. Humpback whales perform haunting solos, lasting from seven minutes to half an hour and ranging from deep basso groans to high soprano squeaks. (What they are "saying" is a matter of conjecture.) The male sage grouse inflates his chest sac, erects the feathers on his neck and face, assumes a strutting posture, and emits a *swish-swish-coo-oo-poink* to attract females during mating season. The sound can be heard by humans a mile away, and the display may continue for hours. Our nearest relative in the animal kingdom, the chimpanzee, communicates by means of some fifteen calls plus a wide range of gestures, postures, and facial expressions. The technical term for these messages is signs.

Signs are global or generalized statements about the animal's current bodily state or emotion. They signal alarm, distress, hostility, recognition, sexual excitement, affection, contentment, and the like. But signs do not convey specific information about what experience caused the alarm or delight. The chimpanzee's *waaaaa*, for example, signals danger. But a chimp cannot communicate nearly the detail contained in the sentence, "Look out for the German fighter at three o'clock!" Signs are responses to the immediate situation. A chimp's *hoot* tells other chimps that it has discovered food. But it cannot tell its offspring about the drought of 1975, the first time it tasted termites, or what to do if it encounters a leopard by a stream. Communication is limited to the here and now. Finally, signs are stereotyped. The form and meaning of the male sage grouse's courtship display never changes. If a male grouse were able to change his call from *swish-swish-coo-oo-poink* to *coo-oo-poink-swish-swish*—a highly unlikely event—he would almost certainly remain a bachelor. In a sense, animal communication is an endless stream of clichés.

Human beings are not above signing. Like other animals, we employ a large vocabulary of gestures, postures, and facial expressions. Just as dogs rub against and lick one another, so

Animals and their mating songs

humans hug and kiss to signal happiness and affection. The baboon's screech at the approach of a leopard has the same function as a person's scream at the approach of a mugger. The wolf's growl when a subordinate member of its pack fails to exhibit proper deference resembles an executive's gruff rebuff of an aspiring assistant who is too friendly. Exclamations such as "Ouch!" and "Yippee!"—stereotyped responses to an immediate situation that let other people know how you feel, but not *why*—are only one step removed from animal calls. (The one step is that non-English speakers would emit other sounds: *"Zut!"* or *"Oolala!"* in French.)

In some ways, human communication depends on signs. Often we learn more about how a person feels from nonlinguistic cues—their posture, the way they sit on the edge of a chair, a twinkle in their eyes, a forced smile—than we do from what the person actually says (see Figure 7-1). But unlike other animals, we are not limited to signs. Language is a unique form of communication that sets humans apart from other species.

A Definition of Language

What makes language unique? **Language** is a set of spoken and often written symbols and rules for combining them in meaningful ways. Roger Brown (1973) has identified three properties that distinguish natural human language from other forms of communication: semantics, productivity, and displacement.

Language is *semantic,* or meaningful. Humans can exchange detailed information on all kinds of objects and events, feelings and ideas—including things that never happened. By comparison, the content of animal signs is quite limited. The honeybee's dance is restricted to two topics: the locations of pollen and hives.

The second distinguishing property of language is *productivity.* Language is based on

morphemes, or units of meaning. (This term applies to whole words [*boy, run, who*] and to parts of words that carry meaning [*un-, -ed, -ing*].) Morphemes can be combined in different ways to produce an infinite number of unique utterances. The form and meaning of a chimpanzee's calls are fixed. Chimps cannot combine elements of one call with elements of another to produce new messages. With the exception of greetings, proverbs, and stock phrases such as "Have a good day," almost every sentence humans utter is original. (Think how difficult it is to repeat *exactly* what you said on the telephone five minutes ago.) We use the same sounds to produce different words (*e, n,* and *d* can produce "den," "end," or "Ned"); use the same words to produce different sentences ("Jonah ate the whale" and "The whale ate Jonah"); use qualifiers, change tenses, and so on ad infinitum. One linguist estimates that it would take *ten trillion years*—two thousand times the age of the earth—to speak all of the twenty-word sentences possible with the English language (Farb, 1974). No other form of communication permits such creativity.

The third unique property of language is *displacement.* Animal signs are tied to the immediate situation. With language, humans can transmit information across time and space to others who did not share the experience. On Tuesday you can talk about the party you attended last Saturday night, or the political situation in Central America, without moving from your seat in a coffee shop in Cleveland. The "power of the word" lies in its ability to call up information. Two people who are knowledgeable about, say, hippopotami, can discuss them at length even if the animals are not loitering in the immediate vicinity.

Language makes it possible to transmit cultural knowledge from one generation to the next. You can tell your children how Grandpa spilled soup all over Grandma at their fiftieth

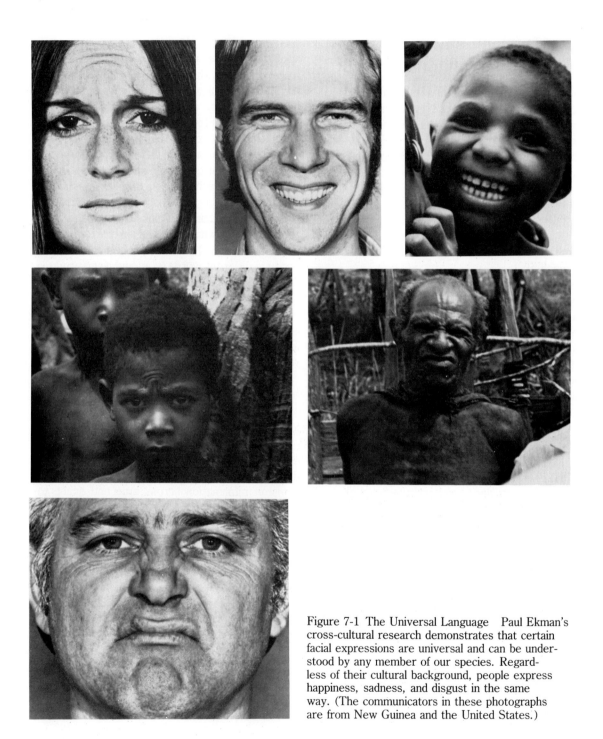

Figure 7-1 The Universal Language   Paul Ekman's cross-cultural research demonstrates that certain facial expressions are universal and can be understood by any member of our species. Regardless of their cultural background, people express happiness, sadness, and disgust in the same way. (The communicators in these photographs are from New Guinea and the United States.)

wedding anniversary party, or how President Nixon expanded the war in Vietnam by bombing Cambodia. As you tell these stories, you may communicate the amusement or distress you felt at the time with your facial expression, gestures, and tone of voice. But signs alone cannot recreate past situations or anticipate future events. It takes language to transmit the specific and historical information that maintains culture. Without language—and by extension without culture—we would be very different animals.

Aping Conversation

Are human beings the only animals who are capable of symbolic communication? The answer is a qualified yes. In recent years researchers have attempted to teach language to a number of chimpanzees and gorillas. An early experiment with a chimp named Vicki failed because chimpanzees do not have the vocal apparatus necessary for speech. Some years later, Allen and Beatrice Gardner set out to teach American Sign Language, a language of gestures designed for the deaf, to another female chimp named Washoe (Gardner & Gardner, 1975). After four years, Washoe had learned more than 130 words and could understand three times that number—about the range of a 2- to 3-year-old child. She could put words together, producing simple sentences: *Listen dog; More tickle; Susan* [a trainer] *stupid.* When Washoe learned the hand-sign for *open* in connection with doors, she extended its use to boxes, briefcases, and even a faucet. She used the novel word combination *water-bird* to describe a swan.

At about the same time, David Premack (Premack & Premack, 1983) was teaching a chimp named Sarah to use an artificial language made up of plastic chips that attached to a magnetic board (a blue triangle for *apple,* an orange rectangle for *same,* and so on). By using a systematic program of rewards, Premack was able to teach Sarah to use symbols for such abstract words as *same, different, color of* and *name of* correctly. Using the plastic words for *same* and *different,* she passed some of Piaget's conservation tests that most 3-year-old children fail. Taught the sentence, *Mary give pear* [*to*] *Sarah,* she produced, *Mary give apple chocolate* [*to*] *Sarah.*

Stanford University psychologist Francine Patterson reports that the gorilla Koko has learned more than 400 signs and combines signs in novel ways to insult her trainer *(You nut),* compose rhymes *(bear, hair, squash, wash),* and invent metaphors *(eye hat* for mask, *finger bracelet* for ring). These researchers are convinced that apes demonstrate a rudimentary capacity for language. They maintain that Washoe, Sarah, and Koko are not simply mimicking their trainers; they are using linguistic symbols productively.

Washoe, shown here making the sign for *drink,* was one of the first chimps to learn sign language. Early reports that she and other chimps made up "sentences" and invented their own signs led some primatologists to proclaim that apes were capable of symbolic thought. But further investigation suggested that chimps are imitating (and manipulating or playing with) their trainers, not learning language.

Other psychologists suspect that they are reading more into the apes' signed communications than the apes themselves understand. Herbert Terrace (1979) is one of the skeptics. Terrace taught another chimp sign language. Nim Chimpsky[1] performed about as well as Washoe. But analysis of videotapes of "conversations" between Nim and his human trainers convinced Terrace that chimps are skillful imitators, not true speakers. When children learn to speak, they progress more or less steadily from simple utterances such as "Daddy eat" to "Daddy eat breakfast," and later to complex sentences such as "Why didn't Daddy finish his cereal?" Although Nim's vocabulary increased, he never progressed beyond the two-word ("Daddy eat") stage. Unlike a child, Nim rarely "spoke" spontaneously. Most of his utterances were responses to questions, imitations of signs his trainers made, or repetitions of words that had produced rewards (bananas or tickles) in the past. With conditioning, Terrace argues, one could train a pigeon to produce "sentences" as grammatical as Sarah's. Chimpanzees use sign language only instrumentally—to get food, to get attention, to get in or out. Unlike humans, they do not use words for reflection, the exchange of ideas, or the sheer fun of communication (Snowdon, 1983). They prefer to operate on the world in a physical, not a verbal, manner. (Terrace adds, however, that his analysis of Nim is not the last word.)

Whether one views the experiments with chimpanzees as a success or a failure, several points stand out. First, it is humans who are attempting to teach language to apes, not vice versa. Neither chimps nor gorillas use symbolic communication in their natural environments. Second, whereas children need little encouragement to speak, apes must be taught. All of the

[1]A play on the name of Noam Chomsky, a linguist who argues that language is part of our species' unique biological heritage and beyond the reach of any other creature.

"talking" chimps and gorillas have had full-time instructors who rewarded them for their efforts. Finally, neither an ape nor a 2-year-old child can understand a complex sentence such as, "This is the dog that chased the cat that ate the rat that lived in the house that Jack built." But the English-speaking child will develop into an adult who can understand this sentence and others that are equally complex. As far as we know, the ape will not (de Villiers & de Villiers, 1979).

We can only speculate about how and why our distant ancestors began to speak (see Bates, 1979a). What we do know is that "the child makes a leap that recapitulates evolutionary developments several eons in the making" in the preschool period (de Villiers & de Villiers, 1979, p. 10). This giant leap consists of many small steps. To become a full-fledged speaker, the child must be able to produce the sounds of his language (phonology), master the rules for combining words and parts of words in meaningful utterances (syntax), grasp the meanings of words and how concepts can be represented in language (semantics), and learn the social rules governing the use of language by speakers and listeners in real-life situations (pragmatics). We consider each of these aspects of language development in turn.

Phonology: From Sound to Sense

Phonology refers to the sound patterns of speech. For infants, language begins with sound. To understand language, the child must be able to discriminate between speech and the innumerable thumps, clicks, and squeaks of objects in her environment, and between speech and the grunts, coughs, "uh's," and other irrelevant sounds that accompany human conversation. She also must master a set of symbols or arbitrary associations between sounds and objects, people, actions, feelings. In some cases (onomatopoeia), the sound of a word reflects the object or event to which it refers. "Brr" imitates the sound of a person shuddering with cold. "Ruff-ruff" imitates the sound of a dog, and "meow" that of a cat. But in most cases the association is arbitrary. A house is a structure you live in, but the structure itself does not produce the sounds "house" or "home." The child must learn these arbitrary associations.

In technical terms, the future speaker must learn to recognize **phonemes,** which are units of sound that indicate changes in meaning. In some English words, the first consonant identifies the word (*f*og, *l*og, *h*og, *d*og); in others, a single vowel signals a change in meaning (p*i*n, p*a*n, p*e*n, p*u*n). What letters or syllables constitute phonemes depends on the language. In English, /z/ and /s/ are phonemes[2]: the word *zip* means something different from *sip*. Spanish does not distinguish these phonemes—one reason why native Spanish-speakers may seem to lisp in English. In English, /r/ and /l/ are different phonemes. In Japanese they are not—one source of the stereotypes of Japanese pronunciations of English (*a red rooster* may be pronounced "a lead looster").

Babies begin listening to voices and recognizing different sounds very early. Infants tested a few days after birth preferred the sound of people talking or singing to nonvocal

[2]Linguists mark phonemes by enclosing them in slashes.

tones (Butterfield & Siperstein, 1974). There is some evidence that newborns prefer female voices, and that neonates can recognize their own mothers' voices within a few weeks of birth (DeCasper & Fifer, 1980). They respond to an adult's tone of voice long before they understand what adults are saying (Menyuk, 1971). Habituation experiments (such as those described in Chapters 3 and 4) indicate that infants can distinguish between "*ba*" and "*pa*" at 1 month; between "*ma*" and "*na*" and even "*bad*" and "*bag*" at 2 months (Eimas & Tartter, 1979; Jusczyk, 1977).

Peter Eimas (1985) used computer-generated speech to determine precisely which sounds adults hear as distinct phonemes. He then played phonemes and subtler changes in sounds that adults do not perceive to 4-month-old infants. Judging by changes in sucking rates, the infants heard the same sounds adults hear and ignored the subtler changes adults ignore (Figure 7-2). Guatemalan infants, born into a Spanish-speaking environment, and Kenyan babies, born into a Kikuyu-speaking environment, demonstrate the same patterns of perception. Eimas concludes that it is difficult to see how learning could account for this special sensitivity to speech. It seems that infants are programmed to pay attention to speech and to make auditory distinctions that are important to understanding language.

"Bunny, eat your dinner!" Babies go through the motions of speech long before they are able to produce meaningful sounds.

Prespeech

The first sound a baby produces is a wail. Crying is a spontaneous expression of discomfort. But it is also an effective means of communication, in that it summons caregivers and initiates social interaction.

At about 2 months, babies begin to coo, producing long strings of vowel sounds. A baby's "uuuuuuuu's" and "aaaaaaaa's" at the end of a meal or the sight of a smiling human face are signs of pleasure. At about 6 months, infants begin to babble, adding consonants to vowels and repeating the same syllable over and over: "gugugugugugu" "bibibibibibi," and the like. Whereas adults have difficulty pronouncing phonemes which are not used in their native language, babies spontaneously produce all kinds of sounds. American, Japanese, and French babies sound alike in this period (Nakazima, 1962).

Babbling seems to be genetically programmed. Even deaf babies babble. And infants of all nationalities begin by producing gutteral sounds such as /g/ and /k/, which come from the back of the mouth, and progress to sounds such as /b/, /p/, and /t/, which are produced by the lips and teeth (de Villiers & de Villiers, 1979). This progression is the result of physical maturation, not exposure to language. At 8 to 10 months, however, environmental influences begin to show. The infant's babbling begins to resemble the cadences of adult speech: He seems to be asking questions, making demands, describing events. And his babbling begins to conform to the phonemes of the language he hears around him. He may not make any sense, but he sounds as if he were trying to speak Japanese, French, English, or another native tongue. This development is the result of learning. He has been listening to a particular language and set of phonemes for some months now. In addition, the people around him are likely to respond to noises that sound like speech to them, but

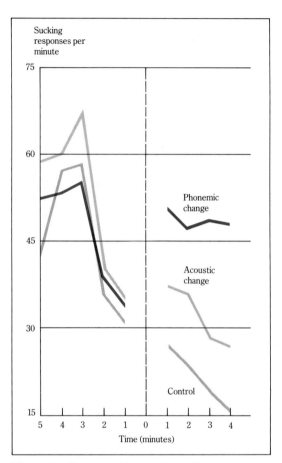

Figure 7-2 Ready to Listen   Peter Eimas found that 4-month-old infants recognize phonemes, but are not impressed by acoustical gradations that adults cannot hear. Sucking rates jumped when infants were played a new phoneme (the dark red line in the chart), but rose only slightly when they were played a meaningless acoustical shift.

(Eimas, 1985)

ignore sounds that have no meaning in their language.

First Words

The shift from babbling to words is a shift from playing with sound to planned, controlled vocalization. Infants babble for the same reason they wiggle their fingers and toes: It is a pleasant sensorimotor experience. And like other sensorimotor activities, it helps the infant gain control over her body (in this case, her mouth and vocal chords). Most babies produce their first words at about 1 year. (Some start talking at 10 months, some at 18 or 20 months; 1 year is an average.) Baby talk bears little resemblance to adult speech. Brenda's "nene," "awa," and "da" are typical. We recognize these as words because the child systematically uses the same sound to refer to the same object or class of objects, or to the same feeling or experience, and because they sound like they might be words. (See Figure 7-3.)

Gradually, the child's words begin to resemble adult words, but they are not perfect copies. Many small children regularize multiple-syllable words by duplicating syllables ("bubba"

Figure 7-3 "No Eat!"   Three scenes from the children's book *Higglety Pigglety Pop!* by Maurice Sendak illustrate the ambiguity of two-word communications. An adventurous dog named Jennie has taken a job as a nurse for Baby. Jennie is told that if she doesn't get Baby to eat, she will be fed to the lion in the basement. In the first scene (A) Baby refuses the food: "No eat" (meaning "I won't eat"). Jennie finally gives up and begins eating the porridge herself in scene B. This makes Baby angry: "No eat!" (meaning "Don't eat my food"). When Jennie continues lapping up the porridge, Baby pushes a button to deliver the dog-nurse to the hungry lion downstairs—and finds himself in the lion's den in scene C. Again Baby cries "No eat!!" (now meaning "Don't eat me").

(From Sendak, 1967, and Gleitman, 1981)

for *button* or *baby*); reduce single-syllable words to a consonant and a vowel ("da" for doll, "be" for bed); and delete parts of words (pronouncing *spoon* as "'poon" or *another* as "'notha"). The words adults use with small children often imitate "baby talk": "Mama," "Dada," "weewee," "choo-choo" (de Villiers & de Villiers, 1979). Even when children begin using adult words, the pronunciation often is off-target (for example, "ephalent" for *elephant*). Children continue to struggle with sound throughout the preschool period.

The Fis Phenomenon

Curiously, preschoolers are often unaware that they are mispronouncing words, as here.

A three-year-old child told me her name was "Litha."
  I answered, "Litha?"
  "No, *Litha*."
  "Oh, Lisa."
  "Yes, Litha."
(Miller, 1964, p. 864)

Another child pronounced the word *puddle* as "puggle," yet pronounced the word *puzzle* as "puddle" (Smith, 1973)! Psychologists refer to this as the *fis phenomenon*. Like Lisa, youngsters who do not pronounce the *sh* in fish correctly become quite indignant when adults imitate their mispronunciations. Clearly, the small child's perception of sound is better than her production of sounds.

John Locke (1979) conducted a series of experiments with phonemes many English-speaking children find difficult to pronounce: /l/ and /r/. (Often preschoolers say "wabbit" for *rabbit*, "weft" for *left,* and so on.) Locke showed 5-year-olds pictures of a ring, a wing, and a king. First he named one of the pictures; then he asked the child to point to it and pronounce the word. The children identified the pictures correctly, but many said "wing" for *ring*. When asked if they said "wing," most said immediately, "No, I said *wing*." Later the children

were played tapes of the experimenter pronouncing the words and then tapes of their own pronunciations. When they heard the experimenter say "ring," they pointed to the ring; when they heard their own pronunciation ("wing") they pointed to the wing. Experiments with *lake, wake,* and *rake* produced similar results.

Children are capable of distinguishing these phonemes in adult speech. Why don't they monitor their own pronunciations? Locke suggests that it is because preschoolers evaluate their speech in terms of their *intentions,* ignoring auditory feedback. They know what they meant to say. Moreover, their pronunciations work in real-life situations: Other people can usually figure out what they mean from the context. Closing the gap between what they mean and what they say is one of the tasks of the preschool period.

Syntax: From Words to Sentences

To become a competent speaker and listener, a child must master **syntax**: the rules for combining and modifying words in meaningful ways. Language is constructed with morphemes (units of meaning, as explained earlier) that can be combined in different ways to produce different meanings. In English, as in many other languages, the meaning of a sentence is often determined by *word order.* "Timmy hit the truck" means one thing; "The truck hit Timmy" means something quite different; and "Hit truck Timmy the" is nonsense. In some cases, the meaning of an utterance is determined by *intonation.* Spoken with a rising tone, "You're coming" is a question; spoken with the accent on the last word, "You're coming" is an order. We also use *grammatical markers*—prefixes and suffixes, such as *un-* to indicate negation and *-s* to indicate the plural—which change the meanings of words. There are rules for posing questions, rules for making negative statements, rules for using the passive voice—and more.

Insight

A NEW LOOK AT STUTTERING

Between ages 2 and 6, nearly all children have trouble speaking smoothly and freely. They hesitate, stumble, repeat words and phrases as they struggle to communicate a thought. These difficulties are a normal part of learning to speak. About one in twenty children have intense or prolonged difficulty speaking. Stuttering is distinguished by multiple repetitions of words or syllables ("sup-sup-sup-sup-supper"); difficulty with the weak vowels ("su-uh-uh-uh-uh-uggest"); prolongation of initial sounds ("mmm-mmmmommy"); a rising pitch and level when a word "gets stuck"; and perhaps facial tics and tremors around the mouth and jaw.

Ideas about the causes and cures for stuttering are changing (Homzie & Lindsay, 1984). At one time, most psychologists believed that it was an emotional problem. Freudians traced stuttering to unconscious conflicts and the fear of uttering unspeakable thoughts. Others saw stuttering as a conditioned response to early speech failures, most likely to occur in families that placed a high value on verbal performance.

Today most psychologists believe that stuttering has an organic basis. First, stuttering appears to be a developmental problem: it may begin as early as 18 months, nearly always appears before age 8, and usually disappears before the end of puberty. (More than 80 percent of children who stutter speak fluently by age 18.) Second, more than three times as many boys as girls stutter: the problem is sex-linked. Third, stuttering runs in families. The likelihood of stuttering is much higher in identical than in fraternal twins. Many psychologists also believe that stuttering is not an isolated problem. About two out of three children who stutter have other, related problems with listening, reading, and writing.

The fact that most people "outgrow" stuttering is little consolation to a child who is frequently tongue-tied. New directions in therapy for children who stutter include indentifying the child's level of speech development (which may not be the same as his or her age); working on pragmatics (the social conventions of speech); establishing fluency with familiar materials (jingles, nursery rhymes, favorite poems and books); and rehearsing situations in which the child frequently stutters in the privacy of individual therapy sessions.

The child hears specific examples of speech in particular situations. How does she acquire general rules for putting words together—rules that enable her to produce original sentences and comment on novel situations? The process begins one word at a time.

Putting Words Together

Children produce their first words near the end of the sensorimotor period. This is the stage in which youngsters begin to perform deferred imitation and to show other evidence of forming mental images of objects, people, and events. The child who makes believe a wooden block is a racing car is using the block to stand for (symbolize) something else. Words, too, are symbols. Brenda used "awa" to stand for *I don't want,* "da" to stand for *dolls,* and so on. Thus, by 19 or 20 months, the child may have a vocabulary of fifty words (Nelson, 1973). But children under 18 months rarely speak more than one word at a time. Toddlers communicate in *holographs,* or one-word utterances, that must "say" everything the child wants to express. And one word may serve different functions. Children in this stage of language development rely on intonation and nonverbal cues to "complete" their sentences. Spoken with a rising intonation, "doggie" is a question: "Is that a dog?" An emphatic "doggie!" may mean "Spot, come here," or "Get away from me." Holographs can only be understood in context.

Between 18 and 24 months, most children begin putting two words together, producing such utterances as "allgone cookie," "my daddy," "Mommy read," "big kitty," and "where ball." There is a telegraphic quality to speech in this stage (Brown, 1973). Small children delete unessential words, much as adults do when they send a telegram. Asked to repeat the sentence, "We are going to the store," a 2-year-old may say "Go store"—leaving out the pronoun (*we*), the auxiliary verb (*are*), the verb ending (*-ing*), the preposition (*to*), and the article (*the*). Most of the child's utterances in the two-word period are either assertions or requests (see Table 7-1).

Language development accelerates at age 2 to 2½. The child begins to use grammatical markers, such as *-ed* for the past tense and *-ing* for ongoing action. She begins to deliver negatives by adding *no* and *not* to her sentences ("I no go," "this not better"); to use auxiliary verbs (*can, do, will, may*); and to use conjunctions and prepositions (*and, 'cause,* and so on). By three or four, she will be able to produce the adult forms of questions and negatives most of the time. Progress in this period is rapid and dramatic. As shown in Table 7-2, the greatest change is not in Eve's vocabulary, but in how she puts words together to express ideas. She does not speak like an adult, but she is far more sophisticated than she was in the one-word stage. As one child (age 2 years 10 months) put it, "When I was a little girl I could go 'geek-geek' like that; but now I can go 'This is a chair'" (Limber, 1973, p. 181).

One way of measuring the child's level of language development in this period is by calculating the *mean length of utterance* (M.L.U.)—or the average number of morphemes in a child's sentences (Brown, 1973).

Table 7-1 Assertions and Requests at the Two-Word Stage

Speech Act	Utterance
Assertions	
Presence of an object	See boy. See sock. That car.
Denial of presence	Allgone shoe. No wet. Byebye hot.
Location of object	Bill here. There doggie. Penny in here.
Possession of object	My milk. Kendall chair. Mama dress.
Quality of object	Pretty boat. Big bus.
Ongoing event	Mommy sleep. Hit ball. Block fall.
Requests	
For action	More taxi. Want gum. Where ball?
For information	Where doggie go? Sit water?
Refusal	No more.

(Clark & Clark, 1977)

Table 7-2 Beyond Two Words

Eve at 18 Months	Eve at 27 Months*
More grapejuice.	This not better.
Door.	See, this one better but this not better.
Right down.	There some cream.
Mommy soup.	Put in your coffee.
Eating.	I go get pencil n' write.
Mommy celery?	Put my pencil in there.
No celery.	Don't stand on my ice cubes.
Oh drop celery.	They was in the refrigerator, cooking.
Open toy box.	I put them in the refrigerator to freeze.
Oh horsie stuck.	An' I want to take off my hat.
Mommy read.	That why Jacky comed.
No mommy read.	We're going to make a blue house.
Write a paper.	You come help us.
Write a pencil.	You make a blue one for me.
My pencil.	How 'bout another eggnog instead of cheese sandwich?
Mommy.	I have a fingernail.
Mommy head?	And you have a fingernail.
Look at dollie.	Just like Mommy has, and David has, and Sara has.
Head.	What is that on the table?
What doing, Mommy?	
Drink juice.	

(de Villiers & de Villiers, 1979)

*Eve was a precocious speaker. Most children do not progress this rapidly.

How Do They Do It?

How do children learn to combine words into meaningful phrases and sentences? Debates over the development of syntax reflect ongoing arguments over how much of human behavior is learned and how much is innate.

IMITATION AND CONDITIONING On one side of the debate are those who maintain that children acquire syntax in the same way they acquire other skills—through learning (Skinner, 1957). This view has intuitive appeal. Common sense suggests that children learn syntax by listening to adults and *imitating* what they hear. Obviously, imitation plays a role in language development. Whereas an American child learns to greet people by saying "hello," a Zulu child learns to say, "tsa bona." Moreover, children sometimes pick up stock phrases from adults' conversations. "How are you," "lemme see," "I dunno," and "once upon a time" are familiar examples. One child learned to parrot the phrase her parents, who were professors, and their friends used to break into a conversation: "I read an article" (de Villiers & de Villiers, 1979). But these are exceptions. Much of what children say is spontaneous and original. Moreover, all children say things they never heard from an adult, such as "nene" and "fis," or "His is gooder than mine" and "I seed two mouses." An explanation of syntax development based on imitation overlooks the originality of children's speech.

Another common belief is that children learn syntax through *conditioning*. Simply put, parents and others reward youngsters for grammatically correct statements and punish or ignore them when they make mistakes. Research does not support this view. Studies show that parents are more concerned with *what* small children say than with *how* they say it. Accuracy and truth come first; grammar, second. When a 2-year-old said, "Mama isn't boy he a girl" (a thoroughly ungrammatical sentence), her mother smiled and said, "That's right." When

another child said, "Walt Disney comes on Tuesday" (a grammatically correct statement), his mother replied firmly, "No, he does not." Walt Disney aired on Thursday (Brown & Hanlon, 1970). On the rare occasions when parents do attempt to correct their children's grammar, youngsters cling stubbornly to their incorrect forms.

> CHILD: My teacher holded the rabbits and we petted them.
> MOTHER: Did you say your teacher held the baby rabbits?
> CHILD: Yes.
> MOTHER: What did you say she did?
> CHILD: She holded the baby rabbits and we petted them.
> MOTHER: Did you say she held them tightly?
> CHILD: No, she holded them loosely.

> (Bellugi, 1970)

We do not mean to suggest that conditioning and social interaction play *no* role in the acquisition of syntax. Children who have few opportunities to talk with others develop language slowly, if at all. But imitation and conditioning alone do not explain how children advance from one-word utterances to complex sentences.

INNATE GRAMMAR On the other side of the debate are those who maintain that human beings are genetically prewired for language. In other words, syntax is innate. From this viewpoint, all that is required for a child to begin speaking is exposure to language—just as all that is required for a child to grow is adequate nutrition and exercise. Linguist Noam Chomsky (1965) is a leading spokesman for this point of view. (See also Lenneberg, 1967.) Chomsky proposed that human infants are equipped by nature with a "language acquisition device," or LAD, which includes a knowledge of the universal principles of language and techniques for discovering how these principles apply to the specific language to which the child is exposed. This position is based on three observations: first, despite surface differences, all human languages have many basic features in common (such as verbs and nouns); second, all normal children, bright or dull, pampered or neglected, learn to speak in a remarkably short time; and third, no other species uses a form of communication that matches human language.

Most psychologists would agree with some of Chomsky's argument. Humans are biologically constructed in a way that enables them spontaneously to learn to speak if they are raised in a normal environment where language is used. But this statement is a tautology[3]; it does not explain *how* children learn to put words together. Chomsky implies that language development is separate from other areas of cognitive development and the child's growing understanding of objects and events in the environment. Many other psycholinguists disagree. Moreover, the development of syntax is not entirely spontaneous. Speech is social behavior, and children develop language in the context of communicating with significant others.

HYPOTHESIS TESTING A third group of psychologists sees the development of syntax as the product of the child's active efforts to understand and be understood by other people. The *hypothesis testing* model of language development is based on the observation that children seem to look for regularities in the speech they hear. When they discover a pattern, they devise a hypothesis. If it works—if people understand them the first time they use it—they apply it to other word combinations and continue using it until they discover a better rule. Why do children do this? The ability to listen to particular sentences (what people around them say), to extract rules, and then to use these

[3]A tautology is a repetition of an idea that does not add new, clarifying information.

rules to produce novel phrases and sentences is probably part of our species' genetic program. But the development of this ability depends on social interaction and overall cognitive development.

Growth errors provide evidence for the hypothesis-testing model. For example, the general rule for forming the past tense in English is to add the suffix *-ed* to the present tense (as in *look/looked* or *play/played*). But many of the most common English verbs do not follow this rule (such as *go/went, see/saw, take/took*). (See Figure 7-4.) Children usually learn these irregular verbs first and, for a time, produce the correct form of the past tense. Then, rather suddenly, they begin saying such things as "Mommy goed to work," "I seed a horsie," and "Billy taked my toy"—using words they never said or heard before. Why? When they learn the past tense of regular verbs, they discover the rule, "Add *-ed* to the present tense." Having learned this rule, they apply it to everything—even producing an occasional double past tense, such as "wented." Small children make the same, regular mistakes with irregular plurals, calling mice "mouses," feet "foots," and so on. Eventually they learn that some verbs and some plurals are irregular and correct these mistakes. Learning unique rules that apply to only a few verbs and nouns takes time, however, and many 5- and 6-year-olds continue to make mistakes.

There is some evidence that children everywhere use the same schemes or operating principles for discovering linguistic rules (Slobin, 1979). One common strategy is to avoid exceptions, such as the irregular plurals and past tenses in English. Another is to pay attention to the ends of words. Children who are learning English often skip the first syllable of multiple-syllable words, pronouncing *tomato* as "'mato" and *giraffe* and "'raffe." This seems natural in English, which often puts the emphasis on word endings. But children who are learning Czech, a language that puts the stress on the first syllable, also skip the first syllable (de Villiers & de Villiers, 1979).

Children seem to avoid interruptions. In English, for example, *wh-* questions (*who, what, when, where, why*) often require the speaker to break up a verb phrase. To ask why Sally is

I have shoes on my **foots.**

'Have shoes on my **feet.**

Figure 7-4 An Example of Growth Error: Avoiding Exceptions Older children make more mistakes in language than younger children do, in part because they overapply grammatical rules such as those for plurals. In time, they learn that some plurals are irregular: *foot/feet,* not *foot/foots.*

laughing, adults say, "Why *is* Sally *laughing?*" Children usually go through a phase of asking "Why Sally is laughing?" and "When we are going?" before they learn the correct form.

Still another common strategy is to interpret noun–verb–noun sequences as expressing an agent–action–object relationship. With active sentences, this is correct: *The truck* [actor] *bumped* [action] *the car* [object]. However, in passive sentences the word order is reversed: The object comes first, the agent last. Most 3- and 4-year-olds systematically misunderstand passive sentences. When asked to demonstrate the sentence, "The car was bumped by the truck" with toys, they show the car bumping the truck (Bever, 1970). (See Figure 7-5.)

The hypothesis-testing model holds that children are equipped with learning strategies. On the way from one-word utterances to complex sentences, they create and discard a number of provisional rules. Their syntax improves because they test their rules, listen to other people put words together, learn more about how well they are understood, and try to sound more adult.

Semantics: From Names to Ideas
Semantics refers to the meanings of words and larger speech segments, and to the content

Plurals
We'll begin with a box and the plus is boxes
But the plural of ox should be oxen not oxes,
Then one fowl is goose and two are called geese
Yet the plural of moose should never be meese.
You may find a lone house, or a whole lot of houses
But the plural of mouse is mice and not mouses.
The masculine pronouns are he, his, and him
Imagine the feminine she, shis and shim!
So English I fancy you all will agree
Is the silliest language you ever did see.
(Anonymous)

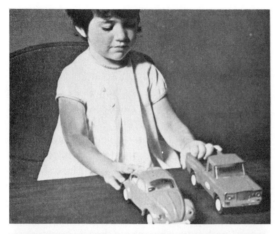

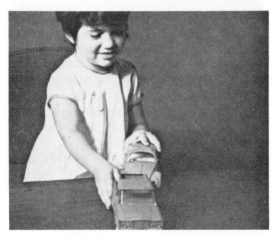

of language. Children are not born with a working vocabulary; every word a baby hears is new. Yet, without formal instruction, the average child acquires a vocabulary of about 14,000 words by the age of 6 (Carey, 1978). The speed with which most small children learn new words is amazing. Preschoolers learn between ten and twenty new words a day (Miller, 1978)!

How do children learn what words mean? When adults encounter a new word, such as *inconcinnous* or *widdershins*, they have several options. They can look the word up in a dictionary, they can ask someone what it means, or they can guess its meaning from the context. Obviously, a 1-year-old or 2-year-old cannot look a word up or even ask what it means. All he can do is observe when and how a word is used, and guess (Clark & Clark, 1977).

First Meanings

Children do not start acquiring meaningful language from scratch. In the first year of life they have learned a good deal about their immediate environment through observation, manipulation, and exploration. Their task now is to connect this sensorimotor knowledge to the words adults use.

Where do children begin? With what interests them most. Katherine Nelson (1973) analyzed 15- to 20-month-old toddlers' vocabularies by sorting their first fifty words into six categories: (1) specific names, which apply to only one person or thing (*Mommy, Spot*); (2) general names, which apply to a class of objects, people,

Figure 7-5 Reversed Word Order   Thomas Bever asked children of different ages to demonstrate passive sentences, such as "The truck was bumped by the car." Small children nearly always get this wrong, and show the truck bumping into the car. This child, however, demonstrates the sentence correctly.

animals (*ball, car*); (3) action words, which are used to describe, accompany, or request activity (*bye-bye, look*); (4) modifiers, which refer to qualities of things (*big, allgone, mine*); (5) personal-social words, which describe the child's feelings about something or someone (*yes, no, please*); and (6) function words, which serve some grammatical purpose (*what, is, for*). Nelson found that over half of children's early words fall into the category of general names. Children talk about the world of objects they have investigated in the sensorimotor period. Moreover, the objects children label first are those that move or make interesting sounds and those that the child can play with or manipulate. *Ball, car,* and *doggie* are far more common than *house* or *tree,* which are familiar but neither act nor invite action from a 1-year-old. What small children notice and remember are the "dynamic, active, and reactive" properties of things in their environment (Nelson, 1979).

Children's very first words are often their own inventions. But even when they begin using adultlike words, they may not use them the same way adults do. In working out the meanings of words, children rely on the context. Guesswork can produce unexpected associations and highly personal definitions.

A mother said sternly to her child, "Young man, you did that on purpose." When asked later what "on purpose" meant, the child replied: *It means you're looking at me.*

A mother said, "We have to keep the screen door closed, honey, so the flies won't come in. Flies bring germs into the house with them." When asked what "germs" were, the child said: *Something flies play with.* (E. E. Maccoby, in Clark & Clark, 1977, p. 486)

One of the most common mistakes children make is to *overextend* a word, applying it to objects or events outside the adult range of meaning (see Figure 7-6). One little girl used the word *moon* to refer to the moon itself, cakes, round marks on the window, postmarks, and a magnetic letter *o,* among other things. At 15 months she learned to use the word *kick* to describe propelling an object forward with her foot. Later she applied it to a picture of a cat with a ball near its paw, a fluttering moth, turtles dancing a can-can on a TV cartoon, and bumping a ball with her tricycle (Bowerman, 1976). Many children extend the word *doggie* or *bow-wow* to horses, cows, cats, and other animals. Other children apply the label *dog* to soft toys, furry slippers, and pictures of people in fur coats. In some cases, children *underextend* a word: for example, by restricting the use of *kitty* to their own pet.

What seems to be happening in such mistakes is this (Clark, 1973): When a child first notices a word, he identifies the meaning with one or two properties of the object (movement, shape, size, sound, texture, or taste). As Piaget would predict, he centers attention on the most attractive features, ignoring other features. When his mother points to a fox terrier and says "doggie," for example, he notes that she is labeling a four-legged object that moves. He may overextend the word because he assumes *doggie* means "four-legged things that move." But he also assumes that every word has a special meaning, and looks for contrasts between words (Clark, 1983). New words call his attention to other features: *cow* means a big animal with horns; *kitty* means a small animal that goes "meow"; and so on. These contrasts help him to refine his definition of *doggie:* dogs are relatively small (size); they bark (sound); they are furry (texture). This more advanced definition leads him to recognize different kinds of animals and apply the right name. A child defines and redefines a word as his experiences teach him more about its applications and uses.

There may be other explanations of the small child's overextensions, however. The child may know that the large, grey animal with

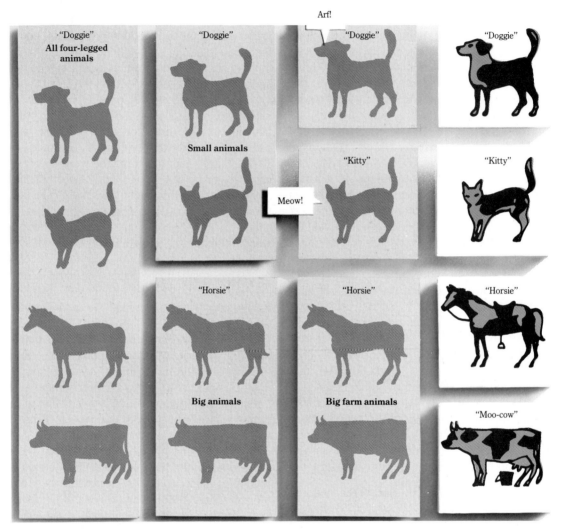

Figure 7-6 Overextensions and Refinements
"What's dat?" Small children often overextend a
term, using the same word for a variety of objects,
animals, or events. Overextensions gradually
disappear as the child learns the names and
distinguishing features of members of the class.

a trunk is not a dog. But she may not have the word *elephant* in her vocabulary. So she chooses the next-best word she knows, the one that comes closest to what she sees. She means that the object is "like a dog." She may use overextension as a strategy for learning the names of things. She is asking, "Is that a dog?" She knows that if she uses a wrong word, her parents supply the right one. In some cases, she may deliberately use the wrong word to call attention to similarities between unrelated things. When she calls a grapefruit a moon, for example, she may mean, "A grapefruit looks like a moon." In other words, some overextensions may be early examples of metaphors. One little boy, who had learned the word *turtle* for a bath toy, noticed his big toe poking through a hole in his sleeper-pajamas. He thrust his foot in the air and exclaimed with delight, "Turtle!" (de Villiers & de Villiers, 1979).

As a general rule, overextensions begin to disappear at about age 2½. This is the age at which children begin to shower adults with "What's this" and "What's that" questions, as if they have suddenly discovered that there are words for everything and want to know them all (Clark & Clark, 1977).

Concept Development

There is more to semantics than knowing which word-label applies to which object, person, or activity. In learning the meanings of words, the child is also learning how the people around him use concepts to organize their perceptions. When a child learns the word *bird,* for example, he has acquired a verbal tool for expressing what he already knows about birds and what he is seeing right now. He also has a tool for finding out how adults think about birds. Language and concepts develop hand in hand.

IS A ROBIN AN ANIMAL? Mastering concepts requires two kinds of knowledge: knowledge of the properties of a concept and knowledge of the relationships among concepts. (See Figure 7-7.)

A concept is a mental category, a general notion that applies to many individual cases (see Chapter 6). The concept *bird,* for example, includes the properties that are common to all or most birds: it has feathers, flies, builds nests, lays eggs, and so on. Some birds are better examples of the concept than others are because they have more of these defining features. A robin is a typical bird. An ostrich is not a good example because it cannot fly and it is too big. A collie is a typical dog: a furry, medium-sized, friendly pet. A Mexican hairless is not a good example of the concept: It is not furry, not friendly, and very small. An elderly person is a good example of the concept *old;* a giant oak is not a good example because it is still growing and has no clear time limit on its existence. The first step in concept development is recognizing common properties and typical examples.

The second step is learning how different concepts are related to one another. Concepts can be arranged in hierarchies, with the narrowest and most specific concepts at the bottom and the most general at the top. Robin is a subset of the category *bird,* and bird is a subset of category *animal.* Fish and people are also animals. Hierarchical relationships among concepts are beyond the cognitive grasp of most preschoolers. Indeed, when presented with the question, "Is a robin an animal?" most adults hesitate for a moment. Answering this question requires two mental steps. ("Let's see, a robin is a bird, and birds are animals, so the answer is yes.") Preschoolers may make the first step, but rarely the second. Most will dismiss the statement, "People are animals," as "stupid."

Concepts link information acquired through real-life experiences to word-labels (Miller & Johnson-Laird, 1976). Hence, first words are a clue to the child's early concepts. Most children learn the word *flower* before they learn the

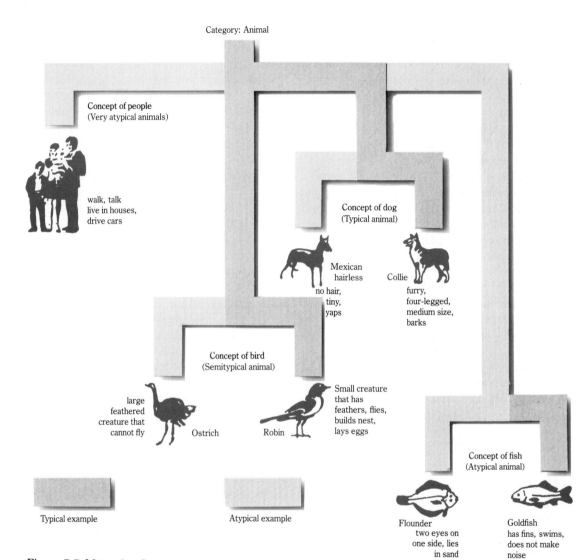

Figure 7-7 Mastering Concepts and Hierarchies

words *rose, daffodil,* or *tulip* (subordinate categories) and before they call flowers, vegetables, trees, and grass *plants* (a superordinate category). Similarly, most children learn the word *car* before they learn the words *convertible* and *station wagon,* or *Volvo* and *Ford* (subordinate categories) or the word *vehicle* (superordinate category that includes everything from tricycles to space ships). Why? The child's early concepts are based on cultural definitions of use (Brown, 1958). Small children class objects together because they have learned or been taught to treat them the same way. There is no reason for a 3-year-old girl to distinguish between tulips and daisies. All she needs to know is that flowers are things she can admire, smell, and pick to put in a vase, but should not eat or step on. The term *plant* is too general for the child's purposes because she is encouraged to run and roll on some plants (grass) and talked into eating others (string beans) (de Villiers & de Villiers, 1979). Early concepts are functional in the evolutionary sense of promoting adaptation to the environment; they are useful to a child at that particular stage of development (Nelson, 1979).

FOUR STAGES IN CONCEPT DEVELOPMENT Nelson (1979) holds that concept development begins before children learn to speak, in the sensorimotor period when they begin noticing similarities and differences in the way things act or react to manipulation. When and how do children connect their own observations to the conventional categories represented in language?

Nelson outlines four stages in the development of a concept. In stage 1, the preverbal child forms concepts on the basis of sensorimotor experiences—that is, he classifies people or objects in terms of what they do or what he can do to them. (Balls roll, cars go "vroom," and so on.) He looks for identifying perceptual features (balls are round; cars are shiny). These functional core concepts lay the foundation for further development.

In stage 2, the child discovers that people and objects have names, and begins to use word labels. But his labels are based on personal experiences and observations; he relies on his own categories. This is why his use of words is different from that of adults. (All animals seem alike to him, so he calls them all "bow-wow," and so on.)

In stage 3, his concepts begin to overlap with those of people in his language community. He begins to use words in a more adult fashion. When asked to define words, however, he falls back on sensorimotor knowledge and personal experience. An apple is "something to eat"; a tiger is "something that runs, growls, and bites," (indirect knowledge acquired from books or television); an uncle is "a funny man" (a definition based on his uncle Bob).

In stage 4, the school-age child separates his personal knowledge of cars, pets, friends, bravery, and other concepts from general properties. His concepts become more conventional and more abstract. A child in this stage will define a tiger as "a striped animal that lives in the jungle," an uncle as "your mother's or father's brother," and an apple as "a kind of fruit." He has mastered the properties of many concepts and begun to understand hierarchies of concepts. This frees him to think about logical relationships among concepts, such as the differences between plants and animals, or the fact that people are animals. He is entering what Piaget called the concrete operational stage (described in Chapter 9).

As Nelson suggests, in the early phases of semantic development the child discovers that language provides tools (words) for expressing ideas he has already formed in his head; in the later stages, language itself becomes a tool for learning new ideas.

Production vs. Comprehension
Small children understand more than they say.

CRIB MONOLOGUES

Many 2-year-olds talk to themselves for several minutes before they fall asleep. Katherine Nelson (1983) used the recordings of one child's crib monologues to study the role of language in developing a personal knowledge of the world.

Emily, an unusually bright and verbal little girl, was 21 months old when her parents began recording her presleep monologues. The first tapes were a jumble of free associations that mixed past, present, and future events. Her chatter did not seem to refer to bedtime conversations with her parents, and they were so inarticulate that transcription was often difficult.

By 23 months, however, Emily had learned to differentiate the past from the present. Besides using the past tense, she had developed such concepts as "yesterday," "now," and "not now." At 24 months Emily also knew the difference between general and specific experience ("usually" as different from "sometimes"), and she distinguished future events from the past and the present. She began to plan for herself and to speculate about what was happening and what would happen. When she heard her father running downstairs, for example, she tried to guess what he was doing. "Is he going to get dinner, or to get a book or a blanket?" she wondered. For the first time in her life, Emily was able to generalize from her previous experience and to project a future probability.

Another striking development took place at about the same age. Emily began to use her crib monologues to "talk over," or resolve problems which had come up in bedtime conversations with her father. One of these problems was the rule that "big kids don't cry." After repeating Daddy's explanation to herself, she questioned the rule by saying, "I big kid but I do cry." Then she seemed to resolve the question by concluding that the other "big kids" she knows don't cry.

At 24 months Emily was actively solving problems. She was able to plan future events on the basis of past experience and she was trying to reconcile inconsistencies between the new information she acquired and her memory of her own past experiences.

Emily's monologues reveal that knowledge is not only passed on through language, it is transformed and internalized through language as well. Before Emily had developed the language skills necessary to "talk things out," or reason about her experiences, her monologues were an undifferentiated stream of consciousness. Once she developed these verbal skills, she was able to distinguish the future from the past and the present, to plan ahead, and to solve problems in the world around her.

A 2-year-old can understand and act on the sentence, "Would you please put your blocks away?" She may not be able to say any of the words in this sentence. Certainly, she cannot produce this complex string of words. Nevertheless, she understands what her mother says. In this example, the child may get the message from the context and from nonverbal cues. The box where she keeps her blocks is on the floor beside her. Her mother picks up a block and points to the box as she speaks. The child doesn't need to know the words to know what her mother wants. When a child who still uses the word *doggie* for all animals is shown a picture of a horse, an elephant, a cat, and a dog, she will point to the dog. When asked to name some examples of the category *animals,* or *clothes, furniture,* or *fruit,* 3- to 5-year-olds produce accurate lists, even though they themselves do not use these category words (Nelson, 1979). Why does production lag behind comprehension?

Eve Clark and Barbara Hecht (1983) suggest that speaking (production) and listening (comprehension) require different information-processing skills. Speakers need programs for retrieving specific words and phrases from memory, procedures for combining words into larger units that express desired meanings, and articulatory programs for pronunciation. Listeners need programs for identifying phonemes (meaningful sounds) in the flow of speech, a recognition vocabulary, and general knowledge about the everyday world of objects, events, and relationships. In speech, the emphasis is on syntax (word order) and phonology (pronunciation). In comprehension, the emphasis is on semantics (meanings). To understand a sentence, all the child need do is pick out key words. Children recognize many more words than they use. (So do adults.) Moreover, if they "look up" a word in their recognition vocabulary and find it isn't "listed," they can fall back on their general knowledge about whatever the other person seems to be talking about. If they get the gist of what is being said, that is enough.

Comprehension precedes, and to some extent guides, production. What children understand sets the standard for what they try to say.

Pragmatics: From Speech to Conversation

People do not always say what they mean. When a mother asks a child, "Would you mind picking up your toys?" or "Could you stop interrupting Grandma?" or "How many times do I have to tell you not to put your tadpoles in the kitchen sink?" she is not asking a question. Rather, she is issuing a command in a polite form. If the child took her literally and answered, "Yes, I would mind," or "Granny is an old bore," the mother would be quite annoyed. Most 3- and 4-year-olds are quite capable of understanding and responding to such indirect or false utterances. They are well on their way to mastering **pragmatics,** the social uses and conventions of language.

Speech is a social act. When a child or an adult says something, it is because he wants to share his observations or feelings with another person or to evoke a response from the other person. Like other social activities, language is governed by numerous rules and conventions. To communicate effectively, the child must learn how to get and hold another person's attention; how to take turns, shifting back and forth between the roles of speaker and listener; and how to judge what the other person can understand and adjust his utterances accordingly. He must know when to take what someone says literally and when someone is joking or hinting. Research shows that children begin to learn the social uses of language very early in their development.

The Emergence of Social Intent

For the first six to eight months of life, the infant's cries and gestures are internally motivated. She is communicating, in the sense that her cries tell caregivers that she is hungry or wet or tired. But she does not seem to realize that the bottle and cuddling she receives are a response to something she did. The infant does not intend her howls as a message.

At about 8 or 9 months, a new pattern emerges. If the infant finds that something she wants is beyond her grasp, she will look at the object, look at a nearby adult, then look at the object again. If the adult does not respond, she will start to fuss. If this nonverbal communication does not work, she will turn up the volume. Now the child *intends* her cries as a signal and expects people to respond. At about the same age, the infant begins to use gestures as signals. Instead of just gazing at a new and attractive object, she points to it, then checks to see if her mother is "listening" to her by looking at the object. Instead of grasping for something she wants, she reaches out with an open hand, signaling "give me." She replaces grunts and other fussing sounds with regular syllables, such as *ba* or *goo*.

Elizabeth Bates (1979b) sees the intent to communicate through conventional signals as "the dawn of language." The child has discovered that mutually agreed-upon signals, such as pointing, can be used for mutually agreed-upon goals. This is a first step toward understanding the social uses of language.

The adults intent to communicate with the infant "emerges" even earlier. During the first months of an infant's life, caregivers often treat burps, yawns, and such as if they were intentional communications.

MOTHER: Hello. Give me a smile then. (*gently pokes infant in the ribs*)
INFANT: (*yawns*)
MOTHER: Sleepy, are you? You woke up too early today.
INFANT: (*opens fist*)
MOTHER: (*touching the infant's hand*) What are you looking at? Can you see something?
INFANT: (*graps mother's finger*)
MOTHER: Oh, that's what you wanted. In a friendly mood, then. Come on, give us a smile.

(Snow, 1977)

When babies are 3 or 4 months old, caregivers begin pointing to objects and parts of the body and naming them. At 7 or 8 months, babies reciprocate by picking up objects and spontaneously showing or giving them to adults (Escalona, 1973).

Games like peek-a-boo introduce the infant to one of the basic rules of conversation: taking turns. In peek-a-boo, two people alternate roles in a joint activity. First one person acts and the other observes; then the roles are reversed. Similarly, conversation is a joint activity in which you talk, I listen, then we reverse roles. In these ways, children are exposed to the social conventions of language well before they utter their first words.

"Motherese": How Adults Talk to Small Children

When adults talk to one another, they string clauses into long, complex, wandering sentences. Relative clauses, conditionals, ungrammatical constructions, unfinished thoughts ("You know what I mean"), and asides are common. This woman is talking to her sister about her feelings for the church:

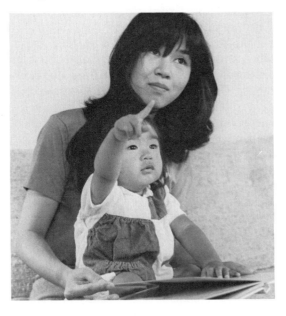

One of the early stages in the development of speech is the emergence of the intent to communicate.

It gives me a certain amount of consolation which allows me to relax my mind and start thinking intelligently an' putting my effort in one y'know force goin' in one direction rather than just y'know continually feeling sorry for yourself. (Slobin, 1979, p. 278)

When adults talk to small children, they speak in short, simple, repetitive sentences. The result is a kind of dialect that linguists call "motherese" (Slobin, 1979). Mothers get and hold a small child's attention by using the child's name ("Susan, what is that?") and prefacing statements with exclamations ("Hey! See the toy?" "Look! That's a foot.") They speak in a higher pitch than they normally use with adults, exaggerating intonations. They slow down, speaking at about half their normal speed and pausing between sentences. They use shorter sentences—an average of about four words—and their sentences are simpler grammatically. They avoid such complicating features as coordinate constructions (*and, but, so*) and subordinate constructions (*when, where, while*). They talk about the here and now, giving the child

opportunities to use the context to guess the meanings of words. They often use sentence frames, such as, "Look at the _____," "That's a _____," and "Where's the _____," to introduce new words within a familiar word setting. And adults frequently repeat themselves, giving the child several chances to grasp what they are talking about.

ADULT: Put the red truck in the box. The *red truck.* No, the red one. In the box. Put the red truck in the box.

The mother speaking above is not only telling the child what she wants him to do, she is also giving him a lesson in sentence structure. She broke the sentence *Put the red truck in the box* into its component phrases (*The red truck / in the box*), repeating each one. Consciously or unconsciously, mothers often build grammar and vocabulary lessons into their conversations with small children. When a child is on the verge of speaking, adults model conversations.

ADULT: Where's the ball?
(*picks up the ball*) *There's* the ball.
ADULT: (*looking at a picture book with a child*) What is the little boy doing?
He is *climbing* up the *tree.*

(Ervin-Tripp, in Clark & Clark, 1977, pp. 324–25)

Games of peek-a-boo introduce children to the idea of taking turns, an essential part of conversation.

When a child has progressed to two-word utterances, mothers often expand or rephrase the child's sentence, filling in grammatical features and information that the child left out.

CHILD: Doggy eat.
ADULT: Yes, the doggie is eating the bone.

CHILD: Doll fell.
ADULT: Oh, dear, the dolly fell over.

(de Villiers & de Villiers, 1979, p. 106)

Mothers also correct children when they use the wrong word.

CHILD: (*points*) Doggie.
ADULT: No, that is a *horsie*.

CHILD: (*pointing to a picture of a bird on a nest*) Bird house.
ADULT: Yes, the bird's sitting on a *nest*.

Note that the mother in the last example told the child that his idea was right, but that he had not used the correct word. It might be an exaggeration to call these conversations "language lessons." Yet the adult is directing interaction with the child in ways that make it easier for the child to understand what is being said and show him how to make himself understood.

Mothers and other caregivers are not the only ones who use motherese. Even preschoolers talk differently when addressing a baby (see Chapter 6):

A.M. TO ADULT: You're supposed to put one of these persons in, see? Then one goes with the other little girl. And then the little boy. He's the little boy and he drives. And then they back up. And then the little girl has the marbles. . . .

A.M. TO A 2-YEAR-OLD: Watch, Perry. Watch this. He's backing in now. Now he drives up. Look, Perry. Look here, Perry. Those are marbles, Perry. Put the men in here. Now I'll do it. . . .

(Shatz & Gelman, 1973)

Like adults, preschoolers use shorter, simpler sentences and numerous attention-getting and attention-holding devices with toddlers.

How Important Is Modeling and Tutoring?

Children must be exposed to language if they are to learn how to speak. But are the kinds of informal instruction we've been describing necessary to language development? One way to answer this question would be to raise half a dozen children with opportunities to listen to adults on radio and TV, but no verbal interaction with accomplished speakers. For obvious ethical reasons, no psychologist would conduct such an experiment. But natural experiments do provide clues.

One team of researchers (Snow, Arlman-Rupp, Hassing, Jobse, & Vorstein, 1976) who were studying parent–child interaction in Holland discovered that the children regularly watched German television. Even though they were exposed to it every day, none of the children had learned any German. Another group of researchers (Bard & Sachs, 1977) studied a normal, hearing child born to two deaf parents. The parents used sign language with each other but thought it inappropriate to sign with their son, Jimmy. Rather, they encouraged him to watch television in the hope that he would pick up speech. Jimmy did not even try to speak until age 2½, when he began producing phrases he had learned from TV jingles and from playmates (such as *Kool-Aid*). When he came to the attention of speech therapists, at age 3 years 9 months, he was beginning to put words together. But his intonation was unemotional and flat, and his syntax was highly irregular. He produced sentences such as "Go downstairs snack" and "Off my mittens." With the aid of regular speech therapy, Jimmy progressed rapidly. In less than a year, he had caught up with other children his age. With Jimmy's help and a small amount of speech therapy, his younger brother, Glenn, was speaking normally by age 2.

These studies suggest that verbal interaction is necessary to language development. Exposure alone is not enough. Children need a *responsive* language environment. The conversations they hear on TV are not linked to familiar objects and events in their environment. The kinds of nonverbal cues that help children discover meanings are absent. TV personalities do not ordinarily speak motherese. Moreover, TV does not respond to what the child says. At the same time, Jimmy and Glenn's story shows that children learn to speak if they have even a minimal amount of verbal exchange. Both boys caught up quickly. Indeed, the brothers were becoming bilingual: both were now learning sign language.

Parallel Talk: How Children Talk to Children

The art of conversation does not develop all at once. A 4-year-old child may produce meaningful, grammatical sentences that other people can understand. But this does not mean that he is a competent conversationalist. One of the most important pragmatic skills is taking into account the listener's knowledge. In some situations, such as talking to a baby, a preschooler may adjust his utterances to the listener. But in many situations he does not take into account what the listener can and cannot know. A 4-year-old may greet his mother after school with the complaint, "He hit me." His mother asks, "Who hit you? How did it happen?" Johnny replies, "I didn't mean it but he said I did and he hit me again." The child does not realize that such indefinite references as *he, it,* and *again* do not convey any information to someone who did not witness the incident. He assumes shared knowledge when it does not exist—another example of the preschooler's egocentrism. This pattern is even clearer when children talk to children.

PIAGET ON EGOCENTRIC SPEECH Piaget (1959) recorded and analyzed the speech of a number of young children. He concluded much of the time that preoperational children talk about themselves, to themselves, and by themselves. Piaget identified three types of egocentric speech. The first is *repetition*. One child says, "John's pants are showing"; another says "My

Although adults do not literally teach children to talk, the way they teach a child to read or ride a bike, verbal interaction is essential.

Insight

THE GESTURAL "LANGUAGE" OF DEAF CHILDREN

Susan Goldin-Meadow and Carolyn Mylander (1983) report that deaf children who have not been exposed to a conventional sign language create a gestural system on their own. The youngsters they studied were children of hearing parents. The parents wanted them to learn to speak and read lips; nevertheless, the children were developing sign languages. They used the same gesture for the same word or grammatical function. Moreover, they strung gestures together in "sentences" and were consistent in the way they ordered their "words." The children were developing their own gestural syntax.

Goldin-Meadow and Mylander videotaped four of the six children they studied in play sessions. They wanted to determine whether the mothers were unconsciously modeling or shaping the children's signs. Nearly all of the youngsters' gestures (90 to 98 percent) were spontaneous. Moreover, their gestural "sentences" were more complex and more regular than their mothers' gestures. Approval (smiles, nods, or compliance with a request or query) or disapproval (head shakes, frowns, or failures to respond) seemed to have little effect on the children's "rules" for gestural syntax. They were developing a rudimentary language without any detectable modeling or shaping.

The spontaneous production of gestural systems in deaf children suggests that children are born with "a strong bias to communicate in language-like ways" (p. 373).

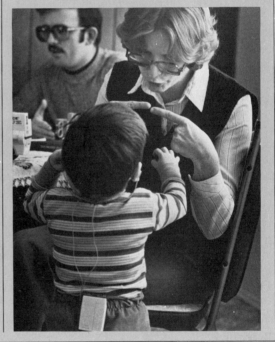

---

pants are showing"; and another, "*My* pants are showing and so is my shirt." The children are mimicking something they just heard. Piaget saw repetition as playing with words. The child is exercising new symbolic skills, much as the infant exercises sensorimotor schemes, repeating an action over and over for the sheer fun of it.

A second type of egocentric speech is the *individual monologue*. The child talks as she plays, describing what she is doing to herself. "I want to make a drawing. I'll put the paper here. Now I'll get some crayons." The child is not attempting to communicate information to another person; she doesn't know or care if anyone is listening. The monologue is part of the action. In some cases, an individual monologue is a form of word magic. If the child finds that a chair that is in her way is too heavy to move, she may *tell* it to move. Again, she makes no attempt to communicate with another person; she doesn't expect a response to her words.

The third and most interesting type of egocentric speech is the *collective monologue.* Two youngsters look as if they are having a conversation. In fact, communication is minimal. They take turns, pausing to let one another speak, but pay no attention to what the other child is saying.

JENNY: They wiggle sideways when they kiss.

CHRIS: (*vaguely*) What?

JENNY: My bunny slippers. They are brown and red and sort of red and white. And they have eyes and ears and these noses that wiggle sideways when they kiss.

CHRIS: I have a piece of sugar in a piece of red paper. I'm gonna eat it but maybe it's for a horse.

JENNY: We bought them. My mommy did. We could't find the old ones. These are like the old ones. They were not in the trunk.

CHRIS: Can't eat the piece of sugar, not unless you take the piece of paper off.

JENNY: And we found Mother Lamb. Oh, she was in Poughkeepsie in the trunk in the house in the woods where Mrs. Tiddywinkle lives.

CHRIS: Do you like sugar? I do, and so do horses.

JENNY: I play with my bunnies. They are real and we play in the woods. They have eyes. We all go in the woods. . . .

CHRIS: I guess I'll eat my sugar at lunch time. I can get more for the horses. Besides, I don't have no horses now.

(Stone & Church, 1973)

A series of experiments provided further evidence of egocentric speech in the preschool years. Piaget would tell one child a story, then ask him to repeat it to a child who was waiting in the next room. A contemporary version of this experiment (Flavell, Botkin, Fry, Wright, & Jarvis, 1968) illustrates the results. Pairs of 6-year-olds were seated on the opposite sides of a screen. The children were given identical sets of pictures. One child was asked to select a pic-

Piaget described the way children talk to children as a collective monologue, full of animated assertions and creative non sequiturs.

ture and tell the other child which one he had chosen. The following "dialogue" was typical.

FIRST CHILD: (*pointing to one of the pictures in front of him*) It's this one.
SECOND CHILD: (*pointing to a picture in front of him*) You mean this one?
FIRST CHILD: (*unable to see, but confident*) Yep!

(Flavell et al., 1968)

Even when two children do focus on the same topic and pay attention to one another, they do not necessarily exchange information. Each may simply assert and reassert his or her point.

HANS: Ruth, look, up there is the railway that goes to heaven.
RUTH: No, there aren't any railway lines up there.
HANS: But there are railway lines.
RUTH: No, there aren't any railway lines up there. There are no railway lines in heaven. God doesn't need any railway lines.
HANS: Yes he does.
RUTH: No, God doesn't need any railway lines nor any trains.
HANS: But there must be a railway line for a train.

(Piaget, 1959)

Although much closer to conversation, this is hardly a discussion.

According to Piaget, the sequence of language development is from sensorimotor "thoughts" to egocentric speech to socialized speech. Typically, egocentric speech begins to fade after age 7 and gradually disappears. Why? Parents and other adults take great pains to understand what a small child is trying to say.

They make every effort to infer what he wants, what is bothering him, or what he thinks from nonverbal and situational clues. Adults assimilate his communications. By 6 or 7, however, the child is spending more and more time with other children. Other children are not as patient as parents and are not willing to devote time and effort to interpreting his unclear statements. To the contrary, they often challenge what the child says and force him to defend himself. Unless he wants to be on the losing end of every argument, the child must learn to make himself understood. He must accommodate listeners. In this way, social pressure forces him to adopt more effective means of communication. In time, Piaget maintained, "socialized speech" takes over and egocentric speech disappears.

VYGOTSKY ON INNER SPEECH The Russian psychologist Lev Vygotsky (1962) viewed egocentric speech quite differently. In sharp contrast to Piaget, Vygotsky held that the child's first attempts to speak are purely social. Her first words and sentences are attempts to establish and maintain social contact and to share feelings and observations. Communication is all-important. At age 3 or 4, she begins to use the verbal skills she developed for social exchanges for personal purposes, to talk to herself about her own activities. Vygotsky found that the amount of egocentric speech doubles when young children are faced with a frustrating situation—for example, when they sit down to draw and find that some of the pencils that they want are missing. Just as a small child counts on her fingers, the young artist solves her problems aloud: "Where's the pencil? I need a blue pencil. Never mind, I'll draw with the red one and wet it with water; it will become dark and look like blue" (Vygotsky, 1962, p. 16). Egocentric speech begins as a problem-solving technique and gradually develops a directing, planning function. In time, the child no longer needs to speak aloud to use words as instruments of thought. Egocentric speech is transformed into *inner speech,* or thinking to oneself.

According to Vygotsky, then, the sequence of development is from social communication to egocentric talk to inner speech. The way children name drawings illustrates this. The small child draws a picture first, decides what to call it afterward. Naming serves the social function of making the drawing meaningful to other people. When slightly older, the child names what he is drawing when he is half finished with it. Here, naming solves a personal problem: "Where shall I go from here?" The older child decides what he will draw before he begins. If asked, he will tell you what he plans, but he does not have to speak out loud to plan his actions. Inner speech is directing his activity. Thus Vygotsky saw egocentric speech as a transitional stage between social communication and independent thought. (See Figure 7-8.)

LANGUAGE AND THOUGHT Underlying this disagreement over the meaning of egocentric speech is a more basic disagreement about the relationship between language and thought. Piaget held that the development of language depends on thoughts. Children have sensorimotor thoughts about objects before they are able to speak. They must have a clear mental representation of an object before they can attach a name to it. Thoughts come first. Vygotsky believed that language and thought develop hand in hand. Learning to speak enables the child to communicate her observations. In turn, her words influence the form and content of her thinking.

Bilingualism: Liability or Asset?

Many children grow up hearing, and in time speaking, not one language but two. Some American children learn to speak Spanish or Korean or Arabic at home and are not exposed to English until they enter day-care or nursery school. Some grow up in bilingual homes, with parents and siblings who speak two languages more or less fluently. Some speak English at home but attend school in French, Hebrew, or another language. What impact does bilingualism have on the development of language and thought?

Studies conducted in the 1950s and 1960s (reviewed in Oren, 1981) reported that bilingualism had damaging effects on a child's intellectual development. Bilingual youngsters did not perform as well on standard intelligence or achievement tests as monolingual youngsters, in either of their languages. Researchers concluded that mastering a second language interfered with cognitive developments in other areas. The child's information-processing capacity was said to be overloaded. However, most of these studies did not control for socioeconomic background. Often the bilingual children's parents had low incomes and little education. Their performance on tests and in school was no better or worse than that of monolingual children from similar socioeconomic backgrounds. Most early studies ignored such factors as different levels of skill in the two languages (could a child read and write as well as speak the second language?), family influences (did one or both parents speak the second language at home?), or the cultural context (did the child grow up in a community of Spanish- or Navajo-speakers?). More recent studies that take these factors into account paint a different picture.

Far from being a disadvantage, bilingualism may have cognitive benefits. Ditza Oren (1981) compared children who had been exposed to two languages from an early age ("true bilinguals") to children who were learning a second language at age 4 or 5 ("two-language children") and to monolinguals. She wanted to know whether children in any one of these groups were more flexible in their use of language. She presented them with a number of tasks that re-

quired them to use nonsense names (*dimp* for dog, *wug* for car) or to misname familiar things (if we call a cow a "dog," does a dog give milk?). (See Figure 7-9). Did they know that a name is merely a label, and that changing the name of an object does not change its properties (an example of object constancy)? Oren found that the true bilinguals consistently outperformed children from the other groups. She concludes that early experience with two languages, with two distinct coding systems, make youngsters more aware of the difference between objects and symbols and of the functions of language. In her view, bilingualism stimulates cognitive flexibility. Other research supports this view. For example, bilingual children often tell more creative stories than do monolingual children of the same

age (Doyle, Champagne, & Segalowitz, 1978).

Bilingualism may create temporary delays and detours in cognitive and language development. A child may transfer syntax from one language to the other (Madrid & Garcia, 1981). For example, in Spanish dropping the subject (as in *no quiero ir*) is grammatically correct. A Spanish-speaking child may apply this rule to English ("no want go"), producing sentences that sound immature. Children who are learning a second language may use stock phrases and clichés more often than other children (Hakuta, 1976). They may have smaller vocabularies in both languages than monolingual children their age (Doyle et al., 1978). They may not perform as well on tests of egocentric speech (Flavell et al., 1968; Meshoulam, 1981).

Figure 7-9 "Dimps" and "Wugs" One way to test comprehension of linguistic rules is to ask children to complete sentences using nonsense or made-up words. "Here is a *wug*. Here is another *wug*. Now there are two _____." The child who says "two *wugs*" understands the rule for plurals.

Figure 7-8 Piaget and Vygotsky: Two Views of Thought and Speech

Taken as a whole, however, current research indicates that bilingualism is more an asset than a liability (Hakuta, 1976). Bilingual education for preschoolers may not only stimulate cognitive flexibility but also enhance self-esteem and pride in different cultural heritages. Acquiring a second language at an early age does not interfere with mastering a primary language. Indeed, the ease with which preschoolers pick up a second language (compared with the difficulties adults experience) is remarkable.

Social class differences in linguistic ability remain, however. With few exceptions, middle-class children (the great majority of whom are English-speaking and white) speak better Standard English than do lower-class children (many of whom are bilingual or black). Some researchers (Hess & Shipman, 1965) believe that this is the result of upbringing: Middle-class mothers require verbal feedback as well as physical compliance from their children; lower-class mothers often do not. Others (Labov, 1972) hold that black youngsters in particular speak a dialect of Standard English with its own conventions and grammar, a dialect that most whites find difficult to understand. Social-class, racial, and ethnic differences in linguistic skills take on new importance when children enter school.

These differences aside, the preschooler has made a giant stride in development. Language greatly increases the possibilities for social exchange, the subject of the next chapter.

SUMMARY

1. All animals have evolved means of communicating alarm, hostility, sexual excitement, and the like to other members of their species. These expressions of "emotion" are called signs.

2. Human language differs from other forms of communication in three ways: We can exchange information as well as express feelings (semantics), combine sounds in new ways to produce new meanings (productivity), and communicate about events that are removed in time and space (displacement).

3. Apes can be taught to use sign language. But they do not develop language spontaneously or progress beyond the two-word stage, and may only be imitating their trainers. Human linguistic ability is unique.

4. Language development depends on mastering the sound patterns of speech (phonology) and recognizing units of sound that indicate changes in meaning (phonemes).

5. Babies respond to the human voice in the first weeks of life, begin babbling at about 6 months, and produce their first "words" (regular sounds they use on similar occasions) around their first birthday. Small children are often unaware of their own mispronunciations (the fis phenomenon), perhaps because they judge their speech in terms of intent.

6. Language development depends on learning rules for combining and altering words in meaningful ways (syntax).

7. Children progress from one-word utterances, to two-word "telegrams," to more complete phrases (at age 2½ or 3). Grammatically correct questions and passive sentences develop last.

8. Some psychologists (such as Skinner) have argued that children learn syntax through imitation; others (such as Chomsky) that they are born with an "innate grammar." A

more plausible explanation is that children listen for regularities in speech, devise tentative rules, then test their hypotheses. This would explain growth errors—why youngsters who use irregular constructions correctly at age 3 make mistakes ("I *seed* two *mouses*") at age 4.

9. Language development depends on understanding the meaning of words and longer segments of speech (semantics).

10. Children's first utterances are words and names that invite action ("Mommy," "bye-bye," "ball"). Often they overextend the meaning of a word (using "doggie" for all animals). Beyond first words, vocabulary develops hand in hand with concepts. According to Nelson, concept development proceeds from sensorimotor images, to personal labels, to socially shared categories, to more abstract notions in middle childhood. But small children understand more than they can say.

11. Language development depends on understanding the social conventions and uses of speech (pragmatics).

12. Adults begin modeling conversations for infants long before the babies utter their first words. They speak to small children in "motherese," simplifying and repeating constructions and building language lessons into their conversations.

13. Children need some social interaction and verbal exchange to learn to speak, but much less than one might think.

14. Children talking among themselves and to themselves reveals other patterns. Piaget held that speech develops from an egocentric activity, to collective monologues, to social dialogues. Vygotsky maintained that speech begins as a social activity, then becomes a device for self-monitoring, and finally is internalized as thought.

15. Many young children learn not one but two languages. Current research indicates that bilingualism may cause temporary disorganization but long-term cognitive benefits.

FURTHER READING

Chukovsky, K. (1968). *From two to five*. Berkeley, CA: University of California Press.

de Villiers, P. A., de Villiers, J. G. (1979). *Early language*. Cambridge, MA: Harvard University Press. A highly readable, delightfully illustrated, research-based description of the development of language.

Dillard, J. L. (1972). *Black English*. New York: Vintage Books. A study of Black English, including its structural and historical resemblance to English spoken in the Caribbean, South America, West Africa, and the Pacific. The book traces the development of Black English to its origins in West African languages. Black English is viewed as a valid dialect, based on normal language changes, rather than being an "inferior" version of Standard English.

Terrace, H. S. (1979). *Nim: A chimpanzee who learned sign language*. New York: Washington Square Press. A behind-the-scenes description of teaching a chimp sign language. The author came to love Nim, but questioned the notion that chimps are capable of symbolic communication.

Sound

Preference for human voice;
may recognize mother's voice

Cooing   Babbling   Babbling   First words
<2–3 mos.>   <6–7 mos.>   resembles   (single or
     language   repeated syllable)
     <8–10 mos.>   <10–14 mos.>

Sense

Vocabulary: 3–50 words   50 + words

           Overextension (All animals called "doggie") (15–30 mos.)

Sentences: One-word "holographs"   Two-word
           <12–18 mos.>   "telegrams"
           <18–24 mos.>

Syntax: Noun/verb   Adds grammatical
           combinations   markers, tenses, and
           adjectives
           <24–30 mos.>

Conversation

[Adults model conversation,   [Adults and older children
e.g., peek-a-boo]   use "motherese"]

     Emergence of intent (looking,
     pointing) <8–9 mos.>

Piaget: Repetition

Vygotsky: Social speech

| | 6 mos. | 12 mos. | 2 yrs. |
Age

HIGHLIGHTS OF LANGUAGE DEVELOPMENT IN THE PRESCHOOL PERIOD

"Fis" phenomenon
("My name is Litha")
(2–6 yrs.)

( ) age range
< > onset or peak
 age extension beyond
that shown on chart

8,000–14,000 words

Three- to four-
word sentences
<3 yrs.>

Seven-word
sentences
<6 yrs.>

Correct forms
of questions
and negatives
<2–3 yrs.>

Growth errors ("I seed two mouses")
(3–6 yrs.)

Compound phrases
and passive
construction
<6–7 yrs.>

Individual
monologue

Collective
monologue

Social speech

Self-directed
monologue

Inner speech

| 3 yrs. | 4 yrs. | 5 yrs. | 6 yrs. |

CHAPTER

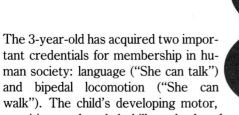

The 3-year-old has acquired two important credentials for membership in human society: language ("She can talk") and bipedal locomotion ("She can walk"). The child's developing motor, cognitive, and verbal skills make her far more capable of getting into mischief than she was at 6 months. She demands independence: *"I'll do it!"* At the same time, her parents require that she exercise more self-restraint and self-control. Her social horizons expand as she begins to play with—not just look at—other children her age. Social play introduces her to new forms of interpersonal conflict as well as new sources of fun and laughter. She catches glimpses of the wider world on trips to the supermarket and the zoo, in picture books and on TV. At the beginning of this period she was a baby; at the end, she will be expected to enter first grade and to begin training for an adult role in her society.

This chapter describes social and emotional changes in the preschool period. We begin by looking at the development of social competence, from both the child's and society's points of view. Then we look at the different ways parents and peers influence the development of social competence. Next we consider two of the most important psychosocial tasks of the preschool period: developing a gender identity and learning sex roles, and controlling aggression. Finally, we examine the emergence of kindness and empathy.

Developing Social Competence

Erik Erikson described the preschooler as suddenly seeming to "grow together" in his body and his person.

He appears "more himself," more loving, relaxed and brighter in his judgment, more activated and activating. He is in free possession of a surplus of energy which permits him to forget failures quickly and to approach what seems desirable (even if it also seems uncertain and dangerous) with undiminished and more accurate direction. (1963, p. 255)

The young child is developing what others have called social competence.

BECOMING A MEMBER OF THE CULTURE

Social Competence

Everett Waters and L. Alan Sroufe (1983) define **social competence** as the ability to use environmental and personal resources "to achieve a good developmental outcome." The emphasis in this definition is on adaptability. The competent child is able to take advantage of the opportunities the environment offers and to cope with most of the difficulties he encounters in the environment. He can adjust to new situations, such as the birth of a sibling or entering nursery school, and enjoys exercising such new skills as running and reading.

Waters and Sroufe also stress the developmental nature of social competence. What is adaptive at one age (for example, dependency in infancy) may be maladaptive at a later age (middle childhood). Moreover, what is adaptive in the immediate situation may be harmful over the long run. A toddler who has been physically abused by a parent may increase his chances of survival by withdrawing from human contact. But if this makes it difficult for him to form relationships with other adults and peers, it is maladaptive in the long run. Social competence is behavior that promotes or does not hinder development.

Waters and Sroufe identify six phases in the development of social competence in early childhood, as shown in Table 8-1. This table is similar to Erik Erikson's description of the psychosocial tasks of early childhood, shown in Table 8-2. Like Erikson, Waters and Sroufe hold that each phase builds on the one before it. The development of social competence is cumulative.

Waters and Sroufe see the basic task for the young infant (phases 1 and 2) as attaining physiological and perceptual regulation—or what Erikson called "basic trust." The competent newborn can hold down her food, focus her eyes on a human face, and adjust in other basic ways to her environment. The older infant (phases 3 and 4) must establish an effective attachment to an adult, or to a few adults, who serves as a

Table 8-1   Phases in the Development of Social Competence

Phase	Age	Issue	Role for Caregiver
1	0–3 mos.	Physiological regulation	Smooth routines
2	3–6 mos.	Management of tension	Sensitive, cooperative interaction
3	6–12 mos.	Establishing an effective attachment relationship	Responsive availability
4	12–18 mos.	Exploration and mastery	Secure base
5	1½–2½ yrs.	Individuation	Firm support
6	2½–4½ yrs.	Management of impulses, sex-role identification, peer relations	Clear roles and values, flexible control

(Based on Sroufe, 1983)

Table 8-2   Erikson's Stages of Psychosocial Development

Age (years)	Issue	Possible Outcomes
1	Trust vs. mistrust	Infant learns to trust, or mistrust, that needs will be met by mother or others.
2	Autonomy vs. shame and doubt	Toddler learns to exercise will, make own choices, and control himself—or becomes doubtful and uncertain that he can do things on his own.
3–5	Initiative vs. guilt	Preschooler acquires direction and purpose, learns to initiate activities and enjoys accomplishments—or feels guilty about attempts at independence.

(Based on Erikson, 1963)

base for exploration. The competent 12-month-old can leave her caregiver's side to explore a new environment; she can also derive comfort from that caregiver in stressful situations. This child has achieved what Erikson called "autonomy."

Individuation, or the desire to master the environment on one's own, is the basic task for the toddler (phase 5). Waters and Sroufe focus on problem-solving style, rather than on specific skills, in this phase. When faced with a task on the edge of her abilities, the competent toddler approaches the problem with enthusiasm and persists despite difficulty. She listens to advice from an adult and requests help when she needs it, but would rather solve the problem herself. The toddler has developed what Erikson termed "initiative." She is willing to venture forth to explore and challenge the world on her own.

The preschooler (phase 6) must learn to manage impulses in order to adapt to social roles (including sex roles) and to operate well in a peer group. Social play is an important measure of competence in this phase. Playing with age-mates requires flexibility. The child must know when to express her own desires and when to suppress them; how to initiate social interaction and how to respond to other children's overtures; when to step up an activity and when a game or joke has gone too far. Competent 4- and 5-year-olds attract other children by making activities fun for everyone.

According to Erikson, developing initiative is the most important psychosocial task of the preschool years.

Socialization

The development of social competence does not take place in a vacuum. The child's parents and other caretakers are members of a society. Their ideas about children and child-rearing reflect their culture. To become a functioning member of that society, the child must become competent in that particular culture.

Socialization is the process of learning the values and rules for behavior of the culture in which one is born and will live (see Chapter 2). It is the child's initiation into his culture. The traditions and technology of a people—what we call their culture—give rhythm and meaning to life's events. Each culture has its own explanation of life and death; its own definitions of right and wrong, good and evil, worthwhile and trivial; its own ideas about when it is appropriate to work or play, laugh or cry, love or hate; its own rules about how young and old, males and females, should behave. Each culture has its own techniques for adapting to the physical environment (its technologies). This design for living is passed from one generation to the next through learning. Parents and others act as *agents of socialization* for the community. Ideally, the child comes to see many of his people's customs and beliefs as "only natural." His hopes and dreams echo theirs.

Socialization may be said to begin at birth. The way parents handle a newborn reflects their culture's norms and values (as well as their own personalities and the baby's temperament). Whether a baby is strapped to a cradleboard, carried in a sling and nursed whenever he fusses, or given his own room and crib and bottle-fed every three hours, for example, is determined largely by cultural beliefs. But parents make few demands on an infant. Babies are not expected to have good manners.

Around the child's second birthday, parents' expectations begin to change. They perceive the youngster as more capable and more intentional or willful than he was before. As a result, they begin to expect at least some obedience and cooperation. Soon parents require that the child exercise modesty, go to bed when told, control temper tantrums, moderate his demands for attention, behave properly at the dinner table, and perhaps "act like a little man or young lady." According to one study of 2-year-olds in their homes (Minton, Kagan, & Levine, 1971), mothers reprimanded their toddlers an average of nine times an hour. Physical or verbal aggression, temper tantrums, or threats to household objects provoked almost half of the mother's communications to the child. At 2 years, socialization has begun in earnest.

Identification

How is socialization accomplished? How is the small human animal transformed into a competent and committed member of the culture? A number of psychologists have focused on the dynamics of adult–child (especially parent–child) interaction in the preschool period.

THE FREUDIAN VIEW Freud saw the preschool years as a turning point in socialization. According to him, the infant is a willful, impulsive, sensual being who seeks instant gratification of every desire. When parents begin to demand that the child exercise self-control, the child becomes angry. He feels he is competing with his father for his mother's love and affection (the Oedipal conflict). A girl has the same feeling toward her parents (the Electra complex). The child's natural impulse is to strike out in rage. But expressing anger toward someone as important and powerful as a parent is dangerous. The child fears not only that he will be punished, but worse, that he will lose both parents' love.

The child resolves this conflict through **identification**: incorporating an image of the parent he or she admires and fears most (the father or mother) into him- or herself. Identification is motivated in part by fear. To avoid punishment, the children adopt their parents' stan-

Learning one's position in life is a central part of socialization, for future kings as well as their subjects.

dards of good and evil as their own. They turn the anger they cannot express toward parents against themselves, and become self-punishing. According to Freud, the conscience (or super-ego) is an internalization of the parent's voice telling the child what he should and should not do. Violations provoke guilt and shame. As a result, the child resists temptation even when the parent is not present. (See Figure 8-1.) Identification is also motivated by love: the child strives to be like the admired parent.

There is more to identification than simple imitation. The development of a conscience involves a fundamental restructuring of the child's psyche. Not until the child has erected a dam to

Figure 8-1 Identification According to both Freudians and social learning theorists, children adopt the standards of the people they love and admire as their own, and become self-policing.

hold back the sexual and aggressive impulses of infancy is he able to concentrate on learning specific cultural skills.

SOCIAL LEARNING THEORY Other psychologists have modified and extended the concept of identification. According to social learning theory (Bandura, 1971), children learn the ways of their culture through reinforcement and modeling. They repeat behavior for which they are rewarded and avoid behavior for which they are punished or ridiculed. They also observe the people around them and imitate behavior for which they see others being rewarded.

Social learning theorists do not maintain that children are simply imitations of, or imitators of, their parents. Often the child gets the "wrong" message, one the parent did not intend. Suppose a mother punishes a child for grabbing a toy away from his little brother. Is the mother: (a) extinguishing aggressive behavior (reducing the likelihood that he will bully his brother again); (b) unintentionally rewarding his aggressiveness by giving him attention; or (c) by spanking him, modeling aggressive behavior (showing him that the way to get what you want is to use physical force on someone smaller than yourself)?

In contrast to Freud, learning theorists maintain that youngsters form not one but many identifications (Mischel & Mischel, 1976). Children identify with people whom they perceive as powerful, nurturant, and more knowledgeable and skillful than they are. Parents are obvious candidates. But older children and other adults may also serve as models. Children are most likely to imitate behavior that they observe often (Bussey, 1981). They seem to develop prototypes based on many different models and numerous observations. When a parent does not fit a child's image of how to dress, how to play a game, or some other behavior, she discards the parent as a model in that area. The children of immigrants, for example, rarely speak with the strong accents of their parents. And like typical American children, they come to love McDonald's.

Contemporary learning theorists also hold that children are to some extent self-reinforcing: They set standards for themselves and respond to their performance with self-praise or self-criticism (Bandura, 1973). One study showed how praise and rewards from adults can backfire (Lepper, Greene, & Nisbett, 1973). When the nursery-school children in the study were given a new set of felt-tip pens, they were enthusiastic. Drawing quickly became a favorite activity. When they were systematically rewarded for producing pictures, however, they lost interest. The drawings they did make were less detailed, thoughtful, and original than their spontaneous creations. Drawing had become work!

Social learning theorists see identification as less dramatic and more wide-ranging than Freudians do. But both would agree that the development of social competence depends on interactions with other people. And both would agree that socialization begins at home.

The Home Front

The family is at the dinner table. Boy gets up.

> FATHER: Hey, sit down! (*yells, but good naturedly*)
> *Boy sits down and finishes milk. Boy gets up.*
> FATHER: What do you say, Todd?
> BOY: Excuse me, please.
> FATHER: What?
> BOY: Excuse me, please.
> FATHER: O.K.
> BOY: (*on the way out*) Tomorrow I'm not going to say it because I said it two times.
>
> *Mother and son are in kitchen.*
> BOY: Can I go out?

> MOTHER: Yes. Oh, no, I guess you can't. I didn't realize how late it was.
> BOY: *Please*, Mother. (*crying, beseeching, pleading*) I never get to go down the street.
> MOTHER: I'll tell you, you can ride your bike on Fall Street.
> BOY: On Spring Street.
> MOTHER: Just once.
> BOY: Why just once?
> MOTHER: You don't really want to go out. *Boy leaves.*

(Baumrind, 1967, pp. 65–66)

All parents work at socializing their children. But the way they go about this varies from parent to parent. What impact do different styles of child-rearing have on the child? Do certain kinds of parenting enhance or impede the development of social competence?

Studying Parent–Child Interaction

Diana Baumrind has been investigating parent–child interaction for more than twenty years. In her first major study, Baumrind and her colleagues (1967) classified a group of 110 nursery-school children into three groups: competent children (who were self-reliant, cheerful, and curious); withdrawn children (who were timid, shy, and often unhappy); and immature children (who were impulsive and clinging). Observers, who did not know how a given child had been classified, made two visits to the home and recorded the parents' and the child's attempts to control one another. (The scenes above are from this phase of the study.) The researchers also observed the mother and child in a laboratory, where the mother was asked to teach the child a number concept, set certain limits on play, and require the child to clean up. The parents were rated in terms of their willingness to exercise control, their demands for mature behavior, their communications with the child, and their nurturance (expressions of tenderness and pride in the child's achievements).

At the time of the study, child-care professionals held that strict child-rearing practices inhibited spontaneity and creativity. Baumrind found the reverse. The parents of competent children exercised firm control over the child and demanded responsible behavior, but were also willing to listen and reason with him.

Three Styles of Child-rearing

After a number of similar studies of parents and children at different ages, Baumrind concluded

that there are three distinct styles of child-rearing. *Authoritarian* parents are parent-centered and demanding. They consider obedience a virtue in and of itself, discourage verbal give and take, and demand that the child accept their decisions without question. Rules are not explained; no one asks the child's opinion. In contrast, *permissive* parents are child-centered and indulgent. They accept the child's desires and impulses, make few demands for responsibility and order in the home, and avoid confrontations, punishments, and control. They let the child have her own way. *Authoritative* parents are child-centered and demanding. They expect the child to conform to household rules but encourage verbal give-and-take. They set high standards and are willing to enforce them, with physical punishment if necessary. But they prefer to reason with the child. These parents believe that both children and their parents have rights and responsibilities.

The three types of parents varied in two critical areas: *warmth,* or the amount of affection parents display for a child, and *discipline,* or the manner in which parents attempt to control a child. Warm parents are sensitive to the child's emotional states, enthusiastic about the child's interests and accomplishments, and like to spend time in joint enterprises that the child has chosen. At the opposite extreme are parents

Confrontations between parents and preschoolers will often occur.

who are cold and rejecting, and who let the child know that they find parenthood a burden and the child unrewarding.

Parents also differ in disciplinary styles. Some parents control their children through the arbitrary assertion of power, invoking their authority and ability to punish. The general message is, "Do it because I say so!" Other parents rely on the firm and consistent enforcement of rules that they have explained to and discussed with the child. Moreover, their use of discipline depends on the child's behavior, not on the parents' moods. Baumrind found that it was neither warmth nor discipline alone that determined the child's behavior, but the combination of the two. Both warmth without discipline and discipline without warmth had negative effects on a child's development.

Other researchers have identified a fourth type, the *uninvolved* parents (Maccoby & Martin, 1983). These mothers and fathers are low in discipline *and* low in warmth; they simply do not want to be bothered. The main effect on children is lowered self-esteem.

The Impact on Children

Children of authoritative parents tend to be independent (assertive, self-reliant, achievement-oriented) and socially responsible (friendly and cooperative). Interestingly, Baumrind found that authoritarian as well as permissive child-rearing contribute to dependency in the child. She suggests that this is because both types of parents have unrealistic notions of childhood. Both see children as driven by primitive, egoistic impulses. Whereas authoritarian parents see these characteristics as something bad that must be eliminated, permissive parents see them as natural behavior that should be encouraged or ignored. Yet neither group seems to take into account the developmental level of the child. Authoritarian parents assign the child the same responsibilities as adults; permissive par-

ents grant the child the same rights as adults. In contrast, authoritative parents try to strike a balance between the two. Baumrind also found that different styles of child-rearing have different effects on males and females (see Table 8-3).

Unanswered Questions

Baumrind's research provided developmental psychologists with a framework for studying socialization and directed attention to the impact of different styles of child-rearing on youngsters' behavior. But her work has raised as many questions as it has answered.

No parent is authoritarian or permissive all of the time, and no child self-reliant or clinging, friendly or shy, all of the time. What situations bring out these tendencies? How much authoritarianism or permissiveness tips the scale?

Baumrind focused on the interaction between parents and a single child. How do parents react to different children with different temperaments? Are some parents permissive with one child, authoritarian with another? Permissive with daughters but authoritarian with sons? Baumrind found that authoritarian child-rearing is associated with defiance in boys. She suggests that the arbitrary, inflexible use of parental power *causes* boys to become hostile. But it may be that aggressive behavior in boys provokes parents to use harsh discipline. Parents may be *responding* to their son.

Do child-rearing styles change over the course of development? Do parents who were permissive with their infant become authoritarian when the child is 2 or 2½ and getting into mischief, authoritative when the child is 6 and better able to listen to reason? Are there other patterns? Does a particular style of child-rearing have the same impact on children of all ages? Is parent–child interaction when the young person is 16 the result of a relationship established in

Table 8-3 The Impact of Different Styles of Child-rearing

Child-rearing Style	All Children	Boys	Girls
Authoritarian	Low in independence Middle range in social responsibility	Sometimes angry and defiant	
Permissive	Low in independence Very low in social responsibility		Tend to set low goals for self and to withdraw out of frustration
Authoritative	High in independence High in social responsibility	More socially responsible than other boys	More self-reliant and achievement-oriented than other girls (also more domineering with peers and rebellious with adults)

(Based on Baumrind, 1973)

the preschool years, or a reflection of current developmental issues?

Baumrind implies, first, that child-rearing styles are stable over time and, second, that socialization is unidirectional (something parents do *to* children). As these questions suggest, other psychologists view socialization as a dynamic process that changes over the course of development, and as a bidirectional or reciprocal process, in which children influence their parents as much as the parents influence them (Bell & Harper, 1977; Maccoby & Martin, 1983). For better or worse, parents and children are in it together.

Peer Power

It is in the preschool period that children discover friends. Infants prefer adult playmates. A baby may follow another baby around, examine the other child with his eyes, and reach out and touch him. But infants behave in much the same way toward inanimate toys. In the first year of life, infants show social interest but lack the skills necessary for social interaction (Hartup, 1983). In the second year this begins to change. When pairs of children aged 10 months to 2 years were observed in a playroom, the older children paid more attention to one another than to their mothers (Eckerman, Whatley, & Kutz, 1975). Often toddlers played with the same toy. But it would be an exaggeration to say that they were having fun together. Although they smiled or laughed at one another occasionally, most of the time their expressions were quite serious.

"It's my turn!"

Insight

"... AND BABY MAKES FOUR"

About 80 percent of American and British children have at least one brother or sister. The birth of a sibling causes dramatic, irrevocable changes in a child's life. Never again will he have his mother all to himself. Suddenly he is confronted with someone who not only competes for his parents' attention, but also does not try to understand *him* (unlike the adults in his life). And the sibling will never simply "go away."

For years, clinical psychologists have viewed the birth of a brother or sister as a traumatic event for a child. They see the relationship that develops between siblings as one based on jealousy and rivalry. Is this picture correct? Judy Dunn and Carol Kendrick (1982) studied 40 British families who were about to have a second child. Interviews and home observations were begun before the baby was born and continued until this child was 14 months old. They found that clinical psychologists are right in part, but only in part.

The arrival of the sibling was greeted by marked changes in the elder child's behavior. Almost all of the mothers said that the child became naughtier and more demanding. "She was always naughty, but now she won't do *anything* I ask." "She's so very selfish—wants everything she can see" (p. 29). Often the misbehavior was a clear message. The researchers saw one child, whose mother was cooing at the baby, pour milk all over a couch. Another child got her mother's attention by running into the garden and lowering a line of fresh laundry into the mud. Some children became clinging and tearful. Some had problems sleeping. Most were bitterly jealous when the father or a grandparent paid attention to the baby. On the positive side, many of the children responded to the baby's arrival by becoming more self-reliant. They began to insist on feeding or dressing themselves. And although many seemed angry at their mother, most expressed interest in and affection for the baby. They were upset when the new sibling cried and eager to help with infant care—whether or not help was wanted.

The child's interactions with the mother also changed. The number of confrontations between the mother and child increased significantly. Joint play, in which the two focused on a common item of interest, decreased. The mothers were less likely to initiate interaction by commenting on the child's activities, suggesting a new activity, or starting a new game or verbal fantasy. Many more of their verbal exchanges began with the mother telling the child to stop doing something. The increase in confrontations may have reflected the child's becoming naughtier; the mother's becoming preoccupied, overburdened, and less patient and more restrictive; or a combination of both.

In some families, however, the presence of a baby added a new and positive element to mother–child exchanges. Prior to the birth, most of their conversations had focused on the child's desires, interests, and intentions. Now their talk included a third party, the baby. The presence of another, smaller person prompted numerous comments about how the elder child was like and unlike the younger sibling in age, gender, size, abilities, and goodness or naughtiness. These comparisons contributed to the elder child's awareness of her own identity. The baby also called attention to development ("Baby can't walk. . . . When she gets bigger she can."). Sometimes the children were triumphant about being ahead ("I was walking before he was"); sometimes they delighted in the baby's accomplishments ("He called you 'Mum!'").

Most of the children were intensely curious about the baby's motives and states. They often explained the younger sibling to the observer ("He wants you to come"; "Callum's crying 'cause he wants his food cold"). And they often corrected their mother's interpretation of the baby's desires. Out of envy or love, or both, the child became highly aware of another person.

A follow-up study, conducted when the older children were about 6 years old, indicated that patterns established in the first years continued. Some sibling relationships were characterized by aggression and hostility. In one mother's words, "It's not very good really—at the moment it's very *bad*. . . . Last week I was pulling my hair out!" Many others are better

described as ambivalent: "It comes down to love and hate, doesn't it? Some days they play so well, then other days . . . fighting about nothing at all, they make it into such a big thing" (p. 208).

Dunn and Kendrick conclude that friendly sibling relationships depend on both the mother and the children. Siblings are most likely to enjoy one another if (1) the mother talks about the baby as a person with special likes and dislikes, and invites the older child to participate in infant care during the first months, (2) if the siblings are the same sex (a surprising finding; one might expect same-sex siblings to display more jealousy of one another), and (3) if the older sibling's immediate response to the birth is positive.

During the preschool period, both positive and negative social interactions increase steadily. The actions of a 3-year-old child depend more on what other children do and how other children respond than do those of a 2-year-old. Four-year-olds are able to construct joint plans for action. There is much more smiling and laughter, imitation, and sharing—and also more hitting, shoving, grabbing, and quarreling—in a group of 5-year-olds than in a group of toddlers. Attention-seeking from peers begins to replace affection-seeking from adults. Is the peer group a "sideshow" to the main events of socialization? Are increases in peer interest and activity simply a by-product of the amount of time the preschooler spends with other children? Or do peers make a special contribution to socialization?

Monkey Business

Peers play an important role in the socialization of nonhuman primates. For example, an infant rhesus monkey spends most of its first month clinging to its mother. In the second month it begins to make tentative explorations of its surroundings, where it normally encounters other young monkeys. By 4 months it is spending most of its waking hours in rough-and-tumble play and games of tag with other youngsters. Interactions with peers continue to occupy much of the monkey's time and interest into adulthood.

Harry Harlow's classic experiments with rhesus monkeys showed that infant monkeys raised in isolation, without "mother love," were social misfits as adults (1958). In another series of experiments, Harlow, Stephen Suomi, and their colleagues demonstrated that peers are also vital to normal development (Suomi & Harlow, 1975). Some infant monkeys were raised with their mother but without contact with peers; others were raised with groups of two or three peers but without their mother. On the whole, members of the second group were better adjusted as adults. As infants, the peer-raised monkeys clung to one another much of the time, engaging in less exploration than young monkeys do under normal conditions (see Figure 8-2). Eventually they parted and developed into more or less socially competent, although cliquish, adults.

In contrast, the infant monkeys raised with mothers but not peers were usually wary of strangers and hyperaggressive when they did make social contact. In other experiments, monkeys who had been totally isolated for their first six or twelve months were given younger monkey "therapists." Although frightened by the other young monkey at first, they soon began to play. In late adolescence they exhibited appropriate social behavior.

To explain these findings, Suomi and Harlow (1975) emphasize the adaptive functions of peer friendships among monkeys. In their natural habitats, monkeys must be able to distinguish members of their own troop from members of other troops, who are likely to attack or even kill them. The ability to tell friends from strangers is a matter of individual survival. In order to survive as a group, members of a troop must know their social positions and behave appropriately. Allies are important. "One's friends determine in large part one's social standing; without any friends one has no social standing other than age and gender" (p. 179). (Sound familiar?) Suomi and Harlow conclude that monkeys are genetically predisposed to behave in appropriate ways, but do so only if such behavior is reinforced. They must learn when, where, and how to exhibit their species' equivalent of good manners. Most of this learning takes place among peers.

These experiments were conducted with monkeys, not humans, for obvious reasons. We know of only one case of "peer-raised" humans. In 1945, six German Jewish 3-year-olds were rescued from Nazi concentration camps and brought to a nursery in England. Separated from their mothers before their first birthday, they had essentially raised themselves. When relocated, the children were alternately hostile or coldly indifferent to adults; they clung to one another. Although their behavior toward outsiders was bizarre, they were not psychologically impaired, according to Anna Freud and her colleague, Sophie Dann (1951). Apparently, they are leading normal lives today (Hartup, 1983). Fortunately this is an isolated case. But there is other evidence of the importance of peer relations in the socialization of a human child.

Figure 8-2 The Choo-Choo Effect   Harlow and his colleagues found that rhesus monkeys raised with peers and no mothers were timid as youngsters, clinging to one another like cars in a choo-choo train. As adults, however, they were better adjusted socially than were rhesus monkeys raised with their mothers but no peers.

Give-and-Take

Willard Hartup (1983) points out that child–child relations differ from parent–child relations in two important ways. First, peer relations are egalitarian. The relationship between parent and child (or between older and younger siblings) is asymmetrical; that between two children, symmetrical. Two 4-year-olds are developmentally equal. They have about the same intellectual and physical capacities, and the same power and status in society. Peers give children opportunities to present their own views of the world, to assert themselves, and to argue more freely than they can with an "all-knowing" adult or older child.

Second, peer relations are not constrained by attachments. A child does not depend on another child the way she depends on her parents and other adults. One child does not have the authority to order another child about. Moreover, peers are not attached to the same set of parents and do not live in the same home. Their relationship is voluntary. A child can choose her friends, but not her parents or siblings. As a result, there is much more freedom to try on new behavior and test the limits of social rules among peers, and much more give-and-take in their relationship. Hartup (1979) puts it this way:

What chance exists, for example, between a . . . boy and his father for effective aggressive socialization—for either the trial-and-error necessary to the acquisition of effective motor behaviors or the internalization of controls over aggressive affect? . . . How can sexual behavior be learned in an environment constrained by authoritarianism? How can one learn to care for the younger generation through interactions with adults? . . . How can the family attachments that enhance the child's survival be maintained during [a parent's] unrestrained aggression? No, parents cannot function as parents and, at the same time, create the give-and-take necessary to foster social competence." (p. 159)

See the profile of Willard Hartup at the end of this chapter.

Observations and experiments show that children are well aware of the differences between peers and adults. There is some evidence that infants are less afraid of preschoolers than of unfamiliar adults in the Strange Situation (Lewis & Brooks, 1975). When preschoolers are asked to complete stories about child or adult dolls, they usually say that adults are "helping" whereas children are "playing" (Edwards & Lewis, 1979). Preschoolers also distinguish between age-mates ("a boy like you"), younger children ("a baby boy"), and older children ("a big boy"). They tend to act dependent with older children, nurturant with younger children, playful and also aggressive toward children their own age (Hartup, 1983). But

the clearest statement on peers comes from children themselves. Why do they like age-mates? "It's fun. . . . Your friends don't tell you to wash your hands all the time, clean up your room, or apologize to your little brother" (Hetherington & Morris, 1978).

Peers As Models

Peers influence the preschooler in much the same way adults do: by reinforcing approved behavior, punishing or ridiculing behavior they consider unacceptable, and acting as models. Peer models can increase altruism. In one experiment, a group of nursery-school children saw a classmate share a prize with a child from another class. (The model knew about the experiment.) When children who had watched the model were rewarded with trinkets for completing a similar task, they gave away more trinkets than those who had not witnessed the model's altruistic act (Hartup & Coates, 1967). Interestingly, popular children gave their presents to children who liked them; unpopular children gave theirs to classmates who ignored them.

Peer models can reduce children's fears. One team of psychologists (Bandura, Grusec, &

Peer interactions involve give as well as take.

Menlove, 1967) worked with children ages 3 to 5 whose mothers said they were frightened of dogs. In the experiment, some of the children watched a fearless child play with a dog, some were exposed to a dog but no model, and some were given other play materials in the same setting. One month after this experience, the children who had observed a confident model were calmer around dogs then those who had not seen the confident model.

Peers can also punish. Several experiments by Michael Lamb and colleagues (Lamb & Roopnarine, 1979; Lamb, Easterbrooks, & Holden, 1980) suggest that small children are intolerant of sex role violations. When 3-year-olds see a child engaging in what they consider inappropriate behavior—a girl playing with a hammer, a boy with a doll—they stop playing with the child. Five-year-olds are more actively critical: they demand that the child stop, try to take an inappropriate toy away, attempt to divert the child with another toy. If this doesn't work, they move away from the child. In most cases, the child abandons the cross-gender play immediately. Thus peers may undermine parents' and teachers' attempts to make children of both sexes well-rounded.

We have considered only some of the people who participate in the preschooler's socialization. The full cast would include grandparents, aunts and uncles, neighbors, friends of parents and siblings, nursery and Sunday school teachers, and fictional characters from TV and movies. The child becomes less dependent on the parents over the preschool years. But parents continue to play an important executive role, mediating the socializing influences of other adults, siblings, peers, and the mass media.

Sex Roles and Gender Identity

Fifteen or twenty years ago, almost all psychologists considered learning sex-appropriate behavior to be an important and desirable goal of socialization. This has changed (Huston, 1983). Today, many professionals and parents believe that our culture's prescriptions for feminine and masculine behavior interfere with the development of social competence in both sexes. Sex stereotyping is thought to be bad for boys as well as for girls. Nevertheless, most would agree that the development of a gender identity and knowledge of sex roles are important elements in the preschooler's development.

The distinction between sex roles and gender identity is an important one. A **sex role** is a set of cultural directions for how males or females are supposed to think, feel, and behave. Usually the two sex roles are defined in terms of opposites: males are supposed to be career-oriented, females family-oriented; males are supposed to be more interested in sex than in love, females the reverse; females are allowed to cry when they're upset, males are not, and so on. A **gender identity** is an inner sense of oneself as male or female. The fact that a person thinks of herself as a girl or woman does not necessarily mean that she prefers dolls to trucks, or cooking to climbing mountains. But knowing whether you are a girl or a boy is a fundamental part of learning to be a member of the culture. Socialization is directed at making children appropriately masculine and feminine, as their culture sees it.

In this section we look first at sex differences and similarities; then we consider the development of both sex roles and gender identity.

Sex Differences: Fiction and Fact

By age 2, most children have made their gender part of their identity (Money & Ehrhardt, 1972). They label themselves "boy" or "girl" long before they are aware of the biological characteristics and the erotic and reproductive functions that differentiate males from females. Two-year-olds may not know anything about "the birds and the bees," but they do know whether they are boys or girls. By age 2½ or 3, they actively avoid toys associated with the opposite sex (guns for girls, dolls for boys). At age 4 or 5 they often express highly stereotyped occupational aspirations. Girls want to be nurses, teachers, or secretaries; boys want to be astronauts, the boss, or firemen (Huston, 1983). From an early age, boys and girls are different—although not as different as many adults imagine.

In 1974, psychologists Eleanor Maccoby and Carol Jacklin published a highly influential book, *The Psychology of Sex Differences*. Maccoby and Jacklin had analyzed more than 2,000 articles and books written between the mid-1960s and the early 1970s. They concluded that many common beliefs about sex differences are myths masquerading as facts. For example, everyone knows that girls are more sociable and more concerned about what their friends think of them than boys are. Right? Wrong. Most studies show that boys are more gregarious than girls are, and more susceptible to social pressure. Boys are physically stronger than girls. Right? Partly true. Through middle childhood, the differences in size and strength between girls and boys are slight. After puberty, males as a group are heavier, taller, and stronger than females. But males are more vulnerable to disease at every age. The one consistent, undeniable difference between the sexes is that males are more aggressive than females. (We discuss aggression later in this chapter.)

The Maccoby and Jacklin report is not the final word on sex differences and similarities. Jeanne Block (1976) reanalyzed some of their data and found serious flaws. For one example, Maccoby and Jacklin concentrated on studies of young children; yet many sex differences do not emerge until adolescence. For another, in adding up the evidence they gave equal weight to studies with small samples and questionable methods and to those that were more general and reliable. But no other researchers have

come as close to pulling together "everything there is to know" about sex differences and similarities as Maccoby and Jacklin did. A summary of their findings, updated and corrected by Carol Tavris and Carole Wade (1984) appears in Table 8-4 on page 316.

The Maccoby and Jacklin review makes two important points. First, the similarities between the sexes far outweigh the differences. Given the controversy about this topic, their most surprising finding is that boys and girls are so *alike*. Second, when psychologists discuss sex differences they mean group *averages*. There is a great deal of variation within each sex. And there are always members of one sex who exceed the average of the other, producing overlapping distributions. On the average, boys spend more time outdoors than girls do, for example. But some girls spend much more time outside than most boys do, and some boys spend considerably less time outside than most girls do (see Figure 8-3 on page 317).

Cross-cultural Perspective

Sex role differentiation is universal. Cross-cultural studies show that all societies view males and females as different in socially significant ways. Despite the diversity of social organizations and rituals among cultures, there are sex-typed consistencies in the tasks that men and women have performed throughout history. Men have been responsible primarily for fighting wars, fishing, hunting, domesticating animals, and pursuing activities that require physical strength, endurance, and sheer brawn (D'Andrade, 1966). By contrast, women have breast-fed their infants, tended young children, gardened, and gathered food. It is not surprising that given these roles by their forebears, males have been expected to develop their assertiveness and independence, while females have been taught to be nurturant and compliant. In a cross-cultural study of 110 societies, Barry, Bacon, and Child (1957) found that girls and boys

Insight

COMMUNAL CHILD-REARING

In the last two centuries, many groups have rebelled against the traditional family and established communities where child care is not the exclusive responsibility of the biological parents. Instead, child care is shared among members of the group and children are raised with their peers (Scarr, 1984).

The best known examples are the kibbutzim, first established in Palestine around 1910 and still flourishing in modern Israel. Kibbutzim are collective settlements that operate as independent villages. The kibbutzim were founded with two goals: to free women from the bonds of traditional marriage and economic dependency, and to liberate children from "emotional enslavement" to their biological parents. The founders believed that the traditional dependency of child on parents fosters selfishness and excessive individualism. Life on the kibbutzim centers around the dining hall, where all adults meet for meals. Couples have their own rooms, but not their own kitchens. Men and women rotate jobs in the kitchen and farm or factories, often crossing traditional sex-role boundaries. Children live in their own houses with professional caregivers.

For the first six weeks after the birth of a child, the mother spends much of her time in the infant house with her baby. Then she returns to work part-time but continues to devote about four hours a day to feeding, bathing, diapering, and playing with her infant. When the child is about 4 months old, routine care is turned over to a nurse and her assistant, who care for four or five infants. Parents usually take the child to their room for about two hours of play in the late afternoon. At about 15 months, the child moves to a toddler house, which has its own dining room, play facilities, and bedrooms for groups of four or five children. The nurse moves with them and begins the business of teaching toilet use, self-feeding, dressing, and other social skills. At about 5 years, three toddler groups are combined into an eighteen-child kindergarten group that will remain together for several years. Caring for a small garden, keep-

ing animals, and some formal instruction are added to the children's day. Parents continue to visit their child every day. Most keep a corner or closet in their room for some of the child's belongings. They might put the child to bed in the children's house each night. But primary responsibility for socialization is in the hands of professional caregivers.

Early critics of the kibbutzim argued that these communally-reared children were no better off than orphans. Freudians, in particular, maintained that children who had not had the opportunity to form an intense emotional attachment to their mothers early in life would be shallow, uncaring, distrustful, and very likely emotionally disturbed as adolescents and adults (Goldfarb, 1955). They were wrong. Comparative studies show that children of the kibbutz are as well-adjusted and smart as children from other Israeli villages or their American peers (Bar-Tal, Raviv, & Shavit, 1981; Rabin, 1965; Rabin & Beit-Hallahmi, 1982). They are no more likely than other children to have emotional problems, or to prefer their peers to their parents. On the other hand, they also are no more likely to be helpful and cooperative. Communal child-rearing has not produced the emotional disasters some predicted—or the high levels of community spirit and unselfishness others dreamed about.

A study of communally reared children in this country came to similar conclusions. The children were part of a study of the impact of alternative lifestyles on youngsters (Eiduson, Kornfein, Zimmerman, & Weisner, 1982). The subjects included 50 single-mother families, 50 unmarried couples who lived together, 50 communal families, and 50 traditional two-parent families. The researchers observed and interviewed the families beginning in the last trimester of pregnancy and continuing until the children were 4 years old. There were vast differences in attitudes toward child-rearing among these groups. Communal parents believed in sharing their babies' upbringing; traditional parents believed that parents should do all

A study of conventional and unconventional families found more similarities than differences in child-rearing strategies.

child-rearing themselves. Some of the families were financially well-off, some were poor, and some—the communal families—were poor by choice. The researchers expected to find that communal parents were casual about daily routines; traditional parents, obsessed with doing everything "by the book"; and single parents, a bit neglectful.

To their surprise, they found that differences in the groups' child-rearing philosophies produced few differences in practices. All of the children were fed regular meals, put to bed at a regular hour, taken for trips to the grocery store and the doctor, and played with about the same amount. Differences in scheduled activities

and disciplinary techniques were greater among individual families within a type than between types of households. Moreover, no significant differences were found in the children's attachment to their parents, intelligence, creativity, emotional maturity, or general social competence. Family lifestyle seemed to have very little impact on either parental behavior or child development. The research team reports that "the children in all groups seem to be developing normally" (p. 344).

Table 8-4   Sex Similarities and Differences

Category	Findings	Category	Findings
Physical Attributes		Emotionality	Self-reports and observations conflict; no convincing evidence that females feel more emotional, but they may express certain emotions more freely.
Strength	Males taller, heavier, more muscular after puberty.		
Health	Females less vulnerable to illness and disease, live longer.		
Activity level	Some evidence that preschool boys more active during play in same-sex groups; school-age boys and girls are active in different ways.	Dependence	Conflicting findings; dependence appears not to be a unitary concept or stable trait.
Manual dexterity	Women excel when speed is important; findings hard to interpret.	Susceptibility to influence	Preschool girls more obedient to parents; boys may be more susceptible to peer pressure; no overall difference in adult susceptibility to persuasion across different settings in laboratory studies.
Abilities			
General intelligence	No difference on most tests.		
Verbal ability	Some evidence that females acquire language slightly earlier; males more often diagnosed as having reading problems; females excel on various verbal tests after age 10 or 11.*	Self-esteem and confidence	No self-reported differences in self-esteem, but males more confident about task performance; males more likely to take credit for success, less likely to blame selves for failure.
Quantitative ability	Males excel on tests of mathematical reasoning from the start of adolescence.*	Nurturance	No overall differences in altruism; girls more helpful and responsive to infants, small children; some evidence that fathers as responsive to newborns as mothers are, but issue of maternal versus paternal behavior remains open.
Spatial-visual ability	Males excel starting in 10th grade, but not on all tests or in all studies.*		
Creativity	Females excel on verbal creativity tests, but otherwise no difference.	Aggressiveness	Males more aggressive from preschool age on; men more violent, more likely to be aggressive in public, more likely to be physically aggressive in situations not involving anger.
Cognitive style	Males excel on spatial-visual disembedding tests starting at adolescence, but no general differences in cognitive style.		
Personality Characteristics		*Values and Moral Perceptions*	Some controversial evidence that males and females approach choice and conflict somewhat differently. Males seem more likely to emphasize abstract standards of justice, fairness, balancing of individual rights. Females seem more likely to emphasize the ethics of care, human attachments, balancing of conflicting responsibilities.**
Sociability	No consistent findings on infants' responsiveness to social cues; school-age boys play in larger groups; women fantasize more about affiliation themes, but there is no evidence that one sex wants or needs friends more.		
Empathy	Conflicting evidence; probably depends on situation and sex of participants in an interaction.		

(Adapted from Tavris & Wade, 1984)
* Differences statistically reliable but quite small.
** See Chapter 12.

are trained to develop these different characteristics in virtually all societies.

The specific tasks assigned to men and women vary among societies. Yet men's work is always regarded as more valuable than women's work. In ancient Greece, for example, marketing was men's work. Buying and selling was thought to be too important and too complicated for women. The Toda of India assign domestic chores, which they consider sacred, to men (Rosaldo, 1974). If the women of a tribe grow sweet potatoes and the men raise taro, taro is the prestige food reserved for special occasions. In all cultures and times, "males have held the most prized offices, controlled the basic resources, and extolled the superiority of their sex" (Tavris & Wade, 1984, p. 21). In virtually every society, the sexes are regarded as not only different but unequal.

We cannot solve the puzzle of gender inequality here, as Tavris and Wade have attempted to do. We can relate what is known about how children learn sex roles and develop a gender identity.

"Like Father, Like Son": Family Influences

Do parents handle boys and girls differently? Do they encourage sex-typed behavior in small chil-

dren? In general, research indicates that they do. The question of why parents do this is difficult to answer, however. Some research suggests that parents push their children toward sex-appropriate interests and activities. Other research suggests that parents are responding to differences in their sons' and daughters' behavior.

Running, jumping, climbing, playing with blocks or dolls, following an adult around, and helping an adult with a task all elicit sex-stereotyped responses from parents (Fagot, 1978). In particular, parents discourage boys from playing with dolls. Fathers react more positively to physical activity in boys than in girls; mothers react more positively to girls' requests for affection and contact than to requests from boys (Tauber, 1979). Parents also give their male and female preschoolers different types of toys, shaping both their activities and their environments (Rheingold & Cook, 1975). It is difficult to say whether this is because parents are trying to mold their children's sex roles or because boys and girls prefer different kinds of toys. A preference for trucks over dolls might reflect either different activity levels in boys and girls or some other biological predisposition.

The way parents teach a preschooler a new skill reveals sex role differentiation (Block,

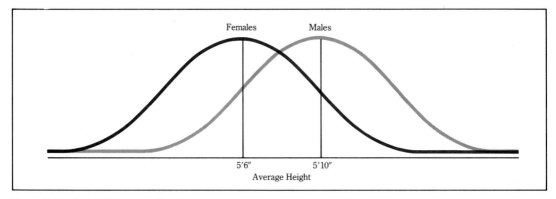

Figure 8-3   Sex Differences Are Averages

1979; Golden & Birns, 1975; Rothbart & Rothbart, 1976). Parents tend to demand more independence of boys than of girls. They also tend to have higher expectations for boys. They are quicker to respond to requests for help, and focus more on the interpersonal aspects of the task, with girls. A quick response may communicate lower expectations and reinforce helplessness to girls; demands for independence may signal confidence in boys' abilities.

Parents punish boys—verbally and, especially, physically—more often than girls (Maccoby & Jacklin, 1974). The explanation may lie in boys' behavior, not in parental sex stereotypes (Maccoby, 1980). As infants, boys demand more attention than girls do. At 12 months, boys are more likely to engage in forbidden activities such as touching delicate or dangerous objects, or climbing on furniture. At 4 or 5 years, boys are less likely than girls to comply with parents' requests. In short, boys resist efforts to teach and train them—and parents respond in kind, with punishment.

Interestingly, fathers seem to be more actively and personally concerned about proper sex role behavior than mothers are. In one study (Langlois & Downs, 1980) researchers observed how fathers and mothers reacted to their preschoolers' playing with stereotypically masculine or feminine toys. Fathers rewarded sex-appropriate play and interfered with sex-inappropriate play, especially with sons. In contrast, mothers rewarded sex-inappropriate play in daughters and were inconsistent with sons.

How do siblings affect the development of sex roles? One hypothesis is that a same-sex sibling encourages sex-typed behavior through modeling and reinforcement. According to this view, a boy who has a brother will be "doubly masculine." By extension, a girl with a brother may be less stereotypically feminine than she would be otherwise. The opposite hypothesis is that a child with a same-sex sibling engages in fewer sex-typed activities in order to establish his or her individuality (Schachter, Gilutz, Shore, & Adler, 1978). A boy with a typically masculine brother might choose indoor activities. By extension, a girl with a tough brother might be especially feminine. A review of the evidence shows that a sibling may have either effect (Huston, 1983). The impact of brothers and sisters on each other is unpredictable.

The family's influence on the development of sex roles is the result of complex interactions among family members. Boys and girls evoke different responses in their parents. Because of their own sex roles and identities, mothers and fathers often have different ideas about sex-appropriate behavior. A parent relates differently to a child of the same sex than to a child of the opposite sex. Siblings may either compound or counteract these parental influences.

Does this photograph make you uncomfortable? As a rule, parents (especially fathers) are much more upset when a boy violates traditional sex roles than they are when a girl acts like a tomboy.

Social Play and Social Pressure

Deanna Kuhn and her colleagues (1978) questioned 2- and 3-year-olds about what girls and boys think, do, and say. Even at this early age, children have different expectations for the sexes. In general, their ideas match adult stereotypes. The children said that girls like to play with dolls, help their mothers, cook dinner, and clean house. Girls never hit, but they talk a lot, say "I need help," and will grow up to be teachers and nurses. According to these preschoolers, boys like to play with cars, build things, and help their fathers. Boys say "I can hit you" and will grow up to be the boss. On this much the boys and girls agreed. But each sex attributed special positive qualities to their own gender and negative qualities to the other. Girls said that girls look nice, give kisses, and never fight, but that boys are mean and like to fight. Boys claimed that boys work hard but that girls are slow and cry a lot. This study illustrates two patterns established already in preschoolers: Both boys and girls prefer members of their own sex, and each sex has its own style of play.

Small children are "guilty" of both sex discrimination and sex segregation. Preschoolers like members of their own sex better than those of the opposite sex and seek them out as playmates—a pattern that continues through middle childhood. As G. Stanley Hall wrote (1904, p. 617) many years ago, "At this age, by almost world-wide consent, boys and girls separate for a time and lead their lives during this most critical period more or less apart. . . ."

Jacklin and Maccoby (1978) studied pairs of unacquainted children in play laboratory, where they were given opportunities to share or compete for toys. Some pairs were of the same sex; some pairs were of opposite sexes. Their mothers were asked to dress them in plain tee shirts and pants, and to remove hair ribbons, holsters, and other gender cues. The mothers had difficulty guessing the sex of the other child. The

children seemed to know the difference between boys and girls, however. Jacklin and Maccoby found that the children were much more likely to play with a partner of the same sex. They also found that girls were more likely to withdraw and watch the other child quietly if he was a boy, and that boy–boy pairs engaged in tugs-of-war over a toy more often than either boy–girl or girl–girl pairs. Observations of nursery-school children confirm the same-sex preference (Fagot, 1982). Two-year-olds paid more attention to members of the same sex. They were also far more likely to respond to positive or negative feedback from a same-sex child than to praise or criticism from a child of the opposite sex.

As the children in Kuhn's study seemed to realize, boys and girls play differently (Hartup, 1983). Small boys' interactions center on blocks and moveable toys. They enjoy boisterous, rough-and-tumble games, competitive activities, and playing outdoors. Small girls' interactions center on dramatic play and table activities, such as drawing or having a tea party. Boys prefer unstructured play that does not require or invite adult assistance, such as tag or "king of the mountain". Thus, boys and girls create different environments for themselves. Boys' games provide more opportunities for leadership, intitiative, and novel use of materials; girls' games allow more opportunities for cooperation and recognition from adults (Carpenter & Huston-Stein, 1980).

Girls are often seen in pairs. Boys tend to congregate in large groups and play more often with boys of different ages. Put another way, girls' social lives tend to be intensive, centering around "best friends"; boys' social lives tend to be extensive, centering around group activities and games (Waldrop & Halverson, 1975).

Peers expect and enforce sex-typed behavior. Children who engage in cross-sex activities are often socially isolated (Fagot, 1977). A boy

who plays with dolls or dresses up will be criticized by other children and left alone when he shifts to masculine activities. Girls who play with trucks or build in the sandbox may be ignored at the time but are not subjected to long-term isolation. Like parents, preschoolers are more tolerant of "tomboys" than of "sissies." But children who choose sex-typed activities are more popular, have more playmates, and get more peer approval than do other children.

It would be only a slight exaggeration to say that most 4- and 5-year olds are "sexists." One explanation of this phenomenon is that preschoolers' concepts of gender are limited by their level of cognitive development. They have learned what adults expect of boys and girls. But their level of cognitive development makes them even more rigid in their stereotypes than adults are.

Gender Identity: A Cognitive View

By the age of 2 or 2½, most children have acquired a gender identity and categorize themselves as boy or girl. But sex is only a label to preschoolers. Most are not aware of the biological or social implications of gender.

> JOHNNY (age 4½): I'm going to be an airplane builder when I grow up.
> JIMMY (age 4): When I grow up, I'll be a Mommy.
> JOHNNY: No, you can't be a Mommy. You have to be a Daddy.

Sex differences in play and friendship styles continue throughout the lifespan. Men's friendships center on shared interests and group activities; women's, on shared confidences and one-on-one conversations.

JIMMY: No, I'm going to be a Mommy.

JOHNNY: No, you're not a girl, you can't be a Mommy.

JIMMY: Yes I can.

(Kohlberg, 1966, p. 95)

In one experiment (Emmerich, Goldman, Kirsch, & Sharabany, 1976) preschoolers were shown a drawing of a girl named Janie. They were asked whether Janie could be a boy if "she really wanted to," and then whether she would be a boy if she cut her hair short, dressed in boys clothing, or played with trucks and did other "boy things." A few of the children said she couldn't change because "She was born a girl" or "'Cause she ain't got no magic" (p. 75). Many of the children thought that changing sex was naughty or weird. But most of the children

Children strive to look, dress, and behave in ways that their society and culture consider appropriate for their sex. Although ideas of what is appropriate vary, almost all cultures use dress and ornamentation to accentuate sex differences.

were convinced that Janie could change if she wanted to. The children gave similar answers to questions about a boy.

By age 6 or 7, few if any children make Jimmy's mistake. They have acquired what Lawrence Kohlberg (1966) calls **gender constancy**: an understanding that gender does not change over time, that gender is not altered by changes in appearance or activities, and that gender cannot be changed by wishing. The development of gender constancy parallels the development of conservation (see Chapter 6). By the end of the preschool period children understand that "just as the amount of water remains the same when it is poured from a short fat glass into a tall thin one, a woman remains a woman when she wears pants" (Tavris & Wade, 1984, p. 216).

What causes this change in the child's understanding? Kohlberg suggests that when children acquire a gender identity, they begin to classify people, activities, and interests as male or female. The concepts male and female help them to organize incoming information. They focus on external signs of gender. The desire for consistency motivates them to fit everyone into one or the other category. This explains the "sexism" of preschoolers. During the period when they are acquiring gender constancy— roughly, ages 2 to 7—sex stereotyping increases. Children tend to see deviations from sex stereotypes as bad behavior. Once they acquire gender constancy, they become less rigid. When they understand that gender is not altered by superficial changes in appearance, they can understand that departures from stereotypes do not alter gender either. They begin to make the distinction between what is right and what is merely customary. They are better able to accept the idea that males and females can share activities and traits.

Kohlberg and other cognitive theorists hold that the child's concepts and level of understanding are as important as modeling and reinforcement in the development of sex roles and identity. To some extent, children socialize themselves, applying masculine and feminine standards without adult instruction. The specific criteria preschoolers use depend on their culture and on what they observe around them. If men in their society wear earrings and paint their faces, they will consider this behavior masculine. But the desire to do "boy things" or "girl things" is universal. Sex-typing results in part from the child's own efforts to make sense of the social world. This is why cultural stereotypes often override the examples parents set for their children. In the United States, small girls whose own mothers are physicians or Ph.D.'s frequently *insist* that women cannot be doctors. In the USSR, where more physicians are female than male, this probably does not occur.

Aggression: Domesticating the Human Animal

Another basic element of the preschooler's social and emotional development is learning to control aggression. **Aggression** is intentional, hostile behavior aimed at a person or object and motivated by the desire to inflict damage, physical pain, or psychological discomfort. The key word in this definition is "intentional." Accidental injury, due to clumsiness or ignorance, does not count. Aggression is designed to harm or at least frighten.

The Development of Aggression

Nothing the infant does in the first year of life qualifies as true aggression. Babies are not in complete control of their bodies and only dimly aware that their behavior has consequences. They do express what adults might call anger or frustration when they are uncomfortable. But these communications are not directed at a particular person or designed to frighten or harm.

A BRIEF HISTORY OF TANTRUMS In a classic study of preschoolers, Florence Goodenough (1931) documented the translation of diffuse rage into aggression over the preschool years. Goodenough asked 45 mothers to keep diaries of their child's outbursts. She found that tantrums almost doubled in the second year, peaked around the second birthday, then gradually declined, falling off sharply after age 4. In contrast, acts of retaliation (revenge for a perceived injury) increased with age. Thus unfocused anger was replaced by focused aggression (see Figure 8-4). Three- and 4-year-olds' outbursts were directed at someone or something. Accompanying these changes Goodenough found an increase in "after reactions," such as sulking or whining, after age 4.

The situations that provoked outbursts changed over the preschool period. The infant's "anger" was related to physical discomfort and needs for attention. Between ages 2 and 3, outbursts centered on "habit training": parents' demands that the child use the toilet, wash his face, go to bed, and the like. Frustration at having a toy taken away also increases at this age (Bronson, 1975). The child is beginning to develop the concept of ownership and a sense of "me" and "mine." He knows what he wants, but may be too young to know how to go about getting it. The result is tantrums. At age 3 or 4, the child is spending more time with peers. Aggression at this age most often results from social difficulties during play.

INSTRUMENTAL AND HOSTILE AGGRESSION Hartup's study of inner-city preschoolers (1974) picks up where Goodenough left off. Hartup distinguished between two kinds of aggression. **Instrumental aggression** is object-oriented. The child's pursuit of a specific goal has been blocked. The resulting aggressive behavior is designed to acquire an object, regain stolen territory, or retrieve a lost privilege. **Hostile ag-**

gression is person-centered. Outbursts are a response to personal threats to the child's ego or self-esteem.

Hartup's team focused on 102 male and female children between the ages of 4 and 7. Every incident of aggression observed in classrooms, corridors, or the playground was recorded.

Marian (a seven-year-old) is complaining to all that David (who is also present) had squirted her on the pants she has to wear tonight. She says, "I'm gonna do it to him to see how he likes it." She fills a can with water and David runs to the teacher and tells of her threat. The teacher takes the can from Marian. Marian attacks David and pulls his hair very hard. He cries and swings at Marian as the teacher tries to restrain him; then she takes him upstairs. . . . Later, Marian and Elaine go upstairs and into the room where David is seated with a teacher. He throws a book at Marian. The teacher asks Marian to leave. Marian kicks David, then leaves. David cries and screams, "Get out of here, they're just gonna tease me." (p. 339)

Hartup found that instrumental aggression declines and hostile aggression increases in the preschool years. Older children were less likely than were younger children to fight over a toy or a place in line. Many more of their outbursts were classified as hostile, person-centered aggression. There were clear age differences in the way aggression was expressed. When younger children were insulted ("My dad is bigger than your dad"; "You the most dumb in the world"), they often responded by hitting the other child. Older children responded more often with a return blow to the other child's self-esteem. They seemed to be operating on the principle of "let the punishment fit the crime" (Maccoby, 1980).

Hartup's description of changes in aggression over the preschool period is consistent with other observations about the young child's social and cognitive development. Preschoolers have

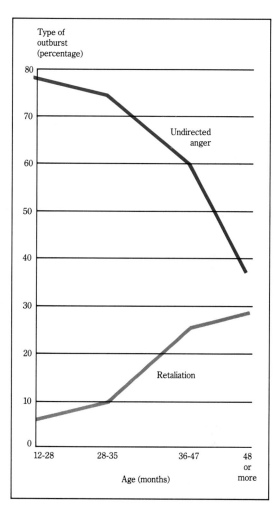

Figure 8-4 From Tantrums to Retaliation   Goodenough found that unfocused anger (or tantrums) decreased during the preschool period, while directed anger (or retaliation) and "after reactions" (sulking and whining) increased.

(Adapted from Goodenough, 1931, in Maccoby, 1980, p. 121)

only a limited ability to understand other people's motives and intentions. When something goes wrong, they strike out at whomever or whatever happens to be in their way (instrumental aggression). Older children are better at identifying the agent of frustration and directing their attack at that person (hostile aggression). Preschoolers have only vague notions of status and self-esteem. For them, stealing a toy is a major crime, but verbal insults may go unnoticed. Older children are more self-aware, more self-conscious, and as likely to fight with words as with their fists. In part, changes in the forms and functions of aggression reflect cognitive development.

"Boys Will Be Boys": Sex Differences

Almost every study reports that boys engage in more physical, verbal, and even fantasy aggression than girls do (Maccoby & Jacklin, 1974, 1980). Indeed, aggression is one of the defining characteristics of masculine behavior (Sears, Maccoby, & Levin, 1957). This sex difference appears as soon as children begin to play with one another (age 2 or 3) and continues into adulthood. Adolescent males are the most violent members of our species. They are also the most likely to be the victims of violence.

Some psychologists question this portrait. After observing first-graders, Seymour and Norma Feshbach (1973) concluded that girls are as aggressive as boys are, but they show it in indirect ways: by ignoring another child, moving away, denying requests for help, and declaring a newcomer unwelcome. They concluded that boys were "nicer." But the Feshbachs are in the minority. Most psychologists do not consider cliquishness aggression.

Why are males more aggressive? One reason may be that boys have higher energy levels than girls do. They are more active, engage in more rough-and-tumble play, play in larger groups, and therefore get into more combative situations. Girls are less active, play in smaller groups, and stay closer to adults. Both sexes echo a primate pattern (Bruner, Jolly, & Sylva, 1976; Fishbein, 1976). In most nonhuman primate species, young females stay close to their mothers and show more interest in observing their younger siblings than in playing with agemates. The playful, aggressive, "macho" male monkeys get into disputes with one another and elicit rough treatment from adults much more often (Poirier, 1973).

Sex differences in aggression may indeed have biological roots. But they are also influenced by socialization. From an early age, boys in our society are taught not to punch girls—and girls are told not to punch anyone (Tavris & Wade, 1984). Moreover, the level of aggression found in different societies and cultures varies. American females are less aggressive than American males, but they are more aggressive than Japanese females, at every age.

In most studies, aggression is defined as physical threats and physical violence. If arguing and other, subtler forms of aggression were included in the definition, sex differences might be smaller.

Dominance Hierarchies:
An Ethological View

Primatologists (for example, Jolly, 1972; Suomi, 1977) maintain that aggressive play among male monkeys serves an adaptive function. Rough-and-tumble games provide opportunities to practice aggressive postures, to test the responses of other monkeys, and to discover what actions will and will not provoke retaliation from this or that peer. Although the young monkeys may appear to be fighting, actual injuries are rare. By the time they mature, members of a troop have worked out a more or less stable dominance hierarchy. Each member knows his place and is therefore able to anticipate and avoid severe aggression. A threat from a dominant monkey nearly always evokes submissive behavior in a subordinate. Dominance hierarchies reduce fighting within the troop and organize the troop for contact and conflict with other troops.

Does rough-and-tumble play among human children serve a similar function? Do youngsters work out stable patterns of dominance and submission among themselves? One team of researchers (Patterson, Littman, & Bricker, 1967) observed nursery-school children for one month at the beginning of the school year and another at the end. They recorded the initiation and the consequences of aggressive acts (whether the victim counterattacked or ran away crying, for example). The researchers found that about three out of four attacks were successful: the young aggressor got what he or she wanted. They also found that children who accepted the role of victim and did not strike back were likely to be attacked again.

Most interesting was a small group of children who were friendly but pacifistic at the beginning of the year. They liked to play with other children but did not like to fight. By the end of the year these youngsters not only refused to be victimized but also initiated ag-

gression themselves. They had earned a high-ranking place in the hierarchy. With this exception, however, the pattern of dominance and submission was stable and predictable. Victims did not become aggressors, or aggressors become victims. Other research confirms this observation (Strayer & Strayer, 1976).

What happens to children at the bottom of hierarchy? Children who are left out of playground "troops"? After observing social networks on two elementary-school playgrounds, Gary Ladd (1983) speculates on the fate of rejected children. Rejected children do not seem to understand the hierarchy that develops among more popular youngsters. They fight in situations where other children would be submissive or conciliatory. They tend to be more aggressive than very popular and average children, to spend less time in social conversation and more time observing or doing nothing, and to play in smaller groups with other unpopular or younger children. Because they play in smaller groups, Ladd suggests, they have fewer opportunities to develop the skills needed to function in larger social contexts. Because they often play with younger children, they have less experience with egalitarian or symmetrical social relationships. They can dominate younger children without fear of retaliation. Because they play with other unpopular, aggressive children, they tend to rely on defensive and retaliatory strategies and may be somewhat paranoid about their peers' motives. (We will say more about rejected and isolated youngsters in Chapter 11.)

Words As Weapons: A Cognitive View

The development of aggression in humans may parallel that in monkeys, but it is not identical. To the extent that aggression is a natural response and seems to follow a roughly developmental timetable, it may be called instinctive (Maccoby, 1980). But its development is also shaped by social learning. To say that behavior is both instinctive and learned is not a contradiction. Modern ethologists do not see aggression as a knee-jerk reaction. Even in monkeys, it depends on the interpretation of social cues. In humans, the expression of aggression depends on still more complex processes of social thinking.

Children have one weapon that other primates lack: words. Both Goodenough (1931) and Hartup (1983) found that the decline with age in physical attacks on the body coincides with an increase in *verbal* attacks on a child's self-esteem. Words add an extra dimension to human aggression. Children can and do cause intentional harm by calling someone "dumb," "ugly," or "weird." Beginning in the preschool period, cognition transforms aggression into something subtler and more complex than the behavior observed in other animals.

In addition, the expression of aggression in humans is governed by cultural rules. To some extent, every culture sends the child mixed messages. In our society, the combat of war, the verbal clashes of politicians, the "friendly" competition of the marketplace, the assertion of one's ideas and convictions, and striving to beat another team or player in sports are all approved by the adult world. Tackles on the football field, violence in the boxing ring, and collisions on the stock-car track are considered recreation. Yet when a motorist cuts us off,

someone trips us in the aisle of a bus, or a neighbor's dog performs on our lawn, we are only permitted to mutter angry epithets under our breath and deliver a scornful look. To complicate matters, cultural rules change according to the situation and the actor. Parents are allowed to hit their own child, for example, but not a strange child. Subcultures add variations to these middle-class themes.

The differences between human and nonhuman aggression have prompted interest in the cognitive dimensions of aggression in recent years (Parke & Slaby, 1983). Taking your older sister's favorite doll when she won't let you play with her magnetic letters, as one 14-month-old did in Dunn and Kendrick's study of siblings (1982), requires thought. As Eleanor Maccoby puts it (1980), to carry out an intentionally hurtful act, the aggressor (called *A*) must know:

1. that another person can help or get in the way of A's own objectives, know what A wants him or her to do, and experience distress;

Some forms of aggression, like boxing, are socially approved, especially for boys.

2. that A's own actions can cause distress;
3. *which* actions can cause distress in *which* other people;
4. how to carry out distress-producing actions;
5. that distress can cause other people to act the way A wants them to;
6. that the distressed person's action can be in A's interests. (p. 118)

A toddler or preschooler may not perform conscious mental calculations: *She won't let me play. How can I hurt her? There's her favorite doll.* But to inflict intentional injury the child must have some understanding of who stands in his way and what can hurt that person. The verbal power-plays toward the end of the preschool

---

Insight

SOCIALIZATION TO AGGRESSION

Even in the preschool years, some children are notably more aggressive than others. Gerald Patterson (1982) studied a group of boys aged 3 to 8½ who had been labeled "out of control" by the school, the parents, or correctional authorities. After studying the boys in their homes, he concluded that aggression is a family problem.

Patterson and his colleagues recorded each time a family member criticized another family member, whined, refused a request or command, yelled, destroyed an object, hit, pushed, shoved, slapped, or threw something at another family member, teased, commanded ("Stop that now!"), or cried. For purposes of the study, all of these acts were labeled "coercive." Events were recorded in time sequence, so that entire episodes could be analyzed later. Families that did not include a problem child were observed for comparison.

Patterson found that "out of control" children engage in almost three times as many coercive acts as other children do. But members of their families also threaten and use force. In other words, family relationships are mutually coercive. Patterson points out that aggressive behavior is not a single act, but a chain of interaction. Once an incident has begun, other participants or observers may attempt to cool down the angry individual or fan the flame. A mild encounter may or may not escalate into a serious fight. Whether a mother separates two siblings who are fighting, yells or throws something at them, or simply ignores them makes a difference in the outcome of the incident. Whether a child who has been scolded or frustrated hits the mother, ignores her, or sulks also makes a difference.

The families of "out of control" children are characterized by lack of mutual responsiveness. Other family members ignore the child's aggressive behavior and hurt feelings. In turn, the child ignores other family members. Most children cease aggressive behavior when they realize that their parents are serious and may punish them. But punishment increases the aggressive behavior in the "out of control" youngsters. The result is a cycle of coercion. No member of the family seems able to de-escalate hostile interactions once they begin: one coercive act leads to another, and another, and so on. Over time, family members begin to avoid one another whenever possible. They engage in joint activities less and less frequently. And they fail to solve ordinary, minor problems.

Patterson has improved such children's behavior by teaching parents to change their own coercive behavior: to be clear and consistent about what they expect; to react firmly but nonviolently when the child fails to obey; to declare "time out" when the child is in a rage and allow him to cool down; to reward good behavior with hugs, praise, and privileges; and to discuss noncoercive ways of solving everyday problems with the child. Patterson treats the child by treating the family.

period require still more complex information processing. To comprehend an insult and retaliate requires a strong sense of one's rights and privileges in relation to others. The child must grasp the cultural rules, make social judgments, and evaluate the consequences of different responses. Anger may come naturally, but being mean takes brains.

Aggression and Play: Drawing the Line

The distinction between aggression and play is subtle at any age. Adults often wonder if a rude remark was an insult or a joke. In the preschool years, this line is even harder to draw. Consider the following episode from Maccoby's files (1980):

Jimmy, a preschooler, stands observing three of his male classmates building a sand castle. After a few moments he climbs on a tricycle and, smiling, makes a beeline for the sand area, ravaging the structure in a single sweep. The builders immediately take off in hot pursuit of the hit-and-run phantom, yelling menacing threats of "come back here, you." Soon the tricycle halts and they pounce on him. The four of them tumble about in the grass amid shouts of glee, wrestling and punching until a teacher intervenes. The four wander off together toward the swings. (p. 125)

Was Jimmy's action aggressive? The teacher responded as though the boys were fighting. Maccoby offers a different interpretation: Jimmy wanted to be part of the action. He gambled on making the others angry, but he won. Perhaps the others could see from his expression that he was looking for fun; perhaps they were not in a mood to fight. We do not know.

We do know, first of all, that the same action may or may not lead to aggression, depending on other children's dispositions and responses. Second, sociable children who like to play, such as Jimmy, exhibit more prosocial *and* more aggressive behavior than do less outgoing children. Their efforts to engage other children make them friends and get them into fights. This is not surprising, given the preschooler's cognitive and linguistic immaturity and social inexperience. In many ways, the preschooler is a Dr. Jekyll and Mr. Hyde. His friendly offering to share a truck with a peer can quickly change into hostility—whacking the friend in the head with the same toy.

Prosocial Behavior: The Beginnings of Conscience

Prosocial behavior is behavior that benefits or aids another person (Radke-Yarrow, Zahn-Waxler, & Chapman, 1983). Showing concern for others, helping, sympathizing, defending, rescuing, sharing, donating, and cooperating all fall into this category. Prosocial behavior illustrates what a Chinese philosopher in the fourth century B.C. called "human-heartedness."

A strict reading of the literature on cognitive development implies that small children are too egocentric, and too impulsive, to show concern and compassion for others. But the growing evidence of prosocial behavior in the preschool years suggests that youngsters' hearts lead their heads. Older infants often show or give objects to adults (Rheingold, Hay, & West, 1976). By age 2 or 3, children use gifts as a way of initiating contact with peers as well as with adults (Stanjek, in Radke-Yarrow et al., 1983). The content of the gift does not seem to matter as much as the act of giving itself. A rock or a piece of wood will do. In a homelike laboratory, 2-year-olds helped their mother or an unfamiliar woman with ordinary household tasks, such as setting a table, without being asked (Rheingold, 1979). In some cases the toddlers imitated the adult, but often they invested their own contributions.

The Development of Empathy

When do children begin to demonstrate empathy or sensitivity to others? Carolyn Zahn-Waxler, Marian Radke-Yarrow, and their colleagues

trained mothers to keep detailed records of their toddlers' responses to another person's anger, fear, pain, sorrow, or fatigue (Zahn-Waxler & Radke-Yarrow, 1982; Zahn-Waxler, Radke-Yarrow, & King, 1979). At age 10 to 12 months, another person's distress often upsets the infant. "*S* somberly watched; tears welled in her eyes and she began to cry. She looked to her mother" (Radke-Yarrow et al., 1983, p. 481). Infants were upset in about half the incidents reported, and simply attentive in another third. Toward the end of the second year, agitation began to decline and active efforts to comfort the distressed person increased. The toddler brought someone who was suffering an object, verbalized sympathy, sought someone else to help, or defended the victim. If one strategy didn't work, the child tried another. Toddlers were not always kind. Signs of distress in another person sometimes made them laugh, attack the sufferer, or flee. But the following entry in one mother's report was not unusual (Zahn-Waxler et al., 1979). Jerry and John were almost two.

Today Jerry was kind of cranky; he just started completely bawling and he wouldn't stop. John kept coming over and handing Jerry toys, trying to cheer him up, so to speak. He'd say things like "Here, Jerry" and I said to John: "Jerry's sad; he doesn't feel good; he had a shot today." John would look at me with his eyebrows kind of wrinkled together like he really understood that Jerry was crying because he was un-

happy, not that he was just being a crybaby. He went over and rubbed Jerry's arm and said "Nice, Jerry" and continued to give him toys. (pp. 321–22)

Mothers may want to believe that their children are well-intentioned. Are they reading something into the youngsters' behavior? Apparently not. Judy Dunn and Carol Kendrick (1982) saw evidence of empathy in the *younger* children in their study of siblings. For example, one stocky 15-month-old could make his parents laugh by pulling up his tee shirt and exposing his large belly. When his elder brother fell out of a tree one day and cried, the little boy did this as if to cheer up his brother. Dunn and Kendrick suggest that the match of perspectives, interests, and abilities between siblings promotes understanding of another person. A small child may realize that a parent is upset but may not know how to comfort the adult. He is better able to understand the feelings of his siblings and to provide remedies for their distress.

Observers report similar behavior in nursery schools (Eisenberg-Berg & Hand, 1979). According to one study, prosocial incidents of sharing, comforting, and cooperation occurred four or five times an hour (Radke-Yarrow & Zahn-Waxler, 1976). The number of antisocial, aggressive acts were about equal. For every child who grabbed someone else's toy there was a child who patted a hurt child on the head; for every child who shoved another out of line for the sliding board, another struggled to help a friend who had tripped tie his shoes. Almost every child observed engaged in at least one prosocial act (and one aggressive act) in a 40 minute period.

Teaching Prosocial Behavior

Must children learn prosocial behavior, or does being kind come naturally? One experiment in training altruism shows that adult models can have an impact (Radke-Yarrow, Scott, & Zahn-Waxler, 1973). The researchers divided nursery-school children into two groups and fit training sessions into their daily routine. Each of the children in group A was shown a series of

pictures and dioramas of people or animals in distress. For example, one scene showed a caged monkey trying to reach a banana that was beyond its grasp. The experimenter modeled helpful behavior, explaining what she was doing and why: "Oh, Mister Monkey, you must be hungry. You can't reach your food. I'll help you. Here's your banana. Now you won't be hungry." The child was then presented with an identical scene and told that it was her turn. If the child gave the monkey a banana, she was told, "I think the monkey feels better because you gave him his food. He isn't hungry now" (pp. 246–47). The children in group B were given this training plus opportunities to observe a staged event in which one adult was kind to another. For example, an adult who was bending over to pick up toys "accidentally" banged her head on the table (p. 247). The experimenter put her hand on the adult's shoulder and said something like, "I hope you aren't hurt. Do you want to sit down for a minute?" An additional condition in the experiment was affection. The experimenters were warm and friendly toward half of the children in each group, displaying interest in their activities, responding to requests for help, and the like. They were cool and matter-of-fact with the other children.

Two days after the training ended, the youngsters were shown similar scenes of people or animals in distress. Children in both groups made more helpful suggestions than they had

Descriptions of preschoolers as egocentric and prone to tantrums obscure how much they want to help others.

before training began. Two weeks later, they were exposed to two situations that had no direct relationship to their training. In one, the experimenter spilled a basket of spools and buttons on the floor. In the other, a baby was confined to a playpen, out of reach of his toys. Would the children generalize their training to the new situations? Or had they learned simply to give a banana to a monkey? This procedure revealed that children who had observed real-life situations (group B) *and* had a warm relationship with the experimenter were most likely to be helpful at a later date. Affection was the key to the learning. All of the children had demonstrated good intentions on the first test. Those who had had a friendly relationship with the experimenter acted more often on their intentions.

Social learning is only one factor in the development of prosocial behavior. There is some evidence that prosocial behavior is spontaneous. When preschoolers were asked why they had done something nice (Eisenberg-Berg & Neal, 1979), most referred to the other person's need ("He's hungry") or said simply that they wanted to do it. Some mentioned friendship, wanting approval, or mutual benefits. Not one mentioned fear of punishment or expectation of rewards from adults.

Temperament may also shape responses to training prosocial behavior. The mothers' reports in Zahn-Waxler and Radke-Yarrow (1982) brought out consistent individual differences. Some children were emotional and compassionate, some were afraid of other people's emotions, and some were cool and detached from infancy on. These differences persisted over time. For example, a child who, at age 2, had pushed another child away to protect his friend, at age 7 confronted an adult who broke into a supermarket line ahead of his grandmother. Attempts to relate these individual differences to patterns of child-rearing have yielded mixed results (Radke-Yarrow et al., 1983).

We consider children's ideas of right and wrong and the development of moral codes in Chapter 12. The key point here is that prosocial behavior appears early in life. To some extent, helping others seems to come naturally to children.

SUMMARY

1. For preschoolers, the development of social competence entails learning to control impulses, to get along with peers, and to manage social roles (especially sex roles).
2. Socialization accelerates around the child's second birthday, as parents step up their efforts to initiate the child into their culture. The child's acceptance of social norms and roles is in part the result of identification.
3. Parents may help or hinder the development of social competence. Baumrind identified three styles of child-rearing: authoritarian (discipline without warmth); permissive (warmth without discipline); and authoritative (warmth and discipline combined). She found that authoritative child-rearing encourages both independence and social responsibility.
4. Other psychologists question the unidirectional model of socialization for failing to consider the impact of the child's temperament and developmental stage on parents.
5. Harlow's experiments with monkeys indicate that peers play a vital role in primate socialization and may compensate for parental absence or neglect. Looking at human children, Hartup concludes that peers provide opportunities for testing limits and for give-and-take that are not possible between parents and their children.

6. Developing a gender identity and learning sex roles are important psychosocial tasks for the preschool years. Research shows that males and females are more alike than different. Nevertheless, all cultures emphasize the differences.

7. Parents (especially fathers) treat sons and daughters differently. Whether they are responding to innate sex differences or creating sex differences through socialization is difficult to say.

8. Peers also enforce sex standards. Boys and girls prefer members of their own sex, ignore or avoid children who engage in sex-inappropriate behavior, and have different styles of play.

9. A cognitive view of gender identity emphasizes the importance of developing gender constancy, and how this influences preschoolers' behavior.

10. Controlling aggression is another psychoso-cial task of the preschool years. Goodenough traced the translation of diffuse rage (or tantrums) in infancy and toddlerhood into aggression (deliberate attempts to harm someone or something) in the preschool years. Hartup documented the shift from instrumental (physical, object-oriented) aggression to hostile (verbal, person-oriented) aggression in early to middle childhood.

11. Sex differences and dominance hierarchies suggest that aggression has an evolutionary history and function. But the expression of anger in humans depends on social learning and cognitive development.

12. The development of prosocial behavior is an important chapter in the preschooler's development. Even infants show signs of empathy. Preschools make active, if awkward, attempts to be helpful.

FURTHER READING

Axline, V. (1964). *Dibs: In search of self.* New York: Ballantine Books. This is the story of a withdrawn, emotionally disturbed 5-year-old boy who was judged mentally retarded by his parents. Through play therapy, he successfully struggles for his identity.

Bronfenbrenner, U. (1970). *Two worlds of childhood: U.S. and U.S.S.R.* New York: Russell Sage Foundation. This summary of a landmark cross-cultural study contrasts the different child-rearing practices in the two countries.

Baumrind, D. (1972). Socialization and instrumental competence in young children. In W. W. Hartup (Ed.), *The young child: Review of research* (Vol. 2). Washington, D.C.: National Association for the Education of Young Children. This offers one of the quickest and easiest ways to be exposed to Baumrind's research on the development of competence in young children.

Maccoby, E. E., & Jacklin, C. N. (1974). *The psychology of sex differences.* Stanford, CA: Stanford University Press. An extensive review of research on sex differences, or everything you ever wanted to know about how men's and women's behaviors do and do not differ.

Parke, R. D. (1981). *Fathers* (part of *The developing child* series). Cambridge, MA: Harvard University Press. This is a guide to psychology's new understanding of the relation between fathers and children; includes a frank discussion of fathering.

Patterson, G. R. (1976). *Living with children: New methods for parents and teachers.* Champaign, IL: Research Press. Written in a programmed instruction format and based on social learning concepts, this book is aimed at helping parents of both normal and problem children to deal with situations that come up in any family.

Tavris, C., & Wade, C. (1984). *The longest war: Sex differences in perspective.* (2nd ed.). San Diego, CA: Harcourt Brace Jovanovich. A witty but serious scientific review of the battle of the sexes and the nature and nurture of sex differences in behavior.

Willard W. Hartup

Professor of Child Psychology
and former Director of the
Institute of Child Development,
University of Minnesota

ANN LEVINE: Dr. Hartup, how did you first become interested in psychology?

WILLARD W. HARTUP: I grew up in Ohio. My parents were both teachers, and learning was highly valued in our home. But we didn't live near a university, and there were only a handful of high schools in the country that offered courses in psychology in the 1940s. Mine wasn't one of them. The idea of a career in higher education or psychology never occurred to me. I didn't know what psychology *was*.

I went into the army directly from high school. The war was almost over, so I wasn't sent to the battlefields. I used my two years in the army to read. I would go on reading jags—the complete works of Hemingway, all of Faulkner's novels, maybe not all of Tolstoy, but quite a bit. I began reading Eugene O'Neill's plays on a short tour of duty in Panama. I was so immersed in his work I even read on guard duty. As you know, some of O'Neill's plays spring from psychoanalytic theory. They deal with the inner workings of the person. A friend of mine who had gone to college before the army told me that, if I liked O'Neill, I ought to read Freud. So I did, helter-skelter. I didn't have access to an extensive library, but there were a few pieces by Freud in a series of paperbacks the Army Information Service published. As far as I knew, this was psychology.

When I got my discharge and enrolled at Ohio State, I had made up my mind about two things: I had an interest in literature, and I wanted to know more about psychology.

AL: And the first thing you learned was that there was more to psychology than the Freudian analysis of dreams.

WWH: Exactly. Delos Wickens, an experimental psychologist at Ohio, taught the introductory course. It was a very basic, very good, intensively experimental course. This shocked me at first, but I thought some of it was interesting and persisted. I knew right off that I wasn't interested in hard-core experimental psychology, in sensation and perception, but in personality and social psychology.

AL: Did you major in psychology?

WWH: In psychology and English. I went through college with the idea that I needed to get prepared for the workplace. Right up to my senior year I expected to begin teaching English in junior high or high school as soon as I graduated. I took courses in educational psychology and child psychology because that seemed appropriate for a teacher-to-be. But I didn't have a very happy experience with student teaching, and I knew I would starve to death as a writer. So I began to think about what possibilities might exist in psychology. I applied for the master's program in educational psychology at Ohio State with vague ideas about becoming a school psychologist.

AL: You were interested in practicing psychology, not in teaching or doing research?

WWH: I guess I was, but it wasn't very focused. School psychology was hardly a field at that point. This was 1950. The educational psychology program at Ohio State dealt with the basic psychology of learning and teaching. I found those courses dusty dry, and wanted to take courses in clinical psychology. Educational psychology students weren't supposed to do that, but I got permission to enroll in the clinical sequence. The clinical program at Ohio State was terribly exciting at that time. George Kelly was the director of the psychological clinic and taught one course; Julian Rotter taught another; Boyd McCandless, another. The students were an exciting bunch, too.

AL: You didn't become a clinical psychologist, though.

WWH: No, I didn't. McCandless, who had been trained at the Iowa Child Welfare Research Station, taught a clinical course on mental retardation and child development. I took his class and did pretty well on the examination. Since I wasn't in the clinical program, he had never heard of me and wanted to know who I was. He called me into his office and asked what I had been doing. When he learned that I had gone right from undergraduate to graduate work at Ohio State, he said, right off, "You need to get out of here." When I told him I didn't plan to go any further than an M.A., he asked if I'd heard of a field called human development. I hadn't. Before I left his office that day he had called Robert Sears at the new Laboratory of Human Development at Harvard. There were still a few research assistantships open, and he recommended me. That's how I gravitated to developmental psychology.

AL: You went to Harvard with a background in literature and training in educational psychology and clinical psychology. What did you do at the Laboratory of Human Development?

WWH: I was immediately put to work on the famous project that resulted in the book, *Patterns of Child-rearing*. I was a research assistant on that project for three years, working partly under Robert and Pauline Sears and partly under Eleanor Maccoby. What the project focused on, and my major interest at the time, was the development of parent–child relations. We call this "attachment" now, but at that time it was called "dependency." Most of my early work was in this area.

AL: Tell me about your doctoral dissertation. How did you study "dependency," as it was called?

WWH: What I did was something of a departure from the kind of study that was being done at Harvard and most other universities in those days. The Searses and Maccoby were interviewing mothers, observing mothers and children, and correlating the two data sets. I designed a laboratory experiment, substituting a graduate student for the mother. The student's task was to create a warm, supportive relationship with some children; an inconsistent relationship with others, by being warm and supportive

one moment, cool and aloof the next. Then we observed the child's behavior with the experimenter. We found that uncertainty, not indulgence, increased dependent behaviors.

AL: This is what Mary Ainsworth would find when she studied mothers and children in the Strange Situation, some years later.*

WWH: Yes, but the research strategy was different. The kind of study I did came to be known as an analog experiment. Rather than study the relationship you are interested in directly, you establish something like it—an analog—in the laboratory. You can't manipulate very many things about the actual parent–child relationship, so you can't be sure what "causes" the child to behave in any given way. But you can create similar conditions in the laboratory and observe their effects. Later, this became a common research strategy among social learning theorists. All of Albert Bandura's studies are analog experiments. But when I did my dissertation, this was new. It was published in 1958, and I'm still quite proud of the design.

AL: Primate studies are another kind of analog experiment. Every textbook, including this one, cites Harry Harlow's studies with rhesus monkeys. Do you think this is appropriate? How much can we learn about human development from studies of other primates?

WWH: Personally, I have found animal studies useful. Let me give you a concrete example. In 1967, Wyndal Furman, Don Rahe, and I published a study in *Child Development* that was a direct replication of Harlow, Suomi, and Novak's studies on rehabilitating isolated monkeys with peer therapists.† After screening some 390 preschoolers, we identified twenty-four social isolates. We didn't know why these kids had become isolates: obviously they were not raised alone in cages like Harlow's monkeys. But they were extremely isolated kids. Eight of these children were taken out of their classroom for a half-hour play session with an ordinary preschooler from another class who was about their own age. Eight had the same kind of play session with a child who was about a year and a half younger than they were. And eight were given a half-hour to play by themselves with

*See the discussion of the Strange Situation in Chapter 5.
†See Chapter 11.

some toys, as a control. After ten play sessions, we observed them back in the day-care center. We saw increases in sociability in all of the children who had had peer "therapists," compared to the control group. But the biggest increase was with the children who had had a younger child for a "therapist." This is exactly what Harlow's team had found with monkeys.

Of course, Harlow was interested in a larger issue: namely, the effects of early experience on development, and whether the impact of deprivation is reversible. We were interested in a narrower question: the contribution of cross-age peer interaction to the development of social skills. We confirmed something many educators had suspected: that a shy, immature child may do better in a group of younger children than with age-mates or older children. So I really am a firm believer in the wise use of animal models.

AL: By "wise use" you mean qualified use?

WWH: Yes. If you are interested in the early-experience question, you have to be careful about drawing conclusions about humans based on a primate study. You see a strong attachment between infants and their caretaker in all primate species, but it looks very different from species to species. You cannot assume that similar experiences will have the same kinds of behavioral consequences in all species. But primate studies perform the necessary service of raising basic issues, for the obvious reason that you can conduct experiments with monkeys that cannot be done with humans.

AL: Let's get back to children. You said that your early work focused on parent–child relations. As I understand it, in the 1950s and 1960s, psychologists saw the family as the crucible of personality and social development. Peer relations were treated as a side issue, if they were mentioned at all.

WWH: That's exactly right.

AL: Today you are known for your work on peer socialization. How did you become interested in children's influences on one another?

WWH: By chance. I had been doing observational work in nursery schools, and had spent a lot of time looking at kids interacting with one another, but I never really regarded this as the center of my interest. I was doing the standard parent–child influence studies that most psychol-

ogists were doing at that time. I stumbled onto the field of peer relations.

One of my own children, Grant, rode to nursery school with a colleague's child named Janet. My wife and Janet's mother began to talk about a recurring theme in their conversations. It seemed that Janet and Grant were thoroughly intimidated by a child named David. They spent most of their time going to and from nursery school dreaming up ways to get back at David, really "cut him up bad." I decided to visit their school to see what was going on. Well, I found that David really was a hell-on-wheels kid. But he was also very competent in lots of ways. He was not only bright, he had a lot of social skill. When he was on good behavior around Janet and Grant, the two of them ate it up. He was somebody very special then. But their feelings were ambivalent because he could also be so aggressive. I began to wonder, what is it about a child that makes other children strive for his attention and approval, even though they are afraid of him?

I took this question back to the office. One of my students asked if we knew anything about how other children motivate the young child. The answer was, we didn't. Any number of psychologists were studying the influence of adult approval and attention on children. But no one had looked at how children influence children. So we did a study, which was published in *The Journal of Experimental Child Psychology* in 1964—and that led to twenty years of research on peer relations!

AL: How has the way developmental psychologists view peer relations changed in those twenty years? As one of the pioneers in the study of peer interaction, what do you see as the major advances?

WWH: One is that we've filled in some gaps. Some important studies of peer relations in nursery school—normative studies comparing three-, four-, and five-year-olds—were done in the 1930s and 1940s. The Sherifs studied school-age children in the 1950s and 1960s.* But it was piecemeal; we didn't know what happened between nursery school and third grade. We also know things today about peer skills in toddlers and two-year-olds that we

* See Chapter 11.

didn't know before. And this has changed the way we think. We can see the larger patterns—how peer interaction changes with age, and the connections between what the child is doing socially and what he is doing intellectually.

The second thing that we have come to appreciate (though we don't understand it fully by any means) is the fact that peer experience, the social world as it involves other kids, is a unique developmental challenge for the child. It is unique in the sense that it confronts the child with a set of circumstances that are different from those presented by the world of adults. With adults, the child has to cope with authority and with vast differences between the "self" and "others" in cognitive maturity and skill. Peers represent not only a world of equals, but a world that is governed by egalitarian expectations and rules of reciprocity. Piaget recognized this early on. But it is only in the last decade or so that we have come to recognize the full implications. Having experience with other immature individuals seems to be a developmental *necessity* for children, not just an "add-on" or luxury as is often thought.

We also used to associate the realm of peer activity with deviance. Peers were the source of all evil in socialization, or at least of a lot of it. In other words, the reason kids go bad is association with the bad apple. What we've learned is, "T'ain't so." For the most part, experience with peers has positive, benign outcomes. Of course, peer influences can be maladaptive. But in the main, peers are a positive force in development, even a necessary one.

Finally, we've learned something about close relationships among kids. We used to take for granted that friendships were nice things to have. . . .

AL: But luxuries, not necessities.

WWH: Yes. The research being done now goes well beyond how kids choose friends, to the significance of having friends, how they serve as protective elements in development, and what they contribute to the development of social skills.

Then there is the whole area of social skills. Once we demonstrated that it is important for kids to have a place in the peer group, we began to see the kid who is left out may be the one to worry about. We're learning which

social skills are important at different ages. In elementary school, for example, it becomes more and more important to know how to enter a group. Competent, successful, popular kids have this skill; isolated kids often do not. What Steven Asher and others have done is to break group entry down into its component parts. Hovering skills turn out to be crucial. To enter a group you have to wait until it's time to make a move, and then you have to make the right move. You don't enter a group by saying, "Look, here I am" or "Guess what happened to me today"; you observe what is happening and say something that is relevant to the ongoing activity. You can't be egocentric.

AL: We discuss Asher's experiments with teaching social skills in the text.* Are these applications still in the experimental stage, or are they being used?

WWH: They are indeed being used—in coaching programs, in social education in schools, and in individual therapy sessions.

AL: Where are the gaps today? What questions would you like to see answered in the near future?

WWH: We need to learn more about friendships. If you look at the literature you see studies of kids who have friends and kids who don't, comparisons of the way children behave with friends and with kids they don't know, that kind of thing. But we don't know anything about different kinds of friendships. We need to look at friendships the way we look at attachments. Every child is attached to his caretaker (if he

*See Chapter 11.

isn't severely damaged). The difference between kids is not that some are attached and some not; the difference is in the quality of the relationship. When we were able to classify different kinds of infant–mother relationships, the whole field of attachment took a giant leap forward. We need to do something like that with friendships. And it's time to think more about children's groups, how they differ from one another, how they change over the course of development. These are two frontiers in peer relations.

AL: What do you see as your major contribution to this field?

WWH: That's difficult to say. The chapter I wrote for the third edition of the Mussen handbook* may have been important. From 1963 until 1970, when that was published, I worked in the field more or less alone. Most developmental psychologists weren't interested in peer relations per se. Since then this has become a very popular area, and attracted numbers of people. I hope this will continue for some time.

AL: That brings us to the subject of publication.

*"Peer interaction and social organization." (1980) In P. H. Mussen (Ed.), *Carmichael's manual of child psychology*, [3rd ed., Vol. 2. New York: Wiley. Hartup also wrote the paper on peers for the most recent edition of this work: "Peer relations." (1983) In P. H. Mussen (Ed.), *Handbook of child psychology*, 4th ed., Vol. 4. New York: Wiley.

In addition to your research and teaching, you are the editor of one of the leading journals in the field, *Child Development*. How do you see your role as a "cultural gatekeeper"?

WWH: I think it's important for students to know that both the funding and the publishing of research depend on a system of peer review that really works quite well. The government may be the main source of research funds, but this does not mean that Washington bureaucrats decide which studies get support. Panels of scientists make those decisions and the government abides by them.

Nearly all scientific journals work the same way. Scientists submit their work to the editor. But the editor, cooped up in his office, doesn't decide which get published by himself. We use consultants. So my job is to select experienced and appropriate scientists, who do not have a conflict of interest, to serve as the jury for a paper. My decision is based on their comments and my reading. It's a pooled decision. *Child Development* serves a number of disciplines. We publish more psychology than anything else, but we also publish work in physiology, psychiatry, and sociology. That's one of the challenges for me.

But the important point is that everyone in the field is busy judging each other's work all of the time. It's a significant part of being a psychologist and scientist.

Psychosocial goals

Erikson: Initiative

Waters & Sroufe: Management of impulses, sex-role identification, peer relations

---

Parental influences (Baumrind)

[Parent]
Authoritarian (controlling, cool) . . .

Permissive (uncontrolling, warm) . . .

Authoritative (controlling, warm) . . .

Peer interaction

Prefer adults as playmates

Social interest (more interest in another child than in mother)

Side-by-side play

Gender

Labels self girl or boy (2 yrs.)

Avoids toys associated with opposite sex

Shuns child who engages in sex-inappropriate behavior

Believes sex can change (2–5 yrs.)

Aggression

Unfocused anger (tantrums) <2nd birthday>

Prosocial behavior

(Neonate may cry when other neonates cry)

Becomes distressed when another person seems hurt

Attempts to comfort someone in distress

Explains nice acts in terms of other person's need or own desire to help

---

| | 1 | 2 | 3 |

Age in years

( ) age range
< > onset or peak

HIGHLIGHTS OF SOCIAL AND EMOTIONAL DEVELOPMENT IN THE PRESCHOOL PERIOD

[Child]
Low in independence, middle range in social responsibility

Low in independence, very low in social responsibility

High in independence, high in social responsibility

Joint activities

Increases in fun and conflict; attention-seeking from children begins to replace affection-seeking from adults

Expresses sex-stereotyped ambitions

[Prefers members of same sex as playmates throughout preschool period, and beyond]

Achieves gender constancy
<6–7 yrs.>

Tantrums decrease; aggression increases

Instrumental, object-oriented, physical aggression decreases; hostile, person-oriented, verbal aggression increases

(Kohlberg's Preconventional Stage of moral reasoning; see Chapter 12)

4	5	6

If not us, whom?
If not now, when?

Developmental psychologists with different theoretical views generally agree that important changes take place in children's intellectual growth and learning at the beginning of middle childhood. This so-called 5-to-7 shift reflects a transition in the ways the young child understands and operates in his environment. The child develops increased competencies in thinking about the world and acting on it. Further, the child comes to understand better that other people think differently, feel differently, and see the world differently from the way he does. The ability to view things from another's perspective is an important accomplishment that paves the way for developing personal and social skills such as empathy and caring for others. The decline of egocentrism in the middle childhood years also allows the youngster to appreciate cooperative group effort and teamwork. With even greater mastery of the environment, the school-age child is able to become more independent. He can establish himself as a being with unique abilities, interests, and personal characteristics. The child expands his network of social relationships to include more peers, as well as other adults: schoolmates, teachers, and members of the community who influence his behavior and attitudes. He also puts into practice the moral code he has assimilated from his culture, distinguishing what is right from what is wrong.

During the early years the young child was equipped with simple psychological tools and provided with opportunities to construct a foundation and a framework for later intellectual and social growth. Throughout middle childhood (about ages 6 to 12), the young person rehearses the competencies he has already acquired and actively pursues new skills that he will need to adapt effectively to his expanding environment. It is during the school years that the child appears more like an adult in how he thinks, behaves, and interacts with the culture of which he has become a junior member. Individual differences become more apparent and more significant in this period. In this part we focus on an important and often misunderstood psychological construct, intelligence. What is it? What role does it play in development? How do individual differences in intelligence affect the child's present and future?

PART 4
THE MIDDLE
CHILDHOOD
YEARS

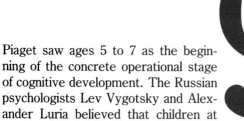

Piaget saw ages 5 to 7 as the beginning of the concrete operational stage of cognitive development. The Russian psychologists Lev Vygotsky and Alexander Luria believed that children at this age are able to control their thoughts and behavior in a way that younger children cannot. Behaviorists focus on the increasing use of language in learning. Freud saw ages 5 to 7 as the beginning of the latency stage, when psychosexual conflicts are dormant and the child is free to concentrate on developing skills. In different ways each of these theorists characterized middle childhood as a period of intellectual revolution. Sheldon White (1965) coined the term 5-to-7 shift to describe this phenomenon.

We begin this chapter by looking at the biological evidence for the 5-to-7 shift. What happens to a child's brain in this period? Next we present Piaget's analysis of the concrete operational stage of cognitive development, and contemporary refinements of his views. Then we discuss changes in attention, memory, and problem-solving strategies by way of information processing theory. In the last sections of the chapter we consider the questions children ask at this stage, the games they play, what makes them laugh, and the demands made on them in school.

Biological Explanations of the 5-to-7 Shift

Between the ages of 5 and 7, there are noticeable changes in the child's physical development (Shonkoff, 1984; Tanner, 1970, 1978). These years add pounds and inches to the child's frame—and gray hair to parents who fight an endless battle to keep their child clothed and shod. As Sheldon White documented, there are many perceptual and cognitive changes in this period as well (see Figure 9-1). Is the 5-to-7 shift the result of sudden, dramatic biological changes?

There is no doubt that the 5-year-old's brain and nervous system are more mature than those of the 2-year-old. At birth, the baby's

THE INTELLECTUAL REVOLUTION OF MIDDLE CHILDHOOD

brain is about 25 percent of its adult weight; by age 5, it has reached 90 percent of its adult weight (Tanner, 1970). But the most significant changes during early childhood are not in the size of the brain, but in its structure. Most important is the development of the outer surface of the brain, the cerebral cortex (see Figure 9-2).

The first areas of the cerebral cortex to develop are the frontal lobes, which control voluntary body movements (chewing, grasping, and so on). This occurs in the first month or two of life. The primary sensory cortex, which responds to sights, sounds, smell, and touch, approaches adult levels by age 6 months. By the end of the first year, the secondary processing areas, which turn sensations into perceptions, are functioning. (Recall the discussion of the primary and secondary visual systems in Chapter 4.) The most important development in the second year is **myelination**—the development of protective sheaths around the nerves that facilitate the transmission of "messages" to and from the brain. The infant has sensations in his trunk, legs, and feet; but until myelination is complete he cannot control those parts of his body.

Perhaps the most significant development of all occurs during the second, third, and fourth years: the growth of *cross-modal zones* that connect one area of the brain with others. These connections enable the child to associate the sound of a bark with the sight of a dog; the sight of an apple with its taste; and eventually the sound of the spoken word "apple" with the sight and taste. Studies of children who have had physical traumas illustrate this (White, 1969). Children who were blinded before age 6 do not have visual memories; children blinded thereafter do. Few children who had a limb amputated before age 4 report sensations from the missing limb; nearly all children who suffered an amputation after age 8 feel the lost limb (the phantom-limb phenomenon). It seems, that the older children have formed lasting sensorimotor connections. Although the brain continues to develop, all major associations are completed between ages 5 and 6 (Fishbein, 1984).

☐ Children who are blinded before the age of 6 have no visual memories; children who are blinded thereafter do.

☐ Up to age 6 or 7, children become increasingly susceptible to classical conditioning; after age 6 or 7, they become increasingly resistant.

☐ Up to age 5 or 6, children cannot tell their right from their left; by about 7 they can.

☐ Five-year-olds have difficulty drawing the "biggest" and the "smallest" possible squares on a piece of paper; 7-year-olds find this task easy.

☐ Children 5 and younger usually respond to word-association tests with a word that follows the cue word (given "dog," they respond "bite"); older children usually respond with a word in the same category ("cat").

☐ Before age 7, most children are not bothered if someone points out that they contradicted themself; after age 7 they avoid self-contradiction.

☐ Before age 6, children are reinforced by praise; after age 6 or 7 being correct is its own reward.

(White, 1965)

Figure 9-1 Changes Associated with the 5-to-7 Shift

Figure 9-2 Brain Maturation The human brain is immature at birth. Myelination (bottom), which is completed in the second year of life, and the development of associational areas in the cerebral cortex (top), which occurs between ages two and five, help to explain the intellectual revolution of middle childhood.

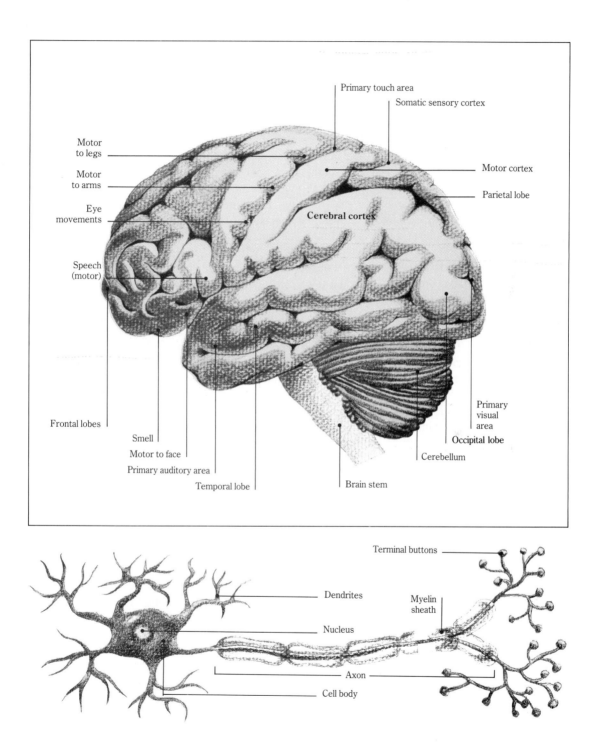

We know that the areas of the brain that develop between birth and age 2 deal with sensorimotor skills; those that develop between ages 2 and 5 pave the way for symbols and concrete operations. However, there is no exact correspondence between brain maturation and cognitive development. Some children begin reading at 3, or even at age 2, when their brains are immature. Moreover, the fact that brain maturation and cognitive development occur at the same time does not demonstrate that the former causes the latter. Cognitive development may cause (or at least accelerate) brain maturation. Most likely, each influences the other. Of course, without a well-developed nervous system, cognitive development could not occur. But there is more to the intellectual revolution of middle childhood than biological maturation.

The Concrete Operational Stage: Becoming a Logical Thinker

Piaget saw the major cognitive achievement of middle childhood (about ages 6 to 12) as the development of logical thinking. In the sensorimotor stage, the infant's actions and expectations show that he has begun to appreciate certain regularities in his environment (see Chapter 4). In the preoperational stage, the child is able to form mental images and to represent and communicate his practical knowledge of the world symbolically (see Chapter 6). The preschooler can talk about people and events, make drawings, reenact events in symbolic play, and invent stories. His verbal explanations of time, space, and cause and effect may be poetic, but they are rarely logical. His thinking is intuitive. He leaps to conclusions and often confuses desires with reality, coincidence with cause and effect. The preoperational child deals in particulars; he has not discovered general rules, and doesn't seem to feel a need for them.

The concrete operational child thinks more like an adult. Adult logic takes the form of deduction and induction. Both modes of thought establish connections between generalizations and particulars. *Deduction* is reasoning from the general to the particular. For example, if we assume that all men have hearts of gold, we deduce that the man to whom we have just been introduced also has a heart of gold. *Induction* is reasoning from the particular to the general. If we meet a number of men with hearts of gold, we may induce that *all* men are as kind as those we have met. In contrast to adults, the preoperational child reasons from particular to particular. As a result, he often assumes connections where none exist. An observation of Piaget's daughter is typical of *transductive reasoning.* "I haven't had my nap so it isn't afternoon" (in Ginsburg & Opper, 1979, pp. 80–81).

The child takes a giant step toward adult thinking in the concrete operational stage. Thought becomes more systematic and planful. She can think ahead, no longer bound by her immediate perceptions and personal experiences. Moreover, the child in this stage can shift mental gears—something the younger child cannot do. The preoperational child's mental world might be compared to scenes viewed from the window of a passing train—a series of unexplored observations flashed before her eyes. The preoperational child is a spectator. The concrete operational child is at the controls. She can speed up or slow down her thinking as the situation requires. She can think about alternative routes from point A to point B and decide which one to take. Most important, the concrete operational child can shift her mind into reverse, retrace her mental route, and perhaps discover where she made a wrong turn.

Piaget called these newfound abilities "operations." An **operation** is a mental activity that organizes or transforms information. The difference between operations and schemes is that operations are mental manipulations of information, not physical and sensory associations. It is the difference between winding up and throwing a baseball and contemplating your next move in chess.

A child in this stage is limited to operations on the concrete or physical world, hence the term **concrete operations.** She thinks about real people, real objects, and possible events. Only later, through formal operations, will she be able to deal with abstractions and hypothetical situations. But concrete operations lead the child to the discovery of logical relationships among objects and actions.

Conservation: The Cornerstone

Mastery of conservation is the major achievement of the concrete operational stage. For the preoperational child, seeing is believing. He doesn't understand that certain properties of a substance remain the same (are conserved) even though their appearance or form has changed. We described the liquid conservation task in Chapter 6. In another version of this, the experimenter shows the child two balls of clay that are the same size and shape. She asks the child if one of the balls has more clay. The child

The ability to manipulate symbols is one of the developments of the concrete operational stage.

says "No, they're the same." Before the child's eyes she rolls one ball of clay into a long, sausage shape, and repeats the question. The 4- to 5-year-old nearly always says that the "sausage" has more clay because it is longer. The experimenter rolls the clay back into a ball and repeats the question again. Amazingly, the child says that the two balls are now equal.

Between ages 5 and 6, the child vacillates. Sometimes he says that the long shape has more clay, sometimes that the round shape has more. He does not focus exclusively on length or height, as before, but he still does not consider the relationship between the two dimensions. Then, rather suddenly, the child "gets it."

There always comes a time (between 6½ years and 7 years 8 months) when the child's attitude changes: he no longer needs to reflect, he decides, he even looks surprised that the question is asked, he is *certain* of the conservation. (Piaget, 1950, p. 140)

The child may give one of several reasons for his new answer. He may say that it is the same clay; the experimenter hasn't added anything or taken anything away (*identity*). He may say that the sausage is longer but it is also thinner (change in one dimension *compensates* for change in the other dimension). Or he may say that you can roll the sausage back into a ball (the transformation is *reversible*). But whichever explanation he gives, he is certain that he is right—and he is!

Conservation takes years to master, and some tasks come more easily than others. As a general rule, children grasp conservation of substances (liquid and matter) before they comprehend conservation of number, length, area, and volume (see Table 9-1). At times, the child accepts conservation for some items but denies it for others (Flavell, 1985). Complete conservation may not develop until adolescence (Piaget,

Table 9-1:
The Development of Conservation

Type	The Child is Shown:	The Experimenter:	The Child Responds:
Liquid	two equal short, wide glasses of water and agrees that they hold the same amount.	pours water from the short, wide glass into the tall, thin one and asks if one glass holds more water than the other.	*Preoperational child:* The tall glass has more. *Concrete operational child:* They hold the same amount.
Matter	two equal balls of clay and agrees they are the same.	rolls one ball of clay into a sausage and asks if one has more clay.	*Preoperational child:* The long one has more clay. *Concrete operational child:* They both have the same amount.
Number	two rows of checkers and agrees that both rows have the same number.	spreads out the second row and asks if one row has more checkers than the other.	*Preoperational child:* The longer row has more checkers. *Concrete operational child:* The number of checkers in each row hasn't changed.
Length	two sticks and agrees that they are the same length.	moves the bottom stick and asks if they are still the same length.	*Preoperational child:* The bottom stick is longer. *Concrete operational child:* They're the same length.
Area	two boards with six wooden blocks and agrees that the blocks on both boards take up the same space.	A B scatters the blocks on one board and asks if one board has more unoccupied space.	*Preoperational child:* The blocks on board B take up more space. *Concrete operational child:* They take up the same amount of space.
Volume	two balls of clay put in two glasses equally full of water and says the level is the same in both.	flattens one ball of clay and asks if the water level will be the same in both glasses.	*Preoperational child:* The water in the glass with the flat piece won't be as high as the water in the other glass. *Concrete operational child:* Nothing has changed; the levels will be the same in each glass.

1970). But the child described above has made that first important step.

Piaget held that conservation reflects a basic reorganization of the child's mind. The conserver thinks differently from the nonconserver. She is able to coordinate different pieces of information in her mind. Whereas the preoperational child centers his attention on one dimension (length), the conserver is able to *decenter* attention and consider two or more dimensions simultaneously. She comprehends the *functional relationship* between height and width: the width of the clay sausage varies as a function of its length. Whereas the younger child focuses on end-states, the older child pays attention to the *transformations* that occur as the clay is rolled into different shapes. Remember also that concrete operational thought is characterized by *reversibility*. The child can mentally undo the transformation by imagining rolling the clay back into its original shape.

Conservation is a milestone in cognitive development because it enables the child to perceive regularities and constancies in a world that would otherwise appear to be in a state of constant flux. She is not so easily misled by superficial changes in appearance.

Putting Two and Two Together: Classification

Conservation is not the only evidence of the child's increasing ability to perform mental operations. He is also beginning to grasp relationships among objects and events. The preoperational child demonstrates simple classification skills (as shown in Chapters 6 and 7). He can sort objects or events that share common characteristics into the same class. As a result, he has mastered such concepts as *sweet, round, red,* and *dog.* By 5 or 6 he is able to add classes together into more general categories: cats, dogs, and rabbits all belong in the superclass *animals.* By age 6 or 7, most children can construct hierarchies such as that in Figure 9-3. They know that the class *people* includes children and adults, and that the class *children* includes boys and girls.

The preoperational child does not understand class inclusion. In another of Piaget's studies, the experimenter shows a child two boxes of wooden beads. One box holds twenty brown beads, the other three white beads. He asks the child if all the beads are made of wood. The child says yes. Then he asks if there are more wooden beads or more brown beads. The child replies, "More brown beads." He asks if the white beads are made of wood. The child agrees that they are. Then he asks again if there are more wooden beads or more brown beads. The child insists that there are more brown beads. Piaget tried the same test with many different kinds of materials, such as flowers, candies, and people, with similar results.

Juil [5 years, 6 months] watched me drawing twelve girls and two boys.
"Are there more girls or more children in this class?"
More girls.
"But aren't the girls children?"
Yes.
"Then are there more children or more girls?"
More girls.   (Piaget, 1965, p. 167)

Solving this problem requires three mental skills. The child must be able to (1) sort individual items into classes (girls and boys), (2) add these together to form a higher-order class (children), and (3) understand that the higher-order class can be broken down again into subclasses (girls and boys). Moreover, the child must be able to do this mentally. When asked whether there are more girls or more boys, the child can compare them visually. When asked whether there are more girls or more children she cannot rely on sight because the girls are members of both categories. The child who cannot perform this mental operation "translates"

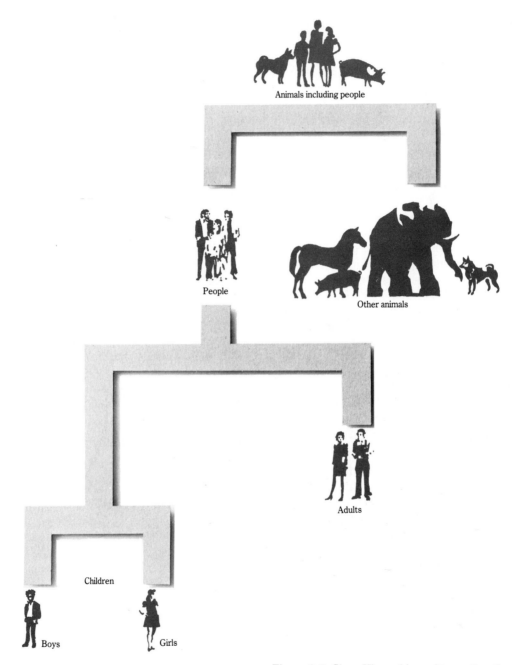

Figure 9-3 Class Hierarchies At age 7 or 8 most children do not understand that people are also animals. Indeed, adults often forget this.

the question into one that she *can* handle and answers as if the experimenter had asked whether there were more girls or more boys.

Piaget found that children master class inclusion between the ages of 7 and 11. He cited the response of one 9-year-old boy to questions about a collection of a dozen yellow tulips, three red tulips, and six daisies.

"Which would make a bigger bunch, one of all the tulips or one of all the yellow tulips?"
All the tulips, of course. You'd be taking the yellow tulips as well.
"And all the tulips or all of the flowers?"
If you take all the flowers, you take all the tulips too.
(Paraphrased from Ginsburg and Opper, 1979, p. 123)

This young man had no problem with the relationships of parts to wholes or wholes to parts.

Getting Things in Order: Seriation

There is one additional set of skills that develop in the concrete operational stage. **Seriation** is the ability to arrange things in a logical order (from shortest to longest, thinnest to fattest, and so on). Preoperational children have difficulty with relational concepts, such as *longer than* and *bigger than*. They do not seem to understand that object A may be bigger than object B but smaller than object C. When preoperational children are asked to arrange a group of sticks according to length, they start typically with a short stick, then pick a long stick, then choose another short stick, another long one, and so on. By age 7, most children are able to accurately arrange six or eight sticks by length (see Figure 9-4).

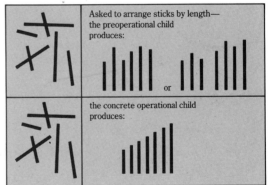

Figure 9-4 Seriation

The development of sensorimotor schemes does not stop in middle childhood. As adults, we continue to use schemes for such activities as playing basketball, driving a car, and typing.

This apparently simple activity lays the foundation for other operations. A child who has mastered seriation can begin to understand *reciprocal* relationships. He can comprehend, for example, that if Sue is taller than Carol, then Carol is shorter than Sue. Later in the concrete operational stage, he will be able to solve the following problem. Sue is taller than Carol, Carol is taller than Jane. Is Sue taller than Jane? The answer depends on *transitive inferences* (or transferring reasoning). The child must be able to compare two isolated relationships ("Sue is taller than Carol" and "Carol is taller than Jane") and also see that Carol supplies the missing link in the question, "Is Sue taller than Jane?" Coordinating these bits of information demonstrates considerable mental agility.

Piaget maintained that conservation, class inclusion, and seriation are all signs of a fundamental reorganization of the child's cognitive structure. Operations have replaced preoperational reliance on schemes and perceptions. The child's thinking is better coordinated (he can think about more than one dimension at a time) and more flexible (he can shift into reverse), and therefore more logical and adultlike. Further, Piaget held that these different skills develop hand in hand. Understanding seriation strengthens the child's grip on conservation, and vice versa. In Piaget's words, "they amalgamate into an organized whole" (1950, p. 141).

Brothers and sisters have I none,
But this man's father is my grandfather's son.
who is he?

Give up? The speaker is talking about himself. Adults sometimes stumble over transductive reasoning.

The child has come a long way. But his thinking is limited to concrete tasks; his mind only operates on the real world. The 8- or 9-year-old cannot deal effectively with abstract concepts based on formal verbal definitions, such as *government, astronomy,* or *social class.* He needs concrete examples. And although he is often able to produce logical, accurate explanations of events, he often lapses into *artificialism,* the belief that people or supernatural beings are responsible for natural phenomena. The transition from artificialism to physical accounts of causality occurs gradually over the years 6 to 12, as the result of accommodation and assimilation.

A Critical Review of Piaget

Piaget's theory of cognitive development and description of the concrete operational stage rests on three questionable predictions (Siegler & Richards, 1983). The first concerns the typical sequence of development; the second, the consistency of a child's thinking in a given stage; and the third, the possibility of teaching young children complex skills. Here we will look at arguments for and against Piaget's claims.

The Sequence of Development

Piaget was explicit about what tasks a child in a given stage can and cannot perform, the order in which skills develop, and the approximate ages at which they are acquired. But his conclusions were based on observations of a small number of children, including his own. Do all children conform to Piaget's stage norms? The answer is yes and no.

Numerous researchers have used modified versions of Piaget's tasks to test what children know and when they know it. Many have found that youngsters who "should be" in the preoperational stage are capable of performing concrete operations (1) if the test materials are familiar (for example, Snoopy dolls); (2) if the researcher takes pains to see that children understand the words being used (such as "more" and "bigger"); and (3) if the number of test materials is relatively small (three checkers instead of eight or ten on conservation of number). Many of these researchers feel that Piaget underestimated preschoolers, as pointed out in Chapter 6. (Many also feel that he overrated adolescents, as we show in Chapter 13.)

Does this mean that Piaget was wrong? Not necessarily. His standards were strict. It was not enough for a child to display *some* understanding of conservation or seriation; Piaget looked for evidence of *complete* mastery. He did not credit a child with conservation of liquid, for example, unless that child was absolutely certain of her answer. One test was the child's reaction to being questioned. True conservers were puzzled or amused by Piaget's questions about brown and wooden beads or tulips and flowers: "Everybody knows that! Why ask stupid questions?" Post-Piagetian studies do suggest that

Insight

ARE CONCRETE OPERATIONS UNIVERSAL?

Piaget's theory of cognitive development is sometimes criticized as being the psychology of the urban, middle-class schoolchild in Geneva, Switzerland. Piaget himself studied only a small number of children, including his own. Most other researchers have used English, Canadian, and U.S. youngsters as subjects. Does Piaget's theory apply to all children? Are concrete operations universal?

Pierre R. Dansen (1972, 1977) reviewed the cross-cultural literature on cognitive development. The empirical evidence overwhelmingly supports the *qualitative* aspects of Piaget's theory—that is, the sequence of stages, the structure of cognitive changes, and the explanations children give for their answers to problems. Evidence for concrete operations is particularly strong. In all cultures studied so far, at least some children reach this stage of cognitive development spontaneously.

Evidence for the *quantitative* aspects of Piaget's theory (the rate of development through stages) is not so strong. The development of specific concrete operations occurs at different ages in different cultures. Children in nomadic hunting cultures (Canadian Eskimos and Australian aborigines) develop spatial concepts more rapidly than do children in sedentary agricultural cultures (the Ebrie of the Ivory Coast).

These African farm children, on the other hand, master the conservation of quantity, weight, and volume at a younger age than do children in the other societies. Dansen reasons that development is most rapid for concepts that people in a culture value highly. Spatial knowledge is particularly relevant or adaptive in a hunting society; understanding quantity and weight is more relevant to people who grow and market produce.

Schooling may affect the development of concrete operations. For example, less than half the unschooled children in a rural community in Zambia had mastered conservation by ages 11 to 13. Social class also seems to influence the rate of development, in Western and non-Western populations. Between 10 percent and 20 percent of lower-class Australian-Europeans had not developed concrete operations at age 12. Some adults never master conservation, seriation, or classification as defined by Piaget.

Dansen draws two conclusions from his survey of cross-cultural data. First, in every culture studied to date, some or all individuals reach the stage of concrete operations, although usually at a later age than in middle-class European populations. Second, the fact that some normal adults never attain this level of reasoning suggests that environmental influences are more important than Piaget originally thought.

the development of operations may *begin* earlier than Piaget thought.

In general, Piaget's description of the content and order of stages has withstood challenges. For example, Neimark (1975) conducted a large-scale, longitudinal study of cognitive development from third to sixth grade. Children were tested on Piagetian tasks once a year. She found that most children either stayed in the same stage or moved up one stage in a given year. It was exceedingly rare for a child to slip backward or to make giant leaps forward. As Piaget predicted, these children developed one stage at a time, in the same order, and without skipping stages.

Consistency within Stages

Piaget held that cognitive development could be divided into four discrete stages. The way a child approaches problems reflects the underlying structure of her thought. Cognitive structure changes from stage to stage, but within each stage the child's performance on a variety of tasks will be consistent. This is because preoperational or concrete operational skills are interdependent, part of a structured whole. A normal 10-year-old is able to pass all (or nearly all) concrete operational tasks, but no (or very few) formal operational tasks.

John Flavell (1982) puts the consistency issue this way. If Piaget is correct, virtually everything an 8-year-old does will illustrate the distinctive style and capacity of the concrete

The concept of stages makes intuitive sense: People are supposed to act their age. We expect 7-year-olds to be giddy and adults in formal dress to be dignified, not the age-role reversal shown here.

operational stage. An observer will find himself thinking, "Always and everywhere the 8-year-old thinker, isn't he?" or "Concrete operational to the very core!" If Piaget is incorrect, the quality and style of the child's thinking will vary from task to task, day to day—as if the toddler in the child answered some questions and the future adolescent handled others. An observer will find himself thinking, "Some grown-up must have told him the answer—he could never have figured it out" one day; "That has to be his little brother's drawing—he couldn't possibly have done anything so primitive" the next day. If Piaget is correct, different skills (conservation, class inclusion, and so on) will develop concurrently. If Piaget is not correct, skills will develop independently and the child's thinking will be uneven.

The boundaries between Piaget's stages and consistency within stages in Piaget's theory are at best overstated (Siegler & Richards, 1982). There is a good deal of evidence of uneven performance on different tasks and even on the same task in all stages. At one point, many psychologists (including Flavell) were ready to abandon the stage approach for a more gradual, continuous model of cognitive development (see Chapter 1). Now they are reconsidering. In the beginning or middle of a stage, children may be erratic in their thinking. They may perform better on some tasks (conservation of liquid) than on others (conservation of number). They may be more consistent in dealing with everyday events than they are with formal tasks in a laboratory. Some children may be more consistent than others. But at the end of a stage the skills they have been developing come together. The idea of stages is useful in identifying these major mental reorganizations.

Teaching Cognitive Skills

Piaget's most controversial claims concern the unlikelihood that cognitive development can be accelerated through training. Piaget called this "the American question." Every time he spoke in this country, the first question he was asked was, "Can we accelerate cognitive development?" For many years he maintained that unless a child had reached a certain level of cognitive development, teaching conservation or other skills was a waste of effort. This position has been challenged.

A large number of studies have shown that children can be taught concrete (and formal) operations before they acquire these skills spontaneously (Siegler & Richards, 1982). Rochel Gelman's work with nonconserving 5-year-olds is an example. Gelman (1969) hypothesized that the main reason why younger children fail conservation tasks is that they focus on a prominent but irrelevant dimension (the height of a glass, the length of a line of checkers). She tested this hypothesis by training children to pay attention to the relevant dimension. One group of children was shown series of three cards. Two of the cards had the same number of dots, but they were spread out on card A and bunched together on card B. On card C, the number of dots was different but the length of the line matched card A (see Figure 9-5). Gelman asked each child which cards had the "same number" of items, calling his attention to the relevant information. The child was rewarded when he gave the correct answer and told when he was wrong. By the end of the training session, the children were giving correct answers most of the time. As controls, a second group of children was shown the cards but not reinforced and a third group was given no training.

The day after the training session, Gelman presented the children with a series of Piagetian conservation tasks. The results were dramatic. Children in the control groups performed poorly. Children who had received training gave correct answers on almost all of the number conservation tests and were able to explain their choices. Even more remarkable, they were able to transfer this newly acquired skill to liquid and length conservation tasks. When tested again after two and three weeks, they retained these skills.

Did these allegedly preoperational children meet Piaget's standard of mastery? Deanna Kuhn (1974) holds that if training studies are to be judged a success they must meet four criteria of genuine understanding:

1. The children must be able to explain their answers in their own words (not simply parrot what they heard in training).
2. They must retain their understanding over time.
3. They must not be confused if the experimenter makes countersuggestions (the certainty criterion).
4. They should be able to apply this understanding to related tasks (generalization).

Gelman's study met three of the four criteria. The children were able to explain conservation; they showed evidence of generalization; and the effects of training lasted. Gelman does not say whether the children resisted countersuggestions. The one "flaw" in her study was that the children were 5 years old and, therefore, near or perhaps at the beginning of the concrete operational stage. Training may have accelerated their development by only a few weeks or months; there is no way of knowing. In other studies, researchers have attempted to accelerate the development of conservation with explicit instruction (Zimmerman & Rosenthal, 1974), peer models (Murray, 1972), and feedback (demonstrating that nonconservation is incorrect) (Gelman, 1969). In varying degrees these studies have met the four criteria of genuine understanding.

In his later years, Piaget softened his position on learning (see Inhelder, Sinclair, & Bovet, 1974). He admitted that his early assertion that training would never accelerate a child's development was overstated. But he held to the view that the degree to which youngsters can benefit from instruction depends on their level of development. Older, more knowledgeable children learn more. In other words, he saw developmental differences in *learning* as additional evidence for stages of cognitive development. (For further discussion of these issues, see the profile of John Flavell at the end of this chapter.)

Information Processing in Middle Childhood

Studies of information processing offer a somewhat different interpretation of the school-age child's intellectual development. Piaget held that

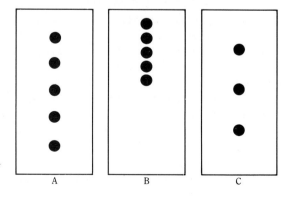

Figure 9-5 Teaching Conservation of Number
Gelman taught children conservation by showing them series of cards like these and reinforcing them when they gave the correct answer to the question, "Which cards have the *same number* of dots?"

advances in attention, memory, linguistic abilities, and other cognitive skills were expressions of structural changes in the child's mind. Simply put, the school-age child thinks better because he has become more logical. Information-processing studies suggest that the development of logic in middle childhood may be due to improvements in attention, memory, and linguistic skills, rather than to a better understanding of logic itself (Siegler & Richards, 1982). Piaget saw the 5 to 7 shift as a metamorphosis: the caterpillar (the preoperational thinker) emerges as a butterfly (a concrete operational thinker). Information-processing theory views the changes in this period as the result of many small improvements in attention, memory, and problem-solving skills the child has possessed for some time.

Paying Attention

One of the major developments in attention during middle childhood is the ability to focus on information that is relevant to the task at hand, or *central learning*. An experiment by John Hagen and Gordon Hale (1973) captures this change. The researchers showed fourth-, sixth-, and eighth-graders a row of picture cards. Each card had one picture of an animal and one of a common household item. They asked the child to try to remember where each of the animals was located. Then, they turned the cards face down. To test for central learning, the researchers asked the children to recall animals. Then they asked the children to locate the household items, a measure of *incidental learning*—called incidental because the children had not been asked to learn the household items. Memory for animals increased more or less steadily with age: eighth-graders gave twice as many correct answers as fourth-graders did. Memory for the household items remained about the same up to age 11 or 12, then *declined*. Were the older children's memories slipping? Not at all. They were told to remember the animals, and they did. The fact that they had trouble recalling household items showed that the children were able to focus on relevant information and screen out incidental information. Put another way, they had developed a strategy to prevent "information overload": Ignore irrelevent details (see Figure 9-6).

The child's ability to recognize visually embedded figures also improves over the school years (see Figure 9-7 on page 359). Older children are better at separating parts from wholes than are younger children. These skills are crucial for learning to read and write, important tasks of the school years.

Remembering to Remember

Four-year-olds often forget where they left their mittens or what happened in nursery school that morning. In contrast, a 6-year-old is like a sponge, soaking up knowledge, assimilating new information to her current understanding and conception of the world. She remembers details about people, places, and things. She re-

In middle childhood youngsters have longer attention spans, and remember more of what they see and hear, than they did as preschoolers.

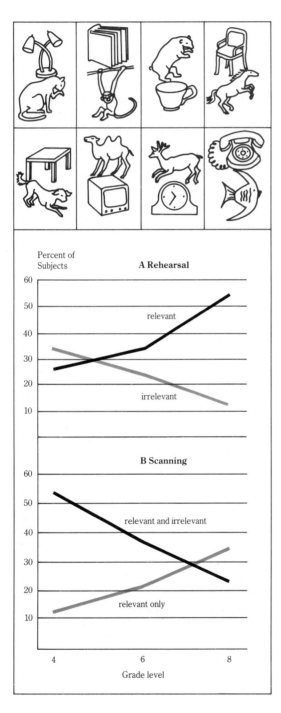

minds adults of unfulfilled promises and of who said what to whom on which occasion. She can remember the addresses and phone numbers of her friends and retrace the path to the neighborhood candy store. In school, children are expected to memorize the multiplication tables and the names of the 50 states, learn the lyrics of songs and verses of poetry, remember the meanings of vocabulary words, and recall their correct spelling. Without prompting, they remember scenes from TV soap operas, advertising jingles, and taboo words. Innumerable studies confirm that school-age children are able to learn (or store in memory) and recall (retrieve from memory) series of numbers, lists of words, arrays of pictures and objects, and other information better than preschoolers are. What accounts for the large increases in memory during middle childhood?

MEMORY STRATEGIES Adults use a number of *mnemonic* (memory-aiding) strategies. One strategy adults use is *rehearsal*. When you repeat a telephone number you obtained from directory information over and over as you dial, you are rehearsing. Do children rehearse?

Some years ago, Flavell and his students watched children who were attempting a memory task (Flavell, Beach, & Chinsky, 1966). Each child was outfitted with a space helmet with a dark visor. Seven pictures of familiar objects were displayed in front of the child. The researcher told the child that he was going to

Figure 9-6 The Development of Selective Attention These are items used in Hagen and Hale's incidental learning study. Chart A shows the percentages of children who named relevant and irrelevant figures as a memory aid. Chart B shows the percentages of children who visually scanned both the relevant and irrelevant figures or only the relevant figures
(Adapted from Hagen, 1972).

point to three pictures that he wanted the child to remember in order; pull down the visor so that the child couldn't see; count to fifteen; then lift the visor so the child could point. During the fifteen-second delay another researcher who was trained in lipreading studied the child. Almost all of the 10-year-olds in the study, but only a few of the 5-year-olds, moved their lips or named the object aloud during the delay period. Those who did were rehearsing their answers. The rehearsers' recall was much better than that of nonrehearsers. In a later experiment, Flavell's team taught first-graders to rehearse (Keeney, Cannizzo, & Flavell, 1967). They found that the children learned this strategy quite easily and performed as well as spontaneous rehearsers when they used it. But they

abandoned rehearsal on other memory tests, in which they were not prompted. Small children can rehearse, but do not do so on their own.

Another study revealed that the *way* children rehearse changes with age (Ornstein, 1978). Groups of 8-, 11-, and 13-year-olds were asked to rehearse aloud items in a list of eighteen unrelated words. The older children added each new word to the list already presented ("cat," "desk," "lawn," "shirt"). The younger children simply repeated the last word they heard ("shirt," "shirt," "shirt")—and recalled many fewer words.

A second memory device is *organization,* or categorizing a list of words or array of objects according to color, use, or some other shared attribute. Suppose the child is asked to memorize the list: shoes, hat, baseball bat, zebra, dress, cow, catcher's mitt, hot dog, raccoon, bus. If he clumps related items together— *clothes* (shoes, hat, dress) *animals* (zebra, cow, raccoon) and *things related to the ball park* (baseball bat, catcher's mitt, hot dog) the words will be easier to recall later. The category labels serve as retrieval cues (Tulving, 1974). The number and kinds of cues a child uses depend on his level of thinking.

Small children do not organize information as older children and adults do (Siegler & Richards, 1982). Younger children tend to use sounds, (such as rhyming patterns) to group items; older children and adults use concepts (meaningful categories). Younger children use associations (saw/wood; hammer/nail) more of-

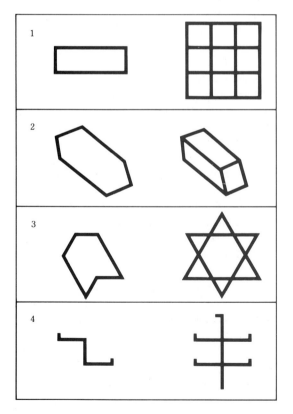

Figure 9-7 Perceiving Embedded Figures
Ghent (1956) asked 4- to 8-year-olds to locate the simple figure on the left in each box in the complex figure on the right, by tracing it with a finger. Ninety percent of the 4- and 5-year-olds made three or four errors on four trials; only 12 percent of the 7- and 8-year-olds made so many errors.

ten than classifications (*tools:* saw/hammer; *materials:* nail/wood). Moreover, small children are less efficient than older children. They divide lists into more categories with fewer items. Here again, children as young as 4 or 5 can be taught organization. But they do not use it without coaching.

A third memory strategy is *elaboration,* or linking items in a meaningful order. The sentence "*E*very *G*ood *B*oy *D*oes *F*ine" makes it easier to remember the lines on the treble clef in music (E-G-B-D-F). We are more likely to recall Mrs. Cardinal's name the second time we meet her if we associate it with her red hair. Another good mnemonic (memory-aiding) device is to locate items to be remembered in familiar places (Luria, 1968). Imagine walking through your front door, down the hall, into the living room, and up to the TV. Then picture each of the items you want to remember in one of these locations. If you are going to the grocery store, you might picture a door the shape of a slice of bread, a pile of eggs on the hall table, and a can of beans on the TV screen. The more associations we make between items and places, the more likely we are to remember them. Older children are far more likely to use elaboration than are younger children (Paris & Lindauer, 1977).

This is not to say that small children have no strategies for remembering. When Mary Anne Kreutzer and colleagues (Kreutzer, Leonard, & Flavell, 1975) asked kindergartners, first-, third-, and fifth-graders how they would remember to take their ice skates the next day, the children had a number of ideas: put the skates where they are easy to see, write themselves a note, tie a string to their finger, or even tie the skates to their body. But small children do not use memory aids deliberately or consistently.

METAMEMORY Knowledge of memory, or *metamemory,* develops during middle childhood.

Even kindergartners and first-graders have *some* knowledge of memory, Kreutzer's interviews of children revealed. They know that it is easier to remember something that happened yesterday than something that occurred a long time go. They realize that it is harder to memorize a long list than a short one. They say it is easier to relearn something you knew before than to start from scratch. And they know and use external memory aids.

The main difference between the memory of preschoolers and that of elementary school children is that the younger children are not aware of their own limitations. When asked, "Do you forget?" about one in three kindergartners will say no (Kreutzer et al., 1975). First-graders know better, because their metamemory is more developed. When shown a set of ten pictures and asked if they can remember all of them, more than half of a group of preschoolers—but only a few older children—said that they could. In fact, they could not. Another group of children was told to take as long as they needed to memorize a set of pictures. When the elementary school children announced that they were ready, they were usually right: They remembered everything. Preschoolers "jumped the gun." They thought they were ready, but only recalled a few items (Flavell, Friedrichs & Hoyt, 1970).

THE KNOWLEDGE BASE A third reason why older children have better memories than younger children do is that they know more to begin with. What they already know—their *knowledge base*—affects what they are able to learn.

Most people think of memory as a tape recorder or camera, and assume that what a person remembers depends on how well the machinery is working. (We describe someone who has almost total recall as having a "photographic memory.") In fact, memory is more like "the archeological reconstruction of an ancient civilization based on building fragments, bits of pottery, and other artifacts, plus a lot of logical inference, conceptual integration, and just plain guessing on the archeologist's part" (Flavell, 1977, p. 192). How well the archeologist does depends on her familiarity with the type of civilization (general knowledge) and her ability to put the bits and pieces together (cognitive skills). So it is with memory. When adults are asked to recall a prose passage, they do not repeat what they read or heard word for word. They retell the story in their own words, leaving out some parts and embroidering others. The result is an interpretive painting, not a photocopy. This view illustrates Piaget's notion of *constructive memory,* and the idea that memory is a cognitive process that draws on general knowledge and intellectual skills.

A clever series of experiments demonstrates the impact of knowledge on memory. William Chase and Herbert Simon (1973) asked a group of chess masters and a group of amateur chess players to reconstruct the arrangement of pieces on a chessboard from memory. On some trials the pieces were arranged at random; on other trials the arrangement was taken from an actual game. The two groups performed equally poorly on the random trials. But the chess masters' memories were far superior on the game-like arrangements. This is hardly surprising: one assumes that chess masters have stored innumerable game plans in memory.

But suppose that the chess masters were only 10 years old and the amateurs were college students. One might assume that in this case, age and cognitive maturity would override experience. They do not. Micheline Chi (1978) repeated the chess experiment with 10-year-olds who were competing in a chess tournament and college students who were chess amateurs. She found that the young chess masters not only outperformed the college students, they also were more accurate in predicting how many

trials they would need to reconstruct the arrangements. Thus the youngsters had better memory and better metamemory in their area of expertise than did the older, presumably wiser, but "nonexpert" college subjects. To be sure that she had not accidentally chosen college students with poor memories, Chi also compared their recall of a series of random numbers. On these tests, the adults "won." (See Figure 9-8.)

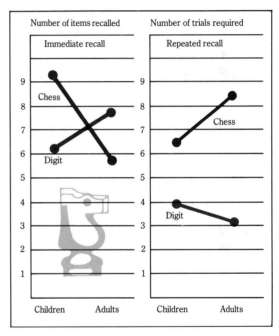

Figure 9-8 Knowledge and Memory: The Chess Test   Chi's experiment demonstrated that knowledge and experience have as much influence on memory as age. Chi asked children who were tournament-level chess players and college students who were chess amateurs to recall the positions of chess pieces on a board and lists of random numbers. The college students outperformed the youngsters on digit recall. On the chess test, however, the young champions recalled more items than the college students did, and required fewer trials to memorize the board.
(Chi, 1978)

Insight

COMPUTER LITERACY

The "computer age" is no longer a fantasy of science fiction writers, even for children. Estimates are that there are at least 300,000 microcomputers, and perhaps 650,000, in classrooms in the United States (Benderson, 1983).

Computers may be used in one of three ways in the classroom. The first is as a tutor. The program presents the child with material, asks the child to respond, then evaluates the response. Computer-aided instruction is similar to using a workbook, with the addition of instant feedback. A sophisticated version asks a student to read a passage, indicate which statements are fact and which opinion, identify hypotheses, and determine whether the author has proven his or her case. Second, computers may be used as tools—for word processing, calculation, even musical composition. Simulation programs fall into this category. For example, a program called *Odell Lake* teaches ecology by casting the student in the role of a rainbow trout that must find food and avoid predators and other dangers in a North American lake. A trout who makes the wrong decision dies. But as in nature, good decisions only increase the odds of survival. Even a smart trout may run into bad luck (Hassett, 1984). Other simulation programs allow chemistry students to simulate experiments that are too dangerous or expensive to perform in the lab. Third, computers may be used to teach programming. Ideally, the effort to program the machine forces the child to master the subject matter. The child becomes the tutor and the computer, the tutee.

Seymour Papert of MIT's Artificial Intelligence Laboratory is one of the leading spokesmen for the third use.

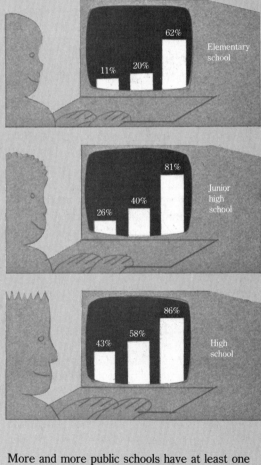

More and more public schools have at least one microcomputer. (Hassett, 1984)

In many schools today, the phrase "computer-aided instruction" means making the computer teach the child. One might say the *computer is being used to program* the child. In my vision, *the child programs the computer* and, in doing so, both acquires a sense of mastery over a piece of the most modern and powerful technology and establishes an intimate contact with some of the deepest ideas from science, from mathematics, and from the art of intellectual model building. (1980, p. 5)

Papert's enthusiasm for computers is based in part on the five years he spent working with Piaget in Geneva. He maintains that programming fosters "Piagetian learning," or learning without being taught.

Papert and his MIT colleagues developed a computer language called LOGO that provides children with a Turtle (either a robot that works on the floor or a light on the computer screen) and commands for moving the Turtle around in space. He claims that LOGO enables youngsters to use their own "body geometry" to discover principles of higher mathematics. For example, the child who wants to draw a square paces a square on the floor, instructs the Turtle to perform the same movements, and discovers that a square is composed of four equal sides. The important point is that the child learns by doing. Papert believes that programming can make formal operations (the most advanced stage of cognitive development in Piaget's theory) both concrete and personal. A child who can program would have little difficulty figuring out all the possible color combinations of beads of assorted colors—a skill Piaget thought developed only in adolescence (see Chapter 14). Papert's hope is that programming with LOGO will not only accelerate development, but overcome widespread "mathophobia."

Critics argue that using computers in elementary school is, at best, overkill. Children do not need sophisticated, expensive equipment to learn to add and subtract, read and write. Moreover, most adults who work with computers do not need to know how to program. There is a "user friendly" (easy to learn) program for almost everything today. Perhaps tomorrow's

adults need to be intelligent consumers of computer software (the programs). But to require students to learn how to program is like requiring every person who wants to learn to drive a car to study engineering. At worst, critics argue, computers may foster a tendency to erase rather than revise, a compulsion for total accuracy, and a lust for control (Howard Gardner, in Hanson, 1983). Computers may accentuate social class differences by dividing the nation's children into two classes: computer literates, whose schools can afford to purchase equipment and train teachers; and computer illiterates, whose schools cannot afford these things. They may also accentuate sex differences: Boys are drawn to computers while girls often shy away from machines, particularly in high school. Computers may create social isolates (the "computer freak" who spends hours alone at the keyboard).

A comprehensive study published by Johns Hopkins University (Becker, in press) suggests that computers have little impact on learning. There is little evidence that programming enhances logical thinking, as Papert and others claim, or that computer-assisted learning accelerates or improves the acquisition of specific skills. One reason may be that most schools use computers for drill-and-practice routines that are little different from the workbooks they imitate, and not for more challenging activities such as simulation.

Although computers may not improve learning, they do seem to boost motivation. Given the chance, many youngsters come to school early or stay late to "play" with different programs. And studies of both elementary school children (Hawkins, Scheingold, Gearhart, & Berger, 1982) and preschoolers (Hanson, 1983) indicate that computers increase rather than decrease sociability. Youngsters talk about their work and collaborate more often when they are using computers than when they are engaged in other classroom activities. Often the computer becomes a "social station," where youngsters gather to observe and advise. In short, classroom computers have not realized the dreams of some psychologists and educators, but neither have they produced the educational nightmares others imagined.

Problem-solving Skills

Improvements in memory and attention alone do not explain the intellectual revolution of middle childhood. As Piaget observed, a child's approach to problems becomes increasingly systematic, inventive, and successful in this stage. But what precisely is it about the child's thought processes that changes? To answer this question we turn to the learning laboratory.

Learning experiments provide clear evidence of a 5-to-7 shift. Consider the *transposition problem* (Stevenson, 1970) (see Figure 9-9). In the training phase, the child is shown two circles, A and B, one larger than the other, and is asked to choose one. If he picks the larger circle, B, he is rewarded. The training phase ends when he has been conditioned to pick the larger circle on every trial. In the test phase, the smaller circle, A, is replaced by a third, still larger circle, C. Which circle does the child select now? According to learning theory, the child should pick circle B—the one he has been rewarded for in the past. Most 3- to-5-year-old children do choose circle B. But 6- and 7-year-old children pick circle C. Apparently they decide that the right answer in the training phase was "the larger one" and *transpose* their rule to the new set of circles.

One of the first psychologists to recognize this 5-to-7 shift was Margaret Kuenne (1946). Because younger children are not capable of verbalizing a relationship such as *larger than,* Kuenne reasoned, they are bound more to the absolute physical properties of the circles. Hence, they choose the *physically* identical circle in the test phase. Older, school-age children recognize a relationship between the two circles in the training phase and can verbalize that relation ("larger than"). This verbal cue guides their performance when confronted with a new stimulus in the test phase. Kuenne held that the older child's behavior is regulated by language—by the ability to identify and label the physical relationship between stimuli. When the child uses a naming strategy to label relationships between stimuli, he is employing a *verbal mediating response.* By generating concepts and applying verbal cues or mediators, the child recodes the stimulus world in symbolic form in his mind, and these symbols direct his behavior.

Howard and Tracy Kendler (1962, 1970) devised another test of the verbal mediating re-

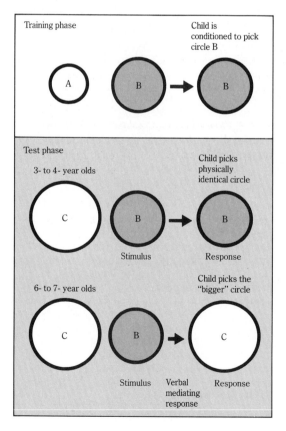

Figure 9-9 Responses to the Transposition Problem

sponse, called the *reversal/nonreversal task* (see Figure 9-10). In the training phase, the child is presented with pairs of stimuli that differ in two dimensions: brightness (red or white) and size (large or small). The child is rewarded for picking the red shape, regardless of size. Then, without warning, the rules are changed. In the test phase, right answers became wrong answers and vice versa. There are two variations in the test phase. In one, the child is rewarded for selecting the white shape, regardless of size. This is called the *reversal shift*, because the same dimension is relevant (brightness) but the correct response (white) is the reverse of what it was before (red). In the second variation, the child is rewarded for choosing the larger shape, regardless of color. This is called the *nonreversal shift*, because responses to the original dimension (brightness) are irrelevant. The new, correct dimension is size.

There are clear age differences in the way children respond to this task. Preschoolers (3- to 4-year-olds) find the nonreversal shift easier; first-graders and older children find the reversal shift easier (Kendler & Kendler, 1970). It seems that preschoolers do not learn a general rule (*Pick the red ones*) in the training phase. Rather, they remember which answers were correct: large red one, small red one. On the nonreversal shift, they have to learn only one new answer: the large white one. The reversal shift is harder for them because they have to learn *two* new responses: the large white one, the small white one.

The older children devised a rule in the training phase: *Pick the red ones, not the white ones.* All they have to do on the reversal shift is to revise the rule: *Now pick the white ones,* or *Do the opposite.* Verbal mediation makes this simple. Faced with the nonreversal shift, however, the child who has trained herself to focus on brightness must, first, change her basic approach (*Now pay attention to size and ignore brightness*) and, second, generate a new rule (*Pick the larger one*). This double twist takes more time and effort to accomplish. Words get in her way temporarily.

Although limited in content to only black and white shapes, these experiments illustrate one of the major changes in middle childhood. The

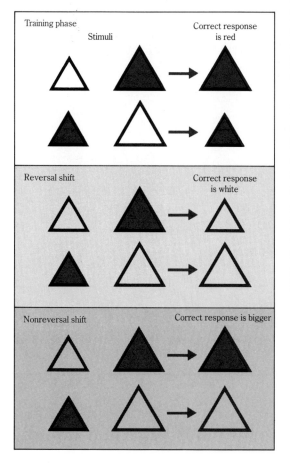

Figure 9-10 The Reversal/Nonreversal Shift

child is using concepts embedded in language—*bigger* and *smaller, light* and *dark,* and *opposite*—to generate rules and to solve problems.

The Child's Everyday World

Laboratory studies of problem solving, memory, attention, and Piagetian tasks are not the only evidence of a 5-to-7 shift. Children "volunteer" evidence by the questions they ask adults, the games they play with one another, and their jokes and riddles.

Asking Questions

Curiosity is an adaptive trait. It leads children (or other animals) to explore and learn about the environment. (Of course, curiosity might lead a small baboon into the jaws of a leopard, or a child to a jar of poisonous cleaning fluid as well as to positive learning experiences.) Children are curious at all ages, but the nature of their investigations changes with development. The infant physically searches his world, exploring shapes, colors, and textures. Preschoolers and

The ability to use computers to solve problems, or to play games, draws on all of the cognitive skills described here: attention, memory, transpositions, and reversals.

older children continue to use their eyes, ears, and hands, but they add verbal inquiries to their explorations. Through spontaneous questioning, the young child not only exercises his curiosity but gives us access to his reasoning and logical activity (Berlyne, 1970). We can learn a lot about children from the questions they ask.

The study of children's questions goes back to the early days of child development. Studying the plentiful collections of questions uttered by children in the course of their daily activities, Piaget (1928) and others differentiated two phases in the nature of children's interrogations about the world around them. The first phase begins about the age of 18 months, when the child has discovered that everything has a name. The child wants to learn *what* objects are called and *where* things are placed. Around the age of 3, the second phase is initiated, characterized by an abundance of *why*-questions and *when*-questions.

The earliest why-questions seem to be expressions of amazement at discovering the unusual (surprise) or frustration at not being able to pursue an activity or object. Apparently these earliest why-questions do not call for answers; sometimes, in fact, the child answers them himself (Berlyne, 1970). Later, the child's why-questions seem to be directed to adults with the hope of receiving an explanation of something. Yet, the child's questions and reactions to answers reflect precausal thought, characteristic of the preschool child (see Chapter 6). Interestingly, it appears that only a small percentage of questions that pass between children are "whys." School-age children evidently reserve causality as the subject of conversation between themselves and adults. Adults can be counted on to have the answers.

Aside from studying the natural spontaneity of children's questions, investigators have also studied questioning by school-age children using

procedures that invite questions. Yamamoto (1962) gave more than 800 children and adolescents between the ages of 6 and 18 an Ask-and-Guess test. The youngsters were instructed to ask as many questions as possible about what they saw in a picture illustrating a familiar nursery rhyme. With age, the number of questions asked tended to increase. Why-questions were the most common, but their incidence dropped after age 9, and what-questions became more frequent. Aikawa and Horiuchi (1962) solicited why-questions from grade school children. The mean number of questions generated reached a peak in grade six (age 11) and then declined. Why-questions about human life increased with age while questions about objects, animals, and plants gradually decreased. Why-questions regarding natural phenomena rose from grades two through four and then declined. Boys asked more why-questions about "heavenly bodies" (the celestial kind) than did girls, who tended to ask more questions about animals and plants.

Other investigators (Zaporozhets & El' Konin, 1964) found that questions are important in directing thinking. Children confronted with practical tasks or problems such as the failure of a toy to work are likely to generate questions about causes: "If this toy car doesn't move, something is wrong. Why isn't it going the way it's supposed to? How do I get it to work?" These questions influence how the child solves a problem. They steer his thoughts in a definite direction and guide his behavior toward a correct solution or course of action. The school-age child, confronted with such practical tasks, is more likely to raise questions that force him to look for causes and to try to "put things right" in an organized way.

As we might expect, the ability to formulate questions that direct behavior in the face of concrete problems (removing candy from a jar, getting a stereo to work) comes earlier than the ability to pose questions in the face of more abstract problems requiring logical inferences. Yet during the school years children are readily able to pose "why" and "how" questions to solve a variety of more complex problems. This ability reflects their expanded cognitive powers.

The Games Children Play

The games children play with one another also change in middle childhood. Hide-and-seek and tag are still popular, but as youngsters become cognitively more mature they are attracted by cognitively more challenging games (Sutton-Smith, 1967). We might not think of baseball or soccer as "intellectual" games. But to play either sport—even badly—the child must under-

stand a complex set of rules. (Try explaining baseball to a foreign visitor who has never seen the game!) To play *well* requires a youngster to develop a game plan, to hold alternative strategies in her mind, to be aware of what other players are doing, and more. Sedentary games—checkers, card games, and word games such as Scrabble—are popular because they offer opportunities for mastery. The child must draw on a wide repertoire of cognitive skills, including attention to detail (the placement of checkers on the board), hypothesis testing ("If I move my man here, he will jump me"), memory (recalling the rules or the cards already on the table), and verbal fluency (in word games).

There are two important differences between the make-believe of younger children and the organized games of older children. First, in make-believe the rules are flexible. Participants are free to change the "plot" of their fantasy, or even to change roles if they wish. Organized games are played by the rules. Rules dictate which roles individuals play and how the game itself will be played. They can only be changed if all participants agree to do so. Second, in make-believe children play for the sheer enjoyment of playing. Competition is minimal; there are no winners or losers. Organized games, in contrast, are goal-oriented—and in most games the aim is to win.

Piaget predicted (1962) that interest in make-believe declines in the late preoperational stage, and interest in organized games picks up when the child is firmly established in the concrete operational stage. In general, research

Changes in the games children play are a sign of cognitive advances, as well as social and emotional development. Preschoolers' games are free-form, improvised, and often messy. In middle childhood children like games with a goal.

supports this (Eifermann, 1971; Hetherington, Cox, & Cox, 1979; Rubin & Krasnor, 1980).

Whether they take place in the school yard or at a game table, organized games require player cooperation as well as cognitive abilities. Because they are social as well as intellectual enterprises, we will look at games again in Chapter 11, when we examine social development in middle childhood.

Tickling the Funny Bone

Humor is another sign of the child's cognitive advances. What children find funny changes with age. In a quite serious consideration of the topic, Paul McGhee (1979) suggests why: We laugh at situations that violate our expectations. Children will not find something incongruous, and therefore funny, until they understand "the way things are." Humor is a cognitive pleasure.[1]

McGhee traces four stages in the development of humor (1979). In stage 1 (roughly 10 to 24 months) children are tickled by *incongruous actions* toward objects. Sucking a cloth as if it were a bottle, or talking into a block as if it were a telephone, is an infant's idea of a great joke. His humor consists of manipulating objects in a silly way—that is, in a way he knows to be at odds with reality.

In stage 2 (about ages 2 to 4) children are amused by applying *incongruous labels* to objects and events. This is the age when children are learning to talk, and once they have grasped the correct labels for things they delight in misusing them. For example, at 27 months Piaget's daughter Jacqueline pointed to a stone.

"It's a dog."
"Where's its head?"

[1]Indeed, the ability to comprehend humor is used on the *Stanford-Binet Intelligence Scale* (1973), in a section called "Verbal Absurdities." Typical items for an 8-year-old child are: "A man had the flu twice. The first time it killed him, but the second time he got well quickly" and "Walter now has to write with his left hand because two years ago he lost both his arms in an accident" (p. 90).

"There" (a lump in the stone).
"And its eyes?"
"They're gone."

Children in this stage think it is hilarious to tell a boy "You're a girl" (and vice versa). They also enjoy distorting words (calling a shoe a "poo" or a "floo") and inventing impossible names ("Mrs. Fool-around" or "Johnny-out-in-the-Grass").

In stage 3 (about ages 3 to 6) children add *conceptual incongruity* to their jokes. They have begun to understand that words refer to classes of objects or events and to learn the defining characteristics of those concepts. Whereas a stage 2 child thinks it is funny to call a cat "doggie," a stage 3 child goes into peals of laughter over a cartoon of a cat with three tails or one eye, or a dog that goes *moo* instead of *whuff*. A stage 2 child finds calling a ball a "pumpkin" a joke; a stage 3 child laughs at a ball that exclaims "ouch" when kicked. Rhyming ("itsy, bitsy, mitsy, pitsy") and nonwords ("lorkel," "vorp," "zwimpy") are also favorites. Note the perceptual bent in these jokes: The child laughs when things look or sound incongruous.

In stage 4 (ages 7 or 8 on) *multiple meanings* (or puns) become a prime source of amusement, and the child's humor begins to resemble an adult's. The child has discovered that the same word can have different meanings in different contexts.

"Hey, did you take a bath?"
"No, is one missing?"

"Order! Order in the court!"
"Ham and cheese on rye, your honor."

Younger children often laugh at these jokes, but for the wrong reasons. They find "Silence! Silence in the court!"/"Ham and cheese on rye" just as funny.

In each of these jokes, a word is presented in one way, then used in another way.

The same is true in riddles, a favorite form of humor in middle childhood.

> "What is black and white and red all over?"
> "A newspaper or an embarrassed skunk or a dalmation with measles."

To understand these jokes, the child must perform the same kinds of operations required on Piagetian tasks. He has to backtrack, comparing the two lines (reversibility). And he has to understand that the same word can have two meanings (much as the same clay can form a ball or a sausage). McGhee cites an old joke that violates the principle of conservation:

> A man went into a restaurant and ordered a whole pizza for dinner. The waiter asked if he wanted it cut into six or eight slices. The man replied, "Oh, better make it six. I could never eat eight!"

McGhee adds that the 7- or 8-year-old's enjoyment of riddles may reflect her experience in school. In school, when a teacher asks a question, he knows the answer. If the child is forced to guess or gives the wrong answer, she is embarrassed or worse. (This experience is repeated many times each day.) With riddles, the tables are turned. The child asks the question and knows the answer; the other person is in the hot seat.

Reading frees a child to explore new worlds and areas of special interest at her own pace.

First Grade

Formal education systems in Western and other cultures recognize the 5-to-7 shift. A child may have attended day-care, nursery school, and kindergarten; but school becomes serious business in first grade. Equipped with newly acquired motor controls, cognitive skills, language abilities, and social competencies, the child launches her academic career.

Children continue to make qualitative advances in cognitive capacities after ages 5, 6, and 7. But they make even more startling *quantitative* leaps in the acquisition of knowledge during the school years. Most school-age children have a natural fascination with how things work

and why natural phenomena occur. Their interest in stars and planets, dinosaurs and cavemen and -women is matched by their need to know why seeds grow into plants and how coal, gasoline, and light are converted into energy. Curiosity about the changing seasons, the processes of birth and death, and life beneath the ocean provides the incentive for new learning. At its best, school provides a host of opportunities for the young learner to stretch her cognitive skills and become more knowledgeable about her world.

Acquiring general knowledge is a central part of the child's education. Advances in cognition make learning and comprehending new

Individual differences in intelligence and motivation become more apparent in middle childhood.

Insight

SCHOOL DAZE:
HYPERACTIVITY

Hyperactivity is the single most common reason why children are referred to clinical psychologists in the United States today. About 6 percent of American schoolchildren are affected. The ratio of boys to girls may be as high as 9:1, or 90 percent boys (Ross & Ross, 1982).*

Hyperactive children perform poorly in school, in spite of average or above-average IQs. They are described as restless, inattentive, distractible, impulsive, explosive, and inappropriate in behavior. In a word, the hyperactive child is a nuisance.

Diane McGuinness (1985) analyzes seven common myths about hyperactivity. (1) *Hyperactivity is a new disease.* On the contrary, Thomas Edison and Winston Churchill, among others, were uncontrollable as children (Goertzel & Goertzel, 1962). What is new is that highly active children are seen as suffering from a disorder that should be treated through psychotherapy or drugs, rather than paddling and expulsion from school. (2) *There is a "normal" child* (in terms of activity level). Judgments of hyperactivity are based on unspoken assumptions about the activity level and attention span of the typical 4- or 8-year-old. In fact, children in any age group vary widely. (3) *Hyperactivity can be diagnosed.* The hyperactive child feels good and has no physical or neurological symptoms. "Diagnosis" is based only on the subjective evaluations of teachers and parents. (4) *Hyperactivity can strike anyone.* It is primarily a male problem, as noted earlier. (5) *The hyperactive child is immature.* On standard measures of ability and achievement these children usually score in the normal range, and sometimes above the average. (6) *Distractibility is bad.* Under many circumstances, parents and professionals consider curiosity, and the desire to experiment and experience, positive characteristics. (7) *Hyperactive children have no opinion.* Indeed, very little *is* known about what these children

think or feel, what they like to do, or whether they consider their own behavior a problem. One study, which reported that hyperactive boys felt depressed and worthless, was conducted several years after the children had been stigmatized as problem children. McGuinness characterizes hyperactivity as "a diagnosis in search of a patient." Determining whether a child is hyperactive is difficult because the disorder or syndrome is defined so vaguely.

What distinguishes children who have been diagnosed as hyperactive from other children? McGuinness begins her review of the research with studies of activity levels. Some neurological disorders (such as Parkinson's disease) and psychological disorders (such as manic psychosis) create uncontrollable, pathological activity. But hyperactive children's behavior does not fall into this category. The main difference between them and other enthusiastic children is that their behavior is situationally or socially inappropriate. Measures of attention span usually do not distinguish between interest, motivation, and the inability to pay attention. McGuinness concludes that children diagnosed as hyperactive are impulsive, but no more so than other children who are considered normal. They are different from other youngsters mainly because they are less willing to do whatever adults ask them to do, and less willing to persist at a task they find uninteresting. Physiological measures of hyperactive children (measures of skin conductance, heart rate, and brain waves) have produced inconsistent findings.

In some cases children are diagnosed as hyperactive because they respond to amphetamines or Ritalin, much as psychotic patients may be diagnosed as manic-depressive because they respond to lithium. These drugs are stimulants that have the effect of calming hyperactive children. The children's concentration improves, although learning may not.

Prescribing drugs for children is controversial. Side effects include insomnia, loss of appe-

*See "Math Gap" in Chapter 14 for another sex-linked learning disorder.

tite, and irritability. Moreover, the drugs are used as diagnostic tools even though no one knows whether they have the same effect on all children. This is because researchers do not use children as subjects in drug experiments.

McGuinness considers the use of drugs for this problem wrong. She suggests that so-called hyperactive children are the victims of an "epidemic" created by drug companies and the media, and accepted by teachers and parents who welcome a medical explanation of a child's misbehavior. In her view most of these children are not sick or bad; they are just boys. Not all psychologists agree with her. Many believe that the label hyperactive is overused. The American Psychiatric Association includes in its diagnostic, however, a label of *attention deficit disorder* (ADA) *with hyperactivity.*

facts possible; the demands of school, in turn, push the child to develop her cognitive skills. Learning to read is crucial.

READERS AND NONREADERS A young child acquires information by asking "What's this?" and "What's that?" An older child can acquire information more efficiently by reading. The printed word has many obvious advantages over the spoken word. The written record allows a culture to retain information about its traditions, history, philosophies, and technology in a way that surpasses human recall. A Chinese proverb says it well: "The palest ink is better than the best memory." The child who can read has access to a vast legacy of cultural knowledge. He can explore areas of special interest, indulge his fantasies, travel, explore, learn about the lives of his heroes. He can move at his own pace, reading and rereading material he finds difficult to comprehend and remember. Reading well is essential to success in school.

Unfortunately, a large number of children—between 10 and 20 percent of schoolchildren in the United States—have difficulties with reading. *Reading disability,* sometimes called dyslexia or "word blindness," is a failure to read at a normal age level that does not result from mental retardation, major brain injury, or severe emotional instability (Gibson & Levin, 1975). Disabled readers seem unable to move beyond the word level. They do not recognize common words they have been exposed to many times, and they make the same errors over and over. They have great difficulty understanding printed material and may have problems writing and spelling as well (Morrison & Manis, 1982). Boys are at least three times as likely as girls to have problems with reading. More than 75 percent of the children in remedial reading classes are male (McGuinness, 1985).

Studies of children with reading disabilities provide indirect evidence of the accomplishment of ordinary children who progress normally in their reading from picture books to "Dick and Jane," simple stories, novels, history texts (not to mention comic books) during the years. Frederick Morrison and Franklin Manis (1982) see reading disability as the result of a chain of failures. The problem begins when a child has difficulty grasping spelling-to-sound correspondences (that is, linking a letter or group of letters to a pronunciation). Spelling-to-sound correspondences are governed by rules (such as $b = $ /b/ and $f = $ /ph/. Pronunciation can depend on the position of a letter in a word, on surrounding letters (*hat* vs. *heat*), or on such things as silent markers (the terminal *e* that changes *pin* to *pine*). The child must learn the rules and the exceptions to the rules, especially in English, a language that has many irregularities. By third or fourth grade, most children are able to pronounce pseudowords such as "cabe" or "prine," which they have never seen before, with ease. Disabled readers find this exceedingly difficult.

A child's failure to master spelling-to-sound correspondences makes it difficult for him to take the next step in learning to read: decoding words for meaning. The accomplished reader has developed rapid, automatic decoding skills. He leaps from the written word to sound and sense without thinking about what he is doing. The good reader is not frightened by unfamiliar words; the poor reader is. When spelling-to-sound translation is effortful and slow, word recognition suffers. One might draw an analogy between the poor reader and an adult who performs long division (9863 ÷ 37 = 266.56756) with paper and pencil. The process is painfully slow and subject to error. Like the adult who has a calculator in her hand, the good reader decodes words in split seconds.

Failure to develop rapid word processing makes it all but impossible for the child to develop the scanning strategies and inferential skills to extract meaning from a text. Comprehension and recall of written material suffer as a result. The disabled reader devotes so much mental energy and processing space to lower-order operations (sound-to-sense correspondences and word decoding) that he has little left for these higher-order operations. Morrison and Manis suggest that if disabled readers seem to have poor attention spans or poor memories, it may be because they rarely progress as far as the meaning. To use an old cliché, the words on the page might as well be Greek. It is as though the child were reading a foreign language.

Analysis of what disabled readers have trouble doing underscores what good readers accomplish. Learning regular and irregular spelling-to-sound correspondences, developing rapid and automatic word recognition, and acquiring the sophisticated processing skills to extract meaning from a text is no small accomplishment.

Learning to read is only one of the challenges of middle childhood. The school environment, the peer group, and the child's family pose new socioemotional tasks. She will be required to use her intelligence in many different settings. Before considering the social and emotional tasks of middle childhood, we will look at intelligence and creativity in Chapter 10.

SUMMARY

1. The intellectual revolution of middle childhood is in part a biological phenomenon. The development of cross-modal zones in the brain lays the foundation for the changes in memory, learning, skill, and motivation that White labeled "the 5-to-7 shift."

2. According to Piaget, thinking becomes more logical in the concrete operational stage. The child is able to manipulate and transform information in her mind (or operate on information). She uses this ability to discover orderly, lawful relationships among objects and events in the real world.

3. Milestones of the concrete operational stage include: *conservation,* which requires the child to decenter attention, reserve his thoughts, and consider functional relationships and transformations; *classification,* which depends on understanding how relationships among things create classes and subclasses; and *seriation,* which involves logical ordering, a grasp of reciprocal relationships, and transitive inferences (realizing that if A is greater than B, and B greater than C, A must be greater than C).

4. Piaget held that concrete operations always develop in the same order. Research supports the sequence of developments he described, but suggests that progress from one stage to the next may vary among children and cultures, and that some cognitive skills can be taught.

5. Information processing becomes more efficient in this period. School-age children pay selective attention to relevant information (incidental learning declines).

6. Memory improves as school-age children learn new memory strategies (rehearsal, organization, elaboration), develop metamemory, and widen their knowledge base.

7. School-age children are able to transpose rules and reverse strategies in solving problems, in part because they are able to verbalize relationships (the verbal mediating response).

8. The intellectual revolution of middle childhood is not confined to scientific and mathematical problems. The questions children ask reveal a new interest in how things work.

9. In their play, children shift from make-believe to organized games with rules.

10. Their sense of humor develops, from hilarity at incongruous actions and labels, to laughter at mixed-up concepts, to an appreciation of multiple meanings (or puns).

11. The major intellectual challenge of first grade is learning to read. Studies of disabled readers show that this accomplishment depends on mastering spelling-to-sound correspondences, developing rapid and accurate word decoding, and acquiring sophisticated techniques for extracting meaning from printed material and remembering what one read.

FURTHER READING

Boehm, A. E., & White, M. A. (1982). *The parents' handbook on school testing.* New York: Teachers College Press. This handy guide provides parents with accurate information about school testing.

Farnham-Diggory, S. (1979). *Learning disabilities.* Cambridge, MA: Harvard University Press. Excellent discussion of learning disabilities by a cognitive psychologist.

Hobbs, N. (1975). *The future of children.* San Francisco, CA: Jossey-Bass. An important book that carefully discusses the problems with categorizing and labeling atypical children.

McGhee, P. E. (1979). *Humor: Its origin and development.* San Francisco, CA: W. H. Freeman. Children's humor and its changes over development make for interesting reading.

Papert, S. (1980). *Mindstorms: Children, computers, and powerful ideas.* New York: Basic Books. This book introduces LOGO, a computer language that enables children to program computers and become involved in the technology. The book has been viewed as revolutionary in its exploration of computers as a learning tool.

John H. Flavell
Professor of Psychology,
Stanford University

ANN LEVINE: Dr. Flavell, what made you decide to become a psychologist?

JOHN H. FLAVELL: Like many people, I went through a series of undergraduate majors. When I went to Northeastern University, I planned to be a chemistry major. But I found college chemistry much harder than high school chemistry. I said to myself, what's the next best thing? Premed. So I became a chemistry-biology major. Then I took an introductory psychology course, which I found very easy compared to all of those hard courses in biology. So I took more psychology—experimental, child (a dull course, actually), social. By the very end of college I had given up premed and decided to go to graduate school in clinical psychology. I applied around and was accepted at Harvard and Clark. Harvard couldn't offer me money, Clark could, so I went there and got my Ph.D. in clinical psychology. This was in the early 1950s, 1951 to 1955.

AL: The emphasis in clinical programs is on applied psychology. Did you plan to become a therapist?

JHF: I didn't quite know what I wanted to do, I just thought clinical was interesting. Well, Clark University was heavily developmental at that time. (To some extent, it still is.) Heinz Werner, one of the first psychologists to develop a theory of cognitive development, was there. He became my teacher and mentor. Because of him I read a little bit about Piaget, which you wouldn't have done at most American universities then, and learned something about European developmental psychology. I did all of the clinical background work too, of course. And I ended up doing my doctoral dissertation on something quasi-developmental. The subject was schizophrenic thinking, viewed from the standpoint of Heinz Werner's developmental theory. The problem wasn't what any one of us would call developmental today. I didn't study kids at all. But studying with Werner had colored my thinking.

My first job was as a clinical psychologist at a tiny VA hospital in the middle of Colorado. I'd been there about nine months when I got a call from someone at the University of Rochester. He said, "The people at Clark think you'd do well here. Do you want a job?" And I said, "Sure." That was it! So I went to Rochester and stayed ten years. Because I had been at Clark, they thought I could teach child psychology. They didn't have anyone else who could. I taught undergraduate and graduate courses in developmental psych. I also taught clinical psychology and had a clinical practice with college students. But I got more and more interested in cognitive development and started doing all of my research in that area. I wrote a book on Piaget, who still wasn't very well known in the United States. Then, in 1965, a straight developmental job came along at the University of Minnesota. I gave up clinical work at that point. Since then, I've been identified completely with developmental psychology.

AL: You are one of the people who brought Piaget to the attention of American psychologists. Before the publication of your book, *The Developmental Psychology of Jean Piaget* [1963], many people thought of him as an obscure Swiss philosopher—if they thought of him at all. What was it about Piaget's work that you found so exciting, so revolutionary?

JHF: Piaget opened our eyes to the possibility that children think in a different way than adults do. Many people had tested kids and found that they don't do as well as adults on this or that test. But they didn't take the next step; they didn't ask themselves why kids think differently, what are the underlying processes. Piaget was fond of saying that he studied children's errors rather than their successes because they revealed something about the quality of the child's thought. He wasn't interested in how many items they got right on a straight IQ test, which is what most psychologists were focusing on long after Piaget began his work in the 1920s.

AL: Freud analyzed adults' slips of the tongue; Piaget analyzed children's errors.

JHF: That's right. In a sense, both Freud and Piaget looked at people's shortcomings and what they tell you about how people think and feel. But Piaget wasn't fixated on errors. He was interested in what we now call "information processing." He tried to analyze the way children thought. And he had the idea that, in many respects and on many topics, children think in a way that is qualitatively different from adult thinking. His work was aimed at showing developmental changes in how children think. *Qualitative* changes. And that was revolutionary.

Piaget ranks with Freud as someone who made an enormous difference by having lived, one of the movers and shakers. He really created the field of cognitive development. It didn't exist before. If he or someone like him hadn't come along, we wouldn't be having this interview and your textbook would be entirely different.

AL: Yet many psychologists whose work is reported in our text have challenged Piaget's descriptions of how children think at different ages and his notion of stages. How well do you think Piaget's theory has held up under research?

JHF: That's complicated to answer. One way of saying it is, first Piaget laid out the problems for us, creating a field out of nothing. He asked the questions and gave some answers. He attracted people to the field and built this enterprise. Then the inevitable process of revision begins. It happens in every science. People start working with a theory and they find what is exactly right and what isn't quite right. Some things go up and others go down.

In a certain sense research has clearly supported Piaget's observations. Piaget often would discover something with a few subjects. If you try it with a lot of subjects you get about the same results. That's an important plus. The conservation tasks, for example, really do work out—even the infancy tasks which Piaget only tried on his own three kids. These turn out to be very replicable when you're dealing with twenty, thirty, forty kids. Obviously Piaget had great intuitions.

But in many cases it turns out that kids actually understand the basic processes earlier than Piaget thought. His tests were drawn out of his head, and he tended to err on the conservative side. Suppose I am interested in whether you can do A. I want to be certain that you grasp A, so I give you a task that demands you to do B, C, and D also. If you flunk B, C, and D, I might think you don't have A. I think that a lot of Piaget's tasks are like that—heavy on performance demands that may be extrinsic to what you are after. It is a harder test than you need to create. With hindsight, we feel that Piaget underestimated what young children can do with their heads.

Other people came along and stripped Piaget's tasks down to the essential task: a simple but fair test, a *child-fair* test. Piaget believed that at age six, seven, or eight, children develop what he called concrete thinking, but you find some pieces of evidence for it down at age three, four, and five. Take conservation of number. You show the child four things here and four things there, then bunch one row up or spread one row out and ask if they are still the same. If you only use a small number of things, a four- or five-year-old can solve the problem, as though she were at the conservational level. But if you present the same problem with a large number of items, she gets confused. To you or me it would be immaterial. But the child may try to count them or do something else that throws her off. So kids may show conservation for small numbers earlier than they do for large numbers. Now, that seems sort of strange if the child really has the principle of conservation.

Here is the tricky part. Everybody says Piaget underestimated what preschool kids can do. Gelman showed this; I guess I did too. But what is it exactly that they have and don't have? Why are they limited by the context? How do you characterize somebody who can do X but can't do it very well or do it generally? What's the true story? Piaget left us a legacy, a problem of trying to characterize in just the right way, the theoretically revealing way, what it is that kids do and do not have. And we're still wrestling with it!

AL: Is this where the information-processing model comes in?

JHF: Yes. The basic idea behind information processing is that we are constrained in the kinds of thinking we can do by our computing apparatus (even if you don't think of the apparatus as being like an actual computer). The emphasis is on real time, getting your head together, and solving a problem without losing things out of memory and attention. Memory and attention create bottlenecks. This is easy to show with adults. I can present you with a problem that floods your memory resources. You can't hold all the information you need in your head at the same time, so your performance goes to pot.

This may account for the differences between children and adults. A lot of psychologists believe that the problem may be not that the child lacks a logical skill (à la Piaget), but rather that the tasks are overwhelming the child with just too much information. Analogies show this. The task is, A is to B as C is to D, E, or X. The answer, of course, is D. Now, to solve an analogy you have to think about the relation of A to B and the relation of C to D, and also the relation of A/B to C/D—the double relation. You have to hold all of that in your head at once. Most adults can do this to some extent. Kids do very poorly on analogies, unless they are very simple. But most adolescents can handle them. Analogies may require a child to juggle too much information.

AL: If you accept an information-processing model of children's cognitive limitations, doesn't the question become "Why doesn't a child have the same memory and attention capacities as an adult?"

JHF: Exactly. And here there are competing explanations. The simplest and most straightforward explanation is that as you grow older, the size of the "memory box" increases physiologically. This is a maturational explanation. Just as

you get bigger and stronger, your ability to process information—even apart from experience—gets bigger and better.

The competing explanation is that if you really know a lot about an area—if you are expert at it—a problem in that area doesn't put as heavy demands on your processing capacity. If I give you familiar symbols to learn, like the letters in the alphabet, you can learn a lot of them. But if I give you unfamiliar symbols, you use up so much energy trying to encode them, you can't learn as many. If you have two people of about equal intelligence and one of them knows a lot about chess and the other doesn't, the image of a chess problem in their heads is much different. You know Michelene Chi's study, in which she compared chess experts with nonexperts. There wasn't any difference in their ability to remember illegitimate chess positions. But on legitimate positions, the experts were much better than the nonexperts. In this study the experts were ten-year-olds who had enrolled in a chess tournament, and the nonexperts were college students. The usual increase in memory with age was reversed.

There have been other studies like that one. Kids' ability to remember Sesame Street characters is excellent. When you get into the child's world, areas in which the child knows more and has more experience, the child's memory may be almost as good as the adult's. This doesn't mean that kids are the same as adults. But at least part of their memory deficit may be because they know much less about the world than adults do, much less about almost everything.

It's a very complicated problem; there's nothing simple about it. But you can see the different lines of reasoning. Both may be right; we really don't know. There may be a physiological increase in memory capacity. There is no reason why our "heads" shouldn't get bigger and stronger with age. But the other idea, which may be true instead of this or in addition to this, is that experience makes things memorable.

AL: What were your most memorable experiences as a researcher? What do you consider your most interesting and significant work?

JHF: Let's see. Clearly I'm proud of having done something with Piaget, even though I didn't know what it meant at the time. It was the right move at the right time, and I was lucky in doing that. The work I did on communication and role-taking in the early 1960s helped to bring social cognition into developmental research. And the work I did on memory development in the later 1960s I'm pretty sure was worth doing. Before that we didn't know what strategies kids were using—or not using—to help themselves remember. Studying strategies made that whole area more interesting. That led almost naturally to the idea of metamemory. Metamemory, broadly speaking, means knowing about memory; knowing memory strategies and when to use them. And this led to metacognition, being aware of your own "cognitive insides," which is something I think is important.

What I have been most interested in for the last couple of years, though, is the development of the appearance/reality distinction. This work is just beginning to be published. We repeated one of the experiments exactly, in its entirety, in the People's Republic of China. They replicated our study at the Peking Normal University nursery school, which is similar to the Stanford University nursery school, and got identical results across these two quite different cultures.

AL: Several times you've mentioned what psychologists don't know. Where are the frontiers in cognitive development today? What are the "big questions" that you would like to see answered?

JHF: I think one of the most important problems in cognitive development, one that people are just beginning to work on, is the really magical transformation of the infant around age one and a half or two. Obviously, babies have minds. They do what Piaget called sensorimotor thinking. But they don't use symbols. And they don't seem to have conscious memories. They think about what is in front of them, or inside them. By age two or thereabouts, the child is a completely different creature. We don't really know how or why this happens. Understanding more about the acquisition of symbolic thinking in little kids is clearly one of the major priorities. That's the really big question, the one for which you'd give the Nobel Prize if you could. The reason I say that is that it's interesting in itself and also, in my opinion, that it is the one change with age that is uncontrovertibly qualitative. The other changes in thinking that come after that, you can always argue, are due to more knowledge or expertise. But this is really an enormous leap.

AL: Would you go as far as saying that it is the leap that makes us human?

JHF: I think so. There is no question but that chimps and other primates can do some symbolic thinking. Where the boundaries are, I don't know. But by the time a kid is five or six years old, he has left the chimp behind. Clearly the whole gigantic venture in the symbolic is one of the things that makes us human. And the transition, the transformation, of the infant is one of the major understudied areas in the field. Not unstudied, but understudied.

Another big issue that we haven't quite settled concerns adult cognition. It is generally true that as people grow older, they get smarter, more sophisticated cognitively. But when you look closely at adults, you see all kinds of cognitive blunders and mistakes. There is a lot of evidence that people have biases in problem solving and gaps in their thinking. We haven't really identified the circumstances under which adults do things well and those in which they don't. How can you track development in children if you don't know where they are heading? The last stages of cognitive development are still problematic. So we have an early-stage problem, becoming symbolic at one and a half or two, and a late-stage problem.

A related issue is whether some kinds of thinking come more easily to us, because of our evolutionary history. A number of people believe that our thinking is not arbitrarily good or bad across different domains. Any animal, any given species, is better at doing some things than other things. It may well be that humans are also born with certain propensities so that some domains of cognition are better established than others. It's not just that human beings are smarter or dumber in some areas, but that they may deal with some cognitive tasks in a different way than they deal with others. Some may be prewired by evolution; others, not. Language is a prime example. There is something very special about language development. People are not all-purpose computers that can learn any language in any old way; I think that's wrong. Human beings are clearly tailored by evolution to learn a human language, and not another *kind* of language, such as bird songs. We all learn language, but we don't all learn to play chess. Chess isn't a species-specific ability. Just what are the biological constraints on specific cognitive areas is an interesting question.

If you ask me what are good problems to study, if you have time and brains enough, this is what I'd answer.

The 5-to-7 shift

Myelination
<2nd yr.>

Cross-modal
zones
<2nd–4th yr.>

Visual & "phantom limb" memories
Resists classical conditioning
Distinguishes own left from right
Avoids self-contradiction

Cognition: **Piaget's Concrete Operational Stage**
Able to organize and transform information mentally

Conservation (may not be complete until adolescence)

Grasps seriation and classification

Artificial, pre-logical reasons . . .

Information processing

Problem-solving:

Able to solve transposition
and reversal problems

Locates embedded
figures

Memory:

Aware of memory limitations

Schoolwork and play

Reading:

Quick word recognition

Grasps spelling-to-
sound correspondences

Efficient scanning strategies

Can "read"
pseudowords

Fun:
Humor based on
incongruity

Make-believe declines

Appreciates jokes with
multiple meanings
(especially riddles)

| | 5 | 6 | 7 | 8 |

Age in years

< > onset or peak
[ ] qualifications
⟨ age extension beyond
⟩ that shown on chart

. . . to logical, physical explanations of concrete events

Incidental (irrelevant)
learning declines

Uses elaboration and classification
(not rhymes or associations) to
organize memory

Uses rehearsal spontaneously
on memory tasks

Uses books to
pursue special interests

Organized games-with-rules increase

| 9 | 10 | 11 | 12 |

10

In Guatemalan villages, it is called *listura*. In the English-speaking world, it is called brightness, smartness, cleverness—intelligence. All languages have terms that describe individual differences in the ways people approach and solve problems. Some people see through the *complexities* of a problem to find an elegant solution. The mechanic who figures out how to rewire a broken starter when several other mechanics have failed is an example. Other people are considered smart because they solve problems so *quickly*. The clerk in the department store who calculates a bill for seven items, including the 6½ percent tax, in her head in two seconds is such a person. Some people are considered smart because they are *articulate* and able to present their point of view in a logical, persuasive manner. They nearly always win arguments. Still other people have an unusual store of *cultural knowledge*. They have learned and retained more information about more topics than most people have. A cousin who is an expert on computer software, North American birds, Italian opera, detective stories, and Chinese cooking seems smart, because so few people are competent in so many fields. Children as well as adults recognize differences in intelligence. By middle childhood, being called "dumb" is grounds for a fight.

In this chapter we stop the developmental film for a closer look at human intelligence. We begin with how and why humans differ from other animals. In the second section we consider the debate among psychologists over the nature of intelligence. What exactly is this quality we value so highly? What is the relationship between intelligence and creativity? Then we turn to psychometrics. What do intelligence tests measure? How reliable are they? What do they tell us about individual and group differences? In the last section of the chapter we look at the special cases of mental retardation and giftedness.

The Evolution of Intelligence

Our uniqueness as a species is due in large part to our brains. *Homo sapiens* has an exceptionally high EQ, or encephalization quotient (Jerison,

INTELLIGENCE
AND CREATIVITY

1982). **Encephalization** refers to an increase in the size of the brain beyond what is necessary to control bodily functions. The ratio of brain size to body size is greater in humans than in other species. An elephant's brain may be larger than that of a human being, but our brain is larger in proportion to the size of our body. The human brain is also more complex than that of other species. A rat's brain has a smooth surface. The surface of the human brain is convoluted, or folded, which permits more information-processing capacity to fit in the same skull space. A species' EQ is based on comparison to the "average mammal." Rats have an EQ of .5, which means that they are about half as intelligent as the average mammal. Wolves have an EQ of 1; they are average mammals. Squirrel monkeys, which have an EQ of 2.1, are about twice as smart as wolves. Humans have an EQ of about 7. How did we get so smart?

The Age of Dinosaurs

According to Harry Jerison (1982), the story begins about 200 million years ago, when the ancestors of today's mammals began to lose the competition for desirable living space to reptiles. During the age of dinosaurs, archaic mammals had two "choices": feed and mate at night, when the cold-blooded super-reptiles were immobile, or become extinct. The twilight hours favored creatures with a keen sense of smell and hearing. Jerison sees the brain development that took place in this period as a response to a "packaging problem." Dinosaurs had enough neurons behind the retinas of their eyes to process visual information and transmit signals for appropriate muscle responses directly throughout their bodies. Because dinosaurs were only active during daylight, this rudimentary system of vision and movement was all they needed for survival. But these neurons could not process sounds and smells as well. The archaic mammals evolved a rudimentary brain to coordinate auditory, olfactory, and visual information.

The Rise of Mammals

The second burst of encephalization began about 50 million years ago, when the dinosaurs became extinct and other animals reclaimed the day. Some mammals began to evolve visual processing in the brain that was vastly superior to that of reptiles. Natural selection favored creatures whose associative systems enabled them to integrate visual with other information. Mammals' ability to analyze information from different senses, and to compare past and present experiences, was the beginning of thought (Konner, 1982). This evolutionary advance occurred more rapidly and more extensively in the primate lineage—our own family tree—than in any other animal line. One of the earliest primates, *Necrolemur,* had a brain-to-body weight ratio of 1:35, compared to a ratio of 1:2,000 for a rhinoceros of the same period. Rhinoceri have not changed much since then; the descendants of the early primates have evolved with larger and more complex brains.

Primates thrived and multiplied in the forests of that period because they evolved stereoscopic vision and grasping hands. They could not only look, see, and hear, but also pick up objects and examine them, and test visual estimates of distance with acrobatic leaps through trees. Unlike most other mammals, they inhabited a three-dimensional world. This idea may strike readers as odd: Don't all animals occupy the same world? Yes and no. Recall the discussion of perception in earlier chapters. Your sensory organs (or those of another animal) pick up waves of light and sound; but what you perceive is what your brain makes of this raw information. The more advanced primate brain constructed a more complex reality.

The Primate Path

A third burst of encephalization began about 1 million years ago. Homonids (ancestral humans) had pursued a distinctive way of life for several million years before. They walked upright, manufactured simple tools, and probably hunted in groups. But their brains were not much larger than that of a chimpanzee. Jerison attributes the evolution of a fully human brain to the development of language. He speculates that language resolved the mismatch that occurred when our forest-dwelling, fruit- and leaf-eating ancestors turned to hunting and gathering on open savannah. The "homonids were trying to make a wolf-like living without adequate sensory machinery" (1982, p. 764). Wolves and other social predators (animals that hunt in groups) have a keen sense of smell. They depend on scent to navigate over large expanses, locate prey, stake out territories, and distinguish friendly from hostile wolves. Among the mammals, primates have an exceptionally poor sense of smell. In the trees, good eyes were more adaptive than a good nose. For a primate to become a social predator was like fitting a round peg into a square hole.

Language enabled humans to construct mental maps of their territories and to communicate verbally the whereabouts of rich food sources, good shelter, and danger. If a baboon spots a leopard, it can warn members of its troop to flee, but it cannot tell them why. Language enabled humans to communicate precisely what the predator was and how best to fight it (see Chapter 7). Language laid the foundation for culture. And culture in effect created a new environment in which individuals who had a greater ability to learn and innovate (that is, a better brain) had a greater chance of surviving to reproduce and of nurturing their offspring to reproductive age.

Human Intelligence Today

The result of this long process of evolution, which we carry in our heads, weighs a little more than three pounds and contains as many as 100 billion cells. Our brains are the epitome of encephalization. *Non*motor, *non*sensory nerve

cells outnumber the nerve cells that control bodily functions by about ten to one (Konner, 1982). Most of these associative cells are found in the cerebral cortex. This is a large sheet of interconnected nerve cells, wrinkled and folded over the older, more primitive parts of the brain and divided into specialized lobes. The cerebral cortex is, quite literally, our "crowning glory." Without it we could not speak, remember, learn, conceptualize, generate ideas and ideals, hypothesize, dream, or even love and hate like humans.

From an evolutionary perspective, intelligence is a uniquely human adaptation. To be sure, we have much in common with other primates, especially the great apes. Like other primates, we are generalists; we have not developed hoofs, fangs, or the highly specialized sensory equipment found in other species. This is why we use pigeons to search for people who are lost at sea (they can see much better at heights of 200 feet than we can) and dogs to sniff out illegal drugs or bombs in innocent-looking packages. Lack of specialization makes primates more flexible than most other mammals. In the first year or two of life, the mental development of a chimpanzee is similar to that of a human infant (Scarr, 1983). Both grasp the object concept, learn to imitate behavior, discover cause-and-effect relations, develop means–ends reasoning, and become self-aware. At age 3, chimps do about as well as human children on intelligence tests that do not require language. Gorilla infants are probably in the same mental league. But human children go on to develop abstract reasoning and language, whereas apes remain in the preoperational stage of practical experimentation. By middle childhood, there is no comparison between the two.

Our bigger brains, symbolic thought, and more complex communications are part of our species' genetic program. The differences in intelligence among humans are *much* smaller than the differences between humans and our nearest relatives, the apes. This is not to say that intelligence is genetically fixed and requires no learning. The development of intellect depends on opportunities to communicate with others, to manipulate objects, to explore and experiment, and to observe and imitate other people. Feral children, if such exist, do not develop normally in the wild. But neither do apes develop into children with human care and tutoring. Intelligence depends both on our species' genetic program and on normal human environments.

What Is Intelligence?

What is intelligence? Robert Sternberg and a colleague (Sternberg & Davidson, 1982) asked this question of commuters waiting for a train, shoppers in a supermarket, and students in the Yale University library. Everyone they questioned had definite ideas about what is and is not smart, including some idiosyncratic notions. One person characterized intelligent people as "fun to be with"; another described them as "bores." But in general, these nonpsychologists agreed that intelligence has three facets: practical problem-solving ability, verbal ability, and social competence. *Practical problem-solving ability* includes such capabilities as reasoning logically, connecting ideas, seeing all sides of a problem, and keeping an open mind. *Verbal ability* takes the form of speaking clearly, being a good conversationalist, and reading often and

well. *Social competence* includes accepting others for what they are, admitting mistakes, displaying interest in the world at large, and thinking before acting.

Sternberg and his colleague asked the same question of 140 authorities: men and women who hold doctorates in psychology, teach at major universities in the United States, and have published several books or articles on intelligence. The correlation between the experts' and the nonexperts' ratings of intelligent behavior was a high .82 (on a scale where zero signifies no relationship and 1 indicates a perfect correspondence). There were two main differences between the answers of the two groups. First, experts consider motivation an important factor in academic intelligence. They often mention dedication, persistence, and studying hard as signs of intelligence. Nonexperts rarely mention motivation. Second, nonexperts place more importance on social competence than experts do. As a rule, experts do not consider sensitivity to others, honesty, and the like as signs of intelligence; nonexperts do. In other words, nonexperts emphasize the display of *inter*personal skills in social settings. Psychologists are more concerned with *intra*personal competence in private settings (reading, thinking deeply, and the like). But there were many more points of agreement than disagreement between the groups. What psychologists study as intelli-

Psychologists' definitions of intelligence emphasize *intra*personal skills (the ability to sit and think); nonpsychologists emphasize *inter*personal skills.

gence turns out to be very close to what non-psychologists mean by intelligence.[1]

The Nature of Intelligence: "Lumpers" and "Splitters"

When psychologists debate the meaning of intelligence among themselves, they are far from unanimous about what it is. In general, psychologists can be assigned to one of two camps: the "lumpers" and the "splitters."

Some psychologists—the lumpers—view intelligence as a *general capacity* for acquiring knowledge, reasoning, and solving problems that is manifest in different ways. According to this view, the 14-year-old Puluwat who is able to navigate a canoe through hundreds of islands in the Caroline chain without a compass, the 13-year-old Iranian who has committed the entire Koran to memory, and the 15-year-old Parisian who has taught herself to program music on a computer with the aid of a synthesizer are demonstrating the same capacity in different ways. French psychologists Alfred Binet and Theodore Simon, the developers of the first useful mental test, took this view.

It seems to us that in intelligence there is a fundamental faculty, the alteration or lack of which is of the utmost importance for practical life. This faculty is judgment, otherwise called good sense, practical sense, initiative, the faculty of adapting oneself to circumstances. To judge well, to comprehend well, to reason well, these are the essential activities of intelligence. (Binet & Simon, 1905, p. 191)

The American psychologist Charles Spearman (1927) arrived at a similar view through factor analysis of scores on intelligence tests. Although the mathematics are sophisticated, the basic principle of factor analysis is simple. If

people who score high (or low) on a vocabulary test also score high (or low) on a test of reading comprehension, we can conclude that performance on both tests reflects a single factor. This conclusion is strengthened if people who do well on these tests do not necessarily do well on tests of mathematical ability or logic. Different scores on the two tests indicate that the tests tap different factors. To simplify a bit, Spearman found that very uneven scores on different tests are unusual. As a rule, people who do well (or poorly) on some intelligence tests also do well (or poorly) on a variety of intellectual tasks (vocabulary *and* mathematics *and* spatial relations). He concluded that all people have a general intelligence factor, which he called *g*. Some people have more of this factor than others; they are generally bright while the others are generally dull. Spearman added that some tests or sections of tests require specific information, and that some people have more information in one area (math) than in another (vocabulary). But he held that intelligence is best represented by *g*, the factor common for all tests. Belief in general intelligence is the main justification for using a single index of intelligence, the IQ, for a variety of purposes.

Other psychologists—the splitters—hold that intelligence is composed of many *separate mental abilities* that operate more or less independently. According to this view, being able to comprehend James Joyce's novel *Ulysses,* perform calculus, or take apart and reassemble an automobile engine require different mental aptitudes. People who are good at one are not necessarily good at the others. The psychologist Louis Thurstone (1938) was a leading spokesman for this point of view. For Thurstone, *g* (and by extension, the IQ) was a meaningless abstraction. He identified seven factors, or "primary abilities," as he called them: verbal comprehension, word fluency, number, space, memory, perceptual speed, and reasoning.

[1]Sternberg adds that more intelligence testing probably goes on in job interviews, on coffee breaks, at cocktail parties and in other settings where people informally "size one another up" than in schoolrooms and psychologists' offices.

Others thought Thurstone was modest: J. P. Guilford listed 120 separate mental abilities. This may be extreme, but many psychologists accept the notion of distinct mental capabilities.

Some psychologists have taken an intermediate position in this debate. For example, Philip Vernon (1971) has proposed a hierarchical model of intelligence in which *g* is divided into two general areas of ability: verbal-educational and practical-mechanical. These areas are divided into such specific skills as reading, mathematics, and mechanics (see Figure 10-1). In Vernon's model, *g* is like the conductor of an orchestra, verbal-educational ability is the first violin, and practical-mechanical ability is the lead horn. Reading is the violin section, spelling the cellos, mathematical ability the saxophones, scientific skills the trumpets, and so on. When a person is reading a newspaper or a chapter in a textbook, the violins are playing the melody, with the guidance of the first violin and the direction of the conductor.

All of these models of intelligence have their uses. Testing often yields a high correlation between an individual's scores on different tests or subtests—supporting the notion of *g*. At the same time, analysis of subtests often shows that an individual is stronger in some areas than in others—supporting the notion of specialized abilities. Which approach a psychologist chooses depends in large part on his or her interests.

The theories of intelligence we have been describing come from psychometrics, the branch of psychology that is concerned with measuring psychological characteristics, such as intelligence (see Chapter 4). Many contemporary psychologists feel that this approach is too narrow (it relies too heavily on analysis of test scores and school performance) and too vague (it does not explain *how* individuals solve intellectual problems). Robert Sternberg's model of intelligence is an attempt to correct these problems.

Intelligence As Adaptive Information Processing

Sternberg might be classified as a lumper. He would argue that if you look closely at any form of intelligent behavior, you will see the same basic processes at work: perception, memory,

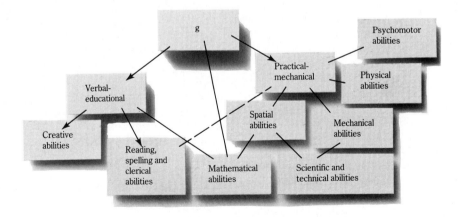

Figure 10-1 Vernon's Hierarchical Model of Intelligence
(Vernon, 1971)

Insight

"FRAMES OF MIND"

Howard Gardner is one of a number of contemporary psychologists who reject the notion of general intelligence and the exclusive use of IQ tests to measure intelligence. Gardner argues that human intelligence is far too complex to be reduced to a single factor, much less a single score (the IQ).

In *Frames of Mind* (1983), Gardner argues for a theory of multiple intelligences. In his view there are at least six intelligences. The first, *linguistic intelligence,* is exemplified by the poet, who is dedicated to finding the exact word or phrase. Poets have the memory for detail and techniques to develop ordinary skills, which all normal humans possess, to an extraordinary degree.

Musical intelligence depends on sensitivity to tone and pitch: Composers hear patterns where others hear only noise.

Logical-mathematical intelligence begins with the exploration of the world of objects and culminates in highly abstract reasoning, divorced from real-world applications.

Spatial intelligence is the ability to perceive the world of objects accurately, imagine transformations and modifications of what one sees, and recreate visual experiences from memory. This is the intelligence that guides great artists and art lovers, engineers, and many scientists.

Bodily-kinesthetic intelligence is "a family of procedures for translating intention into action" (p. 209), exemplified by the French mime Marcel Marceau, who can fill an empty stage with imagined props and tell a story with his body alone.

Personal intelligences include both access to one's own feelings (exemplified by novelists such as Marcel Proust) and understanding other people's motivations (exemplified by charismatic leaders such as Gandhi).

Why does Gardner view these as separate intelligences? Each follows, he says, a somewhat different developmental path. Musical intelligence often appears quite early: Many great composers and performers were child prodigies. In contrast, poets usually go through

Gardner cites the Balinese as an example of a people and culture that develop bodily-kinesthetic intelligence to an extraordinary degree.

a period of apprenticeship and imitation before they find their own voice. Logical-mathematical intelligence peaks in late adolescence and early adulthood: Mathematicians and physicists often consider themselves "burned out" by age 35 or 40. But many painters and composers do some of their finest work in their eighties.

There are group as well as individual differences in these abilities. Different cultures emphasize different intelligences. Virtually everyone on the island of Bali, where great attention is paid to every movement and gesture, would qualify as a dancer by Western standards.

Further evidence of multiple intelligences comes from *idiots savants.* Some children who seem mentally retarded in most respects perform complex mathematical calculations in their heads that most adults would find impossible.

Finally, brain damage often causes highly

(Continued)

specific dysfunctions. An injury to one part of the brain causes an adult to communicate in short, concrete sentences—a caricature of Ernest Hemingway's style. An injury to another area causes adults to speak in long, intricate passages whose meaning is obscure—almost a parody of William Faulkner's style. Specific, localized language impairments suggest to Gardner that the idea of multiple intelligences is not merely a metaphor; it is grounded in physiology.

Gardner's analysis of exceptional skills makes intuitive sense. It appeals to common stereotypes of the absent-minded scientist, impractical poet, and illiterate athlete. The main criticism of *Frames of Mind* is that Gardner overextends the term "intelligence." Dancing, understanding people, painting, or playing cello extraordinarily well do require skills that are not well represented on standard intelligence tests. But most psychologists would not call these talents "intelligence."

and combining and comparing bits of data. The mechanics of information processing are universal—whatever the task, whoever the performer.

Like other psychologists who study information processing, Sternberg is interested in the minute details of problem-solving. But he is also concerned with the practical applications of intelligence in real-world situations. His model of intelligence links internal information processing to external adaptation to social and cultural contexts (1984). According to Sternberg, the full exercise of our brains depends on contextual knowledge, the combination of "cleverness" and "expertise," and information-processing skills.[2]

CONTEXTUAL KNOWLEDGE Sternberg begins by stating that intelligence cannot be understood

[2]These are our terms, not Sternberg's.

outside a sociocultural context. What is intelligent in one environment may be irrelevant or considered stupid in another. The chances are that an African pygmy would not do very well on a North American intelligence test. Most North Americans would not pass the test of the pygmy's Ituri forest, either. Our lifestyles require and foster different abilities. One need not travel to an exotic society to make this point. Until quite recently, mathematical computation was an essential ingredient of intelligence in our society. Calculators have made this skill less and less important. Being able to add, subtract, mul-

In this cultural setting, being able to pack a llama with goods for the market and come home with a profit represent the adaptive use of intelligence.

tiply, and divide will not help you get a good job today; knowing how to program a computer will certainly help.

Sternberg argues that part of intelligence is the ability to adapt to one's environment. This may mean fitting into existing circumstances, reshaping the environment to fit one's needs, or selecting an environment in which one works well. Success in real-world pursuits depends as much on knowing the ins and outs of an occupation as on the cognitive skills measured by IQ and other tests. Richard Wagner and Sternberg's interviews of successful business managers and psychologists (in press) illustrate this. Those who do well have a good deal of tacit knowledge of their field—information that is never explicitly taught or even verbalized. They know how to manage themselves (how to motivate themselves, set priorities, increase their productivity); how to manage others (how to assign tasks and reward subordinates); and how to manage their careers (how to establish a good reputation and convince superiors of their worth). The role of tacit knowledge in adapting to environments explains why some people who were A-students have undistinguished careers in later life—and some with poor grades become successful.

"CLEVERNESS" AND "EXPERTISE" In Sternberg's view, intelligence is purposeful, goal-oriented, relevant behavior. All adaptive behavior does not qualify as intelligent behavior, however. Eating is purposeful and relevant, but most people would not consider eating a sandwich a mark of high intelligence. Sternberg holds that intelligence consists of two general skills: the ability to deal with novel tasks and the ability to automatize information processing. In everyday language, we call the first "cleverness," the second "expertise."

Novelty is a mental challenge. Consider a practical example. It does not take much intelligence to drive to work along the same route you have taken every morning for two years. It does take some intelligence to find your way to a museum in a foreign city if you do not speak the language and the street signs are printed in an unfamiliar alphabet such as Greek. One sign of cleverness is being able to grasp and apply new concepts. To apply the concept of *conservation* to a young child's mistaken ideas about quantity, for example, a student must change the way she thinks about preschoolers' errors. Another sign of cleverness is the ability to distinguish relevant from irrelevant information. The riddles and puzzles in adult game books tap this ability (Sternberg & Davidson, 1982):

If you have black and brown socks in your drawer, mixed in the ratio of 4:5, how many socks will you have to take out to make sure of having a pair of the same color?

Give up? The answer is three. Many people are stumped by this question because they focus on the 4:5 ratio. People who solve it easily realize that this information is irrelevant. If the ratio were 1:2 or 2:7, the answer would be the same. Coping with novelty requires this kind of discrimination.

Developing expertise is also part of intelligence. The difference between a novice and an expert is that the former has to use all of his mental energy to perform a task, whereas the latter is able to perform the same mental task almost effortlessly. When you are learning to drive a car, for example, you have to think about putting on the turn signal, checking the rearview mirror, and what a flashing yellow light means. When you are an experienced driver, you perform these tasks (that is, process this information) automatically. Driving no longer consumes your full attention; you are free to think about other things. So it is with academic, occupational, and other mental tasks. When you are learning a new language, you must translate every word. As you become fluent, you can produce and understand whole phrases without referring to the dictionary in your hand (or even the one in your mind). You can concentrate on what you want to say, not how to say it. Learning to play chess, you must think about the moves you might make and your opponent's possible responses, one at a time. A chess master sees the whole board at a glance and imagines how the game might develop over the next five or six moves. Exposure does not guarantee expertise. Many people study French for years without ever becoming fluent, and few people become chess masters.

Sternberg sees coping with novel tasks and being able to automatize information processing as equally important. One without the other is limiting. Some people can perform a familiar task in a familiar setting brilliantly, but they are totally disoriented by any change. Others seem to learn new information easily but do not "absorb" enough to move to higher levels of performance. Intelligence requires both cleverness and expertise.

INFORMATION-PROCESSING SKILLS All novel or automatic tasks do not require the same degree of intelligence. Almost anyone can learn to drive a car, but not everyone can master calculus. Ultimately, intelligence depends on information processing: on what happens between the time a person receives information and the time the information is acted upon. Simply put, some people process information more effectively than others do. As a result, they are able to deal with the kinds of complex problems presented in calculus.

Analysis of thought processes on this level reveals the many small components of intelligence. Sternberg distinguishes among executive processes (recognizing what the problem is, selecting an approach or strategy, deciding how much time and effort are required, and monitoring one's performance); knowledge acquisition (sifting relevant from irrelevant information, combining bits of information into meaningful wholes, and comparing newly acquired data with data already in the memory); and performance (using knowledge to carry out a strategy).

Sternberg and others have begun to trace differences in intelligence to differences in information-processing skills and strategies. As a general rule, bright people devote more time to executive processes than to performance (Sternberg & Davidson, 1982). They do more planning. On an analogy problem such as that in Figure 10-2, people who spend time encoding the question (step 1) are more likely to pick the correct answer than are people who move rapidly from step 1 to step 6. They also tend to have higher IQs. Being quick is not necessarily smart; making sure you have all the necessary information to solve the problem is.

Sternberg's model suggests that individual differences in intelligence are three dimensional, reflecting differences in information-processing skills, the ability to deal with novelty and develop expertise, and contextual knowledge. Usually the three go together. Good information-processing strategies are essential to other expressions of intelligence. But they do not guarantee that a person will learn the ins and outs of marketing securities on Wall Street, hunting and gathering in the Kalahari desert, or any other occupation.

Cognitive Style and Tempo

Sternberg touches on two issues that some psychologists consider central to the exercise of intelligence: cognitive style and tempo. Ask a group of children or adults to solve a problem. Some jump to a solution, volunteering a quick answer. Others take time to work out a careful solution. Some have an analytical approach; they

QUESTION:
WASHINGTON IS TO <u>ONE</u> AS LINCOLN IS TO:

A.) <u>FIVE</u> B.) <u>TEN</u> C.) <u>FIFTEEN</u> D.) <u>FIFTY</u>

The steps required to solve this analogy problem are:

1. *Encoding:* Identifying the terms in the analogy and retrieving from long-term memory information that might be relevant to a solution. (Washington was a president, a hero in the Revolutionary war; Lincoln was a president, a hero in the Civil War; both appear on currency.)
2. *Inferring:* Thinking about possible relationships between the first and second terms in the analogy. (Washington was our *first* president; his portrait appears on a *one*-dollar bill.)
3. *Mapping:* Tracing the higher-order relationship between the first and second halves of the analogy. (Washington and Lincoln were both presidents; both appear on currency; both provided the names for cities.)
4. *Applying:* Using inferences about the relationship between *Washington* and *one* to test relationships between *Lincoln* and the answer choices. (If the problem-solver did not encode the presidents' portraits on the currency, she may guess that there are five Washingtons in the United States and ten Lincolns. Or the list of numbers may bring currency to mind.)
5. *Justifying:* Explaining to oneself why this answer is better than the others. (Suppose the problem-solver has not thought about currency. She may think that Lincoln was the sixteenth president, but conclude that her memory is wrong and that *Fifteen* must be the right answer.)
6. *Responding:* Supplying the answer that seems to be the best completion of the analogy.

ANSWER:

B.) <u>FIVE</u>   (Washington appears on a one-dollar bill, Lincoln on a five-dollar bill.)

Figure 10-2 Processing an Analogy
(Based on Sternberg, 1979)

take the problem apart and examine each part. Others have a more global approach; they turn the whole problem around in their heads or in their hands until they find a solution. People have different cognitive styles.

According to one school of thought, people actually see problems in two different ways. Herman Witkin (Witkin, Dyk, Faterson, Goodenough, & Karp, 1962) coined the term *field dependent* (FD) to describe those who have difficulty perceiving the parts of a field as separate from the whole. Others who are *field independent* (FI) are able to analyze the field into separate parts.[3] Field-independent people think like scientists; field-dependent people think more like artists. On a perceptual level, the test of field independence is the ability to discover the diamond or triangle hidden in a more complex pattern (the Embedded Figures Test; see Figure 9-7). On a cognitive level, field independence is linked to the ability to restructure the elements of a problem to arrive at a solution. Thinking about whether the ratio of black to brown socks in your drawer is relevant to finding a matching pair is an example. In this case, one element of the problem can be discarded.

On a social and emotional level, field independence is associated with autonomy and self-direction; field dependence is linked to other-direction and reliance on external cues for self-evaluation. Field-independent children tend to be task-oriented; field-dependent children are usually people-oriented. Given the opportunity to observe a model complete a puzzle, field-independent children watched the model's hands, whereas children who are field-dependent checked the model's face (Ruble & Nakamura, 1972).

Field independence increases with development. The older children become, the less likely

[3]Field dependence and field independence are not the only cognitive styles. We cite them here because there has been more research on these two styles than on others.

they are to be captured by external appearances (field dependence) and the more likely they are to analyze the components of a problem (field independence). But some children develop this ability more quickly and more fully than others do. A large body of research (summarized in Kogan, 1983) indicates that field-independent people are better at intellectual tasks than are field-dependent people—especially in a culture such as ours, which values scientific thinking more than artistic ability. However, there is some evidence that field-dependent people have

Recent studies suggest that the impulsive child who cannot sit still is not "bad" and overreactive, but bored and understimulated.

superior social skills (Nakamura & Finck, 1980). They pay more attention to people. This may not translate into better grades or higher test scores; but on tasks requiring social sensitivity, field-dependent youngsters excel.

Individuals also vary in their conceptual tempo. *Reflective* people take time to evaluate a problem. They consider different strategies, monitor their own progress, and change directions if necessary. In a word, they are thoughtful. *Impulsive* people leap to a solution. They may use the first strategy that comes to mind, skip steps, and disregard contrary evidence; but they are quick. Reflective people are more concerned with accuracy than speed; impulsive people value speed over accuracy. The standard measure of reflection/impulsivity is the Matching Familiar Figures Test (MFFT) that requires a person to match a standard figure of a common object, such as a leaf, ship, or lamp, to six slight variations on the figure (Kagan, Rosman, Day, Albert, & Phillips, 1964). Scores on this test are based on both accuracy and speed.

Which cognitive strategy is "best"? Zelniker and Jeffrey (1979) argue that it depends on the task. They suggest that reflective children are field-independent children who take more time to solve a problem because they analyze its components. These children excel on tasks requiring attention to detail. Impulsive children are field dependent and take less time because they focus on the problem as a whole. These children excel on tasks requiring global solutions, such as quickly identifying a picture. In general, however, Western education rewards detailed information processing and analytic thinking. Hence, reflective children have an advantage (Kogan, 1983).

Cognitively impulsive children are not necessarily behaviorally impulsive in the classroom. One group of researchers, (Moore, Haskins, & McKinney, 1980) found that they tend to be more cautious and self-doubting, more patient and more responsible, than are reflective children. This is the opposite of what one might expect. Perhaps these children are impulsive on intellectual tasks because they fear they are not competent and want to escape the task as quickly as possible (Kogan, 1983). Attempts to train impulsive youngsters to think reflectively, through incentives (Bush & Dweck, 1975) or instruction (Barstis & Ford, 1977), have been moderately successful. The children do take their time but their test scores do not match those of children who are reflective by nature. A longitudinal study (Gjerde, Block, & Block, 1985) found that conceptual tempo may change over time, but that error rates are relatively stable. This suggests that reflectivity and impulsivity are not matters of style, but indirect measures of intelligence: To be sure, the way a person approaches problems influences his or her performance; but people who are more intelligent select more intelligent strategies.

Creativity: Unique or Universal?

Are intelligent people creative? Are creative people intelligent? Is creativity a necessary ingredient of intelligence? Is intelligence essential to creativity? To our knowledge, no one has conducted a survey of how the average person defines creativity. But we imagine they would find that most people believe that creativity and intelligence are related but separate—cousins, not Siamese twins.

Psychologists define **creativity** as the ability to use familiar materials in unfamiliar but interesting and useful ways. Writing an original short story or musical composition, inventing a new machine or scientific theory, and solving a personal dilemma or a mathematical paradox are all examples of creativity.

Psychologists have approached creativity in one of two ways (Feldman, 1980). The *trait approach* assumes that creativity is an unchanging potential that will find expression under almost any condition. The aim of research is to discover the characteristics that distinguish creative people from those who are not creative. The *process approach* assumes that all behavior, including creativity, is the result of interaction between the individual and the environment. The goal of research is to identify the circumstances that enable a person to express his or her creative potential.

The Trait Approach

The trait approach dominated research on creativity for many years. One result was the construction of creativity tests. The subject responds to questions for which there are no right or wrong answers. For example, she may be asked, "How many uses can you think of for a brick (or a paper clip or toothbrush)?" (Guilford, 1954). Scores are based on the "fluency of ideas," or the number of answers the subject gives (paper clips can be used as fishhooks, strung into a necklace, and the like). Scores also are based on the unusualness of the responses (A brick can be used as a bug trap: Put it down, pick it up the next day, and you'll find a collection of insects) (Tavris & Wade, 1984, pp. 52–53). Questions from other creativity tests are shown in Figure 10-3).

As a general rule, people who score high on creativity tests also score high on intelligence tests. Above an IQ of 120, however, this correspondence fades. Some individuals with quite high IQs score low on creativity tests, while some with only above-average IQs score quite high on creativity tests. There seems to be an intelligence threshold for creativity, but a high IQ does not guarantee originality (Crockenberg, 1972).

One criticism of creativity tests is that they measure only the subject's ability to give novel answers. Being different is not, by itself, creative. Mixing chemicals in a novel way may produce a mess or an explosion, not a scientific insight. It takes more than originality to create an *aesthetic* painting, a *moving* short story, a theory that *fits* the facts, or a *useful* invention. Creativity seems to require a certain amount of intelligence.

A second criticism of creativity tests is that inventing uses for a paper clip bears little relationship to real-world creativity. High scores on these tests do not predict achievements in art, breakthroughs in science, or leadership in politics (see Pankove & Kogan, 1968).

Another line of research based on the trait approach focused on "the creative personality." How does the creative person differ from her plodding (although perhaps equally intelligent) neighbor? Frank Barron (1980) discovered that art students whom their teachers considered particularly creative preferred complex or ambiguous patterns to simple ones; their less creative classmates did not. Other psychologists have given batteries of psychological tests to architects, physicists, and others whom their

---

1 Ingenuity (Flanagan, 1963)

a A very rare wind storm destroyed the transmission tower of a television station in a small town. The station was located in a town in a flat prairie with no tall buildings. Its former 300-foot tower enabled it to serve a large farming community, and the management wanted to restore service while a new tower was being erected. The problem was temporarily solved by using a _____.

b As part of a manufacturing process, the inside lip of a deep cup-shaped casting is machine threaded. The company found that metal chips produced by the threading operation were difficult to remove from the bottom of the casting without scratching the sides. A design engineer was able to solve this problem by having the operation performed _____.

2 Unusual uses (Guilford, 1954)

Name as many uses as you can think of for:

a a toothpick
b a brick
c a paper clip

3 Consequences (Guilford, 1954)

Imagine all of the things that might possibly happen if all national and local laws were suddenly abolished.

4 Fable endings (Getzels and Jackson, 1962)

Write three endings for the following fable: a moralistic, a humorous, and a sad ending.

THE MISCHIEVOUS DOG

A rascally dog used to run quietly to the heels of every passerby and bite them without warning. So his master was obliged to tie a bell around the cur's neck that he might give notice wherever he went. This the dog thought very fine indeed, and he went about tinkling it in pride all over town. But an old hound said. . . .

5 Product Improvement (Torrance, 1966)

The subject is presented with a series of objects, such as children's toys or instruments used in his or her particular occupation, and asked to make suggestions for their improvement.

6 Pattern meanings (Wallach and Kogan, 1965)

The subject is shown a series of patterns of geometric forms (like the samples shown below) and asked to imagine all the things each pattern could be.

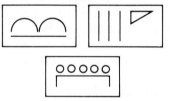

7 Remote associations (Mednick, 1962)

Find a fourth word which is associated with each of these three words:

a rat—blue—cottage
b out—dog—cat
c wheel—electric—high
d surprise—line—birthday

8 Word association (Getzels and Jackson, 1962)

Write as many meanings as you can for each of the following words:

a duck   c pitch
b sack   d fair

Figure 10-3 Items Used in Creativity Tests

colleagues considered highly creative. The researchers found that these creative individuals tended to be open-minded, independent, enthusiastic, ambitious, self-centered, exhibitionistic, and introspective—a seemingly contradictory array of traits. The assumption behind these studies is that the root causes of creativity lie deep within the individual. The researchers take special talents for granted, as if a creative person could just as easily become a violinist or a sculptor as a chemist. Opportunities to be creative are also taken as given. According to this view, creativity works from the inside out.

The Process Approach

The process approach, in contrast, views creativity as part talent, part hard work, and part opportunity. Even highly creative people (such as Albert Einstein or Pablo Picasso) are not creative all of the time; they have their dull moments. Moreover, brilliance takes time and effort to develop. Studies of child prodigies (8-year-old chess masters, 9-year-old composers) indicate that extraordinary achievements early in life depend on intensive training (Feldman, 1980). Child prodigies usually have exceptionally dedicated parents and teachers. To be sure, they are gifted. But they are not "born musicians" or "born chess players." Rather they are born with an unusual capacity to learn these media. Without support and opportunities, their gifts would not be realized.

David Feldman (1980) suggests that psychologists examine creativity from the outside in. The place to begin, in his view, is with the work itself. What makes a work creative? Feldman cites four criteria (from Jackson & Messick, 1965) that apply equally well to a piece of music or a scientific theory. A work is creative if it is: (1) innovative (unusual or rare); (2) appropriate (a solution that fits the problem so well, or painting that expresses emotions so clearly, that it provokes a "shock of recogni-

tion"); (3) transformational (work that challenges accepted ideas about the creator's medium—for example, an abstract photograph); and (4) condensational (a simple, elegant summation of complex phenomena—for example, Einstein's formula for relativity, $E = mc^2$).

Focusing on creative *works,* rather than on creative traits, eliminates the paper-clip problem as useless novelty. To date, this research strategy has hardly been used. In one small pilot study, the individual who gave the most creative responses, judged by these four criteria, on a standard creativity test ranked only 57th out of 87 on the basis of test scores. Having a lot of ideas does not necessarily produce *good* ideas.

To investigate the creative process, Feldman turns to case studies and autobiographies. Picasso described the creation of a painting as "the crystallization of a dream." He began with a vision, something in his mind's eye. His first attempts to put that image on canvas were only crude renditions. As he continued to work, he came closer and closer to his original image until he felt that the painting was right. But he had not known how the image would develop until he began painting. The medium of canvas and paint transformed Picasso's vision into tangible form. Mastering the medium (or the discipline, such as mathematics) is central to the creative process. (See Figure 10-4.)

The Artist and the Child

Feldman draws an analogy between the creative adult and the developing child. The experience of creativity is similar to the experience of advancing from one of Piaget's stages of cognitive development to the next. The achievement of new rules of thought is a profound experience for a child. Piaget was present on several occasions when a child had a sudden insight—into conservation, for example. The youngster has been struggling for some time to assimilate observations and experiences that do not fit into his current way of thinking. He feels as though he were being pulled toward a solution. Suddenly he understands. He may state the principle of conservation without realizing what he is saying, then exclaim, "But it's obvious!" When he grasps the new principle, it seems both obvious and necessary. He experiences what Jerome Bruner (1962) calls "effective surprise." The child may add, "Once you know, you know for ever and ever." He has attained a new equilibrium.

Great insights and intuitions have much the same impact on the person who experiences them. Feldman suggests that creative breakthroughs occur when the artist or scientist is at the limits of a craft and must invent new techniques to realize a vision. Like the child, the creative genius feels pulled toward a solution (be it a new musical form or an equation). When the breakthrough occurs, the creator feels effective surprise: "Why didn't I see that before?" The person's whole way of thinking and performing changes. If many other people who read

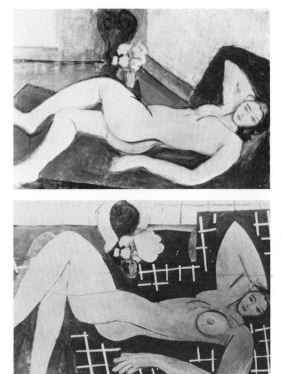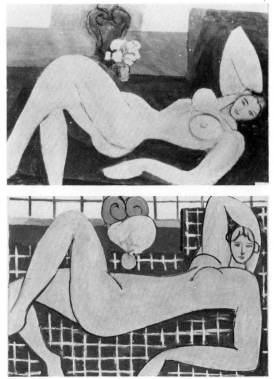

Figure 10-4 The Crystallization of an Image
Henri Matisse made twenty-two sketches before he was satisfied with his painting *Pink Nude*. He began by drawing a voluptuous nude reclining on a couch in the corner of a room (1), then flattened the background (2), enlarged the figure so that her feet and elbow run off the canvas (3), and changed her face and posture before he finished (4).

the theory or hear the composition have the same reaction—"Aha, that's it"—the new approach may spread through society, causing a reorganization of thinking on a cultural level.

Feldman does not mean to suggest that every child is an artist. But the universal experience of attaining new levels of cognitive development is similar to the unique experience of creative breakthroughs. To this extent, creativity is both universal and unique.

Measuring Intelligence

Intelligence or IQ tests are designed to *measure* or quantify intellectual ability and to *rank* individuals in terms of their intellectual skills. An individually administered standard IQ test takes one to one and a half hours to give. The psychologist asks the child a series of questions designed to assess his store of information ("Who discovered America?" "What does the stomach do?"), his vocabulary ("What does *nonsense* mean?" "*belfry?*"), his skills with arithmetic ("If one candy bar costs eight cents, how much will five cost?"), his ability to remember a series of numbers ("5, 1, 7, 4, 2, 8, 3"), his capacity to see similarities between different objects or concepts (such as elbow and knee), and his reasoning ("Is the following sentence sensible or foolish? 'Mrs. Smith has no children, and I understand the same was true of her mother' "). The child may also be asked to solve a maze, or to arrange a series of pictures so that they tell a story. Later the psychologists scores the child's responses and calculates his IQ. This scene is repeated thousands of times a day in the United States alone. IQ tests are as much a part of modern societies as are opinion polls, television, and frozen orange juice.

Tests of general intelligence are our best guides to later academic achievement. Historically, IQ tests have been used to place individuals in educational programs, make adoptive home placements, and make other important decisions. But they are far from the end of the intelligence story.

The Making of Intelligence Tests

The first intelligence test was created by the French psychologist Alfred Binet and his colleague Théodore Simon.

THE BINET–SIMON MENTAL SCALE France made public education compulsory for all children in 1881. The ministry of education asked Binet to devise a test that would identify slow learners at an early age so that they could be

Alfred Binet with his daughters.

given special instruction. He and Simon took a commonsense approach. They measured intelligence by testing memory, reasoning, and judgment, the qualities most people associate with intelligence. On their first test, published in 1905, children were asked to point to their nose, copy a square, name four colors, count backward from 20 to 0, and so on. In all, there were thirty questions arranged in order of difficulty. The more questions a child could answer, the higher her score.

Binet and Simon soon realized that a child's score reflected chronological age as well as intellectual abilities. Older children know more than younger children do, and can perform more complex intellectual tasks. For example, most 9-year-olds can name the months of the year and make change for 20 francs; many 7-year-olds and most 5-year-olds cannot. The idea of regular mental growth was the key to a useful diagnosis of slow learners. Binet reasoned that "dull" children think like normal children at younger ages. A slow 10-year-old may be able to solve the problems an average 7-year-old can solve, but not those most 8-, 9-, and 10-year-olds can handle. A bright 10-year-old can answer questions that baffle most 11- and 12-year-olds. This observation led to the concept of mental age. **Mental age** is a child's ranking on an age-graded scale of intelligence. A slow child's mental age is below her chronological age; a bright child's mental age is above her chronological age.

Binet's major contribution was to measure intelligence in terms of the regular development of mental abilities with age. His test provided educators with a concrete measure of intellectual ability that was relatively easy to translate into appropriate teaching strategies. In retrospect, the ideas that knowledge and reasoning improve with age and that slow children think like younger children seem obvious. At the time, they were revolutionary. Soon the Binet–Simon scale was adopted in other countries.

CONTEMPORARY IQ TESTS Lewis Terman and his colleagues at Stanford University published the major revisions of the Binet–Simon scale in 1916 and 1937. They used the score known as the **intelligence quotient** or **IQ**. An IQ was calculated from the ratio of mental age (MA) to chronological age (CA). The formula was MA ÷ CA × 100. A child with a mental age of 10 and a chronological age of 8 earned an IQ of 125 (10 ÷ 8 × 100), while a child with a mental age of 8 and a chronological age of 10 received an IQ score of 80. An IQ of 100 is average (10 ÷ 10 × 100). The scoring of the Stanford–Binet, as Terman's revision was called, was refined further in 1960 and again in 1972. (See Figure 10-5.) Today, mean IQ scores are established for each age group; an IQ number indicates how far above and below the mean a person scores.[4]

Another American psychometrician, David Wechsler, disagreed with Binet's global approach. A splitter, Wechsler sees intelligence as a composite of related abilities. The Wechsler Adult Intelligence Scale (the current revision of which is known as the WAIS-R) and the Wechsler Intelligence Scale for Children (WISC-R) are divided into verbal and performance scales, which in turn are divided into specific subscales (see Figure 10-6 on p. 402). The content of these tests is similar to the Stanford–Binet, but the individual receives verbal and performance IQs as well as an overall score.

The Kaufman Assessment Battery for Children (K-ABC) is based on theories of cerebral specialization and the different functions of the left and right hemispheres of the brain. This test has two scales. The Sequential Processing Scale is designed to measure children's ability to mentally arrange items in order (for example, to re-

[4]The reason for this adjustment is that mental growth, like physical growth, does not continue indefinitely. People reach a plateau in their mid-twenties. Although their chronological age continues to increase, their mental age remains about the same. If adult intelligence were calculated with the IQ formula, it would appear that people become less intelligent as they grow older. The new scoring system corrects this distortion.

peat a series of digits backward or perform a series of hand movements in the order the examiner performed them). The Simultaneous Processing Scale is designed to measure children's ability to process spatial problems and analogs (for example, recognizing faces or assembling triangles in a pattern to match a model). The K-ABC is intended to help educators determine a child's style of cognitive processing. Published in 1983, it has already attracted criticism concerning the theory underlying the test and the data offered to support the validity of the test. (See Jensen, 1984, and Sternberg, 1984, for critiques, and Kaufman's reply, 1984.)

The Stanford–Binet, Wechsler, and Kaufman scales are individual tests. The psychologist examines one person at a time, rating that person's concentration, effort, and persistence as well as right and wrong answers. The psychologist's clinical judgments are included in the interpretation of the score. Answers are given orally or by pointing. Because these tests are expensive to give, group paper-and-pencil tests (such as the Lorge–Thorndike or the Primary Mental Abilities tests) are often substituted.

THREE AIMS OF INTELLIGENCE TESTS Whatever the format, all contemporary intelligence tests measure differences in the *rate* at which individuals learn, the *quantity* of past learning, and the *quality* of present learning skills. All general IQ tests have timed sections that measure the rate at which a person solves problems. The rationale for speed performance is that nearly everyone has extensive experience in intellectual

Age	Task
2	**Naming parts of the body.** Child is shown a large paper doll and asked to point to various parts of the body.
3	**Visual-motor skills.** Child is shown a bridge built of three blocks and asked to build one like it. Can copy a drawing of a circle.
4	**Opposite analogies.** Fills in the missing word when asked: "Brother is a boy; sister is a _____." "In daytime it is light; at night it is _____." **Reasoning.** Answers correctly when asked: "Why do we have houses?" "Why do we have books?"
5	**Vocabulary.** Defines words such as *ball, hat,* and *stove.* **Visual-motor skills.** Can copy a drawing of a square.
6	**Number concepts.** Is able to give the examiner nine blocks when asked to do so.
8	**Memory for stories.** Listens to a story and answers questions about it.
9	**Rhymes.** Answers correctly when asked: "Tell me the name of a color that rhymes with Fred." "Tell me a number that rhymes with free."
12	**Verbal absurdities.** Tells what is foolish about statements such as, "Bill Jones' feet are so big that he has to put his trousers on over his head."
14	**Inference.** Examiner folds a piece of paper a number of times, notching a corner with scissors each time. Subject is asked the rule for determining how many holes there will be when the paper is unfolded.
Adult (15 years and older)	**Differences.** Can describe the difference between "misery and poverty," "character and reputation." **Memory for reversed digits.** Can repeat six digits backward (that is, in reverse order) after they are read aloud by the examiner.

Figure 10-5 Items from the Stanford–Binet
Intelligence Scale
(Terman & Merrill, 1986)

Information (30 questions)
How many legs do you have?
What must you do to make water freeze?
Who discovered the North Pole?
What is the capital of France?

Similarities (17 questions)
In what way are pencil and crayon alike?
In what way are tea and coffee alike?
In what way are inch and mile alike?
In what way are binoculars and microscope alike?

Arithmetic (18 questions)
If I have one piece of candy and get another one, how many pieces will I have?
At 12 cents each, how much will 4 bars of soap cost?
If a suit sells for 1/2 of the ticket price, what is the cost of a $120 suit?

Vocabulary (32 words)
ball   poem
summer   obstreperous

Comprehension (17 questions)
Why do we wear shoes?
What is the thing to do if you see someone dropping her packages?
In what two ways is a lamp better than a candle?
Why are we tried by a jury of our peers?

Digit Span
Digits Forward contains seven series of digits, 3 to 9 digits in length (Example: 1-8-9).
Digits Backward contains seven series of digits, 2 to 8 digits in length (Example: 5-8-1-9).

Picture Completion (26 items)
The task is to identify the essential missing part of the picture.
☐ A picture of a car without a wheel.
☐ A picture of a dog without a leg.
☐ A picture of a telephone without numbers on the dial. . . .
An example of a Picture Completion task is shown here.

Picture Arrangement (12 items)
The task is to arrange a series of pictures into a meaningful sequence. An example of a Picture Arrangement item is shown in the photograph of the WISC-R.

Block Design (11 items)
The task is to reproduce stimulus designs using four or nine blocks. An example of a block design item is shown here.

Object Assembly (4 items)
The task is to arrange pieces into a meaningful object. An example of an object assembly item is shown here.

Coding
The task is to copy symbols from a key. An example of the coding task is shown below.

Mazes
The task is to complete a series of mazes.

tasks such as simple arithmetic. Such skills are "overlearned"; most people have learned the tasks. Individuals differ only in the facility with which they can solve similar problems. Facility is measured in terms of speed.

The quantity of past learning is usually tested by the relative rarity of the information a person has. The rationale here is that someone who has learned a great deal possesses all of the information that most people have, plus information that few others have learned. On vocabulary tests the difficulty of words is defined by their rarity in everyday conversation (*enigma* vs. *shoe*).

The quality of learning skills is often measured in terms of the complexity of problems a person can solve. For example, it is more difficult to figure out the dimensions of a rectangle with an area of 9,324 square feet than to figure out how many apples one can buy for fifty cents if each one costs a dime. Speed, rarity, and complexity are the typical criteria of difficulty on intelligence tests.

What IQ Tests Do (and Do Not) Measure

What is most important to know about intelligence tests is what they do and do not measure.

THE TEST AS A SAMPLE Many IQ test items seem arbitrary and even ridiculous. Why should the way a person traces a maze or arranges a series of pictures, knowledge of the capital of Greece,

Figure 10-6 Youngster Taking the Wechsler Intelligence Scale for Children, Revised (WISC-R)
(Adapted from Sattler, 1982)

and the ability to define the word *ballast* be used to measure his intelligence? The rationale is that a person who knows the capital of Greece is also more likely to have other kinds of rare information; one who can repeat six digits backward can also manipulate other kinds of information mentally; and one who can abstract the similarities between farming and manufacturing can also think abstractly about other problems. The test is a sample of the person's abilities. While no one item is crucial to the measurement of his intelligence (why not ask for the capital of Italy?), the many items on a test give a person repeated opportunities to show that he has the knowledge and skills appropriate to his age.

In the usual test construction procedure, numerous items are tried out on a large, representative sample of people to find those items that best discriminate among people of different ages. Often, test-makers must discard items that discriminate unnecessarily between males and females, rural and urban groups, and among races and socioeconomic groups. The goal is to build a test that samples all people fairly. To be an adequate sample of intelligence, the test must also be a reliable and valid sample of intellectual performance.

RELIABILITY A test is considered reliable if it yields a consistent, reproducible measure of an individual's performance. If a person takes the test twice during a relatively short period (a year or two), she should receive about the same score each time (test-retest reliability). She should obtain about the same score on odd-numbered and even-numbered questions (split-half reliability). The reliability of the Stanford–Binet and Wechsler scales is a high .90+ (1.00 indicates perfect reliability). The standard error (deviation of the test score from the person's "true" score) is not more than five IQ points, on the average. Whatever IQ tests measure, they do so reliably for all groups.

VALIDITY AND FAIRNESS The validity of a test depends on whether it actually measures what it was designed to measure. IQ tests were originally constructed to predict success in school. A large body of data from many years of testing show that they have good predictive validity. Those who receive high (or low) IQs usually do well (or poorly) in school and in jobs that require academic abilities. In other ways, however, the validity of IQ tests is questionable. A major criticism of IQ tests is that they are not a fair sample of a person's entire repertoire of intelligent behaviors.

One source of possible unfairness is the *testing situation* itself, which can be frightening to inexperienced subjects (Zigler, Abelson, & Seitz, 1973). Testing is also an artificial situation, one that some people may not take seriously or that may not evoke their best performance. On individual tests (the Stanford–Binet and WISC-R or WAIS-R), the examiner tries to build rapport before beginning the test. It is not always possible to reassure an anxious subject or motivate an indifferent one, however. In some cases the examiner may decide that the test was not a valid measure of the subject's information and skills. These precautions are not possible on a group paper-and-pencil test.

Another potential source of unfairness is the *cultural content* of the test. Most IQ tests contain items that depend on knowledge of a particular language and culture. As a result, they may discriminate against groups that are not familiar with the cultural content of the test. Non-English-speaking children, for example, may not understand the instructions or the questions. Poor black children may be unfamiliar with words from the standard English vocabulary if these words are not used in their homes. Children in isolated rural areas may not be familiar with some of the material. (There are more questions about literature than about farming or hunting on intelligence tests.) Therefore, it may be unfair to consider their IQ scores a measure of their "natural" ability. They might score much higher on a test based on their native language or more familiar subjects. But standard tests are a fair (or valid) measure of their probable success in school. Success in school, like scores on an intelligence test, depends on competence in the majority culture.

This young boy may be a future architect. But his score on an IQ test will not predict everything about his career success.

Raymond Cattell (1949) and others have attempted to construct "culture-fair" intelligence tests, using nonverbal materials that should be equally familiar or unfamiliar to everyone (see Figure 10-7). These tests did not succeed in eliminating average group differences, as hoped. In some cases minority children score higher on the culturally loaded standard tests than they do on tests designed to be culture-fair (Jensen, 1980). Moreover, scores on culture-fair tests do not correlate as highly with school performance as do conventional IQs. In other words, they lack predictive validity.

Another criticism of IQ tests is that they measure only a limited *sample* of intelligent behaviors. For the most part, they do not measure interpersonal skills, for example, or what Sternberg calls contextual knowledge. They do not credit a ghetto child for knowing how to escape arrest, a midwestern youngster for being able to milk a herd of cows in 30 minutes, an Appalachian child with skill at finding her way home through ten miles of West Virginia woods, or an upper-class child for his discriminating taste in gourmet food. They do not credit any child for being able to understand other people or resolve disputes among peers. IQ tests primarily measure *school-learning* ability, not general adaptation to life—an extremely important distinction.

Individual Difference in IQ

Intelligence tests show that individuals differ at every age, in every group. What accounts for these differences? Is a person's IQ established at an early age? Are people "born" smart or slow?

STABILITY AND CHANGE IN IQ Intelligence measures taken at age 2 are not very good predictors of the IQ score a child will achieve at age 10 or 15. As explained in Chapter 4, both the nature of intelligence and the structure of intelligence tests change in the preschool years. By the time children enter school, their IQs are more stable (Bloom, 1964). The correlation between IQ at age 6 and age 18 is between .70 and .80 (see Table 10-1). A child with a score of 130 is almost sure to have an above-average IQ as an adult. A child with a score of 70 is almost certain to be below average as an adult. And a child with an IQ of 100 is unlikely to test as

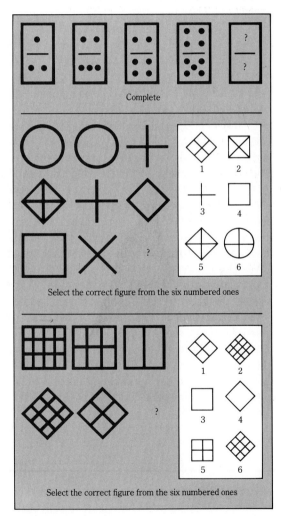

Figure 10-7 A Selection of "Culture-Fair" IQ Test Items

Table 10-1   Correlation of Mental Test Scores across Ages

Approximate Age at First Test	Name of First Test	Years Elapsed between First and Second Test			
		1	3	6	12
3 months	California First-Year	0.10	0.05	−0.13	0.02
1 year	California First-Year	0.47	0.23	0.13	0.00
2 years	California Preschool	0.74	0.55	0.50	0.42
3 years	California Preschool	0.64	—	0.55	0.33
4 years	Stanford–Binet	—	0.71	0.73	0.70
6 years	Stanford–Binet	0.86	0.84	0.81	0.77
7 years	Stanford–Binet	0.88	0.87	0.73	0.80
9 years	Stanford–Binet	0.88	0.82	0.87	—
11 years	Stanford–Binet	0.93	0.93	0.92	—

(Adapted from Bayley, 1949)

retarded (IQ of 70 and below) or as a genius (IQ of 140 and above) in later life.

The developmental path from age 6 to 18 is not necessarily a smooth one, however. Longitudinal studies show that IQ scores often fluctuate by twenty points or more during this period (Bayley, 1970; McCall, Applebaum, & Hogarty, 1973). The long-term stability but short-term fluctuations in IQ puzzle researchers. One explanation is that each child has his own, unique developmental path, with spurts and lags (Wilson, 1983). IQ tests are standardized so that the average is 100 at every age. As a result, the growth curve in IQ is a neat, sloping line. But individual children may have sharp rises, plateaus, and even temporary declines in intellectual skills. A child of 5 who is tested just after she made a great leap forward will score higher relative to her age-mates than she will at age 7 if she happens to be on a plateau at that time.

HEREDITY, HOMES, AND IQ In 1869 the English scientist Sir Francis Galton (1822–1911) published the results of a study of prominent British citizens. Galton found that eminent lawyers, scientists, and artists often had many equally illustrious relatives,[5] and concluded that genius runs

[5]Galton himself was Charles Darwin's cousin.

in families. Critics quickly pointed out that great men are able to provide their offspring with intellectual stimulation and innumerable other advantages. Genius might depend on opportunity. So began one of the longest debates in the history of psychology. Where does the matter stand today?

The simplest way to measure the inheritance of IQ is to examine the correlations in IQ between people of different degrees of relatedness. As shown in Table 10-2, the closer the genetic relationship, the higher the correlation. Identical (monozygotic) twins, who share all their genes, are more alike than siblings or fraternal (dizygotic) twins, who share half their genes. Even when they are reared apart, the scores of identical twins are as close as the scores of the same person tested on two different occasions. Judging by IQ tests in adolescence, adopted children reared in the same home are no more alike than two complete strangers (Scarr & Weinberg, 1978).

This is not to say that the environment has *no* impact on IQ. Identical twins, and parents and children, who live together are more alike than those who live apart. Moreover, adopted children reared in advantaged homes score significantly higher, on the average, than one would expect on the basis of heredity alone. As a rule, their scores are higher than those of their biological parents. But on the whole, genetic influences on individual IQ scores seem stronger than environmental forces.

The solution to the gene/environment controversy is found in the concept of *reaction range* (see Chapter 2). Genes determine the responsiveness of an individual to various environments. In an intellectually impoverished environment, a child's IQ may hover near the bottom of his range. With excellent care and continuous intellectual stimulation, he may develop his full intellectual potential (Scarr & McCartney, 1983).

Race and IQ

The evidence on racial differences in IQ is more complicated—and more controversial. Just as there are individual variations in IQ within groups, so there are *average* differences among groups in IQ. Differences among groups take the form of overlapping curves (see Figure 10-8). This means that some members of a low-average group have *higher* IQs than most members of a high-average group, and that some in a high-average group have *lower* IQs than most in a low-average group.

On the average, Asian-Americans score highest on IQ tests, followed by whites, Hispanics, and blacks. The average IQ for whites in the United States is ten to fifteen points higher than that for blacks (Jensen, 1980; Kamin, 1974). On

Table 10-2   IQ and Degrees of Relatedness: Similarities of Genetically Related and Unrelated Persons Who Live Together and Apart

Relationship	Correlation	Number of Pairs
Genetically identical		
Identical twins together	.86	1,300
Identical twins apart	.76	137
Same person tested twice	.87	456
Genetically related by half of the genes		
Fraternal twins together	.55	8,600
Biological sisters & brothers	.47	35,000
Parents & children together	.40	4,400
Parents & children apart	.31	345
Genetically unrelated		
Adopted children together	.00	200*
Unrelated persons apart	.00	15,000

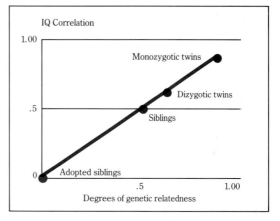

(Table adapted from Plomin & DeFries, 1980)
* Based on data from Scarr and Weinberg (1978) and Teasdale and Owen (1984) on older adolescents, who are comparable in age to other samples in this table. Younger adopted children resemble each other to a greater degree with correlations around .24, based on samples of 800 pairs.

The more closely related people are, the more alike they are in IQ—and perhaps interests. (The Koralja triplets are all members of the Jersey City police force.)

this nearly all psychologists agree. But there is less agreement on what this statistic *means*. On one hand are those who argue that racial differences in IQ are the result largely of heredity. On the other hand are those who argue that these differences are the result of social inequality and discrimination.

THE HERITABILITY QUESTION Given the evidence that genes play a role in creating individual variations in IQ, it seems logical to conclude that heredity also plays a role in creating racial differences. The psychologist most closely associated with this point of view is Arthur Jensen. Jensen's review of a number of twin studies led him to conclude that the heritability of IQ is about +.80. If this is so, he reasoned, it is "a not unreasonable hypothesis that genetic factors are strongly implicated in the average Negro–white intelligence difference" (1969). Jensen estimated that one-half to three-quarters of the dif-

ference between blacks and whites might be attributed to heredity.

One of the main criticisms of Jensen's position relates to his interpretation of the heritability of racial differences. The *heritability ratio* is an estimate of how much of the variation in IQ (or another trait) within a group is due to heredity and how much to the environment. There are three important things to know about the heritability ratio.

First, heritability is a population statistic that applies to groups, not individuals. If the heritability ratio for IQ is +.50, this does *not* mean that 50 percent of each child's IQ is determined by genetic factors. Rather, it means that 50 percent of the variation in a group can be traced to genetic differences among members of that group.

Second, the heritability ratio is not fixed. It applies to a particular group at a particular time. Like the birth rate, the infant mortality rate, and

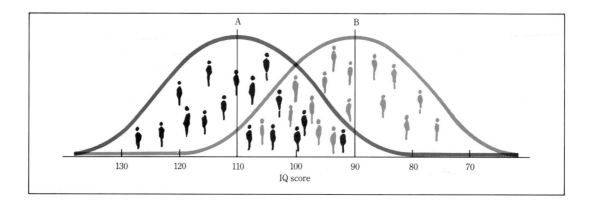

Figure 10-8 Group Averages in IQ Form Overlapping Curves Some people in group A score below the mean IQ for group B and some people in group B score above the mean IQ for group A.

other population statistics, it can and does change.

Third, heritability estimates alone do not explain differences *between* groups. Even if the heritability of a trait is high for two groups, the difference between them may be due largely to the environment. For example, height has a high heritability ratio. Tall parents have taller children than short parents do. If you visit a village of subsistence farmers who have barely enough to eat, you might find that the men's heights vary from 4 ft. 10 in. to 5 ft. 6 in. Most of this variation is due to heredity. If you visit another village where people eat well, you might find that men's heights vary from 5 ft. 4 in. to 6 ft. These variations are also due to heredity. But the difference between the villages is the result of diet, or the environment, not genes. (See Figure 10-9).

SOCIAL AND ECONOMIC INFLUENCES Several recent studies indicate that the racial "IQ gap" is largely the result of social and cultural differences. For example, one team of researchers (Nichols & Anderson, 1974) compared the IQs of black and white children from families of very similar socioeconomic status (SES). Fifty thousand children born at ten major hospitals were followed from the prenatal stage to 8 years of age. In Boston, both black and white children came from high-SES families. In Baltimore and Philadelphia, both came from quite low-SES families. When tested at age 4 with the Stanford–Binet, the Boston children scored an average IQ of 105, regardless of race. The Baltimore and Philadelphia children scored an average of 93, again regardless of race. The twelve-point difference betweem them was correlated with social class. When tested again at age 7, racial differences did appear, but they were small. These findings suggest that the difference between white and black average IQ scores may be the result of social class differences, not race.

A French study supports this view (Schiff et al., 1978). Researchers compared working-class children who had been adopted by upper-middle-class families to their siblings who lived with their biological parents. The average IQ of the adoptees was 110.6; that of the children who remained in working-class environments, 94.7. Whereas 55 percent of the nonadopted children had failing grades in school, 85 percent of their adopted siblings passed.

The Minnesota Adoption Study (Scarr & Weinberg, 1976) supported this conclusion. The subjects of the study were 99 black and interracial children who had been adopted by economically advantaged white parents of above-average intelligence. The question was whether

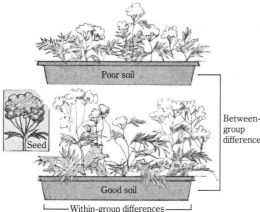

Between-group differences

Within-group differences

Figure 10-9 Between-Group Differences and Within-Group Differences The same seeds planted in poor and good soil show average differences in plant height and number of flowers. Genetic variations in seeds planted within each box produce plants of different heights and flowers, even though they are raised in the same environment.
(After Gleitman, 1983)

Insight

THE POLITICS OF INTELLIGENCE TESTING

Alfred Binet saw his mental scale as an instrument for identifying children who needed to learn how to learn. He believed that intellectual ability, like athletic ability, responds to training and practice. Indeed, he outlined a program of "mental orthopedics" to increase the mental age of slow learners. Commenting on the notion that intelligence is a fixed quantity, Binet declared, "We must protest and react against such brutal pessimism" (1909, p. 126). Ironically, it was the view that intelligence is fixed that fueled enthusiasm for the new mental tests in the United States.

The Binet–Simon scale was published at a time when many Americans were alarmed by the increasing numbers of Europeans coming to this country. In 1912, the U.S. Public Health Service asked the psychologist Henry Goddard to devise a method for screening new arrivals (Kamin, 1974). Despite differences in language and culture, Goddard believed the Binet scale could be adapted for the task. Over the next decade, thousands of immigrants were deported because Goddard's tests found that they were "feeble-minded." Conveniently for the racists of the day, the tests indicated that the least popular immigrants—Jews, Russians, Hungarians, Italians—were also the least intelligent.

Unlike Binet, Goddard held that intelligence is a fixed, hereditary trait, and that some ethnic groups were more intelligent than others. He thought it might be possible to train some members of these groups for simple manual jobs. But he saw no point in offering all of them education or citizenship. Goddard was not alone. Psychologists who analyzed the results of intelligence tests the Army gave to nearly two million draftees during World War I declared "Nordics" genetically superior to southern and eastern Europeans. In fact, differences in IQ scored reflected how long immigrants had been in this country, and how familiar they were with the language and culture. But the idea that intelligence (or the lack of it) was hereditary appealed to nativists. Where Binet saw intelligence tests as a tool for including youngsters with learning problems in the educational system, many American psychologists and politicians saw them as scientific justification for excluding the unwanted.

Such flagrant misuse and misinterpretation of IQ scores is rare today. Still, intelligence tests remain controversial. In 1969, Arthur Jensen published a long, scholarly article in which he concluded that the *average* difference between the IQ scores of whites and blacks might be due to genetic factors. Jensen took pains to explain that this hypothesis did not apply to *individuals*. But his position was simplified and exaggerated in the press and by some scientists (Shockley, 1971). There were flaws in his interpretation. But the attack on Jensen went beyond normal scientific debate. Whereas genetic explanations of group differences had been cheered in the 1920s, genetic hypotheses were taboo in the 1960s and 1970s.

The IQ controversy reached the courts in California in the 1970s. Larry P. was one of six black children who had been assigned to special programs for the educable mentally retarded (EMR). In *Larry P. v. Wilson Riles,* his lawyers argued that a disproportionate number of minority children were assigned to EMR classes; that EMR placement was based primarily on IQ tests; and that EMR classes were an academic dead end that stigmatized children for their entire school career. California's use of IQ tests to assign children to special classes was undermining Public Law 94-142 guaranteeing handicapped children equal education, lawyers argued.

Although Larry P. was suing the state of California, psychological measurement was on trial. Larry P.'s main argument was that IQ tests are culturally (if not racially) biased. Nadine Lambert (1981) summarized the arguments for the defense of IQ testing. First, the state of California banned the use of IQ tests in placing children in classes for the mentally retarded shortly after the trial began. Although the number of students placed in such classrooms dropped substantially, the proportion of minority children remained about the same. (Lambert notes that males are also overrepresented in special classes, but that no one has filed a sex discrimination suit on their behalf.) Second, IQ tests usually are given to determine why a child has repeatedly failed in school, not to determine whether a child *will* fail. And the test is usually part of an overall assessment that includes interviews with the child's parents and teachers. Third, there is no evidence that placement in a special education program has lasting negative effects on a child. Indeed, some studies have shown that low-IQ adults who were enrolled in special education programs as children are more likely to be financially independent, self-sufficient, and successfully married than are similar adults who attended a regular school program.

In *Larry P. v. Wilson Riles,* the California courts ruled in favor of the plaintiff—and against psychometrics. Intelligence tests are no longer used to help decide whether a child requires special education in California. In a related case in Illinois, however, the courts ruled that IQ tests are a valid measure of intellectual ability and are less likely to be biased than clinical evaluations. Given these contradictory rulings, it seems probable that the IQ controversy will reach the U.S. Supreme Court in the near future.

black children reared in culturally advantaged environments would score higher IQs than children raised in a lower-class black environment. They did: The average IQ of the adopted children was 110, compared with an average IQ of 90 for other black children in the same region. As their IQs predicted, the adoptees also scored above average on school-administered achievement tests.

Many of the families in the study had natural or biological children as well as adopted children. The biological children had higher IQs than the adopted children. This is not surprising. The biological offspring had the double advantage of their bright parents' genes and a stimulating environment. (The biological mothers of the adopted children were about average in intelligence, as judged by their levels of education.) Although the adopted children scored below the natural offspring, they scored *above* the average of *white nonadopted* children their age.

This study suggests, first, that explanations of racial differences in IQ must take the social environment into account. Black children in an advantaged environment develop more of their potential than do white children in an average environment, and considerably more than do black children in an impoverished environment. Second, intelligence (as measured by IQ tests) is not a fixed trait; it responds to stimulation or deprivation. Finally, if all black parents were able to provide the cultural milieu and social advantages these adoptive parents offered, the average IQ for blacks might be ten to twenty points higher than it is.

PREDICTIONS FOR GROUPS IQ tests provide useful predictive information about success in school and in many jobs for all groups. Low IQ scores predict low achievement in school, whomever the scorer, and high IQ scores predict success in school, regardless of the social class, race, or ethnic group to which a person belongs. Like IQ test performance, school and job performance are based on the standards of the majority group. The predictor (the test) and the criteria (school or job requirements) have the same underlying bias.

IQ scores cannot predict anyone's future exactly, however; some children defy the statistics. Nor do IQ scores tell psychologists what a child *could* have achieved in a different environment. But in some cases one can make an educated guess. When presented with an otherwise well adjusted child with an IQ of 80 from a white, middle-class family, one can guess that the home environment has not stunted the child's intellectual development. A black child from an urban slum with an IQ of 80 probably has more potential for intellectual development. In the second case, the child's environment is both culturally different and less intellectually stimulating. Both of these factors would lower his IQ score. His future environment is likely to be similar to his past environment, so one should not expect changes in his IQ. Nor should one expect him to excel in school, unless he has extraordinary teaching. Outside school, however, he may function normally. The first child probably will not adapt as well as the second child to his social setting.

Testing *for* Children: Some Alternatives

Intelligence tests would not be as controversial if so much did not depend on them. The IQ is often treated as a "magical number." A child's score on this one test may influence what her teachers expect from her, what educational opportunities she will be offered, and thus, indirectly, her life chances. Some psychologists defend intelligence tests as an objective measure that eliminates personal bias from education selection (Jensen, 1973). This may be true. But does it justify the *exclusive* use of tests in deciding a child's scholastic future? Many psychologists think not.

Schools have a responsibility to educate children, not just their minds (Scarr, 1981). This means that schools must foster social competence. *Social competence* is the ability to make good developmental use of environmental and personal resources (see Chapter 8). It is the ability to adapt to social circumstances (or to change them) and to fill social roles, including the role of student. Social competence depends not only on cognitive abilities, but also on physi-

cal health and well-being, achievement in school, and such personality factors as achievement motivation, self-image, and creativity (Zigler & Seitz, 1982).

IQ tests measure only part of social competence. Whenever psychologists measure a child's intelligence, they are measuring the child's motivation and adjustment as well. The child's performance on a test—and in school—depends on such things as cooperation, attention, persistence, social responsiveness, and even the ability to sit still. The child's score reflects her motivational history and current state. During one test, the psychologist asked a child, "What is an orange?" The child said that he didn't know. Was the youngster retarded? Was his environment so impoverished that he lacked such common knowledge? (He lived in an institution.) Neither was true: Further questioning revealed that he did not answer the question because he wanted to prolong the interaction with the psychologist. The child was lonely. For once, he had an adult's undivided attention (Zigler & Seitz, 1982). Individual tests may uncover motivational reasons for poor performance; group tests do not. Neither type of test measures youngster's health, home life, or success in making friends.

Several alternatives to the exclusive use of intelligence tests are gaining support among psychologists and educators. The first is a *battery of tests* with explicit measures of health and psychological and social well-being. SOMPA, Jane Mercer's System of Multicultural Pluralistic Assessment for 5- to 11-year-olds, is an example (Mercer & Lewis, 1978). SOMPA uses the WISC-R to measure cognitive ability, then adds: (1) a two-hour interview with parents to provide background on the child's social and economic circumstances; (2) an adaptive behavior inventory, which includes such questions as "Does your child prepare his or her own lunch?" and "How many pupils in his or her class does your child know?"; and (3) a thorough medical examination and history. The child's IQ score is adjusted in light of the results of these three assessments. However, many psychologists are seriously concerned about using different sets of norms for different racial and ethnic groups to predict the same outcomes.

IQ tests measure what a child already knows. *Dynamic assessment* is designed to measure what a child is capable of learning. This approach is based on the Russian psychologist Lev Vygotsky's concept of "the zone of proximal development" (see Chapter 7). In Vygotsky's words, this zone includes

those functions that have not yet matured but are in the process of maturation, functions that will mature tomorrow but are in the embryonic state. These functions could be termed the "buds" and "flowers" rather than the "fruits" of development. (1978, pp. 86–87)

Dynamic tests often use problems from standard IQ tests, such as copying a block design. But if the child cannot copy the design on the first try, the psychologist provides him with a clue. If he still does not grasp the solution, the psychologist provides another clue, and another. When they have solved the problem together, the psychologist presents the child with a similar task and again provides as many clues as he needs to complete the task. This form of testing provides a measure of the child's learning speed and his ability to transfer skills from one problem to another. (See Budoff, 1974; Campione, Brown, & Ferrara, 1982; Feuerstein, Rand, Hoffman, & Miller 1979.)

Criterion-referenced tests are still another alternative. Standard intelligence tests are norm referenced. That is, the score indicates the child's rank among other children, regardless of how much material or which material he has mastered. On criterion-referenced tests, the child's performance is compared with an accepted standard in a particular area. The basic idea is: If you want to know whether a child can

tie her shoes, ask her to tie her shoes. These tests have begun to replace intelligence tests in personnel placement, on the grounds that the kinds of scholastic aptitudes IQ tests measure do not necessarily predict success in an occupation (McClelland, 1973). With children, criterion-referenced tests are used to identify specific areas of educational need.

The growing popularity of criterion-referenced tests is part of a general move away from using tests to classify and sort children, toward using tests as diagnostic tools. This shift reflects a return to Binet's commitment to improving educational programs for those youngsters whose current skills are not well developed—or testing *for* children.

Exceptional Children

Few children score exactly 100 on IQ tests. But two out of three score between 85 and 115 (± 1 standard deviation from the mean), and nine in ten receive IQs between 70 and 130 (± 2 standard deviations from the mean). At the opposite extremes of this are two special groups of children: the mentally retarded and the intellectually gifted.

The Mentally Retarded

Estimates are that 2–3 percent of the United States population—about six million Americans—are mentally retarded (Gearheart, 1980). Psychologists distinguish between two broad categories of mental retardation: organic and familial. *Organic retardation* refers to severe mental limitations caused by genetic defects or environmental traumas. Down's syndrome (described in Chapter 3) is an example. *Familial retardation* refers to milder forms of mental disorders whose causes are unknown. For no apparent physiological reason, these children have IQs that are much lower than average. This form of mental retardation tends to run in families. As shown in Figure 10-10 on p. 415, the risk of mental retardation is highest in families

Insight

ABILITY VS. EFFORT: CROSS-CULTURAL VIEWS OF ACHIEVEMENT

Harold Stevenson and his colleagues James Stigler, C. C. Hsu, and S. Kitamura recently completed a study (discussed in Cunningham, 1984) of 5,000 first- and fifth-graders from Japan, Taiwan, and the United States. They found that Japanese and Taiwanese students outperform their American peers as early as first grade.

If achievement were distributed evenly among these three populations, 33 of the poorest 100 readers would be found in each group. But American first-graders received 47 of the lowest 100 scores on vocabulary tests, 57 of the lowest 100 scores on reading comprehension, and 58 of the lowest 100 math scores. In fifth grade, 67 Americans numbered among the poorest 100 math students and only one ranked in the top 100 in math. These differences in achievement could not be attributed to "native intelligence": The children's performances on basic cognitive tasks were similar. Social factors were also ruled out: A much higher proportion of the American mothers and fathers had attended college than was true of either the Taiwanese or Japanese parents.

Stevenson traces this "achievement gap" to parents' attitudes and behavior. American mothers tend to explain their child's success in school (or the lack of it) in terms of ability, not achievement. They believe parents should encourage a child and be aware of school experiences, but not interfere. Most parents are happy with their child's school performance; indeed, 40 percent said that they were "very satisfied." In contrast, Japanese mothers believe that hard work and effort, not ability, determine whether a child will do well in school. They devote considerable time to their preschoolers, structuring learning experiences, and helping older children with homework. Only about 10 percent of the Japanese and Taiwanese mothers said that they were "very satisfied" with their child's achievements. Many Japanese parents and educators object to the use of IQ tests. In their view, the tests put too much emphasis on individual differences, discourage group effort, and undermine group harmony.

Differences in parents' attitudes, standards, and behavior translate into concrete differences in students' behavior. Japanese first-graders spend an average of 37 minutes a day doing homework, Taiwanese first-graders spend 77 minutes, and American first-graders spend an average of 14 minutes. Japanese children pay attention to their teachers. American youngsters are often seen talking to classmates, wandering around the room, or staring vacantly into space.

By high school, the average Japanese student devotes several hours a day to schoolwork and scores much higher on achievement tests than the typical American student. Critics argue that the pressure to achieve in the Japanese educational system stifles creativity. Stevenson disagrees. "Go to Fifth Avenue [in New York City]. Look at the [Japanese] innovations in fashion, in film. Look at the avant-garde dancers. Look at Nikon cameras. . . . Look at robotics. Look at computers . . ." (Cunningham, 1984).

Down's syndrome is an example of organic retardation. Children with this genetic disorder have pleasant personalities and respond to care and training. There is a limit to what they can achieve intellectually, however. (This woman's second child is a normal, healthy baby.)

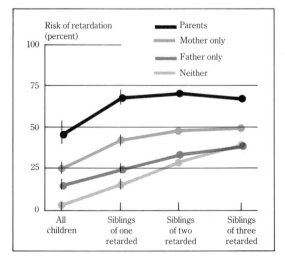

Figure 10-10 Risk of Mental Retardation The risk that a child will be mentally retarded increases if the child's mother, mother and father, and one or more siblings are mentally retarded—in that order. (Anderson, 1974)

where both parents and one or more siblings are retarded. Although the incidence of organic retardation is about the same for all social classes, familial retardation is more common in the lower classes (Zigler & Seitz, 1982). This may be because mentally impaired adults drift down into the lower classes and transmit genes for lower IQs to their children; and because impoverished environments lower mental functioning in parents and children or both.

Are retarded youngsters able to adapt to ordinary home life and regular schools? Or are they better off in specialized facilities? One comparison of retarded children who are institutionalized with similar children living at home found that both treatments have costs and benefits (Harter & Zigler, 1974). The noninstitutionalized children displayed more curiosity and exploratory behavior than did the institutionalized children. But they were less confident of their own abilities—presumably because they often found themselves in situations in which they were at an intellectual disadvantage. This suggests that there is no one way to guide retarded children through school. The right decision depends on the specific child, the family, and the resources the community provides.

The Debate over "Mainstreaming" Children with IQs of 70 to 85 are classified as educable mentally retarded (EMR) or minimally handicapped (Ysseldyke & Stevens, in press). These children may function adequately at home yet perform far behind their age-mates at school.

Joseph Campione and his colleagues (Campione, Brown, & Ferrara, 1982) see this milder form of retardation as a problem in information processing. In their view, there are two main differences between intellectually normal youngsters and youngsters with this learning handicap. First, mildly retarded children have difficulty learning new strategies for solving problems. With normal children, much learning is incidental. The youngsters "pick up" techniques for processing information without formal instruction. For example, without being taught, most children discover that it is easier to remember a series of numbers (1, 5, 6, 7, 9, 3) if they "chunk" them (15, 67, 93) than if they commit them to memory one at a time. Retarded children do not develop such strategies on their own; they require explicit instruction. Second, retarded children have difficulty transferring old learning to new situations. When intellectually normal children develop the knack for chunking, they apply it spontaneously to different problems (such as remembering a series of pictures, phone numbers, and grocery lists). Mentally retarded youngsters tend to treat each problem as a new one, ignoring prior experience. They do not generalize on their own, but have to be taught step-by-step what other youngsters grasp with effort or explanation. Campione and colleagues suggest that the extent to which a person needs instruction in how to learn is a measure of his or her mental retardation.

These inherent learning difficulties contribute to the debate over how much mildly retarded students benefit from placement in classrooms with students of normal intelligence. Public Law 94-142 requires states to provide "free appropriate public education" in the "least restrictive environment" for all handicapped children, including the mentally retarded. As a result many mildly retarded children who would have been placed in special classes or special schools ten years ago are now in regular classrooms. *Mainstreaming,* as this is called, is con-troversial. Advocates of mainstreaming argue that placing mildly retarded children in special classes stigmatizes them. Being labeled slow lowers a child's self-esteem and motivation to learn. A simplified curriculum denies the child the opportunity to learn what other children learn in regular academic programs. Opponents of mainstreaming counter that placing mildly retarded children in classrooms with children of average intelligence exposes them to continual stress and frustration. They will always be at the bottom of their class. Other children may avoid or tease them.

Do mildly retarded children learn more in regular classrooms? One team of researchers (Goldstein, Moss, & Jordan, 1965) found that retarded youngsters achieved more in regular classrooms than similar youngsters did in special classrooms the first year, but that the difference faded after three years. Other researchers (Kaufman, Agard, & Semmel, 1978) found that these children pay more attention to academic tasks in special classrooms than they (or normal children) do in regular classes. But increased attention did not translate into higher achievement scores. The available research indicates that mainstreaming does not improve school performance, but neither does it lower achievement. The youngsters perform at about the same level in either environment (Semmel, Gottlieb, & Robinson, 1979).

How does mainstreaming affect social adjustment? Do mainstreamed youngsters have a better self-image than their peers in special classes? Do they find it harder or easier to make friends? Again, the data are inconclusive (Semmel, Ballard, & Sivasailam, 1979). Being in a regular or a special class seems to have little effect on a child's self-esteem and self-confidence. An early study (Thurstone, 1959) found that retarded children can be "stars" in special classes for learning-disabled youngsters but never stand out—often becoming "isolates"—in regular classrooms. This remains true. However, there is some evidence that other children accept a mentally retarded classmate better when the teacher carefully arranges group activities to include the child (Kaufman et al., 1978).

Most research on mentally retarded youngsters focuses on their adjustment to school. Often overlooked is that many of these children function adequately outside school. Their problems may be confined largely to school hours. One sociologist (Mercer, 1973) calls this "six-hour retardation"; "16-year retardation" might also apply. Mentally retarded adults have mental ages in the 9- to 12-year-old range. By comparison, adults with IQs of 100 have a mental age of 16. Mildly retarded adults may not be able to attend college or to work at white-collar jobs. But they are capable of getting dressed, traveling to and from work, performing undemanding jobs, shopping for themselves, talking with friends, enjoying movies, and other routines of daily life. Just as a high IQ does not guarantee that a person will be socially competent (much less happy), so a low IQ does not dictate that a person will be socially incompetent. In mild cases, mental retardation is primarily a handicap in the school years.

The Gifted

Teachers, pediatricians, child psychologists, and others who work with children occasionally encounter a youngster whose knowledge, logic, or special skills are unusual for her age, or perhaps for any age. A 5-year-old who understands calculus, an 8-year-old poet, a chess master of 10, an elementary school child who composes fugues are exceptional children!

"Precocity," "brightness," and "genius" are closely related concepts. *Brightness* means very high ranking on IQ tests. *Precocity* means the early attainment of advanced forms of cognitive development (Inhelder, 1965). Precocious children surprise us with the advanced level, the depth, and the breadth of their cultural knowledge, logical powers, and special talents. *Ge-*

nius is best defined as the general recognition of a person's unusual contribution to society (Montour, 1977). Children are not candidates for the term *genius;* a child's brightness and precocity may or may not be translated into socially significant accomplishments worthy of the label *genius* in adulthood. Brightness is necessary but is insufficient to cause genius; precocity is a frequent companion to it.

The early histories of adult geniuses are often marked by precocity. Science abounds with precocious children. As a boy, the famous French mathematician and philosopher Blaise Pascal single-handedly reconstructed most of Euclid's proofs in geometry and went on to reinvent large portions of higher mathematics. For unknown reasons, Pascal's father had forbidden the boy to talk about mathematics.

Pascal, however, began to dream [about] the subject and . . . he used to mark with charcoal the walls of his playroom, seeking a means of making a circle perfectly round and a triangle whose sides and angles were all equal. He discovered these things for himself and then began to seek the relationship which existed between them. He did not know any mathematical terms and so he made up his own. . . . Using these names he made axioms and finally developed perfect demonstrations . . . until he had come to the thirty-second proposition of Euclid. (Gardner, 1983, p. 152)

The renowned pianist Arthur Rubinstein came from a family that, in his own words, lacked "the slightest musical gift." Nevertheless, Rubinstein's parents bought a piano for their older children. He was not given lessons. But

half in fun, half in earnest, I learned to know the keys by their names and with my back to the piano I would call the notes of any chord, even the most dissonant one. From then on it became mere child's play to master the intricacies of the keyboard, and I was soon able to play first with one [hand], later with both, any tune that caught my ear. . . . (Gardner, 1983, p. 113)

Child's play indeed. Rubinstein had reached the advanced age of 3!

TERMAN'S "GENIUSES" In 1925, Lewis Terman, the American psychologist who translated Alfred Binet's intelligence test into English, began a longitudinal study of 1,500 youngsters whose IQs were 140 or higher. Terman found that, contrary to popular belief, intellectually gifted children were neither social misfits nor physically frail. Indeed, these youngsters were bigger, healthier, and better adjusted than were their less gifted age-mates. Follow-up studies conducted every five or ten years (Oden, 1968; Terman, 1925; Terman & Oden, 1947, 1959)

revealed that they have lived unusually successful lives in nearly every sphere. Many are intellectuals, humanitarians, and social leaders. They have written hundreds of books, tried thousands of law cases, become judges on supreme courts, eminent physicians, deans and presidents of universities. Most are happy with their social and family lives. None of them has made a major creative breakthrough—which supports the view that IQ tests do not measure creativity. But they are outstanding adults by almost any measure.

The Terman children seem to show that those with unusual native intelligence cannot fail. David McClelland (1973), among others,

Rubinstein is one child prodigy who lived up to his early promise.

questions this conclusion. McClelland points out that most of the Terman youngsters were white, middle- and upper-class children from economically and intellectually superior families. He argues that their achievements as adults were as much the result of opportunity as of high IQs. We conclude that very bright children, given opportunities, are often very successful later in life.

STANLEY'S YOUNG MATHEMATICIANS Julian Stanley and his colleagues at Johns Hopkins University (Stanley, Keating, & Fox, 1974) studied 35 mathematically talented boys, ages 12 to 14. In seventh and eighth grades 31 of these boys scored 600 or higher on their College Entrance Examination S.A.T. for mathematics—which placed them in the 89th percentile for male *high school seniors*. Many had had no formal training in mathematics beyond arithmetic. Like Pascal, they had taught themselves. Stanley found that these young mathematicians were above the average of their age-mates for most "good" personality traits: maturity, stability, sense of well-being, flexibility, and leadership (as measured by the California Psychological Inventory). Bored and frustrated with their grade, some needed only to be given senior high school work. Others went from eighth grade into a selective college curriculum without faltering.

While still 13, . . . Bill enrolled at [Johns] Hopkins for honors calculus, physics, and computer science, a 12-credit load. He made A's in both calculus and physics and a B in computer science. (The next semester he took the second course in computer science and made an A.) His GPA for that initial semester was 3.75. His parents had indeed been right. He was fully ready intellectually to do splendid work at a selective college.

Bill is now a 16-year-old senior. After performing brilliantly the first two years, he has encountered adjustment problems which are taking some time to solve. Fortunately he is three years accelerated, so there is no need to hurry.

Leaving junior high school for Hopkins "cured" Bill's academic and personal maladjustment for two splendid years. Few students or faculty members at Hopkins paid much attention to his long blond hair or his dirty field jacket and nobody threw rocks at him, literally or figuratively. He was keenly attuned to the Hopkins atmosphere intellectually ("Seems like a bright, highly articulate graduate student," one faculty member told me). During his first year he commuted from home (requiring some five miles of walking daily), but since that wasted so much time he moved into a dormitory on campus in October of his sophomore year. This seemed to work out well. Bill is neater now and appears to have friends on campus and also in the Sierra Club for hiking and mountain climbing. (Stanley et al., 1974, p. 15)

Stanley holds that opportunity alone does not explain such youngsters' gifts. They were "born mathematicians."

FELDMAN'S PRODIGIES David Feldman, whose interest in child prodigies we mentioned earlier, amplifies Stanley's interpretation. Feldman (1980) has studied prodigies directly and indirectly, through biographies and case histories. He concedes that prodigies reach relatively advanced levels of achievement on their own but require instruction to excel. One of the young chess masters he is studying asked his father to teach him the game when he was 4. The child was able to beat anyone at his family's swim club before he reached his fifth birthday. At this point his father found an instructor for the boy at a New York chess club. Without formal instruction, Feldman argues, the boy would never have become a chess master at age 8, or perhaps at any age. The 9-year-old composer and violinist Feldman studied was taking weekly classes in theory and composition, violin, solfège, chamber music, and piano, plus a monthly master class in violin. Feldman believes these children are born with a remarkable capacity to learn in a specific area, not with innate understanding of the field. They are "preorganized," not preformed.

In some ways, the prodigies Feldman studied conform to Piaget's notions of cognitive development. Their development in their particular field took place in stages; each stage was marked by a new level of understanding and mastery. Their instructors taught them in stages, leading them through the history of chess or music step-by-step. In other ways they violated Piaget's theory, however. Clearly they had attained the level of formal operations in their own field, but they did not use formal operations in other areas. When tested outside their specialty (on cognitive measures of map drawing, moral judgment, role-taking, and hypothetical reasoning), they were well within the normal range—bright but not extraordinary. Feldman adds that away from the chess tournament or the music room, they acted like normal children.

Feldman sees prodigies as the product of a remarkable coincidence: the matching of a specialized individual and a specialized environment. He goes on to speculate about why such extraordinary and specialized gifts are rare.

The fact that there are not more examples of prodigious achievement suggests that, on the whole, Nature is a conservative gambler. I am not suggesting by this statement that Nature has a game plan, but rather that the few prodigies produced means relatively few chancy situations. Since the risks—as well as the likely payoffs—of producing a specialized organism are greater than the risks of producing a flexible one, and since a complex, subtle set of environmental forces is required for the pretuned organism to express its potential, it makes sense that relatively few astounding coincidence[s] of this sort would occur. To produce a large number of specialized individuals, limited in the range of environments to which they might respond, would seem to go against the grain of evolution. (Feldman, 1980, p. 152)

SUMMARY

1. Human evolution is in part the story of the evolution of our brains (encephalization). As our ancestors moved from forests to savannah, they developed language and what we call "intelligence."

2. Nonexperts' definitions of intelligence are similar to psychologists' definitions, but nonexperts emphasize social skills whereas psychologists emphasize private thinking.

3. Psychologists who study intelligence can be divided into two groups. "Lumpers" (such as Spearman) maintain that intelligence is general ability, or *g*, that governs performance in many different areas. "Splitters" (such as Thurstone and Guilford) argue that intelligence is composed of many abilities, and that an individual may be smarter in some areas than in others. Both views are based on psychometrics.

4. Robert Sternberg's model of intelligence links adaptation to the sociocultural environment and information-processing strategies common to any form of intelligent behavior. In his view, intelligence depends on contextual knowledge (or adaptability), the ability to deal with novelty (or "cleverness"), and the ability to perform familiar though difficult intellectual tasks automatically ("expertise"), as well as specific information-processing skills.

5. How well an individual performs an intellectual task may also depend on cognitive style (for example, field dependence or independence) and tempo (impulsive or reflective thinking).

6. Creativity—using ordinary materials in unusual and interesting or useful ways—requires intelligence. However, intelligence does not guarantee creativity.

7. There are two ways to look at creativity. The trait approach, which relies on tests of novel ideas or personality assessments, takes opportunities to develop creativity for granted. The process approach focuses on the environmentals that foster creativity and on the creative process itself. Feldman suggests that breakthroughs in art and science are not unlike the breakthroughs a child experiences moving from one stage of cognitive development to the next.

8. Intelligence tests are a quantitative measure of a person's cultural knowledge and mental skills. Binet's work led to the concept of mental age; Terman used the IQ to establish a person's rank among peers; Wechsler devised performance and verbal scales for children and adults.

9. All intelligence tests measure differences in the rate, quantity, and quality of learning. Although only a sample of the individual's abilities, IQ tests are a reliable and valid measure of probable achievement in school. Whether these tests are fair to all groups is controversial, however.

10. Analysis of individual scores suggests that after age 4 or 5, IQ is relatively stable. In large part, this is because heredity establishes an intellectual reaction range. But analysis of group differences (especially studies of children in different socioeconomic circumstances and adopted children) shows that IQ is not fixed, but responds to environmental stimulation.

11. The use of test batteries, dynamic assessment, and criterion-referenced tests reflects the belief that social competence is as important as IQ to a child's intellectual development.

12. Because of organic or familial retardation, some youngsters cannot perform at normal levels in school. The question of whether children who have mild intellectual handicaps should be assigned to special classes or placed in regular classes (mainstreaming) has not been resolved.

13. Some children are exceptionally bright for their age, or for any age. Terman's study of "geniuses," Stanley's work with young mathematicians, and Feldman's case studies of child prodigies all suggest that gifted children require nurturing (good homes and intensive training) for them to reach their potential.

FURTHER READING

Block, N. J., & Dworkin, G. (Eds.) (1976). *The IQ controversy.* New York: Pantheon Books. A collection of important papers written by psychologists, sociologists, and political scientists.

DuBois, P. H. (1970). *A history of psychological testing.* Boston: Allyn & Bacon. A short yet comprehensive overview of the development of psychological tests and the field of psychometrics.

Forrest, D. W. (1974). *Francis Galton: The life and work of a Victorian genius.* New York: Taplinger. A well-written biography of this pioneer who contributed to the development of psychological testing and formulated the major genetic principle of the segregation of inherited characteristics.

Jensen, A. R. (1982). *Straight talk about tests.* San Francisco: Freeman. A readable and scientifically accurate account about intelligence testing and the major results.

Sternberg, R. J., & Davidson, J. E. (1982, June). The mind of the puzzler. *Psychology Today,* pp. 37–44. Puzzles and games are seen through the eyes of a cognitive psychologist.

CHAPTER

Between the ages of 6 and 12, many children in the world go to work, contributing to their family's survival by caring for small children, laboring in the fields, herding livestock, and the like (Rogoff, Sellers, Pirotta, Fox, & White, 1975). In Western societies, this is the age when children embark on an educational journey that may take from ten to twenty years. The first day of school is a landmark in every Western child's life. In school the child must develop ways of relating to new adults (teachers and other staff) and children, and ways of dealing with new standards of behavior ("stay in your seat," "raise your hand," "do not talk out of turn," "get in line"). For the first time in his life, the child's performance will be graded. For the first time, he is on his own. But the friends he makes, his family life, and perhaps the TV he watches help to determine his adjustment to school. We begin this chapter by looking at the social dynamics of school, then consider friendships, different family situations, and the impact of television on behavior.

Becoming a Student

The school is a social institution, designed to transmit to the young a cultural ethos and worldview, as well as specific knowledge and skills. A school is also a small society, with its own membership, tasks, and rules. The average American child spends five hours a day, 180 days a year, for twelve years or more in school. Much of the youngster's development occurs in this unique social context.

The School As a Small Society

School is the child's introduction to an impersonal, bureaucratic organization in which power and privileges are distributed unequally (Parsons, 1959). One of the functions of school is to wean children from the intimate environment of the family and to prepare them for the more impersonal world of adults. Ideally, relationships in the family are based on affection and mutual obligations. The child is valued for who she is. Rules and schedules are adjusted to her needs and temperament. Once in school, the child must learn that what counts is what she does,

THE SOCIAL
WORLDS
OF CHILDHOOD

not who she is. Relationships in school are supposed to be based on the tasks at hand, not affection and liking. The same rules apply to everyone, regardless of personal qualities. How the child ranks in class depends on how she performs. The emphasis is on individual achievement. At home, cooperation and helpfulness are considered virtues; in school, cooperating with another child on a test and collaborating on homework are usually defined as "cheating." These lessons are part of school's hidden curriculum. Not stated directly to the child, they are implied in the structure of the classroom and embedded in daily regulations.

The school environment changes as the child moves from preschool programs to the elementary and secondary levels (Minuchin & Shapiro, 1983). Nursery school and kindergarten resemble home life. Preschoolers do not think of their class as a social unit. Most of their interactions are with teachers (who are usually female), individual peers, or small groups. The elementary classroom is more structured and complex. Children in the middle years usually see teachers as authority figures and leaders, not as friends. Teachers establish the climate in the classroom, set conditions for interaction among children, and build relationships with individual children and with the class as a whole.

But the real "social frontier" in the elementary classroom is the peer group. In elementary school, peer groups develop norms and a structure of their own, independent of adults. Friendships, belonging, and status in this group become increasingly important. In high school, students are oriented toward the school as a whole, rather than toward a particular classroom. They have different teachers (male and female) for different classes, are offered a variety of extracurricular activities, and are members of a number of peer groups. Behavior is oriented not only toward teachers and peers, but also toward the community (for example, in sports competitions with other schools). It is in this stage that students may begin to think of the school as a social organization—and to question the system.

Teaching Styles

Teachers determine the climate in a classroom by establishing and enforcing rules for interaction. What impact do different styles of teaching have on youngsters? In a classic study, Kurt Lewin and his colleagues (Lewin, Lippitt, & White, 1939) assigned groups of five 10-year-old-boys three different types of teachers. *Authoritarian* teachers dictated rules for behavior, made all the decisions (who was responsible for which tasks, who could work together, and so on), and praised good work, but were otherwise aloof and impersonal. *Democratic* teachers discussed the rules and regulations with their stu-

In most societies, education begins around age 6—even if it does not entail formal schooling. In Morocco, young Berber girls are taught the art of weaving by skilled adolescents.

dents, encouraged group participation in decisions, let the boys choose their activities and teammates, and often joined in group activities. *Laissez-faire* or permissive teachers gave the group complete freedom, offered advice and supplied materials only when requested, and refrained from praise, criticism, or any other interference. Lewin found that democratic teachers were most effective. The boys in their groups were more productive, worked better on their own, and had fewer quarrels among themselves than the boys in other groups did. Boys with authoritarian teachers were sometimes passive, sometimes rebellious, and generally unmotivated. Laissez-faire teaching led to boredom, inactivity, hostility, and fights.

A study by the British psychiatrist Michael Rutter and colleagues (Rutter, Maughan, Mortimore, & Ouston, 1979) provides more details

In first grade children get their first taste of regimentation.

on the impact of different teaching styles. The Rutter team followed the careers of London boys of similar socioeconomic backgrounds from their last year of primary school through third year of secondary school. The aim was to determine whether some schools were more successful than others, and if so, why. Success was measured in terms of school attendance; whether the boys remained in school beyond the age that they are legally required to do so; behavior in school; behavior outside school (shown by incidents of delinquency); and scores on a national examination.

Rutter's team found that the most successful schools were those in which the faculty held a consistent set of high standards for students and provided a model of commitment to learning. Teachers in the successful schools took education seriously. They started classes on time, gave regular homework assignments, and conveyed the expectation that their students would do well. They spent more time addressing the class as a whole than they did interacting with individual students. They gave their students immediate feedback, using praise more often than criticism. They treated students as responsible people, putting them in charge of study periods and the like. And they demonstrated concern for the students' needs and problems. Effective teaching paid off: Boys in the lowest ability group at the best school obtained about the same scores on national examinations as did boys in the highest ability group at the worst school. The delinquency rate at the worst school was three times that at the best school.

Teachers' Pets?

Teachers do not treat all students alike. Research consistently shows that they are attached to youngsters who achieve and conform; are concerned about youngsters who make demands they consider appropriate in the classroom; reject youngsters who make illegitimate demands as "behavior problems;" and are indifferent to youngsters who are quiet and shy (Minuchin & Shapiro, 1983).

What impact do teachers' attitudes and expectations have on students? Some years ago Robert Rosenthal and Lenore Jacobson (1968) told elementary school teachers that IQ tests had identified some of their students as "intellectual bloomers," who could be expected to make significant progress in the coming year. In fact, the bloomers were chosen at random from lists of first-through sixth-graders who had all been given IQ tests. Rosenthal and Jacobson hypothesized that high expectations would function as a self-fulfilling prophecy. If teachers expected certain children to do well, they would devote more attention to those children. As a result, the children would excel. Like Pygmalion, whose love and attention brought the ivory statue of a maiden to life, high expectations would cause children to bloom intellectually. The authors claimed to find the Pygmalion effect. But their methods and conclusions have been questioned (for example, Snow, 1969). Alas, teachers are not as powerful as Pygmalion. But this does not mean that they have no impact on students.

Other researchers have studied the ways in which teachers' expectations for different students translate into different treatment in the

Perhaps teachers cannot perform miracles, but their attitudes toward the children and toward schoolwork can make a difference.

classroom (Cooper, 1979; Good, 1980). High achievers are given more opportunities to participate, more time to respond to questions, and more praise when they give the right answers than low achievers are. If high achievers are criticized, it is for lack of effort, not lack of ability. Teachers' treatment of low achievers is less logical. Low achievers receive less praise than high achievers do; when they are praised—or criticized—it is often for their behavior rather than for their work. Teachers may not create important differences in achievement, as Rosenthal and Jacobson suggested, but they may sustain patterns of unequal performance.

Social Class and the Classroom

Clearly some youngsters are better students than others. The best predictor of high achievement, other than IQ, is social class. There are many exceptions to the rule, but children from middle-class homes are much more likely to do well in school than lower- and working-class children. Describing the educational career of a lower-class child, one author calculates that "by third grade he is approximately one year behind academically, by sixth grade two years behind, by grade eight two and one-half to three years retarded academically and by ninth grade a top candidate for dropping out" (Rioux, 1968, p. 92). Why is this true?

Schools are middle-class institutions, staffed by middle-class teachers who apply middle-class standards. For a middle-class child, school is a continuation of his preschool life, which included books, trips to the zoo, and many other learning experiences. He knows how people who are like his parents expect a child to behave. For a lower-class child, school may consist of a series of puzzling demands made by strange people in an unfamiliar setting. Socialization prepares the middle-class child for school; the lower-class child may require *re*socialization.

There is some evidence that teachers assume that middle-class students are brighter and act accordingly. Rist (1970) followed a group of thirty black youngsters from their first day in school through the first half of second grade. The kindergarten teacher assigned the children to three different reading tables on the eighth day of school. It was obvious that her assignments were based on her perception of which children could be expected to learn and which could not. Her time was divided among the tables accordingly. The children's behavior toward one another reflected the teacher's attitudes. Children at the "fast learner" table made frequent derogatory remarks about the children at the "slow learner" tables, who withdrew and expressed hostility toward one another. Assignment to ability groups was self-perpetuating, continuing into second grade. Rist holds that the teacher's initial assignments were based not on students' demonstrations of ability but on their social class. Children who spoke well, were neat and clean, seemed at ease with adults, and came from educated families were assumed to be fast learners. Children whose mothers were on welfare were assumed to be slow learners.

Teacher bias is not the only reason for class differences in school achievement. Parents from different social classes instill different attitudes toward school in their children (Kohn, 1976). When lower-class parents were asked what personal qualities they valued in their children, they mentioned good manners, neatness, obedience, and good grades. Middle-class parents asked the same question emphasized self-control, responsibility, consideration for others, and curiosity. Where lower-class parents emphasize conformity to rules and external appearances, middle-class parents emphasize self-control and self-direction. Lower-class parents try to teach their children how to avoid trouble by obeying authorities. They stress neatness and manners—qualities that are valued in elementary school. Middle-class parents encourage their children to explore the world around them and

to learn on their own—qualities that are valued in high school college-preparatory programs. When asked what they would advise their child on the first day of school (Hess & Shipman, 1967), lower-class mothers issued orders—"sit down," "don't holler," "mind the teacher"—without explanations. Middle-class mothers were more likely to explain to the child *why* they would have to learn new rules for behavior. "You have to wait your turn, because if everyone talked in class, no one could hear the teacher." All parents want their children to do well in school. But middle-class parents, who are more knowledgeable about school themselves, are better able to help their children learn to play the role of student. They not only *hope* that their children will excel, they *help* them set realistic goals and develop strategies for achieving them.

Social class compounds the individual differences in ability among children, making it easier for middle-class youngsters—and harder for lower-class youngsters—to adjust to the new world of school.

Peers and Pals

By age eleven, children spend nearly half of their waking hours with other children (Barker & Wright, 1951). The number of peers a child knows from school, the neighborhood, church groups, scouting, summer camp, and the like increases in middle childhood. But the most significant change is not in the number of acquaintances, but in the importance of friendship.

Friendships

INTERVIEWER: Why is Caleb your friend?
TONY: Because I like him.
INTERVIEWER: And why do you like him?
TONY: Because he's my friend.
INTERVIEWER: And why is he your friend?
TONY: (*with mild disgust*): Because . . . I . . . choosed . . . him . . . for . . . my friend.   (Rubin, 1980)

Children do not want company for company's sake; they want to be with Caleb, or Joan, or Juan (Hartup, 1983). Friendships are special attachments. In some ways, they resemble the attachment between an infant and her mother. Friends like to maintain proximity; they provide security in strange situations. But childhood friendships are fragile. They are not embedded in community organizations, work relations, and other social contexts, as are adult friendships. Friends may feel an obligation to one another; but that obligation must be reaffirmed continually by both parties.

Kenneth Rubin's interview with Tony reveals that young children have few explanations for why they are friends. Thomas Berndt (1981) questioned kindergartners, third-graders, and sixth-graders. Like Tony, most children said "We're friends because we're friends." But further questioning brought out *defining attributes*

In middle childhood, friends provide a secure base—much as parents did in infancy.

("He's nice"; "She's funny"); *frequent association* ("He plays with me"; "She calls me all the time"); sharing, helping, and other *prosocial behavior;* and *not fighting,* calling the child names, or other aggressive behavior. One child defined a friend as someone who does *not* "put dynamite next to my house and blow it up." Frequent association and *in*frequent aggression were important elements of friendship for children of all ages. Sixth-graders added *intimacy* and *trust* ("We can talk"; "I can tell secrets to her"); *loyal support* ("She won't talk behind my back"; "He'll stick with me when I'm in a fight"); and *faithfulness* (not deserting the child for another friend). Girls were more likely to emphasize intimacy and exclusivity than boys were. Older children may also include more psychological traits in their descriptions of their friends.

To illustrate developmental changes in conceptions of friendship, Berndt quotes two children's responses to the question, "How do you know that someone is your best friend?" (Different categories of responses are printed in brackets.) A kindergartner answered:

I sleep over at his house sometimes [play or association]. When he's playing ball with his friends he'll let me play [prosocial behavior]. When I slept over he let me get ahead of him in 4-squares [a playground game—prosocial behavior]. He likes me [defining features]. (p. 6)

A sixth-grader answered this way:

If you can tell each other things that you don't like about each other [intimacy]. If you get in a fight with someone else, they'd stick up for you [loyal support]. If you can tell them your phone number and they don't give you crank calls [aggressive behavior]. If they don't act mean to you when other kids are around [loyal support]. (p. 6)

As Berndt points out, the concern with intimacy in older children reflects the understanding that friends can share feelings and thoughts as well as toys and activities. This is part of the general shift from an emphasis on appearances in the preoperational stage of cognitive development to a concern for underlying reality in the concrete operational stage.

Popularity: "Stars," "Isolates," and "Rejects"

As early as kindergarten, some children are more popular with their peers than others are. Psychologists measure popularity by asking children to indicate which of their peers they like and dislike, and which they would choose as playmates, work partners, and best friends. This procedure identifies three peer types: "stars," children who are well liked and sought after); "isolates," children who are seldom mentioned by others, in either positive or negative terms; and "rejects," children whom others dislike and avoid (Peery, 1979). A child's status, or standing, in a group is relatively stable over time (Coie & Dodge, 1983). Changes do occur; but rejects rarely become stars. Moreover, most children in a group agree about who is the smartest, who is the best athlete, who is the most popular, and so on.

Why are some children more popular than others? Research shows that names, physical attractiveness, race, sex, and personality all influence peer preferences.

What's in a *name?* Apparently quite a bit when it comes to selecting friends. McDavid and Harari (1966) obtained popularity ratings for four classes of 10- to 12-year-olds. They also asked youngsters who did not know any of the children personally to rate the attractiveness of their first names. The two ratings were similar. Children with desirable names were more popular than those with odd names. Why is difficult to say. It may be that children avoid Herberts, Henriettas, and Seymours simply because their names are strange. Or it may be that parents who pick "odd" names lack social skills, and so do their children. The importance of names should not be overestimated, however. The

first names of U.S. presidents have included Theodore, Warren, Calvin, Dwight, Lyndon, and Ronald. "It may be that Americans will vote for a man they would not want as a friend; a more plausible interpretation is that names are not everything" (Asher, Oden, Gottman, 1977, p. 35).

Looks matter to school-age children. *Physical attractiveness* is one source of popularity. Most people in the United States agree about who is and who is not good-looking (Cross & Cross, 1971). Even preschoolers seem to act on the assumption that "beauty is good." When elementary school children are shown photographs of attractive and not-so-attractive children, they rate the better-looking youngsters as smarter, nicer, less aggressive, and better prospects for friends than unattractive children (Cavoir & Dokecki, 1973; Langlois & Stephen, 1977). Their choice of friends and selection of popular classmates reflect these prejudgments. Good looks may function as a self-fulfilling prophecy: Children (and adults) respond positively to attractive children; positive experiences enhance the child's social skills and self-esteem; and this, in turn, confirms the belief that attractive children are nicer and more friendly.

Children use *race* as another criterion in selecting friends. Although cross-race friendships do develop among schoolmates, children seem to prefer "their own kind." In February and again in June of the school year, Shaw (1973) asked fourth-, fifth-, and sixth-graders whom they liked to be with. Eighty percent of the children in these classes were white and 20 percent were black. If youngsters had chosen friends at random, without regard to race, 80 percent of the black children's selections would have been white and 20 percent of the white children's choices would have been black. This was not the case. Both blacks and whites chose members of the other race: 33 percent of the black children's selections were white and 6 percent of the white children's selections were black. But both clearly preferred members of their own race. Moreover, there was little change over the spring semester. By itself, interracial contact does not seem to lead to unbiased friendship selections. (We should point out, however, that in studies of this kind it is difficult to separate the effects of race from the effects of social class.)

A far more important factor in friendship selection is *sex*. Numerous studies document the existence of two separate peer cultures: boys' and girls'. During the school years, children's allegiance to their own sex is seen on the playground, in seating patterns in the school lunchroom, and in invitation lists for birthday parties. Of the 97 friendship choices registered in one study (Duck, 1975), only two were cross-sex—and those were unreciprocated.

By far the most important qualification for popularity is *being friendly and outgoing* (Hartup, 1983). Peers describe popular children as kind, helpful, enthusiastic, accepting, and good sports. Stars know how to make friends. But

Youngsters much prefer members of their own sex as friends and playmates at this age.

the association of popularity and friendliness does not necessarily demonstrate cause and effect. It may be that the child is popular because she is outgoing, or that she is outgoing because she is popular, or that both of these characteristics are caused by a third variable, such as high intellectual ability.

Friendless Children

Researchers who ask a classroom of children to name their friends find that about 10 percent of the students are always left out. No one picks them (Asher & Renshaw, 1981). Most of these children are not loners by choice. They are no more likely than other children to say that they enjoy solitary hobbies or reading. And the older they become, the unhappier they are. Friendless children are lonely and adrift (Hymel, Asher, Renshaw, & Geraci, 1981).

An explanation of why some children do not make friends provides insight into how other children do make friends (Asher, Renshaw, & Hymel, 1982; Dodge, Schlundt, Schocken, & Delugach, 1983). Unpopular children lack social skills for initiating contact with peers, maintaining relationships, and resolving conflicts. When unpopular children attempt to join an ongoing activity, they tend to make critical comments, state their own opinions, ask questions, and otherwise call attention to themselves. Popular children wait for a break in the conversation or action, then edge in by focusing on the activity rather than on themselves. In about two out of three cases, a child's attempt to join a group fails. Popular children try another strategy; unpopular children either persist in their ineffective attempts to get attention or give up. Whereas popular children attribute temporary rejections to misunderstandings or to not trying hard enough, friendless children tend to blame themselves: "It's hard for me to make friends."

To maintain peer acceptance, a child must know how to reward others with attention and approval, how to cooperate, and how to share.

Other children want to know that a classmate or neighbor can be counted on to be a good sport. Friendless children have acquired reputations for spoiling games with disruptive behavior, derogatory remarks, and physical aggression. They tend to misinterpret other children's behavior as hostile (Dodge, Murphy, & Buchsbaum, 1984). Moreover, when another child needs help, unpopular children tend to make inappropriate responses—such as telling a child who is being teased to "do something."

All children run into conflicts over what to do, whom to include in a game, who is responsible for breaking a neighbor's window, and the like. Popular children have prosocial strategies for dealing with conflict. Suppose one child is watching TV and another comes over and changes the channel. Popular children are likely to tell the intruder to "turn it back," say they were watching first (invoking the norm of "first come, first served"), suggest taking turns or another compromise, or summon an adult. Unpopular children more often resort to verbal or physical aggression.

Groups and Gangs

Clearly the changes that occur in child–child relationships during the middle school years are closely linked to changes in cognitive skills, especially role-taking abilities (see Chapter 12). The cooperation necessary for a group of children to play together or to plan other joint activities also depends on how well the children understand the points of view and feelings of others (Hartup, 1983).

Isolated, friendless children are at risk. But youngsters can be taught how to enter a group, cooperate, and make friends.

Insight

"WHAT MY GRANDMOTHER ALWAYS KNEW"

Richard Lerner (1982) describes returning to the Brooklyn apartment his mother shared with his grandmother after defending his doctoral dissertation at the City University of New York.

With a Yiddish accent that remains strong despite her over sixty years in this country she asked, "So tell me, Sonny, what did you write your book about?"

While my grandmother is a very bright woman, she has no formal education, especially in the technology (and jargon) of psychology. I immediately recognized that I would have to communicate the main findings of my work without recourse to the vocabulary of my profession. My dissertation dealt with topics that today fall under the headings of "child influences" and "reciprocal socialization." . . . [It] assessed whether children and adolescents who differed in their physical characteristics (i.e., their body types) elicited different, stereotyped reactions from their peers and, if so, whether these children and adolescents had body and self-concepts consistent with the appraisals of their peers. This explanation was not, however, the one I related to my grandmother. Rather, my jargon-free account went something like: "Well, Grandma, I found out that children don't like fat kids as much as they do average build kids, and that fat kids don't like themselves very much either."

My grandmother let go of my arm. She took a step back and her eyes narrowed. "Tell me, boychick" (I knew something was wrong . . .), "how long did it take you to find this out?"

"Well, Grandma, it took me about a year and a half to complete the whole thing."

Her hand flew up and *klopped* the side of my head. "Stupid," she said, "if you would have asked me I would have told you in two minutes!" (p. 343)

Looking back, Lerner considers what he might have said to his grandmother. In a sense, it is the social scientist's job to deal with the obvious. In some cases research has shown that common sense is dead wrong. In many instances research shows that common sense oversimplifies the case. For example, who would think that preschoolers have absorbed their culture's standards of beauty and handsomeness and prefer good-looking children? Lerner adds that today's scientific discoveries often become tomorrow's conventional wisdom. The concepts of *adolescence, socialization,* and *hyperactivity*—among many others—originated in social science.

A group is composed of interacting individuals who have common goals or motives and are guided by shared values and norms (the group code). A collection of people going home together on a bus or subway is not a group, according to this definition. A crowd watching a fire or people marching down the street in a rally might meet some of the qualifications. But a *stable group* is more than a cluster of interacting individuals. It has social organization based on a status hierarchy, or "pecking order." For it to function as a group, leaders and followers must emerge and group tasks must be divided among members. Shared goals and status hierarchies are as important to children's peer groups as to any other human group.

The Robbers Cave experiment conducted by Sherif and colleagues (Sherif, Jarvey, White, Wood, & Sherif, 1961) is a classic study of the dynamics of peer groups. White, middle-class, Protestant fifth-grade boys were recruited for a summer camp, divided into two sets, and assigned to different campsites in the Oklahoma woods. Within a short time, both sets had become groups. Status hierarchies formed, leaders emerged, and the boys developed norms for behavior and shared attitudes toward each other, camp activities, and the like. One group called itself the Rattlers; the other, the Eagles. Neither knew about the other group.

In the second phase of the experiment, the counselors arranged an "accidental" meeting. Then they suggested a series of "friendly" competitions (baseball games, tugs-of-war, and the like). The games were rigged so that both groups experienced losses. Relations between the two groups quickly deteriorated. It was "us against them." Conformity and solidarity within each group increased. Intergroup hostilities escalated. When the Eagles lost one series of games, they stole the Rattlers' flag and burned it. When the Rattlers lost the next series, they stole a pair of pants from an Eagle, painted them orange, and displayed them as their flag. Counselors barely managed to prevent a serious rock fight. In short, the groups became gangs. During this hostile period, the internal structure of both groups changed. Boys who excelled in competition rose in the status hierarchy; those who did not fell in status.

In the third phase of the experiment, counselors tried to negotiate a peace. Their first attempts—bringing the Eagles and the Rattlers together for a movie and fireworks—were disasters. Then they contrived a series of crises that required the boys to work together. On a particularly hot day, the water system broke down; then the truck used to haul food developed engine problems and had to be pushed. Faced with urgent, common problems, the boys had no choice but to join forces. Negative stereotypes fell into disuse and friendships developed across group lines. In effect, the two groups became one.

The central message of Sherif's study—that competition promotes aggression—remains controversial. But there are several conclusions we can draw from this experiment. First, peer groups depend in part on in-group–out-group contrasts. There are always insiders and outsiders. Fortunately, in middle childhood group boundaries and friendship patterns change frequently in response to new activities. Only a few children are left out most of the time.

Second, all peer groups develop status hierarchies. Other studies confirm what Sherif found. For example, in an observational study of older children at another summer camp, Ritch Savin-Williams (1979) found that girls as well as boys quickly established dominance hierarchies. Girls were less likely than boys to admit status differences. But female leaders controlled those in their cabins by giving advice and information to some bunkmates and shunning others. Male leaders more often asserted dominance by arguing and threatening. Leaders of both sexes regularly got the best sleeping sites at campfires and the biggest piece of pie at dinner. Echoing Suomi's analysis of dominance hierarchies in monkey troops (see Chapter 8), Savin-Williams concluded that dominance hierarchies make interaction within a group stable and predictable, and reduce actual fights.

Finally, changes in group goals often produce changes in leadership. Other studies reveal that the characteristics required for leadership also change with age. Hartup (1983) finds that children who can keep possession of toys and know how to use them wield social power in preschool groups; those who are good at initiating and directing play and games become leaders in middle childhood; early maturers with athletic and social skills take over in early adolescence; and those who are bright and well liked become group leaders in late adolescence.

Competition and Cooperation, Sportsmanship and Scholarship

According to the ethologist Konrad Lorenz, competition is cathartic: it reduces aggression by providing an outlet for "fighting instincts" that might otherwise explode. According to

Insight

TEACHING CHILDREN HOW TO MAKE FRIENDS

Popularity is not necessarily a gift that some children have and other children lack. Children can be taught how to make friends, hence how to become more popular, step by step. In a recent paper, Steven Asher and his colleagues (Asher, Renshaw, & Hymel, 1982) evaluated three strategies teachers and parents can use to teach friendless children social skills.

One way to promote friendly behavior is to *reinforce* it with praise and other rewards. For example, Brown and Elliott (1965) succeeded in reducing aggressive behavior in preschool children simply by having the teacher praise each child whenever the child was cooperative. However, other researchers who attempted to "treat" shyness by praising individual children each time they played with others were less successful (Hops, Walker, & Greenwood, 1977). The problem with the reinforcement strategy is that youngsters often revert to unfriendly behavior when the rewards are stopped.

A second way to teach children how to make friends is to demonstrate, or *model*, appropriate social behavior. For example, O'Connor (1969) developed a twenty-minute film for preschoolers showing children of the same age modeling specific social skills. In one sequence, the narrator describes how to be accepted into a play group:

> Now another child comes up to watch. She wants to play too. She waits for them to see her. Now she gets a chair and she sits down with them so they will play with her. She starts to do what they are doing so they will want to play with her.

Teachers have also used real-life models successfully. In one study (Csapo, 1972), six disruptive elementary school children were seated next to six well-behaved classmates and told to watch their neighbors and do as they did.

The disruptive children's behavior improved dramatically.

A third strategy for building social skills is *coaching:* showing the child an appropriate way to behave and then allowing him to practice what he has observed. Oden and Asher (1977) devised a four-week program for third- and fourth-graders who were among the least liked children in their classes. Each child received individual instruction in four skills: *participation* (getting to know others and paying attention to them); *cooperation* (sharing materials and taking turns); *communication* (talking and listening); and being *"friendly, fun, and nice"* (offering others help or encouragement). The children were given a chance to practice these skills in six play sessions with another child, then discuss what happened with an adult. Evaluations conducted a few days after the sessions ended showed significant gains in peer acceptance.

A follow-up study conducted a year later indicated that the once-disliked children were even more popular. The children gained confidence in the coaching sessions; they were able to try out their new social skills with new classmates without the handicap of a bad reputation; successes with the new classmates led to greater confidence. Children in a control group did not change in social status or acceptance over the year. Asher and Ogden conclude that without help, unpopularity is "a rather stable condition."

The few studies undertaken with younger children indicate that coaching can be effective with preschoolers as well. In a classic study, Chittenden (1942) used two dolls named Sandy and Mandy to teach highly aggressive preschoolers prosocial skills. She began by teaching the children to distinguish happy endings (sharing and having fun) from unhappy endings (fighting over a toy). In some scenes, Sandy and Mandy were domineering and uncooperative: they snatched toys, bossed others around, and hurt each other. In other scenes, they shared, took turns, and played happily together. In later sessions Chittenden used the dolls to model conflicts, then discussed ways of resolving those conflicts. The children were asked to show how the dolls could have more fun together. Observations in two-person games and in the classroom showed definite improvements.

Making friends and becoming accepted by peers are crucial developmental tasks in middle childhood. Children give each other emotional support in dealing with new school experiences.

They provide each other with partners for symbolic play and teach each other all kinds of physical, social, and cognitive skills. Difficulties in making friends in childhood have been linked to adjustment problems in later life: dropping out of school, delinquency, mental health problems, bad-conduct discharges from the military, and suicide. Because making friends in childhood is so important, Asher and his colleagues urge that researchers continue to develop and apply strategies to help friendless children learn this skill in the classroom. In answer to the question, "Is it right to intervene?" they ask, "Is it right to do nothing?"

frustration-aggression theory, competition promotes aggression by creating frustration—in winners, who are subjected to the threat of defeat, as well as in losers. There is some evidence for the second point of view. In one observational study (Rausch, 1965), about 90 percent of the interactions of 10- to 12-year-old boys were usually friendly. When the same boys were playing competitive sports, however, over 40 percent of their encounters were unfriendly, and 30 percent of friendly overtures were rebuffed.

Donna Gelfand and Donald Hartman (1982) argue that it is not sports per se that promote aggression, but models of unsportsmanlike behavior. Their own experiments show that children who have watched an adult model aggression become more aggressive themselves during a competitive game, but that children who see an active but nonaggressive adult model simply become more active. What models does our society offer children who play competitive sports? Parents who attend Little League and other games place a high value on their offsprings' winning. Often they get into loud, angry disputes with officials. "No one in the stands is shouting to encourage players to have sympathy, concern, and compassion for their opponents, or even advising them to be

good sports" (p. 200). In professional sports, fistfights among spectators and players are common events. Although broadcasters may verbally deplore this behavior, they reinforce "unnecessary roughness" and rule violations with instant replays and jokes. These lessons are not lost on children.

Many parents and educators worry that competitive sports expose children to excessive, unhealthy levels of stress. A large body of research on stress and sports (summarized in Passer, 1982) shows that athletic competition is no more anxiety-provoking for children than other activities in which their performance is evaluated. In general, individual sports (such as gymnastics or wrestling) produce more anxiety than team sports. But most children find playing a solo with the school band far more stressful than playing on a varsity team (see Figure 11-1 on page 437).

Sports are not the only arena in which American children are encouraged to compete. Even small children perceive school as being competitive. Preschoolers know about winning and losing and who got first prize. The longer children are in school, the more competitive and rivalrous they become (Bryan, 1975; Nelson, 1970; Nelson & Kagan, 1972). Many Americans believe that competition is good for children.

David Johnson and Roger Johnson (1975) challenge four popular myths about the value of competition.

1. *The myth:* "Our society is highly competitive, and a child must be able to function in a 'survival of the fittest' world." *The challenge:* Most human interaction in our society is cooperative, not competitive. Even during wars and other combative activities, cooperative agreements exist concerning how the competition or conflict will be conducted. Competition is only a small part of social interaction with individuals.

2. *The myth:* "Achievement, success, drive, ambition, and motivation depend on successfully competing with others." *The challenge:* Success in achieving a goal does not depend on winning over others, just as failing to achieve a goal does not mean losing to others. Cooperative groups can succeed or fail at accomplishing a task just as competitive individuals can.

3. *The myth:* "Competition builds character and toughens the young for life in the 'real world.'" *The challenge:* There is no evidence that competition builds character and toughens a person for success in future competition. Ogilvie and Tutko

In May 1985, 38 soccer fans were killed and 250 were injured in a riot at a game in Brussels. Whether these young players develop good sportsmanship depends in part on adult models.

Figure 11-1 Strike up the Band
Simon and Martens (1979) compared 9- to 14-year-old boys' normal or "resting" scores on anxiety tests to their scores ten minutes before the start of athletic competitions, a school test, and group and solo band competitions. Surprisingly perhaps, they found that playing a band solo was much more stressful than playing football.

(1971), studying the effect of competition on personality, found no evidence that competition in athletics builds character.

4. *The myth:* "Students *prefer* competitive situations in peer groups and at school." *The challenge:* Although children may enjoy competitive reward situations as long as they are winning and can exhibit mastery of a task, students prefer cooperative situations to competitive ones, when given the choice (Greenberg, 1932, in Johnson & Johnson, 1975).

Cooperative experiences result in more positive interpersonal relationships among peers—including mutual liking, positive attitudes toward one another, friendliness, feelings of obligation to other children, and a desire to win the respect of others (Johnson & Johnson, 1975).

Ecological Perspectives

Up to this point we have been talking as though all friendships and peer groups in middle childhood were alike. They are not. The variations in peer subcultures in the United States are as diverse as the range of living conditions and lifestyles among adults. Consider some examples.

☐ A 10-year-old boy, Charles, lives on a small farm in Nebraska, ten miles from the nearest household. He is bussed to a district school, where he joins his fifteen classmates, then returns to the isolation of his home. On weekends, he has an opportunity to go to a nearby town with his parents to do grocery shopping and participate in a meeting of a 4-H group with six age-mates. He sees a few children of his own age at church on Sunday and at

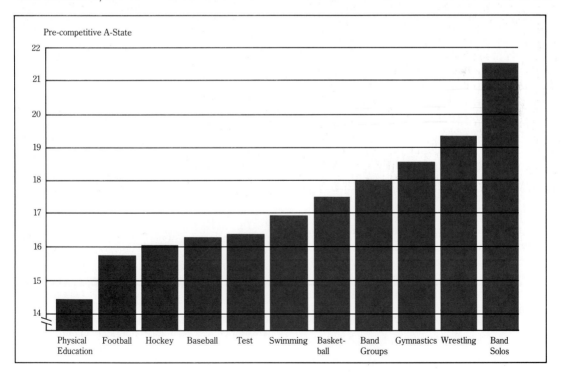

occasional social gatherings of family and friends.

☐ A 12-year-old girl, Susan, who lives in Chicago, is bussed to a private school about five miles from her home. Once a week she stays after school to participate in the school band; her mother picks her up, since the school bus service does not accommodate after-school activities. Her family belongs to a country club, and she is a member of a clique of friends whom she sees regularly at the club. There are three age-mates within a few blocks of Susan's home, and she socializes with two of them on overnight stays, in record sessions after school, and during trips to the "in" boutiques. She also sees children her own age at church on Sunday and at social gatherings of family friends. The church has a youth group that provides opportunities for ski trips and other outings.

☐ An 11-year-old boy, Jason, lives in a third-floor walk-up tenement apartment in New York City. He walks five blocks to school, which most of the other neighborhood children also attend. On his block there are over 50 children, at least ten of whom are within a year or two of his age. The children have access to a community recreation center, and the local church provides Saturday afternoon programs. Madison Square Garden and Yankee Stadium, the ferry to the Statue of Liberty, and the American Museum of Natural History, with its dinosaurs and model whale, are only a subway ride away. Yet when the weather is nice Jason hangs out on the corner or on the front steps of his building with his buddies.

Clearly, the kinds of peer relationships these three children develop and the group activities in which they become involved will differ because of their different opportunities.

In the preschool years, the sociocultural environment affects the child indirectly. The social class and ethnic background of the child's parents shape their ideas about how to rear children, what hours they work, how many people share their living quarters, and so on. As the child begins to spend more on her own, away from home, the neighborhood and community have a more direct impact on her development. The school age child's friends, popularity, and group affiliations depend on her particular interests, preferences, and skills; the neighborhood

Poor children often grow up in chaotic, overcrowded homes with less supervision and more responsibilities than middle-class children have. A child who babysits every afternoon has little time to study.

in which she lives; the social structures within her community; and the expectations for a girl of her social class.

The number of children in the neighborhood and the size of the school a child attends can create or limit opportunities. A child who lives in a neighborhood with many other children has more opportunities to make friends than does a child in a neighborhood with few his own age. The probability is greater that children with similar interests will find one another. This also holds true in a large school. But a small school may offer a child more opportunities to participate in activities, and make friends, because the ratio of students to activities is smaller. In small schools, the glee club, the soccer team, the student newspaper, and other clubs and groups may be understaffed. Students who might be ignored in a larger school, because they lack social or other skills, are encouraged to join (Baird, 1969).

The socioeconomic composition of a school can affect the child's social standing. One study (Asher, Oden, & Gottman, 1977) found that the most popular students in a middle-class school were those who engage in positive *verbal* exchanges. The best-liked children in a working-class school, however, were given to positive *nonverbal* social interactions. These data imply that to gain acceptance, children must "psych out" the environment and figure out what kinds of behavior lead to peer acceptance (Asher, Oden, & Gottman, 1977; Gottman, Gonso, & Rasmussen, 1975). Making friends is one of the most challenging and rewarding tasks of the school years.

Children and Their Families

When John was 4, his mother picked him up at the day-care center, walked him home, fixed him a snack, and set him up with his paints, the TV, or a friend she had invited for the afternoon. Now, at age 9, John bangs open the kitchen door, grabs an apple, and rushes out again, barely acknowledging her questions about homework and suppertime. This simple, familiar scene highlights the changes in parent–child relations in middle childhood.

Parent–Child Relations: Coregulation

The most visible change in parent–child relations during this period is in the amount of interaction. Parents spend about half as much time supervising, entertaining, and caring for children aged 6 to 12 as they do with preschoolers (Hill & Stafford, 1980).

The content and style of parent–child interaction change during this period as well (Maccoby, 1984). With preschoolers, the basic issues for parents are establishing routines, controlling temper tantrums and sibling fights, and teaching them to care for themselves. Middle childhood raises a whole new set of issues (Newson & Newson, 1976). What chores should children be required to do, and should they be paid for work they do around the home? How can parents encourage a child to entertain himself and at the same time keep track of his whereabouts and activities? To what extent should they monitor a child's social life, encourage or discourage relations with certain other children? How much should they become involved in the child's schoolwork? What should they do if the child is having academic or social problems in school? When does interest in the child's achievement become pressure to succeed?

The techniques parents use to correct or control youngsters change in this period. In general, the use of physical punishment decreases and reasoning with the child increases. This can be a mixed blessing, however, for school-age children become skilled at pointing out parents' inconsistencies and seem to have an unlimited capacity for arguing. They are not as easy to distract as they were in their preschool days.

Insight

HOW CHILDREN SPEND THEIR TIME

How do children spend their days? How much time do they spend playing, studying, reading, watching television, helping with housework, talking to their parents? Two recent studies addressed these questions.

The first was a national time-allocation survey of American households, begun in 1975 and repeated each year (Timmer, Eccles, & O'Brien, in press). Household members are asked to keep a 24-hour diary of their activities on two weekdays and two weekend days, six months apart. Mothers kept diaries for their preschoolers and helped young children to keep theirs; older children kept records for themselves.

The results of this survey are shown in the table. On weekdays, children spend about two-thirds of their time on obligatory activities—sleeping, eating, bathing, dressing, and going to school. On weekends, they spend about half of their time this way and the other half on discretionary activities: playing, watching TV, sports, studying, or helping with housework.

According to this survey, sex differences are slight—until children reach adolescence. Teenage girls spend much more time than teenage boys do on personal care and housework; teenage boys devote much more time to sports. Curiously, 11- and 12-year-old boys spend more time watching TV than do either girls or boys in any other age group.

Maternal employment has surprisingly little impact on children's activities. Children whose mothers work do not spend more time on

Children's Major Activities (hours : minutes)

	Weekday			Weekend		
Activity	3–5 yrs	9–11 yrs	15–17 yrs	3–5 yrs	9–11 yrs	15–17 yrs
Market work	—	0:08	0:28	—	0:10	0:48
Personal care	0:41	0:40	1:00	0:47	0:44	0:51
Household work	0:14	0:18	0:34	0:17	0:51	1:00
Eating	1:22	1:13	1:07	1:21	1:18	1:05
Sleeping	10:30	9:08	8:19	10:34	9:56	9:22
School	2:17	5:15	5:14	—	—	—
Studying	0:02	0:29	0:33	0:01	0:12	0:30
Church	0:04	0:09	0:03	0:55	0:53	0:37
Visiting	0:14	0:10	0:20	0:10	0:13	0:56
Sports	0:05	0:21	0:46	0:03	0:42	0:37
Outdoors activities	0:04	0:08	0:11	0:08	0:39	0:26
Hobbies	0:00	0:02	0:06	0:01	0:03	0:03
Art activities	0:05	0:03	0:12	0:04	0:04	0:10
Other passive leisure	0:09	0:02	0:04	0:06	0:07	0:18
Playing	3:38	1:05	0:14	4:27	1:32	0:21
TV	1:51	2:26	1:48	2:02	3:05	2:37
Reading	0:05	0:09	0:12	0:04	0:10	0:18
Being read to	0:02	0:00	0:00	0:03	0:00	0:00
Other	0:30	0:23	0:07	0:52	0:14	0:09

(Adapted from Timmer, 1983)

housework, more time watching TV, or any other "compensation" one might imagine.

The most significant differences among children related to their parents' education. Children of college-educated parents watch less television and spend more time reading and studying than other children do. (The same was true of their parents.) They devote more time to personal care—perhaps because their parents engage in a wider range of leisure-time activities and the children are often getting ready to go out. Children of college-educated parents also sleep less than other children do, perhaps because their parents allow them to decide for themselves when to go to bed. The most surprising finding concerned sports. One might expect that highly educated parents would make a conscious effort to reduce sex-stereotyped activities. But their daughters spent only about six minutes a day in sports, compared to their sons' 40 minutes. Daughters and sons of *less* well-educated parents spent the same amounts of time on sports: about 30 minutes a day.

The researchers conclude that children of college-educated parents spend more time on activities that develop the skills they need for high levels of educational achievement. In other words, children "seem to use their time in ways that make it more likely that they will grow up to be like their parents" (p. 13).

The second study (Ziegler, 1983) was designed to measure the quality as well as the quantity of time children spend with their parents. The children in this study were third- and fourth-grade boys and girls from middle-class, two-parent families. After an interview, the parents were asked to keep independent diaries of the time they spent with their children on the following Tuesday, Thursday, and Saturday. They were also asked to indicate how close their contact with a child had been during a given time period. *Direct time* meant that the parent and child were engaged in the same activity and no one else was present. *Indirect time* meant that the parent and child were together but they were engaged in different activities or another person was present. *Available time* meant that the parent was accessible but not offering much attention to the child.

The researchers found that the amount of time parents spend with a child varies widely from family to family. On the average, the mother spends much more time with the child than the father does during the week. But on the weekends, the father spends more direct time with the child than the mother does. On the whole, the children spend about half of their waking hours in contact with the mother, about a third with the father. But parent and child spend very little time (only 4–5 percent of the day) in what might be called "quality interaction," such as talking over a problem or reading together. The most common joint activity is watching TV.

How does the time children spend with their parents affect intellectual and social development? Teachers were asked to rate each youngster for cognitive ability (overall success in comprehension and learning), classroom skills (attentiveness, eagerness to participate, persistence, and organization), and personal-social skills (cooperativeness, self-reliance, and curiosity). The researchers found that the amount of the mother's and the father's available time and the father's education accounted for almost half (46 percent) of the individual variations in cognitive ability among the children.

Although we cannot claim that parents' time causes children to be smarter in school, we can say that better-educated families spend more time together and have smarter children.

But a parent can appeal to the child's self-esteem ("That's not like you"), play on guilt, invoke humor, or withdraw privileges.

The amount of anger in parent–child interaction usually decreases in the school years. There are fewer disciplinary confrontations. Children are less likely to use such coercive measures as whining, yelling, and hitting to get what they want. When they do get angry, however, they take longer to recover than preschoolers do. Parents must learn to live with sulking, moping, the silent treatment, and various forms of passive noncompliance—evidence of older children's more sophisticated understanding of relationships.

There is a gradual shift from parental control to *coregulation* during middle childhood (Maccoby, 1984). Parents continue to supervise, but turn many daily decisions over to the child. This means that parents must work out methods of guiding the child from a distance, using the time they do have together to reinforce mutual standards of right and wrong, safe and unsafe, behavior. This also means that the child must be willing to keep parents informed of plans and problems. Coregulation depends on cooperation. Parents often complain that it is difficult to know what a school-age child is thinking or feeling. The desire for approval, which motivates youngsters to adhere to the rules, can also make them secretive.

Of course, the child is not the only one who is developing during these years. The parents are also changing. At the very least, they are becoming more experienced as parents, especially if they have another child or two. The mother may be going back to work full-time or starting graduate school. The father may have been promoted to a job that requires most of his concentration—or he may be drinking too much because he was not promoted. The parents' relationship with each other is changing, for better or worse. And their child-rearing values may change as the result of a new occupation, income, home, or perhaps marital status. The parents' own developmental stages and relationship with one another must be factored into the family equation.

Different Family Lifestyles

Ten or fifteen years ago, when psychologists talked about "the American family" they meant a husband and wife with their 2.2 children, living in a home of their own with a white picket fence. They also meant a family in which the father was the only breadwinner, or the principal one, and the wife was devoted to homemaking. Any child who was not being reared in a nuclear family was considered at risk. To some extent, this ideal family was always a myth. Poor and minority women have always worked to support their families. They often raised children by themselves or with the help of female kin. Years before "women's lib" entered the language, many middle- and upper-class women worked at volunteer jobs or for "pin money." But two-career families were rare, and divorce even rarer. Family norms have changed dramatically in the last decade. Different family life-styles are becoming more common and more accepted at all levels of society (see Table 11-1).

WORKING MOTHERS At least half of all mothers of school-age children hold jobs today. What im-

"Here comes the enigma."

Table 11-1   In One Decade: Ten Ways American Families Have Changed

	1970	1980	Percent Change
Marriages performed	2,159,000	2,317,000	Up 7.3%
Divorces granted	708,000	1,170,000	Up 65.3%
Married couples	44,728,000	47,662,000	Up 6.6%
Unmarried couples	523,000	1,346,000	Up 157.4%
Persons living alone	10,851,000	17,202,000	Up 58.5%
Married couples with children	25,541,000	24,625,000	Down 3.6%
Children living with two parents	58,926,000	48,295,000	Down 18.0%
Children living with one parent	8,230,000	11,528,000	Up 40.1%
Average size of household	3.3	2.8	Down 15.2%
Families with both husband and wife working	20,327,000	24,253,000	Up 19.3%

(*U.S. News & World Report,* June 16, 1980, p. 50.)

pact does maternal employment have on children? It depends, first, on the family's socioeconomic status. Children of poor, young, single women with little education seem to benefit from their mother's working. This may be because their family income rises, their mother's self-esteem improves, and they attend preschool programs.

The impact of a mother's working depends on the child's sex. Daughters of working mothers show more achievement motivation than do girls whose mothers are full-time housewives (see Chapter 8). In middle childhood and adolescence they tend to be more independent, higher in self-esteem, better adjusted socially, more likely to do well in school, and more likely to aspire to a career than other girls are (Hoffman, 1980). A study of girls reared by their fathers alone found that they were less independent and more demanding than girls who were reared by their mothers (Santrock & Warshak, 1979). Sons of working mothers are also more independent; but there is no evidence that they are more or less masculine or do better in school than other boys.

The impact of maternal employment also depends on such variable factors as how much help the family can afford, how much the father pitches in, and how flexible the working hours of

both parents are. Unfortunately, most studies of working mothers do not distinguish between those who work full-time and those who work part-time, or between women with low-paying, low-prestige jobs in, say, factories or fast-food chains and women with successful careers in business, the professions, or the arts. But overall, there is no reason to believe that these school-age children suffer because their mothers work.

We know less about the opposite phenomenon, "house-husbands." One study found that children whose fathers were full-time homemakers with primary responsibility for child-rearing are intellectually ahead of children reared in traditional families (Radin, 1982). We suspect that this is because these nontraditional men and their wives were better educated and more creative than average parents—not because the children had "male mothers."

SINGLE-PARENT FAMILIES The proportion of single-parent families in the United States has doubled in the last twenty years. About one-fifth of children aged 6 to 12 live with only one parent today. Estimates are that two out of five will live in a single-parent home at some point in their childhood (Child Care Action Campaign, 1985). Over 90 percent of these children live with their mothers. Studies of children whose mothers *never* married are difficult to interpret because of socioeconomic differences. A very small percentage of single mothers are highly educated, self-supporting women who carefully planned their pregnancies. Most are young, poor, undereducated women who did not anticipate or welcome pregnancy and who depend on public assistance or relatives for support. It is all but impossible to separate the effects of low income, low education levels, minority group membership, and other disadvantages from the effects of single parenthood on their children. However, there are reliable studies of children who live with a single parent after the parents' divorce.

DIVORCE Separation and divorce cause emotional distress for everyone involved, including children. In the first year following a separation, newly single parents tend to be self-preoccupied, less attentive to their children, inconsistent, and irritable. Often they spend less time with their children and are less concerned about household routines such as providing regular meals and doing laundry. One effect of divorce, then, is diminished parenting. How children themselves react to a divorce depends in part on their age (Wallerstein & Kelly, 1981). Children 6 to 8 years old express grief and fear, and long to reunite their parents. Children 9 to 12 years old react more often with shame and anger. They are more likely than younger children are to express hostility toward the parent they blame for the divorce. Older children may be drawn into an alliance of one parent against the other and are more likely to resent a stepparent than are younger children.

Studies by Mavis Hetherington and colleagues (Hetherington, Cox, & Cox, 1982) suggest that the women who are hit hardest by

In many families today, "Father's Day" is every other Sunday when Dad has visitation rights.

divorce are those who have not worked for several years. Suddenly they are faced with becoming a single parent, joining the social world once more as a "single," and reentering the workforce, all at once. Going to work can help the woman get back on her feet, emotionally and socially as well as financially. But her children may act as though they had lost both their father *and* their mother. Almost all children have trouble with school, friends, and parents in the aftermath of a divorce (see Figure 11-2). Children of newly employed mothers are doubly disturbed. Many are resistant or excessively dependent on teachers at school. At home, they nag, whine, demand attention, reject affection, and disobey. One mother described her relationship with her children in the first year after a divorce as "getting bitten to death by ducks" (Hetherington et al., 1982, p. 258).

Although there has not been much research on the long-term effects of divorce, the evidence suggests that how quickly mothers recover depends on support systems—a network of family and friends who are helpful, sympathetic, and who do not choose sides. How quickly children adjust seems to depend in build-

ing, or rebuilding, good relationships with *both* parents. Some children remain sad. But some gain self-confidence from having survived the experience and seem more independent than their peers in traditional families.

ABSENTEE FATHERS In some ways, the father's impact on a child's development is best revealed by his absence. This can occur due to death, divorce, or occupational separation such as military service. The effects of separation from the father depend on the child's age and sex (Hetherington, 1972; Hetherington, Cox, & Cox, 1978). Boys who were separated from their dads at age 4 or younger are more dependent on peers than are boys who live with their fathers. They have lower scores on measures of masculine aggression, are less involved in competitive contact sports, and spend more time in nonphysical activities (such as reading or working at a computer). Boys who were separated from their fathers after age 6 do not show these effects. It seems that early separation makes it more difficult for a boy to acquire typically masculine traits.

Early separation from the father also has more impact on girls than does later separation. But these effects do not appear until the girls reach puberty (Hetherington, 1972). Adolescent girls whose fathers died early in their life often have problems establishing relationships with the opposite sex. They are anxious about boys and often behave in inappropriate ways. Adolescent girls who lost their father through divorce early in their life tend to be more seductive than are other girls their age. This may be because of a visiting relationship with the father, which resembles dating in some ways, or the fact that the mother is dating.

STEPFAMILIES Most adults who are divorced remarry within three or four years. As a result, millions of children have a stepfather, stepmother, stepbrothers and -sisters, and half-sisters and -brothers (who share one of their biological parents). Although little research has been done on the impact of second families on children, we can point to some of the ways in which stepfamilies differ from other households (Vishner & Vishner, 1978). First, some or all

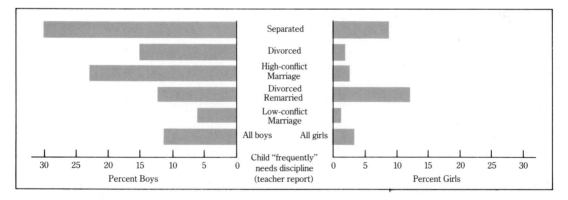

Figure 11-2 Staying Together for the Children's Sake? Popular opinion once held that parents should stay together for the children's sake, no matter how much they hated one another. Today popular opinion holds that children are better off in a single-parent home than they are in a home where parents are fighting. Which view is correct? Zill and Peterson's analysis (1982) of teacher's reports indicates that boys are more likely to act out when their parents are fighting than when their parents are divorced, but that the reverse is true for girls. (Zill & Peterson, 1982)

the members of a stepfamily have experienced a disruption in a close relationship. The child may have lost the full-time attention of her father; the stepfather may be separated from his children; both adults may have gone through a divorce. Second, the relationship between the mother or father and the child predates that between the parent and his or her new spouse. Parent and child have a history the new spouse does not share. Third, the child usually belongs to two households, the mother's with her spouse and the father's with his. Therefore, the parent and the new spouse do not have exclusive control over the child. Disputes about rules between the two sets of parents, and comparisons between the two homes, are probably inevitable. Finally, there are no legal ties between a stepparent and stepchild, and no clearly established norms to guide their behavior toward one another. For example, what should the child call the new spouse? Dad or Mom? Sam or Barb? This is one area in which children can help one another by sharing information on their parent with a stepsibling, or confiding in a friend about what happens when your dad remarries.

The effects of absentee fathers may be different when everyone else is in the same boat. During World War II, most young children here and abroad went several years without seeing their fathers.

All family forms have strengths and weaknesses. There is no one answer to what is best for children in this regard. Traditional two-parent families are usually adept at controlling and monitoring a child. This is good for young children: Three-year-olds should not be trusted to decide whether to cross a street or what to wear outside on a cold day. But 12-year-olds do not want or need to be told what to wear, eat, or do with their free time. Traditional families have difficulty letting go of older children. Full-time homemakers "need to be needed" and may be overprotective and intrusive with teenagers. Single parents typically require a great deal of independence from their children. This may be good for older children but difficult for small children to handle. On the other hand, an intelligent, mature single mother may devote more time and attention to a child than she would if she had a husband in the home to distract her. (The same applies to single fathers.) Moreover, her ability to cope depends in part on whether her family and community view the decision to bear and raise a child alone or her divorce as a sin, a failure, or simply as a personal choice. Children can thrive in many different family arrangements (Scarr, 1984).

Brothers and Sisters

In most countries in the world, children aged 6 to 12 are given major responsibilities for the care and training of their younger brothers and sisters. The United States is one of the few nations in which the sibling relationship is primarily recreational. But having brothers and sisters is not all fun and games; siblings provide a lesson in ambivalence (also see Chapter 8).

The relationship between siblings differs from that between parent and child in that siblings are developmental and social equals. One may be a few years older than the other, but in the eyes of their parents and the world at large, both are children. The sibling relationship differs from peer friendships in the frequency and amount of interaction, accessibility, durability, and the number of common experiences. Friends may come and go, but siblings are there to stay (at least through childhood and adolescence). There is an uninhibited, emotional quality to sibling interaction in childhood that parent–child and peer relations often lack. Boys who have learned not to cry in front of their friends, and girls who have learned not to hit, may lose this self-control with a brother or sister. Siblings delight in making one another laugh and cry.

Sibling interaction provides a special context for advances in social understanding, interpersonal problem-solving, and self-definition (Bryant, 1982). Social comparisons between the child and his older or younger brothers and sisters are inevitable. On one hand, siblings compete for their parents' attention and approval. Rivalry is built into their relationship. On the other hand, siblings act as models who reinforce one another. Teaching a younger sibling to ride a bicycle can be as rewarding as learning to ride a two-wheeler oneself. The child's developing identity reflects the standard set by brothers and sisters.

Siblings help one another to work on dependency issues—that is, to learn how skillful they are at giving others help and how comfortable they feel accepting help. One study (Bryant & Crockenberg, 1980) found that older sisters tend to encourage dependency, sometimes by force. The more the older sister tried to help, the angrier her younger sister became—suggesting that nurturance requires practice!

Siblings provide opportunities to learn techniques for resolving conflicts. Aggressive encounters between siblings are common. Children say that their brothers and sisters use physical force to control them more often than either their fathers or mothers do (Devereaux, Bronfenbrenner, & Rodgers, 1969). A fight with a peer may end a friendship; a fight with a sibling does not terminate the relationship. This may be the one social context in which children learn that expressing anger need not threaten positive feelings and later friendly interaction.

There is some evidence that later-born children are more friendly and sociable, and less jealous and demanding, than are firstborn children (summarized in Bryant, 1982). One hypothesis is that firstborns can overpower younger siblings and do not have to develop skills in negotiation and accommodation. Another hypothesis is that parents are more relaxed with a second or third child. But overall, the evidence

Parents may not know the latest steps; older siblings do.

on the effects of birth order is not compelling. What we do know is that siblings influence one another—directly through their interactions, and indirectly through their different relationships with their parents.

. . . And the Family Pet

A description of the traditional American family that did not include the cat, dog, or parakeet would be incomplete. Some psychologists might not take the family pet seriously. But other psychologists, and many children, do. Levenson (1972) has argued that a pet is part of the sibling generation. Children see Spot, Lion, or Gertrude as "one of us." Bryant (1982) found that over 80 percent of school-age children say they have a pet who is a "special friend." They talk to their pet about their feelings and secret experiences about as often as they do to a sibling. Bryant observed further that for 10-year-olds, the more intimate the talks they had with pets, the greater their empathy was for their peers.

One research team (Mason & Kennedy, 1974) gave pet dogs to monkeys who were fearful and antisocial because they had been reared in isolation. The monkeys developed deep attachments to their canine mother surrogates and became more sociable with other monkeys.

While it might be an overstatement that "dog is man's best friend," we can award pets a role in the social and emotional development of children.

TV or Not TV?

By the 1950s, no student of the American family could ignore the presence of still another family member in the home: the television set. Over 99 percent of American families with children possess at least one TV set. Recent studies (Singer, 1983) show that children as young as 9 *months* spend an hour and a half a day watching TV (although not necessarily comprehending it). By age 3 or 4 years, children average four hours of viewing a day. TV viewing peaks in the preteen to early teen years, then declines slowly (Murray, 1980; Murray & Salomon, 1984). How much time youngsters spend in front of the "tube" depends on a number of variables, including age and intelligence (among young children, bright youngsters tend to spend more time watching than their less intelligent peers, but this pattern reverses in the school years); socioeconomic status (the higher the child's social class, the fewer hours spent in front of the flickering screen), and parental and family viewing patterns, which provide models for the child (Murray and Salomon, 1984). But all American children are exposed to at least some television. Summarizing almost twenty years of research and more than 3,000 studies of the impact of TV on young people, a report issued by the National

Boy's best friend.

Institute of Mental Health (Pearl, Bouthilet, & Lazar, 1982) concluded:

Television can no longer be considered as a casual part of daily life, as an electronic toy. Research findings have long since destroyed the illusion that television is merely innocuous entertainment. While the learning it provides is mainly incidental rather than direct and formal, it is a significant part of the total acculturation process.

How does TV affect a child's daily life? Cross-cultural research has shown that when television is first introduced to a community, children spend less time listening to radio, going to the movies, reading (even comic books), and playing outdoor or indoor games. However, television does not seem to displace these activities permanently. Once TV has been assimilated as a "member of the family," it becomes part of the background of daily life. People, sports, hobbies, and music continue to occupy the foreground. In this country, TV often functions as a "baby-sitter" (Rubinstein, 1983). Most parents do not watch TV with their children or discuss shows with them. And although most express concern about violence and sex on television, they do not control what their children watch.

Many of the shows youngsters view were designed for an adult audience. Do children understand what they are watching? Seven- and 8-year-olds grasp about two-thirds of the essential information in a show (who did what and why) (Collins & Westby, 1981). Often they do not see the connection between one scene and the next, particularly if two scenes are interrupted by commercials. As a result, they often fail to appreciate a character's motives, or what feelings cause people to behave as they do. When they are watching a western, for example, and see a rancher shooting at a group of men riding up to his house, they may not recall whether the rancher is defending his home or protecting stolen goods. All they see is a shooting. The distinction between "good guys" and "bad guys"

may be lost on them. Children's attitudes toward the behavior, and their own behavior after a show, depend on how much information they process.

Models of Aggression

The issue that has provoked the most controversy and research is the impact of televised violence on a child's behavior. On the average, the school-age child is bombarded by eight violent acts during each hour of television (Gerbner & Gross, 1976). Television violence ranges from the escapades of fantasy figures such as Batman and Robin, Wonder Woman, and Bugs Bunny; to westerns, detective stories, and adventure dramas; to the "soaps," which have added rape, assault, and murder to their portrayal of "real life." Does this barrage of violence encourage violence and aggression in children?

Almost all of the research summarized in the 1982 NIMH report concludes that watching violence on TV encourages aggressive behavior. Liebert and Baron's experiment (1972) is a classic. The researchers showed groups of 5- and 6-year-olds and 8- and 9-year-olds either a short segment from the gangster series "The Untouchables" or a videotaped track meet. The three and a half minutes of the gangster segment included a chase, two fistfights, two shootings, and a knifing. The track-meet segment was active but nonviolent viewing. After the show, the children were put in a situation in which they could either help or hurt another child playing in the next room. If they pushed a green button when the light on their panel came on, they would help the child win a game. If they pushed the red button, the handle in the game next door would get hot, making it hard for the child to win. The green button was specifically labeled the "help" button and the red button the "hurt" button. Liebert and Baron found that children who had watched the aggressive segment decided to hurt the other child more often and for longer periods. When the children were later observed during a free-play period, those who had viewed the aggressive tape also exhibited a preference for playing with weapons and aggressive toys.

Children are more likely to push, shove, or hit another child or attack property after they watch a violent show than they were before the show. They are also more likely to disobey rules and requests, and to become frustrated when they don't get what they want right away. Pre-adolescents and adolescents who regularly watch violent programs are more likely to have a reputation for aggression than those who do not (Collins & Westby, 1981). When youngsters repeatedly see violence used to resolve conflicts, they are less likely to be alarmed by aggression or to take steps to prevent or stop aggression. Their inhibitions against acting aggressively may be reduced. They may learn new ways of getting back at someone.

It is impossible to say precisely how television violence affects the way all children think and behave. It is also difficult to pin down cause and effect: aggressive youngsters may select more violent programs than peaceful youngsters do. Variables such as age, sex, socioeconomic status, preexisting aggressive tendencies, and self-esteem need to be entered into the watching-violence–acting-aggressively equation (Murray, 1980). In 1972 the Surgeon General of the United States testified before the U.S. Senate committee that inaugurated an investigation of violence:

While the committee report is carefully phrased and qualified in language acceptable to social scientists, it is clear to me that the causal relationship between televised violence and antisocial behavior is sufficient to warrant appropriate and immediate remedial action. . . . [T]here comes a time when the data are sufficient to justify action. That time has come. (Murray, 1980, p. 29)

Nothing much has changed since 1972.

A Good TV Diet

While public attention has focused on the effects of television violence, other effects have been ignored. It seems reasonable to assume, for example, that prosocial or socially valued behavior such as sharing, cooperating, or helping could be learned as easily as violent behaviors. Stein and Friedrich (1975) found that even a relatively brief exposure to a dozen episodes of "Mister Rogers' Neighborhood," a program that stresses themes of sharing and cooperation, was associated with increases in cooperation, nurturance, and verbalizing one's feelings. Using the same program, other studies have shown that by observing "Mister Rogers" young children demonstrated increased learning of prosocial concepts such as sharing, task persistence, and empathy. On the basis of detailed content analyses, other programs judged to be high on prosocial themes include "Lassie," "I Love Lucy," "Gilligan's Island," and "The Brady Bunch" (Rubinstein, Liebert, Neale, & Poulos, 1974). These programs are often rerun in the late afternoon as part of the networks' after-school programming for children.

In another study, children were presented with a diet of either prosocial or neutral television programs for one-half hour per day, five days per week, for four weeks. Children who had viewed the prosocial diet displayed significant increases in helping behavior in contrast to their age-mates who had viewed the control programs (Ahammer & Murray, 1979).

Undoubtedly, television plays a role in most children's lives never even imagined just thirty years ago. The generation that has grown up with TV has been exposed to many events that these children would have never experienced in their daily lives. They have witnessed men walking on the moon, they have seen the assassinations of world leaders, the inaugurations of presidents, and royal weddings. They have joined photo safaris through Africa and seen the migration of whales. They have ventured to major cities of the world, seeing the Eiffel Tower close up, the pyramids in Egypt, and Red Square. They have attended performances by the world's great musicians, dancers, and actors. They have been spectators at the Olympic Games, the Super Bowl, and the World Series. They have seen other children from different cultures in places around the world they might never visit.

As an agent of socialization, television supplements the media of books, movies, and radio, providing the child with social role models and opportunities to observe fantasies being enacted, skills being developed, and tasks being accomplished. The range of social situations and interpersonal relationships that a child might directly experience is expanded widely as a result of watching television. Never before have so many children been exposed to social worlds beyond their own, personal experiences.

Who Is Responsible?

Despite many prosocial and enriching programs, the potential influence of televised violence, enticing advertisements, and sex-role stereotypes cannot be ignored. What can be done? Who should guide children?

On one end of the continuum are those who believe that parents can monitor their children's exposure to TV in the same way they watch their children's diets, by balancing the amount and kind of programs the youngsters watch. It is up to them to decide when the set will be turned on or off and which programs to tune in. To do this effectively, parents must establish a dialogue with their children, become familiar with what their children watch, and explore what family members have learned from television. Together, parent and child can become discriminating viewers.

Given the difficulty young children have processing the information on TV, Andrew Collins and Sally Westby (1981) recommend reviewing the plot of a show with a child, to make sure the child understands the "meanings that fall between the actions . . . on the screen" (p. 2); discussing any unusual or troubling episodes in the show; talking about the reality of the portrayal and making sure that the child distinguishes between reality and fantasy; and asking about the child's own attitudes and values so that they see TV portrayals as something to question, not as straight fact. This approach might avoid the following scene, reported by Alice Honig (1983):

"There was a guy and he raped this girl on TV last night," cheerfully reported Matt, four years old, to his day-care teacher. She murmured, "How terrible! That must have hurt the girl and scared her awfully." "Oh no," assured Matt, "my sister's boyfriend was watching with us and he said that girls love rape. You just don't know about that," the four-year-old responded in superior tones. (p. 63)

The moral of research on the effects of television is clear: Parents should monitor their children's TV diets as closely as they supervise what their children eat and when they go to bed.

Further along the continuum are private action groups organized to help parents and children make choices. Consumer groups such as Action for Children's Television provide critical reviews of children's programs, prime-time shows, and related advertising for concerned parents.

At the extreme other end of the continuum are those who hold the government and other large organizations responsible. Just as the Federal Communications Commission (FCC), major networks, and major advertisers regulate the amount of nudity and sexually explicit scenes shown on television, so they should regulate the level of violence, kinds of advertisements, and degree of sex-role stereotyping during children's hours. Protecting children is in the public interest. If necessary, the government should institute formal regulations of the television industry (Murray, 1980). Of course, this raises the issues of government censorship and of controls on private enterprise.

The debate over TV or not TV continues. Meanwhile, the child has acquired a degree of self-direction that may be overlooked. In the middle years children select for themselves the television shows and movies they want to see, and the books and magazines they want to buy or borrow from the library. They are developing hobbies and general interests in science fiction, mysteries, or history. They are acquiring their own taste in music and clothes, perhaps emulating an older sibling's choices. They are interested in current events and compete with other family members for first look at the front page, the sports section, the daily horoscope, or the comics. By her eleventh or twelfth birthday, the child has established a personal repertoire of interests and tastes that define her as a unique yet assimilated member of her family and society.

SUMMARY

1. Youngsters in Western societies spend much of their time in school. School influences development in direct and indirect ways.

2. School is the child's first experience of an impersonal, bureaucratic organization in which individuals are graded for their performance.

3. Teaching styles affect student achievement. There is little evidence that teachers can transform an average student into a superior one (the "Pygmalion effect"). But they may perpetuate individual differences in achievement.

4. Social class differences in attitudes toward learning and classroom behavior compound individual differences in ability.

5. In middle childhood opportunities to be with peers increase, friendships become more intimate, and descriptions of friends more psychological.

6. Children prefer children who are friendly, not aggressive, physically attractive, members of their own race, and the same sex. It is rare for a girl and boy to be best friends in middle childhood.

7. Some youngsters are "stars," and others are "isolates" or "rejects," at an early age. Friendless children lack skill in joining a group, cooperating with and rewarding other children, and solving conflicts peacefully.

8. The Robbers Cave experiment showed that competition affects relationships within and

between groups; that children's groups develop a social hierarchy or pecking order on their own; and that leadership changes with the situation and with age.

9. Children's opportunities to make friends, and the kinds of friendships they form, depend in part on their social environment and such factors as school size.

10. There is a gradual shift from parental control to coregulation in middle childhood, as youngsters develop ideas and activities of their own and as parents also change.

11. Most youngsters in the United States do not spend their entire childhood in what we think of as a traditional family. Many mothers work, which seems to have positive effects on poor children and daughters, mixed effects on boys. Many parents get divorced; this is always a sad event for chil-

dren, one which often leads to temporary behavior problems. Girls and boys react to the loss of a full-time father in different ways and at different ages. The impact of stepfamilies on children's development is not known.

12. Ambivalent relationships with siblings continue during middle childhood, with opportunities for learning how to help and how to hurt. A pet is a more adoring friend.

13. Television is also part of the child's social world. In general, research supports the view that violence on television encourages aggression in real life. But TV can also model prosocial behavior and widen a child's horizons. Ultimately the impact of TV depends on who chooses which shows, a controversial issue for parents and children— and for society.

FURTHER READING

Asher, S., & Gottman, J. (Eds.). (1981). *The development of childrens' friendships.* Cambridge, MA: Cambridge University Press. A series of papers on the development of friendship during childhood and adolescence.

Murray, J. P. (1980). *Television and youth: 25 years of research and controversy.* Boys Town, NE: The Boys Town Center for the Study of Youth Development. This comprehensive research review of the impact of television on children includes a 3,000-citation bibliography.

Mussen, P., & Eisenberg-Berg, N. (1977). *Roots of caring, sharing, and helping.* San Francisco: Freeman. An excellent review of the literature on prosocial behavior that suggests adults should concentrate on teaching youngsters what they should do, rather than focusing on what they must not do.

Rutter, M. (1983). School effects on pupil progress: Research findings and policy implications. *Child Development, 54,* 1–29. A review of how students' achievement is affected by the schools they attend.

Shure, M. B., & Spivack, J. (1978). *Problem-solving techniques in child-rearing.* San Francisco: Jossey-Bass. Aimed at helping parents deal with the social adjustment of their children, this book offers parental tactics that enhance children's ability to think through their social problems and decide what to do on their own.

Wallerstein, J., & Kelly, J. (1974). The effects of parental divorce: The adolescent experience. In E. Anthony & A. Koupernik (Eds.), *The child in his family: Children as a psychiatric risk* (Vol. 3). New York: Wiley. A discussion of the effects of divorce on adolescent development.

Zimbardo, P. G., & Radl, S. L. (1982). *The shy child.* Garden City, NY: Doubleday. A pioneer in the study and definition of shyness, Zimbardo suggests ways that parents can embolden their shy children—and perhaps themselves.

School

Enters first grade:

First exposure to impersonal rules, schedules, and grades

Individual differences in intellectual ability compounded by social class differences in ability to play the role of student

---

Relations with peers

Friendships based on shared activities—and on *not* fighting

[Differences in social skills make some children "star," and others "isolates" or rejects]

Leaders control toys (up to 6 yrs.)

Leaders good at initiating and directing games (7–12 yrs.)

[Group membership and group activities may turn friends into enemies, and vice versa]

Relations with parents

Gradual shift from parental regulation to parent-child *co*-regulation

Parents attempt to establish routines, reduce aggression, and teach self-care

Physical punishment and disciplinary confrontations decrease

Child expected to do chores and schoolwork, allowed to choose activities and friends within limits

Working mother: benefits daughters and poor children of both sexes
Divorce: temporary behavior problems at home and in school; outcome depends on good relations with both parents

Fear, grief, longing to reunite parents <6–8 yrs.>

Absentee father (early separation): Boys more dependent on peers, less aggressive in middle childhood [if separated before age 5]

TV

Average 4 hrs. per day

Does not grasp connections between scenes, or characters' motives

---

6   7   8   9

Age in years

HIGHLIGHTS OF SOCIAL DEVELOPMENT IN MIDDLE CHILDHOOD

( ) age range
< > onset or peak
[ ] qualifications

⌇ age extension beyond
that shown on chart

Friendships based on
shared ideas and feelings
and on loyal support

(Spends half the day with peers)

⌇ Leaders early
maturers with
athletic and social
skills (12–15 yrs.)

Reasoning, appeals to
self-esteem increase;
so does pouting

Shame, anger, taking sides
<9–12 yrs.>

⌇ Girls more anxious or
seductive with males
in adolescence

TV viewing peaks, then
declines <11–13 yrs.>

| 10 | 11 | 12 | 13 |

12

Can you remember how you first became aware of yourself as an individual? What events or experiences contributed to your realizing that you are a separate person? Bannister and Agnew (1976) asked a number of adults to answer these questions by thinking back to their childhood. Several recurrent themes emerged from their essays.

The feeling of separateness. "I was playing blindman's bluff . . . and the lost feeling when I had been blindfolded seemed to set up a very much I-Them situation. The isolation of what I felt as a lost feeling made me aware of what it was like to be outside of, or in a sense 'not belonging to,' the group. . . . With this feeling of separateness came a feeling of power and independence." (pp. 116–17)

The privacy of consciousness. "The first time I had been away from home alone . . . I very easily remembered thinking, after a couple of days, that I had done all sorts of odd things which, even if my mother was thinking of me, she wouldn't know until I had told her." (p. 117)

Possessions—the meaning of "mine." "Perhaps the first time I remembered that I had a vague feeling of self was when playing with one of the children and we exchanged toys. On returning home, the distinction between my toys and the toys belonging to others was pointed out, and it became obvious that life was not so simple as it had appeared. There was a difference between what others had and what I had, and there was therefore a distinction between them and me." (p. 118)

Being a causal agent. One writer described an experience at age 5, when she was to take part in a school play and was overcome with stage fright and couldn't go on stage: "Panic stricken, I bawled my eyes out and my sister took me backstage to Miss W. She came up to me and almost pleadingly asked would I do it (i.e., go on stage) and I remember the feeling that I could say yes or no. I could decide as me, not just what I was told to do. This lady was asking *me*, not my sister, who was usually volunteered into pacifying me at school. I felt very surprised and also felt that I had been treated as a person and somehow felt a person." (p. 118)

COMING OF AGE

Realization of how one appears to others. One man describes being mocked by his father because he could not correctly wire up a radio he had been given for Christmas. "It was from incidents like this that I learned I was a stupid and ignorant person." (pp. 121–22). . . .

"Another memory of a discovery of a separate 'me' was the day when I deliberately tripped my younger brother and then pretended to my parents that this silly child kept falling. My deceit was discovered, and this seemed to be the first appreciation that I wasn't just the 'good little girl' which seemed to be an imposed character; she had a nasty side too. Though it wasn't pleasant to have this nasty bit made known, there was a positive side and that was that this was definitely "me" and not what others saw me as. It seems that it was important for me to differentiate myself from my brother in the eyes of my parents." (p. 119)

These memories of middle childhood were filtered through adult consciousness. We do not know if all or most children have a sudden, aha! experience of "I'm me." But we do know that children exhibit a growing awareness of the self and others in middle childhood.

This chapter examines **social cognition** in middle childhood—the development of thinking about oneself and others. We begin by looking at the development of self-concepts and self-esteem. In the second section we explore the school-age child's attitudes and feelings toward other people. Then we turn to moral development and changes in the child's ability to reason about and cope with moral dilemmas and social conflict.

Becoming a Person

Children are not born with a sense of "me" and "mine." Their image of themselves, their ideas about where they fit in their social world, and their feelings of self-worth develop gradually during childhood—and continue to change throughout life.

"Who Am I?"

We have described the beginnings of self-awareness in earlier chapters. To review: The first sign that children have a self-image appears in the second year of life (Bertenthal & Fischer, 1978). When 24-month-olds look in a mirror and see a spot of bright red rouge on their nose, they are surprised and embarrassed (see Chapter 5). Children less than 18 months old often do not notice. The infant's awareness of her continuing identity develops along with object permanence; her image of herself reflects her new ability to form mental representations. As far as we know, the great apes are the only other animals that develop self-consciousness. Chimps react to a red spot on their face much the way children do; gibbons, baboons, and monkeys do not (Gallup, 1977).

Self-portraits by a 9-year-old (far right) and a 16-year-old (near right) illustrate changes in self-concept over middle childhood. The younger child fills her head with favorite objects (her cat) and activities (drawing, jumping); school subjects; coughs and sneezes near the nose; and a special "wishing room." The older artist draws an intense psychological portrait that shows how he sees himself, as serious, somber, and sensitive. (Most adolescents do not draw as well as he does. This young man's parents are both painters and he himself is a budding artist).

The child's awareness of a separate identity expands when he begins to talk, learns his name, and masters the pronouns that describe himself (*I* and *me*) and others (*you*). Using these pronouns correctly requires an inversion: When an adult says "you," she means the child; when the child says "you," he refers not to himself but to the other person. Amazingly, most children grasp this immediately and never refer to themselves as "you" or another person as "me" (Clark, 1976).

A study by John Flavell and his colleagues (Flavell, Shipstead, & Croft, 1978) showed that 4-year-olds have some conception of an inner, private, *psychological self* that is different from their bodies and hidden from other people. The researcher showed the child a doll and pointed out that dolls are like people in some ways—they have arms, legs, and so on. The child was asked how dolls are different from people and whether they know their names and think like

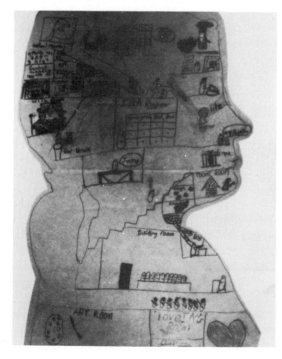

people do. Most of the children said that they did not. Then the children were asked, "Where is the part of you that knows your name and thinks about things?" This stumped some children, but a number of them pointed to their heads. "Can I see you thinking in there?" Most of the children said no. They gave concrete, physical explanations: " 'cause the skin's over it" and " 'cause I don't have any big holes." But they were aware of an inner, private self.

During middle childhood, youngsters' definitions of themselves are elaborated and refined (Rosenberg, 1979). When children of 7 or 8 are asked "Who are you?" they describe concrete, physical features and activities. ("I'm Susan. I'm eight. I have blue eyes. I live on Grove Street. I have a brother. I roller skate."). They may also mention possessions ("I have a kitty"), likes and dislikes ("I don't like spinach"), and grown-up behavior ("I read books" or "I help my Mommy"). As children mature, they begin to add personality traits to their self-descriptions: "I'm cheerful"; "I'm honest"; "I lose my temper." Still later they include *inter*personal traits, characterizing themselves as friendly, outgoing or shy, considerate, a leader, and the like. In late adolescence self-descriptions become more abstract, focusing on values, beliefs, private thoughts, and motivations.

During middle childhood, the basis of the youngster's self-image shifts from concrete, observable characteristics to internal psychological processes (Rosenberg, 1979). When young children look at themselves, they focus on the exterior. Like a census taker, they are only interested in objective facts. Adolescents are more like psychoanalysts, probing the inner world of thoughts and feelings, dreams and fantasies.

The discovery of the *me* depends in part on recognition of the *not me* (McGuire, McGuire, Child, & Fujioka, 1978). When children talk about themselves, they include characteristics that make them stand out. The youngest child in a large family mentions age or size; redheads list hair more often than brunettes or blondes do; a minority child in a predominantly white school is more likely to mention race than white children are. At the same time children are differentiating themselves from others, they are developing a *social identity* based on the groups (the Smith family, first grade at P.S. 24) and categories (male or female, white or black) to which they belong.

"Where Do I Belong?"

The child's image of himself depends in part on how other people respond to him. As Charles Horton Cooley put it (1982) near the turn of the century, each of us has a *looking-glass self*. The "looking glass" is society, which acts as a mirror in which we can observe other people's reactions to our appearance and behavior: "Each to each a looking glass / Reflects the other that doth pass." Our image of ourselves is based in large part on this reflection. The looking-glass self has three parts: how we imagine others see

Comparisons of the self and others, the "me" and "not me," may make a child more aware of her ethnic identity.

us; how we imagine others judge what they see; and how this makes us feel. According to Cooley, there is no self without society, no *I* without *they*. The most striking evidence for the role others play in the development of the self comes from apes. Chimps raised in isolation do not pass the nose test of self-recognition. They react to their image in a mirror as if it were a strange animal (Gallup, 1977).

Elaborating on Cooley's idea, George Herbert Mead (1925) proposed that there are two stages in the development of the social self. In the *play stage* (early childhood), children try on other people's roles. They walk around in their parents' shoes, pretend to be an adult scolding a doll, play "doctor" and "house." Role-playing enables them to see the world—and more importantly, themselves—as though through another person's eyes. In the *game stage* (middle childhood), children participate in games-with-rules. To play baseball, for example, a child must not only play his role (pitcher) but also be aware of other people's roles (as catcher or batter), know how they are likely to respond to his moves, and understand the rules of the game. Through organized games, children develop a "generalized other"—a mental image of how society is put together and what people expect from one another.

Mead went on to suggest that some people have more impact on a child's self-image than others do. "Significant others" are those whose opinion the child values and respects. The people who serve as significant others change over development. Small children see themselves largely in their parents' eyes. In middle childhood, teachers and peers join parents as significant others.

There is no precise way to measure how much a person's *self-concept* is derived from other people's opinions. But we do know that youngsters become increasingly sensitive to the expectations and evaluations of others during

Insight

HOW CHILDREN FEEL ABOUT THEIR LIVES

American society has changed rapidly over the past two decades. There has been a great deal of speculation—mostly pessimistic—about how urban decay and suburban sprawl, crime in the streets, overcrowding and/or understaffing of schools, and such things as maternal employment, divorce, and single parenthood affect children. But until quite recently no one asked children how they feel about their lives (Zill & Peterson, 1982).

The National Survey of Children was designed to give youngsters a chance to speak for themselves. In the fall of 1976, 2,200 children aged 7 to 11, and 1,700 of their parents, were interviewed. The children were shown a set of five faces, ranging from very happy to very sad, and asked to say which face showed how they felt about their family or their schoolwork. They were asked to pick one of the five sentences— "I love it!" "I like it." "I'm not sure." "I don't like it." "I hate it!"—to describe their feelings about various activities. They were also asked how often they felt bored, lonely, or afraid, and what specific situations made them feel ashamed or angry.

How children feel about themselves. Most of the children in the survey said they were happy about themselves. Eight out of ten picked a happy face to "show how you feel about yourself" and to "show how things are going in your life." Over 75 percent agreed that "I am lucky" and 90 percent said "I like being the way I am." But some also said that they "often get angry" (16 percent), "worry about things a lot" (15 percent), or "often get scared" (13 percent). About 8 percent of all children—and 16 percent of black youngsters—said they often felt lonely.

What children fear most. More than two-thirds of the children said they were afraid "that somebody bad might get into [my] house." This fear was so widespread, cutting across all residential, economic, and ethnic groups, that it

suggests the children were reacting to what they had seen on TV, not to real-world experiences. Indeed, children who watched a lot of television (four hours or more on an average weekday) were twice as likely as other children to say they "get scared often."

One in four answered yes to the question, "When you go outside, are you afraid someone might hurt you?" Was this fear real or imaginary? Children from low-income families, and whose parents described their neighborhood as dangerous, were more likely than other children to fear being hurt. But the neighborhood does not seem to be as important as the child's own experience. More than 40 percent of the youngsters said they had been bothered by older children, a third had been threatened with a beating, and 13 percent described at least one occasion when they actually had been beaten up. One in four said they had been robbed of something "like a ball or a toy," and 5 percent had had money taken from them. In short, many children have reason to feel afraid.

When asked whom they feared most, a third of the children mentioned a specific child or adult who had threatened them in the past, or a class of frightening people, such as "strangers" or "burglars." About 15 percent mentioned a member of their own family (most often "my father"). Another 15 percent named imaginary figures such as the devil, Frankenstein, or Dracula. But all children's fears cannot be dismissed as imaginary.

How children feel about their families. Nine out of ten children picked a happy face to show how they felt about their families. The vast majority thought that their parents were proud of them, and nearly two-thirds announced that their parents treated them "more like a grown-up [than] like a baby."

At the same time, however, eight out of
Continued

ten said that they worry about their families. This figure rose to 100 percent in families whose mothers described their marriages as "not too happy." Half of the youngsters who were living with both of their parents said that they felt afraid when their parents had an argument. Nearly half said that they felt angry "when no one pays attention to you at home." And half wished that their fathers spent more time with them. About a third wanted more time with their mother.

What children think of their schools and neighborhoods. Surprisingly perhaps, three out of four children surveyed said that they "loved" or "liked" going to school; less than one in ten said, "I hate it!" Nine out of ten liked their teachers and most of their classmates, and three out of four said that they found schoolwork interesting "most of the time."

Nevertheless, school can be a source of anxiety and frustration for children. About two in three said that they worried about tests and felt ashamed when they made mistakes in school. One in five said that they would rather go to another school. Almost as many picked a sad face to show how they felt about their own schoolwork.

The children in this survey were more critical than their parents about their neighborhoods. Sixty percent of the parents described their neighborhood as a "very good" place to grow up; less than a third of the children agreed. Not surprisingly, children who live in poor urban neighborhoods were most unhappy about their surroundings. But only 40 percent of the children who lived in affluent suburbs rated their neighborhoods as "very good."

Whom children want to be like. "Can you tell me the name of a famous person you want to be like?" Most children answered this question by naming a popular entertainer (Cher, Marie Osmond, Elvis Presley) or an athlete (O. J. Simpson, Muhammad Ali) they had seen on TV. Fewer than one in ten choose an American political figure (George Washington or Abraham Lincoln), an artist or author, a scientist or physician, or a humanitarian. One out of five children could not think of anyone!

middle childhood. The school-age child puts enormous time and effort into making herself as much *like* her peers as possible. Some 9-year-olds will not get dressed until they know whether their friends are wearing jeans or dresses to school that day. (We say more about peer conformity later in this chapter.) Fitting in with the peer group provides both a sense of belonging with age-mates and a feeling of differentiation from adults. The *us* is defined through contrasts with *them.*

"What Am I Worth?"

Erik Erikson (1963) saw the major psychosocial task of middle childhood as developing industry—and the major risk as developing feelings of inferiority and inadequacy. A child needs to become skilled in order to gain credibility in his own eyes as well as in those of society. Learning to read and write, to use tools, to play mu-

sical instruments, to play basketball and chess affect the school-age child's self-image and feelings of self-worth. In societies that emphasize formal education, the child may feel that "I am what I learn."

During middle childhood, youngsters internalize the standards others have set for them and become more self-critical. Susan Harter (1982) asked children of different ages to define a list of emotion words. Three- to 4-year-olds were able to give definitions of happy, sad, mad, and scared, but not of proud and ashamed. Four- to 5-year-olds were vague: Pride is a "good" feeling and shame a "bad" feeling. The first adequate definitions appeared between ages 5 and 7. But children this age focused on how *others* felt about the self. "My Mom was ashamed of me for doing something I wasn't supposed to," or "Dad was proud of me when I took out the trash." Not until age eight or older did children describe being proud or ashamed of *yourself,* in the absence of surveillance by others—"When you throw milk at someone, the next day you're ashamed of yourself"; "Like when you pass a test or do a good deed, you feel proud of yourself" (Harter, 1983, p. 304). This is not to say that younger children do not feel shame or pride; they do. But they do not step back and judge themselves, for themselves.

ACHIEVEMENT MOTIVATION The desire to succeed at difficult tasks and to avoid failure is called **achievement motivation.** Carol Dweck and Elaine Elliott (1983) trace this development to middle childhood. Infants display *mastery motivation,* or an urge to understand and manage their environment. Unless restricted, they play naturally in ways that promote learning. They do not need to be instructed, encouraged, or rewarded to learn to walk and talk. But one would not describe infants and toddlers as "success-oriented."

Children's attitudes toward achievement begin to change around the time they enter first grade. Up to about age 7, most children define ability in terms of specific skills: If you complete a puzzle, you're smart. After age 7, children begin to think of ability as a more general, stable

A new activity, a new style of dressing, or a new place to eat or dance can set off a chain reaction in middle childhood.

personality trait (Rholes & Ruble, 1984). This change is part of the developmental shift away from focusing on concrete, physical attributes to thinking about psychological attributes. Once children begin to think of ability as a personality trait, they become more aware of individual differences and more inclined to use social comparisons in evaluating themselves.

Children's estimates of their own abilities also change. In kindergarten and first grade, nearly all children rank themselves at the top of their class (Stipek, 1981). They tend to have high—often unrealistic—expectations of success, no matter what the problem or task (Weisz, 1981). Failure does not faze them; they keep on trying (Ruble, Parsons, & Ross, 1976). The reason may be that small children have had many experiences of sudden breakthroughs after a long series of complete misses—when they learned to tie a bow, ride a bike, swim, whistle, and so on. In middle childhood, youngsters tend to become more cautious, self-conscious, and vulnerable (Harter, 1983). Performance goals ("How good am I?") may replace learning goals ("Let's try this"). Small children generally approach problems with the attitude, "How can I do it?" and perhaps, "What will I learn?" Older children are more likely to ask themselves, *"Can* I do it?" and *"Will* I look smart?" (These are general trends. Some small children are inhibited, and some older children are excited by challenges.)

The demands placed on children change in this period as well. Prior to entering school, youngsters' efforts to achieve mastery focus on physical skills. Children choose these activities largely for themselves. Moreover, success is visible. Either you caught the ball (or tied your shoe or rode the bike) or did not. In school, children are required to work at intellectual skills in a serious, sustained matter. Adults choose goals for them. The value of arithmetic and spelling may be far from obvious to the child. The steps necessary to solve the problem may not be visible. Consider a typical third-grade math problem: "The train from Chicago to Minneapolis leaves at noon and takes six hours to reach its destination. The plane leaves at five o'clock and takes one and one-half hours to reach Minneapolis. Which gets there first, the train or the plane?" The child may not know how to go about solving this problem, or even whether she has succeeded, until she consults an adult. In short, school creates ambiguities.

The photographer has captured this boy's vulnerability as well as his pride in winning the blue ribbon.

"On intellectual tasks children are less likely to know what they are aiming for, why they are aiming for it, how to get there, and when they have gotten there" (Dweck & Elliott, 1983, p. 877). And this shift occurs at a time when children are becoming more aware of self-image and more vulnerable to criticism. If the child receives recognition and praise, his achievement motivation is likely to remain high. If the feedback is negative or his efforts at mastery are ignored, his intrinsic interest in learning may fade (Harter, 1981). He may begin to avoid challenges. And he may come to think of himself as "dumb."

SELF-ESTEEM Is *self-esteem,* or feelings of self-worth, tied to industry in middle childhood? Is self-esteem a stable personality trait, as Erikson implied?

Stanley Coopersmith (1967) asked hundreds of fifth- and sixth-grade boys to complete a Self-Esteem Inventory, indicating whether statements were "like me" or "unlike me."[1] The statements referred to the children's feelings about themselves, their parents, and their friends: "I'm pretty sure of myself"; "My parents understand me"; "I find it hard to talk in front of the class"; and so on. Coopersmith asked teachers to rate the same children on their reactions to failure, relations to peers, needs for reassurance, and the like.

In-depth clinical assessments and numerous observations in different situations convinced Coopersmith that the outstanding characteristic of boys who were rated as high in self-esteem by both themselves and their teachers was lack of self-consciousness. They expected to be well received and successful; they were willing to advance unpopular opinions; and they were generally more independent and creative than other boys were. In addition, Coopersmith found that

[1]Coopersmith did not include girls in this phase of the research, to eliminate the possibility that variations were due to sex differences.

the level of self-esteem was stable over the school years. The correlation between original scores on the Self-Esteem Inventory and scores three years later was a high .70.

Why does one child have a positive self-image, another child a negative self-concept? Part of the explanation may lie with parents. Coopersmith's interviews of mothers indicated that boys who were high in self-esteem got positive feedback from significant others. Their parents showed genuine affection and concern for their interests and problems, used noncoercive forms of discipline, considered the child's opinion, and enforced strict rules. (Recall Baumrind's analysis of authoritative parenting, in Chapter 8.) Coopersmith suggests that strict rules help the child evaluate his performance by clarifying the ambiguities he confronts in this period. Simply put, good parenting enhances self-esteem. We should qualify this point, however. Perhaps the parents were democratic because the boys themselves were "easy" youngsters who did not provoke either harsh punishment (authoritarian parenting) or resignation and permissiveness. Coopersmith does not consider the impact of the child's temperament and behavior on the parents.

Coopersmith also found that boys who were high in self-esteem had a history of doing well in school and popularity with peers. Success had led to success. Those who were low in self-esteem had been loners and suffered academic failures earlier in life. Thus Coopersmith confirmed the importance of other people's opinions (the looking-glass self), but added that objective criteria are important: Good grades make a boy feel good about himself.

Many studies (for example, Uguroglu & Walberg, 1979) have shown that children who do well in school attribute their successes to ability ("I got an A because I'm smart") and their failures to lack of effort ("I got a D because I didn't study hard enough"). They assume that they will succeed if they try harder. In contrast, children who do poorly in school attribute their successes to chance ("I was just lucky") or to other external factors ("The test was easy"). But they attribute their failures to lack of ability ("I got a D because I'm stupid"). They expect to fail—and often do. Put another way, successful children have an *internal locus of control:* They believe that they are in control of what happens to them. Unsuccessful children often have an *external locus of control:* They feel that outside forces (luck, the difficulty of a test, or being "born dumb") control them. One response to repeated failure, to the conclusion that nothing you do matters, is to stop trying. Martin Seligman (1975) called this "learned helplessness."[2]

In short, although it is difficult to say whether self-esteem is a cause or result of industry and achievement, it does seem to be a stable personality trait.

SEX DIFFERENCES Self-esteem is not distributed evenly through the school-age population. Girls tend to have lower expectations for success than boys do, even in areas where they outperform boys. Moreover, whereas boys usually attribute their successes to ability, girls more often attribute their failures to lack of ability (Dweck & Elliott, 1983).

Carol Dweck and her colleagues (Dweck, Davidson, Nelson, & Ehna, 1978) believed that this phenomenon is the result of learned helplessness. Specifically, they hypothesized that teachers treat boys and girls differently. When boys fail at a task, teachers criticize them for lack of effort, inattention, and general sloppiness. When girls fail, however, they often point

---

[2]This concept is derived from animal studies. When a rat is shocked for crossing to the right side of its cage or for pressing a lever, it learns to avoid these places. When a rat is shocked at random, when the shocks are not contingent on the animal's behavior, it learns that there is nothing to do to avoid pain, and gives up. The animal's helplessness is learned.

out the error but praise the girls for trying hard and turning in a neat paper. The message? Boys fail because of lack of effort; girls fail because of lack of ability. Dweck tested this hypothesis by exposing one group of boys and girls to boy-type criticism and another group to girl-type criticism on a series of difficult word problems. When children in the first group made errors, they were told to stop fooling around and try harder. When children in the second group failed, they were told such things as "Too bad, I know you tried, but you didn't get it right." Toward the end of the session all of the children were given tests they could perform and praised lavishly.

As predicted, the children's self-evaluations reflected the teacher's approach to criticism, not gender. Eighty percent of the girls and 50 percent of the boys who had been treated "like boys" attributed their failure to lack of effort, not lack of ability. But most of the children in the group that had been treated "like girls" attributed their failure to lack of ability: "I'm not very good at it." Yet despite different treatment and lower expectations, girls often outperform boys in elementary school.

The finding that girls tend to be lower than boys in self-esteem does not mean that all girls are content with moderate success. Tracy Austin won her first major tennis championship at age 16.

Seeing It Someone Else's Way

The youngster's ability to imagine what other people are thinking and feeling is also developing. Moving beyond the egocentric and family-centered orientations of early childhood, he is better able to look at the world from different perspectives and understand that others might have different needs and desires.

Just as the young child cannot think about more than one dimension at a time on Piaget's test of liquid conservation ("Which glass has more, the fat one or the tall one?"), so she has difficulty considering more than one person at a time. She does not always distinguish clearly between the self and others. Sometimes she acts as if other people can see what she sees and have the same wishes, desires, and emotions. On the conservation test, the older child does not center on height *or* width; she considers both. In much the same way, the older child can coordinate more than one point of view: "I want to climb the tree. She wants to play dolls. We can take a doll up into the tree." The younger child tries on other roles in games of make-believe, pretending that she is a mommy or a baby. The older child can think about her mother and baby brother's needs and wishes without confusing her own wishes with those of the characters she is playing. Babies need their diapers changed; mommies need to fix dinner.

Concrete operations and social competency develop hand in hand. New cognitive abilities enable the child to think about people in a new way; social experiences accelerate and consolidate cognitive advances. Conflicts with other children who also want the biggest slice of pizza, or who have their own ideas about how to play doctor, force the child to recognize different perspectives.

Although the two may overlap, it is useful to distinguish between *cognitive role-taking* (the child's conceptions of what other people think) and *affective role-taking* (the child's conceptions of how other people feel).

Cognitive Role-taking

An experiment by John Flavell and his colleagues (Flavell, Botkin, Fry, Wright, & Jarvis, 1968) illustrates developments in the school-age child's ability to think about what others are thinking. The experiment focused on communication skills. To communicate information effectively, the speaker must infer how much the listener already knows or take the role of the listener. Flavell asked children in grades 2 through 8 to explain a simple board game to someone who was blindfolded. To do this, a child must form an image of the listener's powers and limitations ("he can't see") and keep this image in mind as he tries to teach the game. The following description is typical of second-graders:

You put that thing in the cup and then you pour it out and you move your pig and then you put it back in and then you move your pig again. And when you put it in there sometimes you can't move it up. (p. 96)

As far as this child was concerned, the listener was only a minor figure in the proceedings. If he had been left in a room alone and was asked to explain the game aloud to himself, the description would probably have been the same. Obviously, the child was not listening to his own message through the ears of his blindfolded audience. Indefinite references—terms like "this" and "there"—could only puzzle someone who cannot see. It is doubtful that the second-grader lacked the verbal skill to explain the game. He simply did not think about the listener. Contrast his explanation to that of an eighth-grader:

The items in this game are a cup, a block with four—three different colors on it—black, blue, and red—two pigs, one's white, one's brown, and there's a board with seven—fourteen squares on it . . . they shake it up and if it happens to turn up blue they go to the blue square. . . . (pp. 98–99)

Older children adapt their message for the listener. They use more detailed verbal descriptions when gestures would not amplify the meaning, and seldom say "this" or "here" to the blindfolded audience.

Robert Selman (1980) has identified five levels in the development of cognitive role-taking. At *level 0* (about ages 3 to 7), children are aware that other people think differently, but either insist "I can't read his mind!" or blithely assume that people in the same situation have the same point of view. At *level 1* (about ages 6 to 8), children realize that two people may see the same situation differently. They become increasingly interested in other people's inner, psychological life. *Level 2* (ages 7 to 12) is marked by the sudden realization that another person can think about what the child is thinking and "tune in" on his thought processes. At *level 3* (ages 10 to 15), the child is able to think about two different viewpoints simultaneously and sees how one influences the other: "She thinks that I think that she wants. . . ." In effect, the child can step back from a two-person relationship and watch how he and another person interact from the viewpoint of a third party. At *level 4* (ages 12 to 15), the child begins to take the role

Posing in dark glasses is one way of dealing with the new realization that other people may see what you are thinking and feeling (Selman's level 2).

of society and to understand the usefulness of social conventions.

Another experiment (Flavell et al., 1968) illustrates the shift to level 3. In the nickel-and-dime game, two children are shown two overturned plastic cups. One cup has a dime taped on the top and a dime underneath; the other, a nickel on top and underneath. The game is for one child to leave the room and the other to remove one of the hidden coins. If the first child guesses which cup still covers a coin, she wins the money; if she guesses wrong, the other child wins the prize. The experimenters' aim is to find out which cup the child who is hiding the coin thinks her opponent will pick. If the child says the opponent will pick the dime cup because it has more money, she is at level 1 or 2. She has not taken into account that the opponent will anticipate *her* thoughts. The child who reasons, "She wants the dime, but she knows I know this, so she'll probably pick the nickel cup," has advanced to stage 3.

The games children play on their own also reflect these developments (Sutton-Smith, 1971). Children of 6 or 8 like tag and dodgeball. These games require a child to understand reciprocal roles: "If he's it, I run; if I'm it, he runs." But the child does not have to think about more than one role at a time, as he does in hockey or baseball. When young children do play organized sports, it often looks like a free-for-all. In soccer, for example, all of the children chase the ball up and down the field in a mob; they rarely think of where their teammates are or of passing the ball. When playing a game like chess, young children have difficulty thinking about attack and defense simultaneously. (So, of course, do many adults.) These skills develop at level 3.

Affective Role-taking

As we described in Chapter 8, prosocial behavior appears early in life. Preschoolers are capable of kindness and generosity. But do they feel what other people are feeling, or are they simply projecting their own emotions onto others? Affective role-taking is the ability not only to share an emotion but also to predict another person's emotional reaction to a situation (Feshbach, 1978; Shantz, 1983). Like other forms of social cognition, it depends on the ability to assume the role of another. But it also depends on the capacity to identify other people's emotional or affective states. The child must be able to read other people's emotions, know the difference between joy and sadness, and know how these emotions are displayed. Tears of pain and sorrow are different from tears of joy and happiness. The same outward responses can have different emotional causes. Can children recognize the relevant cues?

Borke's Interpersonal Perception Test (1971) is designed to measure how well children identify other people's emotions. The child is read stories about a lost toy, getting a favorite snack, and the like. Then she is asked to select one of four stylized drawings of faces showing fear, anger, happiness, or sadness. Preschoolers identify happy or sad situations, but rarely those that produce fear or anger. By age 6 or 7, children are more aware of a range of emotions but are most responsive to people like themselves. They empathize more with someone who is the same age, sex, and race as they are than with someone who is different.

Children are better able to identify others' emotions in familiar situations, such as happiness at a birthday party, than in unfamiliar situations, such as a summit meeting between heads of governments. Indeed, when children see scenes of people displaying unexpected or inappropriate emotions—unhappiness at a birthday party, for example—they often "correct" what they saw and describe the participants as happy. Surprisingly, the ability to identify incongruous emotions does not increase during middle childhood; if anything, it declines (Iannotti, 1978). The reason may be that school-age children are busy absorbing the norms of their culture and do not see, or do not want to see, violations. In reading emotions, they continue to rely on situational cues (Shantz, 1983).

"Why Is He Doing That?"

Small children do not seem concerned with motives (Shantz, 1983). As a general rule, children age 4 and younger do not distinguish between accidental and intentional acts. They tend to assume that all behavior is intentional, including the "actions" of inanimate objects. When small children are asked to talk about a film they saw, they describe what happened but rarely attempt to explain the actors' motives. If intentions are assumed, they are not worth mentioning. Between the ages of 5 and 6, most children show rapid improvement in their ability to distinguish between unintended and intended acts, and gradual improvement in their ability to differentiate between intentional and accidental effects. (We discuss this further when we consider moral codes, later in this chapter.)

Youngsters' descriptions of other children demonstrate increasing awareness of other people's motives and personalities (Livesley & Bromley, 1973). Up to about age 7, children focus on concrete, observable characteristics—as if a person is what he wears, where he lives, what he owns. Young children also tend to use global, all-encompassing evaluative terms, such as "good" *or* "bad," "mean" *or* "nice."

"Max sits next to me, his eyes are hazel and he is tall. He hasn't got a very big head. He's got a big pointed nose." *Age 7½.* (p. 213)

Around age 8, children begin to use more abstract terms and to focus on behavioral regularities (personality traits, abilities, and the like.) But they tend to assume a person is whatever they see in him. They do not entertain the possibility that other people may see the person differently, or that a person may have contradictory traits.

"He smells very much and is very nasty. He has no sense of humor and is very dull. He is always fighting and is very cruel. He does silly things and is very stupid. He has brown hair and cruel eyes. He is sulky and 11 years old and has lots of sisters. I think he is the most horrible boy in the class. He has a croaky voice and always chews his pencil and picks his teeth and I think he is disgusting." *Age 9 years, 11 months.* (p. 217)

Between ages 12 and 14, youngsters add explanations to their descriptions. They use more qualifying terms ("sometimes," "tends to be") and recognize that the same person may behave in different ways in different situations.

"Andy is very modest. He is even shyer than I am when near strangers and yet is very talkative with people he knows and likes. He always seems good tempered and I have never seen him in a bad temper. He tends to degrade other people's achievements,

Eight-year-olds talk about what another child did that day; 12-year-olds spend hours talking about *why*.

and yet never praises his own. He does not seem to voice his opinions to anyone. He easily gets nervous." *Age 15 years, 8 months.* (p. 221)

Thus youngsters progress from surface descriptions to more abstract, relative considerations of others in middle childhood. Understanding motivations and personality traits is the result of both cognitive development and social experience. At what point does a child begin to translate empathy for others into ethical principles?

Learning Right from Wrong
In many schools around the country, children stand at their seats each morning before classes

School-age children confront an array of rules and regulations.

begin and recite the Pledge of Allegiance, which concludes, ". . . with liberty and justice for all." We doubt that many children think about the meaning of *justice* as they recite the Pledge. But certainly, they are dealing with issues of justice and fairness in their day-to-day exchanges. They are members of athletic teams and play games that require taking turns and following rules. They question the fairness of how parents, teachers, and others treat them: "Why can't I stay up later than Joel? I'm older than him." "Why should the whole class be punished for what one person did? It's not fair!" "You cheated!" School-age children are immersed in the give-and-take that results from being members of a society with standards, rules, and sanctions (rewards for conformity to rules and punishments for nonconformity).

Why People Behave Morally
Harold Fishbein (1976) answers the question of why humans behave morally from evolutionary and developmental perspectives. If humans are moral animals, it is in part because we are social animals. The mutual regulation of behavior, or what we call *morality,* is essential to group survival. When reciprocal obligations are known and followed, when promises and contracts are kept, the group thrives. When moral standards are either not known or not followed, the group falls apart.

Human beings are not born with moral instincts, however. Fishbein points out that English common law and the teachings of the Roman Catholic church do not consider morality an issue for children under seven. This is also the age at which Piaget and others believe that children begin to grasp the norms of reciprocity and to make moral judgments on the basis of a person's intentions. The emergence of morality is the result of both cognitive and social-emotional developments.

Fishbein identifies five general factors that govern moral action. Although all five continue to operate throughout the lifespan, their influence on behavior changes dramatically during middle childhood.

1. *Authority-acceptance.* In the second year of life, children begin to act upset when they see evidence that someone has been naughty and to test their parents' rules (Kagan, 1981; see Chapter 5). The tendency to obey authority figures has obvious survival value for a mobile toddler, who might otherwise cause herself and others harm. This moral influence is not confined to early childhood. When an adult stops at a red light, even though there are no other cars or pedestrians in sight, he is obeying authority, abiding by the rules.

2. *External reward and punishment.* A second reason why people act morally is because such action generally leads to rewards (praise, smiles, medals of honor), while immoral behavior often leads to punishment (spankings, demotions, imprisonment). Fishbein suggests that without concrete reinforcements, "our mutual regulation would be sorely strained" (Fishbein, 1976, p. 269). But no society or family can police all of its members all of the time.

3. *Internalized standards of right and wrong.* Social life depends on people wanting to do good and to avoid acts that their culture labels as bad. The development of moral codes begins in the preschool years and continues through middle childhood and beyond. Social learning theorists hold that children avoid committing bad acts because fear of punishment has been conditioned to those acts. Youngsters perform good acts because good feelings have been associated with the acts through external reinforcement.

As pointed out in Chapter 8, Freudian psychologists see the development of self-regulation and self-control as more complex. Identification leads children to adopt their parents' moral standards. The development of a superego or conscience enables a child to resist temptation, delay gratification, and otherwise control "bad" impulses. The mere thought of transgression may produce guilt and shame.

4. *Norms of reciprocity.* A fourth influence on moral behavior are norms of reciprocity: "You scratch my back, I'll scratch yours." Human social life is based in part on the belief that people have an obligation to help (and not injure) those who have helped them. They also have a right to hurt those who have harmed them: "An eye for an eye, a tooth for a tooth." The Golden Rule—"Do unto others as you would have them do unto you"—states that acts of kindness should not be based on the expectation of reward. However, most adults feel uncomfortable if they are unable to reciprocate, and few like to feel indebted to another person. We are embarrassed when we receive an extravagant gift or extraordinary favor from someone whose affection and interest we do not return.

The development of norms of reciprocity begins in the preschool years, when children learn to take turns—and to hit back. Full development of reciprocity depends on the cognitive ability to take the role of another and predict their thoughts and perceptions. It may also depend on empathy and sharing another's joys and sorrows. Mutual role-taking increases the child's awareness that the effects of her actions on others are similar to the effects of their actions on her.

Ultimately, this leads to recognition of the rights of the self and others.

5. *Cognitive judgments.* Finally, moral behavior depends on the cognitive ability to make moral decisions. To act morally, a person must be able to understand right from wrong, verbalize the rules of his culture, and reason about these rules. The cognitive influences on moral behavior become increasingly important with age. In adolescence, ideals become a motivating force. Ordinarily we think of ideals as good and positive. Saying "He has high ideals" is paying a compliment. But as Fishbein points out, as much blood has been shed in the service of ideals as in the pursuit of wealth. Most theory and research on moral development has focused on the last factor, the development of moral *thinking* during childhood.

Piaget on Moral Judgment

Jean Piaget's landmark book *The Moral Judgment of the Child* (1965) laid the foundations for our current knowledge about the systematic development of moral reasoning in childhood. Piaget was interested in how rules develop among children, what children mean by "lies" or "telling the truth," and how they develop concepts of authority and legitimacy. His conclusions were based on observations of, and conversations with, Swiss children aged 6 to 12 from a variety of social backgrounds.

Piaget used two techniques for studying moral development. The first was to watch children playing, join their game (his specialty was marbles), then question them about the rules of the game: what the rules were, who invented them, whether they could be changed, and so on. The second approach was to present children with pairs of stories of childlike transgressions. For example:

I. A little boy who is called John is in his room. He is called to dinner. He goes into the dining room. But behind the door there was a chair, and on the chair there was a tray with 15 cups on it. John couldn't have known that there was all this behind the door. He goes in, the door knocks against the tray, "bang" into the 15 cups and they all get broken!

II. Once there was a little boy whose name was Henry. One day when his mother was called out he tried to get some jam out of the cupboard. He climbed up on a chair and stretched out his arm. But the jam was too high up and he couldn't reach it and have any. But while he was trying to get it, he knocked over a cup. The cup fell down and broke. (1965, p. 122)

He then asked the child which action was naughtier and why.

These procedures led Piaget to the conclusion that there are three stages in moral development. Up to age 4 or 5, children are essentially *premoral:* They are not concerned about rules. When two 3-year-olds play marbles, for example, each plays according to his or her own, idiosyncratic rules. The point is to have fun. Moreover, parents and others are generally tolerant when small children break the rules. If a 3-year-old touches a sculpture in a museum when the sign says "Do not touch," or talks aloud during the preacher's sermon, no one is outraged.

At about age 5, children develop what Piaget called a *morality of constraint.* They now take rules quite seriously, view actions as either right or wrong, and assume that everyone views behavior the same way. The morality of constraint is based on admiration and fear of adults, who are seen as all-powerful and all-knowing. When a 5-year-old declares, "My mommy says . . ." the issue is settled!

Children at this stage of moral development tend to judge behavior in terms of its consequences ("objective responsibility"), not in terms of the actor's intentions ("subjective responsibility"). They say that the boy in the story who broke fifteen cups was naughtier than the boy who broke one cup, disregarding the fact that John's behavior was accidental while Henry was trying to sneak some jam. They feel a child who tells his mother that he saw a "dog as big as a cow" is naughtier than one who tells his mother that he received a high mark in school when he didn't. Why? Because a dog could never be as big as a cow. Just as children at this age do not distinguish between accidents and misdemeanors, so they do not differentiate between deliberate lies and unintentional misstatements.

According to Piaget, children in this stage of moral development also believe in "immanent justice." Even objects have the power to punish. Cutting your finger while playing with a knife is automatic punishment for disobeying the rule, *Don't play with knives.* In short, they see the rules as outside of themselves. Wrong is whatever adults forbid and punish. Rules must not be questioned.

At about age 7 or 8, children begin to move toward a third level of understanding that Piaget called the *morality of cooperation.* Peer interaction is crucial to this change. Working and playing with peers, on an equal basis, frees the child from adult authority. She has to negotiate, argue for her own view, cooperate, participate in joint decisions. Gradually, the child comes to see moral obligations as based on *mutual respect and exchange,* and rules as social agreements that provide a basis for cooperative action and justice. Rules are no longer followed simply because they are rules; they can be changed if everyone agrees. People are not evaluated solely on the objective consequences of their

acts. By age 11 or 12, the child weighs the actor's intentions before making a moral judgment.

In short, the child's conception of morality shifts from submission to the power of adults to self-control.

Kohlberg on Moral Reasoning

Building on Piaget's foundation, Lawrence Kohlberg (1969, 1976) extended the study of moral development into adolescence and young

The morality of constraint is based on fear of punishment.

adulthood. Kohlberg's technique is to present subjects with moral dilemmas in which acts of obedience to laws, rules or commands of authority conflict with the needs or welfare of others. The most famous is the case of Heinz:

In Europe, a woman was near death from a special kind of cancer. There was only one drug that doctors thought might save her. It was a form of radium that a druggist in the same town had recently discovered. The drug was expensive to make, but the druggist was charging ten times what the drug cost him to make. He paid $200 for radium and charged $2000 for a small dose of the drug. The sick woman's husband, Heinz, went to everyone he knew to borrow money, but he could only get together about $1000, which is half of what it cost. He told the druggist that his wife was dying, and asked him to sell it cheaper or let him pay later. But the druggist said, "No, I discovered the drug and I'm going to make money from it." So

Heinz got desperate and broke into the man's store to steal the drug for his wife. Should the husband have done that? Why?" (1969, p. 379)

Kohlberg was interested not in whether the youngsters thought Heinz was right or wrong, but in how they explained their judgments. He believed that their explanations provided evidence of changes in the structure of their moral thinking.

Kohlberg identified three general levels of moral development—preconventional, conventional, and postconventional—each divided into two stages. Thus there are six stages of moral development in all (see Figure 12-1). At the *preconventional level,* moral decisions are based on the consequences of an act for the individual. In stage 1, children argue that "might makes right." Some say Heinz should not steal the drug

Preconventional Level	*Stage 1: Obedience and Punishment Orientation* (or "Might Makes Right") Obeys rules and defers to powerful or prestigious people (such as parents) to avoid punishment.
	Stage 2: Instrumental Orientation (or "Marketplace Morality") Obeys rules in order to get rewards; is kind to others so that they will be kind in return.
Conventional Level	*Stage 3: "Good Boy/Nice Girl" Morality* Conforms to rules to seek approval from family and friends.
	Stage 4: "Law-and-Order" Morality Conforms blindly to social conventions and rules, in the belief that without law and order society would fall apart.
Postconventional Level	*Stage 5: Social-Contract Morality* Committed to individual rights and democratic standards ("the greatest good for the greatest number"). Sees laws as based on a social contract that can be modified through mutual agreement.
	Stage 6: Universal Ethical Principles (a hypothetical stage) Bases decisions on a personal belief in such abstract principles as the value of life, liberty, and equality. Conforms to avoid self-condemnation, not to avoid criticism or even to uphold the social contract. May risk jail or social ostracism rather than violate personal ethics.

Figure 12-1 Kohlberg's Stages of Moral Development

(Adapted from Kohlberg, 1969)

because he will be caught and sent to jail. Others say he should take the drug because he will get in trouble if he lets his wife die. Children in this stage concentrate on avoiding punishment. Stage 2 might be described as the "morality of the marketplace." Children in this stage weigh the possible costs of stealing the drug against the benefits of saving the wife. They believe in a fair exchange. Often they say that Heinz should steal the drug for his wife because his wife might save *his* life some day.

At the *conventional level* of moral development, decisions are based on social rules and expectations. In stage 3, children base judgments on how they imagine others would feel about their action. This is sometimes called the "good boy/nice girl" stage of morality. Children

are most concerned about the opinions of their family and friends. In stage 4, youngsters become advocates of law and order. Their concern for their family and friends is extended to society as a whole. Some youngsters in stage 4 say Heinz should steal the drug because it is his duty as a husband. Letting her die would be a violation of his marriage vows. Others say he should not steal because stealing is against the law, and the law is sacred. As one youngster explained,

There are laws in this society and whether or not they are fair, there is something to be said for obeying them while they are still laws. Stealing is against the law. Although two wrongs don't make a right is an old cliché, I feel it is a valid one. The druggist was certainly wrong—he was putting the value of money higher than the value of life. Heinz was wrong for

Girl- and boy-scout troops attract youngsters in the conventional stage of morality, who are concerned about being seen as good citizens.

Martin Luther King's philosophy of nonviolent resistance is an example of stage 6 reasoning: breaking the law for the sake of universal principles of justice. Kohlberg now believes that few people ever attain this level of moral development.

breaking the law that was made for everyone's good. (Kohlberg, Colby, Gibbs, & Speicher-Dubin, 1978)

In this stage youngsters see the law as maintaining the common good by protecting the rights of the individual.

At the *postconventional level* of moral development decisions are based on personal conviction in ethical principles. People who are in stage 5 view the law as a social contract. A contract is something that was created through mutual agreement and can be changed by democratic processes. As members of a society, individuals have an obligation to live up to that contract. But laws can be wrong, and an individual's rights may override the law. In the United States civil rights movement and in Mahatma Gandhi's peaceful protest against British rule in India, civil disobedience broke the law but resulted in more moral societies. People in this stage appeal to higher principles.

One criticism of Kohlberg's theory and methods is that they do not deal with real-life temptations and conflicts.

By the law of society [Heinz] was wrong but by the law of nature or of God the druggist was wrong and the husband was justified. Human life is above financial gain. Regardless of who was dying, if it was a total stranger, man has a duty to save him from dying. (Kohlberg, 1969, p. 244)

In stage 6, individuals make moral decisions on the basis of universal ethical principles. These are principles they have developed themselves, not cultural rules they accepted as given.

In Kohlberg's early descriptions of moral development, he suggested that only about 20 percent of the population attains postconventional levels of reasoning, usually in their twenties (see Figure 12-2). He has since amended this view. In a recent book (Colby, Kohlberg, Gibbs et al., 1983), he concluded that stage 6 is a hypothetical construct. Only a very few, exceptional people ever demonstrate this level of "saintliness": people such as Mahatma Gandhi, Mother Teresa of Calcutta, and Dr. Martin Luther King. In addition, he has found that stage 5 reasoning is not universal, but depends in part on advanced education.

The key point in Kohlberg's theory is that moral development occurs in stages. Although the rate of moral development and the level attained vary from person to person, the order of development through the stages is constant. People do not leap from stage 2 to stage 5. He sees the attainment of moral maturity as the result of cognitive development on one hand, and "sociomoral experiences" on the other (1969, 1973). By sociomoral experience Kohlberg means exposure to conflict situations and opportunities for leadership, communication, decision making, and responsibility.

Kohlberg's model is based on a cross-sectional study of boys ages 10 to 16, who were presented with ten moral dilemmas; a longitudinal study, which followed boys ages 10 to 16 over a twelve-year period; and cross-cultural studies of youth in the United States, Mexico, Taiwan, Turkey and the Yucatan. No other work in the field of moral development has generated as much research, commentary, and controversy as has Kohlberg's (Rest, 1983).

Critics have pointed to a number of flaws in Kohlberg's theory. Scoring individuals on the basis of intensive, open-ended interviews is extremely difficult. How, for example, would you score the following response?

It is the husband's duty to save his wife. The fact that her life is in danger transcends every other standard you might use to judge his action. Life is more important than property. (Kohlberg, 1976, p. 38)

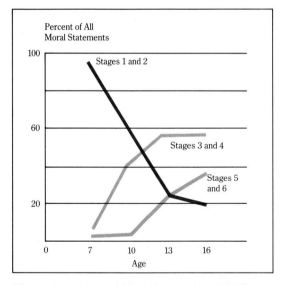

Figure 12-2 Age and Moral Reasoning   Kohlberg found that at age 7, all moral judgments are preconventional and based on the fear of punishment or hope for praise. At age 10, about half of children's responses are conventional and based on the desire for social approval or belief in a rigid system of law and order. From age 13 on, about 20 percent of young people refer to the social contract or abstract ethical principles, signs of postconventional reasoning.
(Kohlberg, 1963)

The idea that life is sacred is a stage 5 response; but the comment that it is Heinz's duty to save his wife is a stage 4 response. Trained scorers sometimes disagree on whether a person is on one level or another (Kurtines & Grief, 1974). Rankings may reflect verbal ability more than moral reasoning. One child might score higher than another because he is more articulate, not because his moral thinking is more advanced. James Rest's Defining Issues Test (1979) which asks subjects to rank a series of statements about moral dilemmas, is one attempt to correct this problem.

Other critics point to a political bias in Kohlberg's stages. Liberals rank in the highest stages of moral development (stages 5 and 6); conservatives, who believe in law and order, are left in stage 4. These rankings may reflect historical circumstances. Kohlberg's major studies were conducted during a period of social upheaval in the United States. The subjects in his longitudinal study came of age during the civil rights movement, student protests over the war in Vietnam, Watergate, and the women's movement (Rest, Davison, & Robbins, 1978). These events focused national attention on the issues of justice and individual rights, and on the possibility of opposing and changing unjust laws. Changes in moral judgments observed over the twelve years of the longitudinal study may have been the result of cultural change, not cognitive development.

All of the subjects in Kohlberg's original studies were male. Do females demonstrate similar patterns in their development of moral reasoning? Should girls and women be judged by a scale based on male samples?

Finally, are Kohlberg's moral dilemmas an accurate measure of moral reasoning? Are the situations real to young people? Would they respond differently to dilemmas that were closer to their everyday experience? After all, few children or adults are put in a position where they

Insight

MORAL REASONING IN DIFFERENT CULTURES

Are Kohlberg's stages of moral development universal? Do young people in other societies and cultures go through the same stages of moral reasoning, in the same order, at about the same ages?

Mordecai Nisan and Lawrence Kohlberg (1982) recently analyzed the responses of young people in Turkey to moral dilemmas. All of the subjects spoke the same language and practiced the same religion, Islam. Some lived in a small, traditional, rural village; others lived in a city. When the young people were first interviewed in 1964, they ranged from age 10 to age 17. Subsequent interviews were conducted in 1966, 1970, and 1974. The moral dilemmas were adapted to the Turkish setting. For example, the Heinz dilemma was translated as follows:

A man and wife have just migrated from the high mountains. They started to farm, but there was no rain and no crops grew. No one had enough food. The wife became sick from having little food and could only sleep. Finally, she was close to dying from having no food. The husband could not get any work and the wife could not move to another town. There was only one grocery store in the village, and the storekeeper charged a very high price for the food because there was no other store and people had no place else to go to buy food. The husband asked the storekeeper for some food for his wife, and said he would pay for it later. The storekeeper said, "No, I won't give you any food unless you pay first." The husband went to all the people in the village to ask for food, but no one had food to spare. So he got desparate and broke into the store to steal food for his wife.

1. Should the husband have done that? Why?

2. Is it a husband's duty to steal the food for his wife if he can get it no other way?

3. Did the storekeeper have the right to charge that much?

3a. (If the subject thought he should steal the food:)
Why is it all right to steal if it is to save a life?

4. If the husband does not feel very close or affectionate to his wife, should he still steal the food?

4a. (If the subject thought the husband should not steal the food:)
Would you steal the food to save your wife's life?

5. Suppose it wasn't his wife who was starving but it was his best friend. His friend didn't have any money and there was no one in his family willing to steal the food. Should he steal the food for his friend in that case? Why?

5a. If you were dying of starvation but were strong enough to steal, would you steal the food to save your own life?

6. (Everyone:)
The husband broke into the store and stole the food and gave it to his wife. He was caught and brought before the judge. Should the judge send him to jail for stealing or should he let him go free?
(Nisan & Kohlberg, 1982, p. 868)

Nisan and Kohlberg found that the sequence of moral development among Turkish youth is the same as that for Western youth. Subjects advanced from preconventional to conventional levels of moral judgment, and in some cases to postconventional reasoning. The rate of moral development was slower in the rural subjects, however, and seemed to stabilize at stage 3. The village youth justified their responses to a dilemma by citing the material consequences or by invoking existing rules ("It's wrong to steal"). Many of the urban subjects spoke of the desire to avoid shame and guilt or to uphold abstract principles of justice.

Why do urban youth demonstrate more complex levels of moral reasoning? Nisan and Kohlberg reason that conventional morality is both necessary and sufficient in a traditional community, where there is a high degree of consensus on what is right and wrong and social order is based on face-to-face relationships. The social ecology of the village does not provide exposure to different moral viewpoints. There is little incentive to question established rules of right and wrong and, indeed, a good deal of social pressure not to do so. Urban youth *are* exposed to different moral stances. There is less pressure to abide by a particular set of standards and more incentive to question existing rules. Developing personal, abstract notions of justice enables a young person to reconcile competing ideas about what is right or wrong in a particular situation.

Nisan and Kohlberg found evidence for the universality of moral development up to a point, and an explanation of variations in moral development beyond that point in different social settings.

---

must steal to save a loved one's life. Children may display more sophisticated moral reasoning in real-life situations than they do when talking to an unfamiliar adult about a hypothetical situation. Or they may use less mature reasoning in real-life situations, because other people's standards of behavior influence their moral actions.

The rest of this chapter adds to Kohlberg's description of moral judgment by examining, first, moral development in females, and then moral *behavior*.

Moral Development in Females: A Different Voice?

In 1925, Freud wrote that women "show less sense of justice than men, that they are less ready to submit to the great exigencies of life, that they are more often influenced in their judgments by feelings of affection or hostility" (1961, pp. 257–58). Piaget held that the legal sense "is far less developed in girls than in boys" (1965, p. 77). Kohlberg has suggested that women define the good as "what pleases or helps others and is approved by them" (1971, p. 164)—Stage 3 reasoning. Are women less likely to attain moral maturity than men are? Or

do they view moral dilemmas and their solutions differently?

One of the most outspoken critics of Kohlberg's theory in recent years is Carol Gilligan (1977, 1982). Gilligan argues that the alleged developmental inferiority of women has more to do with the standard by which moral development is measured than with the quality of female thinking. Kohlberg defines the highest stages of moral development in terms of such traditionally masculine values as individuality, rationality, detachment, and impersonality—epitomized in the stage 6 concept of universal ethical principles. Such traditionally feminine values as caring and responsibility for the welfare of others are assigned to stages 3 and 4.

Gilligan compares the responses of two children to Heinz's dilemma. Amy and Jake are bright, articulate youngsters. Their social backgrounds, education, and scores on intelligence tests are similar. At 11 years old, both resist sex-role stereotyping: Jake is more interested in English than in math, and Amy wants to be a scientist. But their moral reasoning is quite different. Jake states unequivocally that Heinz should steal the drug to save his wife. Why?

For one thing, a human life is worth more than money, and if the druggist only makes $1,000 he is still going to live, but if Heinz doesn't steal the drug, his wife is going to die.
Why is life worth more than money?
Because the druggist can get a thousand dollars later from rich people with cancer, but Heinz can't get his wife back again.
Why not?
Because people are all different and so you couldn't get Heinz's wife again. (1982, p. 26)

Jake is in the conventional phase of moral development on Kohlberg's scale, between stages 3 and 4. By comparison, Amy's responses seem hesitant and confused.

Should Heinz steal the drug?
Well, I don't think so. I think there might be other ways besides stealing it, like if he could borrow the money or make a loan or something, but he really shouldn't steal the drug—but his wife shouldn't die either.
Why shouldn't he steal the drug?
If he stole the drug, he might save his wife then, but if he did, he might have to go to jail, and then his wife might get sicker again, and he couldn't get more of the drug, and it might not be good. So, they should really just talk it out and find some other way to make the money. (1982, p. 28)

Her apparent reluctance to challenge authority, to apply logic to the problem, or to take action places her a full stage below Jake on Kohlberg's scale, between stages 2 and 3.

What Kohlberg would see as two different levels of development, one more advanced than the other, Gilligan sees as two different, but equally sophisticated and valid moral viewpoints. Jake emphasizes individual rights; Amy stresses interpersonal relationships. He believes that the world is held together by a system of rules and consensus; she sees a world held together by human relationships and caring. Jake views the Heinz dilemma as a problem of competing rights (life vs. property; Heinz vs. the druggist) that can be resolved through logic. He translates an interpersonal problem into an abstract equation ("sort of a math problem with humans") and seeks a rational solution.

Amy sees the Heinz dilemma as a fracture of human relationships that can be resolved through communication. Rather than abstract the problem, she thinks about the context. She considers Heinz's ongoing relationship with his wife, her need for him, and the druggist's needs as well. The puzzle for her is not, "Should Heinz steal the drug?" but "What should Heinz do?" and "Why isn't the druggist responding?" She is confident that "if Heinz and the druggist had talked it out long enough they could reach something besides stealing" (p. 29). Rather than answer yes or no to the question of whether Heinz should steal, she looks for other solutions. Amy scores lower than Jake does on Kohlberg's scale because she is answering a different question.

Gilligan argues that the reason Amy (and by implication other females) seems to score lower on Kohlberg's scale is that the scale was based on an all-male sample. "[By] implicitly adopting the male lifespan as the norm, [psychologists] have tried to fashion women out of masculine cloth" (1982, p. 6). Amy's way of thinking "falls through the sieve"; Kohlberg's scoring system does not "hear" what she is saying. Females place a higher priority on maintaining valued relationships and on being "good" and "nice." It is a morality of caring and concern for others. But they do not remain fixed at gate 3, as some writers on moral development have implied. Rather they follow a different developmental path that leads from exclusive concern for serving the needs of others to responding to their own needs as well.

Some recent papers (Baumrind, in press; Haan, in press) offer empirical support for this position. Others do not. Lawrence Walker (1984) reviewed data on sex differences in a recent paper. Walker analyzed 39 studies (which involved more than 8,000 subjects) in detail. Most studies of children and adolescents report that sex differences are small, if they exist at all. When differences did occur, girls were slightly more advanced in their moral

If women were not capable of principled reasoning, they could not work as lawyers and judges. Women may apply more personalized standards in their private lives, however.

thinking than boys were. Most studies of later adolescents and young adults find that sex differences are rare. Some studies report that males are more mature than females in their moral reasoning. But again, the differences are small, less than half a stage. Most studies of adults find *no* differences between the sexes in their moral reasoning. Citing Gilligan's book *In a Different Voice* (1982), Walker concludes that sex bias in Kohlberg's theory and measures of moral development is a myth.

Catherine Greeno and Eleanor Maccoby (1984) take a moderate position. There is some evidence that females show greater empathy and altruism than males do. There also is evidence that females and males have different styles of interacting with others, and different concepts of friendship, at every age. But in these authors' view, the evidence for distinctive styles of moral thinking is slim. While it *may* be true that women follow a different path of moral development, the case has not been proved. Yet Gilligan would claim that as long as moral development is assessed by the Kohlberg measure, the question about differences in moral orientation between males and females cannot be answered. (A profile of Carol Gilligan appears at the end of this chapter.)

Doing "Right" vs. Thinking "Right"

Piaget and Kohlberg were interested in moral reasoning. But knowing the difference between right and wrong, and *acting* morally, are not the same. Children are no more likely than adults are "to practice what they preach."

The evidence suggests that unlike moral reasoning, moral behavior does not follow a predictable developmental course. Early work on children's cheating (Hartshorne & May, 1928) illustrates the point. Children between the ages of 9 and 14 were provided opportunities to cheat on a classroom achievement test (for example, to peek at an answer key or to keep working after the time was up) and to cheat on a test of athletic ability and strength. They found that cheating on achievement tests actually increased with age, particularly between ages 9 and 10. Cheating on measures of athletic ability and strength, however, did not change with age. Why is difficult to say. But if moral behavior were a direct expression of development in moral reasoning, the two curves would be the same (Mischel & Mischel, 1976).

In confidential interviews, Damon (1977) presented children with hypothetical situations, such as the following: Suppose you and some friends are given a job of making bracelets. You have an hour to work. One member of the group makes many more bracelets than the others do. When the hour is up, you are given ten candy bars for your work. How would you divide up the candy? Later Damon compared their responses in the interview with their behavior in real-life situations with real chocolate candy bars. The children's behavior was one or two levels below their reasoning. Children who said they would give more candy to the child who did the most work tended to distribute the candy bars equally in real life. Those who said in the interview that they would distribute the candy evenly usually kept the lion's share for themselves in real life ("one for you, two for me"). Self-interest overcame standards of fairness.

Self-interest comes in many forms. More candy bars, increased power in the peer group, and star status on the basketball court do not cover the full range. In some situations, self-interest is in direct conflict with moral values. Reasoning alone does not determine what the child will do (Carroll & Rest, 1981).

MORAL SOCIALIZATION The older a child gets, the more time she spends away from adults (alone or with peers), the more chances she has to give in to temptation and to break adult rules.

Morals have been internalized only when the child *voluntarily* obeys the rules, even though no one is watching. Freudians hold that children internalize their parents' moral standards in order to avoid loss of love. Non-Freudians also believe parents play a key role in moral development, influencing the child in direct and indirect ways.

Martin Hoffman (1979) links moral internalization to different child-rearing strategies. The best strategy for enhancing moral maturity, according to Hoffman, is to *reason* with a child, pointing out the harmful effects of misbehavior on others, appealing to the child's pride and desire to be thought grown-up. Children are most likely to listen to reason if the parent points out the effect of the child's behavior on *peers,* not on parents or other adults. School-age children do not respond as well to appeals to rules ("Eight-thirty is your bedtime") or to generalizations ("All children have to go to school"). Pointing out the consequences of behavior for others draws on the child's capacity for empathy and stimulates cognitive development, by creating opportunities for role-taking.

Hoffman stresses that reasoning must be combined with affection. Affection makes the child more receptive to discipline, more admiring of the parent, and secure enough to consider other people's needs and feelings. In contrast, *power-assertive discipline* may impede moral development. The constant use of physical punishment, deprivation of privileges, and threats is associated with a lower level of moral development, one based on fear of punishment. Morals are less likely to be internalized. Thus parents who are very strict with a child may achieve the opposite of what they intend.

In actual practice, most parents use a combined strategy (Grusec & Kuczynski, 1980). They use power-assertive techniques to deal with an immediate situation (a fight between siblings, a child who is excessively noisy, or one who is kicking a soccer ball around the living room) but reasoning to achieve long-term goals (when they learn that their child has teased an old man, stolen change from a parent's wallet, or left the backyard without permission). Parents seem to sense that reasoning works better over the long run, but that occasional power plays are necessary.

The school setting may also have a significant impact on the ways children are socialized into the rule systems of the community (Tapp & Levine, 1977). Through its policies and programs, the school sets the tone for the child to understand rule making and justice seeking. Beyond formal social-studies curricula, "legal socialization" occurs indirectly in the classroom. Silberman (1970) has stressed that

children are taught a host of lessons about values, ethics, morality, character, and conduct every day of the week, less by the content of the curriculum than by the ways schools are organized, the ways teachers

and parents behave, the way they talk to children and to each other. (p. 9)

During middle childhood, the various agents of socialization contribute to the child's assimilation of cultural standards and a code of moral sanctions to guide daily life.

Conformity: Peers vs. Parents?

To what extent is the child's moral or immoral behavior a result of conformity—of "following the leader" or "going along with the crowd"? Piaget's and Kohlberg's theories predict that conformity will increase in middle childhood, as children become less egocentric and more concerned about pleasing others and obeying social rules (Kohlberg's stages 3 and 4), then decline in late childhood when youngsters begin to understand that rules are social creations.

Most conformity experiments are based on a technique devised by Solomon Asch (1951). A child, the subject, is introduced to a group of

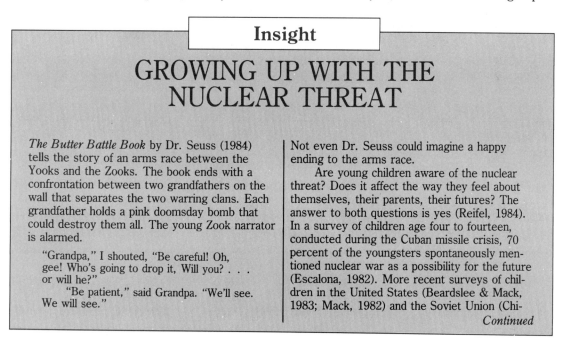

Insight

GROWING UP WITH THE NUCLEAR THREAT

The Butter Battle Book by Dr. Seuss (1984) tells the story of an arms race between the Yooks and the Zooks. The book ends with a confrontation between two grandfathers on the wall that separates the two warring clans. Each grandfather holds a pink doomsday bomb that could destroy them all. The young Zook narrator is alarmed.

"Grandpa," I shouted, "Be careful! Oh, gee! Who's going to drop it, Will you? . . . or will he?"

"Be patient," said Grandpa. "We'll see. We will see."

Not even Dr. Seuss could imagine a happy ending to the arms race.

Are young children aware of the nuclear threat? Does it affect the way they feel about themselves, their parents, their futures? The answer to both questions is yes (Reifel, 1984). In a survey of children age four to fourteen, conducted during the Cuban missile crisis, 70 percent of the youngsters spontaneously mentioned nuclear war as a possibility for the future (Escalona, 1982). More recent surveys of children in the United States (Beardslee & Mack, 1983; Mack, 1982) and the Soviet Union (Chi-
Continued

vian, Mack, & Waletzsky, 1983) reveal similar patterns of awareness and fear. In both countries, children as young as 7 have learned about nuclear weapons from television and from school. Over 98 percent of Soviet children, and 58 percent of American children, say that they are "worried" or "very worried" about nuclear war. In the words of one Soviet child,

> When I watch films or listen to the radio, I can imagine immediately how bombs will fall on my village. And sometimes at night, I cover myself with the blankets, because I am afraid. (Chivian et al., 1983, p. 6)

Young children do not seem to think about themselves dying. Their main worry is that they will lose love, care, and support. Soviet children say, "We can't imagine life without our parents, friends, brothers and sisters, and relatives" (Chivian et al., 1983, p. 6). An American child has the same thought: "The death of people important to me would be too great a thing to bear" (Beardslee & Mack, 1983, p. 81). Older children and adolescents usually realize that no one would survive a nuclear war.

Escalona (1982) holds that awareness and fear of nuclear war in childhood may erupt into a sense of hopelessness in adolescence. The nuclear threat may undermine positive identification with adult role models. Teenagers may see adults as unwilling or unable to control the dan-gers. Whether adults ignore the nuclear issue, deny that the stockpiling of nuclear arms implies the possibility of their use, or argue that nuclear weapons are a legitimate means of maintaining national security, "youth are denied a strong, reality-based pattern of adult action with which they can identify" (Reifel, 1984, p. 77). One study (Schwebel, 1982) found that many young people resent the adults that have made decisions about nuclear arms and feel hopeless and powerless to improve the situation in the future.

The nuclear threat may also undermine "the adolescent's pull to maturity" (Reifel, 1984, p. 77). The desire to assume adult roles implies a belief that *there will be a future* and opportunities to achieve one's dreams. More than half of the youth in one study (Beardslee & Mack, 1983) said that the nuclear threat was causing them to reconsider plans for marriage and a family. Most believed that their own lives would be shortened because of radiation from nuclear waste (in a peaceful use of nuclear technology). One possible response to fears about the future is to live for the present.

Researchers do not know precisely how many young people actively fear nuclear war, and how this influences their feelings, behavior, and plans for adulthood. Today's children are the first generation to grow up with the knowledge that all social and natural life on earth is threat-ened.

contemporaries. The children are presented with a series of questions. For example, the researcher may show them a single line, the standard, then ask which of three other lines is the same length as the standard. After several trials, the other children, who have been coached beforehand, give the same wrong answer. In most cases their answer is obviously wrong. The question is whether the subject will go along with the group and give the wrong answer also.

This procedure supports Piaget and Kohlberg in part. Conformity to peers (and others) first appears at about age 5 or 6. But thereafter, children's behavior does not support their theories (Allen & Newton, 1972). In some cases, as Piaget and Kohlberg predicted, school-age children go along with the crowd more readily than do older children. But in other cases, school-age children are more independent than either younger or older children (see Hartup, 1983). This supports James Rest's view that a variety of personal and social motives influence the child's decisions (Rest, 1983).

Common sense holds that the more time children spend with their peers, the more likely they are to conform to their friends' standards and to disobey or disregard their parents. By adolescence, rebellion against parental standards is expected. Is common sense correct?

Thomas Berndt (1979) conducted two studies on peer conformity in childhood and adolescence. In the first, 250 third-, sixth-, ninth-, and combined eleventh- and twelfth-graders were questioned about everyday behavior. First they were asked to rate ten antisocial acts on a four-point scale from "not bad at all" to "very bad." Then they were asked whether they would go along with their peers in 30 different situations. Some were antisocial—for example, "You are with a couple of your best friends on Halloween. They're going out to soap windows, but you're not sure whether you should or not. Your friends all say you should, because there's no way you could get caught. What would you really do?" (p. 4). Some of the situations were

School-age children tend to conform with peers on matter of style, but follow their parents' advice on bigger questions.

Figure 12-3 Going along with the Crowd? Berndt (1979) found that peer conformity, and especially readiness to join peers in antisocial activities, increases steadily during middle childhood, peaks in ninth grade, then gradually declines.

morally neutral, such as deciding whether to go bowling with friends when you really want to go to the movies. And some were prosocial helping a new classmate make friends or tutoring a younger brother. Berndt found that conformity on all three types of activity peaked between sixth and ninth grade. The greatest increase was in conformity to antisocial suggestions, especially by boys (see Figure 12-3).

Berndt used the same questionnaire for the second study but added questions about conforming to *parents*' advice about prosocial and neutral behavior. This study, too, found that peer conformity peaks in ninth grade then gradually declines. Conformity to parents, on the other hand, decreased with age. There were interesting patterns within these curves. The "generation gap" was already evident in third grade, but children this age usually sided with their parents (suggesting that there is more bark than bite in third-grade rebellion). Peer influence increased between third and sixth grades, but parent–child conflict did not. Thus a child might conform to her parents' wishes in neutral situations but go along with her peers on prosocial choices, or vice versa.

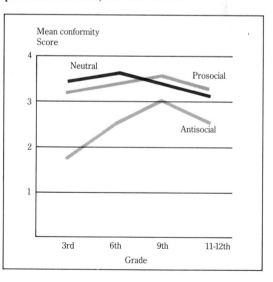

The youngsters in Berndt's second study seemed to inhabit two social worlds, one within the family and another composed of peers. In ninth grade, parents and peers were often in direct opposition, and youngsters usually sided with their peers. Many disagreements with parents at this age concerned how much time a child spent with friends and how much with her family. By the end of high school, parents and children seemed to have negotiated a truce. Fewer conflicts with parents were reported, perhaps because peer conformity had decreased. Older adolescents were less likely to go along with the crowd, no matter what, and more committed to social conventions.

The exchange "Where did you go?" *"Out."* "What did you do?" *"Nothing"* may characterize middle childhood. But family and friends are not necessarily mutual enemies. In some cases, such as fashion, music, and social activities, peer norms dominate; in others, adult influences prevail. Adolescence, however, raises new issues between parents and young people.

SUMMARY

1. Self-awareness begins in late infancy, but changes form in middle childhood. School-age children's descriptions of themselves include personality characteristics and interpersonal skills, as well as concrete facts. They differentiate the *me* and the *not me* in terms of membership in social groups and categories.

2. Erikson saw the major psychosocial task of middle childhood as the development of industry, or a feeling of competence based on acquiring skills. Other psychologists have analyzed the components of industry.

3. Achievement motivation (choosing activities on the basis of whether one expects to succeed and not fail) develops in middle childhood. School-age children begin to think of ability as a stable trait. They are more aware of individual differences and perhaps become self-conscious.

4. Self-esteem becomes linked to industry in middle childhood. Boys who have democratic parents and a history of achievement and popularity in school are most likely to be high in self-esteem. They feel in control (an internal rather than external locus of control). Girls often score lower than boys do on measures of self-esteem, but this does not affect achievement.

5. School-age children's understanding of other people reflects new cognitive skills. They are able to reason, *He thinks that I think that he thinks* (Selman's level 3 of cognitive role-taking). They become aware of a wider range of emotions, which emotions are socially appropriate in a given situation, and other people's motives (affective role-taking).

6. The development of morality can be viewed from an evolutionary perspective or from a cognitive perspective. Most research on moral development has focused on reasoning. Piaget held that children advance from a premoral stage to a morality of constraint and later a morality of cooperation.

7. Kohlberg has identified three levels of moral reasoning: preconventional (in which children move from "might makes right" to a "marketplace morality"); conventional (in which youngsters advance from a "good boy/nice girl" orientation to belief in "law and order"); and postconventional (a belief in "the greatest good for the greatest number," which *may* lead to a personal commit-

ment based on universal ethical principles). Responses to Heinz's dilemma illustrate these stages.

8. Kohlberg's theory has been challenged. Other researchers have found that very few adults reach Kohlberg's final stage of moral development (universal ethical principles). Gilligan argues that females follow a different developmental path, in which responsibility for others precedes and overrides concerns for individual rights.

9. Moral reasoning is the product of socialization, as well as cognitive development. Different child-rearing strategies (power assertive vs. reasoning) may convey different moral lessons.

10. In general, research shows that moral behavior is often one or two stages behind moral reasoning. Conformity to peers' antisocial suggestions peaks around ninth grade, but parents are an important influence throughout middle childhood.

FURTHER READING

Coles, R. (1978). *Children of crisis: A study of courage and fear.* New York: Dell. A sensitive study of the first black children to attend schools in the South that had been desegregated by court order. Coles, a psychiatrist, suggests how and why these remarkable children were able to cope with an extremely stressful environment.

Elkind, D. (1981). *The hurried child: Growing up too fast too soon.* Reading, MA: Addison-Wesley. Elkind argues that the "spoiled" child of days gone by has been replaced by the "hurried" child of today. In pushing preschoolers to read, asking school-age children to care for themselves while their parents work, and encouraging preteens to dress and act like small adults, we are robbing young people of their childhood.

Gilligan, C. (1982). *In a different voice: Psychological theory and women's development.* Cambridge, MA: Harvard University Press. A feminist critique of psychological theory, based on three studies of moral development in women.

Murphy, L. B., & Moriarty, A. E. (1976). *Vulnerability, coping, and growth: From infancy to adolescence.* New Haven, CT: Yale University Press. This summary of the results of a longitudinal study of children growing up in Topeka, Kansas, in the 1950s and 1960s considers how many stresses normal children experience and how they cope with them.

Piaget, J. (1965). *The moral judgment of the child.* New York: The Free Press. Piaget's classic analysis of moral development, which ranges from observations on how children decide the rules of marbles and think about moral issues, illustrated with quotations from children themselves, to adults' ethical theories. Challenging reading.

Taylor, B. W. (1982). *Case studies in child development.* Monterey, CA: Brooks-Cole. Taylor presents vignettes about children faced with real problems during their school years. She highlights the uniqueness of each child while analyzing the problems through different theoretical lenses.

Carol Gilligan
Harvard Graduate School
of Education

ANN LEVINE: How did you first become interested in psychology, Dr. Gilligan?

CAROL GILLIGAN: As an undergraduate at Swarthmore I took a course in perception with Hans Wallach, the Gestalt psychologist. He would demonstrate all kinds of illusions—illusions of the moon, lights that seemed to be moving in a darkened room. When you turn on the lights, you realize that nothing had moved. The lights were stationary but you saw them move.* In retrospect, I think that course was the taproot of my interest in psychology: how things can look different from what they really are, what makes people see things as they do, how they come to see through illusions. . . .

AL: How you turn on the lights.

CG: Yes, so that what they have seen before as reality becomes illusion. I was absolutely fascinated by that course, although I don't think I knew why at the time. I didn't decide there and then, "I want to go into psychology." I majored in literature. Reading novels and Shakespeare deepened my interest in human motivation and in the ways people deal with conflict and choice.

AL: Why did you decide to become a psychologist?

CG: Because I wanted to work in "the real world," as we called it in college. I wanted to deal directly with people and their troubles. So I went to Harvard as a graduate student in clinical psychology. When my first child was born, I wanted to stay home with him. I didn't want to do a full-time clinical internship. But writing a thesis fit nicely with taking care of a baby. So I

* When two stationary lights are turned on and off sequentially, it looks as though a single light has moved from one position to the other. This apparent movement is known as the *phi phenomenon*. The moon illusion refers to the fact that the moon appears much larger when it is near the horizon than when it is higher in the sky. However, if you bend over and look at the moon upside down, through your legs, this illusion disappears.

switched from the clinical program to personality.

AL: And your dissertation?

CG: It was called "Responses to Temptation: An Analysis of Motives." At the time, most psychologists looked at morality in terms of the superego. If you had a strong superego, you would resist temptation, no matter what it was; if you had a weak superego, you probably wouldn't. I didn't accept the idea that morality was an entity inside the person. So I divided a group of children into "cheaters" and "noncheaters." I read the noncheaters a story about Andrew Carnegie and the robber barons, and the cheaters a story about children in a club and their loyalty to one another. I found that you could turn cheaters into noncheaters, and the reverse, by altering the motive and the situation. I got highly significant results without fiddling with toilet training, or weaning, or other Freudian notions.

AL: Your dissertation was written; where did you go from there?

CG: I had another child, three eventually, and taught part time. I taught sections for Erik Erikson, a course on the life cycle. It was during this time that a friend introduced me to Larry Kohlberg.

AL: You've said most psychologists approached morality from a Freudian perspective. Was Kohlberg the exception?

CG: Definitely. Larry really opened up the field. It's impossible to appreciate what he did unless you know what was happening before. His approach was based on Piaget—not so much Piaget's studies of morality, but his cognitive theories. In 1971, Kohlberg organized a course on moral and political choice. It was an unusual class. Students had to fill out all kinds of forms on moral dilemmas, how they felt about the Vietnam war, and so on, before they could sign up. I taught one section.

AL: Was this when you became interested in female moral development?

CG: I never set out to study women specifically. I was interested in judgment in action; in what people do, not what they say they should do or would do. The decision to have an abortion is a real-world dilemma. It seemed like an obvious opportunity to study judgment in action.

AL: Other researchers had used Kohlberg's dilemmas to assess moral thinking in women. What did you do that was different?

CG: I made a decision not to start right off talking about morality. Can you imagine sitting with a woman who is pregnant and thinking about whether to have an abortion and asking her how she feels about the value of life?

AL: What tack did you take?

CG: My question was, Would *they* use moral language in talking about this decision, would *they* see it as a moral question? So I began by asking, "How did you get pregnant? How have you been dealing with it so far? What alternatives have you considered? Who is involved in these decisions?" If a woman used evaluative terms—*should, good, bad, right, wrong*—then I would ask what she meant. The only time I introduced moral language myself was near the end of the interview, when I asked, "Is there a difference between what you want to do and what you think you should do?" and "Is there a right thing to do in this situation?" So you see, the moral structure wasn't taken from an external, a priori notion of the moral problem in abortion; rather, it was taken from an analysis of where women introduced moral language themselves.

AL: What did their language tell you?

CG: When I sat with the interviewees, I began to see how often they used the word *selfish*. These women were defining morality as responsibility. It was good to be responsible. And what responsible meant was perceiving and responding to the other person's need. It was seen as irresponsible to have a child when you couldn't care for the child. That made sense. But then there was a funny contradiction. The opposite of being good was being "selfish."

AL: Doing what I want is bad.

CG: Exactly. The same responsiveness which was considered so valuable when turned toward other people was condemned when directed to the self. To do what *they* want is moral; to do what *I* want is immoral. Whether it was wanting the abortion or wanting the baby, that was branded selfish. "I should have the abortion because everyone wants me to finish college and it would be selfish not to." Now that stopped me. I asked some of the women, "If it is moral to respond to someone else's needs, why is it immoral to respond to your own needs"? They would say, "Good question!"

AL: How did this desire to please affect the women's decisions, their relationships with the men in their lives?

CG: The ideal of selflessness imposes on indirection on relationships. All action must be disguised. You have to see your wants as somebody else's wants in order to consider them legitimate. If you have no wants, you also have no responsibilities. Everything you do, you do for someone else.

AL: That could make a person very angry.

CG: It does. It makes people furious, men as well as women, for good reasons. Some of the women in the abortion study told the baby's father, "I'll do anything you want," to keep the relationship together. Those relationships broke up, because they held the man responsible for their decision.

AL: How did the abortion study change your thinking about development in general?

CG: I began to make sense out of other observations. A graduate student and I had interviewed some of the students in their senior year who took Kohlberg's course on moral and political choice as sophomores. We'd also interviewed students who dropped the course, most of whom were women. The women seemed to be confusing moral problems with problems in interpersonal relationships. After the abortion study I began to think that this was not a lesser form of moral thinking—it was a different orientation, a different voice. It was then that I noticed that Kohlberg had based his theory on an all-male sample.

AL: It's hard to believe that you hadn't seen that before, that someone hadn't questioned this.

CG: Isn't it? Now you see why I said perception and illusion were so important in my thinking. Once you notice that Kohlberg's sample was all male, you begin to see how widespread this is:

Piaget's work on moral development, Erikson's theory of identity, Levinson's description of stages of adult life. Offer's book on adolescent development was called *The Psychological World of the Teenager*—subtitled "A study of 175 boys"!

AL: And no one saw the omission of women as significant?

CG: A few did—Jim Marcia,* David McClelland, and others. But they were exceptions.

AL: This will sound like a naive question, but how do we know the omission of women *is* significant?

CG: It's an empirical question. Half of psychology's population is female. If you selected a sample at random, you'd get both sexes. Any study that leaves out half of the population and generalizes to the whole population is flawed in its methodology. As I see it, the selection of an all-male sample reflects a presumption of gender difference. But it is a presumption that was never tested, never examined. You say, I've studied men and what I've learned can be applied to women. That may be true. But what have you *missed* by leaving women out?

There is something girls and women are saying that isn't heard, that is picked up as noise in Kohlberg's system. That's why I introduced Jake and Amy in my book. To me Jake is a confirmation, a validation of Kohlberg's work. Using Kohlberg's theory, Jake's reasoning is immediately clear. You understand what he's said, where he is coming from, where he is going—thanks to Kohlberg. Then you listen to Amy and you say, "What?" I've tried to take this "nonsense" and explicate it, show that what seems totally illogical has a logic of its own. Kohlberg's theory misses this. Using Kohlberg's schedule, the interviewer only hears what she is *not* saying, instead of what she says.

AL: And what is she saying? What have psychologists missed?

CG: It's much too soon to tell, but I think we have a clue. We've left out the realm of attachment, the issues of intimacy, nurture, and affiliation across the lifespan.

AL: Attachment is usually associated with infancy . . .

CG: . . . and therefore with dependence and

inequality. Psychologists have focused on the move away from family attachments toward individual freedom. Maturity is defined as being separate and detached. Attachment is associated with all kinds of negatives (bonding, fusion, being mired in relationships).

AL: Attachment is seen as infantile and devalued.

CG: Yes. But girls place a very high value on attachments, at every age. So you get this funny statement: Attachment is bad—but it's okay for girls.

AL: Are you saying that if theory builders had listened to girls, psychologists would have a different view of attachment?

CG: I think so. With a group of graduate students, I'm doing a study of adolescent girls. The first thing we want to do is to describe the world of the female adolescent as seen through her own eyes. We're finding that girls try to work out the transitions in life so that attachments can be reformed, rewoven, not broken. In adolescence, they work very hard at coming to terms with sexuality, morality, the self in ways that do not involve *de*tachment.

But this is not just in adolescence. I think we need to study attachment over the life cycle, how it changes and evolves. There is strong evidence that people are at a tremendous risk when they are unattached or detached. The isolated adolescent, the man who is divorced, the friendless child, the old person who doesn't have friends, not even a pet, are extremely vulnerable. The ongoing story of attachment hasn't been told. And this distorts the portrayal of men as well as women.

AL: Let's get back to moral development and the issue of women versus men. The major criticism of your work is that you are attacking a straw man; there are no significant sex differences in moral development.

CG: Are you referring to Lawrence Walker's paper in *Child Development?*

AL: Yes, I am.*

CG: Walker misread my work. I've never said that females score lower than males do on Kohlberg's scales. In fact, I wrote an article in *Human Development* that reports no gender differences in Kohlberg's scores. It's not my argument. Norma Haan, Diana Baumrind, and others do believe that there are gender differ-

---

* See the profile of James Marcia at the end of Chapter 14.

*See pp. 480–81.

ences in Kohlberg's levels of moral reasoning, and they've replied to Walker. Baumrind makes an interesting point. She says that highly educated females are capable of reasoning at Kohlberg's principled, postconventional stages, but choose not to do so. So we are talking about a difference in use, not in capacity. The best statement of this I ever heard was by a woman I was interviewing with Kohlberg's schedule. She said to me, "Do you want to know what I think, or do you want to know what I *really* think?"

AL: How would you like your work to be seen?

CG: In the best sense, I would describe my work as looking for the anomaly, showing that what seemed incoherent is coherent if you analyze it carefully enough. I think my work, rather than being attacked for raising the question of gender, should be seen as one way the field moves ahead. People in successive generations come along and because of the times in which they live, and because of who they are, they see things that other people hadn't seen.

AL: Do you think girls' and women's voices are getting the attention they deserve today?

CG: I'm not sure that I can answer that. There is still a sense that it's not quite legitimate to study women. But among those of us who do there is a feeling of suddenly becoming aware.

AL: Illusion and reality again.

CG: Exactly. The discovery of a problem that wasn't seen as a problem before. When psychologists discovered the active role infants play in attachment, their ability to engage in complex patters of social interaction, the power babies have to affect adults, our whole view of development changed, right down the line. I believe that including girls and women in theory-building samples will have the same kind of impact. That's what I see as happening. Without going into the complications and politics of it, it's very exciting from a research point of view. For a student who is interested in making a real contribution, this is an area that is wide open.

AL: One reviewer described your book *In a Different Voice* as "feminism at its best." Do you consider yourself a feminist?

CG: If being a feminist means to take seriously the omission of women in psychological theory, and to consider women's experience as valid and worthy of attention, then I'm a feminist. How could one not be?

Self-image

Some sense of
psychological self
<4 yrs.>

Defines shame and guilt in
terms of other people's
reactions

Describes self in terms of
physical features and concrete
activities

Shame and guilt based on
self-evaluation

Industry*

[Infancy]
Unself-conscious
mastery motivation

Defines ability in
terms of specific
skills

Sees ability as a stable trait; becomes
more aware of individual differences

[Self-esteem linked to parental support, a history of popularity and success,

---

Role-taking

Selman:

Level 0 (3–7 yrs.)
Cannot imagine other
viewpoints

Level 1 (6–8 yrs.)
Wonders what others think

Does not distinguish
between intentional and
accidental acts
<up to age 4>

Begins to
think about
motives

Distinguishes
personality traits

**Moral
development**

Piaget:
Premoral

Morality of
constraint

Morality of cooperation

Kohlberg:

Preconventional level
("Might makes right" and
"You scratch my back . . .")

Conventional level
("Good boy/nice girl" to "law and order")

[Moral *behavior* may depend on socialization or the situation]

Conformity

Conformity to peers (especially on antisocial suggestions)
increases (8–14 yrs.)

| 6 | 7 | 8 | 9 |

Age in years

*Erikson's term for the school-age child's desire to acquire knowledge and
skills. In this chapter, we focused on achievement motivation and self-
esteem.

( ) age range
< > onset or peak
[ ] qualifications
‹ age extension
‹ beyond that shown
on chart

HIGHLIGHTS OF PSYCHOLOGICAL AND MORAL DEVELOPMENT IN MIDDLE CHILDHOOD

Adds personality traits
to self-descriptions

‹ Defines self in terms of
values, beliefs, private
thoughts, and motives
<Adolescence>

an internal locus of control, and teachers' expectations]

Level 2 (7–12 yrs.)
Suddenly realizes that another
person can think about
what you are thinking

Level 3 (10–15 yrs.)
Can think about two points
of view simultaneously

Level 4 (12–15 yrs)
Takes the role of
society

Reconciles conflicting
motives and contradictory
traits

Morality of mutal respect

Postconventional level
("Greatest good for
greatest number"; perhaps
universal ethical principles)

‹ Conflicts with parents
peak <13–15 yrs.>

Conformity to peer
standards decreases
(14–18 yrs.)

10   11   12

*When I was a boy of fourteen, my father was so
ignorant I could hardly stand to have the old man
around. But when I got to be twenty-one, I was
astonished at how much the old man had learned in
seven years.*
—Mark Twain

Adolescence is marked by rapid and dramatic changes in the way young people look, how they think, and the social roles they are expected—and want—to play. In the space of about six years, from ages 12 to 18, a child becomes an adult—in appearance at least. The days of playing doctor are over; sex is serious business now. Thinking grows more logical, reflective, and abstract. Educational choices and career aspirations take on a new reality.

These primary changes in physiology, cognition, and social expectations provoke secondary developmental issues. John Hill (1980) lists the psychosocial challenges of adolescence:

Attachment: Transforming childhood social bonds to parents to bonds acceptable between parents and their adult children.

Autonomy: Extending self-initiated activity and confidence in it to wider behavioral realms.

Sexuality: Transforming social roles and gender identity to incorporate sexual activity with others.

Intimacy: Transforming acquaintanceships into friendships; deepening and broadening capacities for self-disclosure, affective perspective taking, altruism.

Achievement: Focusing industry and ambition into channels that are future-oriented and realistic.

Identity: Transforming images of self to accommodate primary and secondary changes; coordinating images to attain a self-theory that incorporates uniqueness and continuity through time. (p. 5)

Do these issues represent a break with the past? Along with Hill (1980), we think not. Each has a history in childhood and a future in adulthood. Autonomy, for example, became an issue as soon as the child could walk and talk. It will become an issue again in middle age, when the adult faces decisions about how to care for aging parents. (Should a couple take a widowed mother into their own home?) The child was aware of her gender before she entered first grade, and has been practicing sex role behavior for some time. Now she must add sexuality to this foundation. Later in life she will have to cope with her declining sexual attractiveness (if she lives in a youth-centered society such as ours). In many ways, then, the continuities between childhood and adolescence and between adolescence and adulthood outweigh the discontinuities.

The aim of the next three chapters is to show how the primary biological, cognitive, and social changes of adolescence shape the ongoing issues of development.

PART 5
ADOLESCENCE
TO ADULTHOOD

13

Adolescence can be a time of emotional highs and lows. A wink from a girlfriend, a perfect shot on the basketball court, the taste of spring in the air, a wisecrack in class that everybody repeats during lunch can make a teenager feel good about himself and about life. But a fight with parents, an accusation of betrayal by a close friend, the fear of not being able to write a lead story for the school newspaper, or the uncertainties of romance may leave the same adolescent devastated.

One boy's mood swings during a single week are shown in Figure 13-1. This record is from *Being Adolescent,* a study of 75 teenagers in a Chicago suburb (Csikszentmihalyi & Larson, 1984). The authors gave their subjects electronic pagers, beeped them at random intervals, and asked them to fill out questionnaires on what they were thinking and feeling at the time. The aim of this study was to put together an insider's view of adolescence. The authors conclude that adolescence is "the age of choice." Adolescents cannot sit back and wait for the passage of time to transform them into adults. Often the adolescent's "instinctive goals" (sexual desire and the needs for dominance, social territory, and peer approval) clash with society's values (demands to attend to school, do chores around the house, and conform to the behavioral expectations of adults and peers). The result can be extreme confusion. A girl is so upset by the idea that she let her family down that she cannot move. A boy is so distracted by thoughts of an upcoming date that he cannot study. Both feel, "This isn't like me."

This chapter focuses on two of the most obvious sources of pride and confusion in adolescence: physical and sexual development. We look first at how the growing person's body changes in adolescence, then at how teenagers (and others) feel about these changes. There are two running themes in this chapter: the contrasts between what adults imagine adolescents are thinking and doing, and the realities; and the differences between girls' and boys' experiences of adolescence.

LET'S GET PHYSICAL: GROWTH, PUBERTY, AND SEXUALITY

The Adolescent Growth Spurt

The body's form and function change markedly during adolescence. Height increases rapidly. Body shape changes: Boys develop wider shoulders and girls, wider hips. Strength and stamina increase, and with them the capacity for work and play. The reproductive organs begin to function. Girls buy their first bras and begin to menstruate; boys begin to shave and may have "wet dreams." Voices deepen, especially those of boys. There are other developments, such as body odor and acne. All of these changes occur in the space of a few years (see Figure 13-2).

The Primate Pattern

The rate and timing of human physical and sexual development are unique to our species. But the shape of the human growth curve is much

	Mood (raw score) Negative −24 −16 −8 0 8 16 24 Positive	What he was doing and thinking about
Monday 12:45 P.M.		Walking down the hall at school with a friend
2:52		Walking to work with a girl
6:40		On a dinner break at work, heading for Arby's; "I'm hungry."
8:30		At work, rearranging women's personal products; "I was hoping I wouldn't get beeped right now."
10:25		Lying in bed, daydreaming about the prom; listening to music
Tuesday 8:44 A.M.		In English literature class, discussing Tennyson's "In Memoriam"
11:00		In chemistry class, watching movie; complaining to teacher that the sound is too loud; "This movie is terrible."
12:35 P.M.		Outside at school; "rapping to a friend"
2:05		In sociology class, listening to teacher talk about "living together"
5:15		At work, cleaning shelves; just dropped wristwatch
7:05		Getting off work; rushing to catch the el train; "I want to get home and eat"
Wednesday 7:30 A.M.		In kitchen, pulling toast from the toaster, talking to sister
10:30		In chemistry class, taking notes on hydrogen and oxygen reactions
12:15 P.M.		"Rapping to friends" on the school mall; admiring graffiti
1:30		In typing class; typing a letter; being bored
3:00		Walking to work alone; staring at a squirrel
4:25		
6:00		At work; making room for new products; listening to the radio
8:55		Doing homework in room; listening to new wave music
Thursday 8:50 A.M.		In English literature class studying the poem "Prospice"
12:30 P.M.		In the cafeteria with friends; looking at girls with blond hair
2:10		In sociology class, daydreaming "Should I call my girlfriend tonight?"
6:00		Eating dinner and talking with brother; watching TV
7:05		In English night class; "I'd like to be an author of children's books"
10:00		Talking to brother in bedroom; listening to stereo
Friday 9:05 A.M.		Walking to gym class; "Will this be another 'drugland weekend'?"
11:30		In chemistry class; "Spacing off"
12:15 P.M.		At home watching "Bozo's Circus," heating a sandwich for lunch
1:20		In sociology class, handing in a test
3:15		Taking out the garbage at work; "Checking out a girl"
4:55		At work, bringing stock out from the back room
6:45		Mopping bathroom at work; thinking about "a lecture on the E.R.A."
8:15		At girlfriend's, watching a game of backgammon; drinking beer
10:20		At girlfriend's, taking a hit from a joint and talking "We're wasted!"
Sunday 1:20 P.M.		Starting on a bike ride; talking with a girl
6:15		At home, watching Arthur Ashe on "60 Minutes"; "I never knew he was black"
8:30		In bedroom, listening to music; "Should I call my girlfriend?"
Monday 7:20 A.M.		Talking to mother in kitchen; "Should I eat pizza with my mother tonight?"
10:30		In chemistry class, daydreaming about the girl and the bike ride

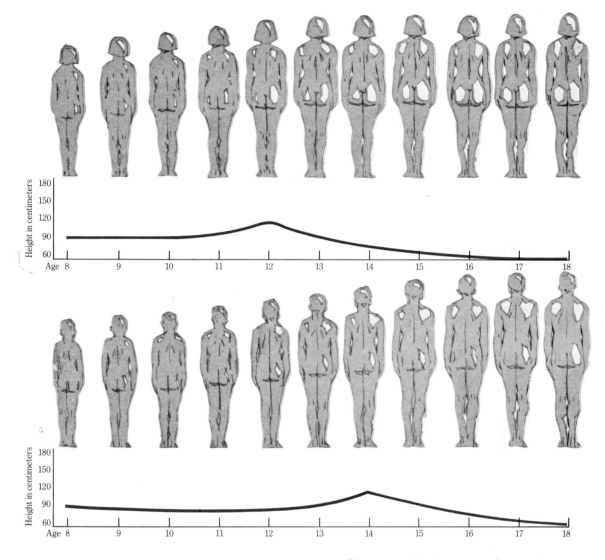

Figure 13-2 The Adolescent Growth Spurt
(Tanner, 1974)

Figure 13-1 The Week of Gregory Stone
(Adapted from Csikszentmihalyi & Larson, 1984)

like that of other primates. Rapid growth in infancy is followed by slower, more gradual development in childhood, and then by a sudden growth spurt at puberty or just before. Rodents and cattle, for example, do not have a pubescent growth spurt; primates, including humans, do. The role genes play in programming this leap into physical maturity is obvious. But the environment also has measurable effects.

Getting Bigger and Bigger: Growth Trends

Young people in North America, Western Europe, and Japan are growing taller and heavier than their parents, grandparents, and great-grandparents did. On the average, a healthy boy will be one or two inches taller and ten pounds heavier than his father when he reaches maturity; a healthy girl will be about an inch taller and two pounds heavier than her mother. Both will be much larger than their distant ancestors. The caskets of Egyptian pharaohs and the armor worn by medieval knights seem designed for 10-year-olds today. The average height of the colonists at Jamestown was reported to be less than 5 feet. Seats in the La Scala opera house, constructed in 1778, were 13 inches wide. Today, comfortable seats need to be 24 inches wide! (Muuss, 1975). According to one estimate (Meredith, 1963), 15-year-olds were 5½ inches taller and 33 pounds heavier in 1955 than they were in 1870. Young people are also maturing earlier. One hundred years ago, males did not reach full adult height until age 25; today, most boys finish growing by age 18 or 19 (Chumlea, 1982).

The acceleration in growth rates and sexual maturation over the last 150 years can be traced in part to improved nutrition and sanitation. Tanner (1971) calls this the "secular trend." Data on **menarche**—a girl's first menstruation—support this. Over the last 150 years or so, the average age of menarche in Western

societies has dropped from about 14 or 15 to 11 or 12. There is evidence to support his view. In technologically simple societies in New Guinea, for example, the average age of menarche is still 15 to 18 years. In developing countries such as Mexico, upper-class girls begin to menstruate at about the same age as girls in the United States and Western Europe do. But in rural Mexican villages, where nutrition and sanitation may be poor, menarche is delayed (Eveleth & Tanner, 1976).

The increased size of today's teenagers may also be the result of genetic mixing. Farmers have long known that inbreeding usually produces small offspring. When farmers mate stock that are only distantly related, the offspring are often bigger and healthier than their parents were—a phenomenon known as *hybrid vigor*. You can see other examples in a Burpee seed catalog. Hybrid vigor could explain growth trends in human populations. Improved transportation and the lowering of many social and religious barriers to marriage between groups make it possible for people to select mates from distant locales and different ethnic groups. As a result, the populations of modern nations are more genetically diverse than those of ancient societies. The greater size and earlier maturation of adolescents are probably the result of both hybrid vigor and improved health standards.

Is there an upper limit to human growth? Are we destined to become a species of giants? Probably not. The age at which boys attain full growth and girls experience menarche in industrial nations began to stabilize in the 1950s. The well-fed segments of these populations seem to have reached their maximum potential (Dreyer, 1982). One physical anthropologist estimates that, under optimal conditions, the average height of the human male will be about six feet. This means that some men will be as short as five feet and some as tall as seven feet

(Krogman, 1970). There should be an ample supply of jockeys as well as basketball centers in the future.

Shoulders, Hips, and Sexual Dimorphism

Boys and girls are remarkably similar in physique during childhood. Up to about age 9, the sexes differ hardly at all in height, weight, strength, speed, agility, and any other measure of physical development. In adolescence this changes. Girls begin maturing earlier than boys do. By age 12, the average sixth-grade girl has spurted three to four inches and is considerably taller than the average boy, whose growth spurt does not begin until age 14. At age 8 she weighs about the same as her male classmates and surpasses them at age 9 or 10. She also reaches sexual maturity earlier than they do. By age 16, she has probably grown as much as she ever will. Boys are slow starters but grow more rapidly (four to five inches a year) than girls do and for a longer period. By age 14 or 15 most boys are taller, heavier, and stronger than most girls—and are still growing.

Why girls mature earlier than boys do is still a mystery. Speculation centers on the theory that the basic pattern for human development, carried on the X chromosome, is "female." It

may take more time for the Y chromosome to direct hormones to override the elemental female pattern. (Recall the discussion of prenatal sexual development in Chapter 3.)

One result of adolescent growth is **sexual dimorphism**: Adult males and females differ in appearance and build. Sexual dimorphism includes many anatomical features. Boys develop broader shoulders, longer arms and legs, and heavier bones than girls do. Girls develop wider hips. Beginning at about age 13, the muscles in boys' shoulders, arms, and trunk develop more rapidly. By the end of adolescence males have more force per gram of muscle, larger hearts and lungs in relation to their size, and a greater capacity for carrying oxygen in the blood than females do. The amount of body fat increases in girls—especially in their breasts, buttocks, thighs, and the back of the arms—but not in boys (Tanner, 1978). Some of this difference may be due to the fact that the average boy exercises more than the average girl, but only some.

Sexual Development

Puberty—the development of reproductive capacity—is a special chapter in the story of adolescent growth. Puberty begins in the brain (Dreyer, 1982). The hypothalamus sends nerve impulses to the pituitary gland; the pituitary secretes hormones that stimulate the development of the gonads (testes or ovaries); the newly mature gonads increase their production of estrogen in females or androgen in males; and these hormones promote the development of secondary sex characteristics such as body hair. (See Figures 13-3 and 13-4.) Puberty may begin

Sexual dimorphism is more pronounced in some primate species than in humans. The mature male orangutan is almost twice the size of the female. His hair is longer. And his face pouches allow him to send calls booming through the jungle.

as early as age 8 or as late as age 13 or 14 in girls; as early as age 10 or as late as age 14 or 15 in boys.

No one knows what causes the hypothalamus to set this process in motion. But we do know the results. For girls, the appearance of "breast buds" is generally the first sign of puberty. Pubic hair usually appears next, and axillary hair about two years later. Meanwhile, the breasts, the uterus, and the vagina are developing. Menarche is a relatively late step in the female sequence of sexual development. It nearly always occurs *after* the peak in the growth spurt. Menarche does not necessarily mean fertility, however. A girl's menstrual cycles may be irregular and she may not ovulate in every cycle for a year, or even several years, after her first menstruation. There may be a period of absent or reduced fertility for males as well (Tanner, 1970).

For boys, the first outward signs of puberty are growth of the testes and scrotum. Pubic hair

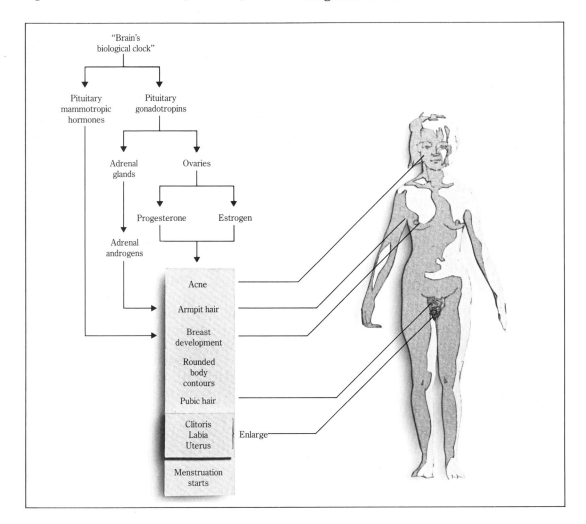

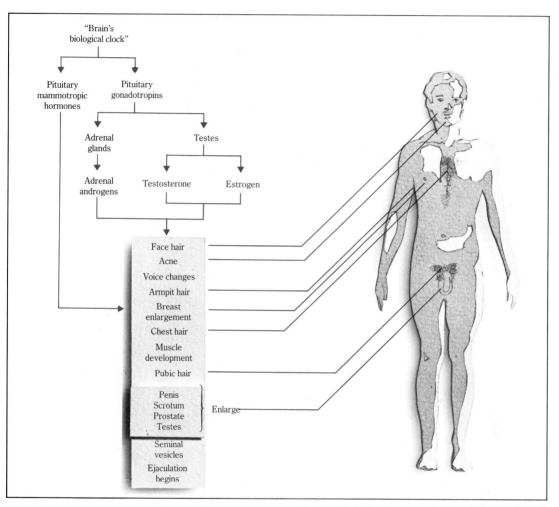

Figure 13-4 Hormones and Sexual Maturation of Males

(Adapted from Allgeier & Allgeier, 1984).

Figure 13-3 Hormones and Sexual Maturation of Females

(Adapted from Allgeier & Allgeier, 1984).

begins to appear at about the same time, or a bit later. The spurt in height and penis growth begin about a year later. The seminal vesicles and prostate are also growing, which makes ejaculation possible. Axillary (underarm) and facial hair begin to appear about two years after pubic hair. A boy's mustache and beard usually appear in a predictable sequence: beginning at the corners of the upper lip, spreading across the lip, then onto the cheeks. As his face becomes hairier,

his hairline begins to recede—a process that continues in the adult years. A boy's voice deepens relatively late in adolescence, as testosterone enlarges the larynx.

From a biological point of view, the most significant aspect of puberty is the development of primary sex characteristics, or the genital equipment for reproduction. From a psychosocial point of view, the development of secondary sex characteristics—those not directly related

---

Insight

THE FEMALE ATHLETE

There is little question that after age 10 or 12, the average male is athletically superior to the average female. The maturing male is bigger, leaner, and stronger than his female age-mate, and possesses greater endurance and superior motor skills. Conventional wisdom attributes the "sports gap" to innate and immutable physiological differences.

Studies of national and world-class female athletes (summarized by Willmore, 1982) suggest a somewhat different picture. At maturity the average female is 30 to 40 pounds lighter than the average male, but also "fatter." Body fat is about 25 percent of body weight in females, compared with 15 percent in males. But female athletes, especially runners who train at distances of 100 miles or more a week, are leaner than most males and almost as lean as male runners. Female marathon runners have about 10 percent body fat, compared with 8 percent for male long-distance runners. They also score about 25 percent higher than the average male on measures of cardiovascular endurance.

At maturity, the average male is roughly 30 to 40 percent stronger than the average female. But female athletes who use weights to train for throwing events in track-and-field competition are considerably stronger (on bench- and leg-press measures) than the average male. Willmore found that a ten-week weight-training

program increased the strength of young, *non*-athletic women by as much as 30 percent—without an increase in muscle bulk, which many women fear. Neither they nor the female athletes approached the strength of male weight lifters. But it seems clear that young women have the potential to be much stronger than they usually are.

Past age 12, males outperform females in virtually every sport. This is true for highly trained athletes as well as nonathletes. World records show that men run about 11 percent faster in the 100-yard dash and 14 percent faster in the mile run; men jump almost 20 percent higher. But in some sports the gap is closing. The female swimmer who held the world record for the 400-meter freestyle in the 1970s swam faster than the world record for males in the mid-1950s. The gender gap for the freestyle dropped from 16 percent difference in winning times in the 1924 Olympic Games, to 12 percent in the 1948 Games, to only 7 percent in 1972. Clearly, earlier generations of female athletes had not developed their full potential.

Does menstruation interfere with the female athlete's performance? Should girls and women cease or reduce vigorous activities when they are having their period? There is no simple answer to either question (Ryan, 1975). Some female athletes report that they perform better during the first fifteen days after their period than at other times, but others report no difference. Some women have established records and won world competitions while they were having their period. Variations among women are as great for athletes as for nonathletes: some experience menstrual difficulties under any conditions, and some never do. Long-distance runners sometimes find that their period ceases (a condition known as dysmenorrhea) when they are in training and running 70 to 100 miles a week. Some gymnasts, dancers, and skaters also lose their menstrual periods, which is probably due to reduced body fat: underweight females often skip periods. Menstruation returns when the athletes stop intensive, precompetition training. There is no evidence that participation in sports has any other effect on reproductive health.

In short, the highly trained female athlete is not very different from her male counterpart, and often leaner, faster, and stronger than the average male. The seemingly vast difference between the sexes by the end of adolescence is

at least in part the result of social and cultural attitudes towards sports. If women are slower, fatter, and weaker than men, it is partly because around age twelve "the average female substitutes piano for climbing in the tree and sewing for chasing boys down the street" (Willmore, 1982, p. 115).

to reproduction—may be more significant. In our society, menstruation and nocturnal emissions (primary sex characteristics) are treated as confidential. Standing taller than your father and shaving, or having curves in the right places (secondary sex characteristics) are public events: Everyone can see these body changes.

Puberty is part of a biological process that began at conception. Basic sexual identity is determined by the chromosomes in the fertilized egg. Whether the egg develops into a physiologically normal male or female depends on the balance of feminizing estrogens and masculinizing androgens during the fetal period. All of the components for mature sexuality are present at birth, in immature form. There is little or no physiological change during childhood; but it is during this period that gender identity is established. In puberty, reproductive capacity matures. Fertility peaks in the late teens and twen-

ties, then begins to decline in the late 30s and 40s (gradually for men, permanently for women). Thus puberty can be seen as one stage in a lifelong sequence (see Figure 13-5). From an adolescent's point of view, however, puberty is a dramatic change. One of the tasks of adolescence is learning to live with a "new" body.

Individual Variations in Growth and Puberty

Knowing that a girl is 12½ or a boy is 15 years old tells you little about that youngster's stage of physical and sexual development. All normal youngsters go through the same stages of growth. But individual variations in the timing and rate of maturation are enormous. If you observe a seventh- or eighth-grade gym class, you will see that some boys or girls are physically and sexually children; some appear fully mature; and others are in various stages of transition (see Figure 13-6). One youngster will complete the steps toward sexual maturity before another the same age begins. Chronological age does not dictate biological age in adolescence. Individual differences are greatest at an age when young people want to *avoid* being different at all costs.

Some Consequences of Physical Growth

As a young person begins to look more grown up, the attitudes of peers, parents, and other important people toward them change. These significant others form new assumptions about the adolescent's overall maturity and interests. Whether the young person is seen as a desirable friend or spurned as "just a kid," viewed as a possible sexual partner or one whom Aunt Sarah can still kiss and cuddle, depends largely on physical appearance. Because the onset and timing of puberty vary greatly among adolescents, young people of the same chronological age but different biological ages live in quite different environments and encounter very different social expectations. Thus the range of *both* biological and psychosocial variations is wider in the junior high school years than at any time

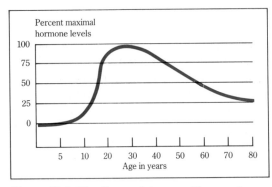

Figure 13-5 The Curve of Average Hormonal Sexual Development

(Adapted from Petersen and Taylor, 1980).

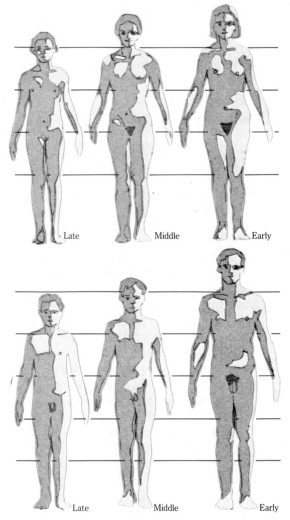

Figure 13-6 Variations in the Rate of Adolescent Development: Early, Middle, and Late Maturers

(Adapted from Tanner, 1974)

before or after (Hill, 1980). Whether adolescents find their new bodies a source of pride, shame, or confusion depends on their own and other people's social evaluations.

Self-evaluations: Am I Okay?

Adolescents who have just been through the growth spurt often seem awkward and self-conscious. Tests of motor performance and athletic ability do not suggest that teenagers are physically awkward or clumsy. But many are socially awkward in their new quasi-adult bodies and roles (Matteson, 1975).

Early adolescents are more concerned about their physical appearance than about any other personal characteristics (Clifford, 1971). In evaluating themselves, adolescents tend to compete with a nearly mythical ideal. Boys want to be built like football players. Girls want to be delicate, graceful, and, above all, thin. Both want to be physically attractive to the opposite sex. In one study of more than 500 tenth-graders (Frazier & Lisonbee, 1950), half of the boys and 80 percent of the girls were unhappy with facial characteristics, such as the size of their nose. Most boys thought that they were about the right weight, but most girls saw themselves as too heavy. Tall girls believed that they were too tall. Short boys considered themselves to be too short. Both boys and girls expressed great concern over skin problems. In all, two-thirds of these adolescents wished for some physical change to improve their appearance. More recent studies indicate that adolescents are no less looks-conscious and no happier with their appearance today than they were then (Matteson, 1975; Simmons & Rosenberg, 1975).

Popularity

The girl who cries herself to sleep because she is too fat or too flat, and the boy who undresses in the darkest corner of the locker room, act as if appearance were a matter of life and death.

Socially, it may be. Social acceptance in junior and senior high school is related to physical development. Boys with superior size, strength, and agility are rewarded with prestige and popularity. Boys who are slow to develop or have less powerful physiques tend to be ignored (Kleck, Richardson, & Ronald, 1974). Throughout adolescence, good looks are the key to popularity with the opposite sex. From fifth grade to college, physical attractiveness is more important in girl-choosing-boy (and vice versa) than similarity in personality, attitudes, self-esteem, or other personal qualities. Adults as well as peers are more likely to attribute desirable personality traits to an adolescent who is physically attractive than to one who is not (Dion, Berscheid, & Walster, 1972). The impact of appearance is strongest at the extremes. Being very attractive or very unattractive may determine popularity. But for the majority of adolescents who fall between these two extremes, other factors (personality, talent, and so on) come into play (Cavior & Dokecki, 1973).

Of course, younger children and adults also care about their looks. What is different about adolescents is that, first, their bodies and physical status among their peers are changing rapidly at this time, and second, they tend to accept stereotypic ideals for their sex. Since most adolescents cannot develop into "ideal specimens," most experience some unhappiness.

Early and Late Maturers

Because adolescents are preoccupied with physical appearance, the timing of puberty has important psychosocial consequences. For boys in particular, maturing slightly ahead of one's peers confers distinct social advantages. Early-maturing boys are better equipped for athletics than their smaller peers and are rewarded for their athletic prowess with social acceptance. Numerous studies show that boys who mature early are poised, relaxed, good-natured, and unaffected, according to peers and adults as well as self-ratings (Jones, 1957, 1965; Mussen & Jones, 1957). They are more popular with their peers, more likely to be social leaders, more self-confident, and psychologically healthier than boys who are slower to develop.

The portrait of late-maturing boys is quite different. For an extended period, they are smaller and weaker than most boys *and girls* their age. Early research suggested that boys who mature late tend to be anxious, tense, talkative, and attention seeking (Jones, 1957; Jones & Bayley, 1950; Weatherly, 1964). They are likely to be rejected by their peers, dominated by their parents, and lacking in self-confidence and leadership. During adolescence, late-maturing boys suffer as many disadvantages as early-maturing boys enjoy advantages.

Longitudinal and in-depth studies have revised this picture somewhat. It now appears that early maturers pay a price later in life for their moment of glory in adolescence, and that late maturers gain important compensations for their agonies (Peskin, 1967, 1973; Siegel, 1982). As adults, early maturers tend to be conventional in personality, lifestyle, and occupation. They are psychologically rigid, bound by rules and regulations, concerned about appearances, and worried about not doing well or not being liked.

On the other hand, late maturers tend to be more expressive, curious, uninhibited, and flexible as adults. They lead less conventional lives and careers, have better senses of humor, and handle ambiguous situations more easily than former high school stars do. One reason may be that the social rewards for early maturation in boys make self-exploration unnecessary. They do not have to work as hard as other boys do at finding a social niche or making friends. In addition, late-maturing boys have more time to prepare for their status as an adult.

The effects of early or late maturation on girls are not as clear-cut. Because girls begin to mature sooner than boys do, the early-maturing girl is likely to be especially conspicuous in sixth and seventh grades (Jersild, Brook, & Brook, 1978). She is also likely to be a bit shorter than other girls in late adolescence. Some researchers (Peskin, 1973) have found that girls who mature early are shyer, more anxious, and lower in self-esteem than their late-maturing peers during junior high school. Perhaps the combination of early development, entering a large, impersonal school, and dating pressure from older boys is stressful. Other researchers

Pictures such as this one from a high school year book capture "great performances" in extracurricular activities. Unfortunately, such performances do not necessarily guarantee comparable success in later life.

(Blyth, Bulcroft, & Simmons, 1981) have found that early-maturing girls are higher in self-esteem and more popular with the opposite sex in junior high school but lose ground in ninth or tenth grade. This may be because they tend to be short and stocky, whereas the ideal North American beauty is tall and slim. Perhaps adolescence in general is more difficult for girls (Siegel, 1982). The early-maturing boy is greeted by the ready-made roles of athlete and school leader. Both peers and parents admire him. In contrast, the early-maturing girl may find that both peers and parents see her outstanding physique as a source of potential sexual trouble. Parents may brag about a son's athletic accomplishments; they are not likely to crow about a young daughter's curvaceous body.

Clearly, how others respond to the presence or delay of physical maturation is important to adolescents. And other people's reactions are shaped by cultural standards. All of the studies we reviewed here are of North American adolescents. Researchers who compared Italian boys with Italian-American boys found no rela-

tionship between physical and personality development (Mussen & Bourterline-Young, 1964). They concluded that physical prowess is simply not as highly prized in Italy. As a result, self-esteem and social standing are less influenced by physical maturation than they are in the United States. This suggests that physical and sexual development are *not* the direct cause of adolescent "growing pains." Rather, it is the cultural meanings attached to these changes, the social roles available to adolescents, and the ways others react to signs of puberty that shape the adolescent's feelings. Figure 13-7 shows the many variables that intervene between the biological event of puberty and the young person's experience of adolescence.

The Development of Sexuality

Sexual feelings and sexual behavior do not suddenly appear full blown in adolescence. The many components of sexuality develop over a long period. Adolescence is not the beginning of sexuality, but the culminating step.

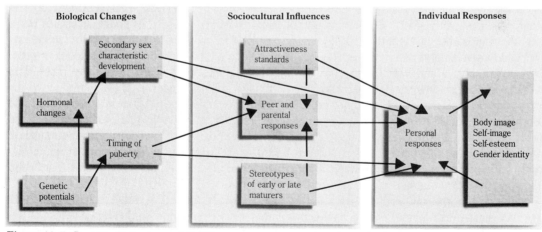

Figure 13-7 Growth, Puberty, and Self-image
How an adolescent responds to the changes in his or her body depends on the interaction of numerous factors, ranging from hormonal changes to cultural standards and stereotypes and how important being physically attractive is to the young person.
(Adapted from Petersen & Taylor, 1980)

Infant Sexuality: Myth or Fact?

No one looms larger in the study of psychosexual development than Sigmund Freud. Freud did not discover infant sexuality. But it was he more than anyone else who made scientists, and ultimately the public, aware of the possibility that infants are pleasure-seekers.

Freud held that sexual energy, or *libido,* is the driving force in all human behavior. Libido is present at birth but takes different forms as the individual matures. He proposed that there are four stages of psychosexual development (1964). In the first year of life the infant discovers that sucking is not only nourishing but also pleasurable. This is the **oral period**. In the **anal period**, which begins at about age 2, children derive pleasure from defecation and urination—provoked in part by their *dis*pleasure at toilet training. The **phallic period**, in which children discover that stimulating their genitals produces pleasant sensations, begins at age 3 or 4. This is also the period in which youngsters discover the anatomical differences between the sexes and become involved in a "love triangle" with their parents. According to Freud, boys desire their mother but fear their father's revenge (the Oedipal conflict). Freud was not as sure about girls, but he hypothesized a similar rivalry between daughter and mother (the Electra complex). Love and hate for the parent of the same sex intertwine. Ideally, the child transforms anger toward the rival parent into positive identification. Freud held that the tumultuous phallic period is followed by a period of *latency,* when sexual desires lie dormant. Sex urges reappear in adolescence. Now primitive, infantile drives must be directed into socially acceptable channels. When the autoerotic (self-stimulating), narcissistic (self-loving) child achieves mutual gratification with a partner of the opposite sex, he or she has reached the **genital period**.

Freud believed that early experience with bodily pleasure, such as physical closeness with parents, is critical to the development of healthy adult sexuality. Some individuals become fixated at an early stage of development, and never learn to give and receive sexual pleasure. All individuals, healthy or not, retain some elements of these earlier stages. The focus of sexual interest changes over development, but arousal is never concentrated in one region of the body to the exclusion of all others. Adult bodies have many erogenous zones.

Freud's theory of psychosexual development was based on analyses of the dreams, fantasies, and projections of adult patients, not on studies of children. The empirical evidence on childhood sexuality suggests that some of his ideas were right, and some were wrong.

Small children are physiologically capable of sexual arousal. The local sensory apparatus and reflexive component of adult sexual responses are present at birth. Both boys and girls are excited by genital stimulation. Male infants have erections from their first days of life. Boys less than one year old have been observed making thrusting pelvic motions that become more rapid and vigorous and culminate in a general spasm quite similar to an adult orgasm (Kinsey, Pomeroy, & Martin, 1948). Although arousal is more difficult to observe in female infants, some parents have observed orgasmic episodes in girls. Male infants do not ejaculate, any more than female infants conceive; their reproductive organs are immature. But genital sensations and reflexes are present in infancy. Indeed, in some societies parents consider genital stimulation the most effective pacifier for an infant in distress (Hyde, 1979). So far, it seems that Freud was right.

The evidence on young children indicates that youngsters may go through a period of secrecy, not latency. In some societies, virtually all youngsters engage in sex play (Merriam, 1971). The Bala, for example, consider masturbation, sex games, and even intercourse between prepubescent children perfectly normal and acceptable. Even in cultures where sexual expression is restricted, sexual games and fantasies are part of childhood (Ford & Beach, 1951; Kinsey, et al., 1948; Sears, Maccoby, & Levin, 1957). Only 12 percent of the female adults and 21 percent of the male adults Kinsey questioned in the United States in the late 1940s and early 1950s recalled masturbating before age 12. On the one occasion when Kinsey's researchers questioned children directly, the percentages were much higher: 56 percent of boys and 30 percent of girls (Elias & Gebhard,

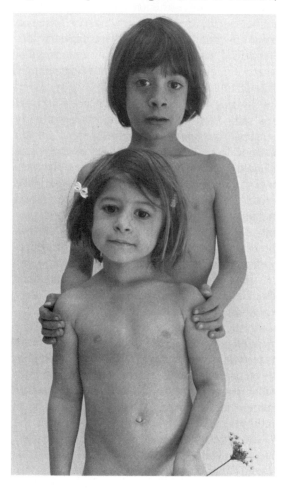

1969). In other surveys (Gebhard, 1971; Hunt, 1974), half or more of the adult males, and almost as many adult females, recalled engaging in heterosexual play before puberty. Playing doctor or house may be nothing more than anatomical show-and-tell, a combination of exhibitionism and exploration. The excitement may come from the fact that undressing and showing private parts are forbidden by adults—not from physiological arousal. But some children are stimulated:

The girl and I were age six. . . . It was my turn to be the patient so I lay on my stomach while she examined me. Then I turned on my back and let her gaze at me a while. She messed around a little bit until I began to get what was for me my first memorable erection. . . . (Martinson, 1973, p. 31)

At best, Freud exaggerated the loss of interest in sex in the school years.

There is much more to human sexuality than pelvic thrusting and erections. Adult sexual behavior includes elaborated *ideas*. The cognitive elements of sexuality, which are shaped by cultural definitions and personal histories, are as important as the physiological equipment. Infants and young children do not understand the social *meaning* of sexuality; they do not recognize the erotic implications of bodily sensations. Consider how the two children playing doctor responded to the boy's erection:

Are these children aware of the erotic implications of posing nude? Probably not.

She started giggling; I couldn't help giggling either so we laughed heartily for a few minutes until she said, almost screaming, "What is that?! What is it!" I blurted out, "I don't know!" (Martinson, 1973, p. 31)

Sexual reflexes might not require learning, but erotic feelings and meanings do.

The Role of Early Sensual Experience

How do children learn whom to feel sexual toward, under what conditions, and how to express it? Studies of nonhuman primates suggest that early experiences with family and peers play a central role in the development of normal adult sexuality.

Some of the most informative studies of sexual development were conducted by accident. We described Harry Harlow and his colleagues' experiments with rhesus monkeys in Chapter 5. Interested in the role of contact comfort and attachment in social development, they reared some infant monkeys alone in cages, some with wire "mothers," some with cloth "mothers," and some with two, three, or more peers but no mother. Laboratory animals are expensive, and when the first round of experiments was completed, Harlow's team hoped to breed a second generation of subjects. To their surprise, they found that the monkeys were unable to breed (Harlow, 1975).

The males who had been reared alone or with wire mothers were sexual failures. They seemed to have no idea of how to mount even cooperative, receptive females. Some tried to copulate with a female's side; some even tried a female's head. Sex therapy—opportunities to observe other monkeys coupling or to interact with an experienced and patient female—had little effect. Similarly, females raised under artificial conditions did not know how to cooperate with an amorous male. When males came courting, they attacked them viciously. One of Harlow's most successful breeding males did manage to overcome the hostilities and fears of a few of the females. But they were totally inept as mothers. The infants had to be taken away from their mothers for their own safety. In short, doing "what comes naturally" does *not* come naturally at all for monkeys reared under abnormal conditions.

Harlow's studies helped to explain what many zoo directors have observed: Animals captured in infancy rarely reproduce in captivity, while those captured as adults are successful copulators, even if they have never observed adult sexual behavior directly. Learning general affectional-sexual responses is essential to later sexual behavior, although early learning need not be specific. Sexual activity must be based on social affection for mothers or peers in early life. Something was missing in Harlow's monkeys— what we might call love—and it was exceedingly difficult to acquire in adulthood.

Judging by animal studies, it seems Freud was right about the critical importance of early sensuality for later sexual development. Infants *do* need to be held, caressed, fed lovingly, and allowed anal and genital pleasures. Sex play with peers can also be important—an experience Freud did not recognize. Harlow's peer-raised monkeys were nearly normal mates and parents, but less affectionate and somewhat less interested in sex than are monkeys raised in normal social environments.

Harlow's work raises interesting questions about human rearing environments. Was the Victorian family of Freud's day, with a distant, authoritarian father and a strict taboo on any mention of sex, a normal environment? Is its descendant, the nuclear family, with its emphasis on privacy (if not prudery) and isolation from wider social networks, a normal environment? Some scientists do not think so. The biological anthropologist Melvin Konner feels that the Western family provides children with much less information and experience with sex, serious or playful, than most preindustrial societies do.

"Little wonder," Konner writes, "that unprecedented numbers of adults are seeking professional help for complaints relating to sex. This is, perhaps, partly a fad, but it is partly the result of real problems" (1982, p. 287). This does not mean that there is one, and only one, correct route through psychosexual development. A review of the cross-cultural literature shows that adult sexuality takes many different forms.

Cultural Scripts

No society leaves sexual decisions entirely to the individual. All cultures have norms, or rules, governing erotic behavior. But what is considered permissible, or even desirable, varies among cultures (Ford & Beach, 1951). In some societies, such as the Samoan culture Margaret Mead studied in the 1920s, girls are expected to have many lovers before they settle down into marriage. A girl who saved herself for her husband would probably have been considered unmarriageable (Mead, 1928). In other societies, such as contemporary Saudi Arabia, the punishment for a female engaging in premarital or extramarital sex is death. In Australia, Aranda couples make love, sleep, make love again, four or five times a night, every night. Couples in the Irish folk community on the island of Inis Beag consider having sexual intercourse once or twice a month more than enough (Messenger, 1971). Husbands and wives never fully undress in front of one another. The men feel that sex is debilitating; the women do not experience orgasms. They are one of the only groups anthropologists have studied that does not have a "dirty joke" tradition.

The Dani of West New Guinea, whom Karl Heider (1976) studied, are a special case: They are not interested in sex. Like many other preindustrial peoples who lack modern birth control, the Dani observe a postpartum taboo. A husband and wife do not engage in sexual intercourse for some time after the birth of the child. In most such societies abstinence lasts one or two years; in Dani society it lasts four to six years. As far as Heider could tell, the taboo was never violated. Are the Dani seething with frustration? No. Do they believe there is a terrible punishment for breaking the taboo? No. When pressed, they say that their ancestors might be annoyed, but the Dani do not take ancestral ghosts very seriously. Do husbands or wives engage in other forms of sexual activity (masturbation or homosexual relations) during the long period of marital abstinence? Again, the answer

Brooke Shields and her mother illustrate that glamour results from the interaction of genes and socialization. The same principle applies to sexuality.

is no. Heider's questions baffled them: What is so important about sex?

To be sure, the Dani are only one small society. But they and other groups who adapt easily to celibacy (priests and nuns, for example) raise questions about a central theme in Freud's theory. Freud saw sexuality as the expression of a powerful innate drive that, like hunger and thirst, demands fulfillment. From this point of view, the development of sexual interests and activities in adolescence is biological in origin. Hormones cause a boy to lust after a girl in the second row of his French class and prevent a girl who is wondering when her date will make his move from concentrating on a play.

John Gagnon and William Simon (1973) question the entire notion of a sex drive and the power of hormones to control social behavior. Yes, many Western adolescents seek sexual relations; but how much of their behavior is due to hormones, and how much is due to social expectations? Parents and peers are watching and waiting. Dating, going steady, falling in love, and lust are part of the script that Western culture writes for adolescents. In pursuing the opposite sex, young people may be performing their social roles, not just obeying their gonads. Adolescents may engage in sexual activity to prove their maturity, establish their independence, win peer approval, confirm their gender identity, or perhaps to rebel against adult authority and social conventions. Gagnon and Simon argue that such social considerations come first and sexual gratification is often secondary.

In short, physiological maturation makes sex possible. Early sensual and affectionate experiences make it probable. But cultural scripts largely determine the who, what, when, where, and why of sexuality.

Sexual Attitudes and Preferences

Attitudes toward sexuality in the United States have changed dramatically in the last 50 years, as everyone knows. When Kinsey conducted his pioneering sex surveys in the late 1940s and early 1950s, most Americans strongly disapproved of a woman having sexual relations outside marriage, although many thought it was permissible for a man to experiment. Today most Americans accept nonmarital sexual relations between adults when both partners consent and no one is harmed. The prohibition against sex without marriage has eroded. So, to some extent, has the double standard which allowed men discrete sexual experiences but required women to remain chaste and virginal. Many myths (women don't enjoy it; masturbation leads to baldness, warts, impotence, or worse) have been laid to rest. Adolescents' attitudes and behavior reflect this revolution in sexual mores.

Masturbation

Guilt and anxiety about masturbation seem to be part of the past (Sorenson, 1973). In recent surveys (for example, Hass, 1979), about 70 percent of the boys and 45 percent of the girls said that they had masturbated by age 15, and about two-thirds of the boys and half of the girls aged 16 to 19 said that they masturbated once a week or more. (The increase may be due to the fact that more young people admit that they masturbate, rather than to a dramatic change in behavior.) Sexually experienced adolescents are more likely to masturbate than are their inexperienced peers. But whereas boys tend to give up self-stimulation when they are involved in an ongoing relationship, girls tend to masturbate more often—perhaps because of heightened sexual awareness, or to release tensions that build up if they do not reach orgasm with their partner. Adolescents are not entirely comfortable with this subject; neither are adults. But although private and somewhat defensive about masturbation, young people do not fear evil consequences.

Heterosexual Behavior

In terms of sex-role behavior, today's adolescents are not as different from previous generations as one might expect. Boys still see their role as persuading their date to have sex, and girls still see their role as avoiding or at least postponing sex (La Plante, McCormick, & Brannigan, 1980). Girls still expect boys to take the initiative, and boys still expect girls to be friendly but passive. Adolescent girls who phone boys for dates or who "go all the way" too early in a relationship sometimes find the boy is shocked.

Sex role stereotypes aside, there is no question that teenagers are more sexually active today than in the past. During adolescence, most young people advance from holding hands and kissing goodnight to necking, petting, and, eventually perhaps, sexual intercourse (DeLamater & MacCorquodale, 1979). The number of adolescents who engage in premarital intercourse increased sharply in the 1960s and 1970s, and continues to climb (Dreyer, 1982). By age 19, 60 percent or more of unmarried girls have had sexual intercourse at least once (Zelnick, Kanter, & Ford, 1981). In a recent poll of children and early adolescents, 12 percent of the fifth-graders and 20 percent of the ninth-graders reported that they had had sexual intercourse (Search Institute, 1984). Although it is possible that the fifth-graders were not entirely sure what sexual intercourse is, we can assume that the ninth-graders knew what they were being asked.

Because males often had premarital sexual experience in past generations, most of this increase is due to changes in females' behavior (see Figure 13-8). Most surveys show that in high school, boys are still more experienced than girls are. By college, however, women have caught up: 74 percent of college women and men are nonvirgins today (Dreyer, 1982). In Kinsey's survey in the late 1940s, only 18 to 19 percent of unmarried women age 19 reported having premarital intercourse (Kinsey, Pomeroy, Martin, & Gebhard, 1953).

Clearly, sexual activity has increased. This is what many parents suspect and fear. But what adolescents say about their sexual experiences might surprise most adults. Surveys confirm Philip Dreyer's observation (1982) that the increase in sexual activity "is more a reflection of an attempt to achieve greater personal identity and fulfillment through physical intimacy than a sort of uncontrolled impulse gratification or wanton promiscuity" (p. 569).

Figure 13-8 Changes in Sexual Behavior, 1925–1980   Most of the increase in sexual activity among young people in recent decades is due to the weakening of the double standard and the fact that girls are becoming sexually active at an earlier age.

(Dreyer, 1982)

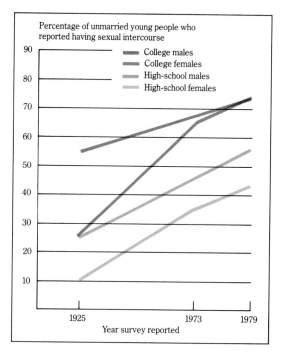

Homosexuality

The gay-rights movement (made up of adult homosexuals who have "come out of the closet") and growing acceptance of homosexuality as an alternate lifestyle have had little effect on adolescents. Most teenagers are tolerant of homosexuality in others but have no interest for themselves. Only about 15 percent of boys and 10 percent of girls have ever had even one homosexual experience, and only 2 to 3 percent report participating in an ongoing homosexual relationship. If anything, homosexuality in adolescence has decreased slightly in recent years (Dreyer, 1982).

How Important Is Sex?

Many adults assume that all adolescents are preoccupied with sex. They are wrong. Sex turns out to be one of the least important concerns in a teenager's life. Aaron Hass (1979) asked 600 boys and girls aged 15 to 18 to rank the following activities in order of importance:

☐ doing well in school
☐ having friendships with members of your same sex
☐ having friendships with members of the opposite sex
☐ having sex with someone
☐ athletics
☐ being romantically involved with someone

Girls ranked sex last, after athletics. Perhaps more surprisingly, boys ranked sex last or next to last. Boys 15 and 16 years old ranked sex ahead of romance, whereas boys 17 and 18 years old ranked romance ahead of athletics and sex. Hass also asked adolescents who had a steady boyfriend or girlfriend how important sex was to their relationship. Most said "moderately important" (as opposed to very or not very important). When questioned further, many indicated that sex was important not for its own

sake, but because it was a way of expressing love and affection.

18-year-old boy: Sex came in second place for me. If I *had* to choose I would rather have the love and affection and companionship than the sex. (p. 21)

16-year-old girl: I think in a relationship it's important to be satisfied emotionally and physically. But the emotional part is stronger and more important. (p. 22)

Love Is Not Sex (and Vice Versa)

Sex is *not* a casual affair for most adolescents. Sexual liberation has not led to promiscuity. Adolescents see nothing wrong with a couple having intercourse *if* they care for one another. In one survey (Sorenson, 1973), half of the boys and three-quarters of the girls said that they would not have sex with someone they did not love. Most agreed that they would not want sex with someone they did not at least like as a person. Some added that they wanted sex because it helped them to get to know another person better and develop a more loving relationship. "The sexual part did bring us closer and help us understand each other more" (Hass, 1979, p. 21). Adolescents subscribe to what one psychologist calls "permissiveness with affection" (Reiss, 1967).

To teenagers, love is emotional, intellectual, and physical closeness. Sex facilitates communication between two people who love each other, but sex is not a substitute for love. Love also comes in two forms: durable and transient. Adolescents believe that "true love lasts a lifetime," but few feel they have experienced such feelings (Sorenson, 1973). True love leads to marriage and family life, something adolescents do not plan on in the near future. Transient love is intense, dramatic, and temporary. Adolescents believe that love can exist "for the time being," whether that time is measured in weeks, months, or even years. They say that breaking off a transient love relationship is painful but morally right when one or both of the partners are no longer happy.

Adolescents prefer sex with love, even if love is transient. A majority oppose having sex for physical pleasure alone (Sorenson, 1973). They consider uncaring, casual sex undesirable—and exploitive or forced sex intolerable. Both boys and girls disapprove of the double standard that allows boys to have sex when girls should not. Most believe sex should be limited to a relationship based on mutual respect, if not love.

Personal Standards

Robert Sorenson's survey of a representative national sample of almost 400 young people between the ages of 13 and 19 (1973) found that adolescents have their own, personal standards for evaluating sexual behavior—an individual ethic. They feel that neither their parents nor society has a right to regulate their intimate behavior. According to them, individuals should decide for themselves what is right and wrong, and act accordingly.

Responses to Sorenson's detailed, anonymous questionnaire indicate that some adolescents are not sexually advanced while some are adventurous. Sorenson classified the teenagers in the survey into four groups.

Sexually inexperienced adolescents, most of whom were under age 16, had not gone beyond kissing. They did not frown on the sexual behavior of others but gave personal reasons for their inexperience: "I'm not ready for it," or "I haven't met a girl/boy whom I would like to have sex with," or "I haven't met a girl/boy who wants to have sex with me."

Sexual beginners, whose average age was 16, engaged in various levels of sexual exploration but had not had sexual intercourse. A majority considered intercourse unnecessary. Their relationships had intimacy, passion, and affection—without the fear of pregnancy or the implied commitment to their current partners. Some advanced sexual beginners had developed petting to climax into an activity they considered more intimate and satisfying than sexual intercourse would be.

Serial monogamists were unmarried nonvirgins who established relationships of uncertain duration with one person. Both partners were sexually faithful for the life of the relationship. There was an unspoken assumption that neither partner was required to consider marriage. Over a period of years, serial monogamists entered into several (or many) exclusive relationships and were faithful to each one in succession. Many of these young people considered this an ethical and convenient way to have sex and affection without marriage.

Serial monogamists were the oldest group (70 percent were 17 or older) and the most satisfied one in Sorenson's sample. They believed that they loved their partners and said that they had a regular and satisfying sexual relationship. Although many were out of school, those in high school and college had higher grades than other groups. They were in conflict with their parents, but not as often as the adventurers.

Sexual adventurers had little or no interest in a monogamous relationship, but sought many sexual partners. The 13- to 19-year-olds in this group had had an average of sixteen partners; nearly half had had sexual intercourse at the age of 13 or earlier. Adventurers, most of whom were boys, were not entirely selfish in their sexual relations. But they sought new excitement and new sensual experiences with a variety of partners. They liked to be praised for their attractiveness and sexual abilities. They valued their sexual freedom, and were not concerned with their partners' deep feelings. The average age of sexual adventurers was 16.8 years. Adventurers had lower school grades than any other group and usually did not get along with their parents. They saw themselves as rebels. About one-quarter of the boys but only 6 percent of the girls in Sorenson's sample fell into this category.

Attitudes vs. Behavior

In general, adolescents seem to be quite tolerant of other people's sexual experiments, but conservative about their own behavior. More adolescents say that they approve of sexual intimacies than engage in them themselves. In Hass' survey (1979), over 80 percent of the girls and 90 percent of the boys said that they approved of heavy (genital) petting, but only 50 percent of the boys and 40 percent of the girls had actually done this. The same was true for oral sex—90 percent of boys and 70 percent of girls said that they approved of it, but only 35 percent had tried it—and for intercourse. This is the exact reverse of the situation 25 or 30 years ago, when the percentage of single people who admitted to premarital intercourse was greater than the percentage who approved of sex without a marriage license (Christensen & Gregg, 1970).

Gender Differences in Romance

Statistics suggest that the gender differences in sexual behavior are disappearing: Virgin brides have become the exception to the rule. But counting virgins does not tell the full story. Although fewer women are "saving themselves" for marriage, many of those who have sex before marriage have only one partner, or at most two (especially if they marry when they are young). Men average about six premarital partners (Hunt, 1974). Studies conducted in the 1970s (Kanter & Zelnick, 1972; Sorenson, 1973) found that most sexually active adolescent girls had sex only once or twice a month. Over half reported that they had had only one sex partner. In Hass' more recent study (1979), a majority of girls aged 17 to 18 (52 percent) said

that they had had sexual experience with only one partner; a majority of boys the same age (60 percent) had had sexual experience with more than two partners. A small minority of girls were "sexual adventurers" (5 percent had had sex with more than ten partners); a minority of boys were monogamous (19 percent had had sex with one partner only).

Males and females may enter into sexual relationships for different reasons (Jessor, Costa, Jessor, & Donovan, 1983) (see Table 13-1). Typically, a girl's first experience of sexual intercourse is with someone she loves and hopes to marry. Typically, a boy's first experience is with someone he does not love. Often it is a one-night stand. He may never see the girl again, or at most date her a few times. Boys talk about their first experience; girls usually do not. These gender differences carry over into young adulthood. College women often say that they agree to sex because they fear they would lose the man if they didn't; men rarely, if ever, use sex to hold a woman. College men often say that they lie about how much they care for a sexual partner; women rarely do this (Bardwick, 1971; Christensen & Gregg, 1970; Tavris, 1973).

Gagnon and Simon (1973) claim that biology makes an indirect contribution to gender differences in sexual development. The increase in male hormones at puberty causes boys to have

---

Table 13-1   His and Her Standards

QUESTION: "At what point in a dating relationship do you consider sexual intercourse permissible?"	girls*	boys*
ANSWER: "After we had gone out for a month or less"	13%	50%
"Only if we were in love"	53%	29%
"Only if we were married"	23%	11%

(Based on Hass, 1979)
* Respondents were 15 to 19 years old

spontaneous erections, even when they are not thinking about sex. They are almost certain to discover, and practice, masturbation. Feelings of guilt or anxiety over self-stimulation may only make the experience more intense. It is much easier for a girl to ignore her genitals. The signs of female arousal are not as obvious as an erect penis. Girls are less likely to discover masturbation or to label vague, new sensations as "sexual."

The social context determines largely what males and females make of their feelings and discoveries. Boys often talk about masturbation with one another. Many hold contests to see who can ejaculate first and farthest. As a result, boys learn to use sex to confirm their social status among peers and to impress their friends.

For the most part, the physical experience of masturbation is divorced from thoughts of intimacy and romance. In contrast, girls rarely talk about masturbation among themselves. They do not brag about reaching orgasm or masturbate in groups. What they talk about is love.

For both biological and social reasons, then, males and females emerge from adolescence with quite different heterosexual skills. Boys know a good deal about the physical aspects of sex but little about romance or intimacy. They have a well-developed vocabulary for physical exploits, but are emotionally inarticulate. In contrast, girls are fluent in the language of love, but inexperienced and often ignorant about the physical aspects of sex.

There seems to be only some truth to the saying that males want a lover while females want love. When Hass (1979) asked adolescents if they had ever been in love, 82 percent of the girls 17 to 18 years old said yes. So did 82 percent of the boys that age. Younger boys (15 to 16 years old) were somewhat *more* likely to say yes than younger girls were (82 percent for boys versus 76 percent for girls). We suspect that Gagnon and Simon's biological explanation of gender differences in sexual development is not so much wrong as dated. More girls masturbate today than in the past, perhaps because girls talk more about the physical aspects of sex

For boys, learning about sex is a social activity.

with each other. At the same time, the decline of the double standard in sexual conduct means that more boys have their first sexual experience with a girl they like, rather than with a girl whom everyone dates but no one respects. A boy is less likely to think only of "scoring" when the girl is a friend.

Sexual Histories

Sex is not just a fantasy for many adolescents. They are both thinking and experimenting with their bodies, their emotions, and their relationships. They often act before they think of the consequences.

First Experiences: Pride and Conflict

How do adolescents feel about losing their virginity? The significance of the event lies not in the physical act, but in its effects on the teenager's self-image. The boys in Hass' study generally reported very positive feelings. They viewed their first experience as an accomplishment. They felt more mature, and more confident about themselves and their relations with girls. No longer would they have to lie to their friends.

16-year-old-boy: "It was like I had become a man and I wanted to tell everyone about it." (p. 73)

Some were merely relieved that they had gotten it over with, but most were exhilarated. Girls were more likely to report mixed emotions. Many felt more mature and closer to their boyfriends. But many were uncertain about how their peers would react: *What will they think of me if I do? What will they think of me if I don't?* Boys know the answers to these questions; girls are unsure. Some viewed sexual intercourse as an irrevocable step, that would change them in some basic way. This led to feelings of anxiety or sadness:

17-year-old girl: "At first I felt hurt and sad because I felt like I had lost the 'little girl' in me."

17-year-old girl: "It was scary—like losing an important part of me which I knew I could never get back." (p. 75).

Others reacted much the way boys did:

15-year-old girl: "I felt beaming, I thought if anyone saw me they would surely know because of the look on my face." (p. 78)

Girls who had their first experience with someone they loved were the least likely to feel guilty. These girls felt that they had given their virginity to someone, not lost it. Hass does not say how many girls felt good, and how many confused or bad, about the experience. But he reports that 70 percent of the girls and 90 percent of the boys said that sex is "very enjoyable."

The available evidence indicates that sexual activity that is part of an ongoing attempt to relate to a caring, supportive peer does not lead to maladjustment or problem behavior—*if* the adolescent accepts his or her sexuality and takes measures to avoid venereal disease and pregnancy (Dreyer, 1982). Unfortunately, many do not take these precautions.

Contraception

Knowledge and use of contraception has not kept pace with the increase in sexual activity among adolescents. Data from four different studies (summarized in Dreyer, 1982) show that only 45 percent of adolescents use any form of contraception the first time they have sexual intercourse, and that only 50 percent of college students and 20 percent of high school students use contraception regularly. Moreover, most adolescents are ill-informed about reproduction. A national survey of 1,300 sexually active girls aged 15 to 19 (Kanter & Zelnick, 1973) revealed that 40 percent did not know at what point in their monthly cycle they stood the greatest risk of becoming pregnant. Most thought that risk was highest during their menstrual period. The same study showed that one out of two girls relied on her partner to use a condom or withdrawal as contraception.

There is no simple answer to the question of why so many adolescents do not protect themselves from unwanted pregnancy. Dreyer (1982) speculates that it is difficult for adolescent girls, and boys, to accept the fact that they are sexually active. To do so means a major revision of the adolescent's self-concept. Using contraception regularly means admitting to oneself, one's partner, and a pharmacist or physician that one is sexually active. Adolescents often rationalize their first sexual experience as an accident, an experiment, or a moment of passion or weakness. They do not expect to repeat the experience regularly—and many do not. This enables them to maintain the fiction of sexual innocence.

A five-year study of the adolescent women at southern California family planning clinics (Oskamp & Mindick, 1981) confirms this view and adds other factors. Researchers found that girls who used contraception erratically or unsuccessfully (1) were unable to accept their sexuality and to assume responsibility for their behavior, (2) were deviant and irresponsible in other ways, (3) felt generally passive, helpless, and incompetent, (4) were slow to acquire and use information about reproduction, (5) did not think about the future or plan for it, (6) felt guilty about sex and unable to communicate with their partner, and (7) were either fearful or ignorant about the use of contraceptives. Of these seven factors, the two that distinguished best between successful and unsuccessful contraceptive users were planning and *sexual* knowledge. Oskamp and Mindick found that general intelligence, as measured by IQ tests, did not correlate significantly with success in avoiding pregnancy; specific sexual knowledge did.

We do not know how adolescent males feel about contraceptives, or how often they use them; virtually no one has studied boys. This double standard in research reflects the unconscious assumption that preventing pregnancy is the female's responsibility. Many adolescent girls assume the reverse—and bear the consequences.

Preaching hasn't stopped teenage pregnancy. Teaching might.

Dressing for a date, this teenager thinks of herself as a young woman. The toy clown shows she has not quite left childhood behind.

Pregnancies, Unwanted and Wanted

The overall birth rate among teenagers declined in the 1970s and early 1980s (Eisen, Zellman, Leibowitz, Chow, & Evans, 1983). Most of this decrease can be traced to the availability of abortions. Between 1973—the year the United States Supreme Court declared laws against abortions in the first trimester of pregnancy unconstitutional—and 1975, the abortion rate among teenagers rose 60 percent (Baldwin, 1976). During this same period, however, the *number* of teenagers who gave birth out of wedlock increased substantially. There were two main reasons for this. First, the so-called baby boom generation had reached childbearing age, so that the number of young fertile women in the population increased.[1] Second, the proportion of pregnant teenagers who decided to become single mothers increased. Fewer teenage girls got married to legitimize their babies or gave the babies up for adoption. Between 1960 and 1980, the number of births out of wedlock among teenagers more than doubled. Nearly half of the teenagers who gave birth in 1980 were unmarried. More than 100,000 adolescents gave birth that year.

Race, social class, education, and the strength of religious belief all affect a teenager's choice of whether or not to keep her child. Black teenagers are more likely to become single mothers than are white teenagers, particularly if their family is receiving public assistance. White, middle-class teenagers are more likely to have an abortion or to get married before the baby is born. The more education a pregnant teenager's mother has (an indirect measure of social class) and the better she herself is doing in school, the more likely she is to decide on an abortion. Whatever a teenager's race or social class, she is more likely to have and keep the baby if she is actively religious than if she is not (Eisen et al., 1983).

Studies of pregnant, unwed teenagers who have already decided to have or not have their baby fill in this socioeconomic sketch. Frank Furstenberg (1976) studied a group of predominantly black, poor, urban teenagers who chose motherhood in Baltimore. He found that 60 percent of these young women were unhappy when they learned they were pregnant, even though they were still seeing the baby's father and expected to marry him someday. About 20 percent had mixed emotions. And 20 percent were happy about the pregnancy, even though they had not consciously tried to conceive. All of these mothers were given instruction in contraception after their baby was born. Two years later, Furstenberg found that they had less than half the pregnancy rate of a group of similar teenagers who had not participated in the program. This suggests that a major factor in teenage pregnancy is lack of information about and access to birth control.

Marvin Eisen and his colleagues (Eisen et al., 1983) interviewed white and Mexican-American teenagers who had come to California clinics for pregnancy tests. The researchers were interested in how and why a teenager made the decision to have a baby. But teenagers do not make this decision alone; they are influenced by the people around them. Teenagers who believed that the baby's father wanted them to have the child were likely to do so, perhaps because his attitude toward pregnancy implied future emotional and financial support. Teenagers whose mothers did not approve of abortion were also more likely to have the baby. Indeed, many were pleasantly surprised by their

[1]The distinction between the birth rate and the number of births is an important one. Suppose that the rate of illegitimate births among teenagers in a population is 5 per 1,000. If there are 2,000 teenage girls in that population, the number of births out of wedlock to young mothers will be 10. Suppose that the birth rate drops to 2 per 1,000 unwed teenagers but the number of adolescent girls in the population increases to 10,000. Even though the birth rate has dropped, the number of babies without legal fathers will increase to 20. Increases in numbers create the impression of an "epidemic" in unwed teenage births, even though the teenage birth rate has declined.

mother's attitude. (Interestingly, the reaction of the girl's own father to the pregnancy had little effect on her decision.) Knowing another teenage mother provided additional social support: Conventional norms had already been broken and the girl had some idea of what to expect.

Other psychologists add that lower-class teenagers might decide that the benefits of motherhood outweigh the costs (Chilman, 1979). The perceived benefits for a teenager might include confirming her identity as a woman, becoming her mother's equal in status, having a dependent child to love, testing the commitment of the child's father, getting attention, and perhaps becoming eligible for welfare. A middle-class girl who becomes pregnant may be giving up, or at least postponing, a college education and a career if she decides to have a baby. A lower-class girl may feel she has little to lose by keeping the child.

Insight

UNPLANNED PARENTHOOD

Cultural norms in the United States hold that the right time for a woman to have her first child is between ages 22 and 32. The approved schedule for the transition from childhood to parenthood is (1) finish school, (2) get a job, (3) get married, and *then* (4) start a family. This sequence allows a young person to adjust to new adult roles one at a time. A teenager who becomes a mother is culturally out of step, whether or not she is married (almost half are not). Often she is pushed onto a "triple-track" pattern of finishing school, getting her first job or getting married, and becoming a parent all at once. She confronts three social and emotional tasks simultaneously: establishing her identity, developing an intimate relationship with the father, and nurturing her child (Russell, 1980).

Becoming a parent for the first time is a difficult transition at any age. In most cases, teenage mothers handle the transition with a good deal of help from their families. In his study of poor, black teenagers in Baltimore, Frank Furstenberg (1976) found that most teenage mothers stayed close to home. Unmarried mothers usually remained with their families; many of those who got married lived with parents or other relatives for a while after the baby was born; and mothers whose marriages broke up often returned to their parents' home. Five years after the birth of their baby, nearly half of the mothers were living with their parents or other older relatives. Although financial considerations were involved, Furstenberg suspects that the main reason for this pattern is that teenage mothers are reluctant to give up the families they know for the uncertainties of an independent household. "Most adolescent[s] . . . do not stop being their parents' children, in the sense of requiring care and support, when they themselves become parents" (Furstenberg, 1980, p. 74).

Joint households and collaborative child-care are the norm in many cultures. In our society, however, there are no clear norms for three-generation households; each family has to negotiate its own rules. If the young mother is also unmarried, families feel the social ambiguities even more sharply. Will the boyfriend be granted the status of father? Should the mother continue to date him? Furstenberg and his colleagues conducted intensive interviews and observations of families whose teenage daughter had presented them with a child (Furstenberg, 1980).

They found that the division of labor varied from family to family. In some families, child-care responsibility resembled a pyramid, with the mother or grandmother at the top; in others it took the form of concentric circles, with a

Continued

number of family members ringed around the child. In some families, one person (usually the mother or grandmother) took care of the child most of the time; in others, several members of the family cared for the child in overlapping shifts. In some, the assignments were clear: "I told her [the adolescent mother] that I was not going to get up in the middle of the night. It was her responsibility" (p. 77). In others, agreements were unspoken: "No, she didn't say anything. I knew that she [the grandmother] would take care of Tania if I went back to school" (p. 77).

Often the birth of a baby brought the whole family closer together. Having an infant to cherish reduced conflict, forestalled a marital breakup, or restored the grandmother's status by refilling an almost empty nest. The teenager's status in the family usually rose when she became a mother. She was treated "less like a girl and more like a woman." In some cases, her relationship with her parents improved. She was surprised and grateful that they accepted her pregnancy; they became more solicitous and protective. In a few cases, the family scapegoat became the favored child. But her gain was usually another child's loss.

Although the family shelters a teenage mother from the full brunt of parenthood, there are liabilities in joint households. First, the teenage mother is cast in the role of apprentice parent. Apprenticeships can be instructive or exploitive. In a few cases, other family members took over infant care, claiming the right of parenthood for themselves. A battle for control of the child seemed inevitable. Second, the teenage mother enjoys a special closeness with her own mother when the two are sharing childcare. But this rapport may make it harder for her to break away from the family and establish her independence in the future. Finally, Furstenberg's observations were made during the "honeymoon" stage of parenthood, when the child was still an infant. As the child grows older and discipline becomes more of an issue, the potential for family conflict increases.

Where is the father while the mother is settling into new household arrangements? Most studies of unmarried teenage mothers suggest that many continue to date the father after their child is born (Parke, Power, & Fischer, 1980). It is not uncommon for the father to visit the child, provide some financial support if he has a job, and then establish a live-in relationship with the mother and child a year or two later. Yet little is known about adolescent fathers themselves. They are missing persons in research on teenage parenthood, as they often are in the lives of mothers and infants.

Few lower-class teenage girls want to become pregnant, however.

Families, Present and Future

Most teenagers expect to get married—but not in the near future. Even those in the oldest group—18- and 19-year-olds—do not think of marriage as one of the next steps in their life, as older adolescents did in the 1950s (Sorenson, 1973). They do not believe that marriage is a precondition for a sexual relationship, as we noted earlier. Indeed, a majority of the teenagers in Hass' study (1979) said that it is important for a couple to find out whether they are sexually compatible before they get married. Many also said that people (female and male) should have sexual experience with different partners before settling down, so that they can develop a better understanding of who is best for them. Some added that a person who has not "played around" before marriage will probably do so after marriage. Nearly three out of four believed that "two people shouldn't have to get married just because they want to live together" (Sorenson, 1973). Most also felt that a couple should not feel compelled to get married if the young woman gets pregnant. Marriage is one option, but only one.

A few of the young people in Hass' sample (6 percent of boys and 3 percent of girls) said that they were disillusioned about traditional marriage. This did not mean that they wanted to run off to communes or establish "open marriages" with no sexual boundaries. They sought commitment and expected to live with their partner, but were not sure that they wanted to get married. Many cited spontaneously the failed marriages of their parents or siblings to prove their point: Marriages do not work.

These and other studies make clear that the social functions of marriage have changed (Dreyer, 1982). In the past, young people were not considered full-fledged adults until they got married, at which time they were assumed to be mature and responsible, whatever their age. Marriage was the dividing line between youth and adulthood. This is no longer true. Many people postpone marriage until their mid- to late-twenties, when they feel settled in a job and career. Others become single again after a divorce in their thirties, forties, or fifties. No longer are youth and singlehood synonymous.

Marriage continues to serve psychological functions. Adolescent sexual behavior and early intimacy can be seen as part of the search for identity; and marriage represents commitment, adult intimacy, and identity resolution. Our society might be evolving toward what Margaret Mead called "practice" marriages and "parenting" marriages. Informal relationships in which two people try themselves out as partners and

Adolescents seek close relationships with members of the opposite sex. Most of today's teenagers do not expect to marry their first love, however.

practice living together may precede formal marriages, which are long-term commitments and often include child-rearing. Mead, among others, believed that two kinds of marriage would serve modern societies better than traditional marriage.

Adolescents see the marriage issue as a major barrier to communicating with their parents about sex. Rightly or wrongly, three-quarters of adolescents believe that their parents consider sex before marriage immoral (Sorenson, 1973). They assume that their parents would disapprove of much of their sexual behavior—if they knew. In Hass' survey (1979), most said that their parents underestimated or overestimated their sexual experience. They would like to be able to talk to their parents about sexuality. But they feel that their conflicting views get in the way. Most adolescents communicate little with their parents about their sexuality or even about sex in general (see Table 13-2). They receive little factual information about sex and even less discussion of the feelings and sexual behaviors that their parents experience.

The one exception to the usual parental silence on sexual matters is menstruation. Most mothers today prepare their daughters for the onset of menses. Unlike a generation ago, contemporary adolescent girls do not fear "the curse" or have only negative feelings about menstruation. Rather, it is a source of pride in growing up (Brooks-Gunn & Ruble, 1982). By contrast, parents do not prepare their adolescent sons for their first ejaculation—or congratulate them if they relate the experience. Perhaps parents can discuss menstruation as a nonsexual bodily event, whereas ejaculation falls under the general taboo on discussing sex in American families (Matteson, 1975).

Table 13-2 Where Teenagers Get Sex Information

	Abor-tion	Con-cep-tion	Contra-ception	Ejac-ula-tion	Homo-sex-uality
Peers	20.0%	27.4%	42.8%	38.9%	50.6%
Literature	32.0%	3.2%	23.8%	22.1%	19.4%
Mother	21.5%	49.4%	13.1%	8.9%	7.5%
Schools	23.7%	16.4%	16.7%	20.7%	16.1%
Experience	.5%	.8%	1.0%	5.2%	2.1%
Father	1.0%	1.2%	2.4%	2.6%	4.3%
Minister	1.0%	.9%	.0%	.7%	.0%
Physician	.3%	.7%	.2%	.9%	.0%

	Inter-course	Mas-tur-bation	Men-stru-ation	Petting	Vene-real Disease
Peers	39.7%	36.3%	21.5%	59.7%	28.2%
Literature	15.2%	25.0%	11.2%	10.0%	21.2%
Mother	23.8%	11.1%	41.5%	4.5%	9.4%
Schools	7.6%	17.5%	15.7%	9.0%	36.8%
Experience	7.5%	8.0%	7.6%	14.0%	1.1%
Father	3.9%	1.3%	1.1%	2.2%	2.1%
Minister	1.0%	.0%	.7%	.2%	.0%
Physician	1.3%	.8%	.7%	.4%	1.2%

(Adapted from Thornburg, 1981)
N = 1152.

On the other hand, most parents apply a double standard to their male and female adolescents (Hass, 1979). What is okay for a son is not necessarily okay for a daughter. Masturbation is more likely to be tolerated in a boy than in a girl. A father may let his son know where to buy condoms. But neither mother nor father casually inform a girl where she can obtain vaginal foam or a supply of birth-control pills.

It seems that the revolution in sexual mores

has left many parents without wisdom to offer their adolescents. Changing norms may have left parents uncertain and uneasy about their *own* sexuality. They may not be able to talk with one another, much less advise an adolescent. Perhaps some parents want to tell their teenagers that sex is an important and wonderful part of love. But they hold back because they do not want to encourage them to experience this too soon: "Enjoy it—but not yet." Teenagers mirror this ambivalence: "I'm only experimenting." Whatever the reasons, adolescents still receive most of their information—and misinformation—about sex from their peers.

Body and Behavior

Physical and sexual development are important background influences on adolescent behavior; but they are not the whole story of adolescence. The adolescent growth spurt and sexual maturation are physiological facts, but culture defines their functional importance. What is noteworthy about adolescence is not just puberty or growth, but how society reacts to the maturing young person. Parents and peers treat adolescents as potential adults. A male who shaves and a female who has curves is no longer a child. He can drive. She might become a lawyer. Both are potential sexual partners. Other people's reactions to the adolescent's physical maturation create new developmental issues for attachment and intimacy, autonomy and identity, as we have shown. In the next chapter we consider how developing cognitive skills and changing social roles shape the adolescent's self-image and public identity.

SUMMARY

1. The adolescent growth spurt follows the typical primate pattern. But increases in height and weight over the last century are the result of cultural and social change: improvements in nutrition and sanitation (the "secular trend") and intermarriage (hybrid vigor).

2. Sex differences in size, strength, and build first appear in adolescence, creating sexual dimorphism. Puberty, or reproductive mat-

uration, usually takes on special emotional and social significance.

3. Individual variations in the rate of physiological and sexual development in adolescence affect self-esteem and popularity. There is some evidence that early maturers (especially boys) enjoy advantages in high school, but that late maturers are more adaptable as adults.

4. The development of sexuality is a lifelong process. Research shows that infants are sensual beings and that early experience is important in the development of mature sexuality (confirming Freud's beliefs). Interest in sexual anatomy and sensations continues through childhood (challenging Freud's notion of latency). But what form adult sexuality takes depends in large part on cultural scripts.

5. Surveys show that adolescents are more sexually active today than teenagers were 15 or 20 years ago. Many more say that they masturbate and that they have had premarital sexual intercourse today. The greatest increase in premarital sexual activity has been among girls.

6. Surveys also show that adolescents are not obsessed with sex; that they distinguish between love and lust; that they believe a person should establish his or her own standards; and that they tend to be more liberated in their attitudes than in their behavior.

7. Although the double standard has faded, adolescent males and females differ in both their behavior and their feelings about sex. According to one theory, these differences are the combined product of biology and socialization.

8. Knowledge and use of contraception has not kept pace with the increase in sexual activity among teenagers. Although the pregnancy rate for teenagers has not increased significantly, the *number* of teenage girls who become single mothers has grown (especially poor and minority girls).

9. Most adolescents expect to make tentative sexual commitments and perhaps live with someone before they get married ("practice" marriages). Rightly or wrongly, they believe that this is one of the issues that prevents them from discussing sex with their parents.

FURTHER READING

Adelson, J. (Ed.). (1980). *Handbook of adolescent psychology*. New York: Wiley. An excellent resource; a collection of articles that summarize research on different aspects of adolescence.

Brooks-Gunn, J., & Petersen, A. C. (Eds.). (1982). *Girls at puberty: Biological and psychological perspectives*. New York: Plenum. Recent articles on the biological, social, and psychological components of puberty in young women.

Gordon, S. (1973). *The sexual adolescent: Communicating with teenagers about sex.* Belmont, CA: Wadsworth. This is an excellent guide for those who are concerned with helping adolescents deal with their sexuality and sex-related problems.

Haas, A. (1979). *Teenage sexuality: A survey of teenage sexual behavior.* New York: Macmillan. The detailed report of a survey on adolescents' sexual attitudes and behavior, with quotations and commentary.

Salinger, J. D. (1977). *Catcher in the rye.* New York: Bantam. A poignant and funny account of a young man's adventures and feelings about being an adolescent.

Physical changes

Female   Height   <Growth spurt peaks age 12>

Menarche

Breast

Pubic hair

Male   Height

Penis

Testes

Pubic hair

(based on Tanner, 1978)

Early and late maturation

Female   Early   Awkward   ? Shy and anxious

? Popular and high in self-esteem

Late   [no research]

Male   Early

Late

Sexual behavior

First experience of sexual intercourse: by age 13   M: 7%

F: 3%

(based on Hass, 1979)

Attitudes toward sex and love

(from Sorenson, 1973)

9	10	11	12	13

Age in years   Early Adolescence

HIGHLIGHTS OF PHYSICAL AND SEXUAL DEVELOPMENT IN ADOLESCENCE

( ) age range
< > onset or peak
[ ] qualifications
≲ age extension beyond
that shown on chart

[Range 11–14 yrs.]

<growth spurt peaks age 14>

? Loses ground because short and stocky

? Popular and high in self-esteem

Poised, confident, popular, social leader . . .

Anxious, talkative, lacking confidence and leadership . . .

≲ (Adulthood)
No differences

≲ Conventional, rigid, other-oriented

≲ Unconventional, flexible, creative

	by age 16	never, age 17–18	never, college age
	M: 42%	M: 44%	M: 26%
	F: 41%	F: 56%	F: 26%

		(15–16 yrs.)	(17–18 yrs.)
Of sexually active adolescents:			
sexual experience with only one partner		M: 23% F: 41%	M: 19% F: 52%
with 2 to 5 partners		M: 31% F: 44%	M: 66% F: 31%
with more than 10 partners		M: 28% F: 7%	M: 19% F: 5%

When is sex permissible?	(ages 15–19)
after dating for a month or less	M: 50% F: 13%
only if you are in love	M: 25% F: 53%
only after marriage	M: 11% F: 13%

Have you ever been in love?	(ages 15–16)	(ages 17–18)
Yes	M: 82% F: 76%	M: 82% F: 82%

14   15   16   17   18

Late Adolescence

CHAPTER

14

The words "adolescence" and "rebellion" are often considered synonyms. And no wonder. Adolescent impatience with the existing social order has a long and venerable history (Braungart, 1980). A 4,000-year-old tablet unearthed in the Biblical city of Ur warns, "Our civilization is doomed if the unheard-of actions of our younger generation are allowed to continue" (Lauer, 1973, p. 176). The Protestant Reformation was in large part a youth movement. When Martin Luther published his ninety-five theses at Wittenberg University in 1517, it had one of the youngest faculties in German history. The Wittenberg Reformers, as Luther's followers became known, included many eminent professors in their early and middle twenties (Moller, 1968).

In his provocative analysis of Luther as a young man, Erik Erikson (1962) argued that Luther's identity crisis coincided with an historical crisis in the Roman Catholic church. His search for personal integrity led to ecclesiastic reform. Adolescents played prominent roles in the French, American, Bolshevik, and Meiji (Japanese) revolutions. In the 1770s, Harvard University all but shut down because most of its students had joined the revolutionary militias. The typical college student in the 1790s was, by one account, "an atheist in religion, an experimentalist in morals, a rebel to authority" (Morison, 1936, p. 185). Student riots erupted at Harvard, Princeton, Yale, and the University of Virginia throughout the nineteenth century (Lipset, 1976). The student movement in the 1960s and 1970s was anything but unique.

Rebellion against the social order reflects important changes in the way adolescents reason and process information; in their concepts of social justice; and in their thinking about themselves and their relationships to society. In this chapter we look at Piaget's model of the development of scientific thinking, or formal operations, and at contemporary revisions of this model. We examine changes in the way adolescents think about society. And we consider how

ADOLESCENT THINKING

adolescents use new cognitive skills and social awareness to form a more coherent sense of self, or ego identity.

Becoming a Scientific Thinker

Most adolescents would be surprised to hear themselves described as scientific thinkers. Most do not count science among their hobbies or favorite subjects, and few will ever be employed as scientists. But many (if not all) adolescents do come to think like scientists. They can reason in abstract as well as in concrete terms, disentangle the influences of different variables on an event, generate and test hypotheses, and weigh probabilities.

Piaget called this stage of cognitive development **formal-operational** thought (Inhelder & Piaget, 1958). He saw formal reasoning as the culmination of the long process of intellectual development that began at birth. In his view, an older adolescent and a nuclear physicist differ only in their expertise, or the content of their thoughts, not the quality of their thinking (Piaget, 1970). Some youngsters take this step as early as age 11, but formal operations are not firmly established until about age 15.

The Real and the Possible

The most important general property of formal-operational thought is the new relation between the *real* and the *possible*. When confronted with a problem, the elementary school child concentrates on the facts at hand. He uses his mental skills to examine the dimensions of the problem, to make comparisons, and to carry out experiments in his head. It is a practical, matter-of-fact, and often effective approach. Like a conservative investor, he does not speculate on unknown quantities or what might be. He treats alternative but unrealized possibilities as belonging to another realm in which logic does not apply. When he is asked what would happen on earth if there were no sun, for example, he may assert simply that the earth *has* a sun. Or he might reply that it would be cold all of the time. But he keeps his feet on the solid ground of empirical facts, exploring hypothetical heights only when pressed to do so. The real world is what matters to him.

The formal-operational thinker approaches problems the other way around, at least when she is in top form (Flavell, 1977, 1985). Possibilities come first and reality second. Faced with a problem, she begins with speculation. Only after considering many possible solutions does she decide on a strategy for determining the best one. A formal-operational thinker would have much more to say about the disappearance of the sun than the child would, because she can apply her logic to hypothetical situations as well as actual events. The adolescent speculates that the only heat would come from volcanos, farming would move indoors, millions would die, survivors might live underground, flowers and birds would be remembered only in poems and pictures, and so on. She knows that a sunless earth is impossible but enjoys the cognitive game nevertheless. She can reason about the *im*possible; her thinking does not stop at real-world experiences of cloudy days and cold nights.

Just as the preschool, preoperational child has difficulty reasoning about the reality underlying appearances, the school-age, concrete-operational child has difficulty reasoning about logical possibilities beyond what she knows or infers. Formal-operational thinkers treat the real, experienced world as only one of many possible realities. In John Flavell's words, "There is nothing trivial about this reversal [of the real and the possible]; it amounts to a fundamental reorientation toward cognitive problems." The adolescent with formal operations is "no longer exclusively preoccupied with the sober business of trying to stabilize and organize just what comes directly to the senses; the adolescent has . . . the potentiality of imagining all that might be there . . . and thereby of much better insuring the finding of all that is there" (1963, p. 205).

Adolescents tend to apply this newfound ability to all areas of life: politics, religion, ethics, love, and so on. Thinking about what could be leads to ideas of what *should* be. Piaget attributed the idealism of adolescence to cognitive development, not to social or psychological causes. Enamored of possibilities, unfettered by practical considerations, adolescents often conjure up images of utopia.

Hypotheses and Deductions

The ability to deal with possibilities lays the foundation for a new style of problem-solving.

Formal operations apply to many areas of thought. A concrete-operational thinker can follow the moves in an actual football game but might have difficulty diagramming alternative plays.

The formal-operational thinker begins by imagining all of the possible solutions to a problem. In other words, he generates *hypotheses,* or possible but not proven explanations. The he *deduces* ways to test each hypothesis in turn. He uses logic to determine what ought to occur (or not occur) if the hypothesis is correct. If this is confirmed experimentally, he includes the hypothesis in his set of real explanations. If it is disconfirmed, he discards it. Piaget called this "hypothetico-deductive reasoning."

Some of the best examples of this approach to problem-solving come from Piaget and Barbel Inhelder's studies (Inhelder & Piaget, 1958). In one, young people ranging from age 8 to age 15 were given materials for making a pendulum (see Figure 14-1). Each youngster was shown how to vary the *length* of the string, to change the *weight* of the object, to release the pendulum from various *heights,* and to push it with different degrees of *force* (Ginsberg & Opper, 1969). The problem was to figure out which of the four factors (length, weight, height, or force), alone or in combination, determines how fast the pendulum swings (its oscillation).

No one factor ever stands alone in the pendulum problem. A particular weight is always combined with a particular length of string, force, and height. The young person must vary each factor systematically while holding the others constant to determine the outcome. For example, the effects of a light weight versus a heavy one can be determined on a long string (no effect), on a short string (no difference), with a hard push (no difference), a soft push (no difference), from a high launch (no difference), and a low launch (no difference). Weight can be eliminated as a factor in oscillation. Similarly, the height from which the pendulum is dropped can be varied while the length of the string, weight, and force are held constant. Eventually, a systematic experimenter will be able to show that the *length* of the string determines the oscillation of a pendulum. Weight, height, and force have no effect.

At the outset of the experiment all of the youngsters guessed that several factors determine oscillation. Many of the younger children Piaget questioned concluded that the length of the string was one of two or more factors in oscillation. But they did not eliminate extraneous variables. Once they found a combination that seemed to work, they stopped experimenting. They looked for confirming evidence but not for *dis*confirming evidence. As a result, their solutions were only half right. Only the older adolescents systematically examined all combinations of causes.

In complex problems like this, it is nearly impossible to arrive at a solution without formal reasoning. One must generate and systematically test all possible hypotheses. Given four variables, the effect can be caused by any one, two, three, or four of the factors, or by none of them. The problem is to find the necessary and sufficient cause or causes. *Necessary* means that the factor is required for oscillation, but others may also be required. *Sufficient* means that the factor or factors identified are all that are required to cause the effect. We already know that the length of the string is both the necessary and the sufficient cause of oscillation.

In another example, suppose you observe that a friend is angry at you. She refuses to speak when you meet. Later she resumes the friendship but will not explain what was wrong. How can you find out what was causing her behavior? Since you are a formal-operational thinker, you generate hypotheses to explain her actions: A. Perhaps you failed to call when you said you would. B. Perhaps you inadvertently passed her without speaking. C. Perhaps she is angry that you earned a better grade than she did in a course. D. Perhaps she resents the fact that you went out with her old boyfriend. You

could generate many other hypotheses, but let us deal with these four.

To solve this puzzle, you must test your hypotheses singly and in combinations. You repeat each event singly: A (you don't call); B (you pretend not to see her); C (you ask what she thought about a course in which you got an A and she got a C); and D (you casually mention that you went to a movie with Jim). If none of these is both necessary and sufficient, she will continue to speak to you—but not explain what was wrong. Then you test each hypothesis in combination with every other hypothesis: A and B (not calling and ignoring her in the cafeteria); A and C (not calling and bringing up the course when she calls you); A and D, and so on. If she is still speaking to you at this point—and still has not told you what is wrong—you try three provocations at a time (A, B, and C; A, B, and D; A, C, and D; and so on). As a next-to-last resort, you try all four. Finally, all four may be wrong: instead, she heard from another friend that you criticized her new haircut! In all, there are sixteen hypotheses to explain her behavior (see Figure 14-2). Formal-operational thought allows adolescents to test for the necessary and sufficient causes of any event.

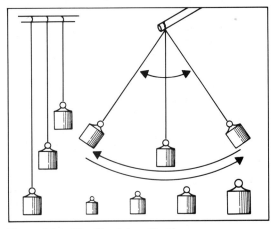

Figure 14-1 The Pendulum Problem
(After Inhelder & Piaget, 1958)

"Pure Logic"

A third characteristic of the formal operations stage is the development of abstract reasoning. Formal operations are logical manipulations of propositions or statements, not operations on concrete observations. An experiment by Osherson and Markman (in Flavell, 1977) illustrates the difference. Subjects were seated at a table strewn with poker chips of different colors. The experimenter explained that he was going to say different things about the chips and ask the subject to indicate whether what he said was true, false, or uncertain ("You can't tell"). On some trials the experimenter hid a chip in his hand and stated, "Either the chip in my hand is green or it is not green" or, "The chip in my hand is green and it is not green." On other trials, he held the chip so that the subject could see its color and made the same statements.

Elementary school children (concrete-operational thinkers) focused on the chips rather than on the statements. When they could see the chip they would say that both statements were true if it was green, and both false if it was red, blue, or another color. When the chip was hidden, they usually said they were uncertain. They judged the statements on the basis of concrete evidence. The adolescents, who were formal-operational thinkers, knew that the experimenter was not asking about the color of the chips; he was asking about the truth or falsity of his statements. Although most of the adolescents probably did not know the formal terms, they recognized that the first statement ("Either the chip in my hand is green or it is not green") was a tautology and always true; the second statement ("The chip in my hand is green and it is not green") was a logical contradiction and always false.

The point here is not that young, concrete-operational thinkers are illogical and adolescent, formal-operational thinkers are logical. Others of Piaget's tasks show that young children can understand, produce, and verify propositions. A 10-year-old will tell you that the amount of liquid you poured from a tall, thin glass into a short, wide one is the same (a proposition) and prove it by pouring the liquid back into the first glass (verification). But young children are not very good at detecting relationships among propositions. The younger child focuses on the *factual* relationship between a proposition and the object or person to which it applies; the older child can also think about the *logical* relationship between two propositions (Flavell, 1985).

A	B	C	D
A and B	A and C	A and D	B and C
B and D	C and D	A, B, and C	A, B, and D
A, C, and D	B, C, and D	A, B, C, and D	0

Figure 14-2 Sixteen Reasons: All Possible Combinations of Four Hypotheses

Insight

LOGIC
ADULT-STYLE

To describe adolescent thought, Piaget proposes two interrelated logical systems. Although most adolescents would be astounded to hear about it, their thought can be described logically by *sixteen binary operations* and the *INRC group*. No adolescent ever describes his own thought in any such formal terms, but his *behavior* in solving complex problems can be abstractly described this way.

The notion of operations in Piaget's theory is that of mental transformations. People over the age of 2 use their heads to change, order, and classify the reality they observe. In other words, they make *cognitive* sense of what they *physically* sense.

Younger children are empiricists. They experiment in order to *discover* the logical structure underlying the physical world. Adolescents *conceive* of that logical structure beforehand and test their propositions empirically afterward. Piaget describes the operations of the concrete operational child as "incomplete lattice-groupings." This means that the child does not have a complete logic system. The adolescent, on the other hand, brings to any empirical problem a complete logic system, which Piaget calls a "lattice-group" (Flavell, 1963, pp. 211–12).

The sixteen binary operations are simply the logically exhaustive associations of any two elements, each one of which can be true or false, present or absent, yes or no (binary choices). The elements of formal reasoning are propositions, such as "a heavier weight makes the pendulum swing faster" or "a heavier weight does *not* make the pendulum swing faster." (The first turns out to be false, the second true.)

In Piaget's pendulum problem, to find out whether or not weight had anything to do with

pendulum oscillation, the adolescent had to generate the logically possible combinations of weight and string length, for example. These associations are expressed formally as the sixteen binary operations. The four basic associations are: heavy weight × short string; not heavy weight × short string; heavy weight × not short string; and not heavy weight × not short string. The other twelve binary operations are logically exhaustive combinations of these four basic associations taken none, one, two, three, and four at a time, and connected by logical relations. While this kind of logic may seem impossibly complex, it does describe what many adolescents are able to do.

To describe the logical relations among formal operations, Piaget uses the INRC group, which consists of four operations: identity (I), negation (N), reciprocity (R), and correlativity (C). *Identity* is a null transformation; it does nothing to change a proposition (A = B is still A = B). *Negation* changes everything in a proposition; all assertions become negations, all negations become assertions, and all relations between elements are changed: A = B becomes A ≠ B; A > B becomes A < B. *Reciprocity* changes the sign or direction of each element: A > B becomes B < A) but does not change the form of the relationship. *Correlativity* changes the form of the relationship (from *and* to *or*, and vice versa) but does not change the sign or direction: A + B becomes A *or* B.

The four transformations, INRC, are related to each other in logical ways. They can be combined and multiplied. The examples, however, become so abstract that the interested and logically sophisticated reader is referred to Flavell (1963, Chapter 6) and Piaget and Inhelder (1958).

Just as algebra is a formalization of arithmetic (a separation of form from content), so formal operations are a formalization of concrete operations. They are logical manipulations freed from the confines of reality. The adolescent can reason with *If . . . then . . .* statements:

> *If* the moon were made of green cheese,
> *then* mice would race to the next spaceship.
> *If* women ran the world *then* there
> wouldn't be any more wars.
> *If* I were the captain of the football team,
> *then* Sally would want to go out with me.

Formal thinkers can complete a line of reasoning, even though they know that the first proposition is false, improbable, or just plain silly. This new cognitive ability leads to the realization that a person does not necessarily have to believe that something is true or fair to argue in its favor. Discovering hypocrisy is one of the "prices" adolescents pay for gaining formal-operational thought.

Correlations

Correlational problems reflect an advanced level of formal operations. They require estimates based on probabilities and do not permit absolute answers. Often Piaget used marbles to observe how young people approach problems for which there is no exact answer. In a variation on his technique, Edith Neimark (1975) gave children and adolescents a shuffled deck of twelve cards: four showing a healthy face and a blank microscopic slide, four showing sick faces and a slide with green germs, two showing healthy faces and green germs, and two showing sick faces and blank slides. The youngsters were told to imagine that they were doctors who had a number of patients complaining of a mysterious malady. Tests for the presence of green germs gave the evidence shown on the cards. On the basis of that evidence, could the doctor conclude that green germs cause the disease? The child was asked to justify his answer: Do green germs always cause the disease, or only sometimes? If sometimes, what probability is there of getting the disease? Finally, he was asked to select the cards from the deck that prove conclusively that green germs *cause* the disease, and then to select the cards showing that green germs do *not* cause the disease.

To answer the first question correctly (Do green germs cause the disease?) the child needs a mental probability table of the following kind:

		Patient Sick?	
		Yes	No
Germs?	Yes	4	2
	No	2	4

There are eight patients who support a correlation between germs and disease (the presence or absence of both) and four who do not. Of the six patients who have the germs, two-thirds (four) are sick. Of those without the germs, two-thirds are not sick. To prove that germs really cause the disease, the youngster can pull the eight cards that fall into the yes/yes and no/no class; to prove that green germs do not cause the disease, he can pull the two yes/no and the two no/yes cards, and two each of the yes/yes and no/no cards. This selection results in a correlation of zero.

Few young people, even at age 15, could reason through this problem. Since older adolescents were not studied, we do not know when correlational thinking becomes available— if it ever does. Most young people do not study correlations and probability until they take statistics courses in college. Since college students are an intellectually select group (and since not all college students seem to understand statistics!), we can surmise that correlational thinking is difficult indeed.

Insight

THE MATH GAP: EXPLAINING SEX DIFFERENCES

Males and females begin school as mathematical equals. Girls are as good as boys at arithmetic. Around age 13, however, girls begin to drop behind in math and never quite catch up. At age 15, their scores on mathematical achievement tests drop below their *own* previous levels (Ross & Simpson, 1971). Many suffer from mild to severe forms of "math phobia." Surveys show that many girls over age 13 or 14 do not like math, are less confident about their mathematical abilities than boys are, and find math more difficult than boys do (Fennoma & Sherman, 1977).

As part of the Johns Hopkins talent search, Camilla Benbow and Julian Stanley (1980) followed seventh- and eighth-graders who scored in the top 2 to 5 percent on mathematical achievement tests for five years. The girls in this select group took as many math courses as the boys did. Unlike many girls, they had a keen interest in mathematics and were more likely than the boys in the study to say that they wanted to major in math in college. They consistently earned higher grades than boys did in geometry and calculus.

Males, however, outperformed females on the math subtests of the Scholastic Aptitude Test (S.A.T.). Five times as many boys as girls scored over 600. The S.A.T. is a college entrance exam given to high school students. It is a test of aptitude, not a test of what students have recently learned in school. By implication, girls who earn higher grades in math work harder for them; boys have more facility with math.

Sex differences in spatial abilities also become more pronounced in adolescence (Harris, 1979). **Spatial ability** is the capacity to imagine or visualize objects in different planes and perspectives. Most studies (summarized in Maccoby & Jacklin, 1974) show that beginning in adolescence, males outperform females on standard tests of spatial skills. Some researchers (for example, Armstrong, 1980) have found little

or no difference in these skills. But there is real-world evidence that males do have an edge (McGuinness, 1985). Boys usually demonstrate a better knowledge of local geography than girls do. Males draw more accurate maps of familiar surroundings (such as their college campus) than females do. Women may supply more detail, but their sense of distance is often poor and they tend to omit paths and roads. Males are also superior at video games, which require a player to anticipate where moving images will appear and to track them with a lever (Rebert, cited in McGuinness, 1985). The ability to remember objects in space and to imagine three dimensions are both useful in higher mathematics, especially geometry.

The math gap is the mirror image of the reading gap between boys and girls in childhood (McGuinness, 1985). At least three times as many boys as girls have reading problems. Sex differences in reading skills are most pronounced at the middle and lower ranges of reading scales. By mid-adolescence (age 15 or so) this difference has disappeared. In childhood, girls are as good at math as boys are. In mid-adolescence, boys move ahead. Sex differences in math skills are greatest at the higher range of the aptitude and achievement scale.

Sex differences in mathematical aptitude and achievement are often attributed to socialization. In our culture, some apologists claim that math is a male domain. Girls are not supposed to "worry their pretty little heads" about numbers. Competing with boys in a male domain is seen as aggressive and unfeminine. A girl who excels in calculus may pay for her success with her popularity. Sex differences appear around puberty, they say, because girls are becoming more aware of traditional sex roles and more concerned with the impressions they make on boys (Tavris & Wade, 1984).

Diane McGuinness (1985), among others, questions this view. Sex-role socialization begins in early childhood, not in adolescence. If girls are taught that math is a male arena, why do they do as well as boys in arithmetic? If they believe that competition is unfeminine, why do they work so hard in biology, history, English composition, foreign languages, and other subjects? Do they receive encouragement from their fathers (and other socializers) for excelling in biology, as girls often do, but not algebra or calculus? This seems unlikely.

McGuinness suggests three alternatives to pinning sex differences on social theories: biological explanations, cognitive theories, and interest. *Biological theories* focus on genetic predispositions. Some scientists have hypothesized that math disabilities are caused by a recessive gene on the X chromosome, which is masked by hormonal influence(s) of the Y chromosome in males. Girls who inherit this gene from both parents would be doubly disadvantaged. Research has not confirmed this view (Scarr & Carter-Saltzman, 1982; Vandenberg & Kuse, 1975). But the fact that identical twins are quite similar in spatial abilities and math aptitude suggests that both have some as yet unidentified genetic component. Attempts to relate math aptitude to the structure and organization of the brain, or to visual acuity, have been suggestive but inconclusive; research continues in these areas.

Cognitive theories draw on Piaget. McGuinness hypothesizes that differences in spatial and mathematical abilities may result from the different ways boys and girls learn. Boys tend to explore the world firsthand—actually using their hands. Physical exploration, combined with visual inspection, may enhance knowledge about objects in space. Boys tend to exercise their gross motor system. Indeed, the males of all mammalian species—not just humans—engage in more rough-and-tumble play than females do; this, too, promotes knowledge of objects in space. Verbally precocious, girls tend to rely more heavily on words to acquire information; in

a sense, they learn about the world secondhand. They are more inclined to exercise their fine motor system, which requires fewer contacts with objects and less negotiation of space. Sewing or drawing, for example, provides less information about object relations than running through a field or playing baseball.

This is not to say that boys and girls do not engage in both sorts of activities. But there is a difference in emphasis and intensity, at least in Western cultures. As a result, girls may have to rely on verbal rules to learn higher mathematics, whereas boys can draw on sensorimotor knowledge. Creating verbal imagery may interfere with manipulating abstract equations.

Finally, whereas from an early age girls exhibit a strong *interest* in people; boys show an equally strong interest in objects. When asked to tell a story, small girls nearly always talk about people (Goodenough, 1957). This is hardly remarkable: Most stories involve people. What is surprising is how many boys invent stories totally *without* people. Objects make them happy, sad, or angry almost as often as people do. While arithmetic books are peopled with real-world examples, algebra, geometry, and calculus texts are not. Perhaps women fall behind in higher mathematics because the material does not capture their interest.

All of these hypotheses are speculative. What seems clear is that many males find reading difficult and require a cognitive boost from the environment. At the same time, many males find higher math relatively easy to learn. In contrast, many females find that reading comes naturally, but that higher math is difficult to learn. But both sexes are capable of learning both subjects. McGuinness holds that girls' difficulties with higher math (and reading problems in boys) are largely the result of society's failure to recognize sex differences and adjust teaching methods accordingly.

Updating Piaget

Do all adolescents become "scientific thinkers"? Is formal-operational thought universal? Does it represent a new stage in cognition, a near-complete reorganization of thought? Or are cogni-

tive advances in adolescence better described as an elaboration of information-processing techniques discovered in childhood? Is formal-operational thought the culmination of cognitive development? More bluntly, does intellectual development *stop* after adolescence? Piaget's description of adolescent thought has proven more controversial than his characterizations of earlier stages.

Wishful Thinking?

Researchers have raised serious questions about whether all healthy, mature human beings attain the level of abstract reasoning we described earlier in this chapter. One of the major criticisms of Piaget is that his portrait of formal operations is too idealistic and his standards for mature thinking too high. As Flavell has commented, "One wishes it were true" (1980).

Researchers who attempt to replicate Piaget's tasks typically find that a significant portion of older as well as younger adolescents "fail" the test (Keating & Clark, 1980; Moshman, 1979; Neimark, 1975). Indeed, a third or more of college students and middle-aged adults do not use formal operations when asked to solve an unfamiliar problem (Keating, 1980). This does not mean that they are incapable of "scientific" thinking, of course. But they do not apply formal operations automatically or consistently.

In general, adults perform better on formal problems when the content is real and concrete than when it is abstract or meaningless (Flavell, 1985). Most adults are not scientists. Even so, they find scientific problems simpler than "pure logic." It is easier to figure out which combination of two, three, or four clear liquids (out of a possible four) produces a yellow liquid (one of Piaget's tasks) than to deduce a rule that generates all possible combinations of the four letters A, B, C, and D. Obviously, concrete problems are more important in everyday life than abstractions are. It is possible, as Flavell has suggested, that our cognitive apparatus has evolved to solve *meaningful* problems. Therefore, Piaget's emphasis on abstract reasoning may have been misplaced.

Another related criticism of Piaget is that his measures of formal operations depend in part on formal schooling. Most of the tasks he devised for formal operations come straight from the physics and chemistry lab and the mathematics classroom. Children who have taken formal science courses usually perform better on Piaget's tasks than do children who have no training (McClosky, Caramazza, & Green, 1980). They have experience in both the language and the techniques of hypothesis testing. One research team (DeLisis & Staudt, 1980) found that physics, political science, and English majors are more likely to use formal operations than are students in fields that do not require the same levels of abstract reasoning. What these studies suggest is that the development of formal operations is not as inevitable or "natural" as Piaget originally believed. Some types of education and some walks of life offer

"Computer freaks," who surprise and confound adults with their ability to invent games, compose music, and break into sophisticated computer networks, have developed formal operations to an exceptional degree.

more training, more practice, and more reasons for formal operations than others do (Flavell, 1977).

Piaget revised his position on this stage of cognitive development in 1972. He agreed that the emergence of formal operations might depend in part on schooling. And he conceded that most adults do not use formal reasoning in all areas of their life, but do so rather in the areas of their greatest interest, experience, and expertise. An auto mechanic, for example, may use hypothesis testing when trying to diagnose an unwanted ping in an engine. He may systematically control variables such as the carburetor setting and compression, while varying the engine speed or the gasoline mixture. But the mechanic may fail to use formal reasoning in other settings, such as a vote on a school bond issue when there is no other legal means to finance necessary construction. A teacher might use formal reasoning in the voting booth but behave like a concrete-operational child when his car breaks down on a deserted country road.

On the whole, the evidence suggests that the formal operations stage allows more individual variations than earlier stages do. All normal humans develop sensorimotor skills and work their way through the preoperational period to concrete operations. Most older adolescents and adults are probably capable of formal operations and think like scientists on occasion. But the level of formal reasoning individuals attain, and when and how they use these skills, vary from person to person. One possible explanation of this is that the earlier stages of cognitive development are genetically less variable than formal operations are. These stages are part of our species' blueprint and are more deeply canalized (see Chapter 2). Both individual genotypes and specific learning experiences have more influence on development in the formal operations stage than on earlier stages. Dulit (1972) illustrates this notion with a tree diagram

(see Figure 14-3) of human knowledge. The first three universal stages of cognitive development form the trunk of the tree. They are "genetically solid." Once formal-operational thought develops, a number of different branches open up, which Dulit represents as specialized talents or areas of expertise. Which branch a person takes depends on her unique genetic makeup and environment.

Cultural Variations

Researchers have also raised questions about whether formal operations are confined to Western, technological societies, which place a high value on scientific reasoning. Perhaps Piaget was observing a cultural phenomenon, not a universal or panhuman development. Some researchers (Berry & Dasen, 1974; Neimark, 1975; Super, 1980) have concluded

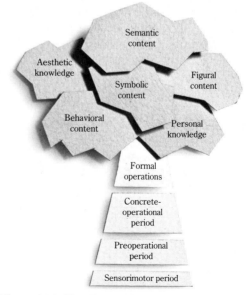

Figure 14-3 The Tree of Knowledge
(After Dulit, 1972)

that abstract logic is not found in nonliterate, technologically simple societies. Patricia Greenfield and Jerome Bruner (1966) have argued that reading, which trains a child to separate thought from real-world experiences, is a prerequisite for formal operations. Michael Cole (1978) suggests that formal education teaches people to classify things in terms of formal rules (cow, donkey, dog) instead of their functions (cow, pasture, milk), and to treat problems as logical puzzles rather than as questions of fact or opinion—two cornerstones of Piaget's description of formal operations. In studies in Africa and rural Latin America, Cole found that some young people develop formal operations after three years of schooling and that most do so after nine years of schooling. According to these researchers, literacy does not guarantee that an individual or group will develop formal reasoning; but it does promote this.

Other social scientists believe that formal operations can be found in all human groups if one looks in the right places: their areas of expertise. Among peoples of the South Seas, for example, formal reasoning is clearly needed to navigate from island to island (Gladwin, 1970). Sighting the stars, taking account of seasonal changes in star locations, and figuring distances, directions, and speed are intricate mental operations that few Westerners could perform mentally. Yet where we use radar and other complex technology, Pacific Islanders use their heads. The anthropologist Melvin Konner (Tulkin & Konner, 1973) was privileged to attend a series of "seminars" on hunting techniques held by the !Kung tribe, who are hunters and gatherers of southern Africa.

As scientific discussions the seminars were among the most stimulating the Western observers have ever attended. Questions were raised and tentative answers (*hypotheses*) were advanced. Hypotheses were always labeled as to the degree of certainty with which the speaker adhered to them, which was related to the type of data on which the hypothesis was based. . . .

The process of tracking, specifically, involves patterns of inference, hypothesis-testing, and discovery that tax the best inferential and analytic capacities of the human mind. Determining, from tracks, the movements of animals, their timing, whether they are wounded and if so how, and predicting how far they will go and in which direction and how fast, all involve repeated activation of hypotheses, trying them out against new data, integrating them with previously known facts about animal movements, rejecting the ones that do not stand up, and finally getting a reasonable fit, which adds up to meat in the pot. (pp. 35, 36)

The !Kung, whom many social scientists consider the best example of our species' ancestral way of life, illustrate the adaptive value of formal operations. Hunting or locating edible roots and

People are most likely to develop formal operations in their areas of expertise. Shown here, !Kung hunters downing a gemsbok.

berries in trackless desert requires more than concrete operations.

On many Western tasks such as Piaget's, nonliterate people do not seem to use formal operations (Dansen, 1972; Cole, Gay, Glick, & Sharp, 1971). But on particularly important, *adaptive* tasks they show clear evidence of formal thought, sometimes in storytelling, sometimes in marketing methods, sometimes in calculating distances and directions that must be traveled. Just as members of a culture differ in the tasks for which they use formal operations, cultures themselves differ in the tasks for which their people use these skills. Moreover, just as some individuals do not seem to use formal operations, some cultures may not, either.

The question of whether formal operations are universal comes down to a matter of definition. If by universal we mean that "all normal adults of all cultures can and will use them skillfully in all applicable problem situations" (Flavell, 1977, p. 146), then clearly formal operations are not universal. But the capacity for formal thought does seem to be widespread. Whether people use formal operations depends on personal interests, cultural guidelines, and environmental incentives.

An Alternative Model

Some psychologists who find Piaget's description of adolescent cognition too abstract and restrictive have turned to information-processing models (Flavell & Wohlwill, 1969; Keating, 1980; Neimark, 1970, 1975; Siegler, 1983; Sternberg, 1977; Sternberg & Powell, 1983). According to this view, the difference between children and adolescents is not absolute. Adolescents are more systematic and therefore more efficient in their approach to problems than children are. They are more likely to plan ahead, anticipating what kind of information will be needed to solve a problem, and more likely to

think about what strategy to use. They are more likely to monitor their own progress. But whether they use concrete or formal operations depends on both the person and the task. Some problems can be solved more simply with concrete operations than with formal operations, or with a combination of the two.

The information-processing approach focuses on the strategies people use to abstract information from, and reduce the memory required for, complex problems. The old game of Twenty Questions illustrates changes in information processing in adolescence (Bruner, Olver, & Greenfield, 1966; Flavell, 1977). For example, ask a child or adolescent to learn what you are thinking about in as few questions as possible. Usually mature thinkers ask categorical questions that progressively narrow the range of possibilities:

Q: Is it living?
A: Yes.
Q: Is it animal (not vegetable)?
A: Yes.
Q: Does it have four legs?
A: No.

In contrast, the preadolescent child usually asks specific questions:

Q: Is it a horse?
A: No.
Q: Is it my mittens?
A: No.

Suppose you are thinking of a chicken. The child could tell you that a chicken has two legs and that it is an animal and alive. She understands categories, and even hierarchies of categories (as described in Chapter 9). But she does not think about using them to solve this problem. The school-age child looks only for confirmation; she wants to hear a "yes." The adolescent looks for confirmation *or* disconfirmation. His logic tells him that it must be either animate or inanimate. A "no" is as informative as a "yes." The school-age child does exactly what you told her to do: guess what you are thinking. The adolescent imposes a structure of his own on the game: eliminating categories. He does not let the task dictate his strategy. Also, notice how concrete the child's questions are, and how *un*concrete (*animate/inanimate, animal/vegetable*) those of the adolescent are (Flavell, 1977).

As this comparison of thinking strategies shows, the information-processing and Piagetian approaches are not necessarily incompatible (Neimark, 1970). Psychologists who use the information-processing model seek to identify the quantitative changes in such things as memory capacity and knowledge base that produce the qualitative changes Piaget observed. But this approach does suggest that the development of formal reasoning is more gradual and cumulative, and less stagelike, than Piaget believed.

Beyond Formal Operations

Piaget held that once formal operations are acquired, further cognitive growth takes the form of refinement rather than structural change, or reorganization of the thought process. Experience in the real world leads the adult to rein in the runaway concern with possibilities that characterizes adolescence. Applying formal operations leads the adult to a deeper understanding of areas of greatest interest. Thus adults continue to *grow* intellectually, in the sense of adding to what they know and appreciate, but they do not *develop* intellectually, in the sense of acquiring new forms of thought.

A number of psychologists have questioned this. Dierdre Kramer (1983) found three themes in contemporary models of adult cognitive development: relativism, contradiction, and integration. Adult thinkers understand that

there are no absolute truths, that knowledge is *relative*. Whereas an adolescent might argue that there can only be one true religion, an adult thinker is able to conceive that many religions have something valid to say about the human condition. Perhaps this is because adults have been exposed to many different viewpoints and are required to play different, sometimes conflicting, social roles. Adult thinkers accept *contradictions* as part of life; they realize that conflicting points of view cannot always be resolved by discarding one or the other. An adolescent might argue that capital punishment is right or wrong. An adult thinker can see the death penalty as *both* necessary and brutal. As novelist F. Scott Fitzgerald wrote in *The Crack-Up*, "the sign of a first-rate intelligence is the ability to hold two opposed ideas in the mind at the same time, and still retain the ability to function." An adult thinker is able to *integrate* or synthesize different, sometimes contradictory, notions into a more or less consistent worldview. An adolescent may feel torn between one group of friends who likes beach parties and dressing "punk" and another group who enjoys marching for nuclear disarmament and listening to classical music. An adult thinker sees serious and fun-loving friends as appealing to different parts of his own personality.

Descriptions of adult cognition have not been subjected to empirical studies that are as rigorous as those of adolescent cognition. On the basis of current evidence, Kramer concludes that the differences between adults and adolescents are a matter of emphasis. Adolescents tend to look for the stability underlying change; adult thinkers are more comfortable with the idea that change is part of life. Adolescents are good at isolating variables to determine cause and effect (*Mr. Jones drinks because he hasn't been able to find a job for months*). Adult thinkers are more at ease with the notion of interdependence (*Mr. Jones drinks because he is unemployed and is unemployed because he drinks*).

What psychologists do not know is why some individuals advance beyond formal operations and others do not, and why some are more advanced in social understanding, some in investment strategies, and others in engineering. These developmental pathways—Kramer emphasizes the plural—remain unexplored. But there is reason to believe that cognition, like sex, continues to improve with age.

Thinking about Society

Formal operations—the ability to entertain alternative hypotheses and to think in propositional terms (*if . . . then*)—have a profound impact on the way adolescents think about politics, the law, and society in general. Formal thinkers are able to line up their beliefs and systematically search through them for inconsistencies. They can compare one set of ideas (religious teachings) to another (political realities). As a result, beliefs that seemed certain during childhood—such as the wisdom of one's parents, the existence of God, or the idea that the law is always just—are called into question.

Political Ideals

In childhood and early adolescence, youngsters' political ideas are a "curious array of sentiments and dogmas, personalized ideas, randomly remembered names and party labels, [and] half-understood platitudes" (Adelson & O'Neil, 1966, p. 295). By the end of adolescence, most people have developed a more or less organized and consistent set of principles that guide their political thinking. According to Adelson and O'Neil (1966), this change in political ideology is a direct result of the shift from concrete to formal operational thought.

Adelson and O'Neil asked 120 fifth-, seventh-, ninth-, and twelfth-graders to imagine that a thousand men and women were dissatisfied with the way things were going in their country and decided to purchase a Pacific island and move there. Once on the island, they had to devise laws and form a government. The adolescents were asked a series of questions about the scope and limit of political authority, the reciprocal obligations of citizens and the state, conceptions of law and justice, and the like.

The researchers found that children and young adolescents emphasize individual rights and interests (as in William Golding's novel *Lord of the Flies*), whereas older adolescents think more in terms of community needs. Younger subjects focus on the immediate consequences of political decisions; older subjects have a greater sense of the future. For example, the adolescents were told a story about a man who was very attached to his land. The state needed that land for a road. The landowner was offered a fair price but refused to sell. Should the man be forced to sell, or should the state have to build a detour? What should the state do if the man threatened violence? The 11- and 13-year-olds sided with the landowner and individual rights. Fifteen- and 18-year-olds believed that the community has preeminent rights in such a dispute. Younger adolescents favored the landowner because his case was concrete, personal, and psychologically immediate. By contrast, the state's position hinged on abstract ideas of public welfare.

Older adolescents usually formulate *general* ethical and political principles, which they then apply to specific cases such as the dispute over the road. Most thought that the other 999 people had a right to the road, that one landowner should not block their access. Some believed in the sanctity of individual property rights. In either case, their position was based on general principles. This is a clear example of a formal (rather than a concrete) approach to problem solving.

Of course, older adolescents are better informed about political matters. They have read more, experienced more, thought more about political issues. But there is more to this shift in political ideology than accumulated knowledge.

Legal Understanding

There are similar patterns in the development of legal understanding. For most young children, the police officer *is* the law. Most children seem

to admire the power to punish and control, and assume that all police are good (Torney, 1971). The exceptions are some minority children and rural youngsters, who may regard all police as bad. But both groups of children personify the law. Cognitive development enables adolescents to separate the concepts of power and authority from the behavior and personal attributes of those who make and enforce the law. Older adolescents usually distinguish between just and unjust laws, fair and unfair enforcement, good and bad police.

Tapp and Kohlberg (1971) have identified three stages in the development of legal thinking. Children think of the law as *prohibitive:* Laws keep bad things from happening. Young adolescents view the law as *prescriptive:* Laws tell people what to do and what not to do. For youngsters at this stage, law and order is a positive good to be maintained at all costs. Compliance with the law is necessary, lest the social order collapse. Many adults around the world would agree. But some late adolescents and adults come to think of the law as *beneficial-rational:* Laws are agreed-upon standards of conduct that facilitate both personal freedom and social welfare. For them, laws are not immutable givens; they are human contracts that can be changed if people agree to change them. Tapp and Kohlberg relate these three stages of legal thinking to Kohlberg's three stages of moral development—preconventional, conventional, and postconventional (see Chapter 12).

Young children personify abstract concepts like the law; more mature thinkers differentiate between the role of police officer and the man or woman in uniform.

Idealism and Alienation

The fact that adolescents can develop a coherent set of principles from which to reason has important consequences for their lifestyles. If we add idealism and alienation to the formula, we can understand much of the adolescent commitment to social, political, and religious movements. When adults call adolescents idealistic, they usually mean that young people have their "heads in the clouds." Many adolescents develop ideal notions of how society and the political and economic systems *should* be run, regardless of what adults perceive as the necessary realities.

Adolescent *idealism* is the application of propositional logic to political and social realities. Aware that the reality they observe is only one of many possible realities, adolescents often come to prefer more ideal, alternative realities—a world without nuclear arms; full sexual equality; an end to poverty and hunger. These ideal alternatives to the current state of affairs have potential reality—which has the same status for a formal thinker as what actually exists.

The other face of adolescent idealism is *alienation:* young people often feel estranged from the realities of society and even from themselves. Often adolescents feel that they are strangers in their own families, that they are adrift in society, that they cannot predict their own emotions and actions. Some psychologists see a period of confusion in adolescents as a necessary and even desirable step toward the formation of an ego identity. (We discuss the translation of idealism and alienation into social activism in Chapter 15.)

Idealism can take many forms. Hitler's youth were among his most ardent followers.

Cultural Differences

All societies and cultures recognize the changes in cognition, physical development, and sexuality we have described; to some extent, all cultures acknowledge transitions from childhood to adulthood (Siegel, 1982). But the social roles available to teenagers vary from culture to culture and from generation to generation. The experience of being an adolescent reflects the cultural setting.

Paths to Adulthood in Traditional Societies

Some traditional societies hold *rites of passage,* or public rituals to mark the transition from childhood to adulthood. The Ndembu of Africa hold ceremonies that transform boys into men (Turner, 1967). After a night of singing, dancing, and sexual adventures, the boys receive their last meal from their mothers. Then they are marched to a camp called "the place of dying," where they are kept in seclusion for four months. There they are circumcised, hazed, harangued, and instructed in the rules of manhood. At the end of this period they are returned to their village, daubed with white clay. Their families bathe them and present them with new clothes, and each performs a war dance to signify his new status as a man. The ceremony gives public recognition to their new rights and responsibilities as adults.

In other traditional societies, the transition from childhood to adulthood is gradual and continuous. Puberty is not seen as a cause for public celebration (or private confusion). Young people are not pressured to assume adult roles, but neither are they prevented from demonstrating maturity. In Samoa, according to Margaret Mead (1928), adolescent girls enjoy sexual and personal freedoms they did not experience as children and will not continue to enjoy as adults. Responsibilities are relaxed for a time, with the assumption that the young girl will ease into womanhood when she is ready. Mead may have idealized Samoa (Freeman, 1983), but similar patterns have been observed in other preliterate societies (Ford & Beach, 1980).

Adolescence—an ambiguous, in-between stage when a young person is no longer a child but not quite an adult—does not exist in these societies, for several reasons. First, there is near-universal agreement about when a child becomes a youth or an adult and what this means. Spheres of authority are clearly defined: Everyone agrees on how teenagers ought to behave toward their elders. Opportunities for autonomy are limited by tradition. Whether the society is sexually permissive or restrictive, everyone knows the rules. Second, there is little question about what and whom a child will become when grown. Most adults earn their livelihoods in the same way. The only significant division of labor is by sex. There is only one way to be a man or a woman, at most a few ways. Often, occupation and social status follow family lines. Individual talents and preferences are not particularly relevant to selection for adult roles. Moreover, there is only one religion, one moral standard, one family life-style. Identity is largely prescribed by tradition, rather than achieved individually. In Mead's words, adolescents are "perplexed by no conflicts, troubled by no philosophical queries, beset by no remote ambitions" (1928, p. 120).

Adolescence in Western Societies

In contrast, adolescents in most Western countries face a diversity of expectations regarding their current conduct and a nearly unlimited set of possibilities regarding their future adult roles. There is little agreement about when a young person becomes an adult. The law determines when adolescents are allowed to leave school, drive a car, work full-time, get married, purchase liquor and cigarettes, be sentenced to adult prisons, and the like. But these secular rites of passage do not all occur at once and do not add up to a new social role. Indeed, there is little consensus on how Western adolescents ought to behave.

Everywhere they turn, young people are confronted with conflicting ethical and social views: in the mass media (ranging from soap-opera dilemmas to advice columns written by doctors); through their parents' personal morals (which they may view as restrictive and unfair or hypocritical); in the different lifestyles of older siblings and other relatives; and in their peers' standards, which they may assume are highly permissive. Religions and political ideologies also compete for their allegiance. They must choose among these alternatives for themselves (Borow, 1973).

Occupational choices are potentially unlimited. Parents and other adults may offer advice; but many jobs available today, such as systems analyst, media consultant, divorce or sex counselor, did not exist when they were young. Most desirable jobs require advanced education, which prolongs the period of preparation for adulthood and financial dependence. Some young people are still students or are going back to school in their mid-twenties; others are raising families, many while they attend school part time. Unlike young people in traditional societies, American adolescents must struggle to find themselves morally, politically, occupationally, sexually, and psychologically.

Some traditional rites of passage are still performed in our society. Cotillions announce that a girl has become a young lady; the Jewish bar mitzvah celebrates a boy's becoming a man.

Ego Identity: Thinking About Oneself

Erik Erikson (1958) was one of the first to call attention to the importance of identity in later adolescence. Erikson proposed that the human life cycle is divided into eight stages, as described in Chapter 1. Each stage is marked by a central problem or crisis that the developing person must resolve. These problems arise from both biophysiological changes in the individual and challenges in the sociocultural environment. As the young person matures, his needs, interests, and abilities change. The standards of conduct and achievement adults and the larger society expect from him also change. When social demands are appropriate to the growing person's needs and abilities, there is a healthy interplay between the two and crises in the life cycle can be resolved. But when too much or too little is expected of a person— when there is a poor match between the individual and his social setting—such crises may remain unresolved and the person may not mature psychologically.

RELIGIOUS CONVERSION

Religious conversion can be seen as a combination of alienation and idealism—alienation from the religion of one's childhood and perhaps from the nonreligious world, and idealism toward a new faith.

Psychologists have offered two competing explanations of religious conversion. The psychoanalytic view attributes a radical change in religion to emotional upheaval, following Freud, who saw conversion as a defensive reaction to unresolved Oedipal conflicts. Young people who experience a revival of childhood anger toward their fathers in adolescence disguise their feelings from themselves and others by submitting to the authority of God or a guru. For psychoanalysts, conversion is a byproduct of emotional needs. The cognitive view of conversion holds that religion offers an explanation of an incomprehensible world by reducing ambiguities. Young people turn to new religions when events challenge their basic beliefs about the nature of reality. For cognitive psychologists, conversion is the byproduct of an intellectual quest.

In a recent study, Chana Ullman (1982) compared forty individuals who had undergone a religious conversion in adolescence to thirty nonconverts. The group of converts included believers in traditional religions (Orthodox Judaism and Roman Catholicism) and members of unconventional religions, or those that are new to our society (Hare Krishna and Bahai). The nonconvert group was composed of Roman Catholics and Orthodox Jews whose religious beliefs and practices had not changed since childhood. (Ullman was unable to locate lifelong members of the Hare Krishna or Bahai religions.)

Ullman hypothesized that if the psychoanalytic view were correct, converts would have experienced more emotional turmoil in childhood than nonconverts had, and more emotional stress and adjustment problems in adolescence, precipitating conversion. If the cognitive view were correct, converts would show a lower tolerance for ambiguity than nonconverts did and would remember going through a period of questioning their own beliefs and attitudes in adolescence, prior to conversion.

She found little support for the cognitive view. Converts were no more or less tolerant of ambiguity than nonconverts were. There was no indication that they had been "seekers" for truth or clarity in adolescence. Only three of the forty subjects said that the new religion had "answered all my questions." Many gave surprisingly concrete, mundane explanations for their

conversion: "the people were nice to me"; "the atmosphere was free of tension"; and even, "the food was out of sight" (reported by two converts to Hare Krishna).

The main difference between the converts and nonconverts lay in their emotional histories, a finding that supported the psychoanalytic view. Converts were much more likely than nonconverts to describe unhappy childhoods punctuated by traumatic events (such as violent fights between their parents or witnessing a parent's suicide attempt). Converts were much more likely to say that they had been troubled as adolescents. Over 80 percent stated that they

had been in emotional turmoil just before their conversion ("I thought I was going crazy") and felt relief from anxiety, depression, or anger when they had converted ("I didn't feel so desperate any more"; "I knew He [Christ] would take care of me"). Three-quarters of the converts suggested that their relationship with their father was problematic ("He did not understand anything you did, you could do nothing right . . . he just did not understand and I started hating him"). In these cases, conversion did seem to be "an attempt to gain the approval, protection, or guidance of an authority figure" (pp. 191–92).

According to Erikson, the major issue for infants is trust; for toddlers, autonomy; in early childhood, initiative; in middle childhood, industry; and in adolescence, identity. In Erikson's view, an **identity crisis** (a period of self-doubt or social alienation) is an integral part of psychosocial development. Successful resolution of this crisis lays the foundation for intimacy in young adulthood, generativity in middle age, and integrity in old age.

"Who Am I?" Revisited

An **identity** is an inner sense of uniqueness and continuity and an outer sociopolitical stance. It combines an awareness of oneself as a distinct person who has a special constellation of needs and abilities with an awareness of how one fits in the social world and where one is headed. It means feeling unique but not alone— connected to other people but not "lost in the crowd."

The formation of an identity does not begin and end in adolescence. The process starts in infancy, when the child learns to distinguish self from objects, and continues into old age, with reflections on the connections between self and society. Identity becomes a crucial issue in adolescence because the biological revolution of puberty, new social pressures to "grow up," and the cognitive ability to consider alternatives combine, all but forcing the adolescent to ask "Who am I?" For the first time, the adolescent is able to sort through childhood experiences and chart a path toward adulthood.

Children do not have consistent identities. Rather, they have identifications with significant others. *Identification,* as we discussed in Chapter 8, is the process of becoming like another person, in both small and large ways.[1] A boy who admires his older brother may adopt his gait, the tilt of his baseball cap, as well as his "philosophy" of life. Childhood identifications are many, varied, and often contradictory, but children generally do not worry about inconsistencies. The sum of childhood identifications could never result in a functioning, adult personality, because one cannot be like Michael Jackson and Reggie Jackson, a Zen Buddhist and a Roman Catholic, a bachelor and a father, a Boy Scout leader and a member of a street gang at the same time.

There is some synthesis of identifications in late childhood, as children begin to wonder what

---

[1]We are following the social learning view of identification here, not the stricter Freudian definition. See Chapter 8.

they will be when they grow up. But the urgency and drive to form a consistent and whole identity does not emerge until adolescence. The teenager must build two bridges: One between the person she has become as a result of childhood experiences and identifications and the person she promises to be as an adult; and one between her private image of herself and what other people see and expect from her (Hill, 1980).

Identity formation is not a neat process. Roles and ways of behaving are tried and discarded, reformulated, and tried again. Commitments are made and unmade. Adolescents' decisions—whether to go to college and which college, whom to date, having sexual intercourse, staying together or breaking up, becoming polit-

ically active, taking drugs, and so on—may have long-term, identity-forming consequences. And there are risks. Forming an identity means giving up what one knows for an unknown and uncertain future: Letting go of one's parents without knowing where one will find love; relinquishing the child's right to take for the give-and-take of maturity; abandoning childhood fantasies of many glamorous life-styles for more realistic and mundane choices. At a bare minimum, forming an identity requires commitment to a sexual identity, an ideological position or worldview, and a vocational direction.

The main danger in this stage, according to Erikson, is *identity diffusion*. Some adolescents are unwilling to take risks and unable to make decisions or commitments. The adolescent who

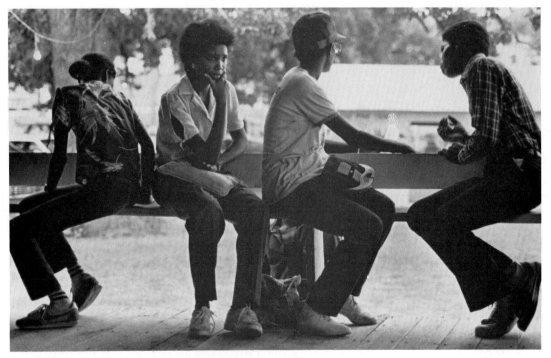

Adolescence is a time of brooding and dreaming. This girl is with her friends, but mentally she is in her own world.

has no consistent sense of self has no standards against which to evaluate his "performance" as a student or worker, friend or lover. Confused about what direction to take, he has difficulty sticking to any one track. He depends on other people or chance to make his decisions and on external cues for an estimate of his self-worth. His identity crisis may be prolonged indefinitely.

This is the adolescent drama according to Erikson. Do most western teenagers go through an identity crisis? In general, the answer is yes. But there are twists and turns in the plot.

Identity Statuses

Erikson described identity and identity diffusion as opposite ends of a continuum, implying that there might be several stages or detours along the way. James Marcia's research on college students in their late teens and early twenties (1966, 1980) has filled in the picture. Marcia designed the semistructured, open-ended interview to be given to adolescents, shown in Figure 14-4. This interview is designed to assess, first, whether a young person has gone through a period of decision-making (or crisis) and, second, his or her level of investment in an occupation, a set of religious values, and a political stance (or commitment).[2] Marcia and his col-

---

[2]Marcia added questions about sexuality for female subjects, for reasons explained later in this chapter.

Introduction
What year are you in?

Where are you from?

How did you decide to come to _____?
Had you considered any other schools?

What does your father do?
Did he go to college? Where?

What does your mother do?
Did she go to college? Where?

Occupation
What are you majoring in? What do you plan to do with it?

When did you decide on this?
Had you considered anything else?

What seems attractive about _____?

Most parents have some plans for their children, things they'd like to see them do or go into. Did yours have any plans like that?

How do your parents feel about what you're going into now?

How willing do you think you'd be to change this if something better came along? (If *S* responds: "What do you mean by 'better'?") Well, what might be better in your terms?

Religion
Do you have any particular religious preference?

What about your parents?

Were you ever very active in your religion? How about now? Belong to any groups? Get into discussions?

Are your beliefs now different from those of your parents? How do they feel about your beliefs now?

Is there any time when you've come to doubt any of your religious beliefs? When? How did it happen? How did you resolve things?

Politics
Do you have any particular preferences?

How about your parents?

Have you ever taken any kind of political action—joined any groups, written letters, protested?

Are there any issues about which you feel strongly now?

Is there any particular time that you decided upon your political beliefs?

Do you have any questions you'd like to ask me?

Figure 14-4 James Marcia's Identity Status Interview

(Marcia, personal communication, 1985)

leagues interviewed males and females, college freshmen and seniors, in the East and Midwest, at small colleges and large universities, in urban and rural settings. On the basis of these interviews, he concluded that there are four **identity statuses** or positions on Erikson's identity-formation continuum: identity achievement, foreclosure, identity diffusion, and moratorium.

IDENTITY ACHIEVEMENT Those in this status have passed through a period of decision making and are committed to an occupation and ideological goals that they have chosen for themselves. They have considered several occupations and have settled on one—often in spite of parental opposition. They think of themselves as a teacher or engineer, not just as someone who is taking courses in education or engineering. They have reexamined childhood concepts of religion and come to their own conclusions. They are interested in politics and usually describe themselves as further left or right than their parents are.

FORECLOSURE Those in this status are also committed to an occupation and ideological position but show little or no evidence of having gone through a crisis period. As one psychologist put it (Blos, 1962), they had "an abbreviated adolescence." In their choice of occupation they seek to live up to their parents' expectations. They have accepted the religion they were taught as children without question. When asked about politics, they preface their answers with "My family has always been _____." At best, Foreclosures seem steadfast, committed, and cooperative; at worst, they appear rigid, dogmatic, and conforming. They give the impression that they would be at a complete loss in a setting where their parents' rules and values did not apply.

IDENTITY DIFFUSION Those in this status lack direction. Some have experienced a crisis; some have not. In either case, they do not seem concerned about their occupational future. They say it might be "nice" to be a doctor or an actor or perhaps both, but they are not taking steps in either direction. They say that they are not interested in religion, or that one religion is as good as another. They are politically uncommitted and socially unconcerned. Society can go its way; they will go theirs. At best, they are blithe spirits who can take or leave both people and ideas; at worst, they seem disorganized, shallow, and confused.

MORATORIUM Those in this status have not made either occupational or ideological commitments, but they are actively seeking answers. They are *in* an identity crisis. Conflicts between their parents' plans for them, their own interests and abilities, and society's requirements seem unresolvable. They think about religion a good deal but have not settled on a set of beliefs or even a stance of disbelief. They are questioning the political views they learned as children but have not yet found anything to replace them. The distinguishing feature of this status is an almost obsessive concern with unresolved questions. At best, they seem sensitive, ethical, and

Conformity to dress codes may help adolescents through a period of mild identity diffusion.

open-minded; at worst, they appear anxiety-ridden, self-righteous, and vacillating.

Marcia had to add a fifth identity status to this list during the Vietnam War years: *Alienated Achievement.* Students in this category had gone through a period of decision making and had come to some definite conclusions. They did *not* want to pursue the kinds of careers society offered and join the "rat race"; they did *not* want to participate in a political system that ignored racial discrimination and waged an immoral war; they did *not* respect the religions that permitted these injustices to continue; they did *not* want traditional marriages and families; and so on. They were uncommitted, not because they could not find their way in the adult world, but because they did not like what they found. These five identity statuses are diagrammed in Table 14-1. For further discussion of identity statuses, see the profile of James Marcia at the end of this chapter.

Table 14-1 Criteria for Identity Statuses

Identity Status	Position on Occupation and Ideology	
	Crisis	Commitment
Identity Achievement	Yes	Yes
Foreclosure	No	Yes
Identity Diffusion	Yes or no	No
Moratorium	In crisis	Yes but vague
(Alienated Achievement)	Yes	Yes but negative

(Adapted from Marcia, 1980)

Many adolescents try on different identities before settling down. In his youth, Jerry Rubin was a leader of the Yippies, one of the most radical antiwar groups of the 1960s. Sticking his tongue out at the world, he fit into the alienated achievement category. Today Rubin works on Wall Street.

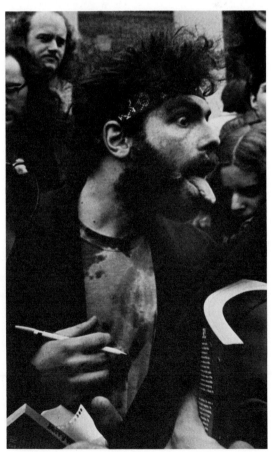

Insight

RESPONSES TO AN IDENTITY INTERVIEW

Identity Achievement, on occupation:

S had been in college for a semester and then went into the Navy. He was originally interested in engineering, but was currently enrolled in a premed program. He had made this choice during the service. "There was no sudden enlightenment, really, I just got interested. I wanted to be involved with people more than an engineer would. I mean help people. . . . I'd be interested in going into general practice. Anything, now, but being a doctor, I don't think I'd like. I'd been pushed into engineering by people in high school and by my parents. That probably had something to do with [my] taking off to the Navy."

Foreclosure, on religion:

"I'm a member of the Baptist church. Everyone in the whole family has been a Protestant. We generally go where we like the minister, if we like the sermons and all, that's what matters most. The whole family goes to the same church."
Ever had any doubts about your religious beliefs?
"No, I don't believe so. We discuss religion sometimes; I find myself pretty much in agreement with them."

Identity Diffusion, on occupation:

"Well, right now it looks as if I might major in history, but if I pull my psych grade up, I'll major in psych. Not too much you can do with a history major. Teach or go into law, I guess. I guess I'd probably teach. With a psych major I don't know what I'd do. I guess I'll have to talk with some psych majors."

What interested you in history?
"I did pretty well in it. Got good grades in it. . . . Don't have any plans for when I get out of school. . . . Folks wanted me to be a lawyer. I imagine it's fine. It's good money. But I don't know enough about it."
What interests you about being a teacher?
"Well, you get two months off in the summer, and I imagine if I taught at college it would be very good money. And I kind of like history. I mean, I take very readily to it."
How willing are you to change if something better came along?
"I'd probably give it up quite rapidly. Any definite choice is pretty much up in the air right now. I wrote home the other day and said that psych might be a good major. But you have to take an awful lot of courses for that—almost fourteen, I guess."

Moratorium, on politics. . . .

"I've looked into it some. . . . My parents were Republicans and so I was a Republican for a long time. I'm kind of in favor of the Democrats just to give them a chance right now. I can't see much difference between the two parties. I'd say I'm a liberal in terms of wanting to modify or change things. I almost believe in a welfare state, I guess. I don't know, though."

and self:

"Other people think I'm jolly and freelancing. Inside, I'm a big knot. I'd just like some peace and quiet. . . . The future seems better than the past, though. I'm not so concerned about what people think, and I can control my temper better." (Marcia, 1985)

Research based on Marcia's typology indicates that the identity crisis usually occurs in late adolescence, at least for white, male college students (Waterman & Waterman, 1972). During the freshman year of college, many students become diffuse or moratorium types. Some are shaken out of a foreclosure status; others have just begun to work on identity. Four years later, most have reached the status of identity achievement and committed themselves to personally chosen occupations and ideologies. But this pattern is not universal. Some individuals begin and end adolescence as foreclosure types; some never seem to attain either an achieved or a foreclosed identity. Like Biff in Arthur Miller's play *Death of a Salesman,* they "just can't seem to take hold." One unanswered question is how much the experience of going to college itself contributes to the identity crisis and its resolution. Almost all studies of identity have used college students as subjects.

Prerequisites for Identity

Identity achievement does seem to be related to other psychosocial achievements. Most researchers have found that students in the identity achievement and moratorium categories score higher on measures of autonomy (Erikson's stage 2) than do those in the foreclosure or identity diffusion categories. The latter tend to attribute their successes and failures to chance or luck. Students who have struggled or are struggling with identity issues feel that they have more control over their lives than do those who have never struggled or have given up (Waterman & Waterman, 1972). Those who have struggled are better able to maintain self-esteem in the face of criticism, to resist group pressure, and to disobey authorities on grounds of conscience (Marcia, 1980).

The connections between identity and trust, initiative, and industry (Erikson's stages 1, 3, and 4) are less clear (Lavoie, 1976; Lerner & Shea, 1982). For example, most *males* who score high on identity also score high on industry, which Erikson saw as a prerequisite for identity. But others score high on industry and low on identity, or vice versa. This may mean that psychosocial development is not as cumulative as Erikson implied: Someone who experiences a good deal of self-doubt (rather than pride and initiative) may develop industry nevertheless. Or it may mean that psychosocial development is not as stagelike as Erikson believed: Identity issues may be postponed or reopened. Some people may not develop industry, for example, until they have established an identity and committed themselves to an occupation.

Identity and Intimacy

Erikson saw identity as a precursor to intimacy. He reasoned that adolescents who have not yet formed a satisfactory identity would have great difficulty becoming involved in an intimate, mutually satisfying relationship. Their preoccupation with themselves would make it difficult to focus on another person's needs, one of the requirements of true intimacy. Orlofsky and colleagues (Orlofsky, Marcia, & Lesser, 1973) interviewed *male* juniors and seniors about their relationships with both men and women. They identified three basic intimacy statuses: intimate, stereotyped, and isolate. *Intimates* were young men who worked at developing relationships, had several close friends, and had a girlfriend with whom they were able to share personal worries and express both affectionate and angry feelings. *Stereotyped* were young men whose relationships with both men and women were numerous and pleasant but lacked depth; they were "Joe College" and "playboy" types. *Isolates* were young men who rarely initiated social contact, dated little, and seemed threatened by any form of closeness.

Orlofsky found strong correlations between degree of ego identity and intimacy. Over 80 percent of those with identity achievement status had intimate relationships, and none were isolates. The majority of moratorium types also were involved in mutually satisfying intimate relationships; less than 10 percent were isolates. Students who were low in identity were most likely to be involved in stereotyped relationships. Foreclosure types and identity diffusion types reported fewer intimate relationships, and more isolation from both male and female peers. Eriskon believes that being able to engage in intimate relationships depends on identity. However, this study shows only that the two are correlated.

Identity and Morality

One would expect that students who have wrestled with personal identity and standards of personal conduct would also have thought through many larger moral issues in a mature fashion. And this is what Marvin H. Podd (1972) found. The majority of *male* identity achievement types argue moral issues on abstract principles of justice and equality. No other identity status has so many people who reason at a postconventional level. Moratorium students are the next most advanced. They are presently grappling with personal standards and are probably struggling with larger moral issues. The diffuse students are primarily conventional. The foreclosure students are overwhelmingly conventional and preconventional. Low in ego identity, the last two

groups are slow in reaching advanced levels of moral reasoning.

The research on moral reasoning and identity statuses points out the close associations among cognitive development, moral reasoning, and identity formation in adolescence. As described in Chapter 12, moral reasoning in Kohlberg's theory is a manifestation of developing intelligence applied to a social-moral context. Similarly, identity is a manifestation of advancing intellectual skills applied to a personal-social context.

With certain adjustments, then, research does confirm Erikson's analysis of identity development in adolescence. There is one major exception, however: *females.*

The Female Pattern: Intimacy and Identity

Like males, females who fall into the identity achievement category demonstrate higher levels of moral reasoning (Poppen, 1974), are more likely to be involved in intimate relationships (Kacerguis & Adams, 1980), choose more difficult college majors (Marcia & Friedman, 1970), and are better able to resist group pressure (Toder & Marcia, 1973), than are their peers whose identities are more diffuse. But here the similarity between males and females ends.

Women depart from the male pattern of identity development in several significant ways. First, sexual relations are more important to females' identity than to males'. Deciding

Identity may become more important to young women as opportunities to become equal members of society open up.

whether to have intercourse usually is not an identity-forming decision for males; for females, it is. Second, identity diffusion among women seems to increase during college, rather than decrease as for men (Constantinople, 1969). Third, female foreclosure types are as advanced in moral development, intimacy, and other measures of psychosocial maturity as are female identity achievers. Indeed, they tend to be high in self-esteem and lower in anxiety than identity achievers—the opposite of the pattern seen in young men. Simply put, foreclosure seems to have the same positive effects as achieving identity for women (Marcia, 1980). During adolescence at least, stability—whether achieved or foreclosed—is the best predictor of overall happiness for women.

Why is this? Marcia (1980) reasons that identity depends on developing a unique, personal style of coping with social expectations—a psycho*social* development. Whereas males in our society are expected to make the kinds of decisions that bring them into conflict with others, promoting identity but postponing intimacy, females are expected to make the kinds of decisions that bring them closer to others, promoting intimacy but postponing identity formation. The order of psychosocial events in males' and females' lives is reversed. Males tend to establish an identity before they risk intimate relationships; females tend to establish intimate relationships before they face identity issues.

Most adolescent girls are not concerned with choosing an occupation and taking an ideological stance, but with establishing and maintaining interpersonal relationships. Intimacy comes first in their lives; identity, second. Girls

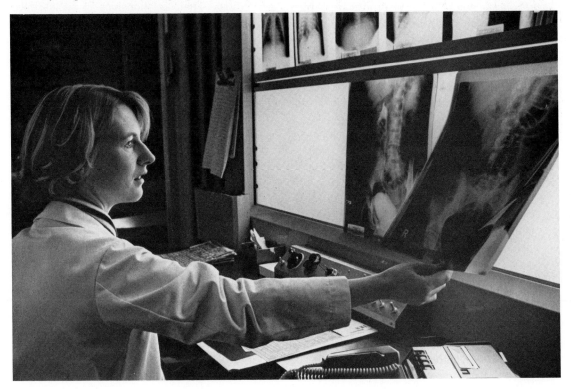

do think about careers, politics, or religion. But those who put these concerns ahead of relationships—who turn down a date to write a term paper, or break off a friendship because of political disagreements—do not receive the same social approval as do foreclosed girls who conform to traditional sex roles. As a result, they are somewhat less sure of themselves than other girls and women are. The exceptional woman can be successful in both "female" terms of relationships and "male" terms of occupational and ideological commitments. But most females, like most males, are not exceptional.

Interviews based on the issues that most concern women reveal subtle differences in identity statuses (Donovan, 1973; Josselson, 1973; Marcia, 1980). Some of the subjects were college-age students; some were in their mid-thirties. In college, those who have reached *identity achievement* status are more concerned about what they might become than with earning their parents' approval. They tend to choose men who are cooperative companions rather than protective fathers. Thirty-five-year-olds in this category recall having adopted a traditional gender role, then discarded it because it did not fit. The person they once were seems like a stranger to them now. Those in *foreclosure* status are most concerned with recreating close family ties in their current relationships during their college years. The adults in this category see their identities as tied to their families. They consider themselves loving, devoted, and nurturant, but also as not very competent outside their homes.

Women who are *identity diffusion* types spend much of their time in college dreaming of Prince Charming but are too afraid of being hurt or betrayed to commit themselves to a relationship wholeheartedly. Adults who remain in this category doubt their femininity and continue to fight infantile battles with their parents. In college, females with *moratorium* status feel guilty about rejecting their mothers by acting independent, and at the same time dream of fulfilling their fathers' ambitions. In a sense, they want everything. Their relationships in adolescence are intense but short-lived. Adults in this category seem to be playing a *yes-but* game: *Yes,* they want to "be themselves," *but* they are afraid, guilty, needy, defiant.

Gender differences in identity formation underscore the influence of cultural guidelines and social expectations on adolescent development.

SUMMARY

1. Piaget saw the major cognitive development in adolescence as the emergence of formal operations: logical manipulations of abstract propositions. The formal thinker differs from the concrete thinker in four main ways: (1) Formal thinkers are able to reason about hypothetical situations. What might be (the possible) interests them as much as what is (the real). (2) Formal thinkers are like scientists in the sense that they generate hypotheses, then systematically test these to discover the necessary and sufficient causes of an event. (3) Formal thinkers recognize abstract, logical relationships among propositions ("This chip is green and is not green" cannot be true), as well as factual connections between events. (4) Advanced formal thinkers can use probabilities and correlations to resolve problems that do not allow absolute answers.

2. Researchers have qualified several points in Piaget's description of adolescent cognition. Formal operations seem to depend in part on formal education. Most people use

higher levels of reasoning only in their area of expertise or in areas that their culture emphasizes. Some of the changes in adolescent thinking are due to more efficient information processing. Finally, there is reason to believe that cognitive development continues beyond adolescence: Many adults are able to think with greater flexibility.

3. The way adolescents think about society provides evidence of cognitive advances. Children focus on individual rights; adolescents on community needs. Children tend to personify the law; adolescents distinguish between the person and the position. Idealism and alienation in adolescence can both be traced to cognitive development.

4. In traditional societies, there is general agreement about when and how a child becomes an adult. The individual's choice of futures is limited. In modern Western societies, adolescence is an ambiguous period with no clear boundaries. The individual must choose among a vast array of life-styles and occupations.

5. Erikson sees the formation of an identity as the major psychosocial task of adolescence. In Erikson's view, most adolescents go through a period of confusion in which they rebel against their parents' social standards and "try on" different identities (an identity crisis). Ideally, the individual is able to come to terms with his or her past and make realistic choices for the future. But some young people are unable to make decisions and commitments (identity diffusion).

6. Marcia's empirical research on Erikson's theory suggests that there are at least four identity statuses: Identity Achievement, Foreclosure, Identity Diffusion, and Moratorium. Individuals in these statuses differ, first, in the extent to which they have considered different life-styles and made their own decisions, and second, in the degree to which they have committed themselves to an occupation and a political stance.

7. Marcia and others who have tested Erikson's theory find that, for males at least, identity formation usually takes place in late adolescence, often during college; that the formation of an identity is a prerequisite for intimacy in young adulthood; and that the struggle for identity is associated with higher levels of moral development.

8. Research suggests that women follow a somewhat different path of psychosocial development. For most women, the quest for intimacy either precedes or is concurrent with the struggle for identity.

FURTHER READING

Erikson, E. (1968). *Identity, youth, and crisis*. New York: Norton. This is a classic description of the alternative routes that identity formation can take. Erikson discusses literary figures, historical contexts, and the identity issues of blacks and women in contemporary America.

Erikson, E. (1958). *Young man Luther*. New York: Norton; *Gandhi's truth*. (1969). New York: Norton. In these fascinating biographies, Erikson applies psychoanalytic concepts to two historical figures and suggests a link between the search for identity and radical historical movements.

McCullers, C. (1974). *The member of the wedding*. New York: Bantam. The story of Frankie Addams, an adolescent girl, and her struggle to achieve identity, set in the South during the 1940s.

Mead, M. (1928). *Coming of age in Samoa*. New York: Morrow. A classic description of the transition from childhood to adulthood in a preindustrial society, which combines ethnography with commentary on American culture.

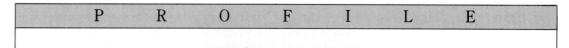

James E. Marcia

Professor of Psychology,
Simon Fraser University

ANN LEVINE: How did you first become interested in psychology, Dr. Marcia?

JAMES E. MARCIA: This sounds like an identity interview!

As an undergraduate I went through a series of majors—English, history, philosophy. I really wanted to find out "the Truth." By my junior year I had narrowed the field down to philosophy and psychology. I majored in psychology because I figured that if you could understand a person, then you could understand why he or she came up with an idea. After I graduated, I went to Ohio State University as a graduate student in clinical psychology, I guess because I thought it was important to *do* something as well as to learn.

AL: Which professors or experiences had the most influence on you during your graduate years?

JEM: When I went to Ohio, the clinical program was at its apex. The emphasis was on Rotter's social learning theory and George Kelly's construct theory. Ed Barker was existential; Al Scodel was psychoanalytic; Doug Crowne and Shep Liverant were sort of all-purpose scientists. It was a little overwhelming. Then I spent a year in Boston as an intern at the Massachusetts Mental Health Center. I came back committed to some form of ego psychology.

AL: Would you explain the difference between ego psychology and traditional psychoanalytic theory?

JEM: The orthodox Freudians are primarily concerned with the impact of sexual and aggressive drives and impulses on behavior, and on how they disrupt behavior. Freud once described the ego as a rider on the horseback of the id. He thought its main function was to rein in primitive urges. Toward the end of his life, though, he became more interested in adaptation. Most people are more or less making it; they are coping pretty well. Most people are not in therapy (except perhaps in New York, and that's partly for educational purposes). Freud's daughter, Anna, picked up on this adaptive emphasis and began writing about defenses as coping mechanisms, not as neuroses. Then Lowenstein, Hartman, Kris, Erikson, Robert White, and others began to say that the adaptational or coping processes of the ego are just as built in as the disruptive impulses. They are part of the human blueprint for development.

AL: So personality has two horses?

JEM: Yes. Ego psychologists are concerned with adaptational processes and how they develop. They don't toss out sex and aggression. But they focus more on adaptation and growth than on the stumbling blocks posed by instincts and drives. Erikson, for example, took Freud's stages of psychosexual development as givens, then added stages of ego development—how individuals' needs and abilities mesh with social supports and social demands.

AL: What led you to Erik Erikson's theories?

JEM: While I was in Boston, I tested a sixteen-year-old boy who seemed to be schizophrenic. All of his tests supported this diagnosis. But he was out of the hospital in six months. That's not supposed to happen! I couldn't understand it. One of my supervisors, Dave Guttman, who was helping Erikson teach a class at Harvard, gave me something of Erikson's to read. Suddenly everything made sense: The boy was going through an identity crisis. I wanted to do my dissertation on something that wasn't in the mainstream of what other people were doing at Ohio State. So I decided to see if you could play the science game with Erikson's theory.

AL: What do you mean by "playing science" with Erikson's theory?

JEM: Erikson's theory, as I understand it, was based largely on his reading and his clinical work. He didn't attempt to measure his constructs empirically. He created a scheme for understanding. When you are dealing in theory, in effect you are talking only to the wise clinician who can nod his head and say "Yes, that's right." When you have to put ideas into a testable format, you reconstruct them so that somebody who is not so wise can use them. So when you do research on a theory you're not just amassing data; you're changing the ideas. You may find mistakes and you may also find new things. You find out things that you wouldn't discover in clinical practice. Also, when you use a theory clinically you learn things you won't find out in empirical research.

I have a foot in both camps. I do research and I also do therapy. I don't think Erikson likes numbers. I sent him a manuscript of one of my books as a gift once, and he never responded.

AL: Your research has focused on Erikson's notion of identity. How did you translate the clinical concept into a testable format?

JEM: When Erikson talks about identity, he implies that either you have an identity and know where you're going, or you are diffuse. (He uses *confused.* I prefer *diffuse,* because most of the people I've interviewed are more spread out than mixed up.) For Erikson, the key to identity is commitment. When I started interviewing students for my dissertation, I began to think that it wasn't an either-or situation. Some people had gone through an exploratory period and made commitments. But I also found some people who were just as committed, but had never thought about who they were or where they were going. They just accepted the labels their parents gave them. So Erikson's dichotomy began to break down. Then, looking at people who were uncommitted, there seemed to be two types again. Some were spread out, hanging loose, careless, uncaring. And some were struggling to find some place where they fit in, something they could believe in.

The next issue was, If there are four types of identity statuses, how do you measure them?

I decided on interviews because they allow you to probe. You aren't limited to particular sentences, as you are with a questionnaire. Of course, the problem with interviews is reliability. You and I could listen to the same interview and interpret the person quite differently. So you have to devise a manual for scoring. You decide that if someone says this and that, you will call it thus and so. If someone else can pick up the manual, give an interview, and come up with essentially the same rating on identity status that I would, you can consider the procedure reliable.

Once that is done, you can reliably sort people into different categories. But does it mean anything? Can you predict anything from identity statuses? So you do a long series of experiments to see how people with different identity statuses behave in different situations. You look into their developmental history. And you look at how they handle intimacy, which is the next stage in Erikson's scheme. What does a rating of Foreclosure, for example, tell you about a person's relationships? So you investigate current conditions, antecedent conditions, and subsequent conditions.

When you've done all this—when you've completed fifteen years of work!—what do you have? You've taken one piece of a theory and shown it makes empirical sense. And you've added something. Without the experiments, we wouldn't have the constructs of Foreclosure or Moratorium.

AL: One criticism of Erikson's theory is that it is culture-bound and only applies to life crises created by Western cultures and societies. How do you respond to this?

JEM: People have done research on identity statuses now in Korea, India, Nigeria, Japan, Denmark, and the Netherlands. Basically, they have found the same patterns we found. So I don't think the constructs are culture-bound. I think it's important to have an identity, wherever you are. If you grow up in a Foreclosure setting, or in a Foreclosure culture, one where you are expected to be what your parents or the tribe tells you to be, having an identity crisis isn't an adaptive thing to do. It isn't adaptive in the sense that there is no social support for you. But if I took a Foreclosure and an Achievement out of the cultures in which they grew up

Continued

and put each of them in an environment that was totally new to them, I don't have any doubt that the Achievement would adapt more easily, be happier, perform more efficiently, than a Foreclosure would. But I don't want to say that Foreclosures are "all bad." They provide continuity of values and culture that may be important.

AL: Most people think of an identity crisis as a phase to be gotten over as quickly as possible, or perhaps as one of the costs of living in a complex society. You talk about an identity crisis as adaptive. Would you explain how a crisis can be adaptive?

JEM: What I am most interested in is ego growth and development, not in adolescence per se. And I think that growth only happens through exploration, taking chances, breaking whatever forms there are and developing new forms for yourself in some way. Social forms are stereotypes, whatever they happen to be, and individuals only more or less fit into those particular molds. So everyone's life is a kind of do-it-yourself project. If you do it well for a while, you work yourself up to a kind of plateau. Once you get there, the problems you face are different from what you faced when you started out.

Solving one set of problems opens up a different set, and that means a new identity crisis. When you get married it's an identity crisis; when you have your first child it's an identity crisis; when you get your first divorce or your second . . . and so on. They are crises, but they lead to some kind of growth or progression. Each involves changes in your definition of yourself, but seldom, I think, a transformation. Old elements are recombined and some new ones added, so that you are different but the same. The first consolidation of identity occurs in late adolescence, because it's the first time all of the parts are there: cognition, sexuality, social skills, social expectations. Identity gets tested, challenged, broken up, and reconstellated all along.

AL: You began working on identity in the 1960s, when there was a lot of social and countercultural support for questioning traditional roles. The 1980s are more conservative. Couples are getting married in white dresses and tuxedos instead of beads and feathers. Are you seeing different identity patterns?

JEM: There are more Foreclosures and more Diffusions now. There were more Moratoriums in the 1960s and 1970s. There was even a fifth status then, which we called Alienated Achievement. These kids would say, "I don't want a job in this screwed-up culture. Who wants to be part of this?" You couldn't say that they had no identity. They knew very well what they didn't believe, what they didn't want to do, and why they didn't want to do it. They were Achievements, but not the ordinary Achievements.

In Eriksonian terms, what the culture provides and what the individual has to offer and needs are supposed to mesh. When a society

asks young people to risk their lives in a war few people understand or support, there's a stripping of the psychological gears.

AL: What about a society that tells you to train for a career but then doesn't provide good jobs or jobs equal to your training?

JEM: You get Diffusions. There is nowhere to go, no social way to define yourself in terms of work. It's a culturally imposed diffusion, because there's nothing to commit to.

We just completed a rather large study here, in British Columbia, where job prospects for college graduates are becoming increasingly dim. We found that 47 percent of the sample were Diffusions—compared to 15 percent in most samples!

AL: Much of your recent work has centered on sex differences. Would you summarize what you are finding?

JEM: I think that beginning in about fourth grade (if not earlier), girls are as concerned with interpersonal relationships as they are with achievement, while boys are concerned with just achievement. If you base your identity on the establishment and maintenance of relationships, it's a lot harder to define success. If you're dealing with grades or sports, it's easy. You know whether you have made it or you haven't. People aren't like that. You have to deal with the complexity, the nuances, the quicksand of relationships. I think that most women achieve their initial identity around age twenty-eight, and most men around age twenty-two. That's not based on research; that comes from therapy. Many women go into therapy between ages twenty-eight and thirty-two. They found the man of their dreams, had lovely children, and now are wondering who they are.

What we have found through research is that women seem to work on identity and intimacy concurrently; men seem to work on identity first and then on intimacy. With the college students we've studied, about the same number of men and women are high in identity. But more women than men are high in intimacy. And some women who are low in identity are high in intimacy. That wouldn't occur if identity always preceded intimacy, as Erikson said. We are also looking at the relationships between masculinity, femininity, androgeny (a combination of masculinity and femininity), and diffusion (a lack of either) and Erikson's stages. I feel fairly safe in saying that masculinity—and I mean psychological, not biological traits—is important for identity; femininity, important for intimacy. This has important implications for child-rearing. What it suggests is that if you rear children to believe that femininity isn't okay for boys and masculinity is wrong in girls, you inhibit a boy's intimacy and a girl's identity.

AL: If you could do anything you wanted, in the best of all possible worlds, where would you go from here?

JEM: I would like to work on other parts of the life cycle, to go back and develop a measure of industry. If I live long enough, I'd like to study each of Erikson's stages, because essentially I think the theory is valid. I think there are mistakes in it. When he talks about industry, it's all about technological skills. He doesn't talk about interpersonal skills. That's what girls are working on, and that's industry and skill, too. And I would like to link psychosocial development to other areas of development. I think we have the theoretical basis for an integrated cognitive-social-psychodynamic theory of personality development.

You see, still looking for "the Truth"!

Cognition:
Piaget's Formal Operational Stage

Hypothetical thinking
(Able to think about what might be and what should be)

Scientific thinking
(Generates hypotheses and deduces necessary & sufficient causes)

Logical thinking
(Reasons at propositional level)

[Formal operations may depend on formal schooling.]

Information
processing

Thinks ahead; selects among alternate problem-solving strategies; monitors own progress

On game of 20 Questions:
    Asks specific questions
    Seeks confirmation

    Asks categorical questions

    Seeks confirmation or disconfirmation

Applying
formal operations

Political ideals:
    Individual rights and interests
    (immediate consequences)
Legal understanding:
    Law prohibits

Community rights and abstract ideals
(long-range consequences)

Law prescribes

Identity

Identifications

Age in years   11   12   13   14
              Early Adolescence

[Individual may use formal operations only in areas of personal and cultural expertise]

[Idealism and alienation]

Law beneficial-rational

Ego identity (or identity diffusion)
Marcia: Identity statuses
Foreclosures   Achievements   Moratoriums   Diffusions

<Young adulthood>

Males: Identity → Intimacy
              [Intimate, stereotyped, or isolated statuses]

Females: Intimacy → Identity
              [Female foreclosures more advanced than male
              foreclosures in other areas; diffusion in late
              college years more common]

| 15 | 16 | 17 | 18 + | Young |
| Late Adolescence | | | | Adulthood |

15

Early adolescence is often an awkward time. Preoccupied with their changing bodies and new social status as semiadults, younger adolescents often assume that other people are constantly monitoring their appearance and actions. They construct what David Elkind (1980) calls an "imaginary audience." Much of their behavior is designed to impress that audience or to conceal information they do not want others to know. To some degree, they are always on stage.

Phoning, dating, and forbidden activities illustrate this. When children or adults make a telephone call, it is primarily to exchange information—if only to say, "I am thinking about you." Adolescents often have a hidden agenda. Phoning and being phoned are signs of popularity. Between classes a 12-year-old girl hints to her friend that she has secret information, a strategy designed to ensure that her friend will call that evening. The call may last an hour or more—because they want to hang out together, by wire. If during this long-winded exchange one adolescent refuses the other's invitation to a party, the latter "plays it cool." She was just asking; she really doesn't care one way or another. Adults consider it rude *not* to express regret that a friend can't come to your party. But most adolescents want to avoid the impression of being lonely and in need of friendship.

When a child wants to go to the movies with another child, he asks. Making a date with a member of the opposite sex is more complex. What if she turns him down? What if she accepts? Older adolescents and adults make a date because they expect to enjoy the other person's company. With young adolescents, much of the enjoyment comes from the idea that everyone knows they have a date that night, not from the pleasure of that person's company. The evening is full of unknowns. Will he make a pass? The boy is expected to "get" as much as he can without forcing himself on the girl. But how is he to know what she wants? Typically, young adolescent boys test the limits physically, by edging

ADOLESCENTS
AND SOCIETY

closer on the couch and, later, trying a hand on the girl's knee. The girl communicates her response nonverbally as well, by moving away or by not removing his hand. Older adolescents and adults may have the same objectives, but they are better able to read subtle cues of sexual attraction or rejection. They learn with their eyes and minds what younger adolescents can only discover through physical groping. The parting gesture of the evening is complicated by the imaginary audience. Each imagines that the next day everyone will be saying, "Look, he kissed her" or "Look, she didn't let him."

Activities that are forbidden to children but permitted to adults hold a special fascination for early adolescents. Elkind recalls "borrowing" the family car for a turn around the block at age 12. Driving is a symbol of maturity; he could not wait until he was old enough to obtain a legal beginner's permit. Every adult has similar memories: smoking tobacco or marijuana and then burning incense to escape detection; trying to look 18 at a liquor store or bar; perhaps shoplifting or shooting out streetlights with an air rifle, "just for the hell of it." Outwitting adults contributes to the adolescent's belief that she is special and unique—what Elkind calls a "personal fable." This fable may include such notions as these: "The rules apply to other people, not to me"; "I'll never get caught" (or "I won't

get hooked on drugs" or "I won't get pregnant"); and "If they could see me now. . . ."

By late adolescence, most young people have outgrown the imaginary audience and personal fable. In this chapter we describe the transition from puberty to adulthood. In the first section we look at changes in the way young people relate to their friends, to their families, and to school during adolescence. In the second section we consider social and psychological problems that appear in the teen years, in part because of new pressures to form an identity. In the last section we put adolescence into historical perspective, giving special attention to recent history.

Social Relations in Adolescence

The search for identity does not occur in a vacuum (Hill, 1980). Adolescents do not discover who they are by staring in a mirror or daydreaming of the future during French class, although they may do both. Their identities are forged in arguments over behavior at the dinner table and the keys to the family car, in marathon telephone calls and in locker-room banter, at parties and hangouts, in classrooms and at band rehearsals. Adolescents experience society and cultural standards indirectly, through their friends, families, schools, and other groups (Elder, 1975).

Cliques and Crowds

The peer group becomes increasingly important during adolescence, for several reasons (J. C. Coleman, 1980). Physiological development forces adolescents to cope with new experiences for which there are few explicit guidelines, such as making or rejecting a pass. Peers who are going through the same transformation provide concrete, if inaccurate, information as well as psychological support. To some extent, all adolescents attempt to sever early emotional ties to their parents. Peers supply techniques and support for challenging adult authority and questioning adult standards. At the very least, they establish ways of dressing and talking that distinguish *us* (adolescents) from *them* (adults). Finally, peers allow adolescents to try on new identities. Parents, who have known the adolescent for years, may ignore or dismiss his efforts to behave like a rock star, a socialist, or an abandoned lover. Peers are more likely to treat such experiments as real. This is not to say that peers are always kind. Far from it. They are often clannish, cruel to outsiders, and rigid in their adherence to in-group norms. But without peer-group experience adolescents could not learn what kinds of behavior their equals find acceptable and unacceptable, and what aspects of their personalities their equals like and reject.

Smoking, drinking, and public sex play are ways of showing your friends that you are too grown up to care what adults think.

In a classic study of young people in Sydney, Australia, Dexter Dunphy (1963) traced the development of cliques and crowds over adolescence. *Cliques* are small (two to nine persons), closed groups of individuals who go places and do things together and identify with one another. *Crowds* are associations of cliques ranging in size from fifteen to fifty. Where cliques specialize in conversation, crowds concentrate on organized social activities such as giving parties. Cliques dominate weekday activities; crowds take over on weekends.

Dunphy identified a clear developmental pattern in group affiliations (see Figure 15-1). In early adolescence, young people formed same-sex cliques. Their first heterosexual contacts usually took the form of getting together with a clique of the opposite sex for a bike trip or other activity. When the leaders of the two cliques went out together alone, others in the cliques also began dating. Eventually, heterosexual cliques developed and joined other cliques to form crowds. For a time, most peer contacts (friendships, dates, group activities) took place under the protective umbrella of this crowd. In late adolescence, as couples began to go steady and think about marriage, the crowd began to drift apart. A more recent study of high-school students in the United States found a similar pattern (Csikszentmihalyi & Larson, 1984). According to self-reports, high-school freshmen like to spend time with same-sex groups; sophomores prefer same-sex dyads; juniors enjoy mixed-sex groups; and seniors prefer being with one person of the opposite sex. Thus peer groups ease the transition from large groups to one-to-one relationships and from same-sex friendships to heterosexual couples.

Other researchers have found that most young people do not leave the shelter of cliques and crowds until late adolescence. For example, John C. Coleman (1974) asked young people to complete the sentence, "If someone is not part of the group. . . ." Nearly all of the 11-, 13-, and 15-year-olds imagined only negative consequences: "He feels inferior" or "He is looked on as an outcast." By age 17, however, many of the young people had begun to see independence from the peer group in a positive light: "He is happy because he is not following sheep" or "He is respected and admired." (See Figure 15-2.) Cliques and crowds provide a ready-made iden-

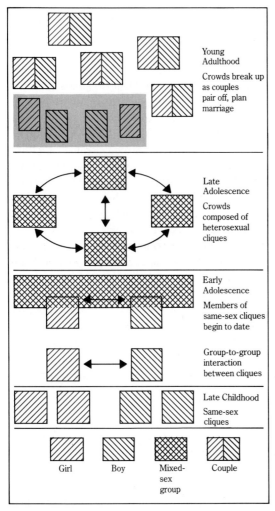

Figure 15-1 From Cliques to Couples
(Adapted from Dunphy, 1963)

Young Adulthood

Crowds break up as couples pair off, plan marriage

Late Adolescence

Crowds composed of heterosexual cliques

Early Adolescence

Members of same-sex cliques begin to date

Group-to-group interaction between cliques

Late Childhood

Same-sex cliques

Girl   Boy   Mixed-sex group   Couple

tity adolescents can wear until they feel comfortable expressing their individuality.

Friendships: His and Hers

Friendships are also transformed during adolescence. The trend is from sharing activities to psychological sharing, from playmateships to discussions and disclosure, at least among girls. Elizabeth Douvan and Joseph Adelson (1966) identified three stages in girls' friendships. In early adolescence (ages 11 to 13), the emphasis is on doing things together rather than on feeling close; on side-by-side activity rather than on face-to-face interaction. A friend is someone who is fun. In middle adolescence (ages 14 to 16), girls' friendships become more emotional. The emphasis is on sharing secrets, especially about friends and dating. A friend is someone you can trust not to betray confidences. In late adolescence (age 17 and older) friendships become more relaxed. No longer haunted by be-

trayal, older girls come to appreciate individual differences in personality and interests. The possessiveness and jealousy that characterized friendships in early adolescence are transferred to relationships with males. In this stage, a friend is someone who is compatible.

Douvan and Adelson found that boys' friendships, in contrast, were action-oriented throughout adolescence. They suggest that this is because boys' identities are based on achievement, assertiveness, and autonomy. "What the girl achieves through intimate connection with others, the boy must manage by disconnecting, by separating himself and asserting his right to be distinct" (1966, p. 348). When asked what they expected from a friend, boys stressed common activities, gang-type alliances, and mutual aid. A friend is someone who helps you when you are in trouble. Other research confirms the existence of sex differences in friendships, in adulthood (Wright, 1982) as well as adolescence (Berndt, 1981; Bigelow & LaGaipa, 1980; J. C. Coleman, 1974). Males seek action; females seek intimacy.

This does not mean that boys or men are insensitive. When asked to describe a friend's personality characteristics (for example, "What does the friend worry about most?"), eighth-grade boys were as likely to give answers that matched the friend's self-report as were eighth-grade girls (Diaz & Berndt, 1981). Neither does it mean boys do not care about others. Friendships are important to both sexes, at all ages.

Families: Aggravation and Approval

Popular wisdom holds that adolescents view their parents as strangers, if not enemies, and that their struggle for identity inevitably creates storm and stress within the family. In fact, large-scale surveys show that adolescence is a peaceful and satisfying time in three out of four families (Hill, 1980). Daniel Offer and his colleagues (Offer, Ostrov, & Howard, 1981) ques-

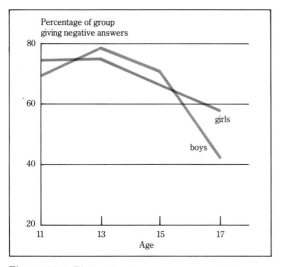

Figure 15-2 Fitting In The percentage of young people who express negative themes (worry, anxiety) when asked how a person who is not part of the group feels rises in early adolescence, then falls in the late teens.

(J. C. Coleman, 1980)

tioned adolescents in the United Stages, Australia, Ireland, and Israel. They found that most of these young people saw their parents as warm and supportive. A majority (70 to 80 percent) agreed with the statements, "Most of the time my parents are satisfied with me," "I can count on my parents most of the time," and "I feel that I have a part in family decisions." Most (55 to 70 percent) conceded that "When my parents are strict, I feel they are right even if I get angry." A minority (10 to 30 percent) felt that "My parents will be disappointed with me in the future," "Understanding my parents is beyond me," or "Usually I feel that I am a bother at home."

Parent–adolescent relations are not trouble-free, however. In most families there is a period of temporary disequilibrium as parents adjust to the "new" person in their midst—new in stature, in reproductive capacity, and in cognitive skills (Hill, 1980). Adolescents themselves are often ambivalent about their new status—demanding to be treated like an adult one minute, whining like a child the next. A group of high-school sophomores were asked to report occasions "either you teased your parent or your parent teased you; you and your parent had a difference of opinion; one of you got mad at the other; you and your parent had a quarrel or an argument; one of you hit the other" (Montemayor, 1982). The adolescents recorded about one argument every three days. Usually the conflict was with their mothers, not their fathers, and girls reported more quarrels than boys did. The average argument lasted only about ten minutes, but most teenagers found them moderately upsetting.

In another study (Csikszentmihalyi & Larson, 1984), negative thoughts outnumbered positive thoughts by about ten to one when adolescents were with their families. The following entries were typical:

"Why my mother manipulates the conversation to get me to hate her."

"The b——t exiting from my sister's mouth."

"Why my brother was scraping the breading off a perfectly good veal Parmesan."

"How much of a b——d my father is to my sister."

"How pig-headed my Mom and Dad are."

"My aunt talks too much."

"About my Mom getting ice cream all over her."

"How f——g stupid my Mom is for making a big f——g fuss." (1984, p. 139)

Complaints about how other family members look and talk and eat may seem trivial to adults; these violations can be aggravating in the extreme to adolescents (see Figure 15-3).

As a rule, the period of confrontation is short-lived. Parent–offspring conflict usually peaks in early adolescence, levels off in middle adolescence, and declines sharply in late adolescence, when the young person leaves home

Boys friendships are sometimes underrated.

Figure 15-3 "I Hate Her Guts!" A teenager describes an angry moment with his family; but angry moments do pass.

(Csikszentmihalyi & Larson, 1984)

Despite all their quarrels over the keys to the car and the decibels on the stereo, adolescents need their parents.

(Montemayor, 1982). A number of psychologists (for example, Cooper, Grotevant, Moore, & Conder, 1982) believe that *some* conflict between adolescents and their parents is a normal, natural part of growing up. Young people who often disagree with their parents may develop stronger identities than those who avoid conflict. But frequent, prolonged combat between adolescents and their parents is the exception to the rule.

The Generation Gap: Fact or Fiction?

Popular wisdom holds that the more time adolescents spend with their peers, the more likely they are to go astray. Peers are said to pressure an adolescent to do things she would never dream of doing on her own. Peer groups allegedly specialize in *negative conformity*: driving fast, smoking, drinking, stealing, vandalizing, and otherwise flouting adult rules simply for the sake of disobeying and scandalizing adults. Engaging in forbidden activities proves (at least to peers) that one is independent of one's parents. Joining radical political groups or unconventional religious cults may serve the same function: demonstrating that one is different from one's parents. During adolescence, peers and parents are thought to be worlds apart.

Yet many studies show that the so-called generation gap has been greatly exaggerated. Contrary to popular belief, adolescents listen to their parents as much or more than they do to their peers. Teenagers tend to follow their parents' advice on issues pertaining to the future (such as educational decisions and career aspirations); they follow their peers on matters related to their current social status (such as choice of language, friends, and activities) (Brittain, 1968; Kandel & Lesser, 1969). Most adolescents agree with their parents on the "big issues" (morality and religious values) but disagree on matters of style (music, clothes, haircuts, neatness, sleeping habits, and so on)

Dressing in ways that shock adults is one way adolescents in every generation demonstrate their independence.

(Lerner & Shea, 1982). Adolescents and their parents most often cross swords ideologically on current controversies such as drugs, sexuality, or the nuclear freeze. But their differences are usually a matter of degree. For example, parents may think that the penalties for using marijuana are too harsh; their adolescents, that marijuana should be legalized. Parents may approve of sex between unmarried adults; adolescents extend this to teenagers.

As a general rule, adolescents see their own attitudes as lying between those of their peers and their parents. In one study (Lerner, Karson, Meisels, & Knapp, 1975), young people were asked to rate their peers' attitudes toward 36 controversial statements, their parents' attitudes, and their own position. Most put their parents on the conservative end of the continuum, their peers on the liberal end, and themselves in the middle. Since most adolescents see themselves as less radical than their peers, they exaggerate their age-mates' liberalism. Interestingly, they overestimate the differences between themselves and their parents, whereas parents underestimate the difference. Adolescents tend to perceive their parents as less influential than they actually are, while parents see themselves as more influential than they are. This perceptual gap can be traced to the adolescent's need to believe that his thoughts and experiences are unique (part of what Elkind called the personal fable).

Of course, parents cannot supervise adolescents 24 hours a day. And in early adolescence especially, young people may give in to peer pressure to engage in antisocial or risky behavior. The following experience is common:

I feel a lot of pressure from my friends to smoke and steal and things like that. My parents do not allow me to smoke, but my best friends are really pushing me to do it. They call me a pansy and a momma's boy if I don't. I really don't like the idea of smoking, but my

good friend Steve told me in front of some of our friends, "Kevin, you are an idiot and a chicken all wrapped up in one little body." I couldn't stand it any more, so I smoked with them. I was coughing and humped over, but I still said, "This is really fun— yeah, I like it." I felt like I was part of the group. (Santrock, 1984, p. 279)

Conformity to peer pressure and willingness to accept dares increase during junior high school, peak in about ninth grade, then decline (Berndt, 1979). By eleventh or twelfth grade, adolescents are better able to resist peer and parental pressure and to make their own decisions.

In short, adolescents do rebel against adults in small and large ways. But the two generations are not necessarily enemies (Conger & Petersen, 1984). The values of peers and parents often overlap, in large part because adolescents choose friends whose families and homes are similar to their own. They are most likely to turn to peers in areas where they believe (rightly or wrongly) that their parents have little experience or expertise, such as drugs, or where their parents are unwilling or unable to provide useful information, such as sexuality.

High School

By the time an adolescent graduates from high school, she has spent 10,000 hours in classrooms (Kaza Lunas, 1978). The question is not whether school influences her development, but *how*. There are two basic ways developmental psychologists can view schools (Hill, 1980). One is to assess them as educational institutions, designed to provide young people with the skills to fill adult roles. The other is to see them as small societies, cut off from the adult world, which develop their own norms and values.

SOCIAL CLASS AND SCHOOL ACHIEVEMENT Americans like to think that school gives all youngsters an equal opportunity to develop their potential. One of the questions that concerns social scientists is whether schools can override the effects of poverty. Put another way, do schools have an impact on achievement (industry) and aspiration (identity) that is independent of parents, neighborhoods, and social class? James S. Coleman, among others, has argued that they do not. He organized a study of 570,000 students at 4,000 schools in the mid-1960s (Coleman, Campbell et al., 1966). He found that lower-class, minority students who attended predominantly white, middle-class schools with small classes, new buildings, up-to-date laboratories and libraries, and many extracurricular activities did not perform better on achievement tests than did similar students who attended run-down schools in poor neighborhoods. The data suggested that social class was a much better predictor of achievement than quality of education: Schools have little impact.

Michael Rutter and his colleagues (Rutter, Maughan, Mortimore, & Ouston, 1979) challenged this in the study described in Chapter 11. To review, Rutter followed the academic careers of British boys who were similar in ability and family background, but attended different schools. He found that schools affect both in-school behavior, measured by attendance and grades, and out-of-school behavior, gauged by acts of delinquency. The most successful schools were those in which teachers took education seriously, treated adolescents as "responsible citizens," and expected students to succeed. Generally, the boys did succeed. According to Rutter, schools do matter. (A more recent report by J. S. Coleman, Hoffer, & Kilgore, 1981, supports this.)

But the jury is still out on this issue. Too little is known about what teachers expect from different pupils; whether they communicate these expectations in subtle or obvious ways; how students respond; which teaching and discipline strategies work best with which students; and how the size and structure of the classroom affect different students.

AN ADOLESCENT SOCIETY? The idea that schools promote the development of an adolescent society or subculture, with its own values and norms, can also be traced to J. S. Coleman (1961). In the 1950s, Coleman gave questionnaires to students at eleven Illinois high schools. He asked them, among other things, how they would like to be remembered: as a brilliant student, an athletic star, an activities leader, or the most popular student in their class. Most boys answered "athletic star"; most girls, "activity leader" or "most popular." Being a brilliant student was the last thing on their minds. Good looks, popularity with the opposite sex, having a car and nice clothes, and knowing how to have a good time counted more with these students than good grades did. Coleman concluded that the adolescent subculture undermines the stated purpose of school (education), as well as parents' hopes and expectations. Coleman's study of the late 1950s took place during a relatively conservative political period, not unlike the 1980s. Results of studies of the adolescent society could be different in periods of greater political upheaval, as in the 1960s and 1970s. For an estimate of how today's teenagers spend their time, see Figure 15-4.

Figure 15-4 An Insider's View of Adolescence According to teenagers' self-reports, they spend more time with friends or alone than with members of their family, yet devote more time to schoolwork and chores than they do to socializing.
(Csikszentmihalyi & Larson, 1984)

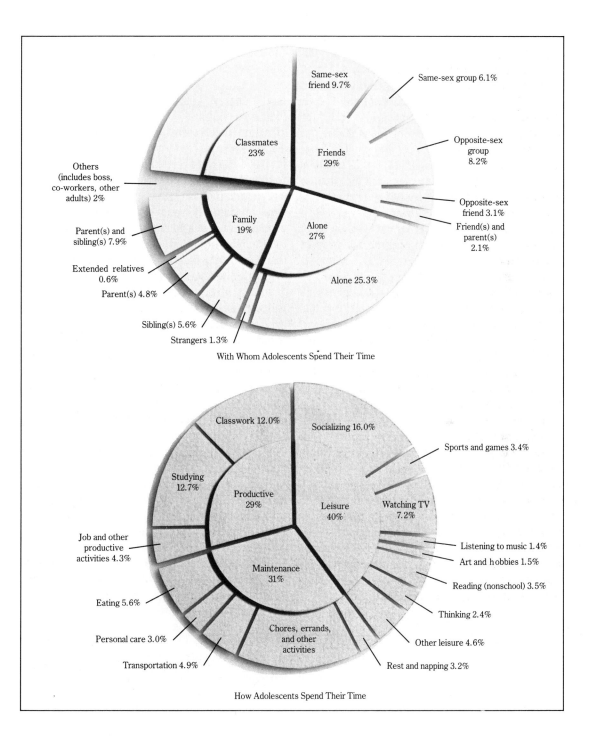

Same-sex
friend 9.7%

Same-sex group 6.1%

Classmates
23%

Friends
29%

Opposite-sex
group
8.2%

Others
(includes boss,
co-workers, other
adults) 2%

Opposite-sex
friend 3.1%

Parent(s) and
sibling(s) 7.9%

Family
19%

Alone
27%

Friend(s) and
parent(s)
2.1%

Extended relatives
0.6%

Parent(s) 4.8%

Alone 25.3%

Sibling(s) 5.6%

Strangers 1.3%

With Whom Adolescents Spend Their Time

Classwork 12.0%

Socializing 16.0%

Sports and games 3.4%

Studying
12.7%

Productive
29%

Leisure
40%

Watching TV
7.2%

Job and other
productive
activities 4.3%

Listening to music 1.4%

Maintenance
31%

Art and hobbies 1.5%

Reading (nonschool) 3.5%

Eating 5.6%

Thinking 2.4%

Personal care 3.0%

Chores, errands,
and other
activities

Other leisure 4.6%

Transportation 4.9%

Rest and napping 3.2%

How Adolescents Spend Their Time

Other research has confirmed but qualified Coleman's description of the adolescent subculture. Eitzen (1975) asked males attending high school in the 1970s the same question Coleman had asked in the 1950s: How would you like to be remembered? Once again, athletic star ranked first and brilliant student last. But the importance of athletics depended on the boy, the school, and the community. Being a sports hero was more important to sophomores than to seniors; to boys who were highly involved in school than to boys who were loners or had friends elsewhere; in small schools than in large schools; and in working-class communities than in upper-middle-class communities with a high percentage of professionals among parents. To some extent, then, the adolescents' values mirrored community values. Friesen (1968) found that although less than 3 percent of a sample of Canadian students thought being an outstanding student admitted one to the leading crowd, 80 percent saw academic achievement as important to their own futures. These students seemed to distinguish between present social success and long-term goals.

To call high school a separate society, with few connections to the adult world, is probably an exaggeration. Nevertheless, schools do influence patterns of peer affiliation, feelings of competence or incompetence, ideas about right and wrong, images of career opportunities, and a concept of how a social system larger than the family works. In short, high school provides some of the ingredients for identity formation.

Problems in Identity Formation

Many adolescents have difficulties in establishing a consistent sense of self, difficulties that are reflected in temporary disruptions in their relations with peers and parents and in their schoolwork. With some teenagers, the normal struggle with identity is exaggerated. When adolescents turn to delinquency, drugs, or even suicide to solve problems and gain attention,

they become social and psychological problems. In this section we look at what can go wrong in adolescence.

Delinquency: Going Through a Phase or Going Wrong?

"Delinquency is presumed to be as endemic to adolescence as acne," write Martin Gold and Richard Petronio (1980, p. 495). In the first textbook on adolescence, G. Stanley Hall (1904) suggested that teenagers "often feel like animals in captivity" and "long intensely for the utter abandon of a wilder life" (p. 339). Although they might find Hall's language a bit flowery, many contemporary adults would agree. Is adolescence the "age of crime"?

The National Survey of Youth (Gold & Reimer, 1975) asked nearly 1,400 young people ages 11 to 18 whether they had committed nontrivial delinquent acts (vandalism, theft, assault, joyriding, and the like). The survey found that delinquency increases more or less steadily over the course of adolescence. Eighteen-year-olds confessed to five times as many violations of the law as 11-year-olds did (see Figure 15-5). Other researchers (summarized in Loeber, 1982) have noted a shift from overt antisocial acts in childhood (such as teasing, bullying, disobeying, fighting, and other open confrontations) to covert antisocial acts in adolescence (stealing, truancy, drug use, vandalism, and other acts committed behind adults' backs).

SEX DIFFERENCES The term "delinquent" usually conjures up images of young, tough males—for good reasons. From age 12 to 18, the rate of violent crimes committed by boys climbs steadily (Cairns & Cairns, 1983). Eighteen-year-old males are, without contest, the most violent group in our society, and in many others. In contrast, the increase with age in violent crimes by females is modest. Ten times as many 18-year-old males as females are arrested for murder each year (Crime in the U.S., 1982). This gender difference is not limited to a particular time or place. A sharp increase in male (but not female) violence during adolescence was recorded in thirteenth century England. The same pattern is observed in rural states and inner cities in every region of the United States today.

This gender gap does not come as a surprise. Most studies have found that males are more aggressive than females are, at every age. But Robert and Beverly Cairns (1983) have uncovered an unexpected pattern. When they asked fourth-graders and their teachers to name the most aggressive children in their class, both picked almost as many girls as boys. Twenty of these "bad" or antisocial youngsters (ten boys

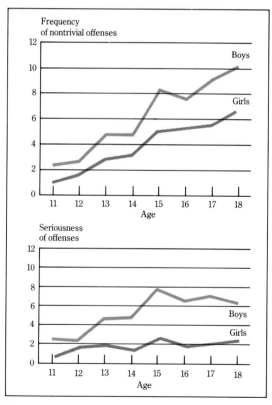

Figure 15-5 Youth and Crime   According to their own reports, males commit more crimes—and more serious crimes—than do females, at all ages.
(Gold & Petronio, 1980)

and ten girls) were followed through seventh grade. In fifth and sixth grades, the differences between the sexes were slight. The girls fought as often and as hard as the boys did. Observations of their behavior confirmed their reputations. Moreover, the girls did not apply a dual standard: When angry, they were as likely to pick boys as girls for their victims. But gender similarities gave way to sharp dissimilarities in seventh grade. While the boys became increasingly violent, the girls rather suddenly became less violent.

Why? By age 13 or 14, males are becoming bigger and stronger, on the average, than females. A girl who started a fistfight with a boy would probably lose. Violence is not as effective for her as it was when she was ten. The girl would also lose socially and psychologically. There is far more peer support among adolescents for males who commit delinquent acts than for females who engage in the same defiant behavior (Cairns & Cairns, 1983; Gold & Petronio, 1980). Aggression—dominance and fighting—enhances a boy's attractiveness to some members of the opposite sex but diminishes a girl's sex appeal. Most girls who were hellions in fourth grade have become flirts by the end of seventh grade.

Official statistics confirm these sex differences. Boys are arrested about five times more often than girls are. Male offenses are most often crimes against property and truancy. Girls are more often brought before the juvenile court as "uncontrollable," which usually means that they are sexually active or have run away from home. Male crimes more often involve nonconsenting others, whose property is stolen or wrecked. Female crimes more often involve the immediate family or consenting males. As a result, males are more likely to become police statistics. In the last decade, the number of females arrested for typically male crimes (auto theft, burglary, vandalism) has increased. But girls have not "achieved" equality in crime.

TYPES OF DELINQUENCY Many adolescents occasionally use a fake identification card, steal lipstick, or smoke marijuana. What distinguishes hard-core, chronic delinquents from occasional delinquents and nondelinquents? In a recent review of the literature, Rolf Loeber (1982) identified a number of distinguishing traits. Delinquency does not appear suddenly, arising out of nowhere, in adolescence. In most cases, chronically delinquent adolescents were antisocial as children. Early lying and stealing often predict future crime. In one study (Mitchell & Rosa, 1981), 67 percent of children whose parents reported that they had stolen things on several occasions committed at least one criminal offense in adolescence, compared with 9 percent of children whose parents said they never stole. Thirty-eight percent of "early liars" later committed a crime, compared with only 8 percent of truthful children. As youngsters, chronic delinquents had not one "bad habit" but committed a variety of antisocial acts (lying *and* stealing *and* vandalism, and so on). They caused trouble at school, in their homes, and in their neighborhoods, not in just one setting. And they got into serious trouble at an early age. One researcher (Farrington, 1982) studied 1,138 youths in Franklin County, Ohio. At age 25, a core group of 23 males had been arrested six times or more and accounted for almost half of the crimes known to have been committed by these 1,138 adolescents. Of this core group, eleven had been arrested for the first time between ages 11 and 12, six between ages 13 and 14, and six at age 15. In addition, Loeber found that once antisocial patterns are established they are rarely abandoned. For some adolescents, then, delinquency is not just a phase.

All delinquents are not alike, even in the hard-core group. Thomas Achenbach (1982) distinguishes between two types: socialized-subcultural and unsocialized-psychopathic. Those in the *socialized-subcultural* category have grown up in communities where some forms of crime are an accepted or tolerated way of life. These lower-class youths join gangs in the same spirit that middle-class adolescents join the YMCA or the scouts. They model their life-style partly on the successful life-styles of adults around them, who may happen to deal in stolen goods or illegal drugs. They are psychologically normal adolescents who have been socialized to a delinquent subculture.

Sociologists (Cloward & Ohlin, 1960; Merton, 1958) explain this type of delinquency in terms of opportunity structures. These youths have the same hopes and dreams as other adolescents (living well, being the head of a household, owning a home). But they *lack* access to legitimate opportunities for achieving these goals, on the one hand, and *have* access to illegitimate opportunities on the other. They may not possess the educational skills, middle-class manners, and connections to get a white-collar job with a bright future, but they do have the know-how and know-who to make their way in the underworld society of drug dealers or the numbers racket.

Is high school a separate adolescent world, or a reflection of the larger society?

Unsocialized-psychopathic (or sociopathic) delinquents are adolescents who lack commitments to other people, persistently defy authority, look for trouble, and fail to respond to rewards or punishments. These youngsters are easily identifiable in late childhood as persistent liars and troublemakers who have no regrets about the effects of their delinquent acts on themselves or others. They are casual about inflicting loss or pain for the sake of immediate gratification. They do not seem to learn to avoid trouble or painful encounters (Eysenck, 1964; Weiner, 1970), unless avoidance brings immediate, material advantage. Long-term commitments to goals, which involve delay of immediate gratification, and lasting relationships to people, which involve mutual interests, are beyond their capabilities. Among other such exploits, one youth defecated into the school piano; sold his father's overcoat to a passerby; joined other youth to break into and vandalize a

summer cottage; stole automobiles with regularity; and abandoned the car his father bought him to steal another inferior model, which he later abandoned also (Cleckley, 1976). Whereas socialized-subcultural delinquents conform to norms (albeit those of which society as a whole does not approve), unsocialized-psychopathic delinquents are amoral.

DELINQUENCY: A RESPONSE TO EXPLOITATION? Perhaps most puzzling are middle-class delinquents, who seem to have every advantage. David Elkind (1967) argues that middle-class delinquency is a response to *exploitation*. We think this applies to some delinquency in other groups as well. Many adolescents and pre-delinquent children feel that their parents and the larger society violate an implicit contract between adults and children. In middle-class families, parents agree to provide for the physical and emotional well-being of their children, who

agree in return to abide by the norms of middle-class society. Although minor infractions of the contract by both parents and children occur occasionally in most families, the contract is generally honored by both adolescents and their parents.

For lower-class delinquents the social contract is often broken by poor housing, too little money, and few opportunities for a better life. The physical and emotional well-being of these children does not receive sufficient protection, either from their parents, who have multiple problems themselves, or from the larger community, which leaves children largely at the mercy of their birthright.

Violations of the implicit contract in middle-class homes take several forms, according to Elkind (1967). Parents may unconsciously ask children to provide *vicarious satisfaction of their own needs*. For example, a sexually frustrated mother may encourage her daughter to provide a vivid description of the daughter's date—"then call the girl a tramp" (p. 81). Another form of exploitation is using adolescents as *slave labor*—expecting an unreasonable and inequitable amount of work. Parents also use their children to *proclaim their own moral rectitude* by holding them to an unreasonable standard of conduct. Children of ministers, principals, and judges are particularly likely to suffer this form of exploitation. Other parents expect their children to *absolve the parent's guilt*, such as the divorced mother whose lover moves into the house, without any explanation to the teenage son. The son's continued residence in the situation appears to condone his mother's behavior. Finally, Elkind observed *ego bolstering* exploitation by parents who pressure their adolescents unreasonably to be star athletes, scholars, or social butterflies, beyond the child's desires or capabilities.

Some adolescent reactions to these forms of exploitation are anger, frustration, and acting out in ways that will get back at the parents or larger society. Elkind draws the parallel between exploited workers and adolescents: "When a worker is exploited he has at least four courses of action open to him. He can either quit, go out on strike, sabotage the plant, or passively submit to the exploitation." In much the same way, some young people simply *quit*. They may quit school and become truant, quit the home and become runaways, or quit the family psychologically and become incorrigible. Other adolescents go on *strike*. They continue to go to school but refuse to perform; they stay in the home but refuse to do their fair share of the chores. They stay out late with a group of whom the parents do not approve. In short, they defy parental authority generally. More serious reactions occur in young people who wish to *sabotage* their parents. These adolescents become pregnant, steal cars, vandalize schools, get drunk, sniff glue, or take drugs. Such reactions cost the parents heavily in worry, time, money, and bad publicity. And some youngsters passively *submit* to parental exploitation in the hope of winning or regaining their parent's love.

Parental exploitation is essentially private and seldom recognized by anyone outside the home. Whereas the worker often has a union to voice his grievances and to stand up for his rights, there are no unions for children. Consequently, the delinquent behavior of adolescents who are being exploited by their parents often serves as a kind of cry for help. Put differently, delinquent behavior is often caused in part by the desire to make the exploitation public, to let the world know what is happening behind the drawn drapes and closed doors. The sad thing about such cries for help is that they are as injurious to the young person as they are to the parents.

Drugs, Legal and Illegal

One form of delinquency deserves special consideration: the use of legal and illegal drugs. According to one estimate (Mervis, 1984) two out

SMOKING PREVENTION

Many adults who smoke began in their teens, when they thought smoking made them look sexy and mature. As adults, they find it difficult or impossible to stop. What can be done to prevent young people from smoking in the first place?

One team of researchers (Evans et al., 1978) designed a smoking prevention program expressly for young adolescents. All teenagers know that smoking is bad for their health, but few take health problems that might develop in 20 or 30 years seriously. To an adolescent, middle age can seem as remote as ancient Greece. The smoking prevention program focuses on negative effects of cigarettes in the here-and-now: Smoking causes bad breath, slows you down on the basketball court, gives you a dull complexion.

Teenagers often have a positive image of the smoker as someone who is sophisticated, willing to take risks, and ready to defy adults. The smoking prevention program attempts to undermine this image by showing young people films on advertising techniques. It suggests that smokers are duped by the tobacco industry, and that people who fall for the Marlboro man or the Virginia Slims woman are suckers. Program leaders do not tell adolescents not to smoke. Rather, they repeat that "the choice is up to you," appealing to adolescents' desire to demonstrate independence.

Often teenagers begin smoking because of social pressure. They do not want their friends to think that they're concerned about their health, afraid to defy adults, and otherwise "chicken." Films in the smoking prevention program model techniques for refusing a cigarette. Then, in workshops, an older adolescent role-plays with the younger students. He or she may act out situations in which the pressure to smoke was strong, or confront younger students with arguments for smoking. This gives the younger students opportunities to practice saying no. The aim of these workshops is "behavioral inoculation," a psychological version of immunization. Immunization (for example, the polio vaccine) is based on the principle that people who are exposed to a weak dose of a germ develop antibodies that protect them when they are exposed to a strong dose. The hope is that young people who are exposed to weak arguments for smoking will develop counterarguments that will protect them when strong pressures are applied.

of five high-school seniors got drunk in the past two weeks, and almost one in three smoked marijuana in the last month. Coming to terms with drugs has become one of the developmental tasks of adolescence.

The most recent data on adolescent drug use come from a survey of 17,500 high-school seniors conducted yearly by Jerald Bachman and his colleagues at the University of Michigan's Institute for Social Research (Bachman, 1982). According to the seniors' responses to anonymous questionnaires, daily use of marijuana peaked in 1978 and 1979 and has declined steadily since then. Nevertheless, 60 percent of the class of 1981 reported having tried marijuana at least once, and over 30 percent had smoked a joint in the preceding month. The percentage of high-school seniors who smoke tobacco regularly has also decreased, although more adolescents smoke cigarettes than marijuana. One of the main reasons for the decline in the use of these drugs is adolescents' concern about their health. A majority of high-school seniors see smoking either drug regularly as a "great risk."

The exception to this pattern is alcohol. Most adolescents do not consider drinking a health risk, and the proportion who consume alcohol has remained more or less steady since 1975 (see Figure 15-6). According to the Institute for Social Research surveys, nearly all adolescents (93 percent) have tried alcohol; half say they drink every week; a surprising 41 percent report that they had five drinks on a single occasion in the last two weeks; and 6 percent admit drinking daily.

There is no simple explanation of why some adolescents abuse drugs, while others experiment but do not make drinking, smoking, or getting high part of their identity. Some psychologists (Bachman, 1982; Jessor, Chase, & Donovan, 1980) stress personality factors as a cause of drug abuse. Adolescents who abuse drugs place a high value on independence, often spend evenings away from home, and are not strongly committed to school, religion, or other adult-run institutions. Other social scientists (Kandel, 1980) emphasize socialization. Adolescents are most likely to drink or smoke if their friends, and their parents, drink and smoke also. Through their own behavior, parents unwittingly socialize young people to think that drugs are acceptable. Peers, who provide the social context for drug use, reinforce family socialization (Barnes, 1977; Brook, Whiteman, & Gordon, 1983).

We believe that there are several explanations why certain adolescents are drug risks. Some adolescents may be drug prone because of personality factors, turning to alcohol or cocaine even though neither their parents nor their peers abuse drugs. Others who do not have the same personality traits may begin to use drugs because of problems in the family—including those caused by a parent who drinks heavily or uses other drugs. In the latter case, there may be a genetic component to substance abuse. And some adolescents whose parents do not smoke or drink, or take sleeping pills or

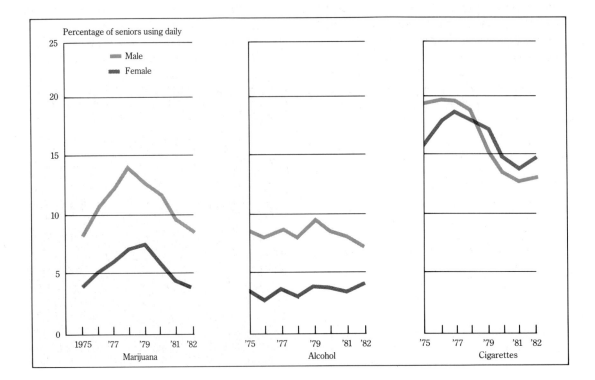

tranquilizers, and who are otherwise conventional themselves may use drugs in order to gain peer acceptance.

Psychopathology: Delusions and Despair

Many forms of psychological disturbance make their appearance in adolescence. Some children who were quiet and very shy in middle to late childhood become overtly schizophrenic adolescents. Others become depressed and suicidal. Still others begin to show signs of anxiety and other disorders that are rare in childhood. Why is there so much psychopathology in adolescence? The evidence that many psychological disorders are based in part on genetic vulnerability and biochemical imbalances is mounting. It may be that psychopathology is governed by a genetic timetable that sounds an alarm at puberty, or that the biological changes that occur in the young person's body at puberty trigger psychological problems. At the same time, the developmental tasks of adolescence—the need to forge an identity, to establish a place in peer groups, to deal with one's emerging sexuality, to think about becoming independent of one's family—may push a young person who is genetically or biochemically vulnerable "over the edge."

SCHIZOPHRENIA The most common of the *psychoses* or severe psychological disorders, schizophrenia is more likely to appear in adolescence or early adulthood than in any other period of life. **Schizophrenia** is characterized by cognitive disorders: by odd and illogical trains of thought, paranoid ideas, hallucinations, avoidance of social contact, and bizarre postures and movements. When this disorder appears in adolescence, it is often mixed with symptoms of other disorders, such as depression or sociopathic tendencies. Often the schizophrenic adolescent did not engage in peer-group activities, had very few friends, and engaged in antisocial behavior in the home (not in school or in the neighborhood) as a child (Weiner, 1982). The prognosis for individuals who develop this disorder early is not as good as for those who develop it later in life.

Why schizophrenia appears in adolescence is a mystery. It does not seem to be related to the much rarer childhood disorders, such as *autism* and so-called *childhood schizophrenia*. The highest-risk period for males is in the late teens

Figure 15-6 Adolescent Drug Use   Surveys show that teenagers are smoking cigarettes and marijuana less, but drinking as much as ever.

According to their own reports on anonymous questionnaires, two out of five teenagers got drunk in the previous two weeks.

to early twenties; for females, it is the thirties. Again, no one knows why.

The alleged causes of schizophrenia range from social to genetic. The strongest evidence supports the idea of genetic vulnerability—that is, some people are genetically more vulnerable to devastation by the stresses in their environment than most people are. Individuals who are biologically related to schizophrenics are far more likely to develop the disorder, even if they are raised in nonschizophrenic adoptive homes (Gottesman, 1983). But this does not mean that the environment plays no role in the disorder. Pressures toward defining oneself, choosing adult roles, managing responsibilities, and forming intimate relationships also occur first in adolescence. It is not accidental, we think, that schizophrenic breakdowns begin to occur in this period. The stresses of adolescence and genetic vulnerability combine to produce the disorder.

DEPRESSION Mild, transient depression is probably the most common form of psychological distress in adolescence; when acute or prolonged, it contributes to a variety of behavior problems (Rutter & Garmezy, 1983; Weiner, 1982). **Depression** is characterized by a sense of loss, related to the real or imagined loss of a loved one, real or imagined failure and loss of self-esteem, or real or imagined disfigurement or loss of physical capacities and bodily integrity. Common symptoms include fatigue, loss of appetite, fears about physical ailments, and poor concentration. Depression takes different forms in younger and older adolescents (Weiner, 1982). Younger adolescents who are depressed constantly seek excitement and companionship, and may use sex, drugs, or delinquent behavior to ward off depression. There are two reasons for this. First, biological changes, learning to become independent from one's parents, and other developmental tasks challenge all adolescents' self-esteem. It may be too painful for

them to admit to themselves or others that they feel hopeless or incompetent. Second, younger adolescents are more inclined to *do* something than to *think* about their situation. Older adolescents who are depressed are more introspective and lethargic. Typically they disavow any long-term hopes or goals and adopt a "what's-the-use-of-it-all" attitude.

SUICIDE Suicide is the third leading cause of death among adolescents, after car accidents and murder. According to one estimate, an adolescent attempts suicide once a minute in the United States; fourteen teenagers succeed each day (Santrock, 1984). (See Table 15-1.) As with adults, female adolescents attempt suicide more often than males, but males succeed in killing themselves more often than females. Most potential suicides let at least one other person know that they are contemplating suicide before they attempt it. And many have learned recently that a relative or schoolmate committed suicide (Weiner, 1982).

Typically, adolescents who decide to take their lives have been struggling with problems they cannot solve for some time (Weiner, 1982). Some are having problems with their parents or suffering from problems their parents are having with each other. Some are alienated from peers, unable to make and keep friends. Some are having trouble in school. Indeed, college students are overrepresented in adolescent suicides. According to one study, these young people did not believe they were doing as well as they should, even though they were better than average students (Bruhn & Seiden, 1965; Weiner, 1982).

Why should bright, talented adolescents with better-than-average opportunities give up on life? College students may be more vulnerable to depression than nonstudents. They are often brighter and more self-questioning than the average adolescent. Their need to define

Table 15-1 Changes in Suicide Rates by Sex and Age

Year		Age Group		
		10–14	15–19	20–24
1960–1977	Males	+78%	+154%	+160%
	Females	+50%	+112%	+152%
1975–1977	Males	+33%	+ 16%	+ 13%
	Females	−25%	+ 17%	+ 7%

(Sheras, 1983)

themselves may involve more intense struggles than the identity crises of other adolescents. In keeping with the old saying, "Nothing ventured, nothing gained," one could conclude that for suicidal students, "Too much ventured, too much lost." When self-esteem becomes too vulnerable and pressures to do well academically and socially grow too strong, they choose to escape through death.

EATING DISORDERS A fourth set of psychological disorders that appear in adolescence are almost exclusively female problems: eating disorders. Some adolescent girls go on periodic binges, stuffing themselves with "forbidden" (high-calorie) foods until they can't eat anymore or they fall asleep. Then they force themselves to vomit, use laxatives and diuretics, or fast to avoid gaining weight (Thompson, 1979). The technical term for this binge–purge syndrome is *bulimia*. Bulimics are obsessed with food: Their entire day revolves around plans to eat or avoid eating. They are also obsessed with their weight and long to be thinner than is normal or healthy for someone their height and age. The inability to control binges creates feelings of in-

The rate of suicide attempts is higher in adolescence than in any other stage of life. This young woman's attempt ended when she landed in a police net.

tense shame, guilt, and self-contempt. Most bulimics are able to hide the disorder from friends and family members, however, and most maintain about normal weight. Because it is a secret disorder, no one knows exactly how many adolescent girls suffer from bulimia. Estimates of the number of college women who periodically gorge themselves, then vomit or fast, range from one in ten to one in four (Halmi, Falk, & Schwartz, 1981).

Anorexia nervosa, or self-starvation, is a more severe eating disorder. Through extreme dieting and constant exercise, these adolescent girls reduce their body weight by 20 to 25 percent in a matter of months. As a result, they often stop menstruating and suffer from mild to severe malnutrition. Without treatment, an estimated 20 percent of anorexics die from self-imposed starvation (Brody, 1982). About half of anorexics also show symptoms of bulimia. The difference between the two is that anorexics succeed in their desire to become super-thin, while bulimics maintain about normal weight.

Anorexia nervosa has been called a disorder of the affluent. Most of the victims are white, above-average college students, from upper-middle-income families. Their drastic attempts to shed pounds have been linked to fear of growing up and becoming a woman; the desire to exercise control over events that are realistically beyond personal control; and the desire to please parents who put exaggerated emphasis on personal appearance, performance, and achievement. Anorexics associate being thin with success but have a distorted body image. Although usually of normal weight when the disorder begins, they are disgusted by the thought that they are fat. They are not satisfied until they have become emaciated, and even then fear becoming fat. Most adolescent girls are unhappy with their weight; anorexia nervosa is an exaggeration of a widespread cultural quest for an unnaturally and, in this case, unhealthily thin shape.

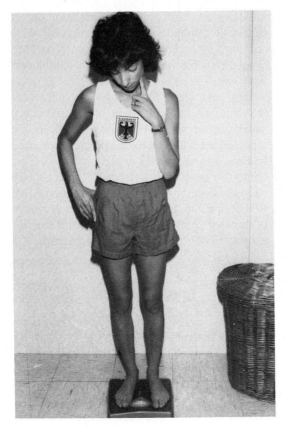

In our culture, concern for body weight has become an obsession for many.

Insight

CHLOROSIS: THE SOCIAL HISTORY OF A FEMALE DISORDER

The history of chlorosis suggests that a physiological or psychological disorder can also be a cultural artifact. Common around the turn of the century (1870–1920), this disorder had disappeared by 1930. Joan Brumberg (1982) traces the rise and fall of chlorosis to social changes, not improved medical diagnosis or treatment.

Like anorexia nervosa and bulimia, chlorosis was a disorder that affected only female adolescents. In *A System of Medicine,* T. Clifford Allport described it in 1905 as a "malady of women, and primarily of young women at or about the age of puberty . . . consisting in a defect of the red corpuscles of the blood" (in Brumberg, 1982, p. 1469). To modern readers this may seem like a description of iron deficiency anemia. But there were other symptoms as well, including palpitations, shortness of breath, inertia, melancholy, headaches, and "caprices and perversions" of the appetite. Chlorotic girls were said to have a passion for eating such repulsive items as chalk or flies, or to adore sweets but become ill at the sight of meat. Diagnosis was based largely on the patient and her family's descriptions, not medical tests. A girl would present herself to the doctor with the statement, "I think my blood must be out of order." Treatment ranged from prescriptions of iron salts to a recommendation of marriage.

Brumberg suggests that chlorosis fit Victorian ideas of womanhood. The pathological condition was also seen as an ideal: Victorians sentimentalized sickly women. It was rare for a woman of the middle or upper classes *not* to suffer from "neurasthenia." Daughters had many opportunities to observe attacks of exhaustion, headaches, palpitations, and indigestion before they reached the age when they were considered at risk for chlorosis. One reason for the idealization of female weakness was that scientists knew little about the female reproductive cycle and generally assumed that menstruation was debilitating. But the idea that women needed to stay indoors, take afternoon naps and medications, also matched Victorian notions of female domesticity.

One of the symptoms of chlorosis—distaste for animal flesh—is particularly telling. Many Victorian physicians associated eating meat with female sexuality. Meat was thought to increase menstrual flow and therefore sexual appetites. A stimulating diet of meat and condiments was recommended for young women whose interest in marriage and motherhood was considered deficient. Conversely, restriction of meat was prescribed as a cure for premature or rampant sexuality. In developing a distaste for meat, a girl was trying to show that she was good, or perhaps to purge herself of unwanted sexual desires. She was also identifying with her mother and other women.

The incidence of chlorosis began to decline rapidly after the turn of the century. Improved nutrition, a better understanding of the female reproductive system, and new techniques for identifying and treating anemia may have contributed to its demise. But Brumberg believes the main reason was social change. More girls were attending public schools, which made afternoon naps an inconvenience. The center of an adolescent girl's life began shifting away from the home to peer group activities and eventually dating, making headaches and melancholy a social drag. New physical education programs demanded vigor, not fainting spells. Moreover, mothers were being urged to practice "scientific nutrition." Now a sickly daughter was an insult, not a validation of womanhood. Under these new social conditions anemia did not disappear (as commercials for Geritol remind us), but chlorosis did.

Storm and Stress for Some

Adolescence is indeed a period of "storm and stress" for some youths—but only some (Offer et al. 1981). We believe that only a minority of adolescents suffer acute growing pains and cause others around them to suffer as well. Most teenagers get along with their parents, although occasionally they disagree and fight. Most work up to their potential in school, with some lapses and flashes of brilliance. Most make a few friends whom they will keep for life, and a few enemies as well. The years between the onset of biological maturity and the achievement of personal and social maturity are not easy ones. But what period of life is free of crisis and problems of adjustment? Is a child's going to school the first time easy? Is turning 40?

Adolescence in Historical Perspective

The experience of being an adolescent reflects historical circumstances. Friendship patterns, family life-styles, and educational opportunities change with the times. Even psychological disorders go in and out of fashion, as with anorexia nervosa and chlorosis. History shapes cultural timetables, establishing appropriate and inappropriate ages to leave school, enter the labor force, set up a home of one's own, get married, and start a family.

Children of the Depression

Depending on the times, one generation's experiences as adolescents may be quite different from those of the following generations. Consider North Americans born in 1920 and those born in 1929 (Elder, 1980). The first of these generations entered the Great Depression as preadolescents. In deprived families—and most families were deprived in the 1930s—girls were old enough to take major responsibility for the household while their mothers worked, and boys were old enough to contribute to the family

income. Many of these boys left high school in the early stages of mobilization for World War II. Service in the military was an opportunity to establish a mature identity without parental interference.

In contrast, most Americans born in 1929 experienced a longer period of family hardship, beginning in their early childhood (the 1930s) and extending into their teens (the 1940s). For two decades they were exposed to the constant emotional strains of downward mobility; fathers who could not fill the role of breadwinner; and overburdened mothers who were preoccupied with maintaining status, if not survival. As adolescents, they watched the war from the home front, with no opportunity to become heroes and often with no father at home. Not all families experienced severe financial and emotional strain during these decades. But these sketches show how the same historical event has different effects on members of adjacent generations.

The Youth Movement of the 1960s and 1970s

Adolescents who came of age in the 1950s (today's 50-year-olds) are often referred to as the "silent generation." Although they had their own styles and rebelled against adults in matters of taste (they invented rock and roll), they were politically silent. Adolescents who came of age in the 1960s and 1970s were anything but silent. Richard Braungart's study of the youth movement of this period (1980) shows how the effects of historical events may be amplified by social and cultural change.

THE POLITICAL CLIMATE Political moods in the United States tend to shift back and forth between periods of liberal reform and periods of conservatism. As shown in Table 15-2, youth movements have been associated with the former. With the election of John F. Kennedy to president in 1960, the pendulum swung left to-

Table 15-2 Temporal Location, Decisive Political Events, and Youth Movements

Temporal Location	Decisive Political Events	Youth Movements
1900–1929	Economic growth and cultural liberalism Industrialization, United States develops favorable balance of trade and becomes world industrial power World War I Isolationism Prohibition Women's suffrage "Roaring Twenties"	Youth culture challenges Victorian social and sexual mores
1930–1940	The Great Depression Poverty Election of FDR—"New Deal" Government economic programs Growth of national socialism in Germany	Youth join antiwar movement, sign Oxford Pledge Campus strikes
1941–1949	World War II Truman administration Atomic bomb Returning GIs Global reconstruction, United Nations	Little youth movement activity
1950–1959	The Cold War–Eisenhower years Growth of "military-industrial complex" Dulles foreign policy Recession McCarthyism 1954 Supreme Court desegregation decision House Un-American Activities Committee	"The silent generation"
1960–1968	Kennedy–Johnson years "New Frontier" Civil rights demonstrations Peace Corps, poverty programs Vietnam escalation Assassinations of Kennedy brothers and Martin Luther King "Great Society" programs Ghetto riots and campus disruption	New Left New Right Civil rights and Black Power Protest demonstrations, strikes, violence
1969–1976	Nixon–Ford years Emphasis on "law and order" Voting Rights Act Vietnam War ends Kissinger foreign policy Inflation, job squeeze Growth of multinational corporations Watergate OPEC and Middle East oil embargo	Women's rights Ecology movement Charismatic religious movements Quiet seventies
1977–1979	Early Carter administration Conciliatory, practical, informal mood in White House Emphasis on government reorganization National energy crisis Inflation, job squeeze continues	"No-Nuke" movement Gay liberation

(Braungart, 1980)

ward government initiatives to reduce poverty and eliminate racial injustice. The students who marched for civil rights, demanded university reform, protested the war in Vietnam, and later supported women's liberation were born in the 1940s. Unlike the so-called silent generation that preceded them, they had not experienced directly either the Depression or World War II. They were the first generation to grow up under the threat of nuclear holocaust. They were also the first generation to become politically aware when the United States was playing the role of superpower.

THE SOCIAL STRUCTURE In the 1960s, the economy in the United States was changing from one based on manufacturing to one centered on service. Many more jobs required advanced education. Between 1946 (the end of World War II) and 1970 (the peak of student activism), the percentage of young people attending college more than doubled, and the absolute number of college students quadrupled (rising from 2 million to almost 8 million). In a sense, this created a "critical mass" on college campuses. The percentage of students who were activists remained small (2 to 5 percent), but their numbers were much larger—and their activities more visible.

CULTURAL CHANGE Youth movements are also associated with periods of cultural change. Polls taken by the American Council on Education, the Carnegie Council, and Yankelovich all showed a steady decline in support for traditional social institutions in the 1960s and early 1970s. More young people approved of sexual freedom. Fewer saw marriage and family as the most important part of life. Fewer subscribed to the work ethic and the ideas that "Hard work pays off," "Competition encourages excellence," and "The boss is always right." Interest in traditional religion declined. So did support for the traditional two-party system: More young people identified themselves as independents.

PERSONALITY FACTORS Countless social scientists attempted to identify the personality traits that distinguished political activists from bystanders in the 1960s and 1970s. Braungart (1980) summarizes their findings as follows. Activists were:

1. spontaneous, impulsive, open to new ideas, and willing—even eager—to take risks
2. strong-willed, assertive, and concerned with dominance and power
3. self-confident and at times self-centered and exhibitionistic
4. idealistic, altruistic, romantic, and nonmaterialistic
5. alienated and distrustful—not because of psychological maladjustment, but because they were shocked by social injustice
6. somewhat more intellectual than non-activists
7. interested in service and creative occupations, rather than such economically motivated and rewarding professions as business, medicine, or law
8. more involved in extra-academic activities (such as social service) than in traditional extracurricular activities (such as sports)

The styles of the conservative 1950s are making a comeback in the conservative 1980s.

A symbol of their times, hippies were romanticized in the press and in early research.

9. majoring in social sciences, humanities, or theoretical sciences
10. the children of parents who were themselves politically liberal and socially conscious.

Perhaps the most surprising finding was that the rebels of the 1960s and 1970s had learned their political values (if not their slogans) at home. Like their parents, they had attained what Kohlberg called the postconventional level of morality. They defined right and wrong in terms of universalistic principles, rather than egocen-

tric (preconventional) perspectives or institutionally supported (conventional) norms.

In many ways, the portrait of student activists that emerged from the first studies was too good to be true: exceptionally bright adolescents from upper-middle-class homes who were practicing the high moral values their parents had preached. Other studies (summarized in Gallatin, 1980) questioned this. Some psychologists found that a disproportionate number of activists were in Kohlberg's primitive, preconventional stage 1—not stage 3. Many students reported conflicts at home and specifically dis-

avowed their parents' political views and life-styles. Some were motivated by hostility toward the police and other authorities, not an idealistic vision of what society should be. Others acted not out of altruistic concern for humankind, but in the egocentric belief that they were destined to innovate and lead. Activists tended to blame their troubles on the Establishment, rather than take responsibility for their own lives. (Theirs was an external locus of control).

Both portraits may be true. Some activists built bombs in their basements and sported machine guns. Others who marched for civil rights and protested the war in Vietnam were pointedly idealistic and nonviolent.

WHY THE 1960S? The question remains why this generation did not accept racial segregation as one of the regrettable facts of life, or the war in Vietnam as an irrevocable government decision. Following Mannheim (1952), Braungart reasons, first, that protest movements usually develop in times when national security and economic growth combine with social and cultural change (due to science and technology, demographics, and so on). Full-scale wars and natural or national catastrophes tend to quell dissent. Second, adolescents are encountering society for the first time. Through formal operations, they are discovering what older generations have come to take for granted. First contact with traditional values and social conditions makes old issues seem new. When contradictions between the value system and real life arise, such as racial discrimination, gender inequality, environmental deterioration, or stockpiling arms, youth take sides.

The adolescent search for identity must be seen against this backdrop. It is no accident that movements for social change attract the segment of the population that is seeking personal integrity.

Middletown Revisited

Where do American youth stand today? Adolescents of the 1980s are neither as numerous nor as politically visible as the preceding generation. As a result, they have not attracted many social researchers. There is one interesting comparative study of yesterday's and today's youth, however.

Over 50 years ago, Robert and Helen Lynd conducted an ethnographic study in the American Midwest. Using the techniques cultural anthropologists use to study preindustrial societies, they set out to compile a portrait of a more or less typical American city. *Middletown* (1929) and *Middletown in Transition* (1937) are classics.

In 1976, Howard Bahr took a research team back to Middletown (a midwestern town) to see what if anything had changed in the intervening years (Bahr, 1980). Middletown III was a study of rich and poor, young and old. Here we will look at Middletown's teenagers, then and now.

Perhaps the most obvious cultural change in Middletown is in what anthropologists call "artifacts." Television, snowmobiles, and Atari did not exist at the time of the Lynds' study. These and many other items are commonplace today. In 1924, two out of three families in Middletown owned a car; today nearly half of all families own two. In 1924, only 12 percent of "business-class" families and 6 percent of working-class

What will tomorrow bring?

families owned a radio. Today every home has at least one television (nearly always a color set), and half of the teenagers surveyed said that they watch four or more hours of TV a day. Clearly, the physical setting of adolescence has changed. In 1924, Middletown was provincial; today it is tuned into a national culture.

The activities of teenage boys in Middletown are not very different from those of boys in 1924; but what girls do with their time has changed. The percentage of boys who work for their spending money, for example, is about the same; the proportion of girls who have jobs has risen from 9 percent to 40 percent. The percentage of boys who said they spent six or seven evenings away from home the preceding week has remained about the same; the proportion of girls who are away from home most nights has doubled.

The sexual revolution has come to Middletown. In the 1920s, the Lynds reported "that God-fearing Middletown is afraid of sex as a force in its midst, afraid it might break loose and run wild . . ." (1937, p. 162). Birth control was highly controversial. Today Middletown has X-rated movie houses and "adult bookstores" similar to those in any other city. The local university has established a birth control information center, and the Planned Parenthood office is crowded with unmarried teenagers.

Some things have not changed, however. Middletown teenagers still endorse many traditional values. Patriotism is as strong today as it was in 1924. When asked if they agreed that the United States is the best country in the world, three out of four teenagers said yes; half ac-

cepted the view, "My country right or wrong." The work ethic also remains strong. Today as in 1924, almost half the teenagers agree that "it is entirely the fault of the man himself if he does not succeed." Now as then, only a third agree with the statement, "The fact that some people have so much more money than others shows that there is an unjust condition in the country which ought to be changed."

Their religious beliefs are much the same as those of their grandparents, although they are more tolerant of people who hold different beliefs. They attend church somewhat more often and more willingly than teenagers did in 1924. And they still quarrel with their parents about what hour they come home at night. Today's teenagers report fewer conflicts with parents about the number of nights they go out and their grades in school, but more arguments about household chores. One of their most common complaints about family life is that they would like to spend more time with their fathers.

Bahr's Middletown III suggests that there has been change in the typical American city. Teenage girls spend more time working and playing away from home, and attitudes towards premarital sex are more tolerant. So are attitudes towards different religions. But these changes are viewed against a background of stability in family values, religious belief, attitudes toward work, and patriotism. Whether these researchers would have obtained the same results in the tumultuous 1960s and 1970s is impossible to say. There may be continuity in Middletown between 1929 and today. Or it may be that the pendulum has swung back and forth.

SUMMARY

1. The development of identity is a social drama, in which the adolescent's peers, family, and school play central roles.

2. Peer groups support experimentation but at the same time demand conformity. Adolescents tend to move from same-sex

cliques, to mixed-sex crowds, to hetero-sexual couples. Girls' friendships develop from sharing activities to sharing secrets; boys' friendships tend to remain action-oriented.

3. Contrary to popular stereotypes, adolescence is a peaceful time for most families. Parent–child conflicts over style, manners, rights, and friends usually peak in early adolescence, then decline. Teenagers tend to overestimate the "generation gap," whereas parents tend to underestimate disagreements.

4. J. S. Coleman found that schools do not override the effects of social class on student achievement, but Rutter found that effective teaching strategies make some difference. From the adolescent's point of view, education is only part of school. Most boys would rather be remembered as sports heroes than as brilliant students, whereas girls want to be remembered as popular and pretty.

5. Rates of delinquency climb during adolescence. Males are much more violent than females (at least after age 14). Chronic delinquents usually established a pattern of antisocial behaviors in childhood. Socialized-subcultural delinquents learn deviant norms and values in their communities; unsocial-ized-psychopathic delinquents appear to have no appreciation of the consequences of their actions, for themselves as well as to others. Both middle- and lower-class delinquents respond to exploitation.

6. Many adolescents use legal and illegal drugs. While smoking tobacco and marijuana have decreased among teenagers, drinking has not. There is no single explanation of drug abuse at this or any other age.

7. A number of psychological problems appear in adolescence: schizophrenia (disordered cognition); depression (an intense feeling of loss); suicide; and eating disorders. Most adolescents cope well with their lives, however.

8. The experience of being an adolescent changes with the times. The Great Depression pushed children born in 1920 into adult roles at early ages but held youngsters born in 1929 in a deprived childhood. The youth movement of the 1960s and 1970s can be traced to a political mood swing and cultural change, as well as to the personality traits of political activists. Each generation of adolescents discovers anew what its elders take for granted. They may accept some of their elders' notions and reject others, as seems to be the case in Middletown today.

FURTHER READING

Bruch, H. (1973). *Eating disorders*. New York: Basic Books. A well-documented sourcebook on obese as well as bulimic and anorexic adolescents.

Elder, G. H., Jr. (1974). *Children of the Great Depression*. Chicago: University of Chicago Press. A classic study of how historical events affect the experience of being an adolescent.

Frank, A. (1981). *The diary of a young girl*. New York: Washington Square Press. The classic wartime diary of a young Jewish girl in hiding from the Nazis: her feelings of being a young woman and of growing up.

Martin, E. C. (1972). Reflections on the early adolescence in school. In J. Kagan & R. Coles (Eds.), *Twelve to sixteen: Early adolescence* (pp. 180–96). New York: Norton. This essay by a teacher provides sensitive insight into the lives of adolescents in schools. The edited volume has many other wonderful essays by a wide range of authors.

**Relations
with peers**

Same-sex
cliques

Heterosexual contacts
through cliques

**Relations
with
parents**

[Confrontations against a backdrop of
mutual acceptance, in most families]

Follow parents' advice on decisions about the future; agree with parents on "big issues"

Follow peers' ideas on current status; agree with peers on matters of style

[Parents see themselves as more influential, and adolescents see
their parents as less influential, than they actually are]

**Social
problems**

Delinquency:

Increases through teen years <18 yrs.>
Males more violent than females (especially after age 14)

Drugs:

Ranges from experimentation (93% have tried alcohol) to regular use
(50% drink every week; 40% have gotten drunk at least once) to abuse
(6% drink every day) [Use of marijuana and tobacco have declined; use
of alcohol has remained steady]

Psychopathology:

Depression takes the form of compulsive activity in early adolescence . . .

Suicide third leading cause of death in adolescence
(after car accidents and murder)

	11	12	13	14

Age in years   Early Adolescence

HIGHLIGHTS OF SOCIAL DEVELOPMENT IN ADOLESCENCE

<   > onset or peak
[   ] qualifications

Mixed-sex crowds   Couples

Schizophrenia most likely to appear in adolescence or early adulthood

. . . lethargy in late adolescence

Eating disorders most common among female, white, upper-middle-class adolescents

15	16	17	18 +

Late Adolescence

 Young Adulthood

ETHICAL STANDARDS FOR RESEARCH WITH CHILDREN

Children as research subjects present ethical problems for the investigator different from those presented by adult subjects. Not only are children often viewed as more vulnerable to stress but, having less knowledge and experience, they are less able to evaluate what participation in research may mean. Consent of the parent for the study of his child, moreover, must be obtained in addition to the child's consent. These are some of the major differences between research with children and research with adults.

1. No matter how young the child, he has rights that supersede the rights of the investigator. The investigator should measure each operation he proposes in terms of the child's rights, and before proceeding he should obtain the approval of a committee of peers. Institutional peer review committees should be established in any setting where children are the subjects of the study.

2. The final responsibility to establish and maintain ethical practices in research remains with the individual investigator. He is also responsible for the ethical practices of collaborators, assistants, students, and employees, all of whom, however, incur parallel obligations.

3. Any deviation from the following principles demands that the investigator seek consultation on the ethical issues in order to protect the rights of the research participants.

4. The investigator should inform the child of all features of the research that may affect his willingness to participate and he should answer the child's questions in terms appropriate to the child's comprehension.

5. The investigator should respect the child's freedom to choose to participate in research or not, as well as to discontinue participation at any time. The greater the power of the investigator with respect to the participant, the greater is the obligation to protect the child's freedom.

From Society for Research in Child Development, "Ethical Standards for Research with Children." In *1982 Directory* (Chicago: Society for Research in Child Development, pp. 257–258).

6. The informed consent of parents or of those who act *in loco parentis* (e.g., teachers, superintendents of institutions) similarly should be obtained, preferably in writing. Informed consent requires that the parent or other responsible adult be told all features of the research that may affect his willingness to allow the child to participate. This information should include the profession and institutional affiliation of the investigator. Not only should the right of the responsible adult to refuse consent be respected, but he should be given the opportunity to refuse without penalty.

7. The informed consent of any person whose interaction with the child is the subject of the study should also be obtained. As with the child and responsible adult, informed consent requires that the person be informed of all features of the research that may affect his willingness to participate; his questions should be answered; and he should be free to choose to participate or not, and to discontinue participation at any time.

8. From the beginning of each research investigation, there should be a clear agreement between the investigator and the research participant that defines the responsibilities of each. The investigator has the obligation to honor all promises and commitments of the agreement.

9. The investigator uses no research operation that may harm the child either physically or psychologically. Psychological harm, to be sure, is difficult to define; nevertheless, its definition remains the responsibility of the investigator. When the investigator is in doubt about the possible harmful effects of the research operations, he seeks consultation from others. When harm seems possible, he is obligated to find other means of obtaining the information or to abandon the research.

10. Although we accept the ethical ideal of full disclosure of information, a particular study may necessitate concealment or deception. Whenever concealment or deception is thought to be essential to the conduct of the study, the investigator should satisfy a committee of his peers that his judgment is correct. If concealment or deception is practiced, adequate

measures should be taken after the study to ensure the participant's understanding of the reasons for the concealment or deception.

11. The investigator should keep in confidence all information obtained about research participants. The participant's identity should be concealed in written and verbal reports of the results, as well as in informal discussions with students and colleagues. When a possibility exists that others may gain access to such information, this possibility, together with the plans for protecting confidentiality, should be explained to the participants as a part of the procedure of obtaining informed consent.

12. To gain access to institutional records, the investigator should obtain permission from responsible individuals or authorities in charge of records. He should preserve the anonymity of the information and extract no information other than that for which permission was obtained. It is the investigator's responsibility to insure that these authorities do, in fact, have the confidence of the subject and that they bear some degree of responsibility in giving such permission.

13. Immediately after the data are collected, the investigator should clarify for the research participant any misconceptions that may have arisen. The investigator also recognizes a duty to report general findings to participants in terms appropriate to their understanding. Where scientific or humane values may justify withholding information, every effort should be made so that withholding the information has no damaging consequences for the participant.

14. Because the investigator's words may carry unintended weight with parents and children, caution should be exercised in reporting results, making evaluative statements, or giving advice.

15. When, in the course of research, information comes to the investigator's attention that may seriously affect the child's well-being, the investigator has a responsibility to discuss the information with those expert in the field in order that the parents may arrange the necessary assistance for their child.

16. When research procedures may result in undesirable consequences for the participant that were previously unforeseen, the investigator should employ appropriate measures to correct these consequences, and should consider redesigning the procedure.

17. The investigator should be mindful of the social, political, and human implications of his research and should be especially careful in the presentation of his findings. This standard, however, in no way denies the investigator the right to pursue any area of research or the right to observe proper standards of scientific reporting.

18. When an experimental treatment under investigation is believed to be of benefit to children, control groups should be offered other beneficial alternative treatments, if available, instead of no treatment.

19. Teachers of courses related to children should demonstrate their concern for the rights of research participants by presenting these ethical standards to their students so that from the outset of training the participants' rights are regarded as important as substantive findings and experimental design.

20. Every investigator has a responsibility to maintain not only his own ethical standards but also those of his colleagues.

21. Editors of journals reporting investigations of children have certain responsibilities to the authors of studies they review: they should provide space where necessary for the investigator to justify his procedures and to report the precautions he has taken. When the procedures seem questionable, editors should ask for such information.

22. The Society and its members have a continuing responsibility to question, amend, and revise these standards.

GLOSSARY

abnormal: May refer to 1. statistically infrequent characteristics or 2. undesirable characteristics, an important distinction. *See also* normal.

accommodation: In Piaget's theory, changing schemes or concepts to take into account new information. *See also* assimilation.

achievement motivation: The desire to succeed at difficult tasks and to avoid failure.

adolescence: The psychological and social changes that accompany puberty in Western societies, where teenagers are seen as being somewhere between childhood and adulthood.

affective role-taking: Putting oneself in another person's position and imagining what he or she is feeling. *See also* cognitive role-taking.

aggression: Intentional, hostile behavior aimed at a person or object and motivated by the desire to inflict physical harm or psychological damage.

alienated achievement: Marcia's term for young people who have gone through a period of decision-making and come to reject the occupational opportunities and ideologies their society offers. This identity status was seen most often during the Vietnam War protest years. *See also* foreclosure, identity achievement, identity diffusion, moratorium.

alienation: The feeling of estrangement from political and social realities, and even from oneself, characteristic of some adolescents who have reached the stage of formal operations. *See also* idealism.

ambivalent attachment: Ainsworth's term describing infants who are not fully attached to their mother. Such infants react to the Strange Situation by sometimes clinging to their mother in fear and sometimes angrily rejecting her approaches. *See also* attachment, avoidant, and secure attachment.

anal period: The stage in Freud's theory of psychological development when children derive pleasure from urination and defecation (about ages 2 to 3). *See also* genital period, latency period, oral period, phallic period.

animism: The belief that inanimate objects have thoughts, feelings, and motives. According to Piaget, this is characteristic of the preoperational thinker.

anorexia nervosa: An eating disorder characterized by extreme, self-induced weight loss, which most often occurs among white, middle-class females in adolescence and early adulthood. *See also* bulimia.

assimilation: In Piaget's theory, the process of taking in experiences by fitting them to already existing schemes or concepts. *See also* accommodation.

attachment: An enduring emotional tie to a specific person.

authoritarian child-rearing: Baumrind's term for parents who use discipline but not warmth, demanding unquestioning obedience from their child. *See also* authoritative child-rearing and permissive child-rearing.

authoritative child-rearing: Baumrind's term for parents who combine discipline with warmth, reasoning with a child whenever possible. *See also* authoritarian child-rearing and permissive child-rearing.

autonomy: Erikson's term for a sense of independence and a readiness to make choices for oneself that develop in the child's second year. The opposite of autonomy is shame and doubt.

avoidant: Ainsworth's term for infants who do not use their mothers as a secure base for exploration in the Strange Situation, may not protest strangers or separation, and ignore the mother on reunion. *See also* ambivalent attachment, attachment, and secure attachment.

basic concepts: Boehm's term for ideas about the location of one thing in relation to others (under, behind, in the middle).

basic trust: Erikson's term for a belief that one's needs will be met by the world; it develops in the first year of life. The opposite of basic trust is mistrust.

brain stem: The lowest section of the brain, near the junction of the head and neck, that controls such functions as heartbeat, digestion, and automatic breathing. This section of the brain appeared earliest in human evolutionary history and is most mature at birth. *See also* midbrain and neocortex.

bulimia: An eating disorder characterized by binges and purges. Occurs most often among white, middle-class females during adolescence and young adulthood. *See also* anorexia nervosa.

canalization: The genetic restriction of development to one, or a few, phenotypic outcomes.

centering: For Piaget, focusing on a single, striking feature of an event or display to the exclusion of other, relevant information. A characteristic of preoperational thinkers.

chromosomes: Long, threadlike strands of genetic material found in the nucleus of every living cell.

classical conditioning: Learning to associate a new stimulus with an existing response. *See also* operant conditioning.

cognition: The mental processes (perceiving, remembering, symbolizing, reasoning, imagining) human beings use to learn about and adapt to their environment.

cognitive role-taking: Putting oneself in another person's position and imagining what he or she is thinking. *See also* affective role-taking.

cohort: People of the same age who are exposed to similar cultural environments and historical events at the same stage of their development.

cohort-sequential study: A study that combines cross-sectional and longitudinal research strategies.

collective monologue: Piaget's term for a conversation in which small children talk at one another but not to one another, each ignoring what the other says.

concept: A generalized idea or notion that applies to many individual cases.

concrete operations: Piaget's term for the ability to think logically about objects and events in the real world, and to discover the relations among them. This is the third stage of cognitive development in Piaget's theory; it begins between ages 7 and 9. *See also* formal operations, preoperational thought, and sensorimotor intelligence.

conditioned response (CR): A response based on a learned association. *See also* unconditioned response.

conservation: The fact that certain properties remain the same (are conserved) even though their shape or physical arrangement has changed. In Piaget's theory, the mastery of conservation is the major achievement of the concrete operational stage.

constructive memory: The idea that memories are not simple recordings, but cognitive re-creations that depend on general knowledge and intellectual skills.

control group: In an experiment, the group of subjects that is not given the treatment whose effects are being studied. *See also* experimental group.

conventional moral reasoning: Kohlberg's second stage of moral development, in which individuals conform to social standards because they want social approval or believe in law and order. *See also* preconventional moral reasoning and postconventional moral reasoning.

correlation: A measure of the strength of the relationship between two variables. If a correlation is positive, the variables tend to occur (or not occur) together; if a correlation is negative, one variable tends to occur when the other does not.

correlation coefficient: A numerical expression of the degree of relationship between two variables, from .00 (no correlation) to ± 1.00 (perfect correlation). This may be expressed as $r =$, or simply as "the correlation. . . ."

creativity: The ability to use familiar materials in unfamiliar but also useful and interesting ways.

criterion-referenced tests: Tests that are scored by comparing the person's performance to an accepted standard in a particular area. *See also* norm-referenced tests.

cross-modal zones: The connections between one area of the brain and others, which permit associations between sights and sounds, sensations and words. These develop between ages 2 and 4.

cross-sectional study: A study of people of different ages at the same point in time. *See also* longitudinal study.

"culture-fair" intelligence tests: Intelligence tests that use nonverbal materials that should be equally familiar or unfamiliar to all people, regardless of their cultural background.

culture: The accumulated knowledge of a people that is passed from one generation to the next through learning.

defense mechanisms: Freud's term for unconscious techniques for dealing with anxiety-provoking conflicts between the id and the superego, between desires and duties.

deferred imitation: Imitation of behavior that one has observed at another time and in another context. For Piaget, it is one of the signs that a child is using mental images.

depression: A sense of inescapable sadness and futility resulting from real or imagined loss or failure.

development: 1. An orderly, cumulative sequence of changes that leads to increasing differentiation, integration, and complexity. 2. In behavioral genetics, the process whereby an individual's genotype comes to be expressed as a phenotype.

difficult: Thomas and Chess' term for infants (and children) who are irregular in body function, negative, and unadaptable. *See also* easy and slow-to-warm-up.

disequilibrium: In Piaget's theory, the times at which a child is unable to assimilate new information into his existing schemes or concepts. *See also* equilibrium.

easy: Thomas and Chess' term for infants (and children) who are regular in body functions, playful, and adaptable. *See also* difficult and slow-to-warm-up.

ecology: The study of the interactions between organisms and their environments.

educable mentally retarded (EMR): Children who may function adequately in their homes but whose performance in school is well behind their peers'; it is sometimes called mild mental retardation and confused with *learning disabled.*

ego: Freud's term for the coping, adapting part of the personality. *See also* id and superego.

egocentrism: The inability to consider another person's point of view. In Piaget's theory this is a cognitive limitation, not a form of selfishness.

elaboration: A memory strategy that entails linking unrelated items in a meaningful order.

embryo: The developing unborn child from 2 weeks to 8 weeks after conception, the period in which different layers of tissue develop specialized functions.

emotions: Feelings that motivate the person and communicate a wide range of nonverbal messages to others.

encephalization: In evolution, an increase in the size of the brain beyond what is necessary to control body functions.

equilibrium: In Piaget's theory, the points at which a child is able to assimilate most of what she encounters into her existing schemes and concepts. *See also* disequilibrium.

ethology: The study of the way animals behave in their natural surroundings.

exosystem: Bronfenbrenner's term for the social structures that have a direct or indirect influence on the growing person's experiences. *See also* macro-, meso-, and microsystems.

experimental group: In an experiment, the group of subjects that is given the treatment whose effects are being studied. *See also* control group.

external locus of control: The belief that external forces beyond your control are responsible for what happens to you. *See also* internal locus of control.

familial retardation: Relatively mild forms of mental limitation whose causes are unknown and which tend to run in families. *See also* organic retardation.

fear of strangers: A baby's wariness of unfamiliar people, beginning at about 8 months and peaking around the first birthday; also called stranger anxiety.

fetus: The developing unborn child from 8 weeks after conception to birth.

5-to-7 shift: White's term for the dramatic cognitive, perceptual, and physical developments that occur at the beginning of middle childhood.

foreclosure: Marcia's term for individuals who accept without question the occupational goals and ideological positions their families chose for them. *See also* identity achievement, identity diffusion, and moratorium.

formal operations: Piaget's term for the ability to think about abstractions, compare what is with what ought to be, generate and test hypotheses, and grasp logical relationships. This is the final stage of cognitive development in

Piaget's theory; it does not develop fully until adolescence, if then. *See also* concrete operations, preoperational thought, and sensorimotor intelligence.

g: Spearman's abbreviation for a general intelligence factor, which he believed was responsible for intelligent behavior in most situations.

gender constancy: Kohlberg's term for the recognition that gender cannot be changed by appearance, activities, or wishes. It is a social application of the principle of conservation.

gender identity: An inner sense of oneself as male or female. *See also* gender role.

gender role: Cultural expectations regarding the different ways males and females ought to behave. *See also* gender identity.

gene: A section of a chromosome that controls a specific aspect of the production of a particular protein.

gene flow: The redistribution of genetic material as a result of intermarriage and the migration of individuals from one population and environment into others.

genital period: The stage in Freud's theory of personality development when the person enjoys mutual sexual gratification with a member of the opposite sex (adulthood). *See also* anal period, latency period, oral period, and phallic period.

genotype: The set of genes an organism inherits from its parents. *See also* phenotype.

goodness of fit: A match between the developing child's temperament and abilities and the environmental opportunities and demands the child encounters.

habituation: A progressive decline in response when a stimulus is presented repeatedly. This simple form of learning is often used in studies of newborns and infants.

heritability ratio: An estimate of how much of the variation in a particular trait (such as height), within a group is due to heredity and how much to the environment.

hostile aggression: Hartup's term for aggression directed toward a person who has threatened the individual's self-esteem. Hostile aggression is person-oriented and usually takes the form of a verbal attack. *See also* instrumental aggression.

id: Freud's term for inborn biological, sexual, and aggressive drives that, he believed, motivated all behavior. *See also* ego and superego.

idealism: The application of abstract logic to political and social realities, characteristic of adolescents who have reached the stage of formal operations. *See also* alienation.

identification: Adopting another person's standards of right and wrong as one's own and striving to be like that person. According to Freud, a child's internalization of parental standards leads to the formation of the superego.

identity: As defined by Erikson, an inner sense of uniqueness and continuity and an outer sociopolitical stance. The opposite of identity is identity diffusion.

identity achievement: Marcia's term for individuals who have gone through a period of decision-making and are committed to an occupation and ideologies they chose for themselves. *See also* foreclosure, identity diffusion, and moratorium.

identity crisis: Erikson's term for the period of self-doubt and alienation, experimentation and exploration, that many adolescents experience during the process of building an identity.

identity diffusion: Erikson's term for individuals who are unable to risk personal and social commitments. (Also used by Marcia.)

identity status: Marcia's term for a position on the continuum from identity achievement to identity diffusion.

idiographic: Explaining individual differences in terms of specific cases. *See also* nomothetic.

imprinting: An attachment formed during an early, critical period that causes the immature animal to follow its mother or a mother figure.

industry: Erikson's term for a sense of competence, and a willingness and eagerness to learn, that develop during middle childhood (ages 6 to 12). The opposite of industry is inferiority.

information processing: 1. A model for studying thought processes based in part on analogies between the human mind and a computer. According to this view, cognitive development involves quantitative as well as qualitative changes. 2. The detailed, step-by-step analysis of cognitive processes by which people acquire, store and retrieve, and use information.

initiative: Erikson's term for a sense of direction and purpose that develops during the third to fifth years of a child's life. The opposite of initiative is guilt.

inner speech: Vygotsky's term for the translation of speech (a social activity) into thought (a private activity); thinking to oneself.

insight learning: 1. Learning based on intuition rather than logical examination of the problem. According to Piaget, this form of thinking is characteristic of the preoperational stage. 2. A solution to a problem found by intuition.

instrumental aggression: Hartup's term for aggression designed to gain or regain a possession, territory, or prestige. Instrumental aggression is object-oriented and usually takes the form of a physical attack. *See also* hostile aggression.

internal locus of control: The belief that you exercise control over what happens to you. *See also* external locus of control.

intimacy: Erikson's term for the ability to form close and lasting relationships that develops in young adulthood. The opposite of intimacy is isolation.

IQ (or intelligence quotient): The ratio of mental age to chronological age. At one time, IQs were calculated by dividing mental age by chronological age and multiplying by 100. Today IQs are based on mean scores for age groups.

knowledge base: A person's mental store of information. The larger someone's knowledge base is, the easier it is for him to learn and remember related information.

latency: The stage in Freud's theory of personality development in which sexual desires are dormant (age 7 or 8 to puberty). *See also* anal period, genital period, oral period, and phallic period.

learning disabled: Term describing a child of normal intelligence (IQ 85 +) who does not learn reading or arithmetic at the normal rate.

libido: Freud's term for sexual energy, which he believed to be the driving force in all human behavior.

longitudinal study: A study of change over time in the same subjects. *See also* cross-sectional study.

macrosystem: Bronfenbrenner's term for the cultural norms and values that people in a society take for granted. *See also* exo-, meso-, and microsystems.

mainstreaming: Integrating handicapped children with normal children in regular classrooms, rather than assigning them to special classes.

mastery motivation: The urge to understand and manage the environment, visible in children from infancy.

mastery standards: Goals a child sets for herself, regardless of adult approval or disapproval. According to Kagan, these develop in the second year. *See also* normative standards.

maturation: Development that occurs because of physiological and neurological growth, not experience and learning.

meiosis: The production of gametes or sex cells (sperm and ova), which have only half the complete set of chromosomes (in humans, 23 pairs).

menarche: A girl's first menstruation.

mental age: A person's ranking on an age-graded scale of intelligence.

memory: A mental record of an object or event.

mesosystem: Bronfenbrenner's term for the groups and settings in which a growing person is involved at different stages of development. *See also* exo-, macro-, and microsystems.

metamemory: Knowing how memory works (mental strategies for remembering, understanding one's capacity, and so on).

microsystem: Bronfenbrenner's term for the immediate environment, including the physical settings and role relationships in which a growing person is involved at the current moment. *See also* exo-, macro-, and mesosystems.

midbrain: The section of the brain that regulates emotions, reflexes, awakeness, the senses, and other involuntary behavior. This section of the brain is almost mature at birth, but does not become adultlike for several months. *See also* brain stem and neocortex.

moratorium: Marcia's term for those who are in the midst of an identity crisis, actively exploring occupational choices and comparing ideologies. *See also* foreclosure, identity achievement, and identity diffusion.

morpheme: A unit of meaning in language. This term may be applied to a word (*cat, think, why*) or to a word fragment that changes meaning (*un-, -ed, -ing*).

"motherese": The use of short, simple, repetitive, attention-getting phrases in talking to small children.

mutation: A random change in the genetic code. These copying errors provide the raw material for natural selection.

myelination: The development of protective sheaths around the nerves that facilitate the transmission of messages to and from the brain. Begins in the second month and continues until the sixth year.

neocortex: The outer layer of the human brain that is associated with language, attention, memory, and spatial understanding. This section of the brain evolved most recently; it continues to develop during the first years of life. *See also* brain stem and midbrain.

nomothetic: Seeking general rules that apply to many or all cases. *See also* idiographic.

norm-referenced tests: Tests that are scored to show the person's rank among age-mates. *See also* criterion-referenced tests.

normal: May refer to 1. statistically frequent characteristics or 2. desirable characteristics, an important distinction. *See also* abnormal.

normative standards: Cognitive representations of what others consider proper and good that evoke an emotional response. According to Kagan, these develop in the second year. *See also* mastery standards.

object concept: Awareness that objects have an independent existence and do not cease to exist when they are out of sight. According to Piaget, this is the major cognitive advance of the sensorimotor period. Sometimes called object permanence.

ontogeny: The development of the individual. *See also* phylogeny.

operant conditioning: Learning to associate behavior with its consequences. *See also* classical conditioning.

operation: Piaget's term for a mental activity that organizes or transforms information.

oral period: The stage in Freud's theory of personality development in which infants derive pleasure from sucking (birth to about age 2). *See also* anal period, genital period, latency period, and phallic period.

organic retardation: Severe mental limitations caused by genetic defects or environmental traumas. *See also* familial retardation.

organization: A memory strategy that entails grouping items according to shared attributes (color, use, and the like).

overextension: A child's tendency to use the name for one object (*doggie*) to refer other objects adults do not consider part of that class (horses, kittens, furry slippers).

perception: The recognition and interpretation of sensory stimuli.

permissive child-rearing: Baumrind's term for parents who use warmth but not discipline, indulging their child and avoiding confrontations over rules. *See also* authoritarian child-rearing and authoritative child-rearing.

phallic period: The stage in Freud's theory of psychological development when children discover that stimulating their genitals is pleasurable (about ages 3 to 7). According to Freud, this is the stage in which boys develop Oedipal conflicts, and girls Electra complexes. *See also* anal period, genital period, latency period, and oral period.

phenotype: An organism's observable characteristics and behavior. *See also* genotype.

phoneme: A unit of sound that indicates a change in meaning.

phonology: The sound patterns of speech.

phylogeny: The evolution of the species. *See also* ontogeny.

placenta: The disc-shaped organ that links the mother's circulatory system to the embryo and, later, to that of the fetus, providing oxygen and nutrients and eliminating wastes.

play: Spontaneous, exaggerated, free-form action for action's sake, which often involves pretense or make-believe.

postconventional moral reasoning: Kohlberg's highest stage of moral development, in which the person is committed to universal ethical principles and believes that behaving morally may require breaking the law. *See also* preconventional moral reasoning and conventional moral reasoning.

pragmatics: The social uses and conventions of language.

precausal thinking: The inability to distinguish between subjective, psychological experience and objective, physical events. According to Piaget, this is a characteristic of preoperational thinkers.

preconventional moral reasoning: Kohlberg's first stage of moral development, in which children obey rules to avoid punishment or to obtain a fair exchange from others. *See also* conventional moral reasoning and postconventional moral reasoning.

preoperational thought: Piaget's term for the ability to use mental images and symbols (especially words), which develops between about ages 2 and 7 and marks the second stage of cognitive development. Piaget did not believe that preoperational thinkers are able yet to perform logical manipulations (or operate) on information. *See also,* concrete operations, formal operations, and sensorimotor intelligence.

primary visual system: According to Bronson, the visual system that is controlled by the neocortex and tells an individual what something is. *See also* second visual system.

primate: A member of the order *Primates,* which includes monkeys, apes, and humans. Primates are distinguished from other mammals by their relatively large brains, flexible arms and five gripping digits, upright or semiupright posture, and keen eyesight but poor sense of smell.

psychometrics: The branch of psychology that is concerned with measuring mental abilities and traits, including intelligence testing.

puberty: The development of reproductive capacity in adolescence, marked by the appearance of secondary sex characteristics, changes in hormone levels, and fertility.

qualitative change: Change that involves reorganization or transformation (as in the metamorphosis of a caterpillar into a butterfly).

quantitative change: Change that involves addition to (or subtraction from), but little reorganization.

reaction range: In behavioral genetics, the range of possible responses to different environmental conditions established by the genotype.

reading disability: A failure to read at a normal age level that is not the result of mental retardation, major brain injury, or severe emotional instability; sometimes called dyslexia or word blindness.

reflex: An automatic, unlearned response to a particular stimulus (such as a sneeze).

rehearsal: A memory strategy that entails repeating material over and over.

reinforcement: Responses that lead an organism to repeat behavior; rewards.

reliability: The extent to which a scientific measure, such as a test, yields consistent results. This may be assessed by giving people the same tests on different occasions (test-retest reliability) or by comparing their scores on odd- and even-numbered questions (split-half reliability). *See also* validity.

replication: The repetition of a study by different researchers, with different subjects, at a different time and place, which yields results that are similar to the original findings.

rites of passage: Public rituals to mark the transition from one socially defined stage of life to another, especially from childhood to adulthood.

sample: The subjects or acts (such as performances on a test) that are chosen to represent a larger class of individuals or behaviors.

scheme: Piaget's term for a sensorimotor action an infant repeats when faced with the same or similar opportunities.

schizophrenia: A form of psychosis, characterized by irrational thought patterns, which may first appear in adolescence.

second visual system: According to Bronson, the visual system that is controlled by the midbrain and tells an individual where something is. *See also* primary visual system.

secular trend: Increases in physical size in Western populations over the last 150 years, due primarily to improved sanitation and nutrition.

secure attachment: Ainsworth's term for infants who use their mother as a base for exploration in the Strange Situation, protest her departure, and welcome her return. *See also* ambivalent attachment, attachment, and avoidant.

semantics: The meaning or content of words and larger speech segments.

sensorimotor intelligence: Piaget's term for the knowledge a child acquires through sensations and motor activities, between birth and age 2. According to Piaget, this is the first stage of cognitive development. *See also* preoperational thought, concrete operations, and formal operations.

separation protest: A baby's distress when a familiar caretaker departs, beginning at about 6 months, peaking around the first birthday, and lasting until about 24 months.

seriation: The ability to arrange things in a logical order (from tallest to shortest, for example). According to Piaget, this ability develops in the concrete operational stage.

sexual dimorphism: Male–female differences in size and appearance.

sign: An expression of an organism's current state or emotion (for example, a smile or clenched fist).

slow-to-warm-up: Thomas and Chess' term for infants and children who tend to withdraw from new people and experiences. *See also* easy and difficult.

social cognition: Thinking about oneself and others.

social competence: The ability to make use of environmental and personal resources "to achieve a good developmental outcome," according to Waters and Sroufe.

social referencing: Using emotional cues from significant others to regulate one's own behavior in uncertain situations.

socialization: The process of learning the values and rules of behavior of the culture in which one is born and will live.

socialized-subcultural delinquents: Youths who have been socialized to a subculture that approves, or does not strongly condemn, certain criminal behavior. *See also* unsocialized-psychopathic delinquents.

Strange Situation: Ainsworth's research procedure for assessing the quality of a child's attachment to the mother or another person.

superego: Freud's term for internalized parental standards of good and evil, or the conscience. *See also* ego and id.

symbol: An image, sound, or gesture that stands for something else.

syntax: The rules for combining and modifying words in meaningful ways.

tabula rasa: Latin for blank slate. John Locke used this term to describe the infant at birth. Locke believed that experience determines whom that infant will become.

temperament: Individual differences in the intensity and duration of emotional responses which influence personality development and social relationships.

transductive reasoning: Piaget's term for reasoning from particular to particular, a characteristic of the preoperational stage. Later the child comes to understand and apply deduction (reasoning from the general to the particular) and induction (reasoning from the particular to the general).

unconditioned response (UR): An automatic or unlearned response. *See also* conditioned response.

unconscious: Thoughts and feelings of which the individual is unaware, even though they influence his or her behavior. (Many consider this Freud's greatest contribution to psychology.)

unsocialized-psychopathic delinquents: Youths who lack feeling for the consequences of their actions, for themselves as well as others; sometimes called sociopaths. *See also* socialized-subcultural delinquents.

validity: The extent to which a scientific measure (such as a test) measures what it claims to measure. *See also* reliability.

verbal mediating response: The use of words to encode information in memory and devise strategies for solving problems. Words mediate, or come between, the stimulus and the response.

zone of proximal development: Vygotsky's term for skills a child has not mastered but can perform with help.

zygote: The new cell formed by the union of a single sperm and an ovum, which will develop into a complete human being.

REFERENCES

Chapter 1

Aries, P. (1962). *Centuries of childhood.* London: Jonathan Cape.

Barker, R. G., & Wright, H. F. (1951). *One boy's day: A specimen record of behavior.* New York: Harper.

Bevington, D. M. (Ed.). (1980). *Complete works of Shakespeare* (3rd ed.). Glenview, IL: Scott, Foresman and Company.

Borstelman, L. J. (1983). Children before psychology: Ideas about children from antiquity to the late 1800s. In P. H. Mussen (Ed.), *Handbook of child psychology* (4th ed.). (Vol. 1, pp. 1–40). New York: Wiley.

Bronfenbrenner, U. (1974). Developmental research, public policy, and the ecology of childhood. *Child Development, 45,* 1–5.

Bronfenbrenner, U. (1977). Ecological factors in human development in retrospect and prospect. In H. McGurk (Ed.), *Ecological factors in human development.* Amsterdam: North-Holland.

Bronfenbrenner, U., & Crouter, A. C. (1983). The evolution of environmental models in developmental research. In P. H. Mussen (Ed.), *Handbook of child psychology* (4th ed.). (Vol. 1, pp. 357–414). New York: Wiley.

Cairns, R. B., & Cairns, B. D. (1983, October 11). *Gender similarities and differences: A developmental perspective.* Paper presented at the Nag's Head Conference, Nag's Head, NC.

Clarke-Stewart, K. A. (1978). And Daddy makes three: The father's impact on mother and young child. *Child Development, 49,* 466–479.

Darwin, C. (1877). A biographical sketch of an infant. *Mind: Quarterly Review of Psychology and Philosophy 2,* 285–294.

Edelman, M. W. (1981). Who is for children? *American Psychologist, 36*(2), 109–116.

Erikson, E. H. (1963). *Childhood and society* (2nd rev. ed.). New York: Norton.

Flavell, J. H. (1982). On cognitive development. *Child Development, 53*(1), 1–10.

Gesell, A. (1928). *Infancy and human growth.* New York: Macmillan.

Hall, G. S. (1904). *Adolescence: Its psychology and its relations to physiology, anthropology, sociology, sex, crime, religion, and education.* New York: Appleton.

Kessen, W. (1965). *The child.* New York: Wiley.

Liebert, R. M., & Barn, R. A. (1972). Some immediate effects of televised violence on children's behavior. *Developmental Psychology, 6,* (3), 469–475.

McGuinness, D. (1985). *When children don't learn: Understanding the biology and psychology of learning disabilities.* New York: Basic Books.

Meehl, P. H. (1972). Second-order relevance. *American Psychologist, 27* (10), 932–940.

Piaget, J. (1965). *The moral judgment of the child.* (M. Gabain, Trans.) New York: Free Press. (First published in 1932; first publication in English, 1935).

Piaget, J. (1963). *Psychology of intelligence.* Paterson, NJ: Littlefield, Adams.

Scarr, S. (1984). *Mother care, other care.* New York: Basic Books.

Scarr, S. (1985). Constructing psychology: Facts and fables for our times. *American Psychologist, 40*(5), 499–512.

Schaie, K. W. (1965). A general model for the study of developmental problems. *Psychological Bulletin, 64,* 92–107.

Sears, R. R. (1975). Your ancients revisited: A history of child development. In M. E. Hetherington (Ed.), *Review of child development research* (Vol. 5, pp. 1–73). Chicago: University of Chicago Press.

Siegel, A. W., & White, S. H. (1982). The child-study movement: Early growth and development of the symbolized child. In H. W. Reese (Ed.), *Advances in child development and behavior* (pp. 234–285). New York: Academic Press.

Semb, G. (Ed.). (1972). *Behavioral analysis and education.* Lawrence, KS: University of Kansas Press.

Skinner, B. F. (1960). Pigeons in a pelican. *American Psychologist, 15*(1), 28–37.

Watson, J. B. (1924). *Behaviorism.* New York: Norton.

Watson, J. B. (1928). *Psychological care of the infant and child.* New York: Norton.

Werner, H. (1948). *Comparative psychology of mental development.* New York: Harper & Row.

White, R. W. (1960). Competence and the psychosexual stages of development. In M. R. Jones (Ed.), *Nebraska symposium on motivation* (pp. 97–141). Lincoln, NE: University of Nebraska Press.

Chapter 2

Beit-Hallahmi, B., & Rabin, A. J. (1977). The kibbutz as a social experiment and as a child-rearing laboratory. *American Psychologist, 32,* 533–541.

Bower, T. G. R. (1979). *Human development.* San Francisco: Freeman.

Bowlby, J. (1969). *Attachment and loss: Vol. 1. Attachment.* New York: Basic Books.

Brim, O. J., Jr., & Kagan, J. (Eds.). (1980). *Constancy and change in human development.* Cambridge, MA: Harvard University Press.

Cadoret, R. (1976). The genetics of affective disorders. In R. G. Grennell & S. Gabay (Eds.), *Biological foundations of psychiatry.* New York: Raven Press.

Clarke, A. M., & Clarke, A. D. (1977). *Early experience: Myth and evidence.* New York: Free Press.

Crowe, R. R. (1972). The adopted offspring of women criminal offenders: A study of their arrest records. *Archives of General Psychiatry, 27,* pp. 600–603.

Darwin, Charles. (1964). *Origin of species: By means of natural selection or the preservation of favoured races in the struggle for life.* New York: New American Library. (Original work published 1859)

Darwin, Charles. (1965). *Expression of the emotions in man and animals.* Chicago, IL: University of Chicago Press. (Original work published 1872)

Dennis, W. (1973). *Children of the crêche.* New York: Appleton-Century-Crofts.

Dobzhansky, T. (1967). On types, genotypes, and the genetic diversity in populations. In J. Spuhler (Ed.), *Genetic diversity in human behavior.* Chicago: Aldine.

Fishbein, H. D. (1976). *Evolution, development, and children's learning.* Pacific Palisades, CA: Goodyear.

Garcia, J., & Koelling, R. A. (1966). Relation of cue to consequence in avoidance learning. *Psychonomic Science, 4,* 123–124.

Ginsburg, B. (1968). Genotypic factors in the ontogeny of behavior. *Science and Psychoanalysis, 12,* 12–17.

Ginsburg, B., & Laughlin, W. (1966). The multiple bases of human adaptability and achievement: A species point of view. *Eugenics Quarterly, 13,* 240–257.

Ginsburg, B., & Laughlin, W. (1971). Race and intelligence, what do we really know? In R. Cancro (Ed.), *Intelligence: Genetic and environmental influences.* New York: Grune & Stratton.

Gottesman, I. (1963). Genetic aspects of intelligent behavior. In N. Ellis (Ed.), *Handbook of mental deficiency.* New York: McGraw-Hill.

Harlow, H. F. (1958). The nature of love. *American Psychologist, 13,* 673–685.

Harlow, H. F., & Suomi, S. J. (1970). The nature of love—simplified. *American Psychologist, 25,* 161–168.

Honzik, M. P. (1957). Developmental studies of parent–child resemblance in intelligence. *Child Development, 28,* 215–228.

Honzik, M. P. (1983). The values and limitations of measurement. In M. Lewis (Ed.), *Origins of intelligence: Infancy and early childhood* (2nd ed.). New York: Plenum, 1983.

Huxley, J. (1965). *Essays of a humanist.* New York: Harper.

Jacob, F., & Monod, J. (1961). Genetic regulatory mechanisms in the synthesis of proteins. *Journal of Molecular Biology, 3,* 318–356.

Lerner, I. M. (1968). *Heredity, evolution, and society.* San Francisco: Freeman.

Martin, R. G., & Aimes, B. N. (1964). Biochemical aspects of genetics. *Annual Review of Biochemistry, 33,* 235–256.

Maurer, D., & Salapatek, P. (1976). Developmental changes in scanning of faces by young infants. *Child Development, 47,* 523–527.

Mayr, E. (1970). *Populations, species, and evolution.* Cambridge, MA: Harvard University Press.

McCall, R. B. (1981). Nature-nurture and the two realms of development: A proposed integration with respect to mental development. *Child Development, 52,* 1–12.

Plomin, R., DeFries, J. C., & Loehlin, J. C. (1977). Genotype-environment interaction and correlation in the analysis of human behavior. *Psychological Bulletin, 84,* 309–322.

Sameroff, A. J. (1983). Developmental systems: Contexts and evolution. In P. H. Mussen (Ed.), *Handbook of child psychology* (4th ed.). (Vol. 1, pp. 237–294). New York: Wiley.

Sameroff, A. J., & Chandler, M. (1975). *Reproductive risk and the continuum of caretaking casualty.* In F. D. Horowitz (Ed.), Review of child development research (Vol. 4, pp. 187–244). Chicago: University of Chicago Press.

Scarr, S., & Kidd, K. K. (1983). Developmental behavioral genetics. In P. H. Mussen (Ed.), *Handbook of child psychology* (4th ed.). (Vol 2, pp. 345–434). New York: Wiley.

Scarr, S., & McCartney, K. (1983). How people make their own environments: A theory of genotype→environment effects. *Child Development, 54,* 424–435.

Scarr, S., & Weinberg, R. A. (1976). IQ test performance of black children adopted by white families. *American Psychologist, 31,* 726–739.

Scarr, S., & Weinberg, R. A. (1983). The Minnesota adoption studies: Malleability and genetic differences. *Child Development, 34,* 260–267.

Scarr-Salapatek, S. (1975). Genetics and the development of intelligence. In F. D. Horowitz (Eds.), *Review of Child Development Research.* (Vol. 4) pp. 1–57. Chicago, IL: University of Chicago Press.

Seligman, M., & Hager, J. (1972). *Biological boundaries of learning.* New York: Meredith.

Skodak, M., & Skeels, H. M. (1949). A final follow-up study of one hundred adopted children. *Journal of Genetic Psychology, 75,* 85–125.

Spitz, R. A. (1945). Hospitalism: An inquiry into the genesis of psychiatric conditions in early childhood. *Psychoanalytic Study of the Child, 1,* 53–74.

Starr, R. H., Dietrich, K. N., Fischhoff, J., Ceresnie, S., & Zweier, D. (1984). The contribution of handicapping conditions to child abuse. *Topics in Early Childhood Special Education, 4*(1), 55–69.

Theissen, D. D. (1972). *Gene organization and behavior.* New York: Random House.

Waddington, C. H. (1957). *The strategy of the genes.* London: Allen & Unwin.

Waddington, C. H. (1966). *Principles of development and differentiation.* New York: Macmillan.

Wohlwill, J. (1973). The concept of experience: S or R? *Human Development, 16,* 90–107.

Chapter 3

Als, H. (1975). The human newborn and his mother, an ethological study of their interaction. Unpublished doctoral dissertation, University of Pennsylvania.

Als, H., Lester, B. M., & Brazelton, T. B. (1979). Dynamics of the behavioral organization of the premature infant: A theoretical perspective. In T. M. Field (Ed.), *Infants born at risk: Behavior and development.* Jamaica, NY: Spectrum.

Anderson, V. E. (1974). Genetics and intelligence. In J. Wortis (Ed.), *Mental retardation (and developmental disabilities): An annual review.* (Vol. 6).

Apgar, V. (1953). A proposal for a new method of evaluation of the newborn infant. *Anesthesia and Analgesia, 32,* 260.

Babson, S. G., Pernoll, M. L., Benda, G. I., & Simpson, K. (1980). *Diagnosis and management of the fetus and neonate at risk: A guide for team care* (4th ed.). St. Louis: Mosby.

Beatty, R. A., & Gluechsohn-Waelsch (1972). *Edinburgh Symposium on the Genetics of the Spermatozoan.* Edinburgh, Scotland, and New York.

Bell, R. Q., & Harper, L. V. (1977). *Child effects on adults.* Hillsdale, NJ: Erlbaum.

Bowlby, J. (1969). *Attachment and loss: Vol. 1. Attachment.* New York: Basic Books.

Bornstein, M. H., Kessen, W., & Weiskopf, S. (1976). Color vision and categorization in young human infants. *Journal of Experimental Psychology: Human Perception and Performance, 2,* 115–129.

Bower, T. G. R. (1974). *Development in infancy.* San Francisco: Freeman.

Brackbill, Y. (1979). Obstetrical medication and infant behavior. In J. D. Osofsky (Ed.), *Handbook of infant development.* New York: Wiley.

Brazelton, T. B. (1969). Behavioral competence of the newborn infant. *Seminars in Perinatology, 3,* 42.

Burns, K. A., Deddish, R. B., Burns, W. J., & Hatcher, R. P. (1983). Use of oscillating waterbeds and rhythmic sounds for premature infant stimulation. *Developmental Psychology, 19*(5), 746–751.

Calhoun, J. A., Grotberg, E. H., & Rackley, W. R. (1980). *The status of children, youth, and families, 1979* (DHHS Publication No. [OHDS] 80-30274). Washington, DC: US Government Printing Office.

Carpenter, G. C., Tecce, J. J., Stechler, G., & Friedman, S. (1968). Differential visual behavior to human and humanoid faces in early infancy. *Merrill-Palmer Quarterly, 14,* 25–46.

Corner, G. W. (1944). *Ourselves unborn.* New Haven: Yale University Press.

Crook, C. K., & Lipsitt, L. P. (1976). Neonatal nutritive sucking: Effects of taste stimulation upon sucking rhythm and heart rate. *Child Development, 47,* 518–522.

Curtis, H. (1975). *Biology* (2nd ed.). New York: Worth.

DeCasper, A., & Fifer, W. (1980). Of human bonding: Newborns prefer their mothers' voices. *Science, 208,* 1174–1176.

DeCasper, A. J., & Sigafoos, D. (1983). The interuterine heartbeat: A potent reinforcer for newborns. *Infant Behavior and Development, 6,* 19–25.

Duchowney, M. S. (1974, August 29). *Interactional influence of infant characteristics and post-partum maternal self-image.* Paper presented at the annual convention of the American Psychological Association, New Orleans.

Edgerton, R. B. (1979). *Mental retardation.* Cambridge, MA: Harvard University Press.

Eimas, P. D., Siqueland, E. R., Jusczyk, P., & Vigorito, J. (1971). Speech perception in early infancy. *Science, 171,* 303–306.

Entwisle, D. R., & Doering, S. G. (1981). *The first birth: A family turning point.* Baltimore, MD: Johns Hopkins University Press.

Fantz, R. L. (1963). Patterns of vision in newborn infants. *Science, 140,* 296–297.

Flanagan, G. L. (1962). *The first nine months* (2nd ed.). New York: Simon & Schuster.

Freire-Maia, N. (1970). Abortions, chromosomal aberrations, and radiation. *Social Biology, 17*(2), 102–106.

Frias, J. L. (1975). Prenatal diagnosis of genetic abnormalities. *Clinical Obstetrics and Gynecology, 18,* 221–236.

Frodi, A. M., Lamb, M. E., Leavitt, L. A., & Donovan, W. L. (1978). Fathers' and mothers' responses to infant smiles and cries. *Infant Behavior and Development, 1,* 187–198.

Goldberg, S. (1982). Some biological aspects of early parent–infant interaction. In S. G. Moore & C. R. Cooper (Eds.), *The young child: Reviews of research* (Vol. 3, pp. 35–56). Washington, DC: National Association for the Education of Young Children.

Ganchrow, J.R., Steiner, J.R., & Daher, M., (1983) Neonatal facial expressions to different qualities and intensities of gustatorial stimuli. *Infant behavior and development, 6,* (No. 2), 189–200.

Green, J. A., & Gustafson, G. E. (in press). Individual recognition of human infants on the basis of cries alone. *Developmental Psychology.*

Gunnar, M., Malone, S., & Fisch, R. (1985). The psychobiology of stress and coping in the human neonate: Studies of adrenocortical activity in response to stress in the first week of life. In T. Fields, P. McCabe, & N. Schneiderman (Eds.), *Stress and coping,* (Vol. 1). Hillsdale, NJ: Erlbaum.

Haith, M. M. (1979). Visual competence in early infancy. In R. Held, H. Leibowitz, & H. L. Teuber (Eds.), *Handbook of sensory physiology.* (Vol. 8). Berlin: Springer-Verlag.

Horowitz, F. D. (1982). The first two years of life: Factors related to thriving. In S. G. Moore & C. R. Cooper (Eds.), *Research on young children.* (Vol. 3, pp. 15–34). Washington, DC: National Association for the Education of Young Children.

Kennell, J. H., Jerauld, R., & Wolfe, H., Chesler, D., Kreger, N. C., McAlpine, W., Steffa, M., & Klaus, M. H. (1974). Maternal behavior one year after early and extended post-partum contact. *Developmental Medicine and Child Neurology, 16,* 172.

Kennell, J. H., & Klaus, M. H. (Eds.). (1976). *Maternal infant bonding.* St. Louis: Mosby.

Klaus, M. H. (1978, March). Invited address to the International Conference on Infant Studies, Providence, RI

Klaus, M. H., Jerauld, R., Kreger, N., McAlpine, W., Steffa, M., & Kennell, J. H. (1972). Maternal attachment: Importance of the first post-partum days. *New England Journal of Medicine, 286,* 460–463.

Kobre, K. R., & Lipsitt, L. P. (1972). A negative contrast effect in newborns. *Journal of Experimental Child Psychology, 14,* 81–91.

Kolata, G. B. (1978). Behavioral teratology: Birth defects of the mind. *Science, 202,* 732–734.

Konner, M. (1982). *The tangled wing: Biological constraints on the human spirit.* New York: Holt, Rinehart & Winston.

Kopp, C. B., & Parmelee, A. H. (1979). Prenatal and perinatal influences on infant behavior. In J. D. Osofsky (Ed.), *Handbook of infant development.* New York: Wiley.

Korner, A. F. (1974). The effect of the infant's state, level of arousal, sex, and ontogenetic stage of the caregiver. In M. Lewis & L. Rosenblum (Eds.), *The effect of the infant on its caregiver.* New York: Wiley.

Lamb, M. E. (1982). Early contact and maternal-infant bonding: One decade later. *Pediatrics, 70,* 763–768.

Lamb, M. E., & Campos, J. L. (1982). *Development in infancy: An introduction.* New York: Random House.

Leboyer, F. (1975). *Birth without violence.* New York: Knopf.

Leiderman, P. H. (1981). The critical period hypothesis revisited: Mother and infant social bonding in the neonatal period. In K. Immelman et al. (Eds.), *Issues in behavioral development: The Bielefeld Interdisciplinary Conference.* Cambridge, Eng.: Cambridge University Press.

Lewis, M., & Goldberg, S. (1969). Perceptual-cognitive development in infancy: A generalized expectancy model as a function of the mother-child interaction. *Merrill-Palmer Quarterly, 15,* 81–100.

Lind, J. (1971). The infant crying. *Proceedings of the Royal Society of Medicine, 64,* 468.

Lipsitt, L. P. (1977). The study of sensory and learning processes of the newborn. Symposium on Neonatal Neurology. *Clinics in Perinatology, 4,* 163–186.

Lloyd-Still, J. D. (1976). Clinical studies on the effect of malnutrition during infancy and subsequent physical and intellectual development. In J. D. Still (Ed.), *Malnutrition and mental development.* Littleton, MA: Publishing Science Group.

Macfarlane, A. (1977). *The psychology of birth.* Cambridge, MA: Harvard University Press.

Macfarlane, A. (1978). What a baby knows. *Human Nature, 1,* 74–81.

Marano, H. (1979, October 29). Breast or bottle: New evidence in an age-old debate. *New York Magazine,* pp. 56–59.

Marquis, D. P. (1931). Can conditioned responses be established in the newborn infant? *Journal of Genetic Psychology, 39,* 479–492.

McAuliffe, K., & McAuliffe, S. (1983, November 6). Keeping up with the genetic revolution. *The New York Times Magazine,* pp. 41–44, 93–97.

Moss, H. A., & Robson, K. S. (1968). Maternal influences in early social visual behavior. *Child Development, 39,* 410–418.

National Natality Survey. (1980).

Needham, J. (with assistance of A. Hughes). (1969). *A history of embryology* (2nd ed.). Cambridge, Eng.: Cambridge University Press.

Otten, A. L. (1984, August 7). Medical efforts to help childless couples pose host of difficult issues. *The Wall Street Journal,* pp. 1, 14.

Parke, R. D. (1981). *Fathers,* Cambridge, MA: Harvard University Press.

Parmelee, A. H., Jr. (1981). Auditory function and neurological maturation in preterm infants. In S. L. Friedman & M. Sigman (Ed.), *Preterm birth and psychological development.* New York: Academic Press.

Ringler, N., Trause, M. A., & Klaus, M. H. (1978). The effects of early post-partum contact and maternal speech patterns on children's IQ, speech, and language comprehension at five. *Child Development, 49,* 862.

Rubin, J. Z., Provenzano, F. J. & Luria, Z. (1974). The eye of the beholder: Parents' views on sex of newborn. *American Journal of Orthopsychiatry, 44,* 512–519.

Saxén, L., & Rapola, J. (1969). *Congenital defects.* New York: Holt.

Scarr, S., & Kidd, K. K. (1983). Developmental behavioral genetics. In P. H. Mussen (Ed.), *Handbook of child psychology* (4th ed.). (Vol. 2, pp. 345–434). New York: Wiley.

Scarr-Salapatek, S., & Williams, M. L. (1973). The effects of early stimulation on low-birth-weight infants. *Child Development, 44,* 94–101.

Schmeck, H. M., Jr. (1983, October 18). Fetal defects discovered early by new method. *The New York Times,* pp. C1, C5.

Schoggen, P. (1963). Environmental forces in the everyday lives of children. In R. G. Barker (Ed.), *The stream of behavior.* New York: Appleton-Century-Crofts.

Smith, R. J. (1978). Agency drags its feet on warning pregnant mothers. *Science, 199,* 748–749.

Sontag, L. W. (1941). The significance of fetal environmental differences. *American Journal of Obstetrics and Gynecology, 42,* 996–1003.

Sontag, L. W. (1944). War and the fetal maternal relationship. *Marriage and Family Living, 6,* 1–5.

Sontag, L. W. (1966). Implications of fetal behavior and environment for adult personalities. *Annals of the New York Academy of Sciences, 134,* 782.

Starr, R. H., Dietrich, K. N., Fischhoff, J., Ceresnie, S., & Zweier, D. (1984). The contribution of handicapping conditions to child abuse. *Topics in Early Childhood Special Education, 4*(1), 55–69.

Steiner, J. E. (1977). Facial expressions of the neonate infant in indicating the hedonics of food-related chemical stimuli. In J. M. Weiffenbach (Ed.), *Taste and development.* Washington, DC: U.S. Department of Health, Education, and Welfare.

Streissguth, A. P., Landesman-Dwyer, S., Martin, J. C., and Smith, D. W. (1980). Teratogenic effects of alcohol in humans and laboratory animals, *Science, 209,* 353–361.

Tanner, J. M. (1974). Variability of growth and maturity in newborn infants. In M. Lewis & L. A. Rosenblum (Eds.), *The effect of the infant on its caregiver* (pp. 77–103). New York: Wiley.

The New York Times News Service. (1981, April 5).

U.S. Department of Health, Education, and Welfare Public Health Service (1979). *Healthy People.* Washington, DC: U.S. Government Printing Office.

Vietze, P. M., Abernathy, S. R., Ashe, M. L., & Faulstich, G. (1978). Contingent interaction between mothers and their developmentally delayed children. In G. P. Sackett (Ed.), *Observing behavior* (Vol. 1). Baltimore, MD: University Park Press.

Wolff, P. H. (1966). The causes, controls, and organization of behavior in the neonate. *Psychological Issues, 5,* 1–105.

Wolff, P. H. (1969). The natural history of crying and other vocalizations in early infancy. In B. M. Foss (Ed.), *Determinants of infant behavior* (Vol. 4, pp. 113–138). London: Methuen.

Chapter 4

Anglin, J. M. (1969). (See Mundy-Castle)

Aronson, E., & Rosenbloom, S. (1971). Space perception in early infancy: Perception within a common auditory-visual space. *Science, 172,* 1161–1163.

Atkinson, R. L., Atkinson, R. C., & Hilgard, E. R. (1983). *Introduction to psychology.* (8th ed.). San Diego: Harcourt Brace Jovanovich.

Banks, M. S., & Salapatek, P. (1983). Infant visual perception. In P. H. Mussen (Ed.), *Handbook of child psychology* (4th ed.). (Vol. 2, pp. 435–571.). New York: Wiley.

Bayley, N. (1969). *Bayley Scales of Infant Development.* Cleveland, OH: Psychological Corporation.

Belsky, J., Steinberg, L. D., & Walker, A. (1982). The ecology of day-care. In M. Lamb (Ed.), *Nontraditional families: Parenting and child development* (pp. 71–160). Hillsdale, NJ: Erlbaum.

Birns, B., & Golden, M. (1972). Prediction of intellectual performance at 3 years from infant tests and personality measures. *Merrill-Palmer Quarterly, 18,* 53–58.

Bower, T. G. R. (1974). *Development in infancy.* San Francisco: Freeman.

Bower, T. G. R., Broughton, J. M., & Moore, M. (1971). Infant responses to approaching objects: An indicator of response to distal variables. *Perception and Psychophysics, 9,* 193–196.

Bringing up superbaby. (1983, March 28). *Newsweek,* pp. 62–68.

Broman, S. H., Nichols, P. L., & Kennedy, W. A. (1975). *Preschool IQ: Prenatal and early developmental correlates.* Hillsdale, NJ: Erlbaum.

Bronson, G. W. (1974). The postnatal growth of visual capacity. *Child Development, 45,* 873–890.

Brooks, J., & Weintraub, M. (1976). A history of infant intelligence testing. In M. Lewis (Ed.), *Origins of intelligence: Infancy and early childhood.* New York: Plenum.

Campos, J., Svejda, M., Bertenthal, B., Benson, N., & Schmid, D. (1981, April). *Self-producing locomotion and wariness of heights: New evidence from training study.* Paper read at the meetings of the Society for Research in Child Development, Boston.

Campos, J. J., Hiatt, S., Ramsay, D., Henderson, C., & Svejda, M. (1978). The emergence of fear on the visual cliff. In M. Lewis & L. Rosenblum (Eds.), *The development of affect.* New York: Plenum.

Charlesworth, W. (1966). Persistence of orienting and attending behavior in infants as a function of stimulus locus uncertainty. *Child Development, 37,* 473–491.

Cicchetti, D., & Sroufe, L. A. (1978). An organizational view of affect: Illustration from the study of Down's syndrome infants. In M. Lewis & L. Rosenblum (Eds.), *The development of affect.* New York: Plenum.

Clarke, A. M., & Clarke, A. D. (1977). *Early experience: Myth and evidence.* New York: Free Press.

Cohen, L. B. (1979, October). Our developing knowledge of infant perception and cognition. *American Psychologist, 34*(10), 894–899.

Cohen, L. J., & Gelber, E. (1975). Infant visual memory. In L. J. Cohen & P. Salapatek (Eds.), *Infant perception: From sensation to cognition* (Vol. 1). New York: Academic Press.

Cravioto, J., & Delicardie, E. (1970). Mental performance in school-age children. *American Journal of Diseases in Children, 120,* 404–410.

Dennis, W., & Najarian, P. (1957). Infant development under environmental handicap. *Psychological Monographs, 71.*

Fagan, J. F. (1984). The intellectual infant: Theoretical implications. *Intelligence, 8,* 1–9.

Fagan, J. F., Fantz, R. L., & Miranda, S. N. (1971). *Infant's attention to novel stimuli as a function of postnatal and conceptual age.* Paper presented at the biennial meeting of the Society for Research on Child Development, Minneapolis, MN

Fantz, R. L. (1961). The origin of form perception. *Scientific American, 204*(5), pp. 66–72.

Fantz, R. L., Fagan, J. F. III, & Miranda, S. B. (1975). Early visual selectivity as a function of pattern variables, previous exposure, age from birth and conception, and expected cognitive deficit. In L. B. Cohen & T. Salapatek (Eds.), *Infant perception: From sensation to cognition. Vol. 1: Basic visual processes.* New York: Academic Press.

Field, T. M., Woodson, R., Greenberg, R., & Cohen, D. (1982, October). Discrimination and imitation of facial expressions by neonates. *Science, 218,* pp. 179–181.

Fischer, K. W. (1980). A theory of cognitive development: The control and construction of hierarchies of skill. *Psychological Review, 87,* 477–531.

Flavell, J. H. (1977). *Cognitive development.* Englewood Cliffs, NJ: Prentice-Hall.

Flavell, J. H. (1985). *Cognitive development* (2nd ed.). Englewood Cliffs, NJ: Prentice-Hall.

Gibson, E. J., & Walk, R. D. (1960). The visual cliff. *Scientific American, 202*(4), pp. 80–92.

Gibson, E. (1969). *Principles of perceptual learning and development.* New York: Appleton-Century-Crofts.

Goldberg, S. (1982). Some biological aspects of early parent–infant interaction. In S. G. Moore & C. R. Cooper (Eds.), *The young child: Reviews of research.* (Vol. 3, pp. 35–56). Washington, DC: National Association for the Education of Young Children.

Golden, M., & Birns, B. (1976). In M. Lewis (Ed.), *Origins of intelligence: Infancy and early childhood.* (pp. 299–351). New York: Plenum.

Goodman, E. (1984, November 11). What's a parent to do? *The New York Times Book Review,* p. 60.

Gratch, G. (1975). Recent studies based on Piaget's view of object concept development. In L. B. Cohen & P. Salapatek (Eds.), *Infant perception: From sensation to cognition* (Vol. 2). New York: Academic Press.

Harris, P. L. (1983). Infant cognition. In P. H. Mussen (Ed.), *Handbook of child psychology* (4th ed.). (Vol. 2, pp. 689–782.). New York: Wiley.

Haviland, J. (1976). Looking smart: The relationship between intelligence and affect in infancy. In M. Lewis (Ed.), *Origins of intelligence: Infancy and early childhood* (pp. 353–377). New York: Plenum.

Hayes, L., & Watson, J. (1979). Neonatal imitation: Fact or artifact? Paper presented at the meeting of the Society for Research in Child Development, San Francisco, March.

Honzik, M. P. (1957). Developmental studies of parent–child resemblance in intelligence. *Child Development, 28,* 215–228.

Honzik, M. P. (1983). The values and limitations of measurement. In M. Lewis (Ed.), *Origins of intelligence: Infancy and early childhood* (2nd ed.). New York: Plenum.

Jacobson, S.W. (1979). Matching behavior in the young infant. *Child Development, 50,* 425–430.

James, W. (1950). *The principles of psychology* (Vol 1). New York: Dover. (Originally published 1890).

Kagan, J. (1984). *The nature of the child.* New York: Basic Books.

Kagan, J., & Klein, R. E. (1973). Cross-cultural perspectives on early development. *American Psychologist, 28,* 947–961.

Kagan, J., & Moss, H. A. (1962). *From birth to maturity.* New York: Wiley.

Lewis, M. (Ed.) (1976). *Origins of intelligence: Infancy and early childhood.* New York: Plenum.

Lipsitt, L. P. (1977). Perinatal indicators and psychophysiological precursors of crib death. In F. D. Horowitz (Ed.), *Early developmental hazards: Predictions and precautions.* Washington, DC: American Association for the Advancement of Science.

Maurer, D., & Salapatek, P. (1976). Developmental changes in scanning of faces by young infants. *Child Development, 47,* 523–527.

McCall, R. B., Kennedy, C. B., & Applebaum, M. I. (1977). Magnitude of discrepancy and the direction of attention in infancy. *Child Development, 48,* 772–785.

McKenzie, B., & Over, R. (1983). Young infants fail to imitate facial and manual gestures. *Infant Behavior and Development, 6,* 85–95.

Meltzoff, A., & Moore, M. K. (1977). Imitation of facial and manual gestures by human neonates. *Science, 198,* 75–78.

Meltzoff, A. N., & Moore, M. K. (1983). Newborn infants imitate adult facial gestures. *Child Development, 54,* 702–709.

Millar, S. (1968). *The psychology of play.* Baltimore: Penguin.

Mundy-Castle, A.C., & Anglin, J. (1969). The development of looking in infancy. Paper read at the meeting of the Society for Research in Child Development, Santa Monica, CA, April.

Nelson, K. E. (1971). Accommodation of visual tracking patterns in human infants to object movement patterns. *Journal of Experimental Child Psychology, 12,* 182–196.

Pick, H. L., Jr., & Pick, A. D. (1970). Sensory and perceptual development. In P. H. Mussen (Ed.), *Carmichael's manual of child development.* (3rd ed.). (Vol. 1). New York: Wiley.

Scarr, S. (1983). An evolutionary perspective on infant intelligence: Species patterns and individual variations. In M. Lewis (Ed.), *Origins of intelligence: Infancy and early childhood* (2nd ed.). New York: Plenum.

Scarr-Salapatek, S. (1976). An evolutionary perspective on infant intelligence. In M. Lewis (Ed.), *Origins of intelligence: Infancy and early childhood* (pp. 165–198). New York: Plenum.

Siegler, R. S., & Richards, D. D. (1982). The development of intelligence. In R. J. Sternberg (Ed.), *Handbook of human intelligence* (pp. 897–971). Cambridge, Eng.: Cambridge University Press.

Skodak, M., & Skeels, H. M. (1949). A final follow-up study of one hundred adopted children. *Journal of Genetic Psychology, 75,* 85–125.

Spelke, E. S. (1978, March). *Perceiving bimodally specified events.* Paper presented at the International Conference on Infant Studies, Providence, RI

Time (1983, August 15). Babies: What do they know? When do they know it? p. 55.

Uzgiris, I. (1976). In M. Lewis (Ed.), *Origins of intelligence: Infancy and early childhood* (pp. 123–163). New York: Plenum.

Wachs, T. D., & Gruen, G. E. (1982). *Early experience and human development.* New York: Plenum Press, 1982.

Werner, E. E., Bierman, J. M., & French, F. E. (1971). *The children of Kauai: A longitudinal study from the prenatal period to age ten.* Honolulu: University Press of Hawaii.

White, B. L., & Castle, P. W. (1964). Visual exploratory behavior following postnatal handling of human infants. *Perceptual Motor Skills, 18,* 497–502.

Yarrow & Pederson (1976). In M. Lewis (Ed.), *Origins of intelligence: Infancy and early childhood* (pp. 379–399). New York: Plenum.

Chapter 5

Ainsworth, M. D. S., Bell, S. M., & Stayton, D. J. (1971). Individual differences in strange-situation behavior of one-year-olds. In H. R. Schaffer (Ed.), *The origins of human social relations.* London: Academic Press.

Ainsworth, M. D. S., Blehar, M., Waters, E., & Wall (1978). *Patterns of attachment.* Hillsdale, NJ: Erlbaum.

Bandura, A. (1969). *Principles of behavior modification.* New York: Holt, Rinehart & Winston.

Bell, S. M., & Ainsworth, M. D. S. (1972). Infant crying and maternal responsiveness. *Child Development, 43,* 1171–1190.

Belsky, J. (1985). Two waves of day-care research: Developmental effects and conditions of quality. In R. Ainslie (Ed.), *The child and the day care setting.* New York: Praeger.

Belsky, J., Steinberg, L. D., & Walker, A. (1982). The ecology of day-care. In M. Lamb (Ed.), *Nontraditional families: Parenting and child development* (pp. 71–160). Hillsdale, NJ: Erlbaum.

Bertenthal, B., Campos, J., & Barrett, K. (1983). Self-produced locomotion: An organizer of emotional, cognitive and social development in infancy. In R.N. Emde & R.J. Harman (Eds.), *Continuities and discontinuities in infant development.* New York: Plenum.

Blehar, M. (1974). Anxious attachment and defensive reactions associated with day care. *Child Development, 45,* 683–692.

Boccia, M., & Campos, J. (1983, April). *Maternal emotional signalling: Its effect on infants' reactions to strangers.* Paper presented to the Society for Research in Child Development, Detroit, MI.

Bowlby, J. (1951). *Maternal care and mental health.* World Health Organization Monograph No. 2. Geneva: World Health Organization.

Bowlby, J. (1969). *Attachment and loss: Vol. 1. Attachment.* New York: Praeger.

Brackbill, Y. (1958). Extinction of smiling response in infants as a function of reinforcement schedule. *Child Development, 29,* 115–124.

Bronfenbrenner, U. (1974). Developmental research, public policy, and the ecology of childhood. *Child Development, 45,* 1–5.

Buss, A. H., & Plomin, R. (1975). *A temperament theory of personality.* New York: Wiley.

Campos, J., Barrett, K. C., Lamb, M. E., Goldsmith, H. H., & Stenberg, C. (1983). Socioemotional development. In P. H. Mussen (Ed.), *Handbook of child development* (Vol. 2). New York: Wiley.

Campos, J. J., Hiatt, S., Ramsay, D., Henderson, C., & Svejda, M. (1978). The emergence of fear on the visual cliff. In M. Lewis & L. Rosenblum (Eds.), *The development of affect.* New York: Plenum.

Caudill, W. A., & Weinstein, H. (1969). Maternal care and infant behavior in Japan and America. *Psychiatry, 32,* 12–43.

Clarke-Stewart, K. A. (1978). And Daddy makes three: The father's impact on mother and young child. *Child Development, 49,* 466–478.

Clarke-Stewart, K. A., & Fein, G. G. (1983). Early childhood programs. In P. H. Mussen (Ed.), *Handbook of child psychology* (4th ed.). (Vol. 2). New York: Wiley.

Cohen, L. J., & Campos, J. J. (1974). Father, mother and stranger as elicitors of attachment behaviors in infancy. *Developmental Psychobiology, 10,* 146–154.

Cohn, J. F., & Tronick, E. Z. (1982). Communicative rules and the sequential structure of infant behavior during normal and depressed interaction. In E. Z. Tronick (Ed.), *The development of human communication and the joint regulation of behavior.* Baltimore, MD: University Park Press.

Darwin, C. (1965). *The expression of emotions in man and animals.* Chicago, IL: University of Chicago Press. (Originally published 1872).

Durrett, M.E., Richards, P., Otaki, M., Pennebaker, J.W., & Nyquist, L. Mother's involvement with infants and her perception of spousal support. *Journal of Marriage and Family,* scheduled February 1986.

Egeland, B. (1979). Preliminary results of a prospective study of the antecedents of child abuse. *International Journal of Child Abuse and Neglect, 3,* 269–278.

Egeland, B., Sroufe, L. A., & Erickson, M. (1983). The developmental consequences of different patterns of maltreatment. *International Journal of Child Abuse and Neglect, 7,* 459–469.

Emde, R. N., & Brown, C. (1978). Adaptation after the birth of a Down's syndrome infant: A study of six cases, illustrating differences in development and the counter-movement between grieving and maternal attachment. *Journal of the Academy of Child Psychiatry, 17,* 299–323.

Emde, R. N., & Harmon, R. J. (1972). Endogenous and exogenous smiling systems in early infancy. *Journal of Personality and Social Psychology, 17,* 124–129.

Ferguson, B. F. (1979). Preparing young children for hospitalization. *Pediatrics, 64,* 656–664.

Field, T. (1978). Interaction behaviors of primary versus secondary caretaker fathers. *Developmental Psychology, 14,* 183–185.

Fraiberg, S. (1974). Blind infants and their mothers: An examination of the sign system. In M. Lewis & L. Rosenblum (Eds.), *The effect of the infant on the caregiver.* New York: Wiley.

Freud, S. (1949). *An outline of psychoanalysis.* New York: Norton. (Originally published 1940).

Goldfarb, W. (1943). Infant rearing and problem behavior. *American Journal of Orthopsychiatry, 13,* 249–265.

Goldsmith, H. H., & Campos, J. J. (1982). Toward a theory of infant temperament. In R. N. Emde & R. J. Harmon (Eds.), *The development of attachment and affiliative systems: Psychological aspects.* New York: Plenum.

Goldsmith, H. H., & Gottesman, I. I. (1981). Origins of variation in behavioral style: A longitudinal study of temperament in young twins. *Child Development, 52,* 99–103.

Gunnarson, L. (1978). *Children in day care and home care in Sweden: A follow-up.* (Bulletin No. 21). Department of Educational Research, University of Gothenburg.

Hebb, D. (1946). On the nature of fear. *Psychological Review, 53,* 259–276.

Hock, E., & Clinger, J. B. (1981). Infant coping behaviors. *Journal of Genetic Psychology, 138,* 231–243.

Izard, C. E. (1971). *The face of emotion.* New York: Appleton-Century-Crofts.

Izard, C. E. (1977). *Human emotions.* New York: Plenum.

Izard, C. E., Huebner, R., Risser, D., McGuinness, G., & Dougherty, L. (1980). The young infant's ability to produce discrete emotion expressions. *Developmental Psychology, 16*, 132–140.

Johnson, W., Emde, R. N., Pannabecker, B., Stenberg, C., & Davis, M. (1982). Maternal perception of infant emotion from birth through 18 months. *Infant Behavior and Development, 5*, 313–322.

Kagan, J. (1974). Discrepancy, temperament and infant distress. In M.L. Lewis & L. Rosenblum (Eds.), *The origins of fear.* New York: Wiley.

Kagan, J. (1981). *The second year: The emergence of self-awareness.* Cambridge, MA: Harvard University Press.

Kagan, J. (1982). *Psychological research on the infant: An evaluative summary.* New York: W. T. Grant Foundation.

Kagan, J. (1984). *The nature of the child.* New York: Basic Books.

Kagan, J., Kearsley, R., & Zelazo, P. (1978). *Infancy: Its place in human development.* Cambridge, MA: Harvard University Press.

Kagan, J., & Moss, H. A. (1962). *From birth to maturity.* New York: Wiley

Kagan, J., Reznick, R. J., Clarke, C., Snidman, N., & Garcia-Coll, C. (1984). Behavioral inhibition to the unfamiliar. *Child Development, 55*, 2212–2225.

Korn, S. J. (1978, September). *Temperament, vulnerability, and behavior.* Paper presented at the Louisville Temperament Conference, Louisville, Kentucky.

Lamb, M. E. (1977). Father–infant and mother–infant interaction in the first year of life. *Child Development, 48*, 167–181.

Lamb, M. E. (1978). Interaction between 18-month-olds and their preschool-aged siblings. *Child Development, 49*, 51–59.

Lamb, M. E. (1979). Separation and reunion behaviors as criteria of attachment to mothers and fathers. *Early Human Development, 3/4*, 329–339.

Lamb, M. E., & Campos, J. L. (1982). *Development in infancy: An introduction.* New York: Random House.

Lewis, M., & Starr, M. (1979). Developmental continuity. In J. Osofsky (Ed.), *Handbook of infant development.* New York: Wiley.

Lewis, M., & Brooks, J. (1978). Self-knowledge and emotional development. In M. Lewis and L. A. Rosenblum (Eds.), *The development of affect.* New York: Plenum.

Lorenz, K. (1970). Companions as factors in the bird's development. In K. Lorenz (Ed.), *Studies in animal and human behavior*, Vol. 1. Cambridge, MA: Harvard University Press. (Originally published 1935)

Maccoby, E. E. (1980). *Social development: Psychological growth and the parent–child relationship.* New York: Harcourt Brace Jovanovich.

Mahler, M., Pine, F., & Bergman, A. (1975). *The psychological birth of the human infant.* New York: Basic Books.

Matas, L., Arend, R. A., & Sroufe, L. A. (1978). Continuity of adaptation in the second year: The relationship between quality of attachment and later competence. *Child Development, 49*, 547–556.

McCartney, K., & Scarr, S. (in press). Day care as intervention. *Journal of Applied Developmental Psychology.*

Mehler, J., Bertoncini, J., Barrière, M., & Jassick-Gerschenfeld, D. (1978). Infant recognition of mother's voice. *Perception, 7*, 491–497.

O'Connell, J. C., & Farran, D. C. (1982). Effects of day care experience on the use of intentional communicative behaviors in a sample of socioeconomically depressed infants. *Developmental Psychology, 18*, 22–29.

Parke, R. D. (1981). *Fathers.* Cambridge, MA: Harvard University Press.

Parke, R. D., & Sawin, D. B. (1980). The family in early infancy: Social interaction and attitudinal analyses. In F. A. Pederson (Ed.), *The father–infant relationship: Observational studies in a family context.* New York: Praeger.

Ramey, C., Dorval, B., & Baker-Ward, L. (1981). Group day care and socially disadvantaged families. Effects on the child and the family. In S. Kilmer (Ed.), *Advances in early education and day care.* Greenwich, CT: JAI Press.

Rothbart, M. J., & Derryberry, D. (1981). Development of individual differences in temperament. In M. E. Lamb and A. L. Brown (Eds.), *Advances in developmental psychology* (Vol. 1, pp. 37–86). Hillsdale, NJ: Erlbaum.

Roupp, R., & Travers, J. (1982). Janus faces day care: Perspectives on quality and cost. In E. Zigler & E. W. Gordon (Eds.), *Day care: Scientific and social issues.* Boston: Auburn House.

Rutter, M. (1981). *Maternal deprivation reassessed* (2nd ed.). New York: Penguin.

Sagi, A., & Hoffman, M. (1967). Empathetic distress in the newborn. *Developmental Psychology, 12*, 175–176.

Scarr, S., & Salapatek, P. (1970). Patterns of fear development in infancy. *Merrill-Palmer Quarterly, 16*(1), 53–90.

Schwarz, C. S. (1983, April). Infant day care: Effects at 2, 4 and 8 years. Paper presented as part of symposium at the meeting of the Society for Research on Child Development, Detroit. Abstract published by ERIC Clearinghouse on Elementary and Early Education, #PS013805.

Schwarz, J. C., Scarr, S., & McCartney, K. (1983). *Center, sitter, and home care before age two: A report on the first Bermuda infant care study.* Paper presented at the annual meeting of the American Psychological Association, Los Angeles, CA.

Simner, N. (1971). Newborn's response to the cry of another infant. *Developmental Psychology, 5*, 136–150.

Sorce, J., Emde, R. N., Campos, J. J., & Klinnert, M. (1981). *Maternal emotional signaling: Its effect on visual cliff behavior of one-year-olds.* Paper presented to the Society for Research on Child Development biannual meeting, Boston.

Sroufe, L. A., & Waters, E. (1976). The ontogenesis of smiling and laughter: A perspective on the organization of development in infancy. *Psychological Review, 38*, 173–189.

Sroufe, L. A., Waters, E., & Matas, L. (1974). Contextual determinants of infant affective response. In M. Lewis & L. Rosenblum (Eds.), *The emergence of fear.* New York: Wiley.

Starr, R. H., Dietrich, K. N., Fischoff, J., Ceresnie, S., & Zweier, D. (1984). The contribution of handicapping conditions to child abuse. *Topics in Early Childhood Special Education, 4*(1), 59–69.

Stern, D. (1977). *The first relationship: Infant and mother.* Cambridge, MA: Harvard University Press.

Thomas, A., & Chess, S. (1977). *Temperament and development.* New York: Brunner-Mazel.

Thomas, A., Chess, S., & Birch, H. G. (1970). The origin of personality. *Scientific American, 223,* 102–109.

Thomas, A., Chess, S., Birch, H. G., Hertzig, M. E., & Korn, S. (1963). *Behavioral individuality in early childhood.* New York: New York University Press.

Thompson, R. A., Lamb, M. E., & Estes, D. (1982). Stability of infant-mother attachment and its relationship to changing life circumstances in an unselected middle-class sample. *Child Development, 53,* 144–148.

Tizard, B., & Hodges, J. (1978). The effect of early institutional rearing on the development of eight-year-old children. *Journal of Child Psychology and Psychiatry, 19,* 98–118.

Trotter, R. J. (1983). Baby face. *Psychology Today, 17*(8), pp. 14–20.

Wachs, T. D., & Gruen, G. E. (1982). *Early experience and human development.* New York: Plenum.

Waters, E., Matas, L., & Sroufe, L. A. (1975). Infants' reactions to an approaching stranger: Description, validation, and functional significance of wariness. *Child Development, 46,* 348–356.

Waters, E., Wippman, J., & Sroufe, L. A. (1979). Attachment, positive effect, and competence in the peer group: Two studies in construct. *Child development, 50,* 821–829.

Watson, J. (1930). *Behaviorism.* Chicago: University of Chicago Press.

Watson, J., & Raynor, R. (1920). Conditioned emotional reactions. *Journal of Experimental Psychology, 3,* 1–14.

Wolff, P. H. (1969). The natural history of crying and other vocalizations in early infancy. In B. M. Foss (Ed.), *Determinants of infant behavior.* (Vol. 4, pp. 81–109). London: Methuen.

Yarrow, L., & Goodwin, M. (1973). The immediate impact of separation: Reactions of infants to changes in mother figures. In L. J. Stone, H. J. Smith, & L. B. Murphy (Eds.), *The competent infant.* New York: Basic Books.

Yogman, M. W., Doxin, S., Tronick, E., Als, H., Adamson, L., Lester, B., & Brazelton, T. B. (1977, March). *The goals and structure of face-to-face interaction between infants and fathers.* Paper presented to the biannual meeting of the Society for Research in Child Development, New Orleans.

Chapter 6

Ball, S., & Bogatz, C. (1972). A summative research of "Sesame Street": Implications for the study of preschool children. In A. Pick (Ed.), *Minnesota symposium on child development* (Vol. 6). Minneapolis: University of Minnesota Press.

Benjamin, L. T., Jr., Langley, J. F., & Hall, R. J. (1979, December). Santa now and then. *Psychology Today,* pp. 36–44.

Black, J. K. (1981, September). Are young children really egocentric? *Young Children,* 51–55.

Bloom, J. B. (1984). *Stability and change in human characteristics.* New York: Wiley.

Boehm, A. E. (1983). Assessment of basic concepts. In K. D. Paget & B. A. Bracken (Eds.), *The psychoeducational assessment of preschool children.* New York: Grune & Stratton.

Briar, D., & Siegler, R. S. (1984). A featural analysis of preschoolers' counting knowledge. *Developmental Psychology, 20*(4), 607–618.

Bronfenbrenner, U. (1974). A report on longitudinal evaluations of preschool programs. Vol. 2. *Is early intervention effective?* (HEW Publication No. [OHD] 74–24). Washington, DC: Office of Child Development.

Brown, A. L., Bransford, J. D., Ferrara, R. A., & Campione, J. C. (1983). Learning, remembering, and understanding. In P. H Mussen (Ed.), *Handbook of child psychology* (4th ed.). (Vol. 3, pp. 77–166). New York: Wiley.

Bruner, J. S. (1972). The nature and uses of immaturity. *American Psychologist, 27,* 687–708.

Carey, S. (1978). The child as a word learner. In M. Halle, J. Bresnan, & G. A. Miller (Eds.), *Linguistic theory and psychological reality.* Cambridge, MA: Massachusetts Institute of Technology Press.

Case, R. (1978). A neo-Piagetian interpretation. In R. Siegler (Ed.), *Children's thinking: What develops?* Hillsdale, NJ: Erlbaum.

Case, R., Kurlind, D. M., & Goldberg, J. (1982). Operational efficiency and the growth of short-term memory span. *Journal of Experimental Child Psychology, 33*(3), 386–404.

Cicirelli, V. (1969, June). *The impact of Head Start: An evaluation of Head Start on children's cognitive and affective development.* Report presented to the Office of Economic Opportunity (OEO Report No. PB 184 328). Westinghouse Learning Corporation for Federal and Scientific and Technical Information. U.S. Institute for Applied Technology.

Collins, R. C. (1983, Summer). Head Start: An update of program effects. *Society for Research on Child Development Newsletter,* pp. 1–2.

Dansky, J. L. (1980). Make believe: A mediator of the relationship between play and associative fluency. *Child Development, 51,* 576–579.

Day, M. (1978). Drawing: The child's own symbol system. *Lyceum, 2*(1), 9–13.

De Vries, R. (1969). Constancy of generic identity in the years three to six. *Monographs of the Society for Research in Child Development, 34*(3) (Serial no. 127), 8.

Eichorn, D. H. (1970). Physiological development. In P. H. Mussen (Ed.), *Carmichael's manual of child development* (3rd ed.). (Vol. 1, pp. 157–283). New York: Wiley.

Elkind, D. (1981). *The hurried child: Growing up too fast too soon.* Reading, MA: Addison-Wesley.

Feitelson, D. (1977). Cross-cultural studies of representational play. In B. Tizard & D. Harvey (Eds.), *Biology of play* (pp. 6–14). London: William Heinemann Medical Books.

Fishbein, H. D. (1976). *Evolution, development, and children's learning.* Pacific Palisades, CA: Goodyear.

Fishbein, H. D. (1984). *The psychology of infancy and childhood: Evolutionary and cross-cultural perspectives.* Hillsdale, NJ: Erlbaum.

Flavell, J. H. (1971). Comments on Beilin's paper. In D. R. Green, M. P. Ford, & G. B. Flanner (Eds.), *Measurement and Piaget* (pp. 189–91). New York: McGraw-Hill.

Flavell, J. H. (1977). *Cognitive development.* Englewood Cliffs, NJ: Prentice-Hall.

Flavell, J. H. (1979). Metacognition and cognitive monitoring: A new area of cognitive-development inquiry. *American Psychologist, 34*(10), 906–911.

Flavell, J. H. (1982). On cognitive development. *Child Development, 53,* 1–10.

Flavell, J. H., Flavell, E. R., & Green, F. L. (1983). Development of the appearance-reality distinction. *Cognitive Psychology, 15,* 95–120.

Flavell, J. H. (1985). *Cognitive development* (2nd ed.). Englewood Cliffs, NJ: Prentice-Hall.

Flavell, J. H., Shipstead, S. G., & Croft, K. (1978). Young children's knowledge about visual perception: Hiding objects from others. *Child Development, 49,* 1208–1211.

Flavell, J. H., & Wellman, H. M. (1977). Metamemory. In R. V. Kail, Jr., & J. W. Hagen (Eds.), *Perspectives on the cognitive development of memory and cognition* (pp. 3–33). Hilldale, NJ: Erlbaum.

Flavell, J. H., Xiao-Dong Zhang, Hong Zuo, Qi Dong, & Sen Qi (1983b). A comparison between the appearance-reality distinction in the People's Republic of China and the United States. *Cognitive Psychology, 15,* 459–466.

Freud, A. (1965). *Feelings and learning.* M. Rasmussen (Ed.). Washington, DC: Association for Childhood Education International.

Gardner, H. (1973). *The arts and human development.* New York: Wiley.

Gardner, H. (1980). *Artful scribbles: The significance of children's drawings.* New York: Basic Books.

Garvey, C. (1977). *Play.* Cambridge, MA: Harvard University Press.

Gelman, R. (1978). Cognitive development. In M. R. Rosenzweig & L. W. Porter (Eds.), *Annual Review of Psychology, 29,* 297–332.

Gelman, R. (1979). Preschool thought. *American Psychologist, 34*(10), 900–905.

Gelman, R., & Gallistel, C. R. (1978). *The child's understanding of number.* Cambridge, MA: Harvard University Press.

Gelman, R., & Shatz, M. (1977). Appropriate speech adjustments: The operation fo conversational constraints on talk in two-year olds. In M. Lewis & L. A. Rosenblum (Eds.), *Interaction, conversation, and the development of language.* New York: Wiley.

Gesell, A., Ilg, F. L. & Ames, L. B. (1974). *Infant and child in the culture of today.* New York: Harper & Row.

Gibson, E. J. (1969). *Principles of perceptual learning and development.* New York: Appleton-Century-Crofts.

Gibson, E. J., & Spelke, E. S. (1983). The development of perception. In P. H. Mussen (Ed.), *Handbook of child psychology* (4th ed.). (Vol. 3, pp. 1–76). New York: Wiley.

Goldhaber, D. (1979). Does the changing view of early experience imply a changing view of early development? In L. G. Katz (Ed.), *Current topics in early childhood education,* (Vol. 2, pp. 117–140). Norwood, NJ: Ablex.

Hawkins, J., Pea, R. D., Glick, J., & Scribner, S. (1984). "Merds that laugh don't like mushrooms": Evidence for deductive reasoning by preschoolers. *Developmental Psychology, 20*(4), 584–594.

Henderson, B., & Moore, S. G. (1979). Measuring exploratory behavior in young children: A factor-analysis study. *Developmental Psychology, 15*(2), 113–119.

Honig, A. S. (1983, May). Television and young children. *Young Children,* pp. 63–76.

Hughes, M. (1975). Egocentrism in preschool children. Unpublished doctoral dissertation, Edinburgh University.

Hunt, J. McV. (1961). *Intelligence and experience.* New York: Ronald Press.

Hutt, C. (1976). Temporal effects on response decrement and stimulus satiation in exploration. *British Journal of Psychology, 58,* 365–373.

Jensen, A. R. (1969). How much can we boost IQ and scholastic achievement? *Harvard Educational Review, 39,* 1–123.

Kellogg, R. (1967). *The psychology of children's art.* New York: CRM/Random House.

Klahr, D., & Wallace, J. G. (1976). *Cognitive development: An information processing view.* Hillsdale, NJ: Erlbaum.

Kohn, M. L. (1976). Social class and parental values: Another confirmation of the relationship. *American Sociological Review, 41,* 538–545.

Laurendeau, M., & Pinard, A. (1962). *Causal thinking in the child: A genetic and experimental approach.* New York: International Universities Press.

Lazar, I., & Darlington, R. (1982). Lasting effects of early education: A report from the Consortium for Longitudinal Studies. *Monographs of the Society for Research in Child Development, 47*(2–3).

Lester, B. M., & Klein, R. E. (1973). The effect of stimulus familiarity on the conservation performance of rural Guatemalan children. *Journal of Social Psychology, 90,* 197–205.

Listen! the children speak: Anecdotes with interpretations. (1979). Washington, DC: United States National Committee, World Organization for Early Childhood Education.

Lorenz, K. (1956). Plays and vacuum activities. In M. Autuori et al. *L'instinct dous le compartement des animaux et de l'homme.* Paris: Masson.

Lorenz, K. (1966). *On aggression.* New York: Harcourt, Brace & World.

Mandler, J. M. (1983). Representation. In P. H. Mussen (Ed.), *Handbook of child psychology* (4th ed.). (Vol. 3, pp. 420–494). New York: Wiley.

Miller, S. N. (1973). Ends, means, and galumphing: Some leitmotifs of play. *American Anthropologist, 75,* 87–98.

Moore, S. G. (1977, November). Old and new approaches to preschool education. *Young Children, 33,* 69–72.

Nelson, K. (1978). Semantic development and the development of memory. In K. E. Nelson (Ed.), *Children's language* (Vol. 1, pp. 39–80). New York: Garden Press.

Norman, D. A. (1969). *Memory and attention.* New York: Wiley.

Perlmutter, M., (Ed.). (1980). *Children's memory: New directions for child development.* San Francisco: Jossey-Bass.

Phillips, J. (1969). *The origins of intellect: Piaget's theory.* San Francisco: Freeman.

Piaget, J. (1960). *The child's conception of physical causality.* Totowa: NJ: Littlefield, Adams.

Piaget, J. (1962). *Play, dreams, and imitation in childhood.* New York: Norton.

Piaget, J., & Inhelder, I. (1963). *The child's conception of space.* F. J. Langdon & J. L. Lunzer (Trans.). London: Routledge and Kegan Paul.

Pick, A. D., Frankel, D. G., & Hess, V. L. (1975). Children's attention: The development of selectivity. In E. M. Hetherington (Ed.), *Review of child development research* (Vol. 5, pp. 325–383). Chicago: University of Chicago Press.

Pulaski, M. A. S. (1971). *Understanding Piaget.* New York: Harper & Row.

Richards, D. D., & Siegler, R. S. (1984). The effects of task requirements on children's life judgments. *Child Development, 55,* 1687–1696.

Rohwer, W. D. (1971). Prime time for early education: Early childhood and adolescence. *Harvard Educational Review, 41,* 316–342.

Rubin, K. H. (1980). Fantasy play: Its role in the development of social skills and social cognition. In K. H. Rubin (Ed.), *Children's play.* San Francisco: Jossey-Bass.

Rubin, K. H., Fein, G. G., & Vandenberg, B. (1963). Play. In P. H. Mussen (Ed.), *Handbook of child psychology* (4th ed.). (Vol. 4, pp. 693–774). New York: Wiley.

Schweinhart, L. J., & Weikart, D. P. (1980). *Young children grow up: The effects of the Perry Preschool Program on youths through age 15.* Monograph No. 3. Ypsilanti, MI: High-Scope Educational Research Foundation.

Shatz, M. (1973). *Preschoolers' ability to take account of others in a toy selection task.* Master's thesis. University of Pennsylvania, Philadelphia.

Siegler, R. S. (1983). Information processing approach to development. In P. H. Mussen (Ed.), *Handbook of child psychology* (4th ed.). (Vol. 1, pp. 129–212). New York: Wiley.

Sprigle, H. A. (1972, December). Who wants to live on Sesame Street? *Young Children, 28,* 91–109.

Sylva, K. (1977). Play and learning. In B. Tizard & D. Harvey (Eds.), *Biology of play.* London: Heinemann.

Thomas, S. B., & Bowermaster, J. (1974). *The continuity of educational development.* (ERIC Document No. PS007 571).

Todd, C. M., & Perlmutter, M. (1980). Reality recalled by preschool children. In M. Perlmutter (Ed.), *New directions in child development,* No. 10. *Children's memory* (pp. 69–85). San Francisco: Jossey-Bass.

Vandenberg, B. (1978, August). Play and development from an ethological perspective. *American Psychologist, 33*(8), 724–738.

Vurpillot, E. (1968). The development of scanning strategies and their relation to visual differentiation. *Journal of Experimental Child Psychology, 6,* 622–650.

Vygotsky, L. (1978). *Mind in society.* Cambridge, MA: Harvard University Press.

Weinberg, R. A. (1979, October). Early childhood education and intervention: Establishing an American tradition. *American Psychologist, 34,* 912–916.

Weisler, A., & McCall, R. (1976). Exploration and play. *American Psychologist, 31,* 492–508.

White, R. W. (1959). Motivation reconsidered: The concept of competence. *Psychological Review, 66,* 297–323.

White, S. H., Pillemer, D. B. (1979). Childhood amnesia and the development of a socially accessible memory system. In J. F. Kihlertrom & F. J. Evans (Eds.), *Functional disorders of memory* (pp. 29–73). Hillsdale, NJ: Erlbaum.

Wolff, M., & Stein, A. (1966). *Factors influencing the recruitment of children into the Head Start program, summer, 1965: A case study of six centers in New York City (Study 2).* New York: Yeshiva University.

Wright, J. C., & Vlietstra, A. G. (1975). The development of selective attention: From perceptual exploration to logical search. In H. W. Reese (Ed.), *Advances in child development* (Vol. 10, pp. 195–239). New York: Academic Press.

Zigler, E., & Berman, W. (1983, August). Discerning the future of early intervention. *American Psychologist, 38,* 894–906.

Chapter 7

Bard, B., & Sachs, J. (1977). *Language acquisition patterns in two normal children of deaf parents.* Paper presented to the 2nd Annual Boston University Conference on Language Acquisition, Boston, MA.

Bates, E. (1979a). *Emergence of symbols: Cognition and communication in infancy.* New York: Academic Press.

Bates, E. (1979b). The emergence of symbols: Ontogeny and phylogeny. In W. A. Collins (Ed.), *Children's language and communication.* The Minnesota Symposium on Child Psychology. Hillsdale, NJ: Erlbaum.

Bellugi, U. (1970). Learning and language. *Psychology Today, 4,* pp. 32–35, 66.

Bever, T. G. (1970). The cognitive bases for linguistic structures. In J. R. Hayes (Ed.), *Cognition and the development of language* (pp. 279–362). New York: Wiley.

Bowerman, M. (1976). Semantic factors in the acquisition of rules for word use and sentence construction. In D. M. Moorehead & A. E. Morehead (Eds.), *Normal and deficient child language* (pp. 99–179). Baltimore, MD: University Park Press.

Brown, R. W. (1958). *Words and things*. New York: Free Press.

Brown, R. W. (1973). *A first language: The early stages*. Cambridge, MA: Harvard University Press.

Brown, R. W., & Hanlon, C. (1970). Derivational complexity and order of acquisition in child speech. In J. R. Hayes (Ed.), *Cognition and the development of language*. New York: Wiley.

Butterfield, E.C., & Siperstein, G.N. (1974). Influence of contingent auditory stimulation upon non-nutritional suckle. In *Proceedings of the Third Symposium on Oral Sensation and Perception: The Mouth of the Infant*. Springfield, IL: Thomas.

Carey, S. (1978). The child as a word learner. In M. Halle, J. Bresnan, & G. Miller (Eds.), *Linguistic theory and psychological reality* (pp. 264–293). Cambridge, MA: Massachusetts Institute of Technology Press.

Chomsky, C. (1965). *Aspects of the theory of syntax*. Cambridge, MA: Massachusetts Institute of Technology Press.

Chomsky, C. (1965). *The acquisition of syntax in children from 5 to 10*. Cambridge, MA: Massachusetts Institute of Technology Press.

Clark, E. V. (1973). What's in a word? On the child's acquisition of semantics in his first language. In T. E. Moore (Ed.), *Cognitive development and the acquisition of language* (pp. 65–110). New York: Academic Press.

Clark, E. V. (1983). Meanings and concepts. In P. H. Mussen (Ed.), *Handbook of child psychology* (4th ed.). (Vol. 3, pp. 787–840). New York: Wiley.

Clark, E. V. & Hecht, B. F. (1983). Comprehension, production, and language acquisition. *Annual Review of Psychology, 34*, 325–149.

Clark, H. H., & Clark, E. V. (1977). *Psychology and language: An introduction to psycholinguistics*. New York: Harcourt Brace Jovanovich.

DeCasper, A., & Fifer, W. (1980). Of human bonding: Newborns prefer their mothers' voices. *Science, 208*, 1174–1176.

de Villiers, P. A., & de Villiers, J. G. (1979). *Early language*. Cambridge, MA: Harvard University Press.

Doyle, A. B., Champagne, M., & Segalowitz, N. (1978). Some issues on the assessment of linguistic consequences of early bilingualism. In M. Paradis (Ed.), *Aspects of bilingualism*. Columbia, SC: Hornbeam Press.

Eimas, P.D. (1985). The perception of speech in early infancy. *Scientific American, 252*, pp. 46–52.

Eimas, P. D., & Tartter, V. C. (1979). On the development of speech perception: Mechanisms and analogies. In H. W. Reese & L. P. Kipsitt (Ed.), *Advances in child development and behavior* (Vol. 13, pp. 155–193). New York: Academic Press.

Ervin-Tripp, S. (1977). Wait for me, roller-skate! In C. Mitchell-Kernan & S. Ervin-Tripp (Eds.) *Child Discourse*. New York: Academic Press.

Escalona, S. K. (1973). Basic Modes of social interaction: their emergence and patterning during the first two years of life. *Merrill-Palmer Quarterly, 19*, 215–232.

Farb, P. (1973). *Word play: What happens when people talk*. New York: Bantam.

Flavell, J. H., Botkin, P. T., Fry, C. C., Wright, J. W., & Jarvis, P. E. (1968). *The development of role-taking and communication skills in children*. New York: Wiley.

Gardner, R. A., & Gardner, B. T. (1975). Teaching sign language to a chimpanzee. *Science, 165*, pp. 664–672.

Gleitman, H. (1981). *Psychology*. New York: Norton.

Goldin-Meadow, S., & Mylander, C. (1983, July). Gestural communication in deaf children: Noneffect of parental input on language development. *Science, 221*, pp. 372–374.

Hakuta, K. (1976). A case study of a Japanese child learning English as a second language. *Language Learning, 26*, 321–351.

Hess, R. D., & Shipman, V. C. (1965). Early experience and the socialization of cognitive modes in childhood. *Child Development, 36*, 869–886.

Homzie, M. J., & Lindsay, J. S. (1984). Language and the young stutterer: A new look at old theories and findings. *Brain and Language, 22*, 232–252.

Jusczyk, P. W. (1977). Perception of syllable-final stop consonants by 2-month-old infants. *Perception and psychophysics, 21*, 450–454.

Lenneberg, E. H. (1967). *Biological foundations of language*. New York: Wiley.

Limber, J. (1973). Representative examples of complex sentences taken from the records of one child between two and three years of age. In T. E. Moore (Ed.), *Cognitive development and the acquisition of language*. New York: Academic Press.

Locke, J. L. (1979). The child's processing of phonology. In W. A. Collins (Ed.), *Children's language and communication*. The Minnesota Symposium on Child Psychology. (Vol. 12, pp. 83–120). Hillsdale, NJ: Erlbaum.

Maccoby, E. E., & Bee, H.L. (1965). Some speculations concerning the lag between perceiving and performing. *Child Development, 36*, 367–377.

Madrid, D., & Garcia, E. E. (1981). Development of negation in bilingual Spanish/English and monolingual English speakers. *Journal of Educational Psychology, 73*, 624–631.

Menyuk, P. (1971). *The acquisition and development of language*. Englewood Cliffs, NJ: Prentice-Hall.

Meshoulam, U. (1981). The role of language skills in referential communication. *Journal of Genetic Psychology, 139*, 151–152.

Miller, G. A. (1978). The acquisition of word meaning. *Child Development, 49*, 999–1004.

Miller, G. A., & Johnson-Laird, P. N. (1976). *Language and perception*. Cambridge, MA: Harvard University Press.

Miller, W. R. (1964). The acquisition of formal features of language. *American Journal of Orthopsychiatry, 34,* 862–867.

Nakazema, S. (1975). Phonemicitization and symbolization in language development. In E.H. Lenneberg and E. Lenneberg (Eds.), *Foundations of language development: A multidisciplinary approach Vol. 1.* New York: Academic Press.

Nelson, K. (1973). Structure and strategy in learning to talk. *Monographs for the Society for Research in Child Development, 38*(1–2, Serial No. 149).

Nelson, K. (1979). Explorations in the development of a functional semantic system. In W. A. Collins, *Children's language and communication.* The Minnesota Symposium on Child Psychology. Hillsdale, NJ: Erlbaum.

Nelson, K. (1983, April 21). *Memories in the crib.* Paper presented at the biennial meeting of the Society for Research in Child Development, Detroit, MI.

Oren, D. L. (1981). Cognitive advantages of bilingual children related to labeling ability. *Journal of Educational Research, 74,* 164–169.

Piaget, J. (1959). *The language and thought of a child* (3rd ed.). (M. Gabain & R. Gabain, Trans.). London: Routledge and Kegan Paul.

Premack, D., & Premack, A. J. (1983). *The mind of an ape.* New York: Norton.

Scollen, R. (1976). *Conversations with a one year old.* Honolulu: University Press of Hawaii.

Sendak, M. (1967). *Higglety pigglety pop!* New York: Harper & Row.

Shatz, M., & Gelman, R. (1973). The development of communications skills: Modifications in the speech of young children as a function of the listener. *Monographs of the Society for Research in Child Development, 38*(5, Serial No. 152).

Skinner, B. F. (1957). *Verbal behavior.* New York: Appleton-Century-Crofts.

Slobin, D. I. (1975). On the nature of talk to children. In E. H. Lenneberg & E. Lenneberg (Eds.), *Foundations of language development* (Vol. 1). New York: Academic Press.

Slobin, D. I. (1979). *Psycholinguistics.* Glenview, IL: Scott, Foresman.

Smith, N. V. (1973). *The acquisition of phonology: A case study.* Cambridge, Eng.: Cambridge University Press.

Snow, C. E. (1977). The development of conversation between mothers and babies. *Journal of Child Language, 4* 1–22.

Snow, C. E., Arlman-Rupp, A., Hassing, Y., Jobse, J., & Vorstein, J. (1976). Mother's speech in three social classes. *Journal of Psycholinguistic Research, 5,* 1–20.

Snowdon, C. T. (1983). Ethology, comparative psychology, and animal behavior. *Annual Review of Psychology, 34,* 63–94.

Stone, L. J., & Church, J. (1973). *Childhood and adolescence: A psychology of the growing person* (3rd ed.). New York: Random House.

Terrace, H. S. (1979). *Nim: A chimpanzee who learned sign language.* New York: Washington Square Press.

Vygotsky, L. S. (1962). *Thought and language.* (E. Hanfmann & G. Vakar, Eds., Trans.). Cambridge, MA: Massachusetts Institute of Technology Press.

Chapter 8

Bandura, A. (1971). Analysis of modeling processes. In A. Bandura (Ed.), *Psychological modeling.* Chicago, IL: Aldine-Atherton.

Bandura, A. (1973). A social learning theory of aggression. In J. F. Knutson (Ed.), *Control of aggression: Implications from basic research.* Chicago, IL: Aldine.

Bandura, A. (1977). *Social learning theory.* Englewood Cliffs, NJ: Prentice-Hall.

Bandura, A., Grusec, J. E., & Menlove, F. L. (1967). Vicarious extinction of avoidant behavior. *Journal of Personality and Social Psychology, 5,* 16–23.

Barry, H. H., III, Bacon, M. K., & Child, I. L. (1957). A cross-cultural survey of some sex differences in socialization. *Journal of Abnormal and Social Psychology, 55,* 327–332.

Bar-Tal, D., Raviv, A., & Shavit, N. (1981). Motives for helping behavior: Kibbutz and city children in kindergarten and school. *Developmental Psychology, 17,* 766–772.

Baumrind, D. (1967). Child care practices anteceding three patterns of preschool behavior. *Genetic Psychology Monographs, 75,* 43–88.

Baumrind, D. (1973). The development of instrumental competence through socialization. In A. D. Pick (Ed.), *Minnesota symposium on child psychology* (Vol. 7, pp. 3–46). Minneapolis, MN: University of Minnesota Press.

Baumrind, D. (1980). New directions in socialization research. *American Psychologist, 35,* 639–652.

Bell, R. Q., & Harper, L. V. (1977). *Child effects on adults.* Hillsdale, NJ: Erlbaum.

Block, J. H. (1973). Conceptions of sex role: some cross-cultural and longitudinal perspectives. *American Psychologist, 28,* 521–526.

Block, J. H. (1976). Debatable conclusions about sex differences. *Contemporary Psychology, 21,* 517–522.

Block, J. H. (1979, September). *Personality development in males and females: The influence of differential socialization.* Paper presented as part of the Master Lecture Series at the Meeting of the American Psychological Association, New York.

Bronson, W. C. (1975). Developments in behavior with age mates during the second year of life. In M. Lewis & L. A. Rosenblum (Eds.), *The origins of behavior: Friendship and peer relations.* New York: Wiley.

Bruner, J. S., Jolly, A., & Sylva, K. (Eds.). (1976). *Play: Its role in development and evolution.* New York: Basic Books.

Bussey, K. (1981, April). *The role of beliefs about self and others in the sex-typing process.* Paper presented at the meeting of the Society for Research in Child Development, Boston, MA.

Carpenter, C. J., & Huston-Stein, A. (1980). Activity structure and sex-typed behavior in preschool children. *Child Development, 51,* 862–872.

D'Andrade, R. G. (1966). Sex differences and cultural institutions. In E. Maccoby (Ed.), *The development of sex differences* (pp. 173–204). Stanford, CA: Stanford University Press.

Dunn, J., & Kendrick, C. (1982). *Siblings: Love, envy, and understanding.* Cambridge, MA: Harvard University Press.

Eckerman, C. O., Whatley, J. L., & Kutz, S. L. (1975). The growth of social play with peers during the second year of life. *Developmental Psychology, 11,* 42–49.

Edwards, C. P., & Lewis, M. (1979). Young children's concepts of social relations: Social functions and social objects. In M. L. Lewis & L. A. Rosenblum (Eds.), *The child and its family: Genesis of behavior* (Vol. 2). New York: Plenum.

Eiduson, B. Y., Kornfein, M., Zimmerman, I. L., & Weisner, T. S. (1982). Comparative socialization practices in traditional and alternative families. In M. Lamb (Ed.), *Nontraditional families: Parenting and child development* (pp. 315–346). Hilldale, NJ: Erlbaum.

Eisenberg-Berg, N., & Hand, M. (1979). The relationship of preschoolers' reasoning about prosocial moral conflicts to prosocial behavior. *Child Development, 50,* 356–363.

Eisenberg-Berg, N., & Neal, C. (1979). Children's moral reasoning about their own spontaneous prosocial behavior. *Developmental Psychology, 15,* 228–229.

Emmerich, W., Goldman, K. S., Kirsch, B., & Sharabany, P. (1976). *Development of gender constancy in economically disadvantaged children.* Report of the Educational Testing Service, Princeton, NJ.

Erikson, E. H. (1963). *Childhood and society* (2nd rev. ed.). New York: W. W. Norton & Company.

Fagot, B. I. (1974). Sex differences in toddlers' behavior and parental reactions. *Developmental Psychology, 10,* 554–558.

Fagot, B. I. (1977). Consequences of moderate cross-gender behavior in preschool children. *Child Development, 48,* 902–907.

Fagot, B. I. (1978). The influence of sex of child on parental reaction to toddler children. *Child Development, 49,* 459–465.

Fagot, B. I. (1982). Adults as socializing agents. In T. Field, A. Huston, H. Quay, & G. Finley (Eds.), *Review of human development.* New York: Wiley.

Feshbach, S. & Feshbach, N. (1973, April). The young aggressors. *Psychology Today, 6,* pp. 90–95.

Fishbein, H. D. (1976). *Evolution, development, and children's learning.* Pacific Palisades, CA: Goodyear.

Freud, A., & Dann, S. (1951). An experiment in group upbringing. In R. S. Eisler, A. Freud, H. Hartman, & E. Kris (Eds), *The psychoanalytic study of the child* (Vol. 6). New York: International Universities Press.

Golden, M. & Birns, B. (1975). Social class and infant intelligence. In M. L. Lewis (Ed.), *Origins of intelligence: Infancy and early childhood* (pp. 299–351). New York: Plenum.

Goldfarb, W. (1955). Emotional and intellectual consequences of psychological deprivation in infancy: A reevaluation. In P. H. Hoch & J. Zubin (Eds.), *Psychopathology of childhood.* New York: Grune and Stratton.

Goodenough, F. L. (1931). *Anger in young children.* Minneapolis, MN: University of Minnesota Press.

Hall, G. S. (1904). *Adolescence: Its psychology and relations to physiology, anthropology, sociology, sex, crime, religion and education.* New York: Appleton.

Harlow, H. F. (1958). The nature of love. *American Psychologist, 13,* 673–685.

Hartup, W. W. (1974). Aggression in childhood: Developmental perspectives. *American Psychologist, 29,* 336–341.

Hartup, W. W. (1979). Peer relations and the growth of social competence. In M. W. Kent & J. E. Rolf (Eds.), *The primacy of prevention of psychopathology. Vol. 3: Promoting social competence and coping in children* (pp. 150–170). Hanover, NH: University Press of New England.

Hartup, W. W. (1983). Peer relations. In P. H. Mussen (Ed.), *Handbook of child psychology* (4th ed.). (Vol. 1, pp. 103–196.). New York: Wiley.

Hartup, W. W., & Coates, B. (1967). Imitation of a peer as a function of reinforcement from the peer group and the rewardingness of the model. *Child Development, 38,* 1003–1016.

Hetherington, E. M., & Morris, W. M. (1978). The family and primary groups. In W. H. Holtzman (Ed.), *Introductory psychology in depth: Developmental topics.* New York: Harper's College Press.

Huston, A. C. (1983). Sex-typing. In P. H. Mussen (Ed.), *Handbook of child psychology* (4th ed.). (Vol. 4, pp. 387–467). New York: Wiley.

Jacklin, C. N., & Maccoby, E. E. (1978). Social behavior at 33 months in same-sex and mixed-sex dyads. *Child Development, 49,* 557–569.

Jolly, A. (1972). *The evolution of primate behavior.* New York: Macmillan.

Kohlberg, L. A. (1966). A cognitive-developmental analysis of children's sex-role concepts and attitudes. In E. E. Maccoby (Ed.), *The development of sex differences.* Stanford, CA: Stanford University Press.

Kuhn, D., Nash, S. C., & Brucken, L. (1978). Sex-role concepts of two- and three-year-olds. *Child Development, 49,* 445–451.

Ladd, G. W. (1983, July). School networks of popular, average, and rejected children in school settings. *Merrill-Palmer Quarterly, 29,* 283–307.

Lamb, M. E., Easterbrooks, M. S., & Holden, G. W. (1980). Reinforcement and punishment among preschoolers: Characteristics, effects, and correlates. *Child Development, 51,* 1230–1236.

Lamb, M. E., & Roopnarine, J. L. (1979). Peer influences on sex-role development in preschoolers. *Child Development, 50,* 1219–1222.

Langlois, J. H., & Downs, A. C. (1980), Mothers, fathers, and peers as socialization agents of sex-typed play behaviors in young children. *Child Development, 51,* 1237–1247.

Lepper, M. R., Greene, D., & Nisbett, R. E. (1973). Undermining children's intrinsic interest with extrinsic rewards: A test of the overjustification hypothesis. *Journal of Personality and Social Psychology, 28,* 129–137.

Lewis, M., & Brooks, J. (1975). Infants' social perception: A constructionist view. In L. Cohen & P. Salapatek (Eds.), *Infant perception: From sensation to cognition (Vol. 2).* New York: Academic Press.

Maccoby, E. E. (1980). *Social development: Psychological growth and the parent-child relationship.* New York: Harcourt Brace Jovanovich.

Maccoby, E. E., & Jacklin, C. N. (1974). *The psychology of sex differences.* Stanford, CA: Stanford University Press.

Maccoby, E. E., & Jacklin, C. N. (1980). Sex differences in aggression: A rejoinder and reprise. *Child Development, 51,* 964–980.

Maccoby, E. E. & Martin, J. A. (1983). Socialization in the context of the family: Parent-child interaction. In P. H. Mussen (Ed.), *Handbook of child psychology* (4th ed.). (Vol. 4, pp. 1–101). New York: Wiley.

Minton, C., Kagan, J., Levine, J. A. (1971). Maternal control and obedience in the two-year-old child. *Child Development, 42,* 1873–1894.

Mischel, W., & Mischel, H. (1976). A cognitive social-learning approach to morality and self-regulation. In T. Lickona (Ed.), *Moral development and behavior* (pp. 84–107). New York: Holt, Rinehart and Winston.

Money, J., & Ehrhardt, A. A. (1972). *Man and woman, boy and girl: The differentiation and dimorphism of gender identity from conception to maturity.* Baltimore, MD: Johns Hopkins University Press.

Parke, R. D., & Slaby, R. G. (1983). The development of aggression. In P. H. Mussen (Ed.), *Handbook of child psychology* (4th ed.). (Vol. 4, pp. 547–641). New York: Wiley.

Patterson, G. R. (1982). *A Social Learning Approach to Family Intervention. Vol. 1: Coercive family processes.* Eugene, OR: Castalia Press.

Patterson, G. R., Littman, R. A., & Bricker, W. (1967). Assertive behavior in young children: A step toward a theory of aggression. *Monographs of the Society for Research on Child Development, 32*(5), Serial No. 113.

Poirier, F. E. (1973). Socialization and learning among nonhuman primates. In S. T. Kimball & J. H. Burnett (Eds.), *Learning and culture.* Seattle, WA: University of Washington Press.

Rabin, A. I. (1965). *Growing up in the kibbutz.* New York: Springer.

Rabin, A. I., & Beit-Hallahmi, B. (1982). *Twenty years later: Kibbutz children grown up.* New York: Springer.

Radke-Yarrow, M. R., Scott, P. M., & Zahn-Waxler, C. (1973). Learning concern for others. *Developmental Psychology, 8*(2), 240–260.

Radke-Yarrow, M. R., & Zahn-Waxler, C. (1976). Dimensions and correlates of prosocial behavior in young children. *Child Development, 47,* 118–125.

Radke-Yarrow, M. R., Zahn-Waxler, C., & Chapman, M. (1983). Children's prosocial dispositions and behavior. In P. H. Mussen (Ed.), *Handbook of child psychology* (4th ed.). (Vol. 4, pp. 469–545). New York: Wiley.

Rheingold, H. L. (1979, March). *Helping by two-year-old children.* Paper presented at the meeting of the Society for Research in Child Development, San Francisco, CA.

Rheingold, H. L., Hay, D. F., & West, M. J. (1976). Sharing in the second year of life. *Child Development, 47,* 1148–1158.

Rheingold, H. L., & Cook, K. V. (1975). The contents of boys' and girls' rooms as an index of parental behavior. *Child Development, 46,* 459–463.

Rosaldo, M. Z. (1974). Woman, culture and society: A theoretical overview. In M. Rosaldo & L. Lamphere (Eds.), *Woman, culture and society,* pp. 17–43. Stanford, CA: Stanford University Press.

Rothbart, M. K., & Rothbart, M. (1976). Birth order, sex of child, and maternal helpgiving. *Sex Roles, 2,* 39–46.

Scarr, S. (1984). *Mother care, other care.* New York: Basic Books.

Schacter, F. F. Gilutz, G., Shore, E., & Adler, M. (1978). Sibling deidentification judged by mothers: Cross-validation and developmental studies. *Child Development, 49,* 543–546.

Sears, R. R., Maccoby E., & Levin, H. (1957). *Patterns of child rearing.* Evanston, IL: Row, Peterson.

Sroufe, L. A. (1983). The coherence of individual development: Early care, attachment, and subsequent developmental issues. *American Psychologist, 34,* 834–841.

Strayer, F. F., & Strayer, J. (1976). An ethological analysis of social agonism and dominance relations among preschool children. *Child Development, 47,* 980–989.

Suomi, S. (1977). Development of attachment and other social behaviors in rhesus monkeys. In T. Alloway, P. Pliner, & I. Kramer (Eds.), *Attachment behavior.* New York: Plenum.

Suomi, S., & Harlow, H. P. (1975). The role and reason of peer relationships in rhesus monkeys. In M. Lewis & L. A. Rosenblum (Eds.), *Friendships and peer relations* (pp. 153–186). New York: Wiley.

Tauber, M. A. (1979). Sex differences in parent-child interaction styles during a free-play session. *Child Development, 50,* 225–234.

Tavris, C., & Wade, C. (1984). *The longest war: Sex differences in perspective* (2nd ed.). San Diego, CA: Harcourt Brace Jovanovich.

Waldrop, M. F., & Halverson, C. F. (1975). Intensive and extensive peer behavior: Longitudinal and cross-sectional analyses. *Child Development, 46,* 19–26.

Waters, E., & Sroufe, L. A. (1983). Social competence as a developmental construct. *Developmental Review, 3,* 79–97.

Zahn-Waxler, C., & Radke-Yarrow, M. (1982). The development of altruism: Alternative research strategies. In N. Eisenberg-Berg (Ed.), *The development of prosocial behavior.* New York: Academic Press.

Zahn-Waxler, C., Radke-Yarrow, M., & King, R. (1979). Child rearing and children's prosocial initiations towards victims of distress. *Child Development, 50,* 319–330.

Chapter 9

Aikawa, T., & Horiuchi, S. (1962). A study in the development of whys: I. Investigations in the areas of whys which arise as a process of cognizing reality. *Japanese Journal of Educational Psychology, 10,* 139–149.

Becker, H. J. (in press). *Microcomputers in the classroom: Dreams and realities.* Baltimore, MD: Center for Social Organization of Schools at Johns Hopkins University.

Berlyne, D. E. (1970). Children's reasoning. In P. H. Mussen (Ed.), *Carmichael's manual of child psychology* (3rd ed.). (Pp. 939–981). New York: Wiley.

Chase, W. G., & Simon, H. A. (1973). Perception in chess. *Cognitive Psychology, 4,* 55–81.

Chi, M. T. (1978). Knowledge structures and memory development. In R. S. Siegler (Ed.), *Children's thinking: What develops?* Hillsdale, NJ: Erlbaum.

Dansen, P. R. (1972, March). Cross-cultural Piagetian research: A summary. *Journal of Cross-Cultural Psychology, 3,* 23–39.

Dansen, P. R. (Ed.). (1977). Introduction. *Piagetian psychology: Cross-cultural contributions* (pp. 1–25). New York: Garden Press.

Eifermann, R. R. (1971). Social play in childhood. In R. E. Herron & B. Sutton-Smith (Eds.), *Child's play.* New York: Wiley.

Fishbein, H. D. (1976). *Evolution, development and children's learning.* Pacific Palisades, CA: Goodyear.

Fishbein, H. D. (1984). *The psychology of infancy and childhood: Evolutionary and cross-cultural perspectives.* Hillsdale, NJ: Erlbaum.

Flavell, J. H. (1963). *The developmental psychology of Jean Piaget.* Princeton, NJ: Van Nostrand Reinhold.

Flavell, J. H. (1977). *Cognitive development.* Englewood Cliffs, NJ: Prentice-Hall.

Flavell, J. H. (1982). On cognitive development. *Child Development, 53,* 1–10.

Flavell, J. H. (1985). *Cognitive development* (2nd ed.). Englewood Cliffs, NJ: Prentice-Hall.

Flavell, J. H., Beach, D. H., & Chinsky, J. M. (1966). Spontaneous verbal rehearsal in a memory task as a function of age. *Child Development, 37,* 283–299.

Flavell, J. H., Friedrichs, A. G., & Hoyt, J. D. (1970). Developmental changes in memorization processes. *Cognitive Psychology, 1,* 324–340.

Gelman, R. (1969). Conservation acquisition: A problem of learning to attend to relevant attributes. *Journal of Experimental Child Psychology, 7,* 167–187.

Ghent, L. (1956). Perception of overlapping and embedded figures by children of different ages. *American Journal of Psychology, 69,* 575–587.

Gibson, E. J., & Levin, H. (1975). *The psychology of reading.* Cambridge, MA: Massachusetts Institute of Technology Press.

Ginsburg, H., & Opper, S. (1979). *Piaget's theory of intellectual development* (2nd ed.). Englewood Cliffs, NJ: Prentice-Hall.

Goertzel, V., & Goertzel, M. G. (1962). *Cradles of eminence.* Boston: Little, Brown.

Hagen, J. W. (1972). Strategies for remembering. In S. Farnham-Diggory (Ed.), *Information processing in children* (pp. 68, 70, 71). New York: Academic Press.

Hagen, J. W., & Hale, G. H. (1973). The development of attention in children. In A. D. Pick (Ed.), *Minnesota symposium on child psychology* (Vol. 7, pp. 117–140). Minneapolis, MN: University of Minnesota Press.

Hanson, J. K. (1983, September 3). *Preschoolers' use of computers overturns myths.* University of Minnesota News Service.

Hassett, J. (1984, September). Computers in the classroom. *Psychology Today,* 22–28.

Hawkins, J., Sheingold, K., Gearhart, M., & Berger, C. (1982). Microcomputers in schools: Impact on the social life of elementary classrooms. *Journal of Applied Developmental Psychology, 3,* 361–373.

Hetherington, E. M., Cox, M., & Cox, R. (1979). Play and social interaction in children following divorce. *Journal of Social Issues, 35,* 26–49.

Inhelder, B., Sinclair, H., & Bovet, M. (1974). *Learning and the development of cognition.* Cambridge, MA: Harvard University Press.

Keeney, T. J., Cannizzo, S. R., & Flavell, J. H. (1967). Spontaneous and induced verbal rehearsal in a recall task. *Child Development, 38,* 953–966.

Kendler, H. H., & Kendler, T. S. (1962). Vertical and horizontal processes in problem solving. *Psychological Review, 69,* 1–16.

Kendler, H. H., & Kendler, T. S. (1970). Developmental processes in discrimination learning. *Human Development, 13,* 65–89.

Kreutzer, M. A., Leonard, C., & Flavell, J. H. (1975). An interview study of children's knowledge about memory. *Monographs of the Society for Research in Child Development, 40*(1, Serial No. 159).

Kuenne, M. R. (1946). Experimental investigation of the relation of language to transposition behavior in young children. *Journal of Experimental Psychology, 36,* 471–490.

Kuhn, D. (1974). Inducing development experimentally: Comments on a research paradigm. *Developmental Psychology, 10*(5), 590–666.

Luria, A. R. (1968). *Mind of the Mnemonist.* New York: Basic Books.

McGhee, P. (1979) *Humor: Its origin and development.* San Francisco: Freeman.

McGuinness, D. (1985). *When children don't learn: Understanding the biology and psychology of learning disabilities.* New York: Basic Books.

Morrison, F. J., & Manis, F. R. (1982). Cognitive processes and reading disability: A critique and proposal. In C. J. Brainerd & M. I. Pressley (Eds.), *Verbal processes in children* (pp. 59–94). New York: Springer-Verlag.

Murray F. B. (1972). Acquisition of conservation through social interaction. *Developmental Psychology, 6,* 106.

Neimark, E. D. (1975). Intellectual development in adolescence. In F. D. Horowitz (Ed.), *Review of Child Development Research* (Vol. 4). Chicago, IL: University of Chicago Press.

Ornstein, P. A. (1978). *Memory development in children.* Hillsdale, NJ: Erlbaum.

Ornstein, P. A., Naus, M. J., & Liberty, C. (1975). Rehearsal and organizational processes in children's memory. *Child Development, 46,* 818–830.

Papert, S. (1980). *Mindstorms: Children, computers, and powerful ideas.* New York: Basic Books.

Paris, S. G., & Lindauer, B. K. (1976). Constructive aspects of children's comprehension and memory. In R. V. Kail, Jr. & J. W. Hagen, (Eds.) *Perspectives on the development of memory and cognition.* Hillsdale, NJ: Erlbaum.

Piaget, J. (1928). *The language and thought of the child.* New York: Harcourt, Brace.

Piaget, J. (1950). *Psychology of intelligence.* London: Routledge and Kegan Paul.

Piaget, J. (1962). *Play, dreams and imitation in childhood.* New York: Norton.

Piaget, J. (1965). *The child's conception of number.* New York: Norton. (First published 1941)

Piaget, J. (1983). Piaget's theory. In P. H. Mussen (Ed.), *Carmichael's manual of child psychology* (Vol. 1, pp. 703–732). New York: Wiley.

Ross, D. M., & Ross, S. A. (1982). *Hyperactivity: Research, theory, action* (2nd ed.). New York: Wiley.

Rubin, K. H., & Krasnor, L. R. (1980). Changes in the play behavior of preschoolers: A short-term longitudinal investigation. *Canadian Journal of Behavioral Sciences, 12,* 278–282.

Shonkoff, J. P. (1984). The biological substrate and physical health in middle childhood. In W. A. Collins (Ed.), *Development during middle childhood: the years from six to twelve.* Washington, DC: National Academy Press.

Siegler, R. S., & Richards, D. D. (1982). The development of intelligence. In R. J. Sternberg (Ed.), *Handbook of human intelligence* (pp. 897–971). Cambridge, Eng.: Cambridge University Press.

Stevenson, H. (1970). Learning in children. In P. H. Mussen (Ed.) *Carmichael's manual of child psychology (Vol. 1).* NY: Wiley.

Sutton-Smith, B. (1967). The role of play in cognitive development. *Young Children, 22,* 361–370.

Tanner, J. M. (1969). Growth and endocrinology in the adolescent. In L. I. Gardner (Ed.) *Endocrine and genetic diseases of childhood.* Philadelphia: Saunders.

Tanner, J. M. (1970). Physical growth. In P. H. Mussen (Ed.) *Carmichael's manual of child psychology (Vol. 1)* NY: Wiley.

Tanner, J. M. (1978). *Fetus into man.* Cambridge, MA: Harvard University Press.

Tepman, L. M., & Merrill, M. A. (1973). *Stanford-Binet Intelligence Scale.* Boston: Houghton-Mifflin.

Tulving, E. (1974). Cue-dependent forgetting. *American Scientist, 62,* 74–82.

White, S. H. (1965). Evidence for a hierarchical arrangement of learning processes. In L. P. Lipsitt & C. C. Spiker (Eds.), *Advances in child development and behavior* (Vol. 2, pp. 187–220). New York: Academic Press.

White, S. H. (1969). *Some general outlines of the matrix of developmental changes between five and seven years.* Paper presented at International Congress of Psychology. London.

Yamamoto, K. (1962). Development of ability to ask questions under specific testing conditions. *Journal of Genetic Psychology, 101,* 83–90.

Zaporozhets, A. V., & El'Konin, D. P. (Eds.). (1964). *The psychology of preschool children.* Moscow: Izdatel'stvo Prosvescenie.

Zimmerman, B. J., & Rosenthal, T. L. (1974). Conserving and retaining equalities and inequalities through observation and correction. *Developmental Psychology, 10,* 260–268.

Chapter 10

Anderson, V. E. (1974). Genetics and intelligence. In J. Wortis (Ed.), *Mental retardation (and developmental disabilities): an annual review.* (Vol. VI). NY: Brunner/Mazel.

Atkinson, R. L., Atkinson, R. C., & Hilgard, E. (1983). *Introduction to psychology.* San Diego, CA: Harcourt Brace Jovanovich.

Barron, F. (1955). The disposition toward originality. *Journal of Personality and Social Psychology, 51,* 478–485.

Barstis, S. W., & Ford, L. H., Jr. (1977). Reflection-impulsivity, conservation, and the development of ability to control cognitive tempo. *Child Development, 48,* 953–959.

Bayley, N. (1949). Consistency and variability in the growth of intelligence from birth to eighteen years. *Journal of Genetic Psychology, 75,* 165–196.

Bayley, N. (1970). The development of mental abilities. In P. H. Mussen (Ed.), *Carmichael's manual of child psychology* (3rd ed.). (Vol. 1). New York: Wiley.

Binet, A. (1971). *Les idées modernes sur les enfants.* Paris: Flammarion. (Original work published 1909)

Binet, A., & Simon, T. (1905). New methods for the diagnosis of the intellectual level of subnormals. *Annals of Psychology, 11,* 191.

Bloom, B. S. (1964). *Stability and change in human characteristics.* New York: Wiley.

Bruner, J. S. (1962). The conditions of creativity. In H. Gruber, G. Terrell, & M. Wertheimer (Eds.), *Contemporary approaches to creative thinking.* NY: Prentice-Hall.

Budoff, M. (1974). *Learning potential and educability among the educable mentally retarded.* Final Report Project No. 312312. Cambridge, MA: Research Institute for Educational Problems, Cambridge Mental Health Association.

Bush, E. S., & Dweck, C. S. (1975). Reflections on conceptual tempo: Relationship between cognitive style and performance as a function of task characteristics. *Developmental Psychology, 11,* 567–574.

Campione, J. C., Brown, A. L., & Ferrara, R. A. (1982). Mental retardation and intelligence. In R. J. Sternberg (Ed.), *Handbook of human intelligence* (pp. 392–490). New York: Cambridge University Press.

Cattell, R. B. (1949). *The culture free intelligence test.* Champaign, IL: Institute for Personality and Ability Testing.

Cook, T. D., & Campbell, D. T. (1979). *Quasi-experimentation.* Boston: Houghton Mifflin.

Crockenberg, S. B. (1972). Creativity tests: A boon or a boondoggle for education? *Review of Educational Research, 42,* 27–45.

Cunningham, S. (1984, September). Cross-cultural study of achievement calls for changes in home. *APA Monitor,* pp. 10–11.

Eysenck, H. J. (1979). *The Structure and measurement of intelligence.* NY: Springer-Verlag.

Feldman, D. H. (1980). *Beyond universals in cognitive development.* Norwood, NJ: Ablex.

Feuerstein, R., Rand, Y., Hoffman, M., & Miller, R. (1979). Cognitive modifiability in retarded adolescents: Effects of instrumental enrichment. *American Journal of Mental Deficiency, 83,* 539–550.

Flanagan, J. C. (1963). The definition and measurement of ingenuity. In C. W. Taylor & F. Barron (Eds.), *Scientific creativity: Its recognition and development.* New York: Wiley.

Gardner, H. (1983). *Frames of mind: The theory of multiple intelligences.* New York: Basic Books.

Getzels, J. W., & Jackson, P. W (1962). *Creativity and intelligence: Explorations with gifted students.* New York: Wiley.

Gjerde, P. F., Black, J., & Black, J. H. (1985). The longitudinal consistency of Matching Familiar Figures Test performance from early childhood to preadolescence. *Developmental Psychology, 21*(2), 262–271.

Gleitman, H. (1981). *Psychology.* NY: Norton.

Goldstein, H., Moss, J. W., & Jordan, L. J. (1965). *The efficacy of special class training on the development of mentally retarded children.* (U.S. Office of Education Project No. 619). Urbana, IL: University of Illinois.

Guilford, J. P. (1954). A factor analytic study across the domains of reasoning, creativity, and evaluation. I: Hypothesis and description of tests. *Reports from the psychology laboratory.* Los Angeles: University of Southern California Press.

Harter, S., & Zigler, E. (1974). The assessment of effectance motivation in normal and retarded children. *Developmental Psychology, 10,* 169–180.

Jackson P., & Messick, S. (1965). The person, the product and the response: Conceptual problems in the assessment of creativity. *Journal of Personality, 33,* 309–329.

Jensen, A. R. (1969). How much can we boost IQ and scholastic achievement? *Harvard Educational Review, 29,* 1–23.

Jensen, A. R. (1973). *Educability and group differences.* New York: Harper & Row.

Jensen, A. R. (1980). *Bias in mental testing.* New York: Free Press.

Jensen, A. R. (1984). The black-white differences on the K-ABC: Implications for future testing. *Journal of Special Education, 18*(3), 377–408.

Jerison, H. J. (1982). The evolution of biological intelligence. In R. J. Sternberg (Ed.), *The handbook of human intelligence* (pp. 723–791). New York: Cambridge University Press.

Kagan, J., Rosman, B. L., Day, D., Albert, J., & Phillips, W. (1964). Information processing in the child: Significance of analytic and reflective attitudes. *Psychological Monographs, 79* (No. 578).

Kamin, L. J. (1974). *The science and politics of IQ.* Potomac, MD: Erlbaum.

Kaufman, M., Agard, J., & Semmel, M. (Eds.). (1978). *Mainstreaming: Learners and their environments.* Baltimore, MD: University Park Press.

Kaufman, A. S. (1984, Fall). K-ABC and controversy. *Journal of Special Education, 18*(3), 409–444.

Kogan, N. (1983). Stylistic variation in childhood and adolescence: Creativity, metaphor, and cognitive style. In P. H. Mussen (Ed.), *Handbook of child psychology* (4th ed.). (Vol. 3, pp. 630–706). New York: Wiley.

Konner, M. (1982). *The tangled wing: Biological constraints on the human spirit.* New York: Holt, Rinehart & Winston.

Lambert, N. M. (1981, September). Psychological evidence in *Larry P. v. Wilson Riles*: An evaluation by a witness for the defense. *American Psychologist, 36,* 937–952.

McClelland, D. C. (1973). Testing for competence rather than for intelligence. *American Psychologist, 28,* 1–141.

McCall, R. B., Applebaum, M. I., & Hogarty, P. S. (1973). Developmental changes in mental performance. *Monographs of the Society for Research in Child Development, 38*(Serial No. 150).

Mednick, S. A. (1962). The associative basis of the creative process. *Psychological Review, 69,* 220–232.

Mercer, J. R. (1973). *Labeling the mentally retarded.* Berkeley and Los Angeles: University of California Press.

Mercer, J. R., & Lewis, J. F. (1978). *System of multicultural pluralistic assessment.* New York: Psychological Corporation.

Montour, K. (1977). William James Sidis, the broken twig. *American Psychologist, 32,* 265–279.

Moore, M. G., Haskins, R., & McKinney, J. D. (1980). Classroom behavior of reflective and impulsive children. *Journal of Applied Developmental Psychology, 1,* 59–75.

Nakaruma, C. Y., & Finck, D. N. (1980). Relative effectiveness of socially-oriented and task-oriented children and predictability of their behavior. *Monographs of the Society for Research in Child Development, 45*(3–4, Serial No. 185).

Nichols, P. L., & Anderson, V. E. (1973). Intellectual performance, race and socioeconomic status. *Social Biology, 20* (4), 367–374.

Oden, M. H. (1968). Fulfillment of promise: 40 year follow-up of the Terman gifted group. *Genetic Psychological Monographs, 77,* 3–93.

Pankove, E., & Kogan, N. (1968). Creative ability and risk taking in elementary school children. *Journal of Personality, 36,* 420–439.

Piaget, J., & Inhelder, B. (1969). *The Psychology of the child.* New York: Basic Books.

Plomin, R., & DeFries, J. C. (1980). Genetics and intelligence: Recent data. *Intelligence, 4,* 15–29.

Ruble, D. N., & Nakamura, C. Y (1972). Task orientation versus social orientation in young children and their attention to relevant social cues. *Child Development, 43,* 471–480.

Sattler, J. M. (1982). *Assessment of children's intelligence and special abilities* (2nd ed.). Boston: Allyn & Bacon.

Scarr, S. (1981). Testing *for* children: Assessment and the many determinants of intellectual competence. *American Psychologist, 36,* 1159–1166.

Scarr, S. (1983). An evolutionary perspective on infant intelligence: Species patterns and individual variations. In M. Lewis (Ed.), *Origins of intelligence: Infancy and early childhood* (2nd ed.). New York: Plenum.

Scarr, S., & McCartney, K. (1983). How people make their own environments: A theory of genotype→environment effects. *Child Development, 54,* 424–435.

Scarr, S., & Weinberg, R. A. (1976). IQ test performance of black children adopted by white families. *American Psychologist, 31,* 726–739.

Scarr, S., & Weinberg, R. A. (1978). The influence of "family background" on intellectual attainment. *American Sociological Review, 43,* 674–692.

Schiff, M., Duyme, M., Dumaret, A., Stewart, J., Tomkiewicz, S., & Feingold, J. (1978). Intellectual status of working-class children adopted early into upper-middle-class families. *Science, 200,* 1503–1504.

Semmel, M. I., Ballard, E. V., & Sivasailam, C. (1976). *The improvement of social status among rejected pupils through the modification of teacher behavior using the computer-assisted training system (CATTS): An inservice training application of CATTS.* Bloomington, IN: Center for Innovation in Teaching the Handicapped, Indiana University.

Semmel, M. I., Gottlieb, J., & Robinson, N. M. (1979). Mainstreaming: Perspectives on educating handicapped children in the public schools. In D. C. Berliner (Ed.), *Review of research in education* (Vol. 7, pp. 223–279). Washington, DC: American Educational Research Association.

Shockley, W. M. (1971). Dysgenics, genecity, raciology: A challenge to the intellectual responsibility of educators. *Review of Educational Research, 41,* 369–377.

Spearman, C. (1927). *The abilities of man.* New York: Macmillan.

Stanley, J. C., Keating, D. P., & Fox, L. H. (Eds.). (1974). *Mathematical talent: Discovery, description, and development.* Baltimore, MD: Johns Hopkins University Press.

Sternberg, R. J. (1979a, September). Stalking the IQ quark. *Psychology Today,* 45.

Sternberg, R. J. (1979b). The nature of intelligence. *New York University Educational Quarterly, 12,* 10–17.

Sternberg, R. J. (1982, April). Who's intelligent? *Psychology Today,* 30–39.

Sternberg, R. J. (1984a). *Beyond IQ: A triarchic theory of human intelligence.* New York: Cambridge University Press.

Sternberg, R. J. (1984b). The Kaufman Assessment Battery for Children: An information processing analysis and critique. *Journal of Special Education, 18,* 269–279.

Sternberg, R. J., & Davidson, J. E. (1982, June). The mind of the puzzler. *Psychology Today,* 37–44.

Tavris, C., & Wade, C. (1984). *The longest war: Sex differences in perspective* (2nd ed.). San Diego, CA: Harcourt Brace Jovanovich.

Terman, L. M. (1925). *Genetic studies of genius.* Stanford, CA: Stanford University Press.

Terman, L. M., & Merrill, M. A. (1986). *Measuring intelligence.* 4th ed. Chicago: Riverside Publishing Co.

Terman, L. M., & Oden, M. H. (1947). *The gifted child grows up: Twenty-five years' follow-up of a superior group.* Stanford, CA: Stanford University Press.

Terman, L. M., & Oden, M. H. (1959). *The gifted group at mid-life: Thirty-five years' follow-up of the superior child.* Stanford, CA: Stanford University Press.

Thurstone, L. L. (1938). Primary mental abilities. *Psychometric monographs* (No. 1). Chicago, IL: University of Chicago Press.

Thurstone, T. G. (1959). *An evaluation of teaching mentally handicapped children in special classes and in regular grades.* U.S. Office of Education, Cooperative Research Program, Project No. 6452. Chapel Hill: University of North Carolina.

Torrance, E. P. (1966). *Torrance tests of creative thinking, verbal forms A and B.* Princeton, NJ: Personnel Press.

Vernon, P. E. (1971). *The structure of human abilities.* London: Methuen.

Wagner, R. K., & Sternberg, R. J. (in press). Practical intelligence in the real world: The role of tacit knowledge in psychology. *Journal of Personality and Social Psychology.*

Wilson, R. S. (1983, April). The Louisville twin study: Developmental synchronies in behavior. *Child Development, 54,* 298–316.

Witkin, H. A., Dyk, R. B., Faterson, H. F., Goodenough, D. R., & Karp, S. J. (1962). *Psychological differentiation.* New York: Wiley.

Ysseldyke, J. E., & Stevens, L. J. (in press). Specific learning deficits: The learning disabled. In C. Reynolds & R. Brown (Eds.), *Psychological perspectives on childhood exceptionality.* New York: Wiley.

Zelniker, T., & Jeffrey, W. E. (1979). Attention and cognitive style in children. In G. A. Hale & M. Lewis (Eds.), *Attention and cognitive development.* New York: Plenum.

Zigler, E., Abelson, W. D., & Seitz, V. (1973). Motivational factors in the performance of economically disadvantaged children on the Peabody Picture Vocabulary Test. *Child Development, 4,* 294–303.

Zigler, E., & Seitz, V. (1982). Social policy and intelligence. In R. J. Sternberg (Ed.), *Handbook of human intelligence* (pp. 586–641). New York: Cambridge University Press.

Chapter 11

Ahammer, I. M., & Murray, J. P. (1979). Kindness in the kindergarten: the relative influence of role playing and prosocial television in facilitatory altruism. *International Journal of Behavioral Development, 2,* 133–157.

Asher, S. R., Oden, S. L., & Gottman, J. M. (1977). Children's friendship in school settings. In K. G. Katl (Ed.), *Current topics in early childhood education* (Vol. 1). Norwood, NJ: Ablex.

Asher, S. R., & Renshaw, P. D. (1981). Children without friends: Social knowledge and social skill training. In S. R. Asher & J. M. Gottman (Eds.), *The development of children's friendships* (pp. 273–296). New York: Cambridge University Press.

Asher, S. R., Renshaw, P. D., & Hymel, S. (1982). Peer relations and the development of social skills. In S. G. Moore & C. R. Cooper (Eds.), *The young child: Review of research–Vol. 3.* Washington, DC: National Association for the Education of Young Children.

Baird, L. (1969). Big school, small school: A critical examination of the hypothesis. *Journal of Educational Psychology, 60,* 253–260.

Barker, R. G., & Wright, H. F. (1951). *One boy's day: A specimen record of behavior.* New York: Harper.

Berndt, T. J. (1981). Relations between social cognition, nonsocial cognition, and social behavior: The case of friendship. In H. J. Flavell & L. D. Ross (Eds.), *Cambridge studies of social and emotional development: Frontiers and possible futures.* New York: Cambridge University Press.

Brown, P., & Elliott, R. (1965). Control of aggression in a nursery school class. *Journal of Experimental Child Psychology, 2,* 103–107.

Bryan, J. H. (1975). Children's cooperation and helping behaviors. In E. M. Hetherington (Ed.), *Review of Child Development Research, Vol. 5.* Chicago, IL: University of Chicago Press.

Bryant, B. K. (1982). Sibling relationships in middle childhood. In M. Lamb & B. Sutton-Smith (Eds.), *Sibling relationships: Their nature and significance across the lifespan.* Hillsdale, NJ: Erlbaum.

Bryant, B. K., & Crockenberg, S. (1980). Correlates and dimensions of prosocial behavior: A study of female siblings with their mothers. *Child Development, 51,* 529–544.

Cavoir, N., & Dokecky, P. R. (1973). Physical attractiveness, perceived attitude similarity, and academic achievement as contributors to interpersonal attraction among adolescents. *Developmental Psychology, 9,* 44–54.

Child Care Action Campaign (1985).

Chittenden, M. F. (1942). An experimental study in measuring and modifying assertive behavior in young children. *Monographs of the Society for Research in Child Development, 7* (Serial No. 31).

Collins, W. A., & Westby, S. (1981, March). *Children and television: What children watch, what they learn.* Institute of Child Development, University of Minnesota.

Coie, J. D., & Dodge, K. A. (1983, July). Continuities and changes in children's social status: A five-year longitudinal study. *Merrill-Palmer Quarterly, 29,* 261–282.

Cooper, H. M. (1979). Pygmalion grows up: A model for teacher expectation, communications, and performance influence. *Review of Educational Research, 49,* 389–410.

Cross, J. F., & Cross, J. (1971). Age, sex, race, and the perception of facial beauty. *Developmental Psychology, 5,* 433–439.

Csapo, M. (1972). Peer models reverse the "one bad apple spoils the barrel" theory. *Teaching Exceptional Children, 5,* 20–24.

Devereaux, E. C., Bronfenbrenner, U., & Rodgers, R. B. (1969). Child-rearing in England and the United States: A cross-national comparison. *Journal of Marriage and Family, 31,* 257–270.

Dodge, K. A., Murphy, R. R., & Buchsbaum, K. (1984). The assessment of intention-cue detection skills in children: Implications for developmental psychopathology. *Child Development, 55,* 163–173.

Dodge, K. A., Schlundt, D. C., Schocken, I., & Delugach, J. D. (1983). Social competence and children's sociometric status: The role of peer group entry strategies. *Merrill-Palmer Quarterly, 29,* 309–336.

Duck, S. W. (1975). Personality similarity and friendship choices by adolescents. *European Journal of Social Psychology, 5,* 351–365.

Gelfand, D. M., & Hartman, D. P. (1982). Some detrimental effects of competitive sports on children's behavior. In R. A. Magill, M. Ash, & F. L. Small (Eds.), *Children in sport* (2nd ed.). Champaign, IL: Human Kinetics.

Gerbner, G., & Gross, L. (1976). Living with television: The violence profile. *Journal of Communication, 26,* 173–199.

Good, T. L. (1980). *Teacher expectations, teacher behavior, student perceptions, and student behavior: A decade of research.* Paper presented at the meeting of the American Educational Research Association.

Gottman, J. M., Gonso, J., & Rasmussen, B. (1975). Social competence and friendship in children. *Child Development, 46,* 709–718.

Greenberg, P. J. (1932). Competition in children: An experimental study. *American Journal of Psychology, 44,* 221–248.

Hartup, W. W. (1983). Peer relations. In P. H. Mussen (Ed.), *Handbook of child psychology* (4th ed.). (Vol. 4, pp. 274–385). New York: Wiley.

Hess, R. D., & Shipman, V. C. (1967). Cognitive elements in maternal behavior. In J. P. Hill (Ed.), *Minnesota symposium on child psychology* (Vol. 1). Minneapolis, MN: University of Minnesota Press.

Hetherington, E. M. (1972). Effects of father absence on personality development in adolescent daughters. *Developmental Psychology, 7,* 313–326.

Hetherington, E. M., Cox, M., & Cox, R. (1978). *Family interaction and social, emotional, and cognitive development of children following divorce.* Paper presented at the Symposium on the Family: Setting Priorities, Washington, DC.

Hetherington, E. M., Cox, M., & Cox, R. (1982). Effects of divorce on parents and children. In M. Lamb (Ed.), *Nontraditional families: Parenting and child development* Hillsdale, NJ: Erlbaum.

Hill, C. R., & Stafford, F. P. (1980). Parental care of children: Time diary estimates of quantity, predictability, and variety. *Journal of Human Resources, 15,* 219–239.

Hoffman, L. W. (1980). The effects of maternal employment on the academic attitudes and performance of school-aged children. *School Psychology Review, 9,* 319–335.

Honig, A. S. (1983, May). Television and young children. *Young Children,* 63–76.

Hops, H., Walker, H. M., & Greenwood, C. R. (1977, March). *PEERS—A program for remediating social withdrawal in the school setting.* Paper presented at Banff 9: The History and Future of the Developmentally Disabled, Banff, Alberta.

Household and family characteristics: March, 1984. U.S. Dept. of Commerce, Bureau of the Census, Washington, DC.

Hymel, S., Asher, S. R., Renshaw, P. D., & Geraci, R. (1981). *Loneliness in children: Development of self-report measures.* Paper presented at the meeting of the American Educational Research Association, Los Angeles.

Johnson, D. W., & Johnson, R. T. (1975). *Learning together and alone: Cooperating, competition, and individualization.* Englewood Cliffs, NJ.

Kohn, M. L. (1976). Social class and parental values: Another confirmation of the relationship. *American Sociological Review, 41,* 538–545.

Langlois, J. H., & Stephen, C. (1977). The effects of physical attractiveness and ethnicity on children's behavioral attributes and peer preferences. *Child Development, 48,* 1694–1698.

Lerner, R. M. (1982). Children and adolescents as producers of their own development. *Developmental Review, 2,* 342–370.

Levenson, B. M. (1972). *Pets and human development.* Springfield, IL: C. C. Thomas.

Lewin, K., Lippitt, R., & White, R. K. (1939). Patterns of aggressive behavior in artificially created "social climates." *Journal of Social Psychology, 10,* 271–299.

Liebert, R. M., & Baron, R. A. (1972). Some immediate effects of televised violence on children's behavior. *Developmental Psychology, 6,* 469–475.

Maccoby, E. E. (1984). Middle childhood in the context of the family. In W. A. Collins (Ed.), *Development during middle childhood: The years from six to twelve.* Washington, DC: National Academy Press.

Mason, W. A., & Kennedy, M. D. (1974). Redirection of filial attachments in rhesus monkeys: Dogs as mother surrogates. *Science, 182,* 1209–1211.

McDavid, J. W., & Harari, H. (1966). Stereotyping of names and popularity in grade-school children. *Child Development, 37,* 453–459.

Minuchin, P. P., & Shapiro, E. K. (1983). The school as a context for social development. In P. H. Mussen (Ed.), *Handbook of child psychology* (4th ed.). (Vol. 4, pp. 197–274). New York: Wiley.

Murray, J. P. (1980). *Television and youth: Twenty-five years of research and controversy.* Boys Town, NE: Boys Town Center for the Study of Youth Development.

Murray, J. P., & Salomon, G. (Eds.). (1984). *The future of children's television: Results of the Markle Foundation/ Boys Town Conference.* Boys Town, NE: Boys Town Center for the Study of Youth Development.

Nelson, L. L., & Kagan, S. (1972). Competition: The star-spangled scramble. *Psychology Today, 6,* 53.

Newson, J., & Newson, E. (1976). *Seven years in the home environment.* New York: Wiley.

O'Connor, R. D. (1969). Modification of social withdrawal through symbolic modeling. *Journal of Applied Behavior Analysis, 2,* 15–22.

Oden, S., & Asher, S. R. (1977). Coaching children in social skills for friendship making. *Child Development, 48,* 495–506.

Ogilvie, B. C., & Tutko, T. A. (1971). Sport: if you want to build character, try something else. *Psychology Today, 5,* pp. 60–63.

Parsons, T. (1959). The school class as a social system. *Harvard Educational Review, 29,* 297–318.

Passer, M. W. (1982). Psychological stress in youth sports. In R. A. Magill, M. J. Ash, & F. L. Smoll (Eds.), *Children in sport* (2nd ed.). (pp. 153–175). Champaign, IL: Human Kinetics.

Pearl, D., Bouthilet, L., & Lazar, J. (Eds.) (1982). Television and behavior: ten years of scientific progress and implications for the 80s. Vol. 1. Washington, DC: National Institute of Mental Health.

Peery, J. C. (1979). Popular, amiable, isolated, rejected: A reconception of sociometric status in preschool children. *Child Development, 50,* 1231–1234.

Radin, N. (1982). Primary caregiving and role-sharing fathers. In M. Lamb (Ed.), *Nontraditional families: Parenting and child development* (pp. 173–204). Hillsdale, NJ: Erlbaum.

Rausch, H. L. (1965). Interaction sequences. *Journal of Personality and Social Psychology, 2,* 487–499.

Rioux, J. W. (1968). The disadvantaged child in school. In J. Helmuth (Ed.), *The disadvantaged child.* New York: Bruner/Mazel.

Rist, R. C. (1970). Student social class and teacher expectations: The self-fulfilling prophecy in ghetto education. *Harvard Educational Review, 40,* 411–451.

Rogoff, B., Sellers, M., Pirotta, S., Fox, N., & White, S. (1975). Age of assignment of roles and responsibilities in children: A cross-cultural survey. *Human Development, 18,* 353–369.

Rosenthal, R., & Jacobson, L. (1968). *Pygmalion in the classroom.* New York: Holt, Rinehart & Winston.

Rubin, Z. (1980). *Children's friendships.* Cambridge, MA: Harvard University Press.

Rubinstein, E. A. (1983). Television and behavior. *American Psychologist, 38*(7), 820–825.

Rubinstein, E. A., Liebert, R. M. Neale, J. M., & Poulos, R. W. (1974). *Assessing television's influence on children's prosocial behavior.* Stony Brook, NY: Brookdale International Institute.

Rutter, M., Maughan, B., Mortimore, P., & Ouston, J. (1979). *Fifteen thousand hours: Secondary schools and their effects on children.* Cambridge, MA: Harvard University Press.

Santrock, J. W., & Warshak, R. A. (1979). Father custody and social development in boys and girls. *Journal of Social Issues, 35,* 112–125.

Savin-Williams, S. R. (1979). Dominance hierarchies in groups of early adolescents. *Child Development, 50,* 142–151.

Scarr, S. (1984). *Mother care, other care.* New York: Basic Books.

Shaw, M. E. (1973). Changes in sociometric choices following forced integration of an elementary school. *Journal of Social Issues, 29,* 143–157.

Sherif, M., Jarvey, O. J., White, B J., Wood, W. R., & Sherif, C. (1961). *Intergroup conflict and cooperation: The Robbers Cave experiment.* Norman, OK: University of Oklahoma Press.

Simon, J. A., & Martens, R. (1979). Children's anxiety in sport and non-sport evaluative activities. *Journal of Sport Psychology, 1,* 160–169.

Singer, D. G. (1983). A time to reexamine the role of television in our lives, *American Psychologist, 38,* 815–816.

Snow, R. (1969). Unfinished Pygmalion. *Contemporary Psychology, 14,* 197–199.

Stein, A. H., & Friedrich, L. K. (1975). Impact of television on children and youth. In E. M. Hetherington (Ed.), *Review of child development research* (Vol. 5). Chicago: University of Chicago Press.

Surgeon General's Scientific Advisory Committee on Television and Social Behavior. (1972). *Television and growing up: The import of televised violence.* Rockville, MD: NIMH.

Timmer, S. G. (1983). *How children use their time: A description of data and methods.* Paper presented at the meeting of the Society for Research in Child Development, Detroit, MI.

Timmer, S. G., Eccles, J., & O'Brien, K. (in press). How children use time. In F. T. Juster & F. P. Stafford (Eds.), *Time, goods, and well-being.* Ann Arbor, MI: Institute for Social Research, University of Michigan.

U.S. News & World Report (1980, June 16), p. 50. (From U.S. Department of Commerce data).

Vishner, E. B., & Vishner, J. S. (1978). Major areas of difficulty for stepparent couples. *International Journal of Family Counseling, 6,* 71–72.

Wallerstein, J. S., & Kelly, J. B. (1981). *Surviving the breakup: How children and parents cope with divorce.* New York: Basic Books.

Ziegler, M. E. (1983). *Assessing parents' and children's time together.* Paper presented at the meeting of the Society for Research in Child Development, Detroit, MI.

Zill, N., & Peterson, J. L. (1982, January). *Trends in the behavior and emotional well-being of U.S. children: Findings from a national survey.* Paper presented at the meeting of the American Association for the Advancement of Science, Washington, DC.

Chapter 12

Allen, W. L., & Newton, D. (1972). Development of conformity and independence. *Journal of Personality and Social Psychology, 22,* 18–30.

Asch, S. (1951). Effects of group pressure upon the modification and distortion of judgment. In M. Guetzkow (Ed.), *Groups, leadership, and man.* Pittsburgh, PA: Carnegie Press.

Bannister, D., & Agnew, J. (1976). The child's construing of the self. In J. K. Cole & A. W. Landfield (Eds.), *Nebraska symposium on motivation.* Lincoln, NE: Nebraska University Press.

Baumrind, D. (in press). Sex differences in moral reasoning: Response to Walker's (1984) conclusion that there are none. *Child Development.*

Beardslee, W. R., & Mack, J. (1983). Adolescents and the threat of nuclear war: The evolution of a perspective. *Yale Journal of Biology and Medicine, 56,* 79–91.

Berndt, T. (1979). Developmental changes in conformity to peers and parents. *Developmental Psychology, 15,* 608–616.

Bertenthal, B. I., & Fischer, K. W. (1978). Development of self-recognition in the infant. *Developmental Psychology, 14,* 44–50.

Borke, H. (1971). Interpersonal perception of young children: Egocentrism or empathy? *Developmental Psychology, 5,* 263–269.

Carroll, J. L., & Rest, J. R. (1981). Development in moral judgment as indicated by rejection of lower-stage statements. *Journal of Research in Personality, 15,* 538–544.

Chivian, E. E., Mack, J. E., & Waletzsky. (1983). *What Soviet children are saying about nuclear war: Project summary.* Mimeograph. The Nuclear Psychology Program, Harvard Medical School.

Clark, E. V. (1976). From gesture to word: On the natural history of deixis in language acquisition. In J. S. Bruner & A. Gartner (Eds.), *Human growth and development.* Oxford: Clarendon Press.

Colby, A., Kohlberg, L., Gibbs, J. C., Kandee, D., Hewer, R., Kaufman, K., Lieberman, M., Power, C., & Speicher-Dubin, B. (1983). *Assessing moral stages: A manual.* New York: Cambridge University Press.

Cooley, C. H. (1982). *Human nature and the social order.* New York: Scribners. (Originally published 1902).

Coopersmith, S. (1967). *The antecedents of self-esteem.* San Francisco: Freeman.

Damon, W. (1977). *The social world of the child.* San Francisco: Jossey-Bass.

Dweck, C. S., Davidson, W., Nelson, S., & Ehna, B. (1978). Sex differences in learned helplessness. II: The contingencies of evaluative feedback in the classroom. III: An experimental analysis. *Developmental Psychology, 14,* 268–276.

Dweck, C. S., & Elliott, E. S. (1983). Achievement motivation. In P. H. Mussen (Ed.), *Handbook of child psychology* (4th ed.). (Vol. 4, pp. 643–691). New York: Wiley.

Erikson, E. (1963). *Childhood and society* (1st ed.). New York: Norton.

Escalona, S. (1982). Growing up with the threat of nuclear war: Some indirect effects on personality development. *American Journal of Orthopsychiatry, 52,* 600–607.

Feshbach, N. (1978, March). *Empathy training: A field study in affective education.* Paper presented at a meeting of the American Education Research Association, Toronto.

Fishbein, H. D. (1976). *Evolution, development, and children's learning.* Pacific Palisades, CA: Goodyear.

Flavell, J. H., Botkin, P. T., Fry, C. L. Jr., Wright, J. W., & Jarvis, P. E. (1968). *The development of role-taking and communication skills in children.* New York: Wiley.

Flavell, J. H., Shipstead, S. G., & Croft, K. (1978). *What young children think you see when their eyes are closed.* Unpublished report, Stanford University.

Gallup, C. (1977). Self-recognition in primates: A comparative approach to the bidirectional properties of consciousness. *American Psychologist, 32,* 329–338.

Gilligan, C. (1977). In a different voice: Women's conception of the self and of morality. *Harvard Educational Review, 47,* 481–517.

Gilligan, C. (1982). *In a different voice: Psychological theory and women's development.* Cambridge, MA: Harvard University Press.

Greeno, C. G., & Maccoby, E. E. (1985, April). *How different is the "different voice"?* Paper presented at the meeting of the Society for Research in Child Development, Toronto.

Grusec, J. E., & Kuczynski, L. (1980). Direction of effect in socialization: A comparison of the parent *vs.* the child's behavior as determinants of disciplinary techniques. *Developmental Psychology, 16,* 1–9.

Haan, H. (in press). With regard to Walker (1984) on sex differences in moral reasoning. *Child Development.*

Harter, S. (1981). A model of intrinsic mastery motivation in children: Individual differences and developmental change. *Minnesota symposium on child development* (Vol. 14). Hillsdale, NJ: Erlbaum.

Harter, S. (1982). *Developmental differences in children's understanding of self-affect labels.* Unpublished manuscript, University of Denver.

Harter, S. (1983). Developmental perspectives on the self-system. In P. H. Mussen (Ed.), *Handbook of child psychology* (4th ed.). (Vol. 4, pp. 274–385). New York: Wiley.

Hartshorne, H., & May, M. A. (1928). *Studies in the nature of character. Vol. 1: Studies in deceit.* New York: Macmillan.

Hartup, W. W. (1983). Peer relations. In P. H. Mussen (Ed.), *Handbook of child psychology* (4th ed.). (Vol. 4, pp. 274–385). New York: Wiley.

Hoffman, M. L. (1979, October). Development of moral thought, feeling, and behavior. *American Psychologist, 34,* 958–966.

Kagan, J. (1981). *The second year: The emergence of self-awareness.* Cambridge, MA: Harvard University Press.

Kohlberg, L. (1963). The development of children's orientations toward a moral order: Sequence of development of moral thought. *Vita Humana, 6,* 11–33.

Kohlberg, L. (1969). Stage and sequence: The cognitive-developmental approach to socialization. In D. A. Goslin (Ed.), *Handbook of socialization theory and research.* Chicago: Rand McNally.

Kohlberg, L. (1971). From is to ought: How to commit the naturalistic fallacy and get away with it in the study of moral development. In T. Mischel (Ed.), *Cognitive development and epistemology.* New York: Academic Press.

Kohlberg, L. (1973). Continuities in childhood and adult moral development revisited. In P. B. Baltes & K. W. Schaie (Eds.), *Life-span developmental psychology: Personality and socialization.* New York: Academic Press.

Kohlberg, L. (1976). Moral stages and moralization: The cognitive-developmental approach. In T. Lickong (Ed.), *Moral development and behavior.* New York: Holt, Rinehart & Winston.

Kohlberg, L., Colby, A., Gibbs, J., & Speicher-Dubin, B. (1978). *Standard form scoring manual.* Cambridge, MA: Center for Moral Education, Harvard Graduate School of Education.

Kurtines, W., & Grief, E. B. (1974). The development of moral thought: Review and evaluation of Kohlberg's approach. *Psychological Bulletin, 81,* 453–470.

Livesley, W. J., & Bromley, D. B. (1973). *Person perception in childhood and adolescence.* London: Wiley.

Mack, J. E. (1982, March–April). But what about the Russians? *Harvard Magazine,* pp. 21–24, 53–54.

McGuire, W. J., McGuire, C. V., Child, P., & Fujioka, T. (1978). Salience of ethnicity in the spontaneous self-concept as a function of one's ethnic distinctiveness in the social environment. *Journal of Personality and Social Psychology, 36*(5), 511–520.

Mead, G. H. (1925). The genesis of the self and social control. *International Journal of Ethics, 35,* 251–273.

Mischel, W., & Mischel, H. (1976). A cognitive-social learning approach to morality and self-regulation. In T. Lickona (Ed.), *Moral development and behavior.* New York: Holt, Rinehart & Winston.

Nisan, M., & Kohlberg, L. (1982). Universality and variation in moral judgment: A longitudinal and cross-sectional study in Turkey. *Child Development, 53,* 865–876.

Piaget, J. (1965). *The moral judgment of the child.* (M. Gabain, Trans.). New York: Free Press. (First published in 1932; first publication in English in 1935).

Reifel, S. (1984, July). Children living with the nuclear threat. *Young Children,* pp. 74–80.

Rest, J. R. (1979). *Development in judging moral issues.* Minneapolis, MN: University of Minnesota Press.

Rest, J. R. (1983). Morality. In P. H. Mussen (Ed.), *The handbook of child psychology* (4th ed.). (Vol. 3, pp. 556–629). New York: Wiley.

Rest, J. R., Davison, M. L., & Robbins, S. (1978). Age trends in judging moral issues: A review of cross-sectional, longitudinal, and sequential studies of the defining issues test. *Child Development, 49,* 263–279.

Rholes, W. S., & Ruble, D. N. (1984). Children's understanding of dispositional characteristics of others. *Child Development, 55,* 530–560.

Rosenberg, M. (1979). *Conceiving the self.* New York: Basic Books.

Ruble, D. N., Parsons, J. E., & Ross, J. (1976). Self-evaluative responses of children in achievement settings. *Child Development, 47,* 990–997.

Schwebel, M. (1982). Effects of nuclear war threat on children and teenagers: Implications for professionals. *American Journal of Orthopsychiatry, 52,* 608–618.

Seligman, M. E. P. (1975). *Helplessness: On depression.* San Francisco: Freeman.

Selman, R. L. (1980). *The growth of interpersonal understanding.* New York: Academic Press.

Seuss, Dr. (1984). *The butter battle book.* New York: Random House.

Shantz, C. V. (1983). Social cognition. In P. H. Mussen (Ed.), *Handbook of child psychology* (4th ed.). (Vol. 3, pp. 495–554). New York: Wiley.

Silberman, C. (1970). *Crisis in the classroom: the remaking of American education.* New York: Random House.

Stipek, D. J. (1981, August). *Children's use of past performance information in ability and expectance judgments for self and others.* Paper presented at the meeting of the International Society for the Study of Behavioral Development, Toronto.

Sutton-Smith, B. (1971). A syntax for play and games. In R. R. Herron & B. Sutton-Smith (Eds.), *Child's play.* New York: Wiley.

Tapp, J. L., & Levine, F. J. (1977). *Law, justice, and the individual in society: Psychological and legal issues.* New York: Holt, Rinehart & Winston.

Uguroglu, M., & Walberg, H. (1979). Motivation and achievement: A quantitative synthesis. *American Educational Research Journal, 16,* 375–389.

Walker, L. J. (1984). Sex differences in the development of moral reasoning: A critical review. *Child Development, 55,* 677–691.

Weisz, J. R. (1981). Achievement behavior, contingency judgments, and the perception of control. Paper presented at the meeting of the International Society for the Study of Behavioral Development, Toronto.

Zill, N., & Peterson, L. (1982, January). *Trends in the behavior and emotional well-being of U.S. children: Findings from a national survey.* Paper presented at the meeting of the American Association for the Advancement of Science, Washington, DC.

Chapter 13

Allgeier, E. R., & Allgeier, A. R. (1984). *Sexual interactions.* Lexington, MA: D. C. Heath.

Baldwin, W. H. (1976). Adolescent pregnancy and childbearing—Growing concerns for Americans. *Population Bulletin, 31,* 1–34.

Bardwick, J. (1971). *Psychology of women: A study of biocultural conflicts.* New York: Harper and Row.

Blythe, D. A., Bulcroft, R., & Simmons, R. G. (1981, August). *The impact of puberty on adolescents: A longitudinal study.* Paper presented at the annual meeting of the American Psychological Association, Los Angeles.

Brooks-Gunn, J., & Ruble, D. N. (1982). The development of menstrual-related beliefs and behavior during early adolescence. *Child Development, 53,* 1567–1577.

Cavior, N., & Dokecki, D. R. (1973). Physical attractiveness, perceived attitude similarity, and academic achievement as contributors to interpersonal attraction among adolescents. *Developmental Psychology, 9,* 44–54.

Chilman, C. (1979). *Adolescent sexuality in a changing American society: Social and psychological perspectives.* Washington, DC: U.S. Government Printing Office.

Christensen, H. T., & Gregg, C. F. (1970). Changing sexual norms in America and Scandinavia. *Journal of Marriage and the Family, 32,* 616–627.

Chumlea, W. C. (1982). Physical growth in adolescence. In B. B. Wolman (Ed.), *Handbook of developmental psychology* (pp. 471–485). Englewood Cliffs, NJ: Prentice-Hall.

Clifford, E. (1971). Body ratification in adolescence. *Perceptual and Motor Skills, 33,* 119–125.

Czikszentmihalyi, M., & Larson, R. (1984). *Being adolescent: Conflict and growth in the teenage years.* New York: Basic Books.

DeLamater, J., & MacCorquodale, P. (1979). *Premarital sexuality: Attitudes, relationships, behavior.* Madison, WI: University of Wisconsin Press.

Dion, K., Berscheid, E., & Walster, E. (1972). What is beautiful is good. *Journal of Personality and Social Psychology, 24,* 285–290.

Dreyer, P. H. (1982). Sexuality during adolescence. In B. B. Wolman (Ed.), *Handbook of developmental psychology.* Englewood Cliffs, NJ: Prentice-Hall.

Eisen, M., Zellman, G. L., Leibowitz, A., Chow, W. K., & Evans, J. R. (1983). Factors discriminating pregnancy resolution decision of unmarried adolescents. *Genetic Psychology Monographs, 108,* 69–95.

Elias, J., & Gebhard, P. (1969). Sexuality and sexual learning in childhood. *Phi Beta Kappan, 50,* pp. 401–405.

Eveleth, P. B., & Tanner, J. M. (1976). *Worldwide variation in human growth.* Cambridge, England: Cambridge University Press.

Ford, C. S., & Beach, F. A. (1951). *Patterns of sexual behavior.* New York: Harper and Row.

Frazier, A., & Lizonbee, L. K. (1950). Adolescent concerns with physique. *School Review, 58,* 397–405.

Freud, S. (1964). Three essays on the theory of sexuality. In S. Freud, *The Standard Edition of the Complete Psychological Works of Sigmund Freud* (Vol. 7). London: Hogarth Press-Institute of Psychological Analysis. (Original work published 1905).

Furstenburg, F. F. (1976). *Unplanned parenthood.* New York: Free Press.

Furstenburg, F. F., Jr. (1980). Impact of early childbearing on the family. *Journal of Social Issues, 36,* 64–87.

Gagnon, J. H., & Simon, W. (1973). *Sexual conduct: The social origins of human sexuality.* Chicago: Aldine.

Gebhard, P. H. (1971). Human sexual behavior: A summary statement. In D. S. Marshall & R. C. Suggs (Eds.), *Human sexual behavior.* New York: Basic Books.

Harlow, H. (1975). Lust, latency, and love: Simian secrets of successful sex. *Journal of Sex Research, 11,* 79–90.

Hass, A. (1979). *Teenage sexuality: A survey of teenage behavior.* New York: Macmillan.

Heider, K. G. (1976, June). Dani sexuality: A low energy system. *Man, 11,* 188–201.

Hill, J. P. (1980). *Understanding early adolescence: A framework.* Chapel Hill, NC: Center for Early Adolescence.

Hunt, M. (1974). *Sexual behavior in the 1970s.* Chicago: Playboy Press.

Hyde, J. S. (1979). *Understanding human sexuality.* New York: McGraw-Hill.

Jersild, J. T., Brook, J. S., & Brook, D. W. (1978). *The psychology of adolescence* (3rd ed.). New York: Macmillan.

Jessor, R., Costa, F., Jessor, L., & Donovan, J. E. (1983). Time of first intercourse: A prospective study. *Journal of Personality and Social Psychology, 44*(no. 3), 608–626.

Jones, M. C. (1957). The later careers of boys who were early- or late-maturing. *Child Development, 28,* 115–128.

Jones, M. C. (1965). Psychological correlates of somatic development. *Child Development, 36,* 899–911.

Jones, M. C., & Bayley, N. (1950). Physical maturing among boys as related to behavior. *Journal of Educational Psychology, 41.* 129–148.

Kanter, J. F., & Zelnick, M. (1972). Sexual experience of young unmarried women in the United States. *Family Planning Perspectives, 4*(no. 4), 9–18.

Kanter, J. F., & Zelnick, M. (1973). Contraception and pregnancy: Experience of young unmarried women in the United States. *Family Planning Perspectives, 5*(no. 1), 21–35.

Kinsey, A. C., Pomeroy, W. B., & Martin, C. E. (1948). *Sexual behavior in the human male.* Philadelphia, PA: Saunders.

Kinsey, A. C., Pomeroy, W. B., Martin, C. E., & Gebhard, P. H. (1953). *Sexual behavior in the human female.* Philadelphia, PA: Saunders.

Kleck, R. E., Richardson, S. A., & Ronald, L. (1974). Physical appearance cues and interpersonal attraction in children. *Child Development, 45,* 305–310.

Konner, M. (1982). *The tangled web: Biological constraints on the human spirit.* New York: Holt, Rinehart & Winston.

Krogman, W. M. (1970). Growth of head, face, trunk and limbs in Philadelphia white and Negro children of elementary and high school age. *Monographs of the Society for Research on Child Development, 35* (3), serial no. 136.

La Plante, M. N., McCormick, N., & Brannigan, G. G. (1980). Living the sexual script: College students' views of influences in sexual encounters. *Journal of Sex Research, 16,* 338–355.

Luker, K. (1975). *Taking chances: Abortion and the decision not to contracept.* Berkeley, CA: University of California Press.

Martinson, F. M. (1973). *Infant and child sexuality: A sociological perspective.* St. Peter, MN: The Book Mark (Gustavus Adolphus College).

Matteson, D. R. (1975). *Adolescence today: Sex roles and the search for identity.* Homewood, IL: Dorsey.

Mead, M. (1928). *Coming of age in Samoa.* New York: Morrow.

Meredith, H. V. (1963). Changes in the stature and body weight of North American boys during the last 80 years. In L. P. Lipsitt and C. C. Spiker (Eds.) *Advances in child development and behavior.* Vol. 1. NY: Academic Press.

Merriam, A. P. (1971). Aspects of sexual behavior among the Bala (Basongye). In D. S. Marshall & R. C. Suggs (Eds.) *Human sexual behavior.* NY: Basic Books.

Messenger, J. C. (1971). Sex and repression in an Irish folk community. In D. S. Marshall & R. C. Suggs (Eds.), *Human sexual behavior.* New York: Basic Books.

Mussen, P. H., & Bourterline-Young, H. (1964). Relationships between rate of physical maturing and personality among boys of Italian descent. *Vita Humana, 7,* 186–200.

Mussen, P. H., & Jones, M. C. (1957). Self-conceptions, motivations, and interpersonal attitudes of late- and early-maturing boys. *Child Development, 28,* 243–256.

Muuss, R. E. (1975). Adolescent development and the secular trend. In R. E. Muuss (Ed.), *Adolescent behavior and society* (2nd ed.). New York: Random House.

Oskamp, S., & Mindick, B. (1981). Personality and attitudinal barriers to contraception. In D. Byrne & W. A. Fisher (Eds.), *Adolescents, sex, and contraception.* New York: McGraw-Hill.

Parke, R. D., Power, T. G., & Fischer, T. (1980). The adolescent father's impact on the mother and child. *Journal of Social Issues, 36,* 88–106.

Peskin, H. (1967). Pubertal onset and ego functioning. *Journal of Abnormal Psychology, 72,* 1–15.

Peskin, H. (1973). Influence of the development schedule of puberty on learning and ego functioning. *Journal of Youth and Adolescence, 2,* 273–290.

Petersen, A. C., & Taylor, B. (1980). The biological approach to adolescence: Biological change and physiological adaptation. In J. Adelson (Ed.), *Handbook of adolescent psychology.* New York: Wiley.

Reiss, I. (1967). *The social context of sexual permissiveness.* New York: Holt, Rinehart & Winston.

Russell, C. S. (1980). Unscheduled parenthood: Transition to "parent" for the teenager. *Journal of Social Issues, 36,* 45–63.

Ryan, A. J. (1975). The female athlete: Gynecological considerations. *Journal of Health, Physical Education, and Recreation, 46,* 40–44.

Search Institute. (1984, July). Young adolescents and their parents. Reported in *Psychology Today,* p. 8.

Sears, R. R., Maccoby, E. E., & Levin, H. (1957). Patterns of child-rearing. Evanston, IL: Row, Peterson.

Siegel, O. (1982). Personality development in adolescence. In B. B. Wolman (Ed.), *Handbook of developmental psychology*. Englewood Cliffs, NJ: Prentice-Hall.

Simmons, R. G., & Rosenberg, F. (1975). Sex, sex roles, and self-image. *Journal of Youth and Adolescence, 4,* 225–258.

Sorenson, R. C. (1973). *Adolescent sexuality in contemporary America*. New York: World.

Tanner, J. M. (1970). Physical growth. In P. H. Mussen (Ed.), *Carmichael's Manual of child psychology*. New York: Wiley.

Tanner, J. M. (1971). Sequence and individual variation in the growth and development of boys and girls aged twelve to sixteen. *Daedalus, 100,* 907–930.

Tanner, J. M. (1974). *Readings from* Scientific American: *Biological anthropology*. San Francisco: W. H. Freeman.

Tanner, J. M. (1978). *Fetus into man*. Cambridge, MA: Harvard University Press.

Thornburg, D. H. (1981). Sources of sex education among early adolescents. *Journal of Early Adolescence, 1,* 174.

Weatherly, D. (1964). Self-perceived rate of physical maturation and personality in late adolescence. *Child Development, 35,* 1197–1210.

Willmore, J. H. (1982). The female athlete. In R. S. Magill, M. J. Ash, & F. L. Smoll (Eds.), *Children in sport* (2nd ed.). (pp. 106–117). Champaign, IL: Human Kinetics.

Zelnick, M., Kanter, J. F. & Ford, K. (1981). *Sex and pregnancy in adolescence*. Beverly Hills, CA: Sage.

Chapter 14

Adelson, J., & O'Neil, R. P. (1966). Growth of political ideas in adolescence: The sense of community. *Journal of Personality and Social Psychology, 4,* 295–306.

Armstrong, J. M. (1980). Achievement and participation of women in mathematics. Final report to the National Institute of Education, Washington, DC.

Benbow, C. P., & Stanley, J. C. (1980). Sex differences in mathematical ability: Fact or artifact? *Science, 210,* 58–59ff.

Berry, J. W., & Dasen, P. (Eds.). (1974). *Culture and cognition: Readings in cross-cultural psychology*. London: Methuen.

Blos, P. (1962). *On adolescence*. New York: Free Press.

Borow, H. (Ed.), (1973). *Career guidance for a new age*. Boston: Houghton Mifflin.

Bruner, J. S., Olver, R. R., & Greenfield, P. M. (1966). *Studies in cognitive growth*. New York: Wiley.

Cole, M. (1978). How education affects the mind. *Human Nature, 1,* 50–58.

Cole, M., Gay, J., Glick, J. A., and Sharp, D. W. (1971). *The cultural context of learning and thinking*. New York: Basic Books.

Constantinople, A. (1969). An Eriksonian measure of personality development in college students. *Developmental Psychology, 1,* 357–372.

Dansen, P. R. (1972, March). Cross-cultural Piagetian research: A summary. *Journal of Cross-Cultural Psychology, 3,* 23–39.

DeLisis, R., & Staudt, J. (1980). Individual differences in college students' performance on formal operational tasks. *Journal of Applied Developmental Psychology, 1,* 201–208.

Donovan, J. M. (1975). Identity status and interpersonal style. *Journal of Youth and Adolescence, 4,* 37–55.

Dulit, E. (1972). Adolescent thinking à la Piaget: The formal stage. *Journal of Youth and Adolescence, 1,* 281–301.

Erikson, E. H. (1969). *Gandhi's truth*. New York: Norton.

Erikson, E. H. (1962). *Young man Luther*. New York: Norton.

Fennoma, E., & Sherman, J. (1977). Sex-related differences in mathematics achievement, spatial visualization, and affective factors. *American Education Research Journal, 14,* 51–71.

Flavell, J. H. (1963). *The developmental psychology of Jean Piaget*. Princeton, NJ: Van Nostrand.

Flavell, J. H. (1977). *Cognitive development*. Englewood Cliffs, NJ: Prentice-Hall.

Flavell, J. H. (1980, October). *Structures, stages, and sequences in cognitive development*. Paper presented at the Minnesota Symposium of Child Psychology, Minneapolis, MN.

Flavell, J. H. (1985). *Cognitive development* (2nd ed.). Englewood Cliffs, NJ: Prentice-Hall.

Flavell, J. H., & Wohlwill, J. F. (1969). Formal and functional aspects of cognitive development. In D. Elkind & J. H. Flavell (Eds.), *Studies in cognitive development: Essays in honor of Jean Piaget* (pp. 000–000). New York: Oxford University Press.

Ford, C. S., & Beach, F. S. (1951). *Patterns of sexual behavior*. New York: Harper & Row.

Freeman, D. (1983). *Margaret Mead and Samoa: The making and unmaking of an anthropological myth*. New York: Oxford University Press.

Ginsburg, H., & Opper, S. (1969). *Piaget's theory of intellectual development: An introduction*. Englewood Cliffs, NJ: Prentice-Hall.

Gladwin, T. (1970). *East is a big bird*. Cambridge, MA: Harvard University Press.

Goodenough, E. W. (1957). Interest in persons as an aspect of sex differences in the early years. *Genetic Psychological Monographs, 55,* 287–323.

Harris, L. J. (1979). Sex differences in spacial ability: Possible environmental, genetic, and neurological factors. In M. Kinsbourne (Ed.), *Asymmetrical function of the brain*. Cambridge, England: Cambridge University Press.

Hill, J. P. (1980). *Understanding early adolescence: A framework*. Chapel Hill, NC: Center for Early Adolescence, University of North Carolina.

Inhelder, B., & Piaget, J. (1958). *The growth of logical thinking from childhood to adolescence.* New York: Basic Books.

Josselson, R. L. (1973). Psychodynamic aspects of identity formation in college women. *Journal of Youth and Adolescence, 2,* 3–52.

Kacerguis, M. A., & Adams, G. R. (1980). Erikson stage resolution: The relationship between identity and intimacy. *Journal of Youth and Adolescence, 9,* 117–126.

Keating, D. (1980). Thinking processes in adolescence. In J. Adelson (Ed.), *Handbook of adolescent psychology.* New York: Wiley.

Keating, D., & Clark, D. V. (1980). Development of physical and social reasoning in adolescents. *Developmental Psychology, 16,* 23–30.

Kramer, D. A. (1983). Post-formal operations? A need for further conceptualization. *Child Development, 26,* 91–105.

Lauer, R. H. (1973). *Perspectives on social change.* Boston: Allyn & Bacon.

LaVoie, J. C. (1976). Ego identity formation in middle adolescence. *Journal of Youth and Adolescence, 5,* 371–385.

Lerner, R. M., & Shea, J. A. (1982). Social behavior in adolescence. In B. B. Wolman (Ed.), *Handbook of developmental psychology.* Englewood Cliffs, NJ: Prentice-Hall.

Lipset, S. M. (1976). *Rebellion in the university.* Chicago: University of Chicago Press.

Maccoby, E. E., & Jacklin, C. N. (1974). *The psychology of sex differences.* Stanford, CA: Stanford University Press.

Marcia, J. E. (1966). Development and validation of ego-identity status. *Journal of Personality and social Psychology, 3,* 551–558.

Marcia, J. E. (1980). Identity in adolescence. In J. Adelson (Ed.), *Handbook of adolescent psychology.* New York: Wiley.

Marcia, J. E. (1985). *Identity status interview.* Unpublished personal communication.

Marcia, J. E., & Friedman, M. L. (1970). Ego identity status in college women. *Journal of Personality, 38,* 249–263.

McClosky, M., Caramazza, A., & Green, B. (1980). Curvilinear motion in the absence of external forces: Naive beliefs about the motion of objects. *Science, 210,* 1139–1141.

McGuinness, D. (1985). *When children don't learn: Understanding the biology and psychology of learning disabilities.* New York: Basic Books.

Mead, M. (1928). *Coming of age in Samoa.* New York: Morrow.

Mollar, H. (1968). Youth as a force in the modern world. *Comparative Studies in Society and History, 10,* 237–260.

Morison, S. E. (1936). *Three centuries of Harvard.* Cambridge, MA: Harvard University Press.

Moshman, D. (1979). Development of formal hypothesis-testing ability. *Developmental Psychology, 15,* 104–112.

Neimark, E. D. (1970). Model for a thinking machine: An information processing framework for the study of cognitive development. *Merrill-Palmer Quarterly, 16,* 345–368.

Neimark, E. D. (1975). Intellectual development during adolescence. In F. D. Horowitz (Ed.), *Review of child development research* (Vol. 1). Chicago: University of Chicago Press.

Orlofsky, J. L., & Marcia, J. E., & Lesser, I. M. (1973). Ego identity status and the intimacy *vs.* isolation crisis of young adulthood. *Journal of Personality and Social Psychology, 27,* 211–219.

Piaget, J. (1970). Piaget's theory. In P. H. Mussen (Ed.), *Carmichael's manual of child psychology* (3rd ed.). (Vol. 1). New York: Wiley.

Podd, M. H. (1972). Ego identity status and morality: The relationship between two developmental constructs. *Developmental Psychology, 6,* 497–507.

Poppen, P. J. (1974). *The development of sex differences in moral judgment for college males and females.* Unpublished doctoral dissertation, Cornell University.

Ross, J. M., & Simpson, H. R. (1971). The national survey of health and development, 1. Educational attainment. *British Journal of Psychology, 41,* 49–61.

Scarr, S., & Carter-Saltzman, L. (1982). Genetics and intelligence. In R. J. Sternberg (Ed.), *Handbook of human intelligence* (pp. 792–898). New York: Cambridge University Press.

Siegel, O. (1982). Personality development in adolescence. In B. B. Wolman (Ed.), *Handbook of developmental psychology.* Englewood Cliffs, NJ: Prentice-Hall.

Siegler, R. S. (1983). Information processing approaches to development. In P. H. Mussen (Ed.), *Handbook of child psychology* (3rd ed.). (Vol. 1, pp. 129–211). New York: Wiley.

Sternberg, R. J. (1977). *Intelligence, information processing, and analogical reasoning: The componential analysis of human abilities.* Hilldale, NJ: Erlbaum.

Sternberg, R. J., & Powell, J. (1983). The development of intelligence. In P. H. Mussen (Ed.), *Handbook of child psychology.* (3rd ed.). (*Vol. 3*). NY: Wiley.

Super, C. M. (1980). Cognitive development: Looking across at growing up. In C. M. Super & S. Harkness (Eds.), *New directions for child development. No. 8: Anthropological perspectives on child development* (pp. 59–69). San Francisco: Jossey-Bass.

Tapp, J. L., & Kohlberg, L. (1971). Developing senses of law and legal justice. *Journal of Social Issues, 27,* 65–93.

Tavris, C., & Wade, C. (1984). *The longest war: Sex differences in perspective* (2nd ed.). San Diego, CA: Harcourt Brace Jovanovich.

Toder, N. L., & Marcia, J. E. (1973). Ego identity status and response to conformity pressure in college women. *Journal of Personality and Social Psychology, 26,* 287–294.

Torney, J. V. (1971). Socialization of attitudes toward the legal system. *Journal of Social Issues, 27,* 137–154.

Tulkin, S. R., & Konner, M. J. (1973). Alternative conceptions of intellectual functioning. *Human Development, 16,* 33–52.

Turner, V. W. (1967). *The forest of symbols: Aspects of Ndembu ritual.* Ithaca, NY: Cornell University Press.

Ullman, C. (1982). Cognitive and emotional antecedents of religious conversion. *Journal of Personality and Social Psychology, 43*(1), 183–192.

Vandenberg, S. G., & Kuse, A. R. (1975). A critical review of the sex-linked major-gene hypothesis. In M. A. Wittig & A. C. Peterson (Eds.), *Sex-related differences in cognitive functioning.* New York: Academic Press.

Waterman, A. S., & Waterman, C. K. (1972). Relationship between ego identity status and subsequent academic behavior: A test of the predictive validity of Marcia's categorization for identity status. *Developmental Psychology, 6,* 179.

Chapter 15

Achenbach, T. M. (1982). *Developmental psychopathology* (2nd ed.). New York: Wiley.

Bachman, J. G. (1982, June 28). *The American high school student: A profile based on survey data.* Paper presented in Berkeley, CA.

Bahr, H. M. (1980). Changes in family life in Middletown. *Public Opinion Quarterly, 44,* 35–52.

Barnes, G. M. (1977). The development of adolescent drinking behavior: An evaluative review of the impact of the socialization process within the family. *Adolescence, 13,* 571–595.

Berndt, T. J. (1979). Developmental changes in conformity to peers and parents. *Developmental Psychology, 15,* 608–616.

Berndt, T. J. (1981). Relationship between social cognition, nonsocial cognition, and social behavior: The case of friendship. In J. H. Flavell & L. D. Ross (Eds.), *Social cognitive development: Frontiers and possible futures.* New York: Cambridge University Press.

Bigelow, B. J., & LaGaipa, J. J. (1980). The development of friendship values and choices. In H. C. Foot, A. J. Chapman, & R. J. Smith (Eds.), *Friendship and social relations in children.* New York: Wiley.

Braungart, R. J. (1980). Youth movements. In J. Adelson (Ed.), *Handbook of adolescent psychology* (pp. 560–597). New York: Wiley.

Brittain, C. V. (1968). An exploration of the bases of peer-compliance and parent-compliance in adolescence. *Adolescence, 2,* 445–458.

Brody, J. E. (1984, July 14). Therapy helps teen-age girls having anorexia nervosa. *The New York Times,* section 4, p. 20.

Brook, J. S., Whiteman, M., & Gordon, A. S. (1983). Stages of drug use in adolescence: Personality, peer, and family correlates. *Developmental Psychology, 19,* 269–277.

Bruhn, J. G., & Seiden, R. H. (1965). Student suicide: Fact or fancy? *Journal of the American College Health Association, 14,* 69–77.

Brumberg, J. J. (1982). Chlorotic girls, 1870–1920: A historical perspective on female adolescence. *Child Development, 53,* 1468–1477.

Carins, R. B., & Cairns, B. D. (1983, October 11). *Gender similarities and differences: A developmental perspective.* Paper presented at the Nag's Head Conference.

Cloward, R. A., & Ohlin, L. E. (1960). *Delinquency and opportunity.* New York: Free Press.

Coleman, J. C. (1974). *Relationships in adolescence.* Boston and London: Routledge and Kegan, Paul.

Coleman, J. C. (1980). Friendship and the peer group in adolescence. In J. Adelson (Ed.), *Handbook of adolescent psychology* (pp. 408–431). New York: Wiley, 1980.

Coleman, J. S. (1961). *The adolescent society.* New York: Free Press.

Coleman, J. S., Campbell, E., et al. (1966). *Equality for educational opportunity.* U.S. Department of Health, Education and Welfare, Office of Education. Washington, DC: U.S. Government Printing Office.

Coleman, J. S., Hoffer, T., & Kilgore, S. (1981). *Public and private schools: Report submitted to the National Center for Education Statistics.* Chicago: National Opinion Research Center.

Conger, J., & Petersen, A. (1984). Adolescence and youth. In J. Adelson (Ed.), *Handbook of adolescent psychology.* (4th ed.). New York: Harper & Row.

Cleckley, H. (1976). *The mask of sanity.* (5th ed.). St. Louis, MO: Mosby.

Cooper, C., Grotevant, H. D., Moore, M. S., & Conder, S. M. (1982, August). *Family support and conflict: Both foster adolescent identity and role taking.* Paper presented at the American Psychological Association, Washington, DC.

Crime in the U.S.: Uniform Crime Reports. (1982). Published annually by the FBI, U.S. Department of Justice, Washington, DC.

Czikszentmihalyi, M., & Larson, R. (1984). *Being adolescent: Conflict and growth in the teenage years.* New York: Basic Books.

Diaz, R. M., & Berndt, T. J. (1982). Children's knowledge of a best friend: Fact or fancy? *Developmental Psychology, 18,* 787–794.

Douvan, E., & Adelson, J. (1966). *The adolescent experience.* New York: Wiley.

Dunphy, D. C. (1963). The social structure of urban adolescent peer groups. *Sociometry, 26,* 230–246.

Eitzen, D. S. (1975). Athletics in the status system of male adolescents: A replication of Coleman's *The adolescent society. Adolescence, 10,* 267–276.

Elder, G. H., Jr. (1975). Adolescence in the life cycle. In S. Dragastin & G. H. Elder (Eds.), *Adolescence in the life cycle.* Washington, DC: Hemisphere.

Elder, G. H., Jr. (1980). Adolescence in historical perspective. In J. Adelson (Ed.), *Handbook of adolescent psychology* (pp. 3–46). New York: Wiley.

Elkind, D. (1967). Middle-class delinquency. *Mental Hygiene, 51,* 80–84.

Elkind, D. (1980). Strategic interactions in early adolescence. In J. Adelson (Ed.), *Handbook of adolescent psychology* (pp. 432–444). New York: Wiley.

Evans, R. I., Rozelle, R. M., Mittelmark, M. B., Hansen, W. B., Bane, A. L., & Havis, J. (1978). Deterring the onset of smoking in children: Knowledge of immediate physiological effects and coping with peer pressure, media pressure, and parental modeling. *Journal of Applied Social Psychology, 8,* 126–135.

Eysenck, H. J. (1964). *Crime and personality.* Boston: Houghton-Mifflin.

Farrington, D. P. (1982). Delinquency from 10 to 25. In S. A. Mednick (Ed.), *Antecedents of aggression and antisocial behavior.* Hingham, MA: Kluwer Boston.

Friesen, D. (1968). Academic-athletic-popularity syndrome on the Canadian high school society. *Adolescence, 3,* 39–52.

Gallatin, J. (1980). Political thinking in adolescence. In J. Adelson (Ed.), *Handbook of adolescent psychology* (pp. 344–383). New York: Wiley.

Gold, M., & Petronio, R. J. (1980). Delinquent behavior in adolescence. In J. Adelson (Ed.), *Handbook of adolescent psychology.* New York: Wiley.

Gold, M., & Reimer, D. J. (1975). Changing patterns of delinquent behavior among Americans 13–16 years old, 1967–1972. *Crime and Delinquency Literature, 7,* 483–517.

Gottesman, I. I. (1983). *Schizophrenia: the epigenetic puzzle.* Boston: Cambridge University Press.

Hall, G. S. (1904). *Adolescence: Its psychology and relations to physiology, anthropology, sociology, sex, crime, religion and education.* New York: Appleton.

Halmi, K. A., Falk, J. R., & Schwartz, E. (1981). Binge eating and vomiting: A survey of a college population. *Psychological Medicine, 11,* 697–706.

Hill, J. P. *Understanding early adolescence: A framework.* Chapel Hill, NC: Center for Early Adolescence, University of North Carolina.

Jessor, R., Chase, J. A., & Donovan, J. E. (1980). Psychosocial correlates of marijuana use and problem drinking in a national sample of adolescents. *American Journal of Public Health, 70,* 604–613.

Kandel, D. B., & Lesser, G. S. (1969). Parental and peer influences on educational plans of adolescents. *American Sociological Review, 34,* 213–223.

Kaza Lunas, J. R. (1978). Sexism in education. *Clearing House, 51,* pp. 388–391.

Lerner, R. M., Karson, M., Meisels, M., & Knapp, J. R. (1975). Actual and preceived attitudes of late adolescents and their parents: The phenomenon of generation gaps. *Journal of Genetic Psychology, 126,* 195–207.

Lerner, R. M., & Shea, J. A. (1982). Social behavior in adolescence. In B. B. Wolman (Ed.), *Handbook of developmental psychology* (pp. 503–525). Englewood Cliffs, NJ: Prentice-Hall.

Loeber, R. (1982). The stability of antisocial and delinquent child behavior: A review. *Child Development, 53,* 1431–1446.

Lynd, R. R., & Lynd, H. M. (1929). *Middletown.* New York: Harcourt, Brace & World.

Lynd, R. R., & Lynd, H. M. (1937). *Middletown in transition.* New York: Harcourt, Brace & World.

Mannheim, K. (1952). The problem of generations. *Essay on the sociology of knowledge.* London: Routledge and Kegan, Paul.

Merton, R. K. (1958). Social structure and anomie. *American Sociological Review, 3,* 672–682.

Mervis, J. (1984, April). Adolescent behavior: What we think we know. *APA Monitor.*

Mitchell, S., & Rosa, P. (1981). Boyhood behavior problems as precursors of criminality: A fifteen-year follow-up study. *Journal of Child Psychology and Psychiatry, 22,* 19–33.

Montemayor, R. (1982, October). *Parent-adolescent conflict: A critical review of the literature.* Paper presented at the first Biennial Conference on Adolescence, Tucson, AZ.

Offer, D., Ostrov, E., & Howard, K. J. (1981). *The adolescent: A psychological self-portrait.* New York: Basic Books.

Rutter, M., & Garmezy, N. (1983). In P. H. Mussen (Ed.), *Handbook of child psychology* (4th ed.). (Vol. 4, pp. 775–911). New York: Wiley.

Rutter, M., Maughan, B., Mortimore, P., & Ouston, J. (1979). *Fifteen thousand hours: Secondary schools and their effects on children.* Cambridge, MA: Harvard University Press.

Santrock, J. W. (1984). *Adolescence: An introduction* (2nd ed.). Dubuque, IA: William C. Brown.

Sheras, P. (1983). Suicide in adolescence. In E. Walker & M. Roberts (Eds.), *Handbook of child/clinical psychology.* New York: Wiley.

Thompson, M. G. (1979). *Life adjustment of women with anorexia nervosa and anorexia-like behavior.* Unpublished doctoral dissertation, University of Chicago.

Weiner, I. B. (1970). *Psychological disturbance in adolescence.* New York: Wiley.

Weiner, I. B. (1982). *Child and adolescent psychopathology.* New York: Wiley.

Wright, P. H. (1982). Men's friendships, women's friendships, and the alleged inferiority of the latter. *Sex Roles, 8,* 1–20.

Text Credits (*continued from page ii*)

Figure Credits

Chapter 10

10-1 adapted from P. E. Vernon, *The Structure of Human Abilities.* London: Methuen, 1971.

10-3 adapted from R. L. Atkinson, R. C. Atkinson, and E. R. Hilgard, *Introduction to Psychology,* 8th ed. New York: Harcourt Brace Jovanovich, Inc., 1983, and: J. C. Flanagan, "The Definition and Measurement of Ingenuity." In C. W. Taylor and R. Barron (eds.), *Scientific Creativity: Its Recognition and Development.* Copyright © 1963 John Wiley & Sons, Inc. Reprinted by permission of John Wiley & Sons, Inc. J. P. Guilford, "A Factor Analytic Study Across the Domains of Reasoning, Creativity, and Evaluation I: Hypothesis and Description of Tests," *Reports from the Psychology Laboratory.* Los Angeles: University of Southern California Press, 1954. Used by permission of the publisher. J. W. Getzels, and P. W. Jackson, *Creativity and Intelligence: Explorations with Gifted Students.* © 1962 John Wiley & Sons, Inc. Reprinted by permission of John Wiley & Sons, Inc. E. P. Torrance, *Torrance Tests of Creative Thinking, Verbal Forms A and B.* Princeton, N.J.: Personnel Press, Inc., 1966. M. A. Wallach and N. Kogan, *Modes of Thinking in Young Children.* Copyright © 1965 by Holt, Rinehart & Winston, Inc. Reprinted by permission of CBS College Publishing. S. A. Mednick, "The Associative Basis of the Creative Process," *Psychology Review, 69.* © 1962 American Psychological Association. Adapted by permission of the author.

10-4 courtesy of The Baltimore Museum of Art: The Cone Collection, formed by Dr. Claribel Cone and Miss Etta Cone of Baltimore, Maryland. BMA 1950.

10-6 James M. Sattler, *Assessment of Children's Intelligence and Special Abilities* (2nd ed.) Boston: Allyn & Bacon, 1982.

10-7 R. B. Cattell, and M. D. Cattell, *Culture Fair Intelligence Test.* Champaign, IL: Institute for Personality and Ability Testing, © 1949, 1960. Reprinted by permission.

Chapter 11

11-2 N. Zill and J. L. Peterson, "Trends in the Behavior and Emotional Well-being of U.S. Children." Paper presented at the annual meeting of the American Association for the Advancement of Science, Washington, D.C., January, 1982.

Chapter 12

12-2 L. Kohlberg, "The Development of Children's Orientations Toward a Moral Order." *Vita Humana, 6,* 1963, pp. 11–33.

12-3 T. Berndt, "Developmental Changes in Conformity to Peers and Parents." *Developmental Psychology, 15,* 1979, pp. 600–616.

Chapter 13

13-1 M. Csikszentmihalyi and R. Larson, *Being Adolescent: Conflict and Growth in the Teenage Years.* New York: Basic Books, 1984.

13-2 adapted from *Readings from Scientific American: Biological Anthropology.* San Francisco: W. H. Freeman, 1974.

13-5, 13-7 adapted from Anne C. Peterson and Brandon Taylor, "The Biological Approach to Adolescence: Biological Change and Psychological Adaptation." In Joseph Adelson (ed.), *Handbook of Adolescent Psychology.* New York: Wiley, 1980.

13-6 J. M. Tanner, "Sequence and Individual Variation in the Growth and Development of Boys and Girls Aged Twelve to Sixteen." *Daedalus,* 1971.

13-8 Adapted from A. Vener & C. Stewart, "Adolescent Sexual Behavior in Middle America Revisited: 1970–1973," *Journal of Marriage and the Family* (November 1974): 728. Copyright 1974 by the National Council on Family Relations, 1910 West County Road B, Suite 147, St. Paul, MN 55113. Reprinted by permission.

Chapter 15

15-1 D. C. Dunphy, "The Social Structure of Urban Adolescent Peer Groups." *Sociometry,* Vol. 26, 1963.

15-2 James C. Coleman, "Friendship and the Peer Group in Adolescence." In Joseph Adelson, (ed.), *Handbook of Adolescent Development.* New York: Wiley, 1980.

15-3, 15-4 M. Csikszentmihalyi and R. Larson, *Being Adolescent: Conflict and Growth in the Teenage Years.* New York: Basic Books, 1984.

15-5 M. Gold and R. J. Petronio, "Delinquent Behavior in Adolescence." In J. Adelson (ed.), *Handbook of Adolescent Psychology.* New York: Wiley, 1980.

15-6 L. D. Johnston, P. M. O'Malley, and J. G. Bachman, *Use of licit and illicit drugs by America's high school students, 1975–1984* (National Institute on Drug Abuse) (Washington, D.C.: U.S. Government Printing Office, 1985), p. 55.

Photo Credits

Preface and Table of Contents

P. 3, © R. V. Eckert/EKM-Nepenthe; p. 5, © Paul Conklin; p. 6, (top left) © Larry Kolvoord/TexaStock; (bottom left) © Bob Daemmrich/TexaStock; (right) © Ralph Barrera/TexaStock; p. 7, (left) © Lennart Nilsson; (right) © David E. Kennedy/TexaStock; p. 9, © R. V. Eckert/EKM-Nepenthe; p. 10, © David R. Frazier; p. 11, (left) © Bob Daemmrich/TexaStock; (right) Michael D. Sullivan/TexaStock; p. 12, (left) © Melanie Kaestner/Zephyr Pictures; (right) © David R. Frazier; p. 13, (left top and bottom) © Michael D. Sullivan/TexaStock; (right)© Dale Ahearn/TexaStock; p. 14, © David E. Kennedy/TexaStock; p. 15, © Jill Cannefax/EKM-Nepenthe; p. 16, © Reed Kaestner/Zephyr Pictures.

Part and Chapter Openers

Part 1, © Peter Menzel/Stock, Boston; Chapter 1, © Strickler/Monkmeyer Press Photo Service; Chapter 2, © Harvey Stein; Part 2, © Erika Stone; Chapter 3, © Joel Gordon; Chapter 4, © Elizabeth Crews; Chapter 5, © Jean-Claude Lejeune/Stock, Boston; Part 3, © Media Vision/Peter Arnold, Inc.; Chapter 6, © Fredrik D. Bodin/Stock, Boston; Chapter 7, © Elizabeth Crews; Chapter 8, © Mel Konner/Anthro-Photo; Part 4, © Ellen Shub/Picture Cube; Chapter 9, © Photo Researchers; Chapter 10, © David R. Frazier; Chapter 11, © Paul Conklin/Monkmeyer; Chapter 12, © Jeanne Tifft/Photo Researchers; Part 5, © Elizabeth Crews; Chapter 13, © Donald Dietz/Stock Boston; Chapter 14, © Patsy Davidson/The Image Works; Chapter 15, © Bob Daemmrich/TexaStock.

Unnumbered photos and illustrations

Chapter 1: p. 6, courtesy The Ferdinand Hamburger Jr. Archives of the Johns Hopkins University; p. 7, Gehr/Life Magazine, © 1947 Time Inc.; p. 12, Arthur Devis: "The James Family." Oil on canvas, 1751. The Granger Collection; p. 13, courtesy the Department of Library Services, American Museum of Natural History, Neg. #326799; p. 14, photo by Lewis Hine, from the Collections of the Library of Congress; p. 17, © Jason Laure/Woodfin Camp; p. 19, courtesy Lyndon Baines Johnson Library/National Archives; p. 26, courtesy Clark University; p. 33, drawing by M. Stevens, © 1981 The New Yorker Magazine, Inc.; p. 35, © Yves de Brane/Black Star; p. 40, © Paul Light/Lightwave; p. 41, © Mark Antman/The Image Works; p. 42, Drawing by Lorenz, © 1984 The New Yorker Magazine, Inc.; p. 47, courtesy Uri Bronfenbrenner.

Chapter 2

(Top left) © Judith Black/Lightwave; (lower left and right) © Elizabeth Crews; p. 54, Colorphoto Hans Hinz, Basle; p. 57, (both) © M. W. F. Tweedie/The National Audubon Society Collection/Photo Researchers, Inc.; p. 62, © UPI/Bettmann Newsphotos; p. 70, courtesy Harlow Primate Laboratory, University of Wisconsin; p. 74, © Marjorie Shostak/Anthro-Photo; p. 75, © Ken Heyman; p. 77, © Elizabeth Crews; p. 78, © Joanne Leonard/Woodfin Camp.

Chapter 3

P. 90 and 92, © Donald Yeager for Camera M. D. Studios, Inc.; p. 91, © H. Cummins, "The Topographic History of the Volar Pads (Walking Pads: Tast Ballen) in the Human Embryo," in *Carnegie Institution of Washington, Contributions to Embryology,* Vol. 20, Carnegie Institution of Washington Publication 394, © 1929; p. 96, © BBC Hulton, Bettmann/UPI Newsphotos; p. 103. © Chuck Kimball/Nanessence; p. 107, © Blair Irwin; p. 109 (left) © Jean Shapiro; (right) © Elizabeth Crews; p. 117, © John Blaustein/Woodfin Camp; p. 122, courtesy Catholic Relief Services; p. 124, © Jean Shapiro.

Chapter 4

P. 137, © Erika Stone; p. 138, © Blair Irwin; p. 142, © William Van Divert; p. 149, © Elizabeth Crews; p. 153, photos courtesy A. N. Meltzoff from A. N. Meltzoff and M. K. Moore, "Imitation of Facial and Manual Gestures by Human Neonates," Fig. 1, in *Science, 198* (October 7, 1977): 75–78; p. 154 © Erika Stone; p. 156, © George Zimbel/Monkmeyer; p. 165, © Three Lions.

Chapter 5

P. 175, © Suzanne Szasz; p. 177, © Erika Stone; p. 190 (left), courtesy H. Van Lawick; (right) © AP/Wide World Photos; p. 194, Neena Leen/Life Magazine © Time, Inc.; p. 196, © Elizabeth Crews; p. 201, © Suzanne Szasz; p. 204, © Erika Stone; p. 213, courtesy Mary Ainsworth.

Chapter 6

P. 221, © Elizabeth Crews; p. 222, © Jacques Low/Woodfin Camp; p. 223, Maurice Sendak, *Where the Wild Things Are.* New York: Harper & Row, 1984; p. 227, courtesy Rheta DeVries; p. 232, © Mark Antman/The Image Works; p.

CHART

NAME INDEX

SUBJECT INDEX